Robert Barclay

An Apology for the True Christian Divinity

Robert Barclay

An Apology for the True Christian Divinity

ISBN/EAN: 9783337404994

Printed in Europe, USA, Canada, Australia, Japan

Cover: Foto ©Lupo / pixelio.de

More available books at **www.hansebooks.com**

AN
APOLOGY

For the

True CHRISTIAN Divinity,

As the same is held forth, and preached by the people,

Called, in Scorn,

QUAKERS;

Being a full explanation and vindication of their Principles and Doctrines, by many arguments, deduced from Scriptur and right Reason, and the testimonys of famous Authors, both antient and modern, with a full answer to the strongest objections usually made against them, Presented to the *KING.*

Written and published in Latine, for the information of Strangers, by

ROBERT BARCLAY.

And now put into our own language, for the benefit of his countrey-men.

Act. 24: 14. —— *after the way, which they call heresie, so worship I the God of my fathers, believing all things which are written in the Law and the Prophets.*

Tit. 2: 11, 12, 13, 14. *For the Grace of God, that bringeth Salvation, hath appeared to all men;*
Teaching us, that denying ungodliness and worldly lusts, we should live soberly, righteously, and godlily in this present world;
Looking for that blessed hope, and the glorious appearing of the great God, and our Saviour Iesus Christ.
Who gave himself for us, that he might redeem us from all iniquity, and purifie unto himself a peculiar people, Zealous of good works.

1 Thess. 5: 21. *Prove all things: hold fast that, which is good.*

Printed in the Year 1678.

UNTO

CHARLES
The SECOND,
KING
OF
GREAT BRITAIN

And the Dominions thereunto belonging,
ROBERT BARCLAY,

A fervant of JESUS CHRIST, called of God to the difpenfation of the Gofpel, now again revealed, and, after a long and dark night of Apoftafy, commanded to be preached to all Nations; wisheth Health and Salvation.

AS the condition of Kings and Princes, puts them in a ftation, more obvious to the view and obfervation of the world, than that of other men, of whom, as *Cicero* obferves, neither any word, or action can be obfcure; fo are thofe Kings (during whofe appearance upon the ftage of this world, it pleafeth the Great *KING of Kings* fingularly to make known unto men

*   the

the wonderfull steps of his *unsearchable Providence*) more signally obferved, and their lives and actions more diligently remarked, and inquired into by posterity, especially if thofe things be fuch, as not onely relate to the outward tranfactions of this world, but alfo are fignalized by the manifeftation or revelation of the knowledg of God in matters Spiritual and Religious. Thefe are the things that rendred the lives of *Cyrus*, *Auguftus Cefar*, and *Conftantin* the Great, in former times, and of C H A R L E S the Fifth, and fome other modern Princes in thefe laft ages fo confiderable.

But among all thefe tranfactions, which it hath pleafed God to permitt, for the Glory of his Power, and the manifeftation of his Wifdom and Providence, no age furnisheth us with things fo *ftrange & marvellous*, whether with refpect to matters Civil or Religious, as thefe, that have faln out within the compafs of thy time, who, though thou be not yet arrived at the fiftieth year of thy age, haft yet been a witnefs of ftranger things, than many ages before produced; fo that, whether we refpect thofe various troubles, wherein thou foundft thy felf engaged, while fcarce got out of thy infancy, the many different afflictions, wherewith men of thy circumftances are often unacquainted, the ftrange and unparallel'd fortun, that befell thy Father, thy own narrow efcape, and banishment following thereupon, with the great improbability of thy ever returning (at leaft without very much paines and tedious combatings) or finally the incapacity thou wert under to accomplish fuch a defign, confidering the ftrength of thofe, that had poffeffed themfelves of thy throne, and the terror they had inflicted upon foreign States: & yet that, after all this, thou shouldft be reftored without ftroke of fword, the help or affiftance of foreign States, or the contrivance and work of humane policy. All thefe do fufficiently declare, that it is the *Lord's doing*, which, as it is marvellous in our eyes, fo it will juftly be a matter of wonder

and.

and aſtoniſhment to generations to come : and may ſufficiently ſerve, if rightly obſerved, to confute and confound
that Athëiſm, wherewith this age doth ſo much abound.

As the vindication of the *Liberty of Conſcience* (which
thy Father, by giving way to the importunat clamors of the
Clergy, the anſwering and fulfilling of whoſe unrighteous
wills has often proved hurtfull and pernicious to Princes,
ſought, in ſome part, to reſtrain) was a great occaſion of theſe
troubles and revolutions: ſo the pretence of Conſcience was
that, which carried it on, and brought it to that pitch it came
to, and, though (no doubt) ſome, that were ingaged in that
work, deſigned good things, at leſt in the beginning, (albeit
always wrong in the manner they took to accompliſh it, *viz*, by
carnal wapons) yet ſo ſoon as they had taſted of the ſweet of
the poſſeſſions of them, they had turned out, they quickly
began to do thoſe things themſelves, for which they had accuſed others: for their hands were found full of oppreſſion, and
they hated the reproofs of inſtruction, which is the way of life. And they
evilly entreated the meſſengers of the Lord, & cauſed to beat
and impriſon his Prophets, and perſecuted his People, whom
he had called & gathered out from among them, whom he had
made to beat their *ſwords into plow-ſhares, & their ſpears into prunn-
ing-hooks*, and not to learn carnal warr any more : but he
raiſed them up, and armed them with *Spiritual weapons*; even
with his own Spirit and Power, whereby they teſtified in the
ſtreets and high-ways, and publik markets and ſynagogues,
againſt the *pride, vanity, luſts*, and *hypocriſy* of that generation,
who were righteous in their own eyes, though often cruelly
entreated therefore, and they faithfully propheſied and
foretold them of their judgment and down-fall, which
came upon them, as by ſeveral warnings and epiſtles delivered to *Oliver* and *Richard Cromwel*, the Parliament, and
other then Powers, yet upon record, doth appear.

And after it pleaſed God to reſtore thee, what oppreſ-

* 2

ſions,

fions, what banishments and evil entreatings they have
met with, by men pretending thy authority, and cloak-
ing their mifchief with thy name, is known to moft men
in this Ifland, efpecially in *England*, where there is fcarce
a prifon that hath not been filled with them, nor a Judge,
before whom they have not been haled, *though they could
never yet be found guilty* of any thing, that might deferve that
ufage, therefore the fenfe of their innocency did no doubt
greatly contribut to move thee three years ago to caufe
fome hundreds of them to be fet at liberty; for indeed their
fufferings are fingular, and obvioufly diftinguishable from
all the reft of fuch as live under thee, in thefe two
refpects.

    Fift, *in that among all the plots, contrived by others againft
thee, fince thy return into Britann, there was never any owned of
that people found or known to be guilty* (though many of them
have been taken and imprifoned upon fuch kind of jeal-
oufys) *but were always found innocent and harmelefs*, (as became the followers of Chrift) *not coveting after, nor contending for, the Kingdoms of this world, but fubject to every ordinance
of man for Confcience fake.*

    Secondly, *in that in the hotteft times of perfecution and the moft
violent profecution of thofe Laws, made againft meetings* (being cloathed with innocency) *they have boldly ftood to their teftimony for
God, without creeping into holes or corners; or once hiding themfelves,*
as all other diffenters have done, *but daily met, according to their
cuftom, in the publik places, appoynted for that end,* fo that none of
thy officers can fay of them, *that they have furprized them in
a corner, overtaken them in a privat conventicle, or catched them
lurking in their fecret chambers: nor needed they to fend out fpies,
to get them whom they were fure daily to find in their open affemblys, teftifying for God and his Truth.* By which thofe, that
have an eye to fee, may obferve their Chriftian patience
and courage, conftancy and fuffering, joyned in one,

more

more than in any other people, that differ from them, or oppofe them: And yet in the midft of thofe troubles thou canft bear witnefs, that, as, on the one part, they never fought to detract from thee, or to render thee and thy Government odious to the people, by namelefs and fcandalous pamphlets and libells, fo, on the other hand, they have not fpared to admonish, exhort, and reprove thee, and have faithfully difcharged their Confciences towards thee, without flattering words, as ever the true Prophets in antient times ufed to do, to thofe Kings and Princes, under whofe Power, violence, or oppreffion was acted.

And albeit it be evident by experience to be moft agreable both to Divine Truth and humane policy, to allow every one to ferve God, according to their Confciences, neverthelefs thofe other Sects, who, for the moft part, durft not peep out in the times of Perfecution, while thefe innocent people ftood bold and faithfull, do now combine in a joynt confederacy (notwithftanding all the former janglings and contention among themfelves) to render us odious, feeking unjuftly to wreft our doctrin and words, as if they were inconfiftent both with Chriftianity and Civil fociety; fo that, to effectuat this their work of malice againft us, they have not been ashamed to take the help, and commend the labors of fome invidious *Socinians* againft us. So do *Herod* and *Pontius Pilat* agree to crucify Chrift.

But our practice, known to thee by good experience to be more confiftent with Chriftianity, and Civil fociety, and the peace and welfare of this Ifland, than that of thofe, that thus accufe us, doth fufficiently guard us againft this calumny, that we may indeed appeal to the teftimony of thy Confcience, as a witnefs for us, in the face of the Nations.

Thefe things moved me to prefent the world with a
b. ief.

brief, but true, account of this Peopls principles in some short Theological Propositions, which, according to the will of God, proving successfull, beyond my expectation, to the satisfaction of severall, and to the moving in many a desire of being further informed concerning us, as being every where evil spoken of, and likewise meeting with publik opposition by some, as such will always do, so long as *the Devil rules in the children of disobedience*, I was thereby further engaged, in the liberty of the Lord, to present to the world, this *Apology* of the Truth held by those People, which, because of thy interest in them, and theirs in thee, as having first appeared and mostly increased in these Nations under thy rule, I make bold to present unto thee.

Thou know'st and hast experienced *their faithfulness towards their God, their patience in suffering, their peaceableness towards the King, their honesty, plainness, and integrity in their faithfull warnings and testimonys to thee*; and if thou wilt allow thy self so much time as to read this, thou mayst find *how consonant their Principles are both to Scriptur, Truth, and right Reason.* The simplicity of their behaviour, the generality of their condition, as being poor men and illiterat, the manner of their procedur being without the wisdom and policy of this world, hath made many conclude them fools and mad men, and neglect them as not being capable of Reason. But though it be to them as their crown thus to be esteemed of the wise and great and learned of this world, and though they rejoyce to be accounted fools for Christ's sake, yet of late some, even such, who, in the world's account, are esteemed both wise and learned, begin to judge otherwise of them, and find that they hold forth things very agreable both to Scriptur, Reason, and true learning.

As it is inconsistent with the Truth I bear, so it is far
from

from me to ufe this Epiftle as an *engine* to *flatter* thee, the
ufual defign of fuch works; and therefore I can neither
dedicat it to thee, nor crave thy patronage, as if thereby I might have more confidence to prefent it to the
world, or be more hopefull of its fuccefs. To God alone
I ow what I have, and that more immediatly in matters
Spiritual, and therefore to him alone and to the fervice
of his Truth I dedicat whatever work he brings forth in-
me, to whom onely the praife and honor appertaines,
whofe Truth needs not the patronage of wordly Princes,
his Arm and Power being that alone, by which it is propagated, eftablished, and confirmed. But I found it upon
my Spirit, to take occafion to prefent this book unto
thee, that, as thou haft been often warned by feveral of
that people, who are inhabitants of *England*, fo thou mayft
not want a feafonable advertifement from a member of thy
antient Kingdom of *Scotland*, and that thou mayft know
(which I hope thou shalt have no reafon to be troubled at)
that God is raifing up and encreafing that people in that
Nation. And the Nations shall alfo hereby knovv that
the Truth we profefs is not a work of darknefs, nor propagated by ftealth, and that vve are not ashamed of *the*
Gofpel of Chrift, becaufe vve knovv it to be *the Power of God*
unto Salvation : and that vve are no vvays fo inconfiftent
vvith Government, nor fuch difturbers of the Peace, as
our enemies, by traduceing us, have fought to make the
vvorld believe vve are, for what to thee I dare appeal as a
Witnefs of our peaceablnefs and Chriftian patience.

Generations to come shall not more admire that fingular ftep of Divine Providence, in reftoring thee to thy
Throne, vvithout outvvard blood-shed, than they shall
admire the increafe and progrefs of this Truth, vvithout all outvvard help, and againft fo great oppofition,
vvhich shall be none of the leaft things rendering thy
memory

memory remarkable. God hath done great things for thee, he hath sufficiently shevvn thee, that it is *by him Princes rule*, and that *he can pull down and set up at his pleasur.* He hath often faithfully vvarned thee by his servants, since he restored thee to thy Royal dignity, that thy heart might not vvax vvanton againſt him, to forget his Mercys and Providence tovvards thee, vvhereby he might permit thee to be soothed up and lulled asleep in thy sins by the flattering of *Court-Parasits*, vvho, by their fawning, are the *ruin* of many *Princes.*

There is no King in the vvorld, vvho can so experimentally teſtify of God's Providence and Goodness, neither is there any, vvho rules so many free people, so many true Chriſtians, vvhich thing renders thy Government more honorable, thy self more conſiderable, than the acceſsion of many Nations filled vvith ſlavish and ſuperſtitious Soules.

Thou haſt taſted of Proſperity and adverſity : thou knovvſt vvhat it is to be banished thy native countrey, to be over-ruled. as vvel as to rule and ſit upon the Throne; and being oppreſsed thou haſt reaſon to knovv, hovv *hatefull* the *Oppreſſor* is, both to God and man. If, after all theſe vvarnings and advertiſements, thou doſt not turn unto the Lord vvith all thy heart, but forget him, vvho remembred thee in thy diſtreſs, and give up thy self to follovv luſt and vanity, ſurely great vvill be thy condemnation.

Againſt vvhich ſnare, as wel as the temptation of thoſe, that may, or do feed thee, and prompt thee to evil, the moſt excellent and prevalent remedy vvill be, to apply thy self to that *Light of Chriſt*, vvhich *shineth in thy Conſcience*, vvhich neither can, nor vvill flatter thee, nor ſuffer thee to be at caſe in thy ſins, but doth and vvill deal plainly and faithfully vvith thee, as thoſe, that are followers thereof have alſo done.   *GOD*

GOD Almighty, who hath so signally hitherto visited thee with his love, so touch and reach thy heart, ere the day of thy visitation be expired, that thou mayst effectually turn to him, so as to improve thy place and station, for his Name. So wisheth, so prayeth

Thy faithfull Friend and subject

ROBERT BARCLAY.

From Ury*, the place of my Pilgrimage,
in my native countrey of* Scotland*, the 2 5
of the Moneth, called* November*, in the*
YEAR 1675.

R. B. Unto the Friendly Reader wisheth Salvation.

*F*Orasmuch as that, which above all things I propose to my self, is to declare and defend the Truth; for the service whereof I have given up and devoted my self, and all that is mine, therefore there is nothing, which for its sake (by the help and assistance of God) I may not attempt. And in this confidence I did sometime ago publish certain Propositions of Divinity, comprehending briefly the chief Principles and doctrines of Truth, which appearing not unprofitable to some, and being, beyond my expectation, wel received both by forreigners, tho dissenting from us, (albeit also opposed by som envious ones) did so far prevail, as, in some part, to remove that false and monstrous opinion. which lying fame, and the malice of our adversaries had implanted in the minds of some concerning us and our doctrines. In this respect it seem'd to me not fit to spare my paines and labor.*

* *

The-

Therefore being acted by the same measur of the Divine Spirit, and the like design of propagating the Truth, by which I published the Propositions, I judg'd it meet to explain them somewhat more largely at this time, and defend them by certain arguments.

Perhaps my method of writing may seem not onely different, but even contrary to that, which is commonly used by the men, called Divines, *with which I am not concerned, for that I confess my self to be not onely no imitator and admirer of the* School-men, *but an opposer and despiser of them, as such, by whose labor I judge the Christian Religion to be so far from being bettered, that it is rather destroyed. Neither have I sought to accommodat this my work to itching ears, who desire rather to comprehend in their head the sublime notions of Truth, than to embrace it in their heart. For what I have written comes more from my heart, than from my head, what I have heard with the ears of my Soul, and seen with my inward eyes, and my hands have handled of the* Word of Life. *And what hath been inwardly manifested to me of the things of God, that do I declare, not so much minding the eloquence and excellency of speech, as desiring to demonstrat the efficacy and operation of* Truth, *and if I err sometime in the former, it is not great matter; for I act not here the* Grammarian *or the* Orator, *but the* Christian; *and therefore in this have followed the certain Rule of the* Divine Light, *and of the* Holy Scripturs.

And, to make an end, what I have written, is written, not to feed the wisdom and knowledge, *or rather* vain pride of this world, *but to starve and oppose it, as the little* Preface *prefixed to the Propositions doth shew, which with the title of them is, as followeth.*

THE.

THESES
THEOLOGICÆ.

To the Clergy of what fort foever, unto whofe hands thefe may come; but more particularly to the Doctors, Profeffors, and Students of Divinity in the Univerfities and Schools of *Great Britain*, whether *Prelatical, Prefbyterian*, or any other : ROBERT BARCLAY, a Servant of the Lord God, and one of thofe (who in derifion are called *Quakers*) wisheth unfeigned Repentance unto the acknowledgement of the Truth :

FRIENDS,

UNto You thefe following Propofitions are offered, in which, they being read and confidered in the fear of the Lord, you may perceive that fimple Naked Truth, which Man by his wifdom hath rendred fo obfcure and myfterious, that the world is even burthened with the great and voluminous Tractates which are made about it, and by their vain jangling and Commentaries, by which it is rendred a hundred fold more dark and intricate, than of it felf it is; which great Learning fo accounted of (to wit) your School Divinity (which taketh up almoft a mans whole life-time to learn) brings not a whit nearer to God, neither makes any man lefs wicked, or more righteous than he was; Therefore hath God laid afide the wife and Learned, and the Difputers of this world, and hath chofen a few defpicable and unlearned Inftruments (as to Letter-learning) as he did Fisher men of old, to publish his pure and naked Truth, and to free it of thefe mifts and fogs, wherewith the Clergy hath clouded it, that the People might admire and maintain them; And among feveral others, whom God hath chofen to make known thefe things, (feing I alfo have received

* * 2

in

in meafure Grace to be a Difpenfer of the fame Gofpel) it feemed good unto me , according to my duty, to offer unto You thefe Propofitions which (tho fhort , yet) are weighty, comprehending much , and declaring what the true ground of knowledge is , even of that knowledge which leads to life Eternal , which is here witneffed of, and the teftimony thereof left unto the light of Chrift in all your Confciences.

Farewel,

R. B.

The Firft Propofition,

Concerning the true Foundation of knowledg.

John 17:3 SEing the height of all happinefs is placed in the true knowledge of God, (*This is life eternal to know the true God, and Iefus Chrift whom thou haft fent*,) the true and right underftanding of this foundation and ground of knowledge, is that, which is moft neceffary to be known and believed in the firft place.

The Second Propofition,

Concerning Immediate Revelation.

Match. 11 27. **Seing** *no man knoweth the Father, but the Son, and he, to whom the Son revealeth him , and feing the revelation of the Son is in and by the Spirit*; therefore the teftimony of the Spirit is that alone, by which the true knowledge of God hath been, is, and can be only revealed, who, as by the moving of his own Spirit, converted the *Chaös* of this world, into that wonderfull order, wherein it was in the beginning, and created man, a living Soul, to rule and govern it, fo, by the revelation of the fame

Spirit,

Spirit, he hath manifested himself all along unto the sons of men, both Patriarchs. Prophets and Apostles, which revelations of God by the Spirit, whether by outward voices and appearances, dreams or inward *objective manifestations in the heart*, were of old the *formal object* of their *faith*, and remaineth yet so to be, since the *object of the Saints Faith is the same in all ages*, though set forth under divers administrations : Moreover these *divine inward revelations*, which we make absolutely *necessary* for the building up of true Faith, neither do nor can ever contradict the outward testimony of the Scriptures, or right and found reason; Yet from hence it will not follow, that these divine revelations are to be subjected to the examination, either of the outward testimony of the Scriptures, or of the natural reason of man, as to a more noble, or certain rule and touch-stone; for this divine revelation and inward illumination is that, which is evident and clear of it self, forceing by its own evidence and clearness the wel-disposed understanding to assent, irresistibly moving the same thereunto even as the common Principles of natural Truths move and incline the mind to a natural assent. Such as are these, (that *the whole is greater than the part*; that *two contradictory sayings can not be both true, or false,*) which is also manifest according to our adversaries Principle, who (supposing the possibility of inward divine revelations,) will nevertheless confess with us, that neither Scripture nor sound reason will contradict it; and yet it will not follow, according to them, that the Scripture, or sound reason, should be subjected to the examination of the divine revelations in the heart.

The Third Proposition,

Concerning the Scripturs.

From these revelations of the Spirit of God to the Saints, have proceeded the Scriptures of Truth, which contain,

1. A faithful hiftorical account of the actings of Gods people in divers ages, with many fingular and remarkable Providences attending them. 2. A Prophetical account of feveral things, whereof fome are already paft, and fome yet to come. 3. A full and ample account of all the chief Principles of the Doctrine of Chrift held forth in divers pretious declarations, exhortations and fentences, which, by the moving of God's Spirit, were at feveral times, and upon fundry occafions fpoken and written unto fome Churches and their Paftors; Neverthelefs, becaufe they are only a declaration of the Fountain, and not the Fountain it felf, therefore they are not to be efteemed the principal ground of all truth and knowledge, nor yet the *adequate primary Rule* of *Faith* and *Manners.* Neverthelefs, as that which giveth a true and faithfull teftimony of the firft foundation, they are and may be efteemed a *fecondary Rule, fubordinate* to the *Spirit*, from which they have all their excellency and certainty; For as by the inward teftimony of the Spirit we do alone truly know them, fo they teftifie that the Spirit is that guide, by which the Saints are led into all truth; Therefore according to the Scriptures the Spirit is the firft and principal Leader; And feing we do therefore receive and believe the Scriptures, becaufe they proceeded from the Spirit, therefore alfo the Spirit is more originally and principally the Rule, according to that received Maxim in the Schools, *Propter quod unumquodque eft tale, illud ipfum eft magis tale.* Englished thus: *That for which a thing is fuch, that thing it felf is more fuch.*

John 16: 13. Rom. 8; 14.

The Fourth Propofition,

Concerning the Condition of Man in the fall.

Rom. 5: 12, 13.

All *Adam*'s Pofterity (or Mankind) both Jews and Gentiles, as to the firft *Adam* (or earthly man) is fallen, degenerated,

rated, and dead, deprived of the fenfation (or feeling) of this inward Teftimony, or *Seed* of God, and is fubject unto the power, nature, and feed of the Serpent; which he fows *in* mens hearts, while they abide in this natural and corrupted ftate, from whence it comes that not their words and deeds only, but all their imaginations are evil perpetually in the fight of God, as procceding from this depraved and wicked feed. Man therefore as he is in this ftate can know nothing aright; yea, his thoughts and conceptions concerning God, and things fpiritual (until he be disjoyned from this evil feed, and united to the *Divine Light*) are unprofitable both to him-felf and others : Hence are rejected the *Socinian* and *Pelagian* Errors, in exalting a natural light, as alfo the Papifts and moft of Proteftants, who affirm *that Man without the true Grace of* Eph. 2: 1. *God may be a true Minifter of the Gofpel.* Neverthelefs this feed is not imputed to infants, until by tranfgreffion they actually joyn themfelves therewith, for they are by Nature the child-ren of wrath, who walk according to the power of the Prince of the Air.

The Fifth and Sixth Propofition,

Concerning the Vniverfal Redemption by Chrift, and alfo the Saving and Spiritual Light, wherewith every man is enlightened.

The Fifth Propofition,

● *God*, out of his Infinite love, *who delighteth not in the death* Ezek. 18: *of a finner, but that all should live and be faved, hath fo loved the* verfe 23. *world, that he hath given his only Son a Light, that whofoever be-* Efai 49:6. *lieveth in him should be faved, who enlighteneth every man, that* John 3:16 *cometh into the world, and maketh manifeft all things that are reprove-* 1:9. *able, and teacheth all temperance, righteoufnefs, and godlinefs;* Tit. 2:11 and this Light enlighteneth the hearts of all in a day in order Eph. 5:13 to falvation, if not refifted; Nor is it lefs *univerfal* than the Hebr. 2:9.
feed

feed of fin, being the purchafe of his death, who *tafted; death for every man; For as in* Adam *all dye, even fo in* Chrift *all shall be made alive.*

The Sixth Propofition,

According to which principle (or *Hypothefis*) all the Objections againft the univerfality of Chrift's death are eafily folved; neither is it needful to recurr to the Miniftery of Angels, & thofe other miraculous means, which, they fay, God makes ufe of, to manifeft the Doctrine and Hiftory of Chrift's paffion unto fuch who (living in thofe places of the world where the outward preaching of the Gofpel is unknown) have wel improved the firft and common Grace; For hence it wel follows, that as fome of the old Philofophers might have been faved; fo alfo may now fome (who by Providence are caft into thofe remote parts of the world, where the knowledge of the Hiftory is wanting) be made partakers of the Divine Myftery, if they receive and refift not that Grace, *a manifeftation whereof is given to every man to profit withal.* This certain Doctrine then being received, (*to wit*) that there is an Evangelical and faving Light and Grace in all, the univerfality of the Love and Mercy of God towards mankind, (both in the death of his beloved Son the Lord Jefus Chrift, and in the manifeftation of the Light in the heart) is eftablished and confirmed againft all the Objections of fuch as deny it. Therefore *Chrift hath tafted death for every man*, not only *for all kinds of men*, as fome vainly talk; but *for every one*, *of all kinds*, the benefit of whofe offering is not only extended to fuch, who have the diftinct outward knowledge of his death and fuffering, as the fame is declared in the Scriptures; but even unto thofe, who are neceffarily excluded from the benefit of this knowledge by fome inevitable accident; which knowledge we willingly confefs to be very profitable and comfortable,

1 Cor. 12 verf. 7.

Hebr. 2:9

but

but not abfolutely needfull unto fuch, from whom God himfelf hath withheld it, yet they may be made partakers of the
myfterie of his death (though ignorant of the Hiftory) if
they fuffer his Seed and Light (inlightning their hearts) to
take place (in which Light communion with the Father and
the Son is enjoyed) fo as of wicked men to become holy, and
lovers of that power, by whofe inward and fecret touches,
they feel themfelves turned from the evil to the good, and
learn *to do to others, as they would be done by*, in which Chrift himfelf affirms all to be included. As they have then falfly and er-
roneoufly taught, who have denyed Chrift to have dyed for
all men, fo neither have they fufficiently taught the truth,
who affirming him to have dyed for all, have added the abfolute neceffity of the outward knowledge thereof in order to
the obtaining its faving effect; Among whom the *Remonftrants
of Holland* have been chiefly wanting, and many other Affertors of *univerfal Redemption*, in that they have not placed the
extent of this falvation in that Divine and Evangelical Principle of Light and Life, wherewith Chrift hath enlightned
every man that comes into the world, which is excellently
and evidently held forth in thefe fcriptures, Gen 6: 3.
Deut. 30: 14. John. 1: 7, 8, 9. Rom. 10: 8. Tit. 2: 11.

The Seventh Propofition,

Concerning Iuftification.

As many as refift not this Light, but receive the fame,
in them is produced, a holy, pure, and fpiritual birth, bringing forth holinefs, righteoufnefs, purity, and all thefe other
bleffed fruits, which are acceptable to God, by which holy
birth (*to wit*) *Iefus Chrift* formed *within* us, and working his
work in us, as we are fanctifyed, fo are we juftified in the
fight of God, according to the Apoftles words, *But ye are*
* * *
                                                        wafhed,

 Therefore it is not by our works wrought in our will, nor yet by good works, considered as of themselves; but by Christ who is both the gift and the giver, and the cause producing the effects in us, who as he hath reconciled us while we were enemies, doth also in his wisdom save us, and justify us after this manner, as saith the same Apostle elsewhere, *according to his mercy he hath saved us, by the washing of Regeneration, and the renewing of the Holy Ghost.*

Titus. 3: vers 5.

The Eighth Proposition,

Concerning Perfection.

In whom this holy and pure birth is fully brought forth, the body of death and sin comes to be crucified and removed, and their hearts united and subjected unto the truth, so as not to obey any suggestion or temptation of the evil one, but to be free from actual sinning, and transgressing of the Law of God, and in that respect perfect; yet doth this perfection still admit of a growth, there remaineth ever in some part a possibility of sinning, where the mind doth not most diligently and watchfully attend unto the Lord.

Rom. 6: vers 14
Rom. 8: vers 13.
Rom. 6. 2, 18.
1 John. 3 vers 6.

The Ninth Proposition,

Concerning Perseverance, and the possibility of falling from Grace.

Although this Gift and inward Grace of God, be sufficient to work out Salvation, yet in those in whom it is resisted, it both may and doth become their condemnation: Moreover in whom it hath wrought in part, to purifie and sanctifie them in order to their further perfection; by disobedience such may fall from it and turn it to wantonefs, making shipwrack of Faith, and *after having tasted of the Heavenly gift, and been*

1 Tim. 1: vers 6.
Heb. 6. 4, 5, 6.

made

made partakers of the Holy Ghost, again fall away, yet such an increase and stability in the Truth may in this life be attained, from which there can not be a total Apostasy.

The Tenth Proposition,

Concerning the Ministery.

As by this Gift, or Light of God, all true knowledge in things spiritual is received and revealed, so by the same as it is manifested and received *in* the heart by the strength and power thereof, every true Minister of the Gospel is ordained, prepared, and supplied in the work of the Ministery, and by the leading, moving, and drawing hereof, ought every Evangelist and Christian Pastor to be led, and ordered in his labour and work of the Gospel, both as to the place where, as to the Person to whom, and as to the times when he is to Minister : Moreover, who have this Authority may and ought to Preach the Gospel, though without humane Commission or Literature; as on the other hand, who want the Authority of this Divine Gift, however Learned or Authorized by the Commissions of Men and Churches, are to be esteemed but as deceivers, and not true Ministers of the Gospel ; also who have received this holy and unspotted Gift, *as they have freely received, so are they freely to give*, without hire or bargaining, far less to use it as a Trade to get Matt. 10. Money by it; yet if God hath called any from their Imployments or Trades, by which they acquire their livelihood, it may be lawfull for such (according to the liberty which they feel given them in the Lord) to receive such Temporals (to wit) what may be needfull to them for Meat and Cloathing, as are freely given them by those, to whom they have communicated spirituals.

The

The Eleventh Propoſition,
Concerning VVorſhip.

All true and acceptable worſhip to God is offered in the *inward* and *immediate* moving and drawing of his own Spirit, which is neither limited to places, times, or perſons; for though we be to worſhip him always, in that we are to fear before him; yet as to the outward ſignification thereof in Prayers, Praiſes, or Preachings, we ought not to do it where and when we will, but where and when we are moved thereunto by the ſecret Inſpirations of his Spirit in our hearts, which God heareth and accepteth of, and is never wanting to move us thereunto, when need is, of which he himſelf is the alone proper Judge: all other worſhip then, both Praiſes, Prayers, and Preachings, which man ſets about in his own will, and at his own appointment, which he can both begin and end at his pleaſure, do or leave undone as himſelf ſees meet, whether they be a preſcribed Form, as a Liturgy or Prayers conceived extemporarily, by the natural ſtrength and faculty of the mind, they are all but Superſtitions, Will-worſhip, and abominable Idolatry in the ſight of God, which are to be denyed, rejected, and ſeparated from in this day of his Spiritual ariſing, however it might have pleaſed him who winked at the times of ignorance, with a reſpect to the ſimplicity and integrity of ſome, and of his own innocent Seed, which lay, as it were, buried in the hearts of men, under the maſs of Superſtition, to blow upon the dead and dry bones, and to raiſe ſome breathings and anſwer them, and that untill the day ſhould more clearly dawn and break forth.

Ezek. 13
Matt. 10
vers 20.
Acts. 2:4
18,5.
John. 3:
6. & 4:
ver. 21.
Jude. 19.
Acts 17:
vers 23.

The Twelfth Propoſition,
Concerning Baptiſm.

Eph. 4:5
1 Pet. 3:
vers 21.

As there is one Lord, and one Faith, ſo there is one Baptiſm, which is not the putting away the filth of the fleſh, but the anſwer of a
good

good Conscience before God, *by the Resurrection of Iesus Christ*, and
this Baptifme is a Pure and Spiritual thing, to wit, the *Ba-*
ptifm of the *Spirit* and *fire*, by which we are buried with him,
that being washed and purged from our fins, we may *walk in*
newnefs of Life, of which the Baptifm of *Iohn* was a figure,
which was commanded for a time, and not to continue for
ever; as to the Baptifm of infants it is a meer humane Tradition, for vvhich neither Precept nor Practice is to be found
in all the Scripture.

Rom. 6:4
Gal. 3:27
Col. 2:12
Joh. 3:30
1 Cor. 1
vers 17.

The Thirteenth Propofition,
Concerning the Communion or participation of the body
and blood of Chrift.

The *Communion* of the Body and Blood of Chrift is *inward*
and *Spiritual*, which is the participation of his flesh and blood,
by vvhich the *inward man* is daily nourished in the hearts of
thofe in vvhom Chrift dvvells, of vvhich things the *breaking*
of bread by Chrift vvith his Difciples vvas a *figure*, vvhich they
even ufed in the Church for a time, vvho had received the
fubftance, for the caufe of the vveak: even as *abftaining from*
things ftrangled, and *from blood*, *the washing one anothers feet*, and
the *anointing of the fick with Oyl*, all which are commanded with
no lefs authority and folemnity than the former; yet feing
they are but the *shaddows* of better things, they ceafe in fuch
as have obtained the *Subftance.*

1 Cor. 10
16, 17,
Joh. 6:
32, 33.
55.
1 Cor. 5:
vers 8.

Acts 15:
vers 20.
Joh. 13:
vers 14.
Ja. 5: 14

The Fourteenth Propofition,
Concerning the Power of the Civil Magiftrate in matters purely
religious and pertaining to the Confcience.

Since God hath affumed to himfelf the power and Dominion of the Confcience, who alone can rightly inftruct and
govern it, therefore it is not lawfull for any whatfoever, by
vertue of any Authority or Principality they bear in the Government of this World, to force the Confciences of others;
and

Luc. 9:
55, 56.
Matth. 7:
12, 29.
Tit. 3:10

and therefore all Killing, Banishing, Fining, imprisoning, and other such things, which men are afflicted with for the alone exercise of their Conscience or difference in Worship, or Opinion; proceedeth from the Spirit of *Cain*, the murtherer, and is contrary to the Truth, providing always that no man, under the pretence of Conscience, prejudice his Neighbour in his life or estate, or do any thing destructive to, or inconsistent with humane Society, in which case the Law is for the transgressor, and Justice is to be administred upon all without respect of Persons.

The Fifteenth Proposition,

Concerning Salutations and Recreations, &c.

Seing the chief end of all Religion is to redeem man from the spirit and vain conversation of this World, and to lead into inward communion with God, before whom, if we fear always, we are accounted happy, therefore all the vain customs and habits thereof both in word and deed are to be rejected and forsaken by those who come to this fear; such as the taking off the Hat to a man, the bowings and cringings of the body, and such other Salutations of that kind, with all the foolish and superstitious formalities attending them, all which man has invented in his degenerate state to feed his pride in the vain pomp and glory of this world, as also the unprofitable Plays, frivolous Recreations, Sportings and Gamings which are invented to pass away the pretious time, and divert the mind from the witness of God in the heart, and from the living sense of his fear, and from that *Evangelical* Spirit wherewith Christians ought to be leavened, and which leads into sobriety, gravity and Godly fear, in which, as we abide, the blessing of the Lord is felt to attend us in these actions which we are necessarily engaged in order to the taking care for the sustenance of the outward man.

Eph. 5:
vers 11.
1 Pet. 1.
vers 14.
Joh. 5:
vers 44.
Jer. 10:3
Acts 10:
vers 26.
Matth.15
vers 13.
Col.2:8.

AN

AN APOLOGY,

For the true CHRISTIAN DIVINITY.

The firſt Propoſition.

Seing the heighth of all happyneſs is placed in the true
knowledg of GOD, (*this is Life eternal, to know the true* Joh. 17:3
God and Ieſus Chriſt, whom thou haſt ſent) the true and
right underſtanding of this foundation and ground of
knowledg is that which is moſt neceſſary to be known
and believed in the firſt place.

H E, that deſireth to acquire any art or ſcience, ſeeketh firſt thoſe means, by which that art
or ſcience is obtained. If we ought to doe ſo in
things natural and earthly, how much more then in
Spiritual ? In this affaire then ſhould our inquiry be
the more diligent, becauſe he, that erres in the entrance, is not ſo eaſily reduced again into the right
way, he, that miſſeth his road from the beginning of his journey, and is
deceived in his firſt marks, at his firſt ſeting forth, the greater his miſtake
is, the more difficult will be his entrance into the right way.

Thus when a man firſt propoſeth to himſelf the knowledg of God,
from a ſenſe of his own unworthyneſs, and from the great wearyneſs of
his mind, occaſioned by the ſecret checks of his Conſcience, and the tender,

A

der, yet real, glances of Gods *Light* upon his heart, the earneſt deſires he has to be redeemed from his preſent trouble, and the fervent breathings he has to be eaſed of his diſordered paſſions and luſts, and to find quiet-neſs and peace in the certain knowledg of God, and in the aſſurance of his love and good-will towards him, makes his heart tender, and ready to receive any impreſſion, and ſo (not having then a diſtinĉt diſcerning) through forwardneſs embraceth any thing, that brings preſent eaſe. If, either through the reverence he bears to certain perſons, or from the ſe-cret inclination to what doth comply with his natural diſpoſition, he fall upon any principles or meanes, by which he apprehends he may come to know God, and ſo doth center himſelf, it will be hard to remove him thence again, how wrong ſoever they may be. For the firſt anguiſh being over, he becomes more hardy, and the enemy, being near, creats a falſe peace, and a certain confidence, which is ſtrengthened by the mind's un-willingneſs, to enter again into new doubtfulneſs, or the former anxiety of a ſearch.

This is ſufficiently verified in the example of the *Phariſees* and *Jewiſh Doĉtors*, who moſt of all reſiſted Chriſt, diſdaining to be eſteemed igno-rant, for this vain opinion, they had of their knowledg, hindered them, from the true knowledg, and the mean people, who were not ſo much preoccupyed with former principles, nor conceited of their own know-ledg, did eaſily believe. Wherefore the *Phariſees* upbraid them, ſaying, *Have any of the Rulers or Phariſees believed in him? But this people, which know not the Law, are accurſed.* This is alſo abundantly proved by the experi-ence of all ſuch, as being ſecretly touched with the call of God's Grace unto them, do apply themſelves unto falſe teachers, where the remedy provs worſe, than the diſeaſe, becauſe, in ſtead of knowing God, or the things relateing to their Salvation aright, they drink-in wrong opinions of him, from which it's harder to be diſ-intangled, than while the Soul remains a blank, or *tabula raſa.* For they, that conceit themſelves wiſe, are worſe to deale with, than they, that are ſenſible of their igno-rance. Nor hath it been leſs the device of the devil, the great enemy of mankind, to perſwade men into wrong notions of God, than to keep them altogether from acknowledging him, the latter taking with few, becauſe odious, but the other having been the conſtant ruine of the world; for there hath ſcarce been a Nation found, but hath had ſome no-tions or other of Religion: ſo that not from their denying any Deity, but

from

from their miftakes and mifapprehenfions of it, hath proceeded all the idolatry and fuperftition of the world, yea hence even Atheifm it felf hath proceeded, for thefe many and various opinions of God and Religion, being fo much mixed with the gueffings and uncertain judgments of men, have begotten in many the opinion that there is no God at all. This and much more, that might be faid, may fhew how dangerous it is to mifs in this firft ftep. *All, that come not in by the door, are* accounted *as thieves and robbers.*

Again, how needfull and defireable that knowledg is, which brings Life eternal, *Epictetus* fheweth, faying excellently wel, cap. 38. ἴσϑι ὅτι τὸ Κυριώτατον· *Know that the main foundation of piety, is this, to have* ὀρϑὰς ὑπολήψεις, *right opinions and apprehenfions of God.*

This therefore I judged neceffary as a firft principle, in the firft place, to affirme, and I fuppofe will not need much further explanation nor defence, as being generally acknowledged by all (and in thefe things, that are without controverfy, I love to be brief) as that, which will eafily commend it felf to every man's reafon and Confcience, and therefore I fhall proceed to the next Propofition, which, though it be nothing lefs certain, yet by the malice of Satan and ignorance of many, comes farr more under debate.

The Second Propofition,

Of Immediate Revelation.

Seing *no man knoweth the Father, but the Son, and he, to whom the Son revealeth him,* Matt. 11: 27. *And feing the revelation* of the Son is *in,* and *by* the Spirit, therefore the teftimony of the Spirit, is that alone, by which the true knowledg of God hath been, is, and can be, onely revealed: who, as by the moving of his own Spirit, he difpofed the *chaos* of this world, into that wonderfull order, wherein it was in the beginning, and created man a living Soul to rule and govern it; fo by the revelation of the fame Spirit, he hath manifefted himfelf all along unto the fons of men, both Patriarchs, Prophets,

A 2

and

and Apostles; which revelations of God, by the Spirit, whether by outward voices and appearances, dreams or inward objective manifestations, in the heart, were of old the formal object of their faith, and remaine yet so to be : since *the object of the Saints faith is the same in all ages, though held forth under divers administrations* : Moreover these divine inward revelations, which we make absolutely necessary for the building, up of true faith, neither do, nor can ever, contradict the outward testimony of the Scripturs, or right and sound Reason ; yet from hence it will not follow that the Divine revelations are to be subjected to the Test, either of the outward testimony of the Scripturs, or of the natural reason of man, as to a more, noble, or certain rule and touch-stone ; for this Divine revelation and inward illumination, is that, which is evident, and clear of it selfe, forcing, by its own evidence and clearness, the wel disposed understanding to assent, irresistibly moving the same thereunto, even as the common principles of natural truths do move and incline the mind to a natural assent. As that *the whole is greater than its part.* That *two contradictorys can neither be both true, nor both false.*

§ I. IT is very probable, that many carnal and natural Christians will oppose this Proposition, who, being wholly unacquainted with the movings and actings of God's Spirit upon their hearts, judge the same nothing necessary, and some are apt to flout at it as ridiculous. Yea to that heighth are the generality of all Christians apostatized and degenerated, that, though there be not any thing more plainly asserted, more seriously recommended, nor more certainly attested to, in all the writings of the Holy Scriptures, yet nothing is less minded, and more rejected by all sorts of Christians, than *Immediate and Divine Revelation*, in so much, that once to lay claime to it is matter of reproach. Whereas of old, none were ever judged Christians, but such as *had the Spirit of Christ*, Rom. 8:9. But now many do boldly call them_

selves

felves *Chriftians*, who make no difficulty of confeffing they are without it, and laugh at fuch as fay they have it. Of old they were accounted *the fons of God, who were led by the Spirit of God*, ibid. vers. 14. But now many averre themfelves Sons of God who know nothing of this leader, and he that affirms himfelf fo led, is, by the pretended orthodox of this age, prefently proclaimed a heretick: the reafon hereof is very manifeft, viz, becaufe many, in thefe dayes, under the name of Chriftians do experimentally find that they are not acted, nor led by Gods Spirit, yea many great *Doctors, Divines, Teachers*, and *Biſhops* of Chriftianity (commonly fo called) have wholly fhut their ears from hearing, and their eyes from feeing this *inward Guide*, and fo are become ftrangers unto it; whence they are, by their owne experience, brought to this ftrait, either to confefs that they are as yet ignorant of God, and have only the fhadow of knowledg, and not the true knowledg of him, or that this knowledg is acquired without immediat revelation.

For the better underftanding then of this propofition, we do diftinguiſh betwixt the certain knowledg of God, and the uncertain, betwixt the fpiritual knowledg and the literal, the faving heart-knowledg and foaring, airy head-knowledg. The laft we confefs may be, divers wayes obtained, but the firft by no other way, then the inward immediat manifeftation and revelation of Gods Spirit, ſhining in and upon the heart, inlightning and opening the underftanding.

§ II. Having then propofed to my felf, in thefe propofitions, to affirm thofe things which relate to the true and effectuall knowledg which brings life eternal with it, therefor I have affirmed, and that truely, that this knowledg is no otherways attained, and that none have any true ground to believe they have attained it, who have it not by this revelation of Gods Spirit.

The certainty of which truth is fuch, that it hath been acknowledged by fome of the moft refined and famous of all forts of Profeffors of Chriftianity in all ages; who being truly upright-hearted and earneft feekers of the Lord (however ftated under the difadvantages and epidemical errors of their feveral fects, or ages) the true feed in them, hath been anfwered by Gods love, who hath had regard to the Good, and hath had of his elect ones among all, who, finding a diftaft and difguft in all other outward means, even in the very principles and precepts more particularly relative to their own forms and focietys, have at laft concluded,

A 3　　　　　　　　　　　　cluded,

cluded, with one voyce, that there was no true knowledg of God, but that which is revealed inwardly by his own Spirit ; whereof, take these following testimonys of the Ancients.

Aug. ex Tract. Epist. Joh. 3.

„ 1. *It is the inward Master* (saith *Augustin*) *that teacheth, it is Christ, that teacheth, it is inspiration, that teacheth: where this inspiration and unction is wanting, it is in vain that words from without are beaten in.* And thereafter: *For he, that created us and redeemed us, and called us by faith, and dwelleth in us by his Spirit, unless he speaketh unto you inwardly, it is needless for us to cry out.*

Lib. 1. Strom.

Pædag.

„ 2. *There is a difference* saith (*Clemens Alexandrinus*) *betwixt that, which any one saith of the Truth, and that, which the Truth it self, interpreting it self, saith. A conjectur of Truth differeth from the Truth it self, a similitud of a thing differeth from the thing it self ; it is one thing, that is acquired by exercise and discipline, and another thing, which by power and faith.* Lastly the same *Clemens* saith, *Truth is neither hard to be arrived at, nor is it impossible to apprehend it, for it is most nigh unto us, even in our houses, as the most wise Moses hath insinuated.*

Lib. de veland. virginibus cap. 1.

„ 3. *How is it,* (saith *Tertullian*) *that since the devil always worketh, and stirreth up the mind to iniquity, that the work of God should either cease or desist to act ? Since for this end the Lord did send the Comforter, that, because humane weakness could not at once bear all things, knowledg might be by little and little directed, formed and brought to perfection by the holy Spirit that Vicar of the Lord.* I have many things yet (*saith he*) *to speak unto you, but ye can not as yet bear them, but when that Spirit of Truth shall come, he shall lead you into all Truth, and shall teach you these things, that are to come. But of his work we have spoken above. What is then the administration of the Comforter, but that discipline be derived, and the Scriptures revealed ? &c.*

Epist. Paulin. 103.

„ 4. *The Law* (saith *Hierom*) *is spiritual, and there is need of a revelation to understand it.* And in his epistle 150 to *Hedibia,* question 11. he saith, *the whole epistle to the* Romans *needs an interpretation, it being involved in so great obscuritys, that for the understanding thereof, we need the help of the holy Spirit, who, through the Apostle, dictated it.*

De incarnatione verbi Dei.

„ 5. *So great things* (saith *Athanasius*) *doth our Saviour daily: he draws unto piety, persuades unto vertue, teaches immortality, excites to the desire of heavenly things, reveales knowledg from the Father, inspires power against death, and shewes himself unto every one.*

„ 6. Gre-

,, 6. *Gregory* the Great, upon thefe words [he fhall teach you all   Hom. 30.
,, things] faith, *that unleß the fame Spirit fit upon the heart of the hearer, in*   upon the
,, *vain is the difcourfe of the doctor, let no man then afcribe unto the man, that*   Gofpel.
,, *teacheth, what he underftands from the mouth of him that fpeaketh, for, un-*
,, *leß he, that teacheth, be within, the tongue of the Doctor, that's without, la-*
,, *boureth in vain.*

,, 7. *Cyrillus Alexandrinus* plainly affirmeth, *that men know that* Jefus   In thefau-
,, is the Lord by the holy Ghoft, *no otherwife than they, who taft honey,*   ro lib 13.
,, *know that it is fweet even by its proper quality.*   cap. 3.

,, 8. *Therefore* (faith Bernard) *we daily exhort you, Brethren, by fpeech,*   In Pfal. 84
,, *that ye walk the ways of the heart, and that your Soul be always in your hands;*
,, *that ye may hear what the Lord faith in you.* And again, *upon thefe words of*
,. *the Apoftle,* [Let him, that gloryeth, glory in the Lord.] *with which*
,, *threefold vice* (faith he) *all forts of religious men are leß or more dangeroußy*
,, *affected, becaufe they do not fo diligently attend with the ears of the heart,*
,, *to what the Spirit of Truth* (which flatters none) *inwardly fpeaks.*

This was the very *bafis* and main foundation, upon which the primitive
Reformers walked.

Luther in his book to the nobility of *Germany* faith. ,, *This is certain,*
,, *that no man can make himfelf a doctor of the holy Scripture, but the holy Spirit*
,, *alone.* And upon the *Magnificat* he faith, *No man can rightly underftand*
,, *God, or the Word of God, unleß he immediately receive it from the holy Spirit,*
,, *neither can any one receive it from the Holy Spirit, except he find it by expe-*
,, *rience in himfelf, and, in this experience the Holy Ghoft teacheth, as in his pro-*
,, *per fchool, out of which fchool nothing is taught but meer talk.*

,, *Philip Melanchton* in his Annotations upon the 6 of John: *Who hear*
,, *onely an outward and bodyly voyce, hear the creatur, but* God is a Spirit,
,, *and is neither difcerned nor known, nor heard, but by the Spirit; and there-*
,, *fore to hear the voyce of God, to fee God, is to know and hear the Spirit : by the*
,, *Spirit alone God is known and perceived.*

,, *Which alfo the more ferious to this day do acknowledg, even all fuch, who fa-*
,, *tisfy themfelves not with the fuperfice of Religion, and ufe it not as a cover or*
,, *art. Yea all thefe, who apply themfelves effectually to Chriftianity, and are*
,, *not fatisfied, untill they have found its effectual work upon their hearts, redeem-*
,, *ing them from fin, do feel that no knowledg effectually prevails to the producing*
,, *of this, but that which proceeds from the warm influence of God's Spirit upon*
,, *the heart, and from the comfortable fhinings of his Light upon their underftand-*
ing :

ing: and therefore to this purpose a late modern Author faith wel,
videlicet, Doctor *Smith of Cambridge* in his felect difcourfes : ,, *To feek*
,, *our Divinity meerly in books and writings, is to feek the Living among the dead.*
,, *We do but in vain many times feek God in thefe, where his Truth is too often,*
,, *not fo much enfhrined as entombed.* Intra te quære Deum, *feek God with-*
,, *in thine own Soul, he is beft difcerned* νοερῳ επαφῃ, *as Plotinus phrafeth it, by*
,, *an Intellectual touch of him.* We muft fee with our eyes, and hear with
,, our ears, and our hands *muft* handle the Word of Life, (*to exprefs it in*
,, *S. John's words*) ὅτι τῆς ψυχῆς ἀισθησις, *&c.* The Soul it felf hath its fenfe as
,, *wel as the body.* And therefore David, when he would teach us to
,, know what the Divine goodnefs is, calls not for fpeculation, but
,, fenfation. *Taft and fee how good the Lord is.* That is not the beft and
,, trueft knowledg of God, which is wrought out by the labour and fweat
,, of the brain, but that, which is kindled within us, by an heavenly
,, warmth in our hearts. And again: there is a knowing of the *Truth as*
,, *it is in Jefus*, as it is in a Chrift-like nature, as it is in that fweet, mild,
,, humble and loving Spirit of Jefus, which fpreads it felf, like a *Morning-*
,, *ftar*, upon the fpirits of good men full of Light and Life. It profits
,, little to know Chrift himfelf after the flefh, but he gives his Spirit to
,, good men, *that fearcheth the deep things of God.* And again: it is but
,, thinne, airy knowledg, that is got by mcer fpeculation, which is
,, ufher'd in by Syllogifms and demonftrations, but that, which fprings
,, forth from true goodnefs is διαπερ τι πάσης ὑποδειξεως, as Origen
,, fpeaketh, *it brings fuch a Divine Light to the Soul as is more clear and con-*
,, *vincing, than any demonftration.*

§ III. That this certain and undoubted method of the true knowledg of God hath been brought out of ufe, hath been none of the leaft devices of the devil, to fecure mankind to his kingdome. For after the
light and glory of the Chriftian Religion had prevailed, over a good part
of the world, and difpelled the thick mifts of the heathenifh doctrine,
of the plurality of Gods, he that knew there was no probability of deluding
the world any longer that way, did then puff man up with a falfe
knowledge of the true God, feting him on work to feek God, the
wrong way, and perfwading him to be content with fuch a knowledg
as was of his own acquiring, and not of Gods teaching. And this device
hath proved the more fuccefsfull, becaufe accommodated to the naturall
and corrupt fpirit and temper of man, who, above all things, affects to

exalt

exalt himfelf ; in which felf-exaltation, as God is moft greatly difhonour-
ed , fo therein the devil hath his end ; who is not anxious how much God
be acknowledged in words , provided him felf be but alwayes ferved , he
matters not how great and high fpeculations the natural man entertains of
God, fo long as he ferves his lufts and paffions , and is obedient to his evil
fuggeftions and temptations. Thus Chriftianity is become an art , acquired by humane fcience and induftry , as any other art or fcience is,
and men have not only affumed unto themfelves the name of Chriftians ;
but even have procured to be efteemed as mafters of Chriftianity, by certain artificial tricks , though altogether ftrangers to the Spirit and Life of
Jefus.   But if we fhall make a right definition of a *Chriftian* , according to
the Scriptur , videlicet , that *he is one* , *that hath the Spirit of Chrift* , *and is led
by it.* How many Chriftians, yea and of thefe great Mafters and Doctors
of Chriftianity, fo accounted, fhall we juftly diveft of that noble title ?

If then fuch as have all the other means of knowledg, & are fufficiently
learned therein , whether it be the letter of the Scriptur , the traditions of
Churches , the works of Creation and Providence, whence they are able
to deduce ftrong and undeniable arguments (which may be true in themfelves) are yet not to be efteemed Chriftians , according to the certain
and infallible definition above mentioned ; And, if the inward and immediate revelation of God's Spirit in the heart, in fuch, as have been altogether ignorant of fome , and but very little skilled in others , of thefe
means of attaining knowledg, hath brought them to Salvation : Then it
will neceffarily and evidently follow , that inward and immediate revelation is the onely fure and certain way , to attain the true and faving knowledg of God.

But the Firft is true :

Therefore the laft.

Now as this argument doth very ftrongly conclud , for this way of
knowledg, and againft fuch as deny it, fo herein it is the more confiderable,
becaufe the Propofitions , from which it is deduced, are fo clear , that our
very adverfarys can not deny them.   For, as to the firft, it is acknowledged, that many learned men may be, and have been, damned. And as to
the fecond, who will deny, but many illiterate men may be , & are, faved ?
Nor dare any affirme, that none come to the knowledg of God, and Salvation, by the inward revelation of the Spirit , without thefe other outward
means, unlefs they be alfo fo bold, as to exclud Abel, Seth Noah, Abraham,

Job, and all the holy Patriarchs, from true knowledg and Salvation.

§ IV. I would however not be understood, as if hereby I excluded those other means of knowledg from any use or service to man, it is farr from me so to judge, as in the next Proposition concerning the Scripturs shall more plainly appear. The question is not, what may be profitable or helpfull, but what is absolutely necessary? Many things may contribute to further a work, which yet are not that main thing, that makes the work go on.

The summe then of what is said, amounts to this, that where the true inward knowledg of God is, through the revelation of his Spirit, there is all, neither is there any absolute necessity of any other. But where the best, highest, and most profound knowledg is, without this, there is nothing, as to the obtaining of the great End of Salvation. This Truth is very effectually confirmed, by the first part of the proposition it self, which in few words, comprehendeth divers unquestionable arguments, which I shall in brief subsume.

First, *That there is no knowledg of the Father, but by the Son.*

Secondly, *That there is no knowledg of the Son, but by the Spirit.*

Thirdly, *That by the Spirit, God hath alwayes revealed himself, to his children.*

Fourthly, *That these revelations were the formal object of the Saints faith.*

And Lastly, *That the same continueth to be the object of the Saints faith to this day.*

Of each of these I shall speak a little particularly, and then proceed to the latter part.

§ V. As to the first, viz, *that there is no knowledg of the Father, but by the Son*, it will not need much probation, being founded upon the plain words of Scriptur, and is therefore a fit *medium* to draw the rest of our assertions from.

For the infinite and most wise God, who is the Foundation, Root and Spring of all operation, hath wrought all things, by his Eternal Word and Son. *This is that WORD, that was in the beginning with God, and was God, by whom all things were made, and without whom was not any thing made, that was made.* This is that *Jesus Christ, by whom God created all things, by whom,*

Joh. 1: 1, 2, 3.

Eph. 3: 9.

whom, and for whom, all were created, that are in heaven, and in earth, visible, and invisible, whether they be thrones, or dominions, or principalitys, or powers, Col. 1 : 16. Who therefore is called *the first-born of every creature,* Col. 1 : vers 15. As then, that infinite and incomprehensible Fountain of Life and motion operateth in the creaturs, by his own eternal Word and Power, so no creatur has accefs again unto him, but in and by the Son, according to his own exprefs words, *No man knoweth the Father, but the Son, and he, to whom the Son will reveal him,* Matth 11 : 27. Luk 10 : 22. And again he himfelf faith, *I am the Way, the Truth, and the Life : no man cometh unto the Father, but by me,* Joh. 14.: 6.

Hence he is fitly called *the Mediator betwixt God and man :* For having been with God from all eternity, being himfelf God, and alfo in time partaking of the natur of man, through him, is the goodnefs and love of God conveighed to mankind, and by him again man receiveth and partaketh of thefe mercys.

Hence is eafily deduced the probation of this firft affertion, thus :

If no man know the Father, but the Son, and he, to whom the Son will reveal him, then there is no knowledg of the Father, but by the Son :

But no man knoweth the Father, but the Son :

Therefore there is no knowledg of the Father, but by the Son.

The firft part of the antecedent are the plain words of Scriptur. The confequence thereof is undenyable, except one would fay, that he hath the knowledg of the Father, while yet he knows him not : which were an abfurd repugnance.

Again : If the Son be the Way, the Truth, and the Life, and that no man cometh unto the Father, but by him, then there is no knowledg of the Father, but by the Son :

But the Firft is true :

Therefore the laft.

The antecedent are the very Scriptur words. The confequence is very evident. For how can any know a thing, who ufeth not the way, without which it is not knowable ? But it is already proved, that there is no other way, but by the Son, fo that whofo ufes not that way, can not know him, neither come unto him.

§ VI. Having then laid down this firft Principle, I come to the fecond, viz, *that there is no knowledg of the Son, but by the Spirit, or that the revelation of the Son of God, is by the Spirit.*

B 2

Where

Where it is to be noted, that I always speak of the saving, certain, and neceſſary knowledg of God, which that it can not be acquired other-ways than by the Spirit, doth alſo appear from many clear Scripturs. For Jeſus Chriſt, in and by whom the Father is revealed, doth alſo reveal himſelf to his Diſciples and Friends, in and by his Spirit, as his mani-feſtation was ſometimes outward, when he teſtifyed and witneſſed for the Truth, in this world, and approved himſelf faithfull throughout. So be-ing now withdrawn, as to the outward man, he doth teach and inſtruct mankind inwardly, by his own Spirit, *he ſtandeth at the door, and knocketh, and whoſo heareth his voyce, and openeth, he comes in* to ſuch, Rev. 3 : 20. Of this revelation of Chriſt in him, Paul ſpeaketh, Gal. 1 : 16. in which he placeth the excellency of his miniſtry, and the certainty of his calling. And the promiſe of Chriſt to his Diſciples, *lo, I am with you to the end of the world,* confirmeth this ſame thing, for this is an inward preſence, and ſpiritual, as all acknowledg. But what relates hereto will again occurr. I ſhall deduce the proof of this Propoſition from two manifeſt places of Scriptur. The firſt is, 1 Cor. 2, 11 : 12. *What man knoweth the things of a man, ſave the ſpirit of a man, which is in him? Even ſo the things of God knoweth no man, but the Spirit of God. Now we have received not the ſpirit of the world, but the Spirit, which is of God, that we might know the things, which are freely given us of God.* The Apoſtle, in the verſes before, ſpeaking of the won-derfull things, which are prepared for the Saints, after he hath declared, that the natural man can not reach them, adds, that *they are revealed by the Spirit of God,* vers 9, 10. giving this reaſon, *for the Spirit ſearcheth all things, even the deep things of God.* And then he bringeth in the compariſon, in the verſes above mentioned, very apt, and anſwerable to our purpoſe and doctrin, that *as the things of a man are onely known by the Spirit of man, ſo the things of God are onely known by the Spirit of God:* that is, that as nothing below the ſpirit of man (as the ſpirit of bruts, or any other creaturs) can properly reach unto, nor comprehend the things of a man, as being of a more noble and higher nature, ſo neither can the ſpirit of man or the na-tural man, as the Apoſtle, in the 14 vers, ſubſumes, receive, nor diſcern the things of God, or the things, that are ſpiritual, as being alſo of a higher nature, which the Apoſtle himſelf gives for the reaſon, ſaying, *neither can he know them, becauſe they are ſpiritually diſcerned.* So that, the Apoſtl's words being reduced to an argument, do very wel prove the matter under debate, thus:

If

If that, which appertaineth properly to man, can not be difcerned by any lower or bafer principle, than the fpirit of man, then can not thefe things, that properly relate unto God and Chrift, be known or difcerned by any lower or bafer thing, than the Spirit of God and Chrift :

But the Firft is true *:*

Therefore alfo the Second.

The whole ftrength of the argument is contained in the Apoftl's words before mentioned, which therefore being granted, I fhall proceed to deduce a fecond argument, thus *:*

That, which is fpiritual, can onely be known and difcerned by the Spirit of God :

But the revelation of Jefus Chrift, and the true and faving knowledg of him, is Spiritual :

Therefore the revelation of Jefus Chrift, and the true and faving knowledg of him, can onely be known and difcerned by the Spirit of God.

The other Scriptur is alfo a faying of the fame Apoftle, 1 Cor. 12 : 3. *No man can fay, that Jefus is the Lord, but by the Holy Ghoft.* The Scriptur, which is full of Truth, and anfwereth full wel to the inlightened underftanding of the Spiritual and real Chriftian, may perhaps prove very ftrange to the carnal and pretended follower of Chrift, by whom perhaps it hath not been fo diligently remarked. Here the Apoftle doth fo much require the holy Spirit in the things, that relate to a Chriftian, that he pofitively averres, we can not fo much as affirme *Jefus to be the Lord without it*, which infinuats no lefs, than that the Spiritual Truths of the Gofpel are as lyes in the mouths of carnal and unfpiritual men, for though, in themfelves, they be true, yet are they not true, as to them, becaufe not known, nor uttered forth, in and by that principle and Spirit, that ought to direct the mind, and actuat it, in fuch things, they are no better than the counterfeit reprefentations of things in a comedy, neither can it be more truely and properly called a real and true knowledg of God and Chrift, than the actings of *Alexander* the Great and *Julius Cæfar*, &c. if now tranfacted upon a ftage, might be called truely and really their doings, or the perfons reprefenting them might be faid truely and really to have conquered *Afia*, and overcome *Pompey*, &c.

This knowledg then of Chrift, which is not by the revelation of his own Spirit in the heart, is no more properly the knowledg of Chrift, than the pratling of a parret, which has been taught a few words, may be

said

said to be the voyce of a man: for as that, or some other bird, may be taught to sound and utter forth a rational sentence, as it hath learned it by the outward ear, and not from any living principle of Reason actuating it. So just such is that knowledg of the things of God, which the natural and carnal man hath gathered from the words or writings of Spiritual men, which are not true to him, because conceived in the natural spirit, and so brought forth by the wrong organ, and not proceeding from the Spiritual Principle, no more than the words of a man, acquired by art and brought forth by the mouth of a bird, not proceeding from a rational principle, are true, with respect to the bird, that utters them. Wherefore from this Scriptur I shall further add this argument.

If no man can say Jesus is the Lord, but by the Holy Ghost, then no man can know Jesus to be the Lord, but by the Holy Ghost:

But the First is true:

Therefore the second.

From this argument there may be another deduced, concluding in the very terms of this assertion: thus,

If no man can know Jesus to be the Lord, but by the Holy Ghost, then can there be no certain knowledg or revelation of him, but by the Spirit:

But the first is true:

Therefore the second.

§ VII. The third thing affirmed is, *That, by the Spirit, God always revealed himself to his children.*

For the making appear of the truth of this assertion, it will be but needfull, to consider God's manifesting himself towards, and in relation to his creaturs, from the beginning, which resolves it self alwayes herein. The First step of all is ascribed hereunto by Moses, Gen. 1: 2. *And the Spirit of God moved upon the face of the waters.* I think it wil not be denyed that God's converse with man, all along from Adam to Moses, was by the immediate manifestation of his Spirit. And afterwards through the whole tract of the Law, he spake to his children no otherwayes: which, as it naturally followeth from the principles above proved, so it cannot be denyed, by such as acknowledg the Scripturs of Truth to have been written by the inspiration of the holy Ghost. For these writings, from Moses to Malachy, do declare that during all that time, God revealed himself to his children, by his Spirit.

But if any will object, *that after the dispensation of the Law God's method of speaking was altered.*   I An-

I Anſwer firſt, that God ſpake alwayes immediatly to the Jewes, in that he ſpake alwayes immediatly to the High-prieſt, from betwixt the Cherubins; who, when he entred into the Holy of Holys, returning, did relate to the whole people the voice and will of God, there immediatly revealed. So that this immediat ſpeaking never ceaſed in any age.

Secondly from this immediate fellowſhip were none ſhut out, who earneſtly ſought after and waited for it : in that many, beſides the High-Prieſt, who were not ſo much as of the kindred of Levi, nor of the Prophets, did receive it and ſpeak from it, as it is written. Num. 11: 25. Where the *Spirit* is ſaid to have *reſted upon* the *ſeventy elders*, which Spirit alſo reached, unto two, that were not in the tabernacle, but in the campe, whom when ſome would have forbidden, Moſes would not, but rejoiced, *wiſhing all the Lord's people were Prophets, and that he would put his Spirit upon them*, vers 29.

This is alſo confirmed Nch. 9. Where the elders of the people, after their return from captivity, when they began to ſanctify themſelves by faſting and prayer, in which, numbring up the many mercys of God towards their Fathers, they ſay, vers 20. *Thou gaveſt alſo thy Good Spirit to inſtruct them*, and vers 30. *Yet many years didſt thou forbear and teſtify againſt them by thy Spirit in thy Prophets.* Many are the ſayings of Spiritual David, to this purpoſe, as Pſal. 51 : 13. *Take not thy Holy Spirit from me, uphold me with thy free Spirit.* Pſal. 139 : 7. *Whither ſhall I go from thy Spirit ?* Hereunto doth the Prophet Iſaiah aſcribe the credit of his teſtimony, ſaying, chap. 48. v. 16. *And now the Lord God and his Spirit hath ſent me.* And that God revealed himſelf to his children under the New Teſtament, to wit, to the Apoſtles, Evangeliſts, and primitive Diſciples, is confeſſed by all. How farr now this yet continueth, and is to be expected comes hereafter to be ſpoken to.

§. VIII. The fourth thing affirmed, is, that *theſe revelations were the object of the Saints faith of old.*

This will eaſily appear by the definition of *Faith*, and conſidering what its object is. For which we ſhall not dive into the curious and various notions of the ſchool-men, but ſtay in the plain and poſitive words of the Apoſtle Paul, who, Hebr. 11. deſcribes it two wayes. Faith (ſaith he) *is the ſubſtance of things hoped for, and the evidence of things not ſeen*: which, as the Apoſtle illuſtrateth it, in the ſame chapter, by many examples, is, no other but a firm and certain belief of the mind, wherby it reſteth,

resteth, and in a sense possesseth the substance of some things hoped for, through its confidence in the promise of God. And thus the Soule hath a most firm evidence, by its faith, of things not yet seen nor come to pass. The object of this faith, is *the promise, word, or testimony of God* speaking to the mind. Hence it hath been generally affirmed, that the object of faith is *Deus loquens,* &c. That is, *God speaking* &c. which is also manifest from all these examples deduced by the Apostle throughout that whole chapter, whose faith was founded neither upon any outward testimony, nor upon the voyce or writing of man, but upon the revelation of God's will, manifest unto them, and in them; As in the example of Noah, vers 7. thus, *By faith Noah being warned of God, of things not seen, as yet moved with fear, prepared an Ark, to the saving of his house; by the which he condemned the world, and became heir of the righteousness, which is by faith.* What was here the object of Noahs faith, but God speaking unto him? He had not the writings nor prophecyings of any going before, nor yet the concurrence of any church, or people, to strengthen him; and yet, his faith, in the Word, by which he contradicted the whole world, saved him, and his house. Of which also Abraham is set forth, as a singular example, being therefore called the Father of the faithfull, who is said *against hope to have believed in hope* : In that he not only willingly forsook his father's countrey, not knowing whither he went : In that he believed concerning the coming of Isaak, though contrary to natural probability: But above all, In that he refused not to offer him up, not doubting but God was able to raise him from the dead : of whom it is said that *in Isaak shal thy seed be called.* And last of all, In that he rested in the promise that his seed should possess the land, wherein himself was but a pilgrim, and which, to them, was not to be fulfilled, while divers ages after. The object of Abraham's faith, in all this, was no other but inward and immediate revelation, or God signifying his will unto him inwardly, and immediatly, by his Spirit.

But because, in this part of the proposition, we made also mention of external voyces, appearances, and dreams in the alternative, I think also fit to speak hereof what, in that respect, may be objected, to wit,

Obj. That those, who found their faith now upon immediate and objective revelation, ought to have also outward voyces or visions, dreams, or appearances for it.

It is not denyed but God made use of the ministry of Angels, who,

in

in the appearance of men, fpake outwardly to the Saints of old, and that he did alfo reveal fome things to them, in dreams and vifions, none of which we will affirme to be ceafed, fo as to limit the power and liberty of God, in manifefting himfelf towards his children. But while we are confidering the object of faith, we muft not ftick to that, which is but circumftantially and accidentally fo, but to that, which is univerfally and fubftantially fo.

Next again, we muft diftinguifh betwixt that, which, in it felf, is fubject to doubt and delufion, and therefore is received for, and becaufe of another; and that, which is not fubject to any doubt, but is received fimply for, and becaufe of it felf, as being *prima veritas* the *very firft* and *original* Truth. Let us then confider how, or how farr thefe outward voyces, appearances, and dreams, were the object of the Saints faith? was it becaufe they were fimply voyces, appearances, or dreams? nay certainly; we know, and they were not ignorant, that the devil can form a found of words, and conveigh it to the outward ear. That he can eafily deceive the outward fenfes, by making things to appear that are not. Yea, do we not fee by daily experience, that the juglars and mountebanks can doe as much as all that, by their legerdemaine? God forbid then, that the Saints faith fhould be founded upon fo fallacious a foundation, as man's outward and fallible fenfes. What made them then give credit to thefe vifions? certainly nothing elfe, but the fecret teftimony of Gods Spirit in their hearts, affuring them, that the voyces, dreams and vifions were of and from God. Abraham believed the angels, but who told him that thefe men were Angels? we muft not think his faith then was built upon his outward fenfes, but proceeded from the fecret perfwafion of Gods Spirit, in his heart. This then muft needs be acknowledged to be originally and principally the object of the Saints faith, without which there is no true and certain faith, and by which many times faith is begotten and ftrengthened, without any of thefe outward or vifible helps. As we may obferve in many paffages of the Holy Scripture, where it is only mentioned, and *God faid*, &c. And *the word of the Lord came* unto fuch and fuch, faying, &c.

But if any one fhould pertinacioufly affirm, that *this did import an outward audible voyce to the carnal ear,*

I would gladly know, what other argument fuch a one could bring, for this his affirmation, faving his own fimple conjecture. It is faid

C

indeed *the Spirit witneßeth with our Spirit* ; but not to our outward ears , Rom. 8: 16. and feing the Spirit of God is within us , and not without us , it fpeaks to our Spiritual, and not to our bodyly ear.   .Therefore I fee no reafon where it's fo often faid in Scriptur , *the Spirit faid , moved , hindered , called* fuch or fuch a one , *to doe,* or *forbear* fuch or fuch a thing , that any have to conclud , that this was not an inward voyce, to the ear of the Soul , rather than an outward voyce to the bodyly ear.   If any be otherwife minded , let them , if they can , produce their arguments , and we may further confider of them.   From all then , which is above declared, I fhall deduce an argument , to conclud the probation of this affertion , thus ,

That , which any one firmly believes , as the ground and foundation of his hope in God , and life eternal , is the formal objeſt of his faith :

But the inward and immediate revelation of God's Spirit , fpeaking in and unto the Saints , was by them believed , as the ground and foundation of their hope in God , and life eternal :

Therefore thefe inward and immediate revelations were the formal objeſt of their faith.

§ IX. That , which now cometh under debate , is , what we have afferted in the laft place , to wit , *That the fame continueth to be the objeſt of the Saints faith unto this day.*   Many will agree to what we faid before , who differ from us herein.

There is neverthelefs a very firm argument confirming the truth of this affertion , included in the Propofition it felf , to wit , *That the objeſt of the Saints faith , is the fame in all ages , though held forth under divers adminiftrations.*   Which I fhall reduce to an argument , and prove , thus ,

Firft : *Where the Faith is one , the objeſt of the Faith is one :*

But the Faith is one :

Therefore , &c.

That the Faith is one , is the exprefs words of the Apoftle , Eph. 4 : 5. who placeth the *one Faith* with *the one God* , importing no lefs than that to affirme *two faiths* is as abfurd , as to affirme *two Gods.*

Moreover , If the Faith of the Ancients were one and the fame with ours , i. e. agreeing , in fubftance , therewith , and receiving the fame definition , it had been impertinent for the Apoftle , Heb. 11. to have illuftrated the definition of our faith, by the examples of that of the Ancients ,

ents, or to go about to move us by the example of Abraham, if Abraham's faith were different in natur from ours. Nor doth hence any difference arise, because they believed in Christ, with respect to his appearance outwardly, as future, and we, as already appeared, For nor did they then, so believe in him to come, as not to feel him present with them, and witness him near, seing the Apostle faith *they all drank of that spiritual Rock, which followed them, which Rock was Christ*: Nor do we so believe concerning his appearance past, as not also to feel and know him *present with us*, and to *feed upon him; except Christ* (faith the Apostle) *be in you, ye are reprobats*, so that both our faith is one, terminating in one and the same thing. And as to the other part or consequence of the antecedent, to wit, that *the object is one, where the faith is one*, the Apostle also proveth it, in the forecited chapter, where he makes all the Worthys of old, examples to us. Now wherein are they imitable, but because they believed in God? and what was the object of their faith, but inward and immediate revelation, as we have before proved? Their example can be no ways applicable to us, except we believe in God, as they did, that is, by the same object. The Apostle clears this yet further by his own example, Gal. 1 : 16. where he faith, *so soon as Christ was revealed in him, he consulted not with flesh and blood, but forthwith believed and obeyed*. The same Apostle Heb. 13 : ver. 7, 8. where he exhorteth the Hebrewes to follow the faith of the Elders, adds this reason, *considering the end of their conversation, Jesus Christ the same to day, yesterday and for ever:* hereby notably insinuating that in the object there is no alteration.

If any now object *the diversity of administration.*

I answer, that altereth not at all the *object*, for the same Apostle mentioneth this diversity three times, 1 Cor. 12 : 4, 5, 6. centreth always in The same object, The same Spirit, The same Lord, The same God.

But further: If the object of Faith were not one and the same, both to us and to them, then it would follow, that we were to know God some other way, than by the Spirit:

But this were absurd:

Therefore, &c.

Lastly, this is most firmly proved from a common and received maxime of the school-men, to wit, *Omnis actus specificatur ab objecto*, every act is specified from its object, from which, (if it be true) as they acknowledg (though, for the sake of many, I shall not recurr to this argument,

as

as being too nice and scholastick. Neither lay I much stress upon those kind of things, as being that, which commends not the simplicity of the Gospel.) *If the object were different, then the faith would be different also.*

Such as deny this Proposition now adays, use here a distinction, granting, that *God is to be known by his Spirit,* but again denying, that *it is immediate or inward, but in and by the Scriptures, in which the mind of the Spirit* (as they say) *being fully and amply expressed, we are thereby to know God, and be led in all things.*

As to the negative of this assertion, that the Scriptures are not sufficient, neither were ever appointed to be the adequate and onely rule, nor yet can guide or direct a Christian in all those things, that are needfull for him to know, we shall leave that to the next Proposition to be examined. What is proper in this place to be proved, is, that *Christians now are to be led inwardly, and immediately by the Spirit of God,* even in the same manner, though it befall not to many to be led in the same measur, as the Saints were of old.

§ X. I shall prove this by divers arguments, and first from the promise of Christ, in these words, Joh. 14: 16. *and I will pray the Father, and he will give you another Comforter, that he may abide with you for ever:* 17. *Even the Spirit of Truth, whom the world can not receive, because it seeth him not, neither knoweth him, but ye know him, for he dwelleth with you, and shall be in you.* Again vers 26. *But the Comforter, which is the holy Ghost, whom the Father will send in my Name, he shall teach you all things, and bring all things to your remembrance.* and 16: 13. *But when that Spirit of Truth shall come, he shall lead you into all Truth, for he shall not speak of himself, but whatsoever he shall hear, he shall speak, and shall declare unto you things to come.* We have here first, who this is, and that is divers ways expressed: to wit, *the Comforter, the Spirit of Truth, the Holy Ghost, the sent of the Father in the Name of Christ.* And hereby is sufficiently proved the sottishness of those Socinians, and other carnal Christians, who neither know nor acknowledg any internal Spirit, or Power, but that, which is meerly natural, by which, they sufficiently declare themselves to be of the world, who can not receive the Spirit, because they neither see him, nor know him. Secondly, where this Spirit is to be. *He dwelleth with you, and shall be in you.* And thirdly, what his work is, *he shall teach you all things, and bring all things to your remembrance, and guide you into all Truth,* ὁδηγήσει ὑμᾶς εἰς πᾶσαν τὴν ἀλήθειαν.

As to the first, most do acknowledg, that there is nothing else understood,

ftood, than what the plain words fignify. Which is alfo evident, by many other places of Scriptur, that will hereafter occurr: neither do I fee, how fuch, as affirme otherways, can avoid blafphemy. For, if the *Comforter*, the *Holy Ghoft*, and *Spirit of Truth* be all one with the Scriptures, then it would follow, that the Scriptures is God, feing it is true, that the Holy Ghoft is God. If thefe mens reafoning might take place, where-ever *the Spirit* is mentioned in relation to the Saints, thereby might be truely and properly underftood *the Scripturs*. Which what a non-fenfical monfter it would make of the Chriftian Religion, will eafily appear to all men. As where it is faid, *a manifeftation of the Spirit is given to every man to profit withall*, it might be rendred thus, a manifeftation of the *Scripturs* is given to every man to profit withall. What notable fenfe this would make, & what a curious interpretation, let us confider by the fequel of the fame chapter, 1 Cor. 12: 9, 10, 11. *to another the gifts of healing by the fame Spirit, to another the working of miracles, &c. but all thefe worketh that one and the felf fame Spirit, dividing to every man feverally, as he will.* What would now thefe great mafters of Reafon, the Socinians, judg, if we fhould place the *Scripturs* here in ftead of the *Spirit?* would it anfwer their reafon, which is the great guide of their faith? would it be good and found reafou, in their Logical fchools, to affirme that the Scripture divideth feverally, as it will, and giveth to fome the gift of healing, to others the work-ing of miracles? If then this Spirit, a manifeftation whereof is given to every man, to profit withall, be no other, than *that Spirit of Truth*, before mentioned, *which guideth into all Truth*, this Spirit of Truth can not be the Scripturs. I could inferr an hundred more abfurditys of this kind, upon this fottifh opinion, but what is faid may fuffice. For even fome of themfelves being at times forgetfull, or afhamed of their own doctrin, do acknowledg, that the Spirit of God is another thing, and diftinct from the Scripturs, to guide and influence the Saints.

Secondly, that this Spirit is inward, in my opinion, needs no interpre-tation, nor commentary. *He dwelleth with you, and fhall be in you.* This in-dwelling of the Spirit in the Saints, as it is a thing moft needfull to be known, and believed fo is it as pofitively afferted in the Scriptur, as any thing elfe can be. *If fo be the Spirit of God dwell in you*, faith the Apoftle to the Romans 8: 9. and again: *Know ye not, that ye are the temple of the Holy Ghoft, and that the Spirit of God dwelleth in you.* 1 Cor. 6: 19. without this the Apoftle reckoneth no man a Chriftian. *If any man (faith he) have not the*

C 3

Spirit

Spirit of Chrift, *he is none of his*. Thefe words immediately follow thofe a-
bove mentioned out of the Epiftle to the Romans, *but ye are not in the flefh,*
if fo be the Spirit of God dwell in you. The context of which fheweth that the
Apoftle reckoneth it the main token of a Chriftian both pofitively and
negatively.　For in the former verfes he fheweth how the *carnal mind is*
enmity againft God, and that fuch, as are in the flefh can not pleafe him.
Where, fubfuming, he adds, concerning the Romans, that they *are not*
in the flefh, if the Spirit of God dwell in them.　What is this, but to affirme, that they, in whom the Spirit dwells, are no longer in the flefh,
nor of thofe, who pleafe not God, but are become Chriftians indeed?
Again, in the next verfe, he concluds negatively, that *if any man have not*
the Spirit of Chrift, *he is none of his*, that is, he is no Chriftian.　He then,
that acknowledges himfelf ignorant, and a ftranger to the inward in-being
of the Spirit of Chrift, in his heart, doth thereby acknowledg himfelf to
be yet in the carnal mind, which is enmity to God; to be yet in the flefh,
where God can not be pleafed: and in fhort (whatever he may other-
ways know or believe of Chrift, or however much skilled, or acquainted
with the letter of the Holy Scriptur, not yet to be) notwithftanding all
that, attained to the leaft defire of a Chriftian, yea not once to have embraced the Chriftian Religion.　For take but away the Spirit, ard Chriftianity remains no more Chriftianity, than the dead carcafe of a man,
when the Soul and Spirit is departed, remains a man; which the living
can no more abide, but do bury out of their fight, as a noyfome and ufelefs thing, however acceptable it hath been, when actuated and moved
by the Soul.　Laftly, *whatfoever is excellent*, *whatfoever is noble*, *whatfo-*
ever is worthy, *whatfoever is defireable* in the Chriftian faith, is afcribed to
this *Spirit*, without which it could no more fubfift, than the outward
world without the Sun.　Hereunto have all true Chriftians in all ages
attributed their ftrength and Life.　It is by this Spirit that they avouch
themfelves to have been converted to God, to have been redeemed from
the world, to have been ftrengthened in their weaknefs, comforted in
their afflictions, confirmed in their temptations, imboldened in their
fufferings, and triumphed in the midft of all their perfecutions. Yea the
writings of all true Chriftians, are full of the great and notable things,
which they all affirme themfelves to have done by the Power and Vertue
and efficacy of the Spirit of God working in them.　*It is the Spirit, that*
quickeneth, Joh. 6 : 63.　It was the *Spirit*, that *gave them utterance*, Act.

c. 2 : 4. It was the *Spirit*, by which *Stephen ſpake*, *that the Jewes were not able to reſiſt*, Act. 6 : 10. It is ſuch as *walk after the Spirit*, *that receive no condemnation*, Rom. 8 : 1. It is *the Law of the Spirit*, *that makes free*, ver. 2. It is by the *Spirit of God dwelling* in us, that we are *redeemed from the fleſh and from the carnal mind*, v. 9 . It is the *Spirit of Chriſt* dwelling in us, that *quickeneth* our mortal bodys, v. 11. It is through this *Spirit*, that the deeds of the body are *mortified*, and Life obtained, ver. 13. It is by this *Spirit*, that we are *adopted*, and *cry ABBA*, *Father*, v. 15. It is this *Spirit*, that *beareth witneſs with our ſpirits*, *that we are the children of God*, v. 16. It is this *Spirit*, that *helpeth our infirmitys*, and *maketh interceſſion for us, with groanings, which can not be uttered*, 26. It is by this *Spirit*, that the glorious things, which God hath laid up for us, which *neither outward ear hath heard*, *nor outward eye hath ſeen*, *nor the heart of man conceived by all his reaſonings*, are revealed unto us, 1 Cor. 2 : 9, 10. It is by this *Spirit*, that both *wiſdom* and *knowledg*, and *faith* and *miracles*, and *tongues* and *prophecys* are obtained, 1 Cor. 12 : 8, 9, 10. It is by this *Spirit*, that we are *all baptized into one body*, v. 13. In ſhort, what thing relating to the Salvation of the Soul, and to the Life of a Chriſtian, is rightly performed, or effectually obtained, without it? And what ſhall I more ſay? For the time would fail me, to tell of all thoſe things, which the holy men of old have declared, and the Saints, of this day, do witneſs themſelvs to enjoy, by the vertue and power of this *Spirit dwelling in them.* Truely, my paper could not contain thoſe many teſtimonys, whereby this Truth is confirmed. Wherefore, beſides what is above mentioned out of the Fathers, whom all pretend to reverence, and theſe of *Luther* and *Melancthon*, I ſhall deduce yet one obſervable teſtimony out of *Calvin*, becauſe not a few of the followers of his doctrine do refuſe and deride (and that, as it is to be feared, becauſe of their own non-experience thereof) this way of the Spirit's in-dwelling, as uncertain and dangerous, that ſo, if neither the teſtimony of the Scriptur, nor the ſayings of others, nor right reaſon can move them, they may at leaſt be reproved by the words of their own maſter, who ſaith in the third book of his Inſtitutions, cap. 2. on this wiſe :

,, *But they alledg, it is a bold preſumption for any one to pretend to an undoub-*
,, *ed knowledg of God's will* ; which (ſaith he) I ſhould grant unto them,
,, if we ſhould aſcribe ſo much to our ſelves, as to ſubject the incomprehenſible counſel of God to the raſhneſs of our underſtandings. But
,, while

,, while we simply say, with Paul, that we have received *not* the *spirit of*
,, *this world, but the Spirit, which is of God*, by whose teaching we know
,, those things, that are given us of God. What can they prate against
,, it, without reproaching the Spirit of God? For, if it be a horrible sacri-
,, ledge, to accuse any revelation, coming from him, either of a lye, of
,, uncertainty or ambiguity; in asserting its certainty, wherein do we
,, offend? But they cry out, *that it is not without great temerity, that we*
,, *dare so boast of the Spirit of Christ.* Who would believe that the sottish-
,, ness of these men were so great, who would be esteemed the masters
,, of the world, that they should so fail in the first principles of religion?
,, Verily I could not believe it, if their own writings did not testify so
,, much. Paul accounts those the sons of God, who are acted by the
,, Spirit of God, but these will have the children of God acted by their
,, own spirits, without the Spirit of God. He will have us call God
,, Father, the Spirit dictating that terme unto us, which onely can wit-
,, ness to our spirits, that we are the sons of God. These, though they
,, cease not to call upon God, do neverthelefs demitt the Spirit, by
,, whose guiding he is rightly to be called upon. He denys them to
,, be the sons of God, or the servants of Christ, who are not led by his
,, Spirit, but these feign a Christianity, that needs not the Spirit of
,, Christ. He makes no hope of the blessed resurrection, unless we feel
,, the Spirit residing in us, but these feign a hope without any such a feel-
,, ing. But perhaps they will answer that they deny not but that it is
,, necessary to have it, onely of modesty and humility we ought to deny
,, and not acknowledg it. What means he then, when he commands
,, the Corinthians to try themselves if they be in the faith, to examine
,, themselves, whether they have Christ, whom whosoever acknow-
,, ledges not dwelling in him, is a reprobate. By the *Spirit, which he*
,, *hath given us*, saith John, *we know, that he abideth in us.* And what doe
,, we then else, but call in question Christ his promise, while we would
,, be esteemed the servants of God without his Spirit, which he declared
,, he would pour-out upon all his? Seing these things are the first
,, grounds of piety, it is miserable blindness to accuse Christians of pride,
,, because they dare glory of the presence of the *Spirit*, without which
,, glorying, Christianity it self could not be. But by their example
,, they declare how truely Christ spake, saying, that his Spirit was un-
,, known to the world, and that those onely acknowledg it, with whom
,, it remains. Thus farr *Calvin.*   If

If therefore it be fo, why fhould any be fo foolifh, as to deny, or fo unwife, as not to feek after this Spirit, which Chrift hath promifed fhall dwell in his children?　They then, that do fuppofe the in-dwelling and leading of this Spirit to be ceafed, muft alfo fuppofe Chriftianity to be ceafed, which can not fubfift without it.

Thirdly: *what the work of this Spirit is*, is partly before fhowen, which Chrift comprifeth in two or three things, *He will guide you into all truth, he will teach you all things, and bring all things to your remembrance.* Since Chrift hath provided for us fo good an inftructor, what need we then lean fo much to thofe traditions and commandments of men, wherewith fo many Chriftians have burthened themfelves? What need we fet up our own carnal and corrupt reafon for a guide to us in matters Spiritual, as fome will needs do? May it not be complained of all fuch, as the Lord did of old, concerning Ifraël, by the Prophets, Jer. 2: 13. *For my people have committed two Evils, they have forfaken me, the Fountain of Living waters, and hewed them out cifterns, broken cifterns, that hold no water.* Have not many forfaken, do not many deride and reject, this inward and immediate Guide, this Spirit, that leads into all truth, and caft up to themfelves other wayes, broken wayes indeed, which have not all this while brought them out of the flefh, nor out of the world, nor from under the dominion of their own lufts, and finfull affections, whereby Truth, which is onely rightly learned by this Spirit, is fo much a ftranger in the earth?

From all then that hath been mentioned concerning this promife and thefe words of Chrift, it will follow, that Chriftians are alwayes to be led inwardly and immediately by the Spirit of God dwelling in them; and that the fame is a ftanding and perpetual ordinance, as wel to the Church, in general, in all ages, as to every individual member, in particular, as appears from this argument,

The *promifes* of Chrift to his children are *Yea* and *Amen*, and can not fail, but muft of neceffi y be fulfilled:

But Chrift hath promifed that the *Comforter*, the *Holy Ghoft*, the *Spirit of Truth* fhall abide with his children for ever, fhall dwell with them, fhall be *in* them, fhall lead them into all Truth, fhall teach them all things, fhall bring all things to their remembrance:

Therefore, *&c.*

Again: No man is redeemed from the carnal mind, which is at enmi-

Joh. 16: vers 13.
&
14, 26.

D

ty

ty with God, which is not ſubject to the Law of God, neither can be; No man is yet in the Spirit, but in the fleſh, and can not pleaſe God, except he, in whom the Spirit of God dwells:

But every true Chriſtian is, in meaſur, redeemed from the carnal mind, is gathered out of the enmity, and can be ſubject to the Law of God, is out of the fleſh, and in the Spirit, the Spirit of God dwelling in him:

Therefore every true Chriſtian hath the Spirit of God dwelling in him.

Again: Whoſoever *hath not the Spirit of Chriſt is none of his*, that is, no child, no friend, no Diſciple of Chriſt:

But every true Chriſtian is a child, a friend, a diſciple of Chriſt:

Therefore every true Chriſtian hath the Spirit of Chriſt.

Moreover: Whoſoever is the Temple of the Holy Ghoſt, in him the Spirit of God dwelleth and abideth:

But every true Chriſtian is the Temple of the Holy Ghoſt:

Therefore in every true Chriſtian the Spirit of God dwelleth and abideth.

But to conclude, He in whom the Spirit of God dwelleth, it is not in him a lazy, dumb, uſeleſs thing, but it moveth, actuateth, governeth, inſtructeth, and teacheth him all things whatſoever is needfull for him to know, yea bringeth all things to his remembrance:

But the Spirit of God dwelleth in every true Chriſtian:

Therefore it leadeth, inſtructeth, and teacheth every true Chriſtian whatſoever is needfull for him to know.

§ XI. But there are ſome, that will confeſs, that *the Spirit doth now lead and influence the Saints, but that he doth it onely ſubjectively, or in a blind manner, by inlightening their underſtandings, to underſtand and believe the Truth delivered in the Scriptures. But not at all by preſenting theſe truths to the mind by way of object*, and this they call *medium incognitum aſſentiendi*, as *that of whoſe working a man is not ſenſible.*

This opinion, though ſomewhat more tolerable than the former, is nevertheleſs not altogether according to Truth, neither doth it reach the fulneſs of it.

1. Becauſe there be many truths, which, as they are applicable to particulars, and individuals, and moſt needfull to be known by them, are no wiſe to be found in the Scriptur, as, in the following Propoſition, ſhall be ſhown.   Be-

Besides, the arguments already adduced, do prove, that the Spirit doth not onely *subjectively* help us to discern truths, elsewhere delivered, but also *objectively* present those truths to our minds. For that, which teacheth me all things, and is given me for that end, without doubt presents those things to my mind, which it teacheth me. It is not said, *it shall teach you how to understand those things, that are written*, but *it shall teach you all things*. Again: That, which brings all things to my remembrance, must needs present them by way of *object*, else it were improper, to say, it brought them to my remembrance, but onely, that it helpeth to remember the objects brought from elsewhere.

My second argument shall be drawn from the nature of the New Covenant, by which, and those that follow, I shall prove that we are led by the Spirit both immediately and objectively; the nature of the New Covenant is expressed in divers places, and

First, Isa. 59: 21. *As for me, this is my Covenant with them, saith the Lord, My Spirit, that is upon thee, and my words, which I have put into thy mouth, shall not depart out of thy mouth, nor out of the mouth of thy seed, nor out of the mouth of thy seed's seed, saith the Lord, from henceforth and for ever.* By the latter part of this, is sufficiently expressed the perpetuity and continuance of this promise, *It shall not depart, saith the Lord, from henceforth and for ever.* In the former part is the promise it self, which is, the Spirit of God being upon them, and the words of God being put *into* their mouths.

First, this was *immediate*, for there is no mention made of any *medium*, he saith not, I shall by the means of such and such writings, or books, conveigh such and such words into your mouths, but *my words, I, even I, saith the Lord, shall put into your mouths.*

Secondly, this must be *objectively*, for [the words put into the mouth] are the *object* presented by him. He saith not, the words, which ye shall see written, my Spirit shall onely inlighten your understandings, to assent unto, but positively, *my words, which I have put into thy mouth, &c.* From whence I argue, thus,

Upon whomsoever the Spirit remaineth always, and putteth words into his mouth, him doth the Spirit teach immediately, objectively, and continually:

But the Spirit is alwayes upon the seed of the righteous, and putteth words into their mouths, neither departeth from them:

Therefore the Spirit teacheth the righteous immediately, objectively, and continually.

Se_

Secondly, the natur of the New Covenant is yet more amply expreſſed, Jer. 31 : 33. which is again repeated and reäſſerted by the Apoſtle,
Heb. 8 : 10. in theſe words, *For this is the Covenant, that I will make with
the houſe of Iſraël in thoſe days, ſaith the Lord, I will put my Laws into their
minds, and write them in their hearts, and I will be to them a God, and they ſhall
be to me a people. And they ſhall not teach every man his neighbour, and every
man his brother, ſaying, Know the Lord, for they ſhall all know me, from the
leaſt to the greateſt.*

The *object* here, is *God's Law* placed in the heart, and written in the
mind; From whence they become God's people, and are brought truely
to know him.

. In this then is the *Law* diſtinguiſhed from the *Goſpel:* The *Law* before
was *outward*, written in tables of ſtone; but now it is *inward*, written *in*
the heart.   Of old the people depended upon their Prieſts, for the knowledg of God; but now they have *all* a certain and ſenſible knowledg of
him : concerning which, Auguſtin ſpeaketh wel, in his book *De Literâ
& Spiritu*; from whom Aquinas firſt of all ſeem to have taken occaſion,
to move this queſtion, *Whether the New Law be a written Law, or an implanted Law? Lex ſcripta, vel Lex indita ?* which he thus reſolves, affirming, that *the New Law, or the Goſpel, is not properly a Law written, as the old
was; but Lex indita, an implanted Law;* and that *the Old Law was written
without, but the New Law is written within, on the table of the heart.*

How much then are they deceived, who, in ſtead of making the Goſpel preferable to the Law, have made the condition of ſuch as are under
the Goſpel farr worſe?   For no doubt it is a farr better, and more deſirable thing, to converſe with God immediately, than onely mediately,
as being a higher and more glorious diſpenſation : and yet, theſe men acknowledg, that many, under the Law, had immediate converſe with
God, whereas they now cry, it is ceaſed.

Again, Under the Law there was the Holy of Holys, into which the
High-Prieſt did enter, and received the Word of the Lord immediately,
from betwixt the Cherubins, ſo that the people could then certainly
know the mind of the Lord; but now, according to theſe mens judgment,
we are in a farr worſe condition, having nothing, but the outward letter
of the Scriptur, to gueſs and divine from, concerning one verſe of which
ſcarce two can be found to agree.   But Jeſus Chriſt hath promiſed us
better things, though many are ſo unwiſe, as not to believe him, even

to

to guide us, by his own unerring Spirit, and hath rent and removed the vail, whereby not onely one, and that once a year, may enter, but *all* of us at all times have accefs unto him, as often as we draw near unto him, with pure hearts. He reveals his will to us by his Spirit, and writes his Laws in our hearts. Thefe things then being thus premifed; I argue,

Where the Law of God is put into the mind, and written in the heart, there the objeꞔt of faith, and revelation of the knowledg of God, is inward, immediate, and objeꞔtive:

But the Law of God is put into the mind, and written in the heart of every true Chriftian, under the New Covenent:

Therefore the objeꞔt of faith, and revelation of the knowledg of God to every true Chriftian, is inward, immediate, and objeꞔtive.

The *affumption* is the exprefs words of Scripture. The *Propofition* then muft needs be true, except that, *which is put into the mind, and written in the heart*, were either not *inward*, not *immediate*, or not *objeꞔtive*, which is moft abfurd.

§ XII. The third argument is from thefe words of John, 1 Joh. 2: vers 27. *But the Anoynting, which ye have received of him, abideth in you, and ye need not, that any man teach you, but the fame Anoynting teacheth you of all things, and is Truth, and no lye, and even as it hath taught you, ye fhall abide in him.*

Firft: This could not be any fpecial, peculiar, or extraordinary priviledg, but that, which is common to all the Saints, it being a general Epiftle, direꞔted to all them of that age.

Secondly: The Apoftle propofeth this Anoynting in them, as a more certain touch-ftone for them, to difcern, and try feducers by, even then his own writings: for, having in the former verfe faid, that he had written fome things to them, concerning fuch as feduced them, he begins the next verfe, *But the Anoynting, &c. and ye need not, that any man teach you*, &c. which inferrs, that, having faid to them, what can be faid, he refers them for all to the inward Anoynting, which teacheth all things, as the moft firme, conftant, and certain bulwark, againft all feducers.

And Laftly: That it is a lafting and continuing thing, the Anoynting, which abideth; if it had not been to abide in them, it could not have taught them all things, neither guided them againft all hazard. From which, I argue thus,

He, that hath an Anoynting abiding in him, which teacheth him all

D 3

things,

things, so that he needs no man to teach him, hath an inward and immediate Teacher, and hath some things inwardly and immediately revealed
unto him:

But the Saints have such an Anoynting:

Therefore, *&c.*

I could prove this doctrin, from many more places of Scriptur, which
for brevity's sake I omitt, and now come to the second part of the Proposition, where the objections usually formed against it are answered.

§ XIII. The most usuall, is that *these revelations are uncertain.*

But this bespeaketh much ignorance in the opposers; for we distinguish betwixt the *thesis* and the *hypothesis*, that is, betwixt the *proposition*
and *supposition.* For it is one thing to affirme *that the true and undoubted revelation of God's Spirit is certain and infallible*; and another thing to affirme
that this or that particular person, or people, is led infallibly, by this revelation, in what they speak, or write, because they affirme themselves
to be so led, by the inward and immediate revelation of the Spirit. The
first is onely by us asserted, the latter may be called in question. The
question is not, Who are, or are not so led? but Whether all ought not,
or may not, be so led?

Seing then we have already proved, that Christ hath promised his Spirit to lead his children, and that every one of them both ought, and may
be led by it. If any depart from this certain Guide, in deeds, and yet in
words pretend to be led by it, into things, that are not good, it will not
from thence follow, that the true Guidance of the Spirit is uncertain, or
ought not to be followed, no more, than it will follow that the Sun sheweth not light, because a blind man, or one, who wilfully shuts his eyes,
falls into a ditch, at noon-day, for want of Light: or that no words are
spoken, because a deaf man hears them not: or that a garden full of fra-
grant flowers has no sweet smell, because he, that has lost his smelling,
doth not savour it; the fault then is in the organ, and not in the object.

All these mistakes therefore are to be ascribed to the weaknes or wick-
ednes of men, and not to that Holy Spirit. Such as bend themselves
most against this certain and infallible testimony of the Spirit, use commonly to alledge the example of the old Gnosticks, and the late monstrous and mischievous actings of the Anabaptists of Munster, all which
toucheth us nothing at all, neither weakens a whit our most true doctrine. Wherefore as a most sure bulwark against such kind of assaults,

was

was subjoyned that other part of our Proposition, thus, *Moreover these divine and inward revelations, which we establish, as absolutely necessary, for the founding of the true faith, as they do not, so neither can they at any time, contradict the Scripturs Testimony, or sound reason.*

Besides the intrinsick and undoubted Truth of this assertion, we can boldly affirme it, from our certain and blessed experience. For this Spirit never deceived us, never acted, nor moved us, to any thing, that was amiss, but is clear and manifest in its revelations, which are evidently discerned of us, as we wait in *that pure and undefiled Light of God* (that proper and fit *organ*) in which they are received. Therefore if any reason after this manner,

(*That, because some wicked, ungodly, devilish men have committed wicked actions, and have yet more wickedly asserted, that they were led into these things by the Spirit of God:*

Therefore *no man ought to lean to the Spirit of God, or seek to be led by it.*)

I utterly deny the consequence of this Proposition, which, were it to be received, as true, then would all *faith in God*, and *hope of Salvation* become uncertain, and the Christian Religion be turned into meer *Scepticism.* For, after the same manner, I might reason thus,

Because *Eva* was deceived by *the lying of the Serpent:*

Therefore she ought not to have trusted to the *promise of God.*

Because the old world was deluded by *evil spirits:*

Therefore ought neither *Noah*, nor *Abraham*, nor *Moses*, to have trusted *the Spirit* of the Lord.

Because a lying spirit spake through the four hundred prophets, that persuaded *Achab* to go up and fight at *Ramoth Gilead:*

Therefore the testimony of the *true Spirit in Micajah* was uncertain and dangerous to be followed.

Because there were *seduceing spirits* crept into the Church of old:

Therefore it was not good, or uncertain, to follow *the Anoynting*, which taught all things, and is Truth, and no lye.

Who dare say, that this is a necessary consequence? Moreover, not onely the faith of the Saints, and Church of God of old, is hereby rendered uncertain, but also the faith of all sorts of Christians now, is liable to the like hazard; even of those, who seek a foundation for their faith elsewhere, than from *the Spirit.* For I shall prove by an inevitable argument *ab incommodo*, i. e. from the inconveniency of it, that if the Spirit

b

be not to be followed upon that account, and that men may not depend upon it, as their Guide, becaufe fome, while pretending thereunto, committ great evils; that then nor tradition, nor the Scripturs, nor reafon, which the Papifts, Proteftants, and Socinians, do refpectively make the Rule of their faith, are any whit more certain. The Romanifts reckon it an errour to celebrate *Eafter* any other wayes, than that church doth. This can onely be decided by tradition. And yet the Greek Church, which equally layeth claim to Tradition with her felf, doth it otherwife. Yea fo *little effectual* is *Tradition*, to decide the cafe, that *Polycarpus* the Difciple of John, and *Anicetus* the Bifhop of Rome, who immediately fucceeded them, (according to whofe example both fides concluded the queftion ought to be decided) *could not agree.* Here of neceffity one behoved to err, and that following Tradition. Would the Papifts now judg we dealt fairly by them, if we fhould thence averr, that Tradition is not to be regarded? Befides, in a matter of farr greater importance, the fame difficulty will occurr, to wit, in the primacy of the Bifhop of Rome, for many do affirme, and that by Tradition, that in the firft fix hundred years the Roman Prelats never affumed the title of *Univerfal Shepheard,* nor were acknowledged as fuch. And, as that, which altogether overturneth this prefidency, there are, that alledg, and that from Tradition alfo, that Peter never faw Rome; and that therefore the Bifhop of Rome can not be his fucceffor. Would ye Romanifts think this found reafoning, to fay, as ye do,

Many have been deceived, and erred grievoufly, in trufting to Tradition:

Therefore we ought to reject all traditions, yea even thofe, by which we affirme the contrary, and, as we think, prove the truth?

Laftly, in the Council of Florence the chief Doctors of the Romifh and Greek Churches, did debate, whole feffions long, concerning the interpretation of one fentence of the Council of Ephefus, and of Epiphanius and Bafilius, neither could they ever agree about it.

Secondly, as to the Scriptur, the fame difficulty occurreth: the *Lutherans* affirme they believe confubftantiation, by the Scriptur, which the *Calvinifts* deny, as that, which they fay, according to the fame Scriptur, is a grofs errour. The *Calvinifts* again affirme *abfolute reprobation,* which the *Arminians* deny, affirming the contrary, wherein both affirm

them-

Eufeb.
Hift.
Ecclefi.
lib. 5.
cap. 26.

Conc.
Flor.
Seff. 5.
decreto
quodam
Concl.
Eph.
Act. 6.
Seff. 11.
& 12.
Concil.
Flor.

Seff. 18: 20. Conc. Flor. Sect. 21 p. 480. & feqq.

themfelves to be ruled by the Scriptur, and Reafon, in the matter. Should I argue thus then to the Calvinifts?

Here the *Lutherans* and *Arminians* grosfly err, by following the Scriptur:

Therefore the Scriptur is not a good, nor certain Rule, and *è contrà.*

Would either of them accept of this reafoning as good and found? What fhall I fay of the Epifcopalians, Presbyterians, Independents, and Anabaptifts of great Britain, who are continually buffeting one another with the Scriptur? To whom the fame argument might be alledged, though they do all unanimoufly acknowledg it to be the Rule.

And thirdly, as to Reafon, I fhall not need to fay much, for whence come all the controverfys, contentions, and debates, in the world, but becaufe every man thinks he followes right Reafon? Hence of old came the jangles betwixt the *Stoïcks, Platonifts, Peripatetiks, Pythagorians,* and *Cyniks,* as of late betwixt the *Ariftotelians, Cartefians,* and other Naturalifts: Can it be thence inferred, or will the *Socinians,* thofe great Reafoners, allow us, to conclude, becaufe many, and that very wife men, have erred, by following (as they fuppofed) their Reafon, and that with what dil·gence, care, and induftry they could, to find out the Truth, that therefore no man ought to make ufe of it at all; nor be pofitive in what he knowes certainly to be rational. And thus farr, as to opinion, the fame uncertainty is no lefs incident unto thofe other principles.

§ X I V. But if we come to practices, though I confefs, I do with my whole heart abhorr, and deteft, thofe wild practices, which are written, concerning the Anabaptifts of Munfter, I am bold to fay, as bad, if not worfe, things, have been committed by thofe, that lean to tradition, Scriptur and Reafon, wherein alfo they have averred themfelves to have been authorifed by thefe Rules. I need but mention all the tumults, feditions, and horrible blood-fhed, wherewith Europe hath been afflicted, thefe divers ages, in which Papifts againft Papifts, Calvinifts againft Calvinifts, Lutherans againft Lutherans, and Papifts affifted by Proteftants, againft other Proteftants affifted by Papifts, have miferably fhed one anothers blood, hiring and forceing men to kill one another, who were ignorant of the quarrel, and ftrangers to one another: All, mean while, pretending Reafon, for fo doing, and pleading the lawfulnefs of it, from Scriptur.

For what have the Papifts pretended for their many maffacres, acted

as wel in France , as elfewhere , but *Tradition, Scriptur,* and *Reafon?* Did they not fay, that *Reafon* perfwaded them, *Tradition* allowed them , and *Scriptur* commanded them, to perfecut, deftroy, and burn
hereriks , fuch as denyed this plain Scriptur, *Hoc eft corpus meum , This is
my body?* And are not the Proteftants affenting to this blood-fhed ? who
affert the fame thing , and encourage them , by burning and bannifhing ,
while their brethren are fo treated , for the fame caufe. Are not the
Iflands of great Britain and Ireland (yea and all the Chriftian world) a
lively example hereof, which were divers years together as a theatre of
blood , where many loft their lives , and numbers of familys were utterly deftroyed , and ruined? For all which, no other caufe was principally
given , than the precepts of the Scriptur. If we then compare thefe actings, with thofe of Munfter, we fhall not find great difference ; for both
affirmed and pretended they were called , and that it was lawfull to kill ,
burn , and deftroy the wicked. We muft kill all the wicked , faid thofe
Anabaptifts , that we, that are the Saints, may poffefs the earth. We muft
burn *obftinate hereriks,* fay the Papifts , that the holy *church of Rome* may be
purged of rotten members, and may live in peace We muft cut-off
feduceing Separatifts, fay the Prelatick Proteftants , who trouble the peace
of the *Church,* and refufe the *Divine Hierarchy* and *religious ceremonys* thereof. We muft kill, fay the Calviniftick Presbyterians , the profane ma-
lignants , who accufe the *holy confiftorial* and *presbyterian government,* and
feek to defend the *Popifh* and *Prelatick hierarchy;* as alfo thofe other *Se-
ctarys,* that trouble the peace of our *Church.* What difference, I pray
thee , impartial Reader , feeft thou betwixt thefe?

If it be faid , *The Anabaptifts went without , and againft the authority of the
Magiftrate , fo did not the other.*

I might eafily refute it, by alledging the mutual teftimonys of thefe
Sects againft one another. The behaviour of the Papifts towards Henry
the third and fourth of France. Their defigns upon James the fixth , in
the gun-powder treafon, as alfo their principle of the Popes power to de-
pofe kings , for the caufe of herefy , and to abfolve their fubjects from
their oath , and give them to others : proves it againft them.

And as to the Proteftants , how much their actions differ from thofe
other above mentioned, may be feen by the many confpiracys and tumults , which they have been active in , both in *Scotland* and *England,* and
which they have acted within thefe hundred years in divers towns and

Pro-

Provinces of the Nether-Lands.   Have they not often times fought,
not onely from the Popifh Magiftrats, but even from thofe, that had begun to reform, or that had given them fome liberty of exercifing their
religion, that they might onely be permitted, without trouble or hin-
derance, to excercife their Religion, promifing they would not hinder
or moleft the Papifts, in the exercife of theirs? and yet did they not on
the contrary, fo foon as they had power, trouble and abufe thefe fellow-
citizens, and turn them out of the city, and, which is worfe, even fuch,
who, together with them, had forfaken the Popifh religion?   Did they
not thefe things, in many places, againft the mind of the Magiftrats? Have
they not publickly, with contumelious fpeeches, affaulted their Magiftrats, from whom they had but juft before fought and obtained the free
exercife of their religion? Reprefenting them, fo foon as they oppofed
themfelves to their hierarchy, as if they had regarded neither God nor
Religion? Have they not by violent hands poffeffed themfelves of the
Popifh Churches, fo called, or by force, againft the Magiftrats mind,
taken them away?   Have they not turned out of their office and authority whole councils of Magiftrats, under pretence that they were addicted
to Popery? Which Popifh Magiftrats neverthelefs they did but a little
before ackowledg to be ordained by God, affirming themfelves obliged
to yeeld them obedience and fubjection, not onely for fear, but for
Confcience fake, to whom moreover the very Preachers and Overfeers
of the reformed Church, had willingly fworn fidelity: and yet afterwards have they not faid, that the people is bound to force a wicked
Prince to the obfervation of Goa's Word?   There are many other in-
ftances of this kind to be found in their Hiftories, not to mention many
wrfe things, which we know to have been acted in our time, and which
for brevity's fake I pafs by.

I might fay much of the *Lutherans*, whofe tumultuous actions againft
their Magiftrats, not profeffing the Lutheran profeffion, are teftifyed of
by feveral Hiftorians worthy of credit.   Among others I fhall propofe
onely one example to the Readers confideration, which fell out at *Berline*,
in the year 1615.   ,, Where the feditious multitud of the Lutheran Ci-
,, tizens being ftirred up, by the daily clamours of their Preachers, did
,, not onely violently take up the houfes of the reformed Teachers, over-
,, turn their librarys, and fpoil their furnitur; but alfo with reproachfull
,, words; yea and with ftones, affaulted the Marquefs of *Brandeburgh*
E 2   ,, the

„ the Elector's brother, while he fought by fmooth words to quiet the
„ fury of the multitude: they killed ten of his guard, fcarcely fparing him-
„ felf, who, at laft, by flight, efcaped out of their hands.

All which fufficiently declares, that the concurrence of the Magiftrat
doth not alter their principles, but onely their method of procedure. So
that, for my own part, I fee no difference, betwixt the actings of thofe of
Munfter, and thefe others, whereof the one pretended to be led by the
Spirit, the other by *Tradition*, *Scriptur* and *Reafon*, fave this, that the former were rafh, heady, and foolifh, in their proceedings, and therefore
were the fooner brought to nothing, and fo into contempt and derifion:
but the other, being more politick and wife in their generation, held it
out longer, and fo have authorized their wickednefs more, with feeming
authority of Law and Reafon.   But both their actings being equally
evil, the difference appears to me to be onely like that, which is betwixt
a fimple filly thief, that is eafily catched, and hanged, without any more
ado, and a company of refolute bold robbers, who, being better guarded,
though their offence be nothing lefs, yet by violence, do, to evite the
danger, force their mafters to give them good terms.

From all which then it evidently follows, that they argue very ill, that
defpife and reject any principle, becaufe men, pretending to be led by it,
doe evil, in cafe it be not the natural and confequential tendency of that
principle, to lead unto thofe things, that are evil.

Again: It doth follow from what is above afferted, that, if the Spirit
be to be rejected, upon this account, all thefe other principles ought, on
the fame account, to be rejected. And, for my part, as I have never a whit
the lower efteem of the bleffed teftimony of the Holy Scripturs, nor do
the lefs refpect any folid tradition, that is anfwerable and according to
Truth, neither at all defpife Reafon, that noble and excellent faculty of
the mind; becaufe wicked men have abufed the name of them, to cover
their wickednefs, and deceive the fimple: fo would I not have any reject
or diffide the certainty of that unerring Spirit, which God hath given his
children, as that, which can alone guide them into all Truth, becaufe
fome have falfly pretended to it.

§ XV. And becaufe the Spirit of God is the Fountain of all Truth
and found Reafon, therefore we have wel faid, that *it can not contradict
neither the teftimony of the Scriptur, nor right Reafon*: yet (as the Propofition it
felf concludeth, to whofe laft part I now come) *it will not from thence follow,*
                                                                    that

that these Divine revelations are to be subjected to the examination either of the outward testimony of Scriptur, or of the humane or natural reason of man, as to a more noble and certain rule and touch-stone; for the Divine Revelation and inward Illumination is that, which is evident by it self, forcing the wel-disposed understanding, and irresistibly moving it to assent, by its own evidence and clearneß, even as the common principls of natural truths do bow the mind to a natural assent.

He that denys this part of the proposition, must needs affirme, that the Spirit of God, neither can nor ever hath manifested it self to man, without the Scriptur or a distinct discursion of Reason: or that the efficacy of this Supernaturall Principle, working upon the Souls of men, is less evident, then natural principles in their common operations, both which are false.

For First, through all the Scripturs we may observe, that the manifestation and revelation of God by his Spirit, to the Patriarchs, Prophets, and Apostles, was *immediate* and *objective*, as is above proved, which they did not examin by any other principle but their own evidence and clearnefs.

Secondly, to say, that the Spirit of God has less evidence upon the mind of man, then natural principles have, is to have too mean and low thoughts of it. How comes David to invite us, to *taft and fee that God is good*, if this cannot be felt and tasted? This were enough to overturn the faith and assurance of all the Saints, both now and of old. How came Paul to be perfwaded, that nothing could feperate him from the love of God, but by that evidence and clearnefs, which the Spirit of God gave him? The Apoftle John, who knew wel, wherein the certainty of faith confifted, judged it no wayes abfurd, without further argument; to afcribe his knowledg and affurance, and that of all the Saints, hereunto, in thefe words, *Hereby know we that we dwell in him, and he in us becaufe he hath given us of his Spirit* 1 Joh. 4: 13. and again 5: 6. it's the *Spirit, that beareth witnefs, becaufe the Spirit is Truth.*

Obferve the reafon brought by him, *becaufe the Spirit is Truth.* Of whofe certainty and infallibility I have heretofore fpoken; We then truft to, and confide in this Spirit, becaufe we know, and certainly believe, that it can only lead us a right, and never mis-lead us, and from this certain confidence, it is, that we affirme, that no revelation coming from it, can ever contradict the Scripturs teftimony nor right

Rea-

Reafon: not as making this a more certain rule to our felves, but as condefcending to fuch, who, not difcerning the revelations of the Spirit,
as they proceed purely from God , will try them by thefe *mediums.*
Yet thofe, that have the Spiritual fences, and can favour the things of
the Spirit, as it were, *in primâ inflantiâ*, i. e. at the firft blufh, can difcern them without, or before they apply them either to Scriptur, or Reafon.   Juft as a good Aftronomer can calculate an eclipfe infallibly, by
which he can conclude, if the order of Natur continue, and fome ftrange
and unnatural revolution interveen not, there will be an eclipfe of the
Sun, or Moon, fuch a day, and fuch an hour: yet can he not perfwade an
ignorant ruftick of this, untill he vifibly fee it.   So alfo a Mathematici-
an can infallibly know by the Rules of Art, that the three fides of a right
triangle are equal to two right angles, yea can know them more certainly, than any man by meafur.   And fome geometrical demonftrations are
by all acknowledged to be infallible, which can be fcarcely difcerned or
proved by the Senfes; yet, if a Geometer be at the pains, to certify fome
ignorant man concerning the certainty of his Art, by condefcending to
meafur it, and make it obvious to his fenfes, it will not thence follow,
that that meafuring is fo certain, as the demonftration it felf; or that the
demonftration would be uncertain without it.

§ XVI. But to make an end, I fhall add one argument, to prove,
that this inward, immediate, objective revelation, which we have pleaded for all along, is the onely, fure, certain, and unmoveable foundation
of all Chriftian faith; which argument, when wel weighed, I hope, will
have weight with all forts of Chriftians, and it is this,

That, which all Profeffors of Chriftianity, of whatfoever kind, are
forced ultimately to recurr unto, when preffed to the laft. That for, and
becaufe of which, all other foundations are recommended and accounted
worthy to be believed; and without which they are granted to be of no
weight at all, muft needs be the onely muft true, certain, and unmoveable
foundation of all Chriftian faith:

But inward, immediate, objective revelation, by the Spirit, is that,
which all Profeffors of Chriftianity of whatfoever kind are forced ultimately to recurr unto, &c:

Therefore, &c.

The Propofition is fo evident, that it will not be denyed.   The affumption fhall be proved by parts.

And

And first : as to *Papists*, they place their foundation in the judgment of the *Church* and *Tradition*. If we press them to say, why they believe, as the *Church* doth ? Their answer is, *because the Church is alwayes led by the infallible Spirit.* So here, the *leading of the Spirit* is the utmost foundation. Again : If we ask them, why we ought to trust *Tradition?* They answer, *Because these Traditions were delivered us by the Doctors and Fathers of the Church, which Doctors and Fathers by the revelation of the Holy Ghost commanded the Church to observe them.* Here again all lands in the Revelation of the Spirit.

And for the *Protestants* and *Socinians*, both which acknowledg the Scriptures to be the foundation and rule of their faith ; the one as subjectively influenced by the Spirit of God, to use them; the other, as manageing them with and by their own Reason. Ask both, or either of them, why they trust the *Scriptures*, and take them to be their Rule ? Their answer is, *Because we have, in them, the mind of God delivered unto us, by those, to whom these things were inwardly, immediately, and objectively revealed by the Spirit of God.* And not because this or that man wrote them, but because the *Spirit of God* dictated them.

It is strange then, that men should render that, so uncertain, and dangerous to follow, upon which alone the certain ground and foundation of their own faith is built. Or that they should shut themselves out from that holy fellowship with God, which onely is enjoyed in the Spirit, in which we are commanded, both to walk and live.

If any, reading these things, find themselves moved by the strength of these Scriptur arguments to assent, and believe such revelations necessary, and yet find themselves strangers to them, which, as I observed, in the beginning, is the cause, that this is so much gainsaid and contradicted Let them know, that it is not, because it is ceased to become the priviledg of every Christian, that they do not feel it, but rather because they are not so much Christians by natur, as by name : and let such know, that the secret *Light*, which shines *in the heart*, and reproves unrighteousness is the small beginnings of the revelations of God's Spirit, which was first sent into the world to reprove it of sin, Joh 16 : 8. And as by forsaking iniquity, thou com'st to be acquainted with that heavenly voyce *in* thy heart, thou shalt feel, as the old man, the natural man, that favoureth not the things of God's Kingdom, is put off, with his evil and corrupt affections and lusts, I say, thou shalt feel the New Man, the

Spi-

Spiritual birth, and Babe, raised, which hath its Spiritual Senses, and can see, feel, tast, handle, and smell the things of the Spirit: but till then, the knowledg of things Spiritual is but as an historical faith, but as the description of the Light of the Sun, or of curious colours to a blind man; who, though of the largest capacity, can not so wel understand it, by the most acute and lively description, as a child can by seing them. So neither can the natural man of the largest capacity, by the best words, even Scriptur words, so wel understand the mysterys of God's Kingdom, as the least and weakest child, who tasteth them, by having them revealed inwardly and objectively, by the Spirit.

Wait then for this, in the smal revelation of that pure *Light*, which first reveals things more known, and, as thou becom'st fitted for it, thou shalt receive more and more, and by a living experience easily refute their ignorance, who ask, how dost thou know that thou art acted by the Spirit of God? which will appear to thee a question no less ridiculous, than to ask one, whose eyes are open, how he knows the Sun shines at noon-day; and though this be the surest and certainest way, to answer all objections, yet by what is above written, it may appear, that the mouths of all such opposers as deny this Doctrine, may be shut by unquestionable and unanswerable reasons.

The Third Proposition,

Concerning the Scripturs.

From these Revelations of the Spirit of God to the Saints have proceeded the Scriptures of Truth, which contain,

    I. A faithfull historical account of the actings of God's People in divers ages, with many singular and remarkable Providences attending them.

    II. A Prophetical account of several things, whereof some are already past, and some yet to come.

    III. A full and ample account of all the chief principles

-ciples of the Doctrine of Christ, held forth in divers pretious declarations, exhortations, and sentences, which, by the moving of God's Spirit, were at several times, and upon sundry occasions, spoken and written unto some Churches, and their Pastors.

Nevertheless, because they are onely a declaration of the Fountain, and not the Fountain it self, therefore they are not to be esteemed the principal ground of all Truth and knowledg, nor yet the *adequate*, *primary Rule* of Faith and manners. Yet, because they give a true and faithfull testimony of the first Foundation, they are, and may be esteemed, a *secondary rule*, *subordinate* to the Spirit, from which they have all their excellency and certainty: for, as by the inward Testimony of the Spirit we do alone truely know them, so they testify, that the Spirit is that Guide, by which the Saints are led into all Truth; Therefore, according to the Scripturs, the *Spirit* is the *First* and Principal Leader. Seing then that we do therefore receive and believe the Scripturs, because they proceeded from the Spirit, for the very same reason, is the Spirit, more originally and principally, the Rule, according to that received maxime, in the Schools, *Propter quod unumquodque est tale, illud ipsum est magis tale*; *That for which a thing is such, the thing it self is more such.*

Joh. 16: vers 13. Rom. 8: vers 14.

§ 1 THe former part of this Proposition, though it needs no apology for it, yet is a good apology for us, and will help to sweep-away that, among many other calumnys, wherewith we are often loaded, as if we were vilifiers and denyers of the Scripturs, for, in that, which we affirme of them, it doth appear, at what high rate we value them, accounting them, without all deceit or equivocation, the most excellent writings in the world, to which not onely, no other writings are to be preferr'd, but even, in divers respects, not comparable thereunto. For, as we freely

F   acknow-

acknowledg, that their authority doth not depend upon the approbation
or canons of any Church or affembly, fo neither can we fubject them to the
faln, corrupt, and defiled reafon of man; and therein, as we do freely
agree with the Proteftants, againft the errour of the Romanifts; fo, on
the other hand, we can not go the length of fuch Proteftants, as make
their authority to depend upon any vertue, or power, that is in the writings themfelves; but we defire to afcribe all to that Spirit, from which
they proceeded.

We confefs indeed, there wants not a majefty in the ftyle, a cohe-
rence in the parts, a good fcope in the whole, but, feing thefe things
are not difcerned by the natural, but onely by the Spiritual man, it is
the Spirit of God, that muft give us that belief of the Scripturs, which
may fatisfy our Confciences. Therefore the chiefeft among Proteftants, both in their particular writings, and publick confeffions, are
forced to acknowledg this.

Hence *Calvin*, though he faith, he is able to prove, that, if there be a
God in Heaven, thefe writings have proceeded from him, yet he concluds another knowledg to be neceffary: Inft. lib. 1. cap. 7. fect. 4.

,, But, if (faith he) we refpect the Confciences, that they be not
,, daily molefted with doubts, and they ftick not at every fcruple,
,, it is requifit, that this perfwafion, which we fpeak of, be taken high-
,, er, than human reafon, judgment, or conjecturs, to wit, from the
,, fecret Teftimony of the Holy Spirit. And again: To thofe, that
,, ask, that *we prove unto them, by Reafon, that Mofes and the Prophets were
,, infpired of God to fpeak,* I anfwer, that the Teftimony of the Holy
,, Spirit is more excellent, than all reafon. And again: Let this re-
,, main a firm Truth, that he onely, whom the Holy Ghoft hath per-
,, fwaded, can repofe himfelf on the Scriptur with a true certainty. And
,, laftly: this then is a judgment, which can not be begotten, but by a
,, heavenly revelation, *&c.*

The fame is alfo affirmed in the firft publick Confeffion of the French
Churches, publifhed in the year 1559. Art. 4. ,, We know thefe
,, books to be Canonick, and the moft certain Rule of our Faith, not fo
,, much by the common accord and confent of the Church, as by the
,, teftimony and inward perfwafion of the Holy Spirit.

Thus alfo in the 5 Article of the Confeffion of faith of the Churches
of Holland, confirmed by the Synod of Dort. ,, We receive thefe
                                                   ,, books

,, books onely, for holy and canonick, not fo much becaufe the Church
,, receives and approues them, as becaufe the Spirit of God renders wit-
,, nefs in our hearts, that they are of God.

And laftly: The *Divines*, fo called, at *Weftminfter*, who began to be
afraid of, and guard againft the Teftimony of the Spirit, becaufe they
perceived a difpenfation beyond that, which they were under, beginning
to dawn, and to eclipfe them, yet could they not get by this, though
they have laid it down neither fo clearly, diftinctly, nor honeftly, as
they, that went before. It is in thefe words, chap. 1. fect. 5. ,, Ne-
,, verthelefs, our full perfwafion and affurance of the infallible Truth
,, thereof, is from the inward work of the Holy Spirit, bearing witnefs
,, by and with the Word in our heart.

By all which it appeareth, how neceffary it is, to feek the certainty of
the Scripturs, from the Spirit; and no where elfe. The infinit janglings
and endlefs contefts of thofe, that feek their authority elfewhere, do witnefs to the Truth hereof.

For the Antients themfelves, even of the firft centurys, were not at
one, among themfelves, concerning them; while fome of them rejected
books, which we approve, and others of them approved thofe, which
fome of us reject. It is not unknown to fuch as are in the leaft acquainted with Antiquity, what great contefts are, concerning the fecond Epiftle
of Peter, that of James, the fecond and third of John, and the Revelations, which many, even very antient, deny to have been written by
the beloved Difciple and brother of James, but by another of that name.
What fhould then become of Chriftians, if they had not received that
Spirit, and thofe Spiritual fenfes, by which they know how to difcern
the *true* from the *falfe*. It's the priviledg of Chrift's Sheep indeed, that
they hear his voyce, and refufe that of a ftranger, which priviledg being
taken away, we are left a prey to all manner of wolves.

§ II. Though then we do acknowledg the Scripturs to be a very
heavenly and Divine writing, the ufe of them to be very comfortable and
neceffary to the Church of Chrift, and that we alfo admire, and give
praife to the Lord, for his wonderfull Providence, in preferving thefe
writings, fo pure and uncorrupted, as we have them, through fo long a
night of apoftafy, to be a teftimony for his Truth, againft the wickednefs
and abominations even of thefe, whom he made inftrumental in preferv-

F 2 ing,

Concil.
Laod.
can. 59.
in cod.
Ecc. 163.
Concil.
Laod.
held in the
Year 364.
excluded
from the
canon Eccl.
the Wif-
dom of
Solomon,
Judith,
Tobias,
the Mac-
cabees,
which the
Council of
Carthage
held in the
Year 399
received.

ing them; so that they have kept them to be a witness against themselves: yet we may not call them the principal fountain of all Truth and knowledg, nor yet the first adequate rule of faith, and manners, because the principal fountain of Truth must be the Truth it self, i. e., that, whose certainty and authority depends not upon another. When we doubt of the streams of any river or flood, we recurr to the fountain it self, and having found it, there we sist, we can go no further, because there it springs out of the bowels of the earth, which are inscrutable. Even so the writing and sayings of all men we must bring to the Word of God, I mean the Eternal Word, and, if they agree hereunto, we stand there, for this Word alwayes proceedeth, and doth eternally proceed from God, in and by which, the unsearchable wisdom of God, and unsearchable counsel, and will, conceived in the heart of God, is revealed unto us; that then the Scripture is not the principal ground of faith and knowledg, as it appears by what is above spoken, so it is provided in the latter part of the Proposition, which being reduced to an argument runs thus,

That, the certainty and authority whereof depends upon another, and which is received, as Truth, because of its proceeding from another, is not to be accounted the principal ground and origin of all Truth and knowledg:

But the Scripturs authority and certainty depends upon the Spirit, by which they were dictated, and the reason, why they were received, as Truth, is, because they proceeded from the Spirit:

Therefore they are not the principal ground of Truth.

To confirme this argument, I added the school maxime *Propter quod unumquodque est tale, illud ipsum est magis tale.* Which maxime, though I confess it doth not hold universally, in all things, yet in this it both doth and will very wel hold, as by applying it, as we have above intimated, will appear.

The same argument will hold, as to the other branch of the position, *That it is not the primary adequate rule of faith and manners,* thus,

That, which is not the rule of my faith in believing the Scripturs themselves, is not the primary adequate rule of faith and manners:

But the Scriptur is not, nor can it be the rule of that faith, by which I believe them, *&c.*

Therefore, *&c.*

But as to this part, we shall produce divers arguments hereafter, as to
what

what is affirmed, That the *Spirit*, and *not the Scripturs*, *is the Rule*, it is largely handled in the former Propofition, the fumme whereof I fhall fubfume in one argument, thus,

If by the Spirit we can onely come to the true knowledg of God; If by the Spirit we be to be led into all truth, and fo be taught of all things, Then the Spirit, and not the Scripturs, is the foundation and ground of all Truth, and knowledg, and the primary rule of faith and manners:

But the firft is true:

Therefore alfo the laft.

Next, the very natur of the Gofpel it felf declareth, that the Scripturs can not be the *onely* and *chief rule* of *Chriftians*, elfe there fhould be no difference betwixt the *Law* and the *Gofpel*. As from the nature of the New Covenant, by divers Scripturs delcribed in the former Propofition is proved.

But befides thofe, which are before mentioned, herein doth the *Law* and the *Gofpel* differ, in that the *Law* being outwardly written, brings under *condemnation*, but hath *not life* in it to *fave*; whereas the *Gofpel*, as it declares and makes manifeft the evil, fo it being an inward powerfull thing alfo gives power to obey, and deliver from the evil. Hence it is called Εὐαγγέλιον, which is *glad tidings*, the *Law* or *letter*, which is *without* us, *kills*: but the *Gofpel*, which is the *inward* Spiritual *Law*, gives *life*, for it confifts not fo much in *words*, as in *vertue*. Wherefore fuch as come to know it, and be acquainted with it, come to feel greater power over their iniquitys, than all outward laws or rules can give them. Hence the Apoftle concluds, Rom. 6:14. *Sin fhall not have dominion over you. For ye are not under the Law, but under Grace.* This Grace then, that is inward, and not an outward Law, is to be the Rule of Chriftians: hereunto the Apoftle commends the Elders of the Church, faying, Act. 20: 32. *And now, Brethren, I commend you to God, and to the Word of his Grace, which is able to build you up, and to give you an inheritance among all thofe, that are fanctified.* He doth not commend them here to outward *lawes*, or *writings*; but to the *Word of Grace*, which is *inward*, even the *Spiritual Law*, which makes free, as he elfewhere affirms, Rom. 8: 2. *The Law of the Spirit of Life in Chrift Jefu hath made me free from the law of fin and death.* This Spiritual Law is that, which the Apoft. declares he preached and directed people unto, which was not outward, as Rom.

c. 10 : v. 8. is manifest, where distinguishing it from the Law, he saith, *The Word is nigh thee, in thy heart and in thy mouth, and this is the Word of Faith which we preach.*   From what is above said, I argue thus,

The principal Rule of Christians, under the Gospel, is not an outward letter, nor law outwardly written and delivered, but an inward Spiritual Law, ingraven in the heart, the Law of the Spirit of Life, the Word, that is nigh in the heart and in the mouth:

But the letter of the Scriptur is outward, of it self a dead thing, a meer declaration of good things, but not the things themselves:

Therefore it nor is, nor can be the chief or principal Rule of Christians.

§ III. Thirdly: That, which is given to Christians for a Rule and Guide, must needs be so full, as it may clearly and distinctly guide and order them in all things, and occurrences, that may fall out:

But in that there are many hundred of things, with a regard to their circumstances, particular Christians may be concerned in, for which there can be no particular Rule had in the Scripturs:

Therefore the Scripturs can not be a Rule to them.

I shall give an instance in two or three particulars, for to prove this Proposition. It is not to be doubted, but some men are particularly called to some particular services, there being not found in which, though the act be no general positive duty, yet, in so farr as it may be required of them, is a great sin to omit, for as much *God* is *zealous* of his *glory*, and every act of disobedience to his will manifested, is enough not onely to hinder one greatly from that comfort and inward Grace, which otherwise they might have, but also bringeth condemnation.

As for instance: Some are called to the ministry of the Word, Paul saith, there was *a necessity upon him to preach the Gospel, wo unto me, if I preach not.*

If it be necessary that there be now Ministers of the Church, as wel as then, then there is the same necessity upon some, more than upon others, to occupy this place, which necessity, as it may be incumbent upon particular persons, the Scriptur neither doth, nor can declare.

If it be said, that *the qualifications of a Minister are found in the Scriptur, and by applying these qualifications to my self, I may know whether I be fit for such a place, or no.*

I answer: The Qualifications of a Bishop or Minister, as they are men-

mentioned, both in the Epiftle to *Tim.* and *Tit.* are fuch as may be found in a private Chriftian, yea which ought in fome meafur to be in every true Chriftian : fo that that giveth a man no certainty, every capacity to an office giveth me not a fufficient call to it.

Next again : By whar Rule fhall I judg if I be fo qualified ? how do I know that I am *fober, meek, holy, harmlefs* ? Is not the teftimony of the Spirit *in* my *Confcience*, that, which muft affure me hereof ? And, fuppofe that I was qualified, and called, yet what Scriptur Rule fhall informe me, whether it be my duty to preach in this or that place in *France* or *England, Holland* or *Germany* ? whether I fhall take up my time in confirming the faithfull, reclaiming heretiks, or converting infidels, as alfo in writing epiftles to this or that Chnrch ?

The general rules of the Scriptur, viz, *to be diligent in my duty, to doe all to the glory of God*, and *for the good of his Church*, can give me no light in this thing. Seing two different things may both have a refpect to that way, yet may I committ a great errour and offence, in doing the one, when I am called to the other. If Paul, when his face was turned by the Lord toward Jerufalem, had gon back to Achaia or Macedonia, he might have fuppofed he could have done God more acceptable fervice, in preaching, and confirming the Churches, than in being fhut up in prifon in Judea ; but would God have been pleafed herewith ? Nay certainly. *Obedience is better than Sacrifice*, and it is not our doing that, which is good fimply, that pleafeth God, but that good, which he willeth us to doe. Every member hath its particular place in the body, as the Apoftle fheweth, 1 Cor. 12 : If then, I being the *foot* fhould offer to exercife the office of the *hand*, or being the *hand*, that of the *tongue*, my fervice would be troublefome, and not acceptable ; and in ftead of helping the body, I fhould make a fchifme in it. So that that, which is good for another to doe, may be finfull to me : for, as mafters will have their fervants to obey them, according to their good pleafur, not onely in blindly doing that, which may feem to them to tend to their mafters profit ; whereby it may chance (the mafter having bufinefs both in the field, and in the houfe) that the fervant, that knowes not his mafter's will, may go to the field, when it is the mind of the mafter he fhould ftay, and doe the bufinefs of the houfe. Would not this fervant then deferve a reproof, for not anfwering his mafter's mind ? And what mafter is fo fottifh and carelefs, as having many fervants, leaves them in fuch

dif-

diforder, as not to affigne each his particular ftation, and not onely the general terme of doing that, which is profitable, which would leave them in various doubts, and no doubt land in confufion?

Shall we then dare to afcribe unto Chrift, in the ordering of his Church and Servants, that, which in man might juftly be accounted diforder and confufion? The Apoftle fheweth this diftinction wel, Rom. c. 12 : v. 6, 8. *Having then gifts differing according to the Grace, that is given us, whether prophecy, let us prophecy according to the proportion of faith, or miniftry, let us wait on our miniftrings, or he, that teacheth, on teaching, or he, that exhorteth, on exhortation.* Now, what Scriptur rule fheweth me, that I ought to exhort rather than prophecy? or minifter rather than teach? Surely none at all. Many more difficultys of this kind occurr in the life of a Chriftian.

Moreover, that, which of all things is moft needfull for him to know, to wit, whether he really be in the faith, and an heir of Salvation, or no, the Scriptur can give him no certainty in, neither can it be a Rule to him. That this knowledg is exceeding defirable and comfortable, all do unanimoufly acknowledg, befides that it is fpecially commanded, 2 Cor. 13: v. 5. *Examine your felves whether ye be in the faith, prove your felves. Know ye not your own felves how that Jefus Chrift is in you, except ye be reprobats?* and 2 Pet. 1 : 10. *Wherefore the rather, Brethren, give all diligence, to make your calling and election fure.* Now I fay, what Scriptur rule can affure me, that I have true faith? that my calling and election is fure?

If it be faid, *by comparing the Scriptur marks of true faith with mine?*

I demand, wherewith fhall I make this obfervation? what fhall afcertain me, that I am not miftaken? It can not be the Scriptur: That's the matter under debate.

If it be faid, *My own heart,*

How unfit a judg is it in its own cafe? and how like to be partial, efpecially if it be yet unrenewed? Doth not the Scriptur fay, that it is *deceitfull above all things?* I find the promifes, I find the threatnings, in the Scriptur, but who telleth me, that the one belongs to me, more than the other? The Scriptur gives me a meer declaration of thefe things, but makes no application; fo that the affumption muft be of mine own making : thus, as for example, I find this Propofition in the Scriptur;

He, that believes, fhall be faved: thence I draw this affumption

But I, *Robert believe:*

Therefore I fhall be faved.   The

The *minor* is of mine own making , not expressed in the Scriptur , and so a humane conclusion , not a Divine position , so that my faith and assurance here , is not built upon a Scriptur Proposition , but upon an humane principle ; which , unless I be sure of elsewhere , the S.riptur gives me no certainty in the matter.

Again , if I should pursue the argument further , and seek a new *medium* out of the Scriptur , the same difficulty will occurr , thus ,

He , that hath the true and certain marks of true faith , hath true faith :
But I have those marks :
Therefore I have true faith.

For the *assumption* is still here of my own making , and is not found in the Scripturs , and by consequence the conclusion can be no better , since it still followeth the weaker proposition.   This is indeed so pungent, that the best of Protestants , who plead for this assurance , ascribe it to the inward testimony of the Spirit (as *Calvin* in that large citation , cited in the former Proposition) so that , not to seek further into the writings of the primitive Protestants , which are full of such expressions, even the *Westminster* confession of faith affirmeth,chap. 18. sect. 12.   ,, This ,, certainty is not bare conjectur and probable perswasion grounded up- ,, on fallible hope , but an infallible assurance of faith , founded upon the ,, Divine Truth of the promise of Salvation , the inward evidences ,, of these Graces , unto which these promises are made , the Testimo- ,, ny of the Spirit of adoption , witnessing to our spirits , that we are the ,, children of God , which *Spirit* is the *earnest* of our *inheritance* , *whereby we are sealed to the day of redemption.*

Moreover , the Scriptur it self , wherein we are so earnestly pressed , to seek after this assurance , doth not at all affirme it self a rule sufficient to give it ; but wholly ascribeth it to the Spirit , as Rom.8:16.*The Spirit it self beareth witness with our spirit , that we are the children of God.* 1 Joh. 4 : 13. *Hereby do we know , that we dwell in him , and he in us , because he hath given us of his Spirit.* and 5 : 6. *and it is the Spirit , that beareth witness , because the Spirit is Truth.*

§ IV. Lastly : That can not be the onely principle nor chief rule , which doth not universally reach every individual , that needeth it to produce the necessary effect , and from the use of which (either by some innocent and sinless defect, or natural , yet harmeless and blameless imperfection) many (who are within the compass of the visible Church , and

may without abſurdity, yea with great probability be accounted of the
Elect) are neceſſarily excluded, and that either wholly, or at leaſt from
the immediate uſe thereof. But it ſo falls out frequently concerning the Scripturs, in the caſe of deaf people, children, and idiots, who
can by no means have the benefit of the Scripturs. Shall we then affirme,
that they are without any rule to God-ward? or that they are all damned?
As ſuch an opinion is, in it ſelf, very abſurd, and inconſiſtent both with the
juſtice and mercy of God, ſo I know no ſound reaſon can be alledged
for it. Now, if we may ſuppoſe any ſuch to be under the New Covenant diſpenſation, as I know none will deny, but that we may ſuppoſe
it without any abſurdity, we can not ſuppoſe them without ſome rule and
means of knowledg, ſeing it is expreſſly affirmed, *they ſhall all be taught
of God.* Joh. 6: 45. *And they ſhall all know me from the leaſt to the greateſt,*
Heb. 8: 11. But ſecondly, though we were rid of this difficulty, how
many illiterat, and yet good men, are there in the Church of God, who
can not read a letter in their own mothers tongue? which imperfection,
though it be inconvenient, I can not tell whether we may ſafely affirme
it to be ſinfull; theſe can have no immediate knowledg of the rule of their
faith; ſo their faith muſt needs depend upon the credit of other mens
reading, or relateing it unto them; where either the altering, adding or
omitting of a little word may be a foundation, in the poor hearer, of a very dangerous miſtake: whereby he may either continue in an iniquity,
ignorantly, or believe a lye confidently. As for example, the Papiſts in
all their catechiſms and publick exerciſes of examination, towards the
people have boldly cut away the ſecond command, becauſe it ſeems ſo
expreſſly to hitt againſt their adoration, and uſe of images. Whereas
many of theſe people, in whom, by this omiſſion, this falſe opinion is fo-
ſtered, are under a ſimple impoſſibility, or at leaſt a very great difficulty
to be outwardly informed of this abuſe. But further, ſuppoſe all could
read the Scripturs in their own language, where is there one of a thouſand
that hath that through knowledg of the original languages, in which they
were written, ſo as in that reſpect immediately to receive the benefit of
them? Muſt not all theſe here depend upon the honeſty & faithfulneſs of
the Interpreters? Which how uncertain it is for a man to build his faith
upon, the many corrections, amendments, and various eſſays, which,
even among Proteſtants have been uſed, whereof the latter hath conſtantly blamed and corrected the former, as guilty of defects and errours,

doth

doth fufficiently declare.   And that even the laft tranflations in the vulgar languages need to be corrected (as I could prove at large, were it proper in this place) learned men do confefs.   But laft of all there is no lefs difficulty even occurrs to thefe skilled in the original languages, who can not fo immediately receive the mind of the Authors in thefe writings, as that their faith doth not at leaft obliquely depend upon the honefty and credit of the Tranfcribers, fince the original coppys are granted by all not to be now extant.

Of which Tranfcribers *Jerom* in his time complained, faying, that *they wrot not what they found, but what they underftood.* And *Epiphanius* faith, that in the good and correct coppys of Luk it was wrttten, that *Chrift wept*, and that *Irenæus* doth cite it, but that the Catholiks blotted it out, fearing leaft heretiks fhould have abufed it.   Other Fathers alfo declare, that whole verfes were taken out of Mark, becaufe of the Manichees.

Hieron.
epift. 28
ad Lucin.
pag. 247.
Epiphan.
in Anchor.
Tom. 2.
oper.

But further, the various lections of the Hebrew character by reafon of the *Points*, which fome plead for as coævous with the firft writings, which others, with no lefs probability, alledg to be a later invention, the difagreement of divers citations of Chrift and the Apoftles, with thofe paffages in the Old Teftament, they appeal to the great controverfy among the Fathers, whereof fome moft highly approve the Greek *Septuagint*, decrying and rendring very doubtfull the Hebrew coppy, as in many places vitiated, and altered by the Jewes, other fome, and particularly *Jerom*, exalting the certainty of the Hebrew, and rejecting, yea even deriding the hiftory of the Septuagint, which the primitive Church chiefly made ufe of, and fome Fathers, that lived centurys before him, affirmed to be a moft certain thing.   Add the many various lections in divers coppys of the Greek, and the great alterations among the Fathers of the firft three centurys, (who had greater opportunity to be better informed, than we can now lay claime to) concerning the books to be admitted or rejected, as above is obferved. I fay, all thefe and much more which might be alledged, puts the minds, even of the Learned, into infinit doubts, fcrupls, and inextricable difficultys.   Whence we may very fafely conclud, that Jefus Chrift, who promifed to be always with his children, to lead them into all Truth, to guard them againft the devices of the enemy, and to eftablifh their faith upon an unmoveable Rock, left them not to be principally ruled by that, which was fubject, in it felf, to many uncertaintys, and therefore he gave them his Spirit, as their

Prin-

Principal Guide , which neither moths nor time can wear out , nor tran-
scribers nor tranflatours corrupt, which none are fo young , none fo illiterate , none in fo remote a place , but they may come to be reached , and
rightly informed by it.

Through and by the clearnefs, which that Spirit gives us, it is, that
we are onely beft rid of thofe difficultys, that occurr to us , concernig the
Scripturs.   The real and undoubted experience whereof I my felf have
been a witnefs of, with great admiration of the love of God to his children in thefe latter days. For I have known fome of my Friends, who
profefs the fame faith with me , faithfull fervants of the moft High God,
and full of the Divine knowledg of his Truth , as it was immediately and
inwardly revealed to them, by the Spirit, from a true and living experience. Who not onely were ignorant of the Greek and Hebrew, but even
fome of them could not read their own vulgar language , who being preffed by the adverfarys with fome citations out of the Englifh tranflation ,
and finding them to difagree with the manifeftation of Truth in their
hearts, have boldly affirmed the Spirit of God never faid fo, and that it
was certainly wrong, for they did not believe that any of the Holy Prophets , or Apoftles, had ever written fo, which , when I on this account,
ferioufly examined, I really found to be errours and corruptions of the
Tranflatours. Who, as in moft tranflations , do not fo much give us
the genuine fignifications of the words, as ftrain them to exprefs that ,
which comes neareft with that opinion and notion they have of Truth.
And this feemed to me to fute very wel with that faying of *Auguftin* ,
Epift. 19. ad Hen. Tom. 2. fol. 14. after he has faid, that he gives onely
that honour to thofe books , which are called *Canonical*, as to believe that
the Authors thereof did, in writing, not err. He adds : ,, And if I fhall
,, meet with any thing in thefe writings , that feemeth repugnant to
,, Truth, I fhall not doubt to fay that either the volume is faulty , or
,, erroneous: that the expounder hath not reached what was faid, or
that I have in no wife underftood it. So that he fuppofes, that, in the tran-
fcription and tranflation there may be errours.

§ V. If it be then asked me , *whether I think hereby to render the Scriptur
altogether uncertain , or ufelefs?*

I anfwer: not at all.   The propofition it felf declares what efteem
I have for them. And provided that, to the Spirit, from which they came,
be but granted, that place, the Scripturs themfelves give it, I do freely.

ly concede to the Scriptur the second place, even whatsoever they say of themselves. Which the Apostle Paul chiefly mentions in two places, Rom. 15 : 4. *Whatsoever things were written aforetime, were written for our learning, that we through patience and comfort of the Scripturs might have hope.* 2 Tim. 3 : 15, 16, 17. *The Holy Scripturs are able to make wise unto Salvation, through faith, which is in Christ Jesus. All Scriptur given by inspiration from God, is profitable for correction, for instruction, in righteousneß, that the man of God may be perfect, throughly furnished unto every good work.*

For, though God do principally and chiefly lead us by his Spirit, yet he sometimes conveighs his comfort and consolation to us, through his children, whom he raises up and infpires, to speak or write a word in season; whereby the Saints are made instruments in the hand of the Lord, to strengthen and encourage one another: which do also tend to perfect, and make them wise unto Salvation, and such as are led by the Spirit, can not neglect, but do naturally love, and are wonderfully cherished by that, which proceedeth from the same Spirit in another; because such mutual emanations of the heavenly Life, tend to quicken the mind, when at any time it is overtaken with heavyneſs. Peter himself declares this to have been the end of his writing, 2 Pet. 1: 12, 13. *Wherefore I will not be negligent to put you always in remembrance of those things, though ye know them and be established in the present Truth. Yea, I think it meet, as long as I am in this tabernacle, to stirr you up, by putting you in remembrance.*

God is Teacher of his People himself, and there is nothing more expreſs, than that such as are under the New Covenant, they *need no man to teach* them: yet it was a fruit of Christ's ascension, to send teachers and pastors, for perfecting of the Saints. So that the same work is ascribed to the Scripturs, as to Teachers; the one to make the man of God perfect, the other for the perfection of the Saints.

As then Teachers are not to go before the teaching of God himself, under the New Covenant, but to follow after it, neither are they to rob us of that great priviledg, which Christ hath purchased unto us, by his *blood*; so neither is the Scriptur to go before the teaching of the Spirit, or to rob us of it.

Secondly: God hath seen meet, that, herein we should, as in a looking glaſs, see the conditions and experiences of the Saints of old, that finding our experience answer to theirs, we might thereby be the more confirmed and comforted, and our hope strengthened of obtaining the same end;

                    that

that obferving the Providences attending them, feing the fnares they were liable to, and beholding their deliverances, we may thereby be made wife unto Salvation, and feafonably reproved, and inftructed in righteoufnefs.

  This is the great work of the Scripturs and their fervice to us, that we may witnefs them fulfilled *in* us, and fo difcern the ftamp of God's Spirit, and ways upon them, by the inward acquaintance we have with the fame Spirit and work in our hearts. The prophecys of the Scriptur are alfo very comfortable, and profitable unto us, as the fame Spirit inlightens us, to obferve them fulfilled and to be fulfilled. For in all this, it is to be obferved, that it is onely the Spiritual man, that can make a right ufe of them, they are able to make the man of God perfect (fo it is not the natural man) and whatfoever was written aforetime, was written for *our comfort*, [*our*] that are the believers, [*our*] that are the Saints, concerning fuch the Apoftle fpeaks; for as for the other, the Apoftle Peter plainly declares, that the *unftable and unlearned wreft them to their own deftruction*: thefe were they, that were unlearned in the Divine and heavenly learning of the Spirit, not in humane and fchool literatur, of which we may fafely prefume that Peter himfelf, being a fifher-man, had no great skill: for it may with great probability, yea certainly, be affirmed, that he had no knowledg of Ariftotles Logick, which both Papifts and Proteftants, now degenerating from the fimplicity of Truth, make hand-maid of Divinity (as they call it) and a neceffary introduction to their carnal, natural and humane miniftry. By the infinit obfcure labours of which kind of men, mixing-in their heathenifh ftuff, the Scriptur is rendered at this day of fo little fervice to the fimple people, whereof if *Jerom* complained in his time, now twelve hundred years ago, *Hieron.* Ep. 134 ad Cypr. tom. 3. faying, *It is wont to befall the moft part of learned men, that it is harder to underftand their expofitions, than the things, which they go about to expound*; what may We fay then, confidering thofe great heaps of commentarys fince, in ages yet farr more corrupted?

  § VI. In this refpect above mentioned then, we have fhown, what fervice and ufe the Holy Scripturs, as managed in and by the Spirit, are of, to the Church of God; wherefore we do account them a fecondary rule. Moreover, becaufe they are commonly acknowledged by all, to have been written by the dictats of the Holy Spirit, and that the errours, which may be fuppofed by the injury of times to have flipt-in,

are

are not such , but that there is a sufficient clear testimony left to all the essentials of the Christian faith; we do look upon them as the onely fit outward judg of controversys among Christians , and that whatever doctrine is contrary unto their testimony , may therefore justly be rejected , as false.   And for our parts, we are very willing , that all our doctrines and practices be tryed by them , which we never refused, nor ever shall , in all controversys with our adversarys , as the judg and Test.   We shall also be very willing to admitt it , as a positive certain maxime, *That, whatsoever any doe , pretending to the Spirit, which is contrary to the Scripturs, be accounted and reckoned a delusion of the devil.* For, as we never lay claime to the Spirit's leadings , that we may cover our selves , in any thing, that is evil , so we know , that , as every evil contradicts the Scripturs , so it doth also the Spirit , in the first place , from which the Scripturs came , and whose motions can never contradict one another , though they may appear sometimes , to be contradictory ; to the blind eye of the natural man , as Paul and James seem to contradict one another.

Thus farr we have shown both what we believe , and what we believe not , concerning the Holy Scripturs , hoping we have given them their due place.   But , since they , that will needs have them to be the onely, certain , and principal Rule , want not some shew of arguments , even from the Scriptur it self (though it no where call it self so) by which they labour to prove their doctrin , I shall briefly lay them down by way of objections , and answer them , before I make an end of this matter.

§ VII. Their first objection is usually drawn from Isaiah 8: 20. *To the Law and to the Testimony , if they speak not according to this Word , it is because there is no Light in them.* Now this *Law* , *Testimony* , and *Word,* they plead to be the Scripturs.

To which I answer that , That is to begg the thing in question , and remains yet unproved.   Nor do I know for what reason we may not safely affirme this *Law* and *Word* to be *inward.*   But suppose it was outward , it proves not the case at all , for them, neither makes it against us ; for it may be confessed , without any prejudice to our cause , that the outward Law was more particularly to the Jewes a Rule , and more principally than to us : seing their Law was outward and literal , but ours, under the New Covenant , (as hath been already said) is expresly affirmed to be *inward* and *Spiritual.*   So that this Scriptur is so farr from making against us , that it makes for us : for, if the Jewes were directed to try all things,

by

by their Law, which was without them, written in tables of ſtone, then, if we will have this advice of the Prophet to reach us, we muſt make it hold paralell to that diſpenſation of the Goſpel, which we are under.   So that we are to try all things (in the firſt place) by that *Word of Faith*, which is preached unto us, which the Apoſtle ſaith is *in the heart*, and by that Law, which God hath given us, which the Apoſtle ſaith alſo expreſſly, is *written* and *placed in the mind.*

Laſtly: If we look to this place, according to the Greek interpretation of the Septuagint, our adverſarys ſhall have nothing from thence to carp, yea it will favour us much; for there it is ſaid, that *the Law is given us for a help*, which very wel agrees with what is above aſſerted.

Their ſecond objection is from Joh. 5: 39. *Search the Scripturs*, &c.

Here, ſay they, *we are commanded*, by Chriſt himſelf, *to ſearch the Scripturs,*

I anſwer Firſt, That the Scripturs ought to be ſearched, we do not at all deny, but are very willing to be tryed by them, as hath been above declared·   But the queſtion is, *Whether they be the onely and principal Rule?*, which this is ſo farr from proving, that it proveth the contrary; for Chriſt checks them here, for too high an eſteem of the Scripturs, and neglecting of him, that was to be preferr'd before them, and to whom they bore witneſs, as the following words declare.   *For in them ye think ye have eternal life, and they are they, which teſtify of me, and ye will not come unto me, that ye may have life.*   This ſhewes, that, while they thought they had eternal life in the Scripturs, they neglected to come unto Chriſt to have life, of which the Scripturs bore witneſs.   This anſwers wel to our purpoſe, ſince our adverſarys now do alſo exalt the Scripturs, and think to have life in them, which is no more, than to look upon them as the onely principal rule, and way to Life, and yet refuſe to come unto the Spirit, of which they teſtify, even the inward Spiritual Law, which could give them Life.   So that the cauſe of this peopl's ignorance and unbelief was not their want of reſpect to the Scripturs, which though they knew, and had a high eſteem of, yet Chriſt teſtifys in the former verſes, that they had *neither ſeen the Father, nor heard his voyce at any time, neither had his Word abiding in them*, which had they then had, then they had believed in the Son.   Moreover, that place may be taken in the Indicative mood, *Ye ſearch the Scripturs*, which interpretation the Greek word will bear, and ſo *Paſor* tranſlateth it, which by the reproof following, ſeemeth alſo

to

to be the more genuine interpretation, as *Cyrillus* long ago hath obſerved.

§ VIII. Their third objection is from theſe words, Act. 17:11.
*Theſe were more noble, than thoſe in Theſſalonica, in that they received the Word
with all readyneſ of mind, and ſearched the Scripturs daily, whether thoſe things
were ſo.*

Here, ſay they, *the Berœans are commended, for ſearching the Scripturs,* Obj.
and making them the Rule.

I anſwer: That the Scripturs either are the principal or onely Rule,
will not at all from this follow, neither will their ſearching the Scripturs,
or being commended for it, inferr any ſuch thing, for we recommend
and approve the uſe of them, in that reſpect, as much as any; yet will
it not follow, that we affirme them to be the principal and onely Rule.

Secondly: It is to be obſerved, that theſe were the Jewes of Berœa
to whom theſe Scripturs, which were the Law and the] Prophets, were
more particularly a Rule, and the thing under the examination was,
whether the birth, life, works, and ſufferings of Chriſt did anſwer to
the prophecys, that went before, of him; ſo that it was moſt proper
for them, being Jewes, to examine the Apoſtles doctrin, by the Scripturs, ſeing he pleaded it to be a fulfilling of them. It is ſaid nevertheleſs, in the firſt place, that *they received the Word, with chearfulneſs*:
and in the ſecond place, *they ſearched the Scripturs*; not that they ſearched the Scripturs, and then received the Word; for then could not they
have prevailed to convert them, had they not firſt minded the *Word abiding in them,* which opened their underſtandings, no more, than the
Scribes and Phariſees, who (as in the former objection we obſerved)
ſearched the Scripturs, and exalted them, and yet remained in their unbelief, becauſe they had not the *Word abiding in* them.

But Laſtly: If this commendation of the Jewiſh Berœans might inferr,
that the Scripturs were the onely and principal Rule to try the Apoſtles
doctrin by, what ſhould have become of the Gentiles? How ſhould they
ever have come to received the faith of Chriſt, who neither knew the
Scripturs, nor believed them? We ſee, in the end of the ſame chapter,
how the Apoſtle, preaching to the Athenians, took another method, and
directed them to ſomewhat of *God within* themſelves, that they might *feel
after* him. He did not firſt go about to proſelyte them to the Jewiſh religion, and to the belief of the Law, and the Prophets, and from thence to

H   prove

prove the coming of Chrilt.   Nay: he took a nearer way.   Now certainly the principal and onely Rule is not different ; One to the Jewes, and another to the Gentiles, but is **univerſal**, reaching both : though ſecondary and ſubordinat rules and means may be various, & diverſly ſuted, according as the people, they are uſed to,. are ſtated .and circumſtantiated.   Even ſo we ſee that the Apoſtle to the Athenians uſed a teſtimony of one of their own poëts, which he judged would have credit with them : and no doubt ſuch teſtimonys, whoſe Autl ors they eſteemed, had more weight with them , than all the ſayings of Móſes and the Prophets, whom they neither knew, nor would have cared for. Now becauſe the Apoſtle uſed the teſtimony of a Poët to the Athenians, will it therefore follow he made that the principal , or onely rule to try his doctrin by ? So neither will it follow, that, though he made uſe of the Scriptures to the Jewes , as being a principle already believed by them , to try his doctrin , that from thence the Scriptures may be accounted the principal or onely rule.

§ I X. The laſt, and which at firſt view ſeems to be the greateſt , objection, is this ,

Obj.   *If the Scriptur be not the adequate, principal, and onely Rule , then it would follow, that the Scriptur is not compleat, nor the canon filled ; that, if men be now immediately led and ruled by the Spirit, they may add new Scripturs of equal authority with the old, whereas every one, that adds, is curſed: yea what aſſurance have we , but that at this rate every one may bring in a new goſpel, according to his fancy ?*

The dangerous conſequences, inſinuated in this objection, were fully anſwered in the latter part of the laſt Propoſition, in what was ſaid a little before, offering freely to diſclaime all pretended revelations contrary to the Scripturs.

But if it be urged , that *it is not enough to deny theſe conſequences, if they
Obj. naturally follow from your doctrin of immediate revelation , and denying the Scriptur to be the onely rule.*

I anſwer: We have proved both theſe doctrines to be true and neceſſary, according to the Scripturs themſelves , and therefore to faſten evil conſequences upon them, which we make appear do not follow , is not to accuſe us, but Chriſt and his Apoſtles, who preached them.

But ſecondly, we have ſhut the door upon all ſuch doctrin, in this very poſition, affirming that *the Scripturs give a full and ample teſtimony to all*
the

the principal doctrines of the Christian faith. For we do firmly believe, that there is no other Gospel or doctrin to be preached, but that, which was delivered by the Apostles, and do freely subscribe to that saying, *Let him, that preacheth any other gospel, than that, which hath been already preached by* Gal. 1:8, 9 *the Apostles, and according to the Scripturs, be accursed.*

So we distinguish betwixt a revelation of a *new gospel* and *new doctrines* and a *new revelation* of the *good old Gospel* and doctrines; the last we plead for, but the first we utterly deny. For we firmly believe, that *no other foundation can any man lay, than that, which is laid already.* But that this revelation is necessary, we have already proved, and this distinction doth sufficiently guard us against the hazard insinuated in the objection.

As to the *Scripturs* being *a filled canon*, I see no necessity of believing it. And, if these men, that believe the Scripture to be the onely rule, will be consistent to their own doctrin, they must needs be of my judgment: seing it is simply impossible to prove the canon by the Scripturs. For it can not be found in any book of the Scriptur, that these books, and just these, and no other, are canonical, as all are forced to acknowledg, how can they then evite this argument?

That, which can not be proved by Scriptur, is no necessary article of faith:

But the canon of the Scriptur, to wit, that there are so many books precisely, neither more nor less, can not be proved by Scriptur:

Therefore, it is no necessary article of faith.

If they should alledg, that *the admitting of any other books to be now written by the same Spirit might inferr the admission of new doctrines,*   Obj.

I deny that consequence, for the principal or fundamental doctrines of the Christian religion are contained in the tenth part of the Scriptur; but it will not follow thence, that the rest are impertinent, or useless. If it should please God to bring to us any of these books, which by the injury of time, are lost, which are mentioned in the Scriptur, as *the Prophecy of Enoch, the book of Nathan*, &c. or *the third epistle of Paul to the Corinthians*, I see no reason, why we might not receive them, and place them with the rest. That, which displeaseth me, is, that men should first affirme, that the Scriptur is the onely and principal rule, and yet make a great article of faith of that, which the Scriptur can give us no light in.

H 2

A

As for inftance, how fhall a Proteftant prove, by Scriptur, to fuch as deny the Epiftle of James to be authentik, that it ought to be received ?

Firft, if he fhould fay, *becaufe it contradicts not the reft,* (befides that there is no mention made of it in any of the reft) perhaps thefe men think it doth contradict Paul, in relation to *faith* and *works.* But, if that fhould be granted, it would as wel follow, that every writer, that contradicts not the Scriptur, fhould be put into the canon. And by this means, thefe men fall into a greater abfurdity, than they fix upon us ; for thus they would equal every one the writings of their own fect with the Scripturs, for I fuppofe they judg their own confeffion of faith doth not contradict the Scripturs. Will it therefore follow, that it fhould be bound up with the Bible ? And yet it feems impoffible, according to their principles, to bring any better argument, to prove the Epiftle of James to be authentik. There is then this unavoidable neceffity, to fay, We know it by the fame Spirit, from which it was written, or otherwife to ftep back to Rome, and fay ; we know by tradition that the Church hath declared it to be Canonical, and the Church is infallible: let them find a mids, if they can, fo that out of this objection we fhall draw an unanfwerable argument *ad hominem*, to our purpofe.

That, which can not affure me concerning an article of faith, neceffary to be believed, is not the primary, adequate, onely rule of faith :

But the Scriptur can not thus affure me :

Therefore, &c.

I prove the *affumption* thus,

That, which can not affure me concerning the canon of the Scriptur, to wit, that fuch books are onely to be admitted, and the Apocrypha to be excluded, can not affure me of this :

Therefore, &c.

Obj.   And laftly : As to thefe words, Rev. 22 : 18. that, *if any man fhall add unto thefe things, God fhall add unto him the plagues, that are written in this book,* I defire they will fhew me, how it relates to any thing elfe, than to that particular prophecy. It faith not, *now the canon of the Scriptur is filled up, no man is to write more from that Spirit.* Yea do not all confefs, that there have been prophecys, and true Prophets, fince? The Papifts deny it not. And do not the Proteftants affirme, that *John Hus* prophecyed of the *reformation?* Was he therefore curfed ? or did he therein evil? I could give many other examples confeffed by themfelves; but moreover the

fame

(ame was in effect commanded long before, *Prov.* 30 : 6. *Add thou not unto his words, left he reprove thee, and thou be found a lyar,* yet how many books of the Prophets were written after? and the fame was faid by Mofes, *Deut.* 4 : 2. *Ye fhall not add unto the word, which I command you, neither fhall ye diminifh ought from it.* So that, though we fhould extend that of the Revelations beyond the particular prophecy of that book, it can not be underftood, but of a new gofpel, or new doctrines, or of reftraining man's fpirit, that he mix not his humane words with the Divine, and not of a *new revelation of the old,* as we have faid before.

The Fourth Propofition,
Concerning the Condition of Man in the fall.

All Adam's pofterity (or mankind) both Jewes and Gentiles as to the firft Adam (or earthly man) is faln, degenerated, and dead, deprived of the fenfation (or feeling) of this inward Teftimony, or Seed, of God; and is fubject unto the power, natur, and feed of the Serpent, which he foweth in mens hearts, while they abide in this natural and corrupted eftate: from whence it comes, that not onely their words and deeds, but all their imaginations, are evil perpetually in the fight of God, as proceeding from this depraved and wicked feed. Man therefore, as he is in this ftate, can know nothing aright, yea his thoughts and conceptions concerning God, and things Spiritual (untill he be disjoyned from this evil Seed, and united to the Divine Light) are unprofitable both to himfelf and others. Hence are rejected the *Socinian* and *Pelagian* errours in exalting a *natural* Light; as alfo the *Papifts* and moft of *Proteftants*, who affirme, *that man, without the true Grace of God, may be a true minifter of the Gofpel.* Neverthelefs this Seed is not imputed to infants, untill by tranfgreffion they actually joyn themfelves therewith, for they are *by natur the children of wrath*, who walk according to

Rom. 5: 12, 13.

H 3

the

the power of the Prince of the air, and the Spirit that now worketh in the children of disobedience, having their conversation in the lusts of the flesh, fulfilling the desires of the flesh, and of the mind. Eph. 2.

§ I. Hitherto we have discoursed how the true knowledg of God is attained, and preserved, also of what use and service the holy Scriptur is to the Saints.

We come now to examin *the state and condition of man, as he stands in the fall; what his capacity and power is, and how farr he is able, as of himself, to advance, in relation to the things of God.* Of this we touch'd a little in the beginning of the second Proposition; but the full, right, and through understanding of it, is of great use and service: because from the ignorance and altercations, that have been about it, there have arisen great and dangerous errours, both on the one hand, and the other. While some do so farr exalt the light of natur, or the faculty of the natural man, as capable of himself, by vertue of the inward will, faculty, light, or power, that pertaines to his natur, to follow that, which is good, and make real progress towards heaven. And of these are the *Pelagians* and *Semi-Pelagians,* of old, and, of late, the *Socinians* and divers others, among the *Papists.* Others again will needs run into another extream, (to whom *Augustin,* among the Antients, first made way in his declining age, through the heat of his zeal against *Pelagius*) not onely confessing men uncapable, of themselves, to doe good, and prone to evil; but that in his very mother's womb, and before he committs any actual transgression, he is contaminate with a real guilt, whereby he deserves eternal death: in which respect they are not afraid, to affirme, that *many poor infants are eternally damned, and for ever endure the torments of hell.* Therefore the God of Truth, having now again revealed his Truth, that good and even way, by his own Spirit, hath taught us to avoid both these extreames.

That then, which our Proposition leads to treat of, is,

First, *What the condition of man is in the fall, and how farr uncapable to meddle in the things of God.*

And Secondly, *That God doth not impute this evil to infants, untill they actually joyn with it,* that so by establishing the Truth, we may overturn the errours on both parts.

And as for that Third thing included in the Proposition it self, concerning

cerning thefe *Teachers*, which *want the Grace of God*, we fhall refer that to the tenth Propofition, where that matter is more particularly handl-ed.

§ 11. As to the *Firſt*, not to dive into the many curious notions, which many have, concerning the *condition of Adam before the fall*, all agree in this, that thereby he came to a very great lofs, not onely in the things, which related to the outward man, but in regard of that true fel-lowfhip and communion he had with God. This lofs was fignified unto him in the command, *for*, *in the day thou eateſt thereof*, *thou ſhalt ſurely dye*, Gen. 2 : 17. This death could not be an outward death, or the diffolu-tion of the outward man, for, as to that, he did not dye yet many hun-dred years after; fo that it muſt needs refpect his Spiritual life and com-munion with God. The confequence of this fall, befides that, which relates to the fruits of the earth, is alfo expreffed, Gen. 3 : 24, *fo he drove out the man*, *and he placed*, *at the eaſt of the garden of Eden*, *Cherubims*, *and a flaming ſword*, *which turned every way*, *to keep the way of the Tree of Life*. Now whatfoever literal fignification this may have, we may fafely afcribe to this Paradife a myſtical fignification, and truely account it that Spiri-tual communion and fellowfhip, which the Saints obtain with God, by Jefus Chriſt, to whom onely thefe Cherubims give way, and unto as many as enter by him, who calls himfelf the *door*. So that, though we do not afcribe any whit of Adam's guilt to men, untill they make it theirs by the like acts of difobedience, yet we can not fuppofe, that men, who are come of Adam naturally, can have any good thing in their natur, as belonging to it, which he, from whom they derive their natur, had not himfelf to communicate unto them.

If then we may affirme, that Adam did not retain in his nature, as be-longing thereunto, any will or light capable to give him knowledg in Spiritual things, then neither can his pofterity. For whatfoever real good any man doth, it proceedeth not from his natur, as he is man, or the fon of Adam: but from the *Seed of God in him*, as a new vifitation of Life, in order to bring him out of his natural condition. So that, though it be *in him*, yet it is not *of him*, and this the Lord himſelf witneffed, Gen. 6 : 5. where it is faid, he *faw*, *that every imagination of the thoughts of his heart was onely evil continually*: which words, as they are very pofi-tive, fo are they very comprehenfive. Obferve the *emphaſis* of them, Firſt, there is *every imagination of the thoughts of his heart*, fo that this ad-mitts

mitts of no exception of any imagination of the thoughts of his heart. Secondly, *is onely evil continually*: it is neither in *some part evil continually*, nor yet *onely evil at some times*; but both *onely evil*, and *always* and *continually evil*: which certainly excluds any good, as a proper effect of mans heart, naturally. For that, which is onely evil, and that always, can not, of its own natur, produce any good thing. The Lord expresseth this again alittle after, chap. 8. v. 21. *the imagination of mans heart is evil from his youth.* Thus inferring how natural and proper it is unto him; From which I thus argue,

If the thoughts of mans heart be not onely evil, but always evil, then are they, as they simply proceed from his heart, neither good in part, nor at any time:

But the First is true:

Therefore also the Last,

Again,

If mans thoughts be always and onely evil, then are they altogether uselefs and ineffectual to him, in the things of God:

But the First is true:

Therefore also the Last.

Secondly, this appears clearly from that saying of the Prophet *Jeremiah*, 17: 9. *The heart is deceitfull above all things, and desperately wicked.* For who can with any colour of reafon imagine, that that, which is fo, hath any power, of it self, or is any wife fit, to lead a man to righteousnefs, whereunto it is, of its own natur, directly oppofit? This is as contrary to Reafon, as it is impoffible in natur, that a ftone, of its own natur and proper motion, fhould flee upwards. For, as a ftone, of its own natur, inclineth and is prone to move down-wards towards the center, fo the heart of man is naturally prone and inclined to evil, Some to one, and fome to another. From this then I also thus argue,

That, which *is deceitfull above all things, and desperately wicked*, is not fit, neither can it lead a man aright, in things, that are good and honeft:

But the heart of man is such:

Therefore, *&c.*

Rom 3:
vers 10.
Pf. 14: 3.
&
53:2, &c. But the Apoftle Paul, defcribeth the condition of men in the fall, at large, taking it out of the Pfalmift, *There is none righteous, no not one : There is none, that underftandeth, there is none that feeketh after God. They are all gone out of the way, they are altogether become unprofitable,*

fitable, there is none, that doth good, no not one. Their throat is an open se-
pulchre, with their tongues they have used deceit, the poyson of asps is under
their lips: whose mouths are full of cursing and bitterneß. Their feet are swift to
shed blood. Destruction and misery are in their wayes: and the way of peace have
they not known. There is no fear of God before their eyes. What more positive
can be spoken? He seemeth to be particularly carefull, to avoid, that
any good should be ascribed to the natural man, he shewes how he is polluted in all his wayes, he shewes how he is void of rightcousnes, of understanding, of the knowledg of God, how he is out of the way, and in
short, unprofitable : than which nothing can be more fully said, to confirme our judgment. For, if this be the condition of the natural man, or
of man, as he stands in the fall, he is unfit to make one right step to
heaven.

If it be said, *That is not spoken of the condition of man, in general, but onely* Ob.
of some particulars, or at least that it comprehends not all.

The text sheweth the clean contrary, in the foregoing verses, where Answ.
the Apostle takes in himself, as he stood in his natural condition, *What*
then, are we better, than they? No, in no wise, for we have before proved
both Jewes and Gentiles, that they are all under sin, as it is written. And so
he goes on, by which it is manifest, that he speaks of mankind in general.

If they object, that, which the same Apostle saith, in the foregoing Obj.
chapter, vers 14. to wit, that *the Gentiles doe by natur the things contained*
in the Law, and so consequently, do, by natur, that, which is good and acce-
ptable in the sight of God.

I answer: This *natur* must not, neither can be understood of *man's* Answ.
own natur, which is corrupt and falln, but of that *Spiritual natur*, which
proceedeth from the *Seed of God in man*, as it receiveth a new visitation of
God's love, and is quickened by it, which clearly appears by the following words, where he saith, *These not having a Law*, (id est) outwardly,
are a Law unto themselves, which shewes the work of the Law written in their
hearts. These acts of theirs then, are an effect of the Law written in their
hearts, but the Scriptur declareth that the writing of the Law in the heart
is a part, yea and a great part too of the New Covenant dispensation,
and so no consequence nor part of man's natur.

Secondly : If this *natur*, here spoken of, could be understood of
man's own natur, which he hath, as he is a man, then would the

I

Apo-

Apoftle unavoidably contradict himfelf, fince he elfewhere pofitively declares, that *the natural man difcerneth not the things of God, nor can.*   Now I hope the Law of God, is among the things of God, efpecially as it's written in the heart.   The Apoftle, in the 7 chap. of the fame Epiftle, faith, vers 12. that *the Law is holy, juft, and good*; and vers 14. that *the Law is Spiritual, but he is carnal.*   Now, in what refpect is he *carnal*, but as he ftands in the fall, unregenerat? Now what inconfiftency would here be to fay, that he is carnal, and yet not fo, of his own natur? feing it is from his natur that he is fo denominated. We fee the Apoftle contra-diftinguifheth the Law, as Spiritual, from man's natur, as carnal and fin-full. Wherefore, as Chrift faith, *there can no grapes be* expected from *thiftles, nor figs of thorns*, fo neither can the fulfilling of the Law, which is Spi-ritual, holy and juft, be expected from that natur, which is corrupt, falln and unregenerat. Whence we conclude, with good reafon, that the *natur* here fpoken of, by which the *Gentiles* are faid to have done the *things contained in the Law*, is not the *common natur* of men, but that *Spiritual natur*, that arifeth from the works of the righteous and Spiritual Law, that's written in the heart. I confefs they of the other extream, when they are preffed with this teftimony by the *Socinians* and *Pelagians*, as wel as by us, when we ufe this Scriptur, to fhew them, how fome of the Heathens, by the *Light of Chrift in* their *heart*, come to be faved, are very farr to feek, giving this anfwer, *that there were fome reliques of the heavenly image left in Adam, by which the Heathens could doe fome good things.*   Which, as it is in it felf without proof, fo it contradicts their own affertions elfe-where, and gives away their caufe. For, if thefe reliques were of force to enable them to fulfill the righteous Law of God, it takes away the neceffity of Chrift's coming, or at leaft leaves them a way to be faved without him: unlefs they will fay, which is worft of all, *that, though they really fulfilled the righteous Law of God, yet God damned them, becaufe of the want of that particular knowledg, while he himfelf withheld all means of their coming to him, from them*; but of this hereafter.

§ 111. I might alfo here ufe another argument, from thefe words of the Apoftle 1 Cor. 2. where he fo pofitively excluds the natural man from an underftanding in the things of God; but becaufe I have fpoken of that Scriptur, in the beginning of the fecond Propofition, I will here avoid to repeat what is there mentioned, referring thereunto. Yet, becaufe the *Socinians*, and others, who exalt the Light of the natural man, or

a naa natural light in man, do object againſt this Scriptur, I ſhall remove it, ere I make an end.

They ſay, *The Greek word ψυχικὸς ought to be tranſlated* animal, *and not* natural, *elſe,* ſay they, *it* would have been φυσικὸς from which they ſeek to inferr, *that it is onely the animal man, and not the rational, that is excluded here, from the diſcerning the things of God.* Which ſhift, without diſputing about the word, is eaſily refuted, neither is it any wiſe conſiſtent with the ſcope of the place, for

Firſt, The *animal* life is no other, than that, which man hath common with other living creatures, for, as he is a meer man, he differs no otherwiſe from beaſts, than by the *rational* property. Now the Apoſtle deduceth his argument in the foregoing verſes, from this *ſimile,* that *as the things of a man can not be known but by the ſpirit of a man, ſo the things of God no man knoweth but by the Spirit of God.* But I hope, theſe men will confeſs unto me, that the things of a man are not known by the *animal ſpirit* onely, i. e. by that, which he hath common with the beaſts, but by the *rational:* ſo that it muſt be the *rational,* that is here underſtood. Again, the ſubſumption ſhewes clearly, that the Apoſtle had no ſuch intent, as theſe mens gloſs would make him to have; viz, *ſo the things of God knoweth no man, but the Spirit of God,* according to their judgment he ſhould have ſaid, *the things of God knoweth no man by his animal ſpirit, but by his rational ſpirit:* for to ſay, *the Spirit of God* here ſpoken of, is no other, than the *rational ſpirit* of man, would border upon blaſphemy, ſince they are ſo often contradiſtinguiſhed. Again, going on, he ſaith not, that they are *rationally,* but *ſpiritually diſcerned.*

Secondly: The Apoſtle throughout this chapter ſhewes how the wiſdom of man is unfit to judg of the things of God, and ignorant of them. Now I ask theſe men, whether a man be called a wiſe man from his *animal* property, or from his *rational?* If from his rational, then it is not onely the *animal,* but even the *rational,* as he is yet in the natural ſtate, which the Apoſtle excluds here, and whom he contradiſtinguiſheth from the *Spiritual,* verſ 15. *But the Spiritual man judgeth all things,* this can not be ſaid of any man meerly becauſe *rational,* or as he is a man; ſeing the men of greateſt reaſon, if we may ſo eſteem men, whom the Scriptur calls *wiſe,* as were the Greeks of old, not onely may be, but often are, enemies to the Kingdom of God, while both the *preaching of Chriſt* is ſaid to be *fooliſhneſs* with the wiſe men of this world, and the

wiſ-

wisdom of this world, is said to be *foolishness with God*. Now whether it be any wayes probable, that either these wise men, that are said to account the Gospel foolishness, are onely so called with respect to their animal property, and not their rational; or that that wisdom, that is foolishness with God, is not meant of the rational, but onely the animal property, any rational man, laying aside interest, may easily judg.

§ IV. I come now to the other part, to wit, that *this evil and corrupt seed is not imputed to infants, untill they actually joyn with it.* For this there is a reason given in the end of the Proposition it self, drawn from Eph. 2: for these *are by natur children of wrath, who walk according to the prince of the power of the air, the spirit, that now worketh in the children of disobedience.* Here the Apostle gives their evil walking, and not any thing, that is not reduced to act, as a reason of their being children of wrath: and this is suteable to the whole strain of the Gospel, where no man is ever threatened or judged for what iniquity he hath not actually wrought. Such indeed as continue in iniquity, and so do homologat the sins of their Fathers, God will visit the iniquity of the fathers upon the children.

Is it not strange then, that men should entertain an opinion so absurd in it self, and so cruel and contrary to the natur, as wel of God's mercy, as justice, concerning the which the Scriptur is altogether silent? But it is manifest, that man hath invented this opinion out of self-love and from that bitter root, from which all errours spring; for the most of Protestants, that hold this, having, as they fancy, the *absolute decree of election*, to secure them, and their children, so as they can not miss of Salvation, they make no great difficulty to send all others, both old and young, to hell. For, whereas self-love (which always is apt to believe that, which it desires) possesseth them with a hope that their part is secure, they are not solicitous how they leave their neighbours, which are the farr greater part of mankind, in these inextricable difficultys. The Papists again use this opinion, as an art to augment the esteem of their Church, and reverence of its Sacraments, seing they pretend it is washed away by baptism, onely in this they appear to be a little more mercifull, in that they send not these unbaptized infants to hell, but to a certain *Limbus*, concerning which the Scripturs are as silent as of the other. This then is not onely not authorised in the Scripturs, but contrary to the express tenor of it. The Apostle saith plainly, Rom. 4: 15. *Where no Law is, there is no transgression.* And again, 5: 13. *But sin is not imputed, where there is no Law.*

Than

Than which teftimonys there is nothing more pofitive, fince to infants there is no Law, feing, as fuch, they are utterly uncapable of it, the Law can not reach but fuch as have in fome meafur, lefs or more, the exercife of their underftanding, which infants have not. So that from thence I thus argue,

Sin is imputed to none, where there is no Law:

But to infants there is no Law:

Therefore fin is not imputed to them.

The *propofition* is the Apoftl's own words, the *affumption* is thus proved.

Thofe, who are under a phyfical impoffibility of either hearing, knowing, or underftanding any Law, where the impoffibility is not brought upon them by any act of their own, but is according to the very order of natur appoynted by God, to fuch there is no Law:

But infants are under this phyfical impoffibility:

Therefore, *&c.*

Secondly: What can be more pofitive, than that of Ezech. c. 18: v. 20. *The Soul that finneth, it fhall dye: the fon fhall not bear the fathers iniquity?* For the Prophet here firft fheweth what is the caufe of mans eternall death, which, he faith, is in his *finning*; and then, as if he purpofed expresfly to fhut out fuch an opinion, he affures us *the fon fhall not bear the fathers iniquity.* From which I thus argue,

If the fon bear not the iniquity of his father, or of his immediate parents, farr lefs fhall he bear the iniquity of Adam:

But the fon fhall not bear the iniquity of his father:

Therefore, &c.

§ V. Having thus farr fhewn how abfurd this opinion is, I fhall briefly examin the reafons its Authors bring for it,

Firft: They fay, *Adam was a publick perfon, and therefore all men finned in him, as being in his loins.* And for this they alledg that of Rom. 5: 12. *Wherefore, as by one man fin entred into the world, and death by fin: and fo death paffed upon all men, for that all have finned &c.* Thefe laft words, fay they, may be tranflated, in *whom all have finned:*   Obj.

To this I anfwer: That Adam is a publick perfon, is not denyed,   An w. and that through him there is a feed of fin propagated to all men, which in its own natur is finfull, and inclines men to iniquity; yet will it not follow from thence, that infants, who joyn not with this feed, are

I 3

guilty.

guilty. As for thefe words in the Romans, the reafon of the guilt there alledged is, *for that all have finned.* Now no man is faid to fin, unlefs he actually fin in his own perfon, for the Greek words ἐφ' ᾧ may very wel relate to θάνατος, which is the neareft antecedent; fo that they hold forth how that Adam, by his fin, gave an entrance to fin in the world, *and fo death entred by fin,* ἐφ' ᾧ i. e. *upon which* [viz, occafion] or, *in which* [viz, death] *all others have finned,* that is, actually, in their own perfons, to wit, all that were capable of finning, of which number that infants could not be, the Apoftle clearly fhewes by the following verfe, *fin is not imputed, where there is no Law:* and fince, as is above proved, there is no Law to infants, they can not be here included.

Obj.   Their fecond objection is from Pfal. 51: 5. *Behold, I was fhapen in iniquity, and in fin did my mother conceive me. Hence,* they fay *it appears, that infants from their conception are guilty.*

Anfw.   How they inferr this confequence, for my part, I fee not. The iniquity and fin here, appears to be farr more afcribable to the parents, than to the child. It is faid indeed, *in fin did my mother conceive me,* not *my mother did conceive me a finner.* Befides, that, fo interpreted, contradicts exprefly the Scriptur before mentioned, in making children guilty of the fins of their immediate parents, (for of Adam there is not here any mention) contrary to the plain words, *the Son fhall not bear the fathers iniquity.*

Obj.   Thirdly: They object that *the wages of fin is death, and that, feing children are fubject to difeafes and death, therefore they muft be guilty of fin.*

Anfw.   I anfwer: That thefe things are a confequence of the fall, and of Adam's fin, is confeffed, but that that infers neceffarily a guilt, in all others, that are fubject to them, is denyed. For though the whole outward *creation* fuffered a decay by Adam's fall, which *groans* under vanity, according to which it is faid, in *Job,* that *the heavens are not clean in the fight* of God, yet will it not from thence follow, that the herbs, earth, and trees are finners,

Next, Death, though a confequent of the fall, incident to mans earthly natur, is not the wages of fin, in the Saints, but rather a fleep, by which they pafs from death to life; which is fo farr from being troublfom and painfull to them, as all real punifhments for fin are, that the Apoftle counts it *gain: To me,* faith he, *to dye is gain,* Phil. 1: 21.

Obj.   Some are fo foolifh, as to make an objection further, faying, That, if

Adam's

Adam's sin be not imputed to those, who actually have not sinned, then it would fol-
low, that all infants are saved.

But we are willing that this supposed absurdity should be the consequence of our doctrin, rather than that, which, it seems, our adversarys reckon not absurd, though the undoubted and unavoidable consequence of theirs, viz, that *Many infants eternally perish, not for any sin of their*
own, but onely for Adam's iniquity; where we are willing to let the controversy sist, commending both to the illuminated understanding of the
Christian Reader.

This errour of our adversarys is both denyed and refuted by *Zwinglius*
that eminent founder of the Protestant Churches of *Zwitzerland*, in his
book *De Baptismô*, for which he is anathematized by the Council of *Trent*, in
the fifth Session. We shall only add this information, that we confess then,
that a seed of sin is transmitted to all men from Adam (although imputed
to none, untill by sinning they actually joyn with it) in which seed he gave
occasion to all to sin, and it is the origin of all evil actions and thoughts
in mens hearts : ἐφ᾽ ᾧ to wit , θάνατω, as it is in the 5 of the Romans ,
i. e. *in which death all have sinned* For this seed of sin is frequently called
death in the Scripturs, and *the body of death*, seing indeed it is a *death* to the
life of righteousness and holyness.   Therefore its seed and its product is
called the *old man*, the *old Adam*, in which all sin is ; for which cause we
use this name, to express this sin, and not that of *original sin*, of which
phrase the Scriptur makes no mention, and under which, invented and
unscriptural Barbarism, this notion of *imputed sin to infants* took place
among Christians.

The Fifth and Sixth Propositions,

Concerning the Vniversal Redemption by Christ, and also the Saving
and Spiritual Light, wherewith every man is inlightened.

The Fifth Proposition

GOD, out of his infinit love, *who delighteth not in the*
death of a sinner, but that all should live and be saved, hath so

Ezech. 18
vers 32.
& 33: 11.

lov-

loved the world, that he hath given his Onely Son a LIGHT, that whosoever believeth in him should be saved, Joh. 3: 16. *who inlighteneth EVERY man that cometh into the world* Joh. c. 1: v. 9. *and maketh manifest all things*, that are reprovable, Eph. 5: 13. and teacheth all temperance, righteousnefs, and godlynefs. And this Light lighteneth the hearts of all in a day, in order to Salvation, and this is it, which reproves the fin of all individuals, and would, work out the Salvation of all, if not refifted: nor is it lefs *univerfal*, than the feed of fin, being the purchafe of his *death who tafted death* for *every man. For, as in Adam all dye, even fo in Chrift all fhall be made alive*, 1 Cor. 15: 22.

The Sixth Propofition.

According to which Principle (or *hypothefis*) all the objections againft the *univerfality* of *Chrift's death*, are eafily folved, neither is it needfull to recurr to the miniftry of Angels, and thofe other miraculous means, which, they fay, God ufeth, to manifeft the doctrin and hiftory of Chrift's paffion, unto fuch (who living in the places of the world, where the outward preaching of the Gofpel is unknown) have wel improved the firft and common grace. For, as hence it wel followes, that fome of the old Philofophers might have been faved, fo alfo may fome (who by Providence are caft into thofe remote parts of the world, where the knowledg of the hiftory is wanting) be made partakers of the Divine myftery, if they receive, and refift not that Grace, a *manifeftation* whereof is *given to every man to profite withall.* This moft certain doctrin being then received, that there is an Evangelical and Saving *Light* and *Grace in all*, the univerfality of the Love and Mercy of God towards mankind (both in the death of his Beloved Son

1 Cor 12: vers 7.

the

the Lord Jeſus Chriſt, and in the manifeſtation of the *Light in* the *heart*) is eſtabliſhed and confirmed, againſt all the objections of ſuch as deny it. Therefore Chriſt hath *taſted death for every man,* not onely for *all kind of men,* as ſome vainly talk, but for *every man of all kinds*; the benefit of whoſe offering, is not onely extended to ſuch, who have the diſtinct outward knowledg of his death and ſufferings, as the ſame is declared in the Scripturs, but even unto thoſe, who are neceſſarily excluded from the benefit of this knowledg, by ſome inevitable accident: which knowledg we willingly confeſs to be very profitable and comfortable, but not abſolutely needfull unto ſuch, from whom God himſelf hath withheld it, yet they may be made partakers of the myſtery of his death, (though ignorant of the hiſtory) if they ſuffer *his Seed, and Light* (*inlightening their hearts*) to take place, (*in which Light communion with the Father and the Son is enjoyed*) ſo as of wicked men to become holy, and lovers of that Power, by whoſe inward and ſecret touches they feel themſelves turned from the evil to the good, and learn to *doe to others, as they would be done by,* in which Chriſt himſelf affirms all to be included. As *They* have then falſly and erroneouſly taught, who have denyed Chriſt to have dyed for all men, ſo neither have *They* ſufficiently taught the Truth, who affirming him to have dyed for all, have added the abſolute neceſſity of the outward knowledg thereof, in order to obtain its ſaving effect. Among whom the *Remonſtrants* of *Holland* have been chiefly wanting, and many other aſſertors of Univerſal Redemption, in that they have not placed the extent of his ſalvation in that Divine and Evangelical Principle of *Light* and *Life,* wherewith *Chriſt hath inlightened Every man, that cometh into the world,*

Heb. 2: 9

K

which

which is excellently and evidently held forth in thefe
Scripturs, Gen. 6:3. Deut. 30:14. Joh. 1:7, 8, 9, 16.
Rom. 10:8. Tit. 2:11.

Hitherto we have confidered mans fallen, loft, corrupted and
uegenerated condition.

Now it is fit to inquire, *how, and by what means he may come
to be freed out of this miferable and depraved condition*; which, in
thefe two Propofitions, is declared and demonftrated, which
I thought meet to place together, becaufe of their affinity, The one
being, as it were, an explanation of the other.

As for that doctrin, which thefe Propofitions chiefly ftrike at, to wit,
abfolute reprobation; according to which, fome are not afraid to affert;
That God, by an eternal and immutable decree, hath predeftinated to
eternal damnation, the farr greater part of mankind, not confidered as
made, much lefs as falln, without any refpect to their difobedience or fin,
but onely for the demonftrating of the glory of his juftice: and that, for
the bringing this about, he hath appoynted thefe miferable Souls neceffarily to walk in their wicked wayes, that fo his Juftice may lay hold on
them: and that God doth therefore not onely fuffer them to be liable to
this mifery, in many parts of the world, by witholding from them the
preaching of the Gofpel, and knowledg of Chrift; but even in thofe
places, where the Gofpel is preached, and Salvation by Chrift is offered: whom, thcugh he publikely invite them, yet he juftly condemnes,
for difobedience, albeit he hath withheld from them all Grace, by which
they could have laid hold on the Gofpel, *viz*, becaufe he hath, by a fecret will unknown to all men, ordained and decreed, (without any refpect had to their difobedience or fin) that they fhall not obey, and that
the offer of the Gofpel fhall never prove effectual, for their Salvation;
but onely ferve to aggravate and occafion their greater condemnation.

I fay, as to this horrible and blafphemous doctrin, our caufe is common with many others, who have, both wifely, and learnedly, according to Scriptur, Reafon, and Antiquity, refuted it. Seing then that fo
much, and fo wel, is faid already againft this doctrin, that little can be
fuperadded, except what hath been faid already, I fhall be fhort in this
refpect. Yet, becaufe it lies fo in oppofition to my way, I can not let
it altogether pafs.

§ I.

§ I. Firſt : We may ſafely call this doctrin a *novelty*, ſeing the firſt four hundred years after Chriſt, there is no mention made of it : for as it is contrary to the Scripturs teſtimony, and to the tenor of the Goſpel, ſo all the antient writers, teachers, and doctors of the Church paſs it over with a profound ſilence. The firſt foundations of it were laid in the latter writings of Auguſtin, who, in his heat againſt Pelagius, let fall ſome expreſſions, which ſome have unhappily gleaned up, to the eſtabliſhing of this errour; thereby contradicting the Truth, and ſufficiently gainſaying many others, and many more and frequent expreſſions of the ſame Auguſtin. Afterwards was this doctrin fomented by Dominicus a frier, and the Monks of his Order; and at laſt, unhappyly, taken up by John Calvin (otherwiſe a man, in divers reſpects to be commended) to the great ſtaining of his reputation, and diffamation both of the Proteſtant and Chriſtian religion : which, though it received the decrees of the Synod of Dort for its confirmation, hath ſince loſt ground, and begins to be exploded by moſt men of learning and piety in all Proteſtant Churches. However we ſhould not quarrel it for the ſilence of the Antients, paucity of its aſſertors, or for the learnedneſs of its oppoſers, if we did obſerve it to have any real bottom in the writings, or ſayings of Chriſt and the Apoſtles, and that it were not *highly injurious to God himſelf, to Jeſus Chriſt our Mediator and Redeemer, and to the Power, Vertue, Nobility, and Excellency of his Bleſſed Goſpel, and laſtly unto all mankind.*

§ 11. Firſt, *It is highly injurious to God*, becauſe it makes him the author of ſin; which, of all things is moſt contrary to his natur. I confeſs the aſſertors of this principle deny this conſequence, but that is but a pure illuſion, ſeing it ſo naturally followes from their doctrin, and is equally ridiculous, as if a man ſhould pertinaciouſly deny that *one* and *two* makes *three.* For if God has decreed that the reprobated ones ſhall periſh, without all reſpect to their evil deeds, but onely of his own pleaſur : and if he hath alſo decreed, long before they were in being, or in any capacity to doe good or evil, that they ſhould walk in thoſe wicked wayes, by which, as by a ſecondary means, they are led to that end, who, I pray, is the firſt author and cauſe thereof, but God, who ſo willed and decreed? This is as natural a conſequence, as any can be. And therefore, although many of the preachers of this doctrin have ſought out various, ſtrange, ſtrained and intricat diſtinctions, to defend their opinion, and evite this horrid conſequence; yet, ſome, and that of the moſt eminent

of

of them, have been so plain in the matter, as they have put it beyond all doubt. Of which I shall instance a few among many passages. * *I say, that by the ordination and will of God, Adam fell. God would have man to fall. Man is blinded by the will and commandment of God. We refer the causes of hardening us to God. The highest or remote cause of hardening is the will of God. It followeth that the hidden counsel of God is the cause of hardening.* These are Calvin's expressions. a *God (saith Beza) hath predestinated not onely unto damnation but also unto the causes of it, whomsoever he saw meet.* b *The decree of God can not be excluded from the causes of corruption.* c *It is certain, (saith Zanchius) that God is the First cause of obduration. Reprobats are held so fast under Gods Almighty decree, that they can not but sin and perish.* d *It is the opinion (saith Paræus) of our doctors, that God did inevitably decree the temptation and fall of man. The creatur sinneth indeed necessarily by the most just Judgment of God. Our men do most rightly affirme, that the fall of man was necessary and inevitable by accident, because of Gods decree.* e *God (saith Martyr) doth incline and force the wills of wicked men into great sins.* f *God (saith Zwinglius) moveth the robber to kill. He killeth, God forçing him thereunto. But thou wilt say, he is forced to sin, I permitt truely, that he is forced.* g *Reprobate persons (saith Piscator) are obsolutely ordained to this twofold end, to undergo everlasting punishment, and necessarily to sin, and therefore to sin, that they may be justly punished.*

If these sayings do not plainly and evidently import, that God is *the author of sin*, we must not then seek these mens opinions from their words, but some way else: it seems as if they had assumed to themselves that monstrous and twofold will they feign of God; one, by which they declare their minds openly, and another more secret and hidden, which is quite contrary to the other. Nor doth it at all help them, to say, that man sins willingly, since that willingness, proclivity and propensity to evil, is, according to their judgment, so necessarily imposed upon him, that he can not but be willing, because God hath willed and decreed him to be so. Which shift is just as if I should take a child uncapable to resist me, and throw it down from a great precipice, the weight of the childs body indeed makes it go readily down, and the violence of the fall upon some rock or stone, beats out its brains, and kills it. Now then, I pray, though the body of the child goes willingly down, (for I suppose it, as to its mind, is uncapable of any will) and the weight of its body, and not any immediate stroak of my hand, who perhaps am at a

great

great diftance, makes it dye, whether is the child or I the proper caufe of its death? Let any man of reafon judg, if Gods part be (with them) as great, yea more immediate, in the fins of men, (as, by the teftimonys above brought, doth appear) whether doth not this make him not onethe author of fin, but more unjuft, than the unjufteft of men?

§ III. Secondly, *this doctrin is injurious to God*, becaufe it makes him delight in the death of finners, yea and to will many to dye in their fins, contrary to thefe Scriptures, Ezech. 33 : 11. 1 Tim. 2 : 3. 2 Pet. 3 : 9. For, if he hath created men onely for this very end, that he might fhow forth his juftice and power in them, as thefe men affirme, and, for effecting thereof, hath not onely withheld from them the means of doing good; but alfo predeftinated the evil, that they might fall into it; and that he inclines and forces them into great fins, certainly he muft neceffarily delight in their death, and will them to dye, feing againft his own will he neither doth, nor can doe any thing.

§ IV. Thirdly, *it is highly injurious to Chrift our Mediator, and to the efficacy and excellency of his Gofpel*: for it renders his mediation ineffectual, as if he had not by his fufferings throughly broken down the middle wall, nor yet removed the wrath of God, or purchafed the love of God towards all mankind; if it was afore decreed, that it fhould be of no fervice to the far greater part of mankind. It is to no purpofe to alledg that the death of Chrift was of efficacy enough to have faved all mankind, if, in effect, its vertue be not fo farr extended, as to put all mankind into a capacity of Salvation.

Fourthly, it makes the *preaching of the Gofpel a meer mock and illufion*, if many of thefe, to whom it is preached, be by an irrevocable decree excluded from being benefited by it : it wholly makes ufelefs the preaching of faith and repentance, and the whole tenor of the Gofpel promifes and threatenings, as being all relative to a former decree, and means before appoynted to fuch, which becaufe they can not fail, man needs doe nothing, but wait for that irrefiftible fnatch, which will come, though it be but at the laft hour of his life, if he be in the decree of election. And be his diligence and waiting what it can, he fhall never attain it, if he belong to the decree of reprobation.

Fifthly, it makes the *coming of Chrift, and his propitiatory Sacrifice*, which the Scriptur affirmes to have been the fruit of God's Love to the world, and transacted for the fins and Salvation of all men, to have been rather a

K 3

teftimony

testimony of God's wrath to the world, and one of the greatest judgments and severest acts of God's indignation towards mankind, it being onely ordain'd to save a very few, and for the hardening, obduring, and augmenting the condemnation of the farr greater number of men, because they believe not truely in it; the cause of which unbelief again (as the Divines [so called] above assert) is the hidden counsel of God: certainly the coming of Christ was never to them a testimony of God's love, but rather of his implacable wrath. And, if the World may be taken for the farr greater number of such as live in it, God never loved the world, according to this doctrin, but rather hated it greatly, in sending his Son to be crucified in it.

§ V. Sixthly, *this doctrin is highly injurious to mankind*: for it renders them in a farr worse condition, than the devils in hell. For these were sometimes in a capacity to have stood, and do suffer onely for their own guilt; whereas many millions of men are for ever tormented, according to them, for Adam's sin; which they neither knew of, nor ever were accessary to. It renders them worse, than the beasts of the field, of whom the master requires not more, than they are able to performe, and if they be killed, death to them is the end of sorrow; whereas man is for ever tormented, for not doing that, which he never was able to doe. It puts him into a farr worse condition, than Pharaoh put the Israelits: for, though he withheld straw from them, yet, by much labour and pains, they could have gotten it. But from men they make God to withhold all means of Salvation, so that they can by no means attain it. Yea they place mankind in that condition, which the Poëts feign of *Tantalus*, who, oppressed with thirst, stands in water up to the chin, yet can by no means reach it with his tongue; and, being tormented with hunger, hath fruit hanging at his very lips, yet so as he can never lay hold on them with his teeth, and these things are so near him not to nourish him, but to torment him. So do these men, they make the outward creation of the works of Providence, the smitings of the Conscience, sufficient to convince the Heathens of sin, and so to condemn and judg them, but not at all to help them to Salvation. They make the preaching of the Gospel, the offer of Salvation by Christ, the use of the Sacraments, of Prayer and good works sufficient to condemn those they account reprobats within the Church. serving onely to inform them to beget a seeming faith, and vain hope, yet, because of a secret impotency, which they

had

had from their infancy, all theſe are wholly ineffectual to bring them the leaſt ſtep towards Salvation, and do onely contribute to render their condemnation the greater, and their torments the more violent and intolerable.

Having thus briefly removed this falſe doctrin, which ſtood in my way, becauſe they, that are deſirous, may ſee it both learnedly and piouſly refuted by many others, I come to the matter of our Propoſition, which is, that *God, out of his infinite love, who delighteth not in the death of a ſinner, but that all ſhould live and be ſaved, hath ſent his Onely-begotten Son into the world, that whoſoever believeth in him might be ſaved;* which alſo is again affirmed in the ſixth Propoſition, in theſe words, *Chriſt then taſted death for every man of all kinds.*   Such is the evidence of this Truth, delivered almoſt wholly in the expreſs words of Scriptur, that it will not need much probation.   Alſo, becauſe our aſſertion herein, is common with many others, who have both earneſtly and ſoundly, according to the Scriptur, pleaded for this Univerſal Redemption, I ſhall be the more brief in it, that I may come to that, which may ſeem more ſingularly and peculiarly ours.

§ V I. This doctrin of Univerſal redemption, or Chriſts dying for all men, is, of it ſelf, ſo evident from the Scriptur teſtimony, that there is ſcarce found any other article of the Chriſtian faith, ſo frequently, ſo plainly, and ſo poſitively aſſerted.   It is that, which maketh the preaching of Chriſt to be truely termed the Goſpel, or an annunciation of glad tydings to all. Thus the Angel declared the birth and coming of Chriſt to the ſhepheards to be Luk. 2: 1 0. *behold I bring jou good tydings of great joy, which ſhall be to all people.* He ſaith not *to a few people.* Now if this coming of Chriſt, had not brought a poſſibility of Salvation *to all,* it ſhould rather have been accounted bad tydings of great ſorrow, to moſt people, neither ſhould the Angel have had reaſon to have ſung *Peace on earth, and good-will towards men,* if the greateſt part of mankind had been neceſſarily ſhut out from receiving any benefit by it.   How ſhould Chriſt have ſent out his to *preach the Goſpel to every creatur,* Mark. 1 6 : 1 5 ? a very comprehenſive commiſſion! that is *to every ſon and daughter of mankind.*   Without all exception, he commands them to preach *Salvation to all, repentance and remiſſion of ſins to all, warning every one, and exhorting every one,* as Paul did, Col. 1 : 2 8.   Now how could they have preached the Goſpel *to every man,* as became the miniſters of Jeſus Chriſt, in much

aſſur-

aſſurance; if Salvation, by that Goſpel, had not been poſſible for all, what if ſome of thoſe had asked them, or ſhould now ask any of theſe doctors who deny the Univerſallity of Chriſt's death, and yet preach it to all promiſcuouſly, *hath Chriſt dyed for me?* How can they with confidence give a certain anſwer to this queſtion? If they give a conditional anſwer, as their principle obligeth them to do, and ſay, *If thou repent, Chriſt hath dyed for thee,* doth not the ſame queſtion ſtill recurr? *Hath Chriſt dyed for me, ſo as to make repentance poſſible for me?* To this they can anſwer nothing, unleſs they run in a circle: whereas *the feet of thoſe, that bring the glad tidings of the Goſpel of Peace,* are ſaid to be *beautifull,* for that they preach the *common Salvation,* repentance unto all, offering a door of mercy and hope to all through *Jeſus Chriſt,* who *gave himſelf a ranſom for all.* The Goſpel invites *all:* and certainly by the Goſpel Chriſt intended not to deceive and delude the greater part of mankind, when he invites and cryeth, ſaying, *Come unto me, all ye, that are weary and heavy laden, and I will give you reſt.* If *all* then ought to ſeek after him, and to look for Salvation by him, he muſt needs have made *Salvation poſſible to all:* for who is bound to ſeek after that, which is impoſſible? Certainly it were a mocking of men, to bid them doe ſo. And ſuch as deny, that, by the death of Chriſt, *Salvation* is made *poſſible to all men,* do moſt blaſphemously make God mock the world, in giving his ſervants a commiſſion to preach the Goſpel of Salvation unto *all,* while he hath before decreed, that it ſhall not be poſſible for them to receive it. Would not this make the Lord to ſend forth his ſervants with a *lye in their mouth,* which were blaſphemous to think, commanding them to bid *all* and *every one* believe, that Chriſt dyed for them, and had purchaſed life and Salvation? Whereas it is no ſuch thing, according to the forementioned doctrin. But, ſeing Chriſt, after he aroſe, and perfected the work of our Redemption, gave a commiſſion to preach repentance, remiſſion of ſins, and Salvation to all; it is manifeſt, that he *dyed for all.* For he, that hath commiſſionated his ſervants thus to preach, is a *God of Truth,* and no mocker of poor mankind, neither doth he require of any man, that, which is ſimply impoſſible for him to doe; for that, *no man is bound to doe that, which is impoſſible,* is a principle of Truth ingraven in every mans mind. And, ſeing he is both a moſt Righteous and mercifull God, it can not at all ſtand neither with his juſtice nor mercy, to bid ſuch men repent or believe, to whom it is impoſſible.

§ VII.

§ VII. Moreover, if we regard the teftimony of the Scriptur, in this matter, where there is not one Scriptur, which I know of, that affirmeth Chrift not to dye for *all*, there are divers, that pofitively and expreſly aſſert he did, as 1 Tim. 2: 1, 3, 4, 6. *I exhort therefore, that firſt of all fupplications, prayers, interceſſions, and giving of thanks be made for all men, &c. for this is good and acceptable in the fight of God our Saviour, who will have all men to be faved, and to come to the knowledg of the Truth, who gave himself a ranfome for all, to be teſtified in due time.* Except we will have the Apoſtle here to aſſert quite another thing, then he intended; there can be nothing more plain, to confirme what we have aſſerted. And this Scriptur doth wel anfwer to that manner of arguing, which we have hitherto ufed : for firſt the Apoſtle here recommends them to *pray for all men.* And to obviate fuch an objection, as if they had faid, with our adverfarys, *Chriſt prayed not for the world, neither willeth he us to pray for all, becaufe he willeth not that all ſhould be faved, but hath ordained many to be damned, that he might ſhew forth his juſtice in them.* He obviats, I fay, fuch an objection, telling them that *it is good and acceptable in the fight of God, who will have all men to be faved,* I defire to know, what can be more expreſly affirmed, or can any two Propoſitions be ſtated in terms more contradictory than thefe two, *God willeth not fome to be faved,* and *God willeth all men to be faved,* or, *God will have no man periſh.* If we believe the laſt, as the Apoſtle hath affirmed, the firſt muſt be deſtroyed ; feing of contradictory Propoſitions, the one being placed, the other is deſtroyed. Whence, to conclude, he gives us a reafon of his willingnefs that *all* men ſhould be faved, in thefe words, *who gave himſelf a ranfom for all,* as if he would have faid, fince Chriſt dyed for all, fince he gave himfelf a ranfom for all, therefore he will have all men to be faved. This Chriſt himfelf gives as the reafon of God's Love to the world, in thefe words, Joh. 3: 16. *God fo loved the world, that he gave his Onely-begotten Son, that whofoever believeth in him, ſhould not periſh, but have everlaſting life.* Compared with 1 Joh. 4: 9. This [*whofoever*] is an indefinit term, from which no man is excluded. From all which then I thus argue,

For whomfoever it is lawfull to pray, to them Salvation is poſſible :   Arg.
But it's lawfull to pray for every individual man in the whole world :
Therefore Salvation is poſſible unto them.

I prove the *major propoſition* thus,

L

No

No man is bound to pray for that, which is impoſſible to be attained :

But every man is bound and commanded to pray for all men :

Therefore it is not impoſſible to be obtained.

I prove alſo this Propoſition further; thus

No man is bound to pray but in faith :

But he, that prayeth for that, which he judges ſimply impoſſible to be obtained, can not pray in faith :

Therefore, *&c.*   Again,

That, which God willeth, is not impoſſible :

But God willeth all men to be ſaved :

Therefore it is not impoſſible.

And laſtly,

Theſe, for whom our Saviour gave himſelf a ranſom, to ſuch Salvation is poſſible :

But our Saviour gave himſelf a ranſom for all :

Therefore Salvation is poſſible unto them.

§ VIII. This is very poſitively affirmed, Heb. 2: 9. in theſe words, *But we ſee Jeſus, who was made a little lower, than the Angels, for the ſuffering of death crowned with glory and honour, that he by the Grace of God, might taſt death for every man.* He, that will but open his eyes, may ſee this truth here aſſerted; if he taſted death for every man, then certainly there is no man, for whom he did not taſt death, then there is no man, who may not be made a ſharer of the benefit of it; for *he came not to condemn the world, but that the world through him might be ſaved*, Joh. 3: 17. *he came not to judg the world, but to ſave the world*, Joh. 12: 47. Whereas, according to the doctrin of our adverſarys, he behoved to come to condemn the world, and judg it, and not that it might be ſaved by him, or to ſave it : for, if he never came to bring Salvation to a great part of mankind, but that his coming, though it could never doe them good, yet ſhall augment their condemnation, from thence it neceſſarily followes, that he came not of intention to ſave, but to judg and condemn the greater part of the world, contrary to his own expreſs teſtimony, and, as the Apoſtle Paul, in the words above cited, doth aſſert affirmatively, that *God willeth the Salvation of all*, ſo doth the Apoſtle Peter aſſert negatively, that *he willeth not the periſhing of any*, 2 Pet. 3: 9. *The Lord is not ſlack concerning his promiſe, as ſome men count ſlackneſs, but is long-ſuffering to us ward, not willing, that any ſhould periſh, but that all ſhould come to repentance.* And this is cor-

reſponrefpondent to that of the Prophet Ezechiel **33:11**. *As I live, faith the Lord, I have no pleafur in the death of the wicked, but that the wicked turn from his way and live.* If it be fafe to believe God, and truft in him, we muft not think that he intends to cheat us, by all thefe expreffions through his fervants; but that he was in good earneft, and that this will and defire of his hath not taken effect, the blame is on our parts, as fhall be after fpoken of, which could not be, if fo be we never were in any capacity of Salvation, or that Chrift had never dyed for us, but left us under an impoffibility of Salvation, what means all thofe earneft invitations? all thofe ferious expoftulations? all thofe regreting contemplations? wherewith the Holy Scripturs are full, as, *Why will ye dye? O houfe of Ifrael! why will ye not come to me, that ye might have life? I have waited to be gracious unto you. I have fought to gather you. I have knocked at the door of your hearts. Is not your deftruction of your felves? I have called all the day long.* If men, who are fo invited, be under no capacity of being faved, if Salvation be impoffible unto them; fhall we fuppofe God, in this, to be no other, but like the author of a Romance, or the mafter of a comedy, who amufes and raifes the various affections and paffions of his fpectators by divers and ftrange accidents, fometimes leading them into hope, and fometimes into defpair, all thofe actions in effect being but a pure illufion, while he hath appoyn-what the conclufion of all fhall be?

Thirdly, this doctrin is abundantly confirmed by that of the Apoftle 1 Joh. 2: 1,2. *And if any man fin, we have an Advocat with the Father Jefus Chrift the Righteous. And he is the Propitiation for our fins, and not for ours onely, but alfo for the fins of the whole world.* The way, which our adverfarys take to evite this teftimony, is moft foolifh and ridiculous. *The* [*World*] *here,* fay they, *is the World of believers.* For this commentary we have nothing, but their own affertion, and fo, while it manifeftly deftroys the text, may be juftly rejected. For Firft, let them fhew me, if they can, in all the Scriptur, where the [*whole world*] is taken for *Believers* onely, I fhall fhew them, where it is many times taken for the quite contrary, as, *the world knowes me not. The world receives me not. I am not of this world.* Befides all, thefe Scripturs Pfalm. 17: 14. Ifa. 13: 11. Matth. 18:7. Joh. 7:7. 8:26. 12:19. 14:17. 15:18,19. 17: 14, 18, 20. 1 Cor. 1:21. 2:12. 6:2. Gal. 6:14. Ja. 1:27. 2 Pet. 2:20. 1 Joh. 2:15. 3:1. and 4:4,5. and many more. Secondly, The Apoftle, in this very place, contradiftinguifheth the *World* from the

                                                         Saints;

Saints, thus, *and not for ours onely, but for the sins of the whole world.* What means the Apostle by [*ours*] here? is not that the sins of Believers? was not he one of those Believers? and was not this an universal epistle written to all the Saints, that then were? So that, according to these mens comment, there should be a very unnecessary and foolish redundancy in the Apostl's words: as if he had said, *he is a Propitiation not onely for the sins of all Believers, but for the sins of all Believers.* Is not this to make the Apostles words void of good sense? Let them shew us, wherever there is such a manner of speaking in all the Scriptur: where any of the pen-men first name the *Believers* in *concretô* with themselves, and then contradistinguish them from some other whole world of Believers. That [*whole world,*] if it be of Believers, must not be the world we live in. But we need no better interpreter for the Apostle, than himself, who uses the very same expression and phrase, in the same epistle, c. 5: 19. saying, *We know that we are of God, and the whole world lieth in wickedneß:* there can not be found in all the Scriptur two places, which run more paralell, seing, in both, the same Apostle, in the same epistle, to the same persons, contradistinguisheth himself, and the Saints, to whom he writes, from the whole world; which according to these mens commentary, ought to be understood of Believers, as if John had said, *We know particular Believers are of God, but the whole world of Believers lieth in wickedneß.* What absurd wresting of Scriptur were this? And yet it may be as wel pleaded for, as the other, for they differ not at all: seing then that the Apostle John tells us plainly, that Christ not onely dyed for him, and for the Saints and members of the Church of God, to whom he wrot, but for the *whole world.* Let us then hold it for a certain and undoubted Truth, notwithstanding the cavills of such as oppose.

This might also be proved from many more Scriptur testimonys, if it were at this season needfull. All the *Fathers,* so called, and *Doctors* of the Church for the first four centurys preached this doctrin, according to which they boldly held forth the Gospel of Christ, and efficacy of his death, inviting and intreating the Heathens to come and be partakers of the benefits of it, shewing them, how there was a door open for them all to be saved, through Jesus Christ, not telling them that God had predestinated any of them to damnation, or had made Salvation impossible to them, by withholding power and Grace, necessary to believe, from them. But of many of their sayings, which might be alledged, I shall onely instance a few.

Augustin, on the 95 Psalm, saith; ,, The blood of Christ is of so
,, great worth, that it is of no less value, than the whole world.

Prosper ad *Gall. c. 9.*   ,, The Redeemer of the world gave his blood for
,, the world, and the world would not be redeemed, because the darkness
,, did not receive the Light. He that saith, the Saviour was not crucified
,, for the redemption of the whole world, looks not to the vertue of the
,, Sacrament, but to the part of infidels, since the blood of our Lord Jesus
,, Christ is the price of the whole world, from which redemption they
,, are strangers, who either delighting in their captivity would not be
,, redeemed, or, after they were redeemed, returned to the same servitud.

The same *Prosper*, in his answer to *Vincentius's* first objection. ,, Seing
,, therefore because of one common natur, and cause in Truth; under-
,, taken by our Lord, all are rightly said to be redeemed, and never-
,, theless all are not brought out of captivity, the property of redem-
,, ption, without doubt, belongeth to those, from whom the prince
,, of this world is shut out, and now are not vessels of the devil, but
,, members of Christ; whose death was so bestowed upon mankind,
,, that it belonged to the redemption of such, who were not to be re-
,, generated. But so, that that, which was done by the example of
,, one for all, might, by a singular mystery, be celebrated in every
,, one. For the cup of immortality, which is made up of our infirmity
,, and the Divine Power, hath indeed that in it, which may profit all,
,, but if it be not drunk, it doth not heal.

The Author *de vocat. Gentium*, lib. 11. cap. 6.   ,, There is no cause
,, to doubt, but that our Lord Jesus Christ dyed for sinners and wicked
,, men, and if there can be any found, who may be said not to be of
,, this number, Christ hath not dyed for all, he made himself a Re-
,, deemer for the whole world.

Chrysostom, on the   1. chap. of John: ,, If he inlightens
,, every man coming into the world, how comes it, that so many men
,, remain without Light? For all do not so much as acknowledg
,, Christ, how then doth he inlighten every man? he illuminats in-
,, deed so farr as in him is, but if any, of their own accord, closing
,, the eyes of their mind, will not direct their eyes unto the beams of
,, this Light, the cause that they remain in darkness is not from the
,, natur of the Light, but through their own malignity, who willingly

L 3

,, have

,, have rendred themselves unworthy of so great a gift. But why be-
,, lieved they not? Because they would not. Christ did his part.

The *Arelatensian* Synod, held about the year 490, pronounced him
,, accursed, who should say that Christ hath not dyed for all, or that
,, he would not have all men tobe saved.

Ambr. on Psal. 118. Serm. 8. ,, The mystical sun of Righteousness
,, is arisen to all, he came to all, he suffered for all, and rose again
,, for all.   And therefore he suffered, that he might take away the
,, sin of the world: But if any one believe not in Christ, he robs him-
,, self of this general benefit, even as if one by closing the windows,
,, should hold out the Sun-beams; the Sun is not therefore not arisen
,, to all, because such a one hath so robbed himself of its heat: but
,, the Sun keeps its prerogative, it is such a ones imprudence, that he
,, shuts himself out from the common benefit of the Light.

The same man in his 11 book of Cain and Abel, cap. 13. saith;
,, Therefore he brought unto all, the means of health, that, who-
,, soever should perish, may ascribe to himself the causes of his death,
,, who would not be cured, when he had the remedy, by which he
,, might have escaped.

§ IX. Seing then that this doctrin of the Universality of Christ's
death is so certain and agreable to the Scripturs testimony, and to the
sense of the purest Antiquity, it may be wondered how so many, some
whereof have been esteemed not onely learned, but also pious, have been
capable to fall into so gross and strange an errour. But the cause of this
doth evidently appear, in that the way and method, by which the vertue
and efficacy of this death is communicated to all men, hath not been
rightly understood; or indeed hath been erroneously affirmed. The Pelagians, ascribing all to man's will and natur, denyed man to have any seed
of sin conveighed to him from Adam.   And the Semi-Pelagians making
Grace as a Gift following upon man's merit or right improving of his natur, according to their known principle, *Facienti quod in se est, Deus non
denegat gratiam.*

This gave Augustin, Prosper, and some others occasion, labouring,
in opposition to these opinions, to magnify the Grace of God, and paint
out the corruption of man's natur, (as the proverb is, of those, that seek
to make straight a crooked stick) to incline to the other extreme. So also
the Reformers, Luther, and others, finding, among other errours, the

strange

ftrange expreffions, ufed by fome of the Popifh Scholaftiks, concerning free will, and how much the tendency of their principles is to exalt man's natur, and leffen God's Grace, having all thofe fayings of Auguftin and others, for a pattern, through the like miftake ran upon the fame extreme. Though afterwards the Lutherans feing how farr Calvin and his followers drove this matter (who, as a man of fubtile and profound judgment, forefeing where it would land, refolved above board to affert, that God had decreed the means as wel as the end (and therefore had ordained men to fin, and excites them thereto, which he labours earneftly to defend) and that there was no avoiding the making God the author of fin, thereby received occafion to difcern the falfity of this doctrin, and difclaimed it; as appears by the latter writings of Melancthon, and the Monpelgartenfian conference, where Lucas Ofiander one of the collocutors termes it *impious*, calls it a making God the author of fin, and a horrid and horrible blafphemy. Yet, becaufe none of thofe who have afferted this Univerfal Redemption, fince the reformation, have given a clear diftinct, and fatisfactory teftimony, how it is communicated to all, and fo have falln fhort of fully declaring the perfection of the Gofpel difpenfation; others have been thereby the more ftrengthened in their errours. Which I fhall illuftrate by one fingular example.

Epit. Hift.
Eccl.
Lucæ
Ofiand.
Cent. 16.
lib. 4.
cap. 32.

The Arminians and other affertors of univerfal Grace ufe this as a chief argument,

 That, which every man is bound to believe, is true:

 But every man is bound to believe that Chrift dyed for them:

 Therefore, &c.

Of this argument the other party deny the *affumption*, faying, that *they, who never heard of Chrift, are not obliged to believe in him, and feing the Remonftrants* (as they are commonly called) *do generally themfelves acknowledg, that, without the outward knowledg of Chrift, there is no Salvation; that gives the other party yet a ftronger argument for their precife decree of reprobation. For, fay they, feing we all fee really and in effect, that God hath withheld from many generations, and yet from many nations, that knowledg, which is abfolutely needfull to Salvation, and fo hath rendered it fimply impoffible unto them, why may he not as wel withheld the Grace neceffary to make a faving application of that knowledg, where it is preached? for there is no ground to fay, that this were injuftice in God, or impartiality, more than his leaving thofe others in utter ignorance; the one being but a withholding Grace to apprehend*
the

the object of faith, the other a withdrawing the object it self. For anſwer to this, they are forced to draw a concluſion from their former *hypotheſis of Chriſt? dying for all*, and God's mercy and juſtice, ſaying, that *if theſe Heathens, who live in theſe remote places, where the outward knowledg of Chriſt is not, did improve that common knowledg they have, to whom the outward creation is for an object of faith, by which they may gather, that there is a God, then the Lord would, by ſome Providence, either ſend an Angel to tell them of Chriſt, or conveigh the Scriptur to them, or bring them ſome way to an opportunity to meet with ſuch as might inform them.* Which, as it gives alwayes too much to the power and ſtrength of man's will, and natur, and favours a little of Socinianiſm and Pelagianiſm, or at leſt of Semipelagianiſm, ſo, ſince it is onely built upon probable conjecturs, neither hath it evidence enough to convince any, ſtrongly tainted with the other doctrin, nor yet doth it make the equity and wonderfull harmony of God's Mercy and Juſtice towards *all*, ſo manifeſt to the underſtanding. So that, I have often obſerved, that theſe aſſertors of Univerſal Grace, did farr more pithily and ſtrongly overturn the falſe doctrin of their adverſarys, than they did eſtabliſh and confirm the Truth, and certainty of their own. And, though they have proof ſufficient from the Holy Scripturs to confirm the Univerſality of Chriſt's death, and that none are preciſely, by any irrevocable decree, excluded from Salvation, yet I find, when they are preſſed, in the reſpects above mentioned, to ſhew how God hath ſo farr equally extended the capacity to partake of the benefit of Chriſt's death unto all as to communicate unto them, a ſufficient way of ſo doing, they are ſomewhat in a ſtrait, and are put more to give us their conjecturs, from the certainty of the former preſuppoſed Truth, to wit, (that becauſe Chriſt hath certainly dyed for all, and God hath not rendered Salvation impoſſible to any, therefore there muſt be ſome way or other, by which they may be ſaved, which muſt be by improving ſome common grace, or by gathering from the works of Creation and Providence) then by really demonſtrating, by convinceing, and Spiritual arguments, what that way is.

§ X. It falls out then, that, as darkneſs and the great Apoſtaſy came not upon the Chriſtian world all at once, but by ſeveral degrees, one thing making way for another, untill that thick and groſs vail came to be overſpread, wherewith the nations were ſo blindly covered, from the ſeventh and eighth untill the ſixteenth centurys, even as the darkneſs

the

of the night comes not upon the outward creation all at once, but by degrees, according as the Sun declines in each horizon; fo neither did that full and clear Light and knowledg of the Glorious difpenfation of the Gofpel of Chrift appear all at once, the work of the firft Witneffes being more to teftify againft, and difcover the abufes of the apoftafy, than to eftablifh the Truth in purity.   He, that comes to build a new city, muft firft remove the old rubbifh, before he can fee to lay a new foundation, and he, that comes to a houfe greatly polluted and full of dirt, will firft fweep away and remove the filth, before he put up his own good and new furnitur.   The dawning of the day difpells the darknefs, and makes us fee the things, that are moft confpicuous; but the diftinct difcovering and difcerning of things, fo as to make a certain and perfect obfervation, is referved for the arifing of the Sun, and its fhining in full brightnefs.   And we can, from a certain experience, boldly affirm, that the not waiting for this, but building among, yea and with the old Popifh rubbifh, and fetting up, before a full purgation hath been to moft Proteftants the foundation of many a miftake, and an occafion of unfpeakable hurt.   Therefore the Lord God, who, as he feeth meet, doth communicate and make known to man, the more full evident and perfect knowledg of his everlafting Truth, hath been pleafed to referve the more full difcovery of this glorious and Evangelical difpenfation to this our age, (albeit divers teftimonys have thereunto been born by fome noted men in feveral ages, as fhall hereafter appear) and, for the greater augmentation of the glory of his Grace, that no man might have whereof to boaft, hath raifed up a few defpicable and illiterate men, and, for the moft part, mechaniks, to be the difpenfators of it, by which Gofpel all the fcruples, doubts, hefitations and objections above mentioned, are eafily and evidently anfwered, and the juftice, as wel as mercy, of God, according to their Divine and heavenly harmony, are exhibited, eftablifhed, and confirmed, according to which certain Light and Gofpel, as the knowledg thereof hath been manifefted to us, by the revelation of Jefus Chrift *in* us, fortified by our own fenfible experience, and fealed by the teftimony of the Spirit *in* our hearts, we can confidently affirm, and clearly evince, according to the teftimony of the Holy Scripturs, the following points.

§ XI. Firft, That *God*, who, out of his infinit love, fent his Son the Lord Jefus Chrift into the world, who tafted death for every man, *hath given to every man*, whether Jew or Gentil, Turk, or Scythian, Indian,

M

dian,

dian, or Barbarian, of whatſoever Nation, countrey, or place, *a certain day or time of viſitation, during which day or time, it is poſſible for them to be ſaved, and to partake of the fruit of Chriſt's death.*

Secondly, *That for this end, God hath communicated and given unto every man a meaſur of the Light of his own Son, a meaſur of Grace, or a meaſur of the Spirit*; which the Scriptur expreſſes by ſeveral names, as ſometimes of *the Seed of the Kingdom,* Matth. 13: 18. 19. *The Light, that makes all things manifeſt,* Eph. 5: 13. *The Word of God,* Rom. 10: 18. *or Manifeſtation of the Spirit given to profite withall,* 1 Cor. 12: 7. *a Talent,* Matth. 25: 15. *a little Leaven,* *The Goſpel preached in every creatur,* Col. 1: 23.

Thirdly, *That God, in and by this Light and Seed, invites, calls, exhorts, and ſtrives with every man, in order to ſave them*; which, as it is received, and not reſiſted, works the Salvation of *all*, even of thoſe, who are ignorant of the death and ſufferings of Chriſt, and of Adam's fall, both by bringing them to a ſence of their own miſery, and to be ſharers in the ſufferings of Chriſt inwardly, and by making them partakers of his Reſurrection, in becoming holy, pure, and righteous, and recovered out of their ſins; by which alſo are ſaved they, that have the knowledg of Chriſt outwardly, in that it opens their underſtanding, rightly to uſe and apply the things delivered in the Scriptures, and to receive the ſaving uſe of them. But *that this may be reſiſted and rejected in both, in which then God is ſaid to be reſiſted and preſſed down, and Chriſt to be again crucified, and put to open ſhame, in and among men,* and to thoſe as thus reſiſt and refuſe him, he becomes their condemnation.

Firſt then, according to this doctrin, *the Mercy of God is excellently wel exhibited,* in that none are neceſſarily ſhut out from Salvation, and his juſtice is demonſtrated, in that he condemns none, but ſuch, to whom he really made offer of Salvation, affording them the means ſufficient thereunto.

Secondly, This Doctrin, if wel weighed, will be found to be the *foundation of Chriſtianity, Salvation, and Aſſurance.*

Thirdly, It agrees and anſwers *with the whole tenor of the Goſpel promiſes and threats, and with the natur of the miniſtry of Chriſt,* according to which the Goſpel, Salvation, repentance is commanded to be preached to every creatur, without reſpect of nations, kindreds, families, or tongues.

Fourthly, *It magnifys and commends the merits and death of Chriſt,* in that it not onely accounts them ſufficient to ſave all, but declars them to be

brought

brought fo nigh unto all as thereby to be put into the neareft capacity of Salvation.

Fifthly, *It exalts, above all, the Grace of God*, to which it attributeth all good, even the leaft and fmalleft actions, that are fo, afcribing thereunto not onely the firft beginnings and motions of good, but alfo the whole converfion and Salvation of the Soul.

Sixthly, *It contradicts, overturns and enervats the falfe doctrin of the Pelagians, Semi-Pelagians, Socinians and others*, who exalt the Light of Natur, the liberty of man's will, in that it wholly excluds the natural man from having any place or portion in his own Salvation, by any acting, moving, or working of his own, untill he be firft quickened, raifed up and acted by God's Spirit.

Seventhly, *As it makes the whole Salvation of man folely and alone to depend upon God, fo it makes his condemnation wholly, and in every refpect, to be of himfelf*, in that he refufed, and refifted fomewhat, that from God wreftled and ftrove *in* his heart; and forces him to acknowledg God's juft judgment, in rejecting him, and forfaking of him.

Eightly, *It takes away all ground of defpair*, in that it gives every one ground of hope and certain affurance, that they may be faved; *neither doth feed any in fecurity*, in that none are certain how foon their day may expire, and therefore it is a conftant incitement and provocation, and lively incouragement, to every man, to forfake evil, and clofe with that, which is good.

Ninthly, *It wonderfully commends as wel the certainty of the Chriftian Religion, among infidels, as it manifefts its own verity to all*, in that it's confirmed and eftablifhed by the experiences of all men, feing there was never yet a man found in any place of the earth, however barbarous and wild, but hath acknowledged that at fome time or other, lefs or more, he hath found fomewhat *in* his *heart*, reproving him for fome things evil, which he hath done, threatening a certain horror, if he continued in them, as alfo promifing and communicating a certain peace and fweetnefs, as he hath given way to it, and not refifted it.

Tenthly, *It wonderfully fheweth the excellent wifdom of God*, by which he hath made the means of Salvation fo univerfal and comprehenfive, that it is not needfull to recurr to thofe miraculous and ftrange ways: feing, according to this moft true doctrin, the Gofpel reacheth all, of whatfoever condition, age, or nation.

M 2

Ele-

Eleventhly, *It is really and effectively*, though not in so many words, yet by deeds, *established and confirmed by all the Preachers, Promulgators and Doctors of the Christian Religion, that ever were, or now are, even by those, that otherwayes in their judgment, oppose this doctrin*; in that they all, wherever they have been, or are, or whatsoever people, place, or countrey, they come to, do preach to the people, and to every individual among them, that they may be saved, intreating and desiring them to believe in Christ, who hath dyed for them; so that what they deny in the general, they acknowledg of every particular: there being no man, to whom they do not preach, in order to Salvation, telling him, Jesus Christ calls and wills him to believe and be saved, and that, if he refuse, he shall therefore be condemned, and that his condemnation is of himself, such is the evidence and vertue of Truth, that it constrains its adversarys, even against their wills, to plead for it.

Lastly, According to this doctrin, the former *argument* used by the *Arminians*, and *evited* by the *Calvinists*, concerning every mans being bound to believe, that Christ dyed for him, is, by altering the assumption, *rendred invincible*: thus,

That, which every man is bound to believe, is true:
But every man is bound to believe, that God is mercifull unto him:
Therefore, &c.

This assumption no man can deny, seing *his mercys* are said to be *over all his works.* And herein, the Scriptur every where declares the mercy of God to be, in that he invites and calls sinners to repentance, and hath opened a way of Salvation for them; so that, though those men be not bound to believe the history of Christ's death and passion, who never came to know of it, yet they are bound to believe, that God will be mercifull to them, if they follow his ways, and that he is mercifull unto them, in that he reproves them for evil, and incourages them to good. Neither ought any man to believe, that God is unmercifull to him, or that he hath from the beginning ordained him to come into the world, that he might be left to his own evil inclinations, and so do wickedly as a means appoynted by God, to bring him to eternal damnation; which, were it true, as our adversarys affirm it to be of many thousands, I see no reason why a man might not believe: for certainly a man may believe the Truth.

As it manifestly appears, from the thing it self, that these good and
cx-

excellent conſequences follow, from the belief of this doctrin, ſo from the probation of them it will yet more evidently appear. To which before I come, it is requiſite to ſpeak ſomewhat, concerning the ſtate of the controverſy, which will bring great light to the matter. For, from the not right underſtanding of a matter, under debate, ſometimes both arguments on the one hand, and objections on the other, are brought, which do no way hit the caſe; and hereby alſo our ſenſe and judgment therein will be more fully underſtood and opened.

§ XII. Firſt then by this *day and time of Viſitation*, which, we ſay, God gives unto all, during which they may be ſaved, *we do not underſtand the whole time of every man's life*, though to ſome it may be extended even to the very houre of death; as we ſee in the example of the thief converted upon the croſs: but, *ſuch a ſeaſon at leſt as ſufficiently exonereth God of every mans condemnation*, which to ſome may be ſooner, and to others later, according as the Lord in his wiſdom ſees meet.. So that, many men may out-live this day, after which there may be no poſſibility of Salvation to them, and God juſtly ſuffers them to be hardened, as a juſt puniſhment of their unbelief, and even raiſes them up as inſtruments of wrath, and makes them a ſcourge one againſt another. Whence, to men in this condition may be fitly applyed thoſe Scripturs, which are abuſed to prove *that God incites men neceſſarily to ſin*: this is notably expreſſ'd by the Apoſtle, Rom. 1: from v. 17. to the end, but eſpecially vers 28. *And even as they did not like to retain God in their knowlodg, God gave them up to a reprobate mind to doe thoſe things, which are not convenient.* That many may out-live this day of God's gratious viſitation unto them, is ſhewn by the example of Eſau, Heb. 12:16, 17. who *ſold his birth-right*, ſo he had it once, and was capable to have kept it; but afterwards when he would have inherited the bleſſing, he was rejected. This appears alſo by Chriſt's weeping over Jeruſalem, Luk 19:42. ſaying, *if thou hadſt known, in this thy day, the things, that belong unto thy peace, but now they are hid from thine eyes.* Which plainly imports a time, when they might have known them, which now was removed from them, though they were yet alive, but of this more ſhall be ſaid hereafter.

§ XIII. Secondly, *by this Seed, Grace and Word of God, and Light, wherewith, we ſay, every man is inlightened*, and hath a meaſur of it, which ſtrives with them, in order to Save them, and which may, by the ſtubborneſs and wickedneſs of man's will, be quenched, bruiſed, wounded,

M 3

preſſ-

preſſed down, ſlain, and crucified; *we underſtand not the proper eſſence and natur of God, preciſely taken, which is not deviſible into parts and meaſurs,* as being *a moſt Pure, Simple Being, void of all compoſition or diviſion* ,. and therefore can neither be refiſted, hurt, wounded, crucified, or ſlain, by all the efforts and ſtrength of men; *But we underſtand a Spiritual, heaven-ly, and inviſible Principle, in which God, as Father, Son, and Spirit, dwells:* a meaſur of which Divine and glorious Life is *in all men*, as a *Seed*, which, of its own natur, draws, invits, and inclines to God, and this we call *Vehiculum Dei*, or *the Spiritual body of Chriſt, the fleſh and blood of Chriſt, which came down from heaven*, of which all the Saints do feed, and are thereby nouriſhed unto eternal Life. And, as every unrighteous action is witneſſed againſt, and reproved by this Light and Seed, ſo, by ſuch actions, it is hurt, wounded, and ſlain, and refiles or flees from them, even as the fleſh of men flees from that, which is of a contrary nature to it. Now, becauſe it is never ſeparated from God, nor Chriſt, but wherever it is, God and Chriſt are as wrapped up therein, Therefore, and in that reſpect, as it is refiſted, God is ſaid to be refiſted; and where it is born down, God is ſaid to be preſſed, as a cart under ſheavs, and Chriſt is ſaid to be ſlain and crucified. And, on the contrary, as this Seed is received *in the heart*, and ſuffered to bring forth its natural and proper effect, Chriſt comes to be formed and raiſed, of which the Scriptur makes ſo much mention, calling it *the New man. Chriſt within, the hope of Glory.* This is that Chriſt within, which we are heard ſo much to ſpeak and declare of, every where preaching him up, and exhorting people to believe in the *Light*, and obey it, that they may come to know *Chriſt in* them, to deliver them from all ſin.

But by this as we do not at all intend either *to equal our ſelves* to that Holy man the Lord Jeſus Chriſt, who was born of the Virgin Mary, in who n all the fulneſs of the Godhead dwell bodily, nor *to deſtroy the reality of his preſent exiſtence*, ſo neither do we, as ſome have falſly calumniat-ed us. For, though we affirm, that Chriſt dwells *in* us, yet not immediately, but mediately, as he is in that *Seed*, which is *in* us, whereas he, to wit, the *Eternal Word*, which was with God, and was God, dwelt immedi-ately in that holy man. He then is as the Head, and we as the members; he the Vine, and we the branches. Now, as the Soul of man dwells other ways, and in a farr more immediate manner, in the Head, and in the heart, than in the hands, or leggs. And as the ſap, vertue and

life

life of the vine lodgeth farr otherwiſe in the ſtock and root, than in the branches; ſo God dwelleth otherwiſe in the Man Jeſus, than in us. We alſo freely reject the hereſy of Appollonarius, who denyed him to have any Soul, but ſaid, the body was onely acted by the Godhead. As alſo the error of Eutyches, who made the manhood to be wholly ſwallowed up of the Godhead;wherefore, as we believe he was a true and a real man, ſo we alſo believe,that he continues ſo to be glorified in the heavens,in Soul and body,by whom God ſhall judge the world, in the great and general day of Judgment.

· § XIV. Thirdly, *we underſtand not this Seed, Light, or Grace, to be an accident, as moſt men ignorantly do, but a real Spiritual Subſtance*; which the Soul of man is capable to feel and apprehend, from which that real, Spiritual, inward birth *in* Believers ariſes, called the *new creatur*, the *new man in the heart.* This ſeems ſtrange to carnaly minded men, becauſe they are not acquainted with it; but we know it, and are ſenſible of it, by a true and certain experience, though it be hard for man in his natual wiſdom to comprehend it, untill he come to feel it *in* himſelf, and, if he ſhould, holding it in the meer notion, it would avail him little. Yet we are able to make it appear to be true, and that our faith, concerning it, is not without a ſolide ground: for it is in, and by, this inward and Subſtantial Seed *in* our hearts, as it comes to receive nouriſhment,and to have a birth or geniture *in* us, that we come to have thoſe Spiritual Senſes raiſed, by which we are made capable of taſting, ſmelling, ſeing, and handling the things of God. For a man can not reach unto thoſe things by his natural ſpirit and ſenſes, as is above declared.

Next, we know it to be a *Subſtance*, becauſe it ſubſiſts *in* the hearts of wicked men, even while they are in their wickedneſs, as ſhall be hereafter proved more at large. Now no *accident* can be in a *ſubject*, without it give the ſubject its own denomination, as where whitneſs is in a ſubject, there the ſubject is called white. So we diſtinguiſh betwixt *Holyneſs*, as it is an *accident*, which denominates man ſo, as the Seed receives a place *in* him, and betwixt this *holy ſubſtantial Seed*, which many times lies *in* man's heart, as a naked grain in a ſtony ground. So alſo,as we may diſtinguiſh betwixt health and medicine; health can not be in the body, without the body be called healthfull, becauſe health is an accident, but medicine may be in a body, that is moſt unhealthfull, for that it is a ſubſtance. And, as when a medicine begins to work, the body may in ſome reſpect be called healthfull, and in ſome reſpect unhealthfull; ſo

we

we acknowledg, as this Divine medicine receives place *in* man's heart, it may denominate him in some part holy and good, though there remain yet a corrupted, unmortified part, or some part of the evil humors unpurged out; for where two contrary accidents are in one subject, as health and sicknefs in a body, the subject receives its denomination from the accident, which prevailes moft; so many men are called Saints, good, and holy men, and that truely, when this Holy Seed hath wrought *in* them, in a good meafur, and hath somewhat leavened them into its natur, though they may be yet liable to many infirmitys and weaknefles, yea and to some iniquitys.   For, as the seed of fin, and ground of corruption, yea and the capacity of yeelding thereunto, and sometimes actual falling, doth not denominate a good and holy man, impious; so neither doth the feed of righteousnefs *in* evil men, and the poffibility of their becoming one with it, denominate them good or holy.

§ XV. Fourthly, *we do not hereby intend any wayes to leffen or derogate from the atonement and facrifice of Jefus Chrift*: But, on the contrary, do magnify and exalt it.   For, as we believe all those things to have been certainly tranfacted, which are recorded in the Holy Scripturs, concerning the *birth, life, miracles, fufferings, refurrection and afcenfion of Chrift*; so we do alfo believe, that it is the duty of every one to believe it, to whom it pleafes God to reveal the fame, and to bring to them the knowledg of it: yea we believe it were damnable unbelief not to believe, when so declared, but to refift that Holy Seed, which, as minded, would lead and incline every one to believe it, as it is offered unto them; though it revealeth not in every one the outwardly and explicit knowledg of it, neverthelefs it alwayes affenteth to it, *ubi declaratur*, where it is declared. Neverthelefs, as we firmely believe it was neceflary, that Chrift fhould come, that by his death and fufferings he might offer up himfelf a Sacrifice to God, for our fins, *who his own felf bore our fins in his own body on the tree*; so we believe, that the remiffion of fins, which any partake of, is onely in, and by vertue of that moft fatisfactory Sacrifice, and no otherwife.   For it is *by the obedience of that One that the Free Gift is come upon all, unto juftification*, for we affirm, that, as all men partake of the fruit of Adam's fall, in that, by reafon of that evil feed, which through him is communicated unto them, they are prone and inclined unto evil, though thousands of thousands be ignorant of Adam's fall, neither ever knew of the eating of the forbidden fruit; so alfo many may come to feel

the

the influence of this Holy and Divine Seed, and Light, and be turned from evil to good, by it, though they knew nothing of Chriſt's coming in the fleſh, through whoſe obedience and ſufferings it is purchaſed unto them. And, as we affirm, it is abſolutely needfull, that thoſe do believe the hiſtory of Chriſt's outward appearance, whom it pleaſed God to bring to the knowledg of it; ſo we do freely confeſs, that even that outward knowledg is very comfortable to ſuch as are ſubject to, and led by the inward *Seed*, and *Light*. For, not onely doth the ſenſe of Chriſt's Love and Sufferings tend to humble them, but they are thereby alſo ſtrengthened in their faith, and incouraged to follow that excellent pattern, which he hath left us, *who ſuffered for us*, as ſaith the Apoſtle Peter, 1 Pet. 2: 21. *leaving us an example, that we ſhould follow his ſteps:* and many times we are greatly edified and refreſhed with the gratious ſayings, which proceed out of his mouth. The hiſtory then is profitable and comfortable, with the myſtery, and never without it : but the myſtery is, and may be, profitable without the explicit and outward knowledg of the hiſtory.

But Fifthly, this brings us to another queſtion, to wit, *Whether Chriſt be in all men, or no?* which ſometimes hath been asked us, and arguments brought againſt it, becauſe indeed it is to be found in ſome of our writings, that *Chriſt is in all men*, and we are often heard, in our publick meetings and declaratio is, to deſire every man to come to know, and be acquainted with, *Chriſt in them*, telling them, that *Chriſt is in them*. It is fit therefore, for removing of all miſtakes, to ſay ſomething, in this place, concerning this matter. We have ſaid before, how that *a Divine, Spiritual, and Supernatural Light is in all men*; how that *that Divine Supernatural Light or Seed is Vehiculum Dei:* how that *God and Chriſt dwelleth in it, and is never ſeparated from it:* alſo how that (*as it is received and cloſed with, in the heart*) *Chriſt comes to be formed, and brought forth.* But we are farr from ever having ſaid, *that Chriſt is thus formed in all men*, or *in the wicked.* For that is a great attainment, which the Apoſtle travelled, that it might be brought forth *in* the Galatians. Neither is *Chriſt in* all men *by way of union*, or indeed, to ſpeak ſtrictly, *by way of inhabitation*, becauſe this *inhabitation*, as it is generally taken, imports *union*, *or the manner of Chriſt's being in the Saints.* As it is written, *I will dwell in them, and walk in them*, 2 Cor 6: 16. But in regard *Chriſt is in all men*, *as in a Seed*, yea and that he never is, nor can be, ſeparate from that *Holy*, *pure*

N

Seed

Seed and *Light*, which is *in all men*; Therefore may it be said, in a larger sense, that he is *in all*, even as we observed before.   The Scriptur saith, Amos 2: 13. God is *pressed down*, as a cart under sheaves, and Christ crucified in the ungodly, though to speak properly and strictly, neither can God be pressed down, nor Christ, as God, be crucified.   In this respect then, as he is *in* the *Seed*, which is *in all men*, we have said *Christ is in all men*, and have preached and directed all men to *Christ in them*; who lies crucified in them, by their sins and iniquitys, that they may *look upon him*, *whom they have pierced*; and repent: whereby he, that now lies, as it were, slain and buried *in* them, may come to be raised, and have dominion *in* their hearts, over all.   And thus also the Apostle Paul preached to the Corinthians and Galatians, 1 Cor. 2: 2. *Christ crucified in them*, ἐν ὑμῖν, as the Greek hath it.   This Jesus Christ was that, which the Apostle desired to know *in* them, and make known *unto* them, that they might come to be sensible, how they had thus been crucifying Christ, that so they might repent and be saved.   And, forasmuch as Christ is called *that Light, that inlightens every man*; *The Light of the world*: Therefore the *Light* is taken for *Christ*, who truely is the Fountain of all Light, and hath his habitation in it for ever.   Thus the *Light* of Christ is sometimes called *Christ*, i. e. that, in which Christ is, and from which he is never separated.

§ XVI. Sixthly, It will manifestly appear, by what is above said, that *we understand not this Divine Principle to be any part of man's natur, nor yet to be any reliques of any good, which Adam lost by his fall*: in that we make it a distinct separate thing from man's Soul, and all the facultys of it. Yet, such is the malice of our adversarys, that they cease not sometimes to calumniat us, as if we preached up a natural light, or the light of man's natural Conscience.   Next, there are, that lean to the doctrin of Socinus and Pelagius, who perswade themselves, through mistake, and out of no ill design to injure us, as if this, which we preach up, were some natural power and faculty of the Soul, and that we onely differ in the wording of it, and not in the thing it self.   Whereas there can be no greater difference, than is betwixt us, in this matter: for we certainly know, that this *Light*, of which we speak, is not onely distinct, but of a different natur from the Soul of man & its facultys. Indeed that man, as he is a rational creatur, hath reason, as a natural faculty of his Soul, by which he can discern things, that are rational.   We deny not, for this is a pro-

perty.

perty natural and effential to him, by which he can know and learn many
arts and fciences, beyond what any other animal can doe, by the meer
animal principle. Neither do we deny, but by this rational principle man
may apprehend in his brain, and in the notion, a knowledg of God, and
Spiritual things : yet, that not being the right organ, as, in the fecond
Propofition, hath more at length been fignified, it can not profit him
towards Salvation; but rather hindereth, and indeed the great caufe of
the Apoftafy hath been, that man hath fought to fathom the things of
God, in and by this natural and rational principle, and to build up a Religion in it, neglecting and overlooking this Principle and Seed of God in
the heart, fo that herein, in the moft univerfal and catholik fenfe, hath
*Anti-Chrift in every man fet up himfelf, and fitteth in the temple of God, as God,
and above every thing, that is called God.* For, *men being the Temple of the Holy
Ghoft*, as faith the Apoftle, 1 Cor. 3 : 16. when the rational principle
fets it felf up there, above the Seed of God, to reign and rule, as a prince,
in Spiritual things, while the Holy Seed is wounded and bruifed, there
is *Anti-Chrift in every man*, or fomewhat exalted above and againft Chrift.
Neverthelefs we do not hereby affirm, as if man had received his Reafon,
to no purpofe, or to be of no fervice unto him ; in no wife : we look upon
Reafon as fit to order and rule man in things natural : for, as God gave
two great Lights to rule the outward world, the Sun and moon, the
greater Light to rule the day, and the leffer light to rule the night; fo hath
he given man the Light of his Son a Spiritual Divine Light, to rule him,
in the things Spiritual, and the light of Reafon, to rule him in things natural. And, even as the moon borrowes her light from the Sun, fo ought
men, if they would be rightly and comfortably ordered in natural things,
to have their Reafon inlightened by this Divine and pure Light. Which
inlightened Reafon, in thofe, that obey, and follow this true Light, we
confefs may be ufefull to man, even in Spiritual things, as it is ftill fubfer-
vient, and fubject to the other: even as the animal life in man, regu-
lated and ordered by his Reafon, helps him in going about things, that
are rational. We do further rightly diftinguifh this from man's natural
confcience; for Confcience, being that in man, which arifeth from the
natural facultys of man's Soul, may be defiled and corrupted, it is faid exprefly of the impure, Tit. 1 : 15. *that even their mind and confcience is defiled.*
But this Light can never be corrupted, nor defiled, neither did it ever confent to evil or wickednefs in any, for it is faid exprefly, that it *makes all*

N 2

things

things manifeft, that are reproveable, Eph. 5 : 13. and fo is a faithfull witnefs for God againft every unrighteoufnefs *in* man. Now, *Confcience,* to
define it truely, comes from [*confcire*] and *is that knowledg, which arifeth in
man's heart.from what agreeth, contradicteth, or is contrary to any thing believed by
him, whereby he becomes confcious to himfelf, that he transgreffeth, by doing that,
which he is perfwaded he ought not to doe.* So that, the mind being once blinded, or defiled with a wrong belief, there arifeth a confcience from that
belief, which troubls him, when he goes againft it. As for example, a
Turk, who hath poffeff'd himfelf with a falfe belief, that it is unlawfull
for him to drink wine, if he doe it, his confcience fmites him for it : but,
though he keep many concubins, his confcience troubls him not, becaufe
that his judgment is already defiled with a falfe opinion that it is lawfull
for him to doe the one, and unlawfull to doe the other. Whereas, if the
Light of Chrift, *in* him, were minded, it would reprove him, not onely
for committing fornication, but alfo, as he became obedient thereunto,
inform him, that *Mahomet* is an *impoftor;* as wel as *Socrates* was informed
by it, in his day of the falfity of the Heathens gods.

 So, if a Papift eat flefh in Lent, or be not diligent enough in adoration
of Saints and images, or, if he fhould contemn images, his Confcience
would fmite him for it ; becaufe his judgment is already blinded with a
falfe belief, concerning thefe things. Whereas the Light of Chrift never confented to any of thofe abominations. Thus then, man's natural
confcience is fufficiently diftinguifhed from it : for Confcience followeth
the judgment, doth not inform it. But this Light, as it is received, re-
moves the blindnefs of the judgment, opens the underftanding, and re-
ctifys both the judgment and Confcience. So we confefs alfo that Confcience is an excellent thing, where it is rightly inform'd and inlightened.
Wherefore fome of us have fitly compared it to a lanthern, and the Light
of Chrift to the candle. A lanthern is ufefull, when a clear candle burns
and fhines in it : but otherwife, of no ufe. To the Light of Chrift then
in the Confcience, and not to man's natural confcience, it is, that we continually commend men, this, not that, is it, which we preach up, and
direct people to, as to a moft certain Guide unto life eternal.

 Laftly, this *Light, Seed,* &c., appears to be no power or natural
faculty of man's mind; becaufe a man, that's in his health, can, when
he pleafes, ftirr up, move and exercife the facultys of his Soul : he is
abfolut mafter of them, and, except there be fome natural caufe or im-
pediment

pediment in the way, he can uſe them, at his pleaſur: but this Light
and Seed of God *in* man he can not move and ſtirr up, when he pleaſeth,
but it moves, blowes, and ſtrives with man, as the Lord ſeeth meet.
For, though there be a poſſibility of Salvation to every man, during the
day of his viſitation, yet can not a man, at any time, when he pleaſeth,
or hath ſome ſenſe of his miſery, ſtirr up that Light and Grace, ſo as to
procure to himſelf tenderneſs of heart, but he muſt wait for it: which
comes upon *all*, at certain times and ſeaſons, wherein it works powerfully upon the Soul, mightily tenders it, and breaks it, at which time,
if man reſiſt it not, but cloſe with it, he comes to know Salvation by it.
Even as the lake of Bethſaida did not cure all thoſe, that waſhed in it,
but ſuch onely as waſhed firſt, after the Angel had moved upon the waters; ſo God moves in love to mankind, in this Seed, in his heart, at
ſome ſingular times, ſetting his ſins in order before him, and ſeriouſly inviting him to repentance, offering to him remiſſion of ſins, and Salvation; Which if man accept of, he may be ſaved. Now, there is no man
alive, and I am confident there ſhall be none, to whom this paper ſhall
come, who, if they will deal faithfully and honeſtly with their own hearts,
will not be forced to acknowledg, but they have been ſenſible of this in
ſome meaſur, leſs or more, which is a thing that man can not bring upon
himſelf, with all his pains and induſtry. This then, O man and woman,
is the day of God's gracious viſitation to thy Soul, which, thou ſhalt be
happy for ever, if thou reſiſt not. This is the day of the Lord, which, as
Chriſt ſaith, is *like the lightening, that ſhineth from the eaſt unto the weſt.* And
the wind or *Spirit, which blowes upon the heart, and no man knowes whither it
goes, nor whence it comes.*

Matth. 24
ver. 27.
Ioh. 3: 8.

§ XVII. And laſtly, this leads me to ſpeak concerning the *manner of
this Seed,* or *Lights operation in the hearts of all men,* which will ſhew yet more
manifeſtly how we differ vaſtly from all thoſe, that exalt a natural power
or light in man; and how our Principle leads, above all others, to attribut
our whole Salvation to the meer Power, Spirit, and Grace of God.

To them then, that ask us, after this manner; *How do ye differ from the
Pelagians and Arminians? For, if two men have equal ſufficient Light and Grace,
and the one be ſaved by it, and the other not, is it not, becauſe the one improves it,
the other not? is not then the will of man the cauſe of the one's Salvation, beyond
the other?* I ſay, to ſuch we thus anſwer, that, as the Grace and Light,
in all, is ſufficient to ſave *all,* and, of its own natur, would ſave *all,* ſo it

N 3   ſtrives

strives and wrestles with all, for to save them ; he, that resists its striving, is the cause of his own condemnation ; he, that resists it not , it becomes his Salvation, so that in him, that is saved, the working is *of the Grace*, and not *of the man*, and it's a passiveness, rather than an act : though afterwards, as man is wrought upon, there is a will raised in him, by which he comes to be a co-worker with the Grace: for, according to that of Augustin, *he , that made us without us , will not save us without us* So that the first step is not by man's working, but by his not contrary working. And we believe, that, at these singular seasons of every man's visitation, above mentioned, as man is wholly unable, of himself, to work with the Grace, neither can he move one step, out of the natural condition, untill the Grace lay hold upon him ; so it is possible to him to be passive, and not to resist it, as it is also possible for him to resist it. So, we say, the Grace of God works in and upon man's natur, which, though of it self wholly corrupted and defiled, and prone to evil, yet, is capable to be wrought upon by the Grace of God, even as iron, though a hard and cold metall, of it self, may be warm'd and softened by the heat of the fire, and wax melted by the Sun. And, as iron or wax, when removed from the fire, or Sun, returneth to its former condition of coldness, and hardness, so man's heart, as it resists, or retires from the Grace of God, returnes to its former condition again. I have often had the manner of God's working, in order to Salvation towards *all* men, illustrated to my mind, by one or two clear examples, which I shall here add, for the information of others.

The First is, of a man heavily diseased ; to whom I compare man, in his falln and natural condition. I suppose God, who is the great Physician, not onely to give this man physik, after he hath used all the industry he can, for his own health, by any skill or knowledg, he hath of his own.   As those, that say, *If a man improve his Reason or natural facultys, God will superadd Grace. Or*, as others say, *that he cometh and maketh offer of a remedy to this man outwardly, leaving it to the liberty of man's will, either to receive it, or reject it.*   But He, even the Lord, this great Physician, cometh, and poureth the remedy into his mouth, and, as it were, layeth him in his bed, so that, if the sick man be but passive, it will necessarily work the effect : but, if he be stubborn and untoward, and will needs rise up, and go forth into the cold, or eat such fruits as are hurtfull to him, while the medicine should operat ; then, though of its natur it tendeth

to

to cure him, yet it will prove destructive to him, because of those obstructions, which it meeteth with. Now, as the man, that should thus undoe himself, would certainly be the cause of his own death; so, who will say, that, if cured, he owes not his health wholly to the physician, and not to any deed of his own? seing his part was not any action, but a passivenefs.

The Second example is, of divers men lieing in a dark pit together, where all their senses are so stupified, that they are scarce sensible of their own misery. To this I compare man, in his natural, corrupt, faln condition, I suppose not, *that, any of these men wrestling to deliver themselves, do thereby stirre up or engage one able to deliver them, to give them his help.* Saying with himself, *I see one of these men willing to be deliver'd, and doing what in him lies, therefore he deserves to be assisted:* As say the *Socinians, Pelagians* and *Semi-Pelagians.* Neither do I suppose, *that this deliverer comes to the top of the pit, and puts down a ladder, desiring them, that will, to come up, and so put them upon using their own strength and will, to come up;* As do the *Jesuits* and *Arminians:* yet, as they say, such are not delivered without the Grace, seing the Grace is that Ladder, by which they were delivered. But I suppose, that the Deliverer comes, at certain times, and fully discovers and informes them of the great misery and hazard they are in, if they continue in that noyfom and pestiferous place, yea forces them to a certain sense of their misery, (for the wickedeft men at times are made sensible of their misery by God's visitation) and not onely so, but lays hold upon them, and gives them a pull, in order to lift them out of their misery, which, if they resist not, will save them, onely they may resist it. This, being applyed as the former, doth the same way illustrate the matter. Neither is the Grace of God frustrated, though the effect of it be divers, according to its object: being the ministration of mercy and love, *in those,* that reject it not, but receive it, Joh. 1 : 12. but the *ministration of wrath and condemnation, in* those, that do reject it, Joh. 3 : 19. Even as the Sun, by one act or operation melteth and softeneth the wax, and hardeneth the clay. The natur of the Sun is to cherish the Creation, and therefore the Living are refreshed by it, and the flowers send forth a good savour, as it shines upon them, and the fruits of the trees are ripened; yet cast forth a dead carcafe, a thing without life, and the same reflexion of the Sun will cause it to stink, and putrify it, yet is not the Sun said thereby frustrat of its proper effect. So every man, during the day of his visitation, is shined upon by the Sun of Rightcousnefs, and

capable

capable of being influenced by it, so as to send forth good fruit and a good favour, and to be melted by it : but, when he has sinned out his day, then the same Sun hardeneth him, as it doth the clay, and makes his wickedness more to appear and putrify, and send forth an evil savour.

§ XVIII. Lastly, As we truely affirm that God willeth no man to perish, and therefore, hath given, to *all*, Grace sufficient for Salvation, so we do not deny, but that, in a special manner, he worketh *in* some, *in* whom Grace so prevaileth, that they necessarily obtain Salvation, neither doth God suffer them to resist. For, it were absurd to say, that God had not farr otherwise extended himself towards the Virgin Mary and the Apostle Paul, than towards many others.   Neither can we affirm, that God equally loved the beloved Disciple John and Judas the Traitour. In so farr neverthelefs, as none wanted such a measur of Grace, by which they might have been saved, all are justly inexcufable. And also, God working *in* those, to whom this prevalency of Grace is given, doth so hide himself, to shut out all security and presumption, that such may be humbled, and the Free Grace of God magnified, and all reputed to be of the Free Gift, and nothing from the strength of Self. Those also, who perish, when they remember those times of God's visitation towards them, wherein he wrestled with them, by his *Light* and *Spirit*, are forçed to confefs that there was a time, wherein the door of mercy was open unto them, and that they are justly condemned, becaufe they rejeéted their own Salvation.

Thus both the Mercy and Juftice of God is eftablifhed, and the will and ftrength of man is brought down, and rejeéted, his condemnation is made to be of himfelf, and his Salvation onely to depend upon God : Alfo by thefe pofitions, two great objeétions, which often are brought againft this doétrin, are wel folved.

The firft is deduced from thofe places of Scriptur, wherein God feems precifely to have decreed and predeftinated fome to Salvation : and for that end to have ordained certain means, which fall not out to others, as in the calling of Abraham, David, and others, and in the converfion of Paul, for, thefe being numbered among fuch, to whom this prevalency is given, the objeétion is eafily loofed.

The fecond is drawn from thofe places, wherein God feems to have ordain'd fome wicked perfons to deftruétion, and therefore to have obdur'd their hearts, to forçe them unto great fins, and to have raifed them

up,

up, that he might ſhew in them his Power: who, if they be numbered amongſt thoſe men, whoſe day of viſitation is paſt over, that objection is alſo ſolved, as will more evidently appear to any one, that will make a particular application of thoſe things, which I at this time, for brevity's ſake, thought meet to paſs over.

§ X I X. Having thus clearly and evidently ſtated the queſtion, and opened our mind and judgment, in this matter, as divers objections are hereby prevented, ſo will it make our probation both the eaſier and the ſhorter.

The firſt thing to be proved, is, *that God hath given to every man a day or time of Viſitation, wherein it is poſſible for him to be ſaved.* If we can prove, that there is a day and time given, in which thoſe might have been ſaved, that actually periſh, the matter is done. For none deny but thoſe, that are ſaved, have a day of viſitation. This then appears by the regrets and complaints, which the Spirit of God, throughout the whole Scripturs makes, even to thoſe that did periſh; challenging them for that they did not accept of, nor cloſe with God's Viſitation and offer of mercy to them. Thus the Lord expreſſes himſelf then firſt of all to Cain, Gen. 4 : 6, 7. *And the Lord ſaid unto Cain, why art thou wroth? and why is thy countenance faln? If thou doſt wel, ſhalt thou not be accepted? If thou doſt not wel, ſin lieth at the door* This was ſaid to Cain, before he ſlew his brother Abel, when the evil ſeed began to tempt him, and work in his heart, we ſee how God gave warning to Cain in ſeaſon, and in the day of his viſitation towards him acceptance and remiſſion, if he did wel : for, this interrogation ; *ſhalt thou not be accepted?* imports an affirmative, *thou ſhalt be accepted, if thou doſt wel.* So that, if we may truſt God Almighty, the Fountain of all Truth and Equity, it was poſſible, in a day, even for Cain, to be accepted. Neither could God have propoſed the doing of good, as a condition, if he had not given Cain ſufficient ſtrength, whereby he was capable to doe good. This the Lord himſelf alſo ſhewes, even that he gave a day of viſitation to the old world, Gen. 6 : 3. *And the Lord ſaid, My Spirit ſhall not always ſtrive in man* ; for ſo it ought to be tranſlated. This manifeſtly implies, that his Spirit did ſtrive with man, and doth ſtrive with them, for a ſeaſon ; which ſeaſon expiring, God ceaſeth to ſtrive with them, in order to ſave them ; for the Spirit of God can not be ſaid to ſtrive with man, after the day of his viſitation is expired, ſeing it naturally, and without any reſiſtance, works its effect then, to wit, con-

O

tinually

tinually to judg and condemn them.   From this day of visitation, that
God hath given to every one, is it, that he is said to *wait to be gratious*,
Isa. 30: 18. and to be *long-suffering*, Exod. 34: 6. Num. 14: 18. Psal.
86: 15. Jer. 15. 15. Here the Prophet Jeremy, in his prayer, lays hold
upon the long-suffering of God, and in his expostulating with God, he
shuts out the objection of our adversarys, in the 18 vers, *why is my pain
perpetual? and my woud incurable? which refuseth to be healed, wilt thou altogether be unto me as a lyar, and as waters, that fail?* Whereas, according to our adversarys opinion, the pain of the most part of men is perpetual, and their wound altogether incurable.   Yea the offer of the Gospel
and of Salvation unto them, is, as a lye, and as waters, that fail, being
never intended to be of any effect unto them.   The Apostle Peter saith
expressely, that this *long-suffering of God waited, in the days of Noah, for
those of the old world*, 1 Pet. 3 : 20. which being compared with that of
Gen. 6 : 3. before mentioned, doth sufficiently hold forth our Proposition.   And, that none may object that this long-suffering or striving of the
Lord was not in order to save them, the same Apostle saith expresly,
2 Pet. 3 : 15. *that the long-suffering of God is to be accounted Salvation,* and with
this long-suffering, alittle before, in the 9 verse, he couples *that God is not
willing any should perish.*   Where, taking himself to be his own interpreter,
as he is most fit, he holdeth forth, that those, to whom the Lord is long-
suffering (which he declareth he was to the wicked of the old world, and is
now to all, *not willing that any should perish*) *they are to account this long-suffering
of God to them, Salvation.* Now, how, or in what respect, can they account it
Salvation, if there be not so much as a possibility of Salvation conveighed
to them therein? For it were not Salvation to them, if they could not be
saved by it.   In this matter Peter further refers to the writings of Paul,
holding forth this to have been the universal doctrin.   Where, it is observable, what he adds, upon this occasion, how there are *some things in Paul's
epistles hard to be understood, which the unstable and unlearned wrest, to their own
destruction*, insinuating plainly this of those expressions in Paul's epistles,
as the 9 to the Romans, *&c.* which some, unlearned, in Spiritual things,
did make to contradict the Truth of God's long-suffering towards all,
in which he willeth not any of them should perish, and in which they all
may be saved.   Would to God many had taken more heed, than they
have don, to this advertisement! That place of the Apostle Paul, which
Peter seems here most particularly to hint at, doth much contribut also

to

to clear the matter, Rom. 2 : 4. *Defpifeft thou the riches of his goodneß and for-bearance and long-fuffering, not knowing that the goodneß of God leadeth thee to repentance?* Paul fpeaketh here to the unregenerat, and to the wicked, *who,* in the following verfe, he faith, *treafur up wrath unto the day of wrath :* and to fuch he commends the riches of the forbearance and long-fuffering of God ; fhewing that the tendency of God's goodnefs leadeth to repentance. How could it neceffarily tend, to lead them to repentance, how could it be called *riches* or *goodneß* to them, if there were not a time, wherein they might repent by it, and come to be fharers of the riches exhibited in it ?   From all which I thus argue,

If God plead with the wicked, from the poffibility of their being accepted ; If God's Spirit ftrive *in* them, for a feafon, in order to fave them, who afterwards perifh ; If he wait to be gratious unto them ; If he be long-fuffering towards them ; And if this long-fuffering be Salvation to them, while it endureth, during which time, God willeth them not to perifh, but exhibiteth to them the riches of his goodnefs and forbearance, to lead them to repentance; then there is a day of Vifitation, wherein fuch might have been, or fome fuch now may be, faved, who have perifhed, and may, if they repent, not perifh :

But the Firft is true :

Therefore alfo the Laft.

§ XX. Secondly, this appeareth from the Prophet Ifa. 5 : 4. *What could I have done more to my vineyard?* for in the 2 vers he faith, *he hath fenced it, and gathered out the ftones thereof, and planted it with the choyceft vine, and yet,* faith he, *when I looked it fhould have brought forth grapes, it brought forth Wild grapes.* Wherefore he calleth the inhabitants of Jerufalem and men of Judea, to judg betwixt him and his vineyard, faying, *what could I have done more to my vineyard, than I have done in it ? and yet,* as is faid, *it brought forth wild grapes.* Which was applied to many in Ifrael, who refufed God's Mercy. The fame example is ufed by Chrift, Matth. 21: 33. Mar. 12: 1. Luk 20 : 9. where Jefus fhewes how to fome a vineyard was planted, and all things given neceffary for them to get them fruit to pay or reftore to their mafter ; and how the mafter many times waited to be mercifull to them, in fending fervants after fervants, and paffing by many offences, before he determined to deftroy and caft them out.   Firft then, this can not be underftood of the Saints, or of fuch as repent, and are faved, for, it is faid expresfly, *he will deftroy them.* Neither would the parable any

   wayes

wayes have anfwered the end , for which it is alledged , if thefe men had not been in a capacity to have done good , yea, fuch was their capacity, that Chrift faith in the Prophet , *what could I have done more ?* So that it is more than manifeft , that by this parable repeated in three fundry Evangelifts, Chrift holds forth his long-fuffering towards men, and their wickednefs , to whom means of Salvation being afforded , do neverthelefs refift , to their own condemnation. To thefe alfo are paralell thefe Scripturs, Prov. 1 : 24, 25, 26. Jer. 18 : 9, 10. Matth. 18 : 32 , 33 , 34. Act. 13 : 46.

Laftly, that there is a day of vifitation given to the wicked , wherein they might have been faved , and, which being expired , they are fhut out from Salvation , appears evidently by Chrift's lamentation over Jerufalem , exprefled in three fundry places , Matth. 23 : 37. Luk 13 : 34. & 19: v. 41, 42. *And when he was come near , he beheld the city , and wept over it , faying , if thou hadft known , even thou, at leaft , in this thy day , the things , that belong to thy peace ; but now they are hid from thine eyes :* Than which , nothing can be faid more evident , to prove our doctrin. For firft , he infinuats, that there was a day, wherein the inhabitants of Jerufalem might have known thofe things , that belonged to their Peace. Secondly, that, during that day, he was willing to have gathered them, even as a hen gathereth her chickens. A familiar example , yet very fignificative, in this cafe, which fhewes, that the offer of Salvation made unto them was not in vain, on his part, but as really, and with as great chearfulnefs and willingnefs , as a hen gathereth her chickens. Such as is the love and care of the hen towards her brood , fuch is the care of Chrift to gather loft men and women, to redeem them out of their corrupt and degenerat ftate. Thirdly, That becaufe they refufed, the things belonging to their Peace were *hid from* their *eyes.* Why were they hid ? becaufe ye would not fuffer me to gather you ; ye would not fee thofe things, that are good for you , in the feafon of God's Love towards you ; and therefore , *now,* that day being expired , *ye can not fee them :* and, for a further judgment , God fuffers you to be hardened in unbelief.

So it is after real offer of mercy and Salvation rejected , that God hardens mens hearts , and not before. Thus, that faying is verified, *To him, that hath, fhall be given, and from him, that hath not , fhall be taken away, even that , which he hath.* This may feem a riddle , yet is, according to this doctrin, eafily folved. He hath not, becaufe he hath loft the

feafon.

feafon of ufing it, and fo to him it is, now, as nothing; for Chrift ufes this expreffion, Matth. 25: 26. upon the occafion of taking the one talent from the flothfull fervant, and giving it to him, that was diligent, which talent was no wayes infufficient, of it felf, but of the fame nature with thofe given to the others; and therefore the Lord had reafon to exact the profit of it, proportionably, as wel as from the reft. So, I fay, it is after the rejecting of the day of vifitation, that the judgment of obduration is inflicted upon men and women, as Chrift pronounceth it upon the Jewes, out of Ifa. 6: 9. which all the four Evangelifts make mention of; Matth. 13: 14. Mar. 4: 12. Luc. 8: 10. Joh. 12: 40. And laft of all, the Apoftle Paul, after he had made offer of the Gofpel of Salvation to the Jewes, at Rome, pronounceth the fame, Act. 28. 26. after that fome believed not, *Welfpake the Holy Ghoft, by Ifaiah the Prophet, unto our Fathers, faying, go unto this people, and fay, hearing ye fhall hear and fhall not underftand, and feing ye fhall fee, and fhall not perceive. For the heart of this people is waxed grofs, and their ears are dull of hearing, and their eyes have they clofed, left they fhould fee with their eyes, and hear with their ears, and underftand with their heart, and fhould be converted, and I fhould heal them.* So it appears, that God would have them to fee, but they clofed their eyes; and therefore they are juftly hardened. Of this matter *Cyrillus Alexandrinus* upon John, lib. 6. cap. 21. fpeaks wel, anfwering to this objection. *But fome may fay, if Chrift be come into the world, that thofe that fee, may be blinded, there blindnefs is not to be imputed unto them, but it rather feems that Chrift is the caufe of their blindnefs, who faith, he is come into the world, that thofe that fee, may be blinded.* But (faith he) *they fpeak not rationally, who object thefe things unto God, and are not afraid to call him the author of evil. For, as the fenfible Sun is carryed upon our Horizon, that it may communicat the gift of its clearnefs unto all, and make its light fhine upon all, but if any one clofe his eye-lids, or willingly turn himfelf from the Sun, refufing the benefit of its light, he wants its illumination, and remains in darknefs, not through defect of the Sun, but through his own fault. So that the true Sun, who came to inlighten thofe, that fat in darknefs, and in the region of the fhaddow of death, vifited the earth, for this caufe, that he might communicat unto all, the gift of knowledg and Grace, and illuminat the inward eyes of all, by a peculiar fplendor: but many reject this Gift of the Heavenly Light, freely given to them, and have clofed the eyes of their minds, left fo excellent an illumination or irradiation of the Eternal Light fhould fhine unto them. It is not then through defect of*

O 3

the

the true Sun, but onely through their own iniquity and hardneß, for, as the wise man saith, (Wisdom 2.) their wickedneß hath blinded them. From all which I thus argue,

If there was a day, wherein the obstinate Jewes might have known the things, that belonged to their Peace, which, because they rejected it, was hid from their eyes; If there was a time, wherein Christ would have gathered them, who, be cause they refused, could not be gathered; Then such as might have been saved, do actually perish, that slighted the day of God's Visitation towards them, wherein they might have been converted and saved :

But the First is true :

Therefore also the Last.

§ XXI. Secondly, That, which comes in the second place to be proved, is, *that whereby God offers to work this Salvation, during the day of every man's visitation,* and that is *that he hath given to every man a measur of saving, sufficient, and supernatural Light and* Grace. This I shall do, by Gods assistance, by some plain and clear testimonys of the Scriptur.

First, from that of John. 1: 9. *That was the true Light, which inlighteneth every man, that cometh into the world.* This place doth so clearly favour us, that, by some, it is called *the Quakers text;* for it doth evidently demonstrat our assertion, so that it scarce needs either consequence or deduction, seing it self is as a consequence of two Propositions, asserted in the former verses, from which, it followeth, as a conclusion, in the very terms of our faith. The first of these Propositions is, *the Life, that is in him, is the Light of men;* the second *the Light shineth in the darkneß,* and from these two, he infers, and *he is the true Light, that lighteth every man, that cometh into the world.*

From whence, I do, in short, observe, that this Divine Apostle calls *Chrift* the *Light* of men, and giveth us this as one of the chief Propertys, at left considerably and especially, to be observed by us, seing hereby, as he is the Light, and, as we walk with him in that Light, which he communicats to us, we come to have fellowship and communion with him, as the same Apostle saith elsewhere, 1 Joh. 1:7. Secondly, that *this Light shineth in darkneß, though the darkneß comprehend it not.* Thirdly, that *this true Light inlighteneth every man, that cometh into the world.* Where the Apostle, being directed by God's Spirit, hath carefully avoided their captiousness, that would have restricted this to any certain number. Where

every

every one is, there is none excluded.   Next, fhould they bee fo ob-
ftinat, as fometimes they are, as to fay, that this [*every man*] is onely
every one of the Elect: thefe words following, *every man, that cometh
into the world*, would obviat that objection. So that, it is plain, there comes
no man into the world, whom Chrift hath not inlightened, in fome meafur, and *in* whofe dark heart this *Light* doth not fhine, though the darknefs comprehend it not, yet it fhineth there, and the natur thereof is to
difpell the darknefs, where men fhut not their eyes upon it.   Now, for
what end this Light is given, is expreffed, vers 7. where John is faid to
come for a *witnefs*, *to bear witnefs to the Light*, *that all men through it might believe*, to wit, through the Light δι' αυτȣ which doth very wel agree with
Φωτός, as being the neareft antecedent; though moft tranflatours have
(to make it fute with their own doctrin) made it relate to John : as if all
men were to believe through John.   For which, as there is nothing directly in the Text, fo it is contrary to the very ftrain of the context. For,
feing Chrift hath lighted every man with this Light, is it not that they
may come to believe through it?   All could not believe through John,
becaufe all men could not know of John's teftimony, whereas every man
being lighted by this, may come therethrough to believe.   John fhined
not in the darknefs, but this Light fhineth in the darknefs, that, having
difpelled the darknefs, it may produce and beget faith.   And laftly, we
muft believe through That, and become believers through That, by
walking in Which, fellowfhip with God is known and enjoyed, but,
as hath been above obferved, it is by walking in this Light, that we have
this communion and fellowfhip, not by walking in John, which were
non-fenfe.   So that this relative δι' αυτȣ muft needs be refer'd to the
Light, whereof John bears witnefs, that, through that Light, wherewith Chrift hath lighted every man, all men might come to believe.
Seing then this Light is the Light of Jefus Chrift, and the Light, through
which men come to believe, I think it needs not be doubted but that it is
a fupernatural, faving, and fufficient Light.   If it were not fupernatural,
it could not be properly called the Light of Jefus, for, though all things
be his, and *of* him, and *from* him, yet thofe things, which are common and peculiar to our natur, as being a part of them, we are not faid in
fo fpecial a manner to have from Chrift.   Moreover, the Evangelift is
holding out to us here the office of Chrift, as Mediator, and the benefits, which, from him, as fuch, do redound unto us.

Second-

Secondly, It can not be any of the natural gifts or facultys of our Soul, whereby we are said here to be inlightened, because this Light is said to shine in the darkness, and can not be comprehended by it. Now, this darkness is no other, but man's natural condition and state, in which natural state he can easily comprehend, and doth comprehend, those things, that are peculiar and common to him, as such. That man in his natural condition is called *darkness*, see Eph. 5 : 8. *For ye were sometimes darkness, but now are ye Light in the Lord.* And in other places, as Act. 26 : 18. Col. c. 1 : 13. 1 Thess. 5 : 5. where the condition of man in his natural state is termed *darkness*: Therefore, I say, this Light can not be any natural property or faculty of man's Soul, but a Supernatural Gift and Grace of Christ.

Thirdly, *It is Sufficient and Saving.*

That, which is given, *that all men through it may believe*, must needs be Saving and Sufficient: That, by walking in which, fellowship with the Saints, and *the blood of Christ, which cleanseth from all sin*, is possessed, must be Sufficient:

But such is the *L I G H T*: 1 Joh. 1 : 7.

Therefore, &c.

Moreover,

That, which we are commanded to believe in, *that we may become the children of the Light*, must be a Supernatural, Sufficient, and Saving Principle:

But we are commanded to believe in this Light :

Therefore, &c.

The proposition can not be denyed. The Assumption is Christ's own words, Joh. 12 : 36. *While ye have the Light, believe in the Light, that ye may be the children of the Light.*

To this they object, that by [*Light*] here is understood Christ's outward person, in whom he would have them believe.

That they ought to have believed in *Christ*, that is, that he was the *MESSIAH*, that was to come, is not denyed; but, how they evince, that Christ intended that here, I see not: nay, the place it self shewes the contrary, by those words *While ye have the Light*, and by the verse going before, *Walk, while ye have the Light, lest darkness come upon you.* Which words import, that, when that *Light*, in which they were to believe, was removed, then they should lose the capacity, or season

of

ofbelieving. Now, this could not be underſtood of Chriſt's perſon, the Jewes might have believed in him, and many did ſavingly believe in him, as all Chriſtians do, at this day, when the perſon, towit, his bodily preſence or outward man is farr removed from them. So that, this Light, in which they were commanded to believe, muſt be that inward, Spiritual Light, that ſhines *in* their hearts, for a ſeaſon, even during the day of man's viſitation; which, while it continueth to call, invite, and exhort, men are ſaid to have it, and may believe in it: but, when men refuſe to believe in it, and reject it, then it ceaſeth to be a Light, to ſhew them the way, but leaves the ſenſe of their unfaithfulneſs, as a ſting in their Conſcience; which is a terror and darkneſs unto them, and upon them, in which they can not know where to go, neither can work any ways profitably, in order to their Salvation: and therefore to ſuch rebellious ones, *the day of the Lord* is ſaid to be *darkneſs, and not Light,* Amos 5: 18.

From whence it appears, that, though many receive not the Light, (as the darkneſs comprehends it not) nevertheleſs this Saving Light ſhines *in all,* that it may ſave them. Concerning which alſo, Cyrillus Alexandrinus ſaith wel, and defends our Principle. *With great diligence and watchfulneſs (ſaith he) doth the Apoſtle John endeavour to anticipate and prevent the vain thoughts of men, for there is here a wonderfull method of ſublime things, and overturning of objections, he had juſt now called the Son the true Light; by whom he affirmed, that every man coming into the world was inlighten-ed, yea, that he was in the world, and the world was made by him. One may then object, if the Word of God be the Light, and if this Light inlighten the hearts of men, and ſuggeſt unto men piety, and the underſtanding of things; if he was alwayes in the world, and was the Creator or Builder of the world; why was he ſo long unknown unto the world? It ſeems rather to follow, becauſe he was un-known to the world, therefore the world was not inlightened by him, nor he totally Light. Leſt any ſhould ſo object, he divinely infers [and the world knew him not] Let not the world (ſaith he) accuſe the Word of God and his Eternal Light, but its own weakneſs: for the Son inlightens, but the creatur rejects the Grace, that's given unto it, and abuſeth the ſharpneſs of underſtanding grant-ed it, by which it might have naturally known God, and, as a prodigal, hath turned its ſight to the creaturs, neglected to go forward, and, through lazyneſſ and negligence, buried the illumination, and deſpiſed this Grace. Which, that the diſciple of Paul might not doe, he was commanded to watch, therefore it is to be*

upon Joh.
lib. 1.
cap. 11.

ins-

imputed to their wickedneß, who are illuminated, and not unto the Light ; for as, albeit the Sun riseth upon all, yet he, that is blind, receiveth no benefit thereby ; none thence can justly accuse the brightneß of the Sun, but will ascribe the cause of not seing to the blindneß : So, I judg, it is to be understood of the Onely-Begotten Son of God, for he is the true Light, and sendeth forth his brightneß upon all, but the God of this world, as Paul saith, hath blinded the minds of those, that believe not, 2 Cor. 4 : 4. that the Light of the Gospel shine not unto them. We say then, that darkneß is come upon men, not because they are altogether deprived of Light ; for Natur retaineth still the strength of understanding divinely given it, but because man is dull'd by an evil habit, and become worse, and hath made the measur of Grace, in some respect, to languish. When therefore the like befalls to man, the Psalmist justly prayes, crying, Open mine eyes, that I may behold the wonderful things of thy Law. For the Law was given, that this Light might be kindled in us, the blearedneß of the eyes of our minds being wiped away, and the blindneß being removed, which detain'd us, in our former ignorance. By these words then, the world is accused as ungratefull and unsensible, not knowing its Author, nor bringing forth the good fruit of the illumination that it may now seem to be said truely of all, which was of old said, by the Prophet, of the Jewes, I expected that it should have brought forth grapes, but it brought forth wild grapes. For the good fruit of the illumination was the knowledg of the Onely-Begotten, as a cluster hanging from a fruitfull branch, &c.

From which it appears, Cyrillus believed, that a Saving illumination was given unto *all*. For, as to what he speaks of natur, he understands it not of the common natur of man by it self, but of that natur, which hath the strength of understanding Divinely given it : for he understands this Universal Illumination to be of the same kind with that Grace, of which Paul makes mention to Timothy, saying, *Neglect not the Grace, that is in thee.* Now it is not to be believed, that Cyrillus was so ignorant, as to judg that Grace to have been some natural gift.

§ XXII. That this Saving Light and Seed, or a measur of it is given to all, Christ telleth expresly, in the parable of the Sower, Matth. 13. from v. 18. Mark 4. and Luk 8 : 11. he saith, that *this Seed* sown *in* those several sorts of grounds is the *Word of the Kingdom,* which the Apostle calls *the Word of Faith,* Rom. 10:8. Ja. 1:21. ὁ Λόγος ἔμφυτος *the implanted ingrafted Word, which is able to save the Soul* ; the words themselves declare that it is that, which is Saving, in the natur of it, for in the good ground, it fructified abundantly.

Let

Let us then obferve, that this Seed of the Kingdom, this Saving Supernatural and Sufficient Word was really fown in the ftony, thorny
ground, and by the way-fide, where it did not profit, but became ufelefs,
as to thefe grounds. It was, I fay, the fame Seed, that was fown in the
good ground. It is then the fear of perfecution, and deceitfulnefs of
riches (as Chrift himfelf interpreteth the parab'e) which hindereth this
Seed to grow in the hearts of many. Not but that in its own natur it is
fufficient, being the fame with that, which groweth up and profpereth *in*
the hearts of thofe, who receive it. So that, though all are not faved by
it, yet there is a Seed of Salvation planted and fown *in* the hearts of *all*,
by God, which would grow up and redeem the Soul, if it were not choaked and hindered. Concerning this parable Victor Antiochenus (on the
4 chap. of Mark, as he is cited by Voffius in his Pelagian hiftory, book 7.)
faith, that *Our Lord Chrift hath liberally fown the Divine Seed of the Word, and
propofed it to all, without refpect of perfons; and, as he, that foweth, diftinguifh-
eth not betwixt ground and ground, but fimply cafteth- in the feed, without diftinction, fo our Saviour hath offered the food of the Divine Word, fo farr as it was his part,
although he was not ignorant what would become of many. Laftly, he fo behaved himfelf, as he might juftly fay, what fhould I have done, than I have not done?* And
to this anfwereth the parable of the the talents, Matth. 25: he, that had
two talents, was accepted, as wel as he, that had five, becaufe he ufed
them to his mafter's profit. And he, that had one, might have done fo:
his talent was of the fame natur with the reft, it was capable to have proportionably brought forth its intereft, as the reft. And fo, though there
be not a like proportion of Grace given to *all*, to fome five talents, to
fome two talents, and to fome but one talent; yet there is given to all
that, which is fufficient, and no more is required, than according to that,
which is given. *For, unto whomfoever much is given, from him fhall much be required*, Luc. 12:48. he, that had the two talents, was accepted, for
giving four, nothing lefs than he, that gave the ten, fo fhould he alfo,
that gave the one, if he had given two, and no doubt one was capable to
have produced two, as wel as five to have produced ten, or two four.

§ XXIII. Thirdly, this Saving Spiritual *Light* is the *Gofpel*, which
the Apoftle faith exprefsly is preached *in Every creatur under heav'n*, even
that very *Gofpel, whereof* Paul was *a minifter*: Col. 1:23. For the *Gofpel*
is not a meer declaration of good things, being *the Power of God unto Sal-
-vation, to all thofe, that believe*, Rom. 1:16. though the outward decla-

                        ·ration

ration of the Gospel be taken sometimes for the Gospel, yet it is but figuratively, and by a *metonymie*. For, to speak properly, the Gospel is this inward Power and Life, which preacheth glad tidings *in* the hearts of *all* men, offering Salvation unto them, and seeking to redeem them from their iniquitys, and therefore it is said to be preached *in every creatur under Heaven*: whereas there are many thousands of men and women, to whom the outward Gospel was never preached. Therefore the Apostle Paul, Rom. 1. where he saith *the Gospel is the Power of God unto Salvation*, adds, that *therein is revealed the Righteousness of God from faith to faith*, and also *the wrath of God against such as hold the Truth of God in unrighteousness*: for this reason (saith he) *because that, which may be known of God is manifest in them, for God hath shewed it unto them*. Now, that which may be known of God, is known by the Gospel, which was manifest *in* them. For those, of whom the Apostle speaks, had no outward Gospel preached unto them, so that it was by the inward manifestation of the knowledg of God *in* them, which is indeed the *Gospel* preached *in* man, *that the righteousness of God is revealed from faith to faith*, that is, it reveals to the Soul that, which is just, good and righteous, and that, as the Soul receiveth it, and believes righteousness, comes more and more to be revealed, from one degree of faith to another. For, though, as the following verse saith, the outward Creation declares the Power of God, yet that which may be known of him, is manifest within: by which inward manifestation, we are made capable to see and discern the Eternal Power and Godhead in the outward Creation; so, were it not for this inward Principle, we could no more understand the invisible things of God by the outward visible Creation, than a blind man can see and discern the variety of shapes and colours, or judg of the beauty of the outward Creation. Therefore he saith, First, *that, which may be known of God is manifest in them*, and *in* and *by* that, they may read and understand the Power and Godhead in those things, that are outward and visible. And, though any might pretend that the outward Creation doth, of it self, without any supernatural, or Saving Principle, *in* the heart, even declare to the natural man, that there is a God: yet, what would such a knowledg avail, if it did not also communicat to me what the will of God is, and how I shall doe that, which is acceptable to him? For, the outward Creation, though it may beget a perswasion, that there is some Eternal Power or Vertue, by which the World hath had its beginning, yet it doth not tell

me,

me, nor doth it inform me of that, which is juſt, holy and righteous, how I ſhall be delivered from my temptations and evil affections, and come unto righteouſneſs : That muſt be from ſome inward manifeſtation *in my heart.*   Whereas thoſe Gentiles, of whom the Apoſtle ſpeaks, knew by that *inward Law* and manifeſtation of the knowledg of God *in* them, to diſtinguiſh betwixt *good* and *evil*, as in the next chapter appears, of which we ſhall ſpeak hereafter. The Prophet Micah ſpeaking of man indefinite-ly, or in general, declares this Mic. 6: 8. *He hath ſhewed thee, O man, what is good. And what doth the Lord requir of thee, but to doe juſtly, and to love mercy, and to walk humbly with thy God ?* He doth not ſay, God requires, till he hath firſt aſſured, that he hath ſhewed unto them. Now, becauſe this is ſhewed unto *all* men, and manifeſt *in* them, therefore, ſaith the Apoſtle, is *the wrath of God revealed againſt them, for that they hold the Truth in unrighteouſneſs,* that is, the meaſur of Truth, the Light, the Seed, the Grace *in* them ;for that they *hide the talent in the Earth,* that is, in the earthly and unrighteous part in their hearts , and ſuffer it not to bring forth fruit, but to be choaked with the ſenſual cares of this life, the fear of reproach, and the deceitfulneſs of riches, as, by the parables above mentioned, doth appear. But the Apoſtle Paul opens and illuſtrats this matter yet more, Rom. 10. where he declares, that the *Word*, which he preached (now the Word, which he preached, and the Goſpel, which he preached and whereof he was a miniſter, is one and the ſame *) is not farr off, but nigh, in the heart and in the mouth* ; which done, he frameth, as it were, the ob-jection of our adverſarys, in the 12 and 15 verſes, *How ſhall they believe in him, of whom they have not heard ? How ſhall they hear without a preacher ?* This he anſwers in the 18 verſe, ſaying *But (I ſay) have they not heard ? yes verily, their ſound went forth into all the earth, and their words unto the end of the world ;* inſinuating, that this Divine Preacher hath founded in the ears and hearts of all men; for of the outward Apoſtles that ſaying was not true, neither then, nor many hundred years after, yea for ought we know, there may be yet great and ſpatious nations and kingdoms, who never have heard of Chriſt, nor his Apoſtles, as outwardly. This inward and Powerfull Word of God is yet more fully deſcribed in the Epiſtle to the Hebrews, c. 4: v. 12, 13. *For the Word of God is quick, and ſharper than any two-edged ſword, piercing even to the dividing aſunder of Soul and Spirit, and of the joynts and marrow, and is a diſcerner of the thoughts and intents of the heart.* The vertues of this Spiritual Word are here enumerated , it is *quick*, becauſe,

it

it searches and tries the hearts of all: no man's heart is exempt from it, for the Apostle gives this reason of its being so, in the following verse; *but all things are naked and opened unto the eyes of him, with whom we have to doe: and there is not any creatur, that is not manifest in his sight.* Though this ultimately and mediately be refer'd to God, yet nearly and immediately it relates to the *Word*, or *Light*, which, as hath been before proved, is *in the hearts of all*, else it had been improper to have brought it in here. The Apostle shewes how every intent and thought of the heart is discerned by the Word of God, because all things are naked before God, which imports nothing else, but it is in and by this Word, whereby God sees and discerns mans thoughts; and so must needs be *in all* men, because the Apostle saith, *there is no creatur that is not manifest in his sight.* This then is that faithfull Witness and Messenger of God, that bears witness for God, and for his righteousness *in the hearts of all men*: for *he hath not left man without a witness*, Act. 14 : 17. and he is said to be *given for a Witness to the people*, Isa. 55 : 4. And, as this Word beareth witness for God, so it is not placed in men, onely to condemn them, for, as he is given for a Witness, so, saith the Prophet, *he is given for a Leader and a Commander. The Light is given, that all through it may believe*, Joh. 1 : 7. *For faith cometh by hearing, and hearing by this Word of God*, which is placed *in* mans heart, both to be a Witness for God, and to be a mean to bring man to God, through faith and repentance. It is therefore *powerfull*, that it may divide betwixt the Soul and the spirit. It is like a two-edged sword, that it may cut off iniquity from him, and separate betwixt the pretious and the vile; and, because mans heart is cold and hard, like iron, naturally, therefore hath God placed this word *in* him, which is said to be like a *fire* and like a *hammer*, Jer. 23 : 29. that, like as by the heat of the fire, the iron, of its own natur, cold, is warmed, and by the strength of the hammer is softened, and framed, according to the mind of the worker, so the cold and hard heart of man is, by the vertue and powerfulness of this Word of God near, and *in* the heart, as it resists not, warmed and softened, and receiveth a heavenly and celestial impression and image. The most part of the Fathers have spoken at large, touching this Word, Seed, and Light, and Saving voyce calling all unto Salvation, and able to save.

Clemens Alexandrinus saith, lib. 2. Stromat. *The Divine Word hath cried, calling all, knowing wel those, that will not obey. And yet, because it is in our power, either to obey, or not to obey, that none may have a pretext of igno-*
rance,

rance, it hath made a righteous call, and requireth but that, which is according to the ability and ſtrength of every one.   The ſelf ſame, in his warning to the Gentiles, For, *as (ſaith he) that Heavenly Ambaſſadour of the Lord, the Grace of God, that brings Salvation, hath appeared unto all, &c.* This is the new ſong, coming, and manifeſtation of the Word, *which now ſhewes it ſelf in us, which was in the beginning, and was firſt of all.* And again, *Hear therefore ye, who are afarr off, hear ye, who are near, the Word is hid from none, the Light is common to all, and ſhineth to all. There is no darkneſs in the Word, let us haſten to Salvation, to the New birth, that we, being many, may be gathered unto the One alone Love.* Ibid. he ſaith, *that there is infuſed into all, but principally into thoſe, that are trained up in doctrin, a certain Divine Jnfluence,* τις ἀπόῤῥοια θεὶη. And again he ſpeaketh concerning the *innate Witneſs worthy of belief, which, of it ſelf, doth plainly chuſe that which is moſt honeſt.* And again he ſaith, that *it is not impoſſible to come unto the Truth, and lay hold of it, ſeing it is moſt near to us, in our own houſes, as the moſt wiſe Moſes declareth, living in three parts of us, viz, in our hands, in our mouth, and in our heart, this, ſaith he, is a moſt true badge of the Truth, which is alſo fulfilled in three things, namely, in Counſel, in action, in ſpeaking.* And again, he ſaith alſo unto the unbelieving nations: *Receive Chriſt, receive Light, receive ſight, to the end thou mayſt rightly know both God & man. The Word, that hath inlightened us, is more pleaſant than gold, and the ſtone of great value.* And again, he ſaith, *Let us receive the Light, that we may receive God, let us receive the Light, that we may be the ſcholars of the Lord.* And again, he ſaith to thoſe infidel nations, *The Heavenly Spirit helpeth thee, reſiſt and flee pleaſur.* Again, lib. Strom. 5. (he ſaith) *God forbid that man be not a partaker of Divine acquaintance,* θείας ἐποίας, *who in Geneſis is ſaid to be a partaker of inſpiration.* And Pæd. lib. 1. cap. 3. *there is (ſaith he) ſome lovely and ſome deſirable thing in man, which is called the in-breathing of God,* ἐμφύτημα θεὶ. The ſame man, lib. 10. Strom. directeth men unto the *Light* and *Water* in themſelves, who have the eye of the Soul darkened or dimmed through evil up-bringing and learning: let them enter-in unto their own *domeſtik Light,* or unto the Light, which is in their own houſe, πρὸς τὸ οἰκεῖον φῶς βαδιζέτω, unto the *Truth,* which manifeſts accurately and clearly theſe things, that have been written.

Juſtin Martyr in his firſt apology ſaith, that *the Word, which was, and is, is in all, even that very ſame Word, which through the Prophets foretold things to come.*

The writer of the calling of the Gentiles, ſaith, lib. 1. cap. 2. *We believe*
accord-

according to the same (viz, Scriptur) and most religiously confess, that God was never wanting in care to the generality of men: who, although he did lead by particular lessons, a people gathered to himself unto godliness, yet he withdrew from no nation of men the gifts of his own goodness, that they might be convinced that they had received the words of the Prophets and legal commands in services and testimonys of the first principles. Cap. 7. he saith, that he believes that the help of Grace hath been wholly withdrawn from no man. Lib. 2. cap. 1. Because, albeit Salvation is farr from sinners, yet there is nothing void of the presence and vertue of his Salvation. Cap. 2. But, seing none of that people, over whom was set both the doctrines, were justified but through Grace by the Spirit of faith, who can question, but that they, who, of whatsoever nation in whatsoever times, could please God, were ordered by the Spirit of the Grace of God: which, albeit in fore-time it was more sparing and hid, yet denyed it self to no ages, being in vertue one, in quantity different, in counsel unchangeable, in operation multifarious.

§ XXIV. The third Proposition, which ought to be proved, is, *that it is by this Light, Seed, or Grace that God works the Salvation of all men, and many come to partake of the benefit of Chrifts death and Salvation purchased by him.* By the inward and effectual operations of which, as many Heathens have come to be partakers of the promises, who were not of the Seed of Abraham after the flesh, so may some now, to whom God hath rendered the knowledg of the history impossible, come to be saved by Christ. Having already proved, that *Chrift* hath *dyed* for *all*, that there is a *day of visitation* given to *all*, during which, Salvation is possible unto them, and that God hath actually given a measur of *Saving Grace* and *Light* unto *all*, preached the Gospel *to* and *in* them, and placed the *Word* of *faith in* their *hearts*, the matter of this Proposition may seem to be proved.   Yet shall I a little, for the further satisfaction of all, who desire to know the Truth, and hold it, as it is in Jesus, prove this, from two or three clear Scriptur testimonys, and remove the most common, as wel as the more strong, objections, usually brought against it.

Our Theam then hath two parts; *First, that those that have the Gospel and Chrift outwardly preached unto them, are not saved, but by the working of the Grace and Light in their hearts.*

Secondly, That by the working and operations of this many have been, and some may be, saved, to whom the Gospel hath never been outwardly preached, and who are utterly ignorant of the outward history of Chrift.

As to the first, though it be granted by most, yet, because it's more

in

in words, than deeds (the more full difcuffing of which will fall-in in
the next Propofition concerning *Juftification*) I fhall prove it in few words.
And firft from the words of Chrift to Nicodemus Joh. 3: 3. *Verily, verily*
I fay unto thee, except a man be born again, he can not fee the Kingdom of God.
Now this birth cometh not by the outward preaching of the Gofpel, or
knowledg of Chrift, or hiftoricall faith in him, feing many have that,
and firmely believe it, who are never thus renewed.   The Apoftle Paul
alfo goes fo farr, while he commends the neceffity and excellency of this
New Creation, as, in a certain refpect, to lay afide the outward knowledg of Chrift, or the knowledg of him after the flefh; in thefe words,
2 Cor. 5: 16, 17. *Wherefore henceforth know we no man after the flefh: yea*
though we have known Chrift after the flefh, yet now henceforth know we him
no more.   Therefore if any man be in Chrift, he is a new creatur, old things are
paffed away, behold all things are become new.   Whence it manifeftly appears, that he makes the knowledg of Chrift after the flefh, but as it
were the rudiments, which young children learn, which, after they
are become better fcholars, are of lefs ufe to them, becaufe they have,
and poffefs the very fubftance of thofe firft precepts, in their minds.   As
all comparifons halt in fome part, fo fhall I not affirm this to hold in every
refpect: yet fo farr will this hold, that as thofe things, that go no further than the rudiments, are never to be accounted learned, and as they
grow beyond thefe things, fo they have lefs ufe of them; even fo fuch as
go no further than the outward knowledg of Chrift, fhall never inherit
the Kingdom of Heaven.   But fuch as come to know this new birth, to be
in Chrift indeed, to be a new creatur, to have old things paft away, and
all things become new, may fafely fay with the Apoftle, *Though we have*
known Chrift after the flefh, yet now henceforth know we him no more.   Now
this new creatur proceeds from the work of this *Light* and Grace *in* the
heart.   It is that Word, which we fpeak of, that is fharp and piercing,
that *implanted* Word, able to fave the Soul, by which this birth is begotten: and therefore Chrift hath purchafed unto us this Holy Seed; that
thereby this birth might be brought forth *in* us, which is therefore alfo called *the manifeftation of the Spirit given to every one to profit withall*; for it is
written, that *by One Spirit we are all baptized into One body.*   And the
Apoftle Peter alfo afcribeth this birth to this Seed and Word of God,
which we have fo much declared of, faying, 1 Pet 1: 23. *Being born again*
not of corruptible Seed, but of incorruptible, by the Word of God, which liveth

Q

and

and abideth for ever. Though then this Seed be small in its appearance, so that Christ compares it to a *grain of mustard-seed, which is the least of all seeds,* Matth. 13: 31, 32. and that it be hid in the earthly part of man's heart, yet therein is Life and salvation towards the sons of men wrapt up, which comes to be revealed, as they give way to it. And in this Seed, *in* the hearts of *all* men, is the Kingdom of God, as in capacity to be produced or rather exhibited, according as it receives depth, is nourished, and not choaked. Hence Christ saith, that *the Kingdom of God* was *in* the very Pharisees, Luk. 17: 20, 21 who did oppose and resist him, and were justly accounted as serpents, and a generation of vipers. Now the Kingdom of God could be no other ways in them, than in a Seed, even as the thirty-fold and the hundred-fold is wrapt up in a small seed, lieing in a barren ground, which springs not forth, because it wants nourishment: and as the whole body of a great tree is wrapt up potentially in the seed of the tree, and so is brought forth in due season; and as the capacity of a man or a woman is not onely in a child, but even in the very *embryo,* even so the Kingdom of Jesus Christ, yea Jesus Christ himself, *Christ within, who is the hope of glory,* and becometh *Wisdom, Righteousness, Sanctification and Redemption,* is *in every* man and womans heart, *in* that little *incorruptible Seed,* ready to be brought forth, as it is cherished and received in the love of it. For there can be no men worse than those rebellious and unbelieving Pharisees were, and yet this Kingdom was thus *within* them, and they were directed to look for it there: so it is neither *lo here, nor lo there,* in this or the other observation that this is known, but as this Seed of God *in* the heart is minded and entertained. And certainly hence it is, (even because this Light, Seed and Grace, that appears *in* the heart of man is so little regarded, and so much overlooked) that so few know Christ brought forth *in* them. The one sort, to wit, the *Calvinists,* they look upon Grace as an irresistible power, and therefore neglect and despise this Eternal Seed of the Kingdom in their hearts, as a low, insufficient, useless thing, as to their Salvation. On the other hand the *Papists, Arminians* and *Socinians* they go about to set up their *natural Power* and *will,* with one consent denying that this little Seed, this small appearance of the Light, is that Supernatural Saving Grace of God given to *every* man, to save him. And so upon them is verified that saying of the Lord Jesus Christ, *This is the condemnation of the world, that Light is come into the world, but men love darkness rather than Light;* the reason is added, *because their deeds are evil.*

All

All confeſs they feel this, but they will not have it to be of that vertue. Some will have it to be *Reaſon*; ſome *a natural conſcience*; ſome *certain reliques of God's Image, that remained in Adam.* So Chriſt, as he met with oppoſition from all kinds of Profeſſors in his outward appearance, ſo doth he now in his inward. It was the meanneſs of his outward man, that made many deſpiſe him, ſaying, *Is not this the ſon of the carpenter? are not his brethren and ſiſters among us? Is not this a Galilean?* and *came there ever a Prophet out of Galilea?* and ſuch like reaſonings. For they expected an outward deliverer, who, as a Prince, ſhould deliver them, with great eaſe, from their outward enemies, and not ſuch a *MESSIAH* as ſhould be crucified ſhamefully, and, as it were, lead them into many ſorrowes, troubles, and afflictions. So the meanneſs of this appearance makes the crafty Jeſuits, the pretended rational Socinians, and the learned Arminians, overlook it, deſiring rather ſomething, that they might exerciſe their ſubtilty, reaſon and learning about, and uſe the liberty of their own wills. And the *ſecure Calviniſts*, they would have a Chriſt to ſave them without any trouble, to deſtroy all their enemies for them, without them, and nothing, or little, within, while they mean while, be at eaſe to live in their ſins ſecure. Whence, when all is wel examined, the cauſe is plain, it is *becauſe their deeds are evil*, that, with one conſent they reject this *Light*: for it checks the wiſeſt of them all, and the learnedeſt of them all, in ſecret, it reproves them, neither can all their *Logick* ſilence it, nor can the ſecureſt among them ſtop its voyce from crying, and reproving them within, for all their confidence in the outward knowledg of Chriſt, or of what he hath ſuffered outwardly for them. For, as hath been often ſaid, in a day it ſtrives with all, wreſtles with all, and it's the unmortified natur, the firſt natur, the old Adam, yet alive in the wiſeſt, in the learnedeſt, in the moſt zealous for the outward knowledg of Chriſt, that denys this, that deſpiſes it, that ſhuts it out, to their own condemnation. They come all under this deſcription, *every one, that doth evil, hateth the Light, neither cometh to the Light, leſt his deeds ſhould be reproved*, Joh. 3 : 20. ſo that it may be ſaid now, and we can ſay from a true and certain experience, as it was ſaid of old, Pſal. 118 : 22. Matth. 21 : 42. Mark 12 : 10. Luk 20: v. 17. Act. 4 : 11. *The Stone, which the builders, of all kinds, have rejected, the ſame is become unto us the Head of the corner.* Glory to God for ever! who hath choſen us a fiſt-fruits to himſelf in this day, wherein he is ariſen to plead with the nations, and therefore hath ſent us forth to preach this

                                                    ever-

everlasting Gospel unto all, Christ nigh to all, the Light *in* all, the Seed sown in the hearts of all, that men may come and apply their minds to it. And we rejoyce that we have been made to lay down our wisdom and learning (such of us as have had some of it) and our carnal reasoning, to learn of Jesus, and sit down at the feet of Jesus in our hearts, and hear him, who there makes all things manifest, and reproves all things by his Light, Eph. 5 : 13. For many are wise and learned in the notion, in the letter of the Scriptur, as the Pharisees were, and can speak much of Christ, and plead strongly against infidels, Turks, and Jewes, and it may be also against some hereticks, who, in the mean time, are crucifying Christ in the small appearance of his Seed *in* their hearts. O! better were it to be stript naked of all, to account it as dross and dung, and become a fool for Christ's sake, thus knowing him to teach thee in thy heart, so as thou mayst witness him raised there, feel the vertue of his cross there, and say with the Apostle, *I glory in nothing, save in the cross of Christ, whereby I am crucified to the world, and the world unto me.* This is better, than to write thousands of commentarys, and to preach many sermons. And it is thus to preach Christ, and direct people to his Pure Light in the heart, that God hath raised us up, and for which the wise men of this world account us fools; because, by the operation of this cross of Christ *in* our hearts, we have denyed our own wisdom and wills in many things, and have forsaken the vain worships, fashions and customes of this world. For these divers centurys the world hath been full of a dry, fruitless and barren knowledg of Christ, feeding upon the husk and neglecting the kernel, following after the shaddow, but strangers to the Substance. Hence the devil matters not how much of that knowledg abounds, provided he can but possess the heart, and rule in the will, crucify the appearance of Christ there, and so keep the Seed of the Kingdom from taking root. For he has led them abroad, lo here, and lo there, and has made them wrestle in a false zeal, so much one against another, contending for this outward observation, and for the other outward observation, seeking Christ in this and the other external thing, as in bread and wine; contending one with another how he is there, while some will have him to be present therein this way, and some the other way : and some in Scripturs, in books, in societys and pilgrimages and merits. But some confiding in an external barren faith, think all is wel, if they do but firmly believe that he dyed for their sins past, present, and to come, while, in the mean time, Christ

lies

lies crucified and flain, and is daily refifted and gainfaid in his appearance *in* their hearts. Thus, from a fenfe of this blindnefs and ignorance, that is come over Chriftendom, it is, that we are led and moved of the Lord, fo conftantly and frequently to call all, invite all, requeft all to turn to the Light *in* them, to mind the Light *in* them, to believe in Chrift, as he is *in* them. And that in the Name, Power and Authority of the Lord, not in fchool arguments and diftinctions, (for which many of the wife men of this world account us fools and mad men) we do charge and command them to lay afide their wifdom, to come down out of that proud, airy, brain-knowledg, and to ftop that mouth, how eloquent foever to the worldly ear it may appear; and to be filent and fit down as in the duft, and to mind the Light of Chrift *in* their own Confciences. Which, if it be minded, they would find as a fharp two-edged fword in their hearts, and as a fire and a hammer, that would knock againft and burn up all that carnal, gathered, natural ftuff, and make the ftouteft of them all tremble and become *Quakers* indeed. Which thofe, that come not to feel now, and *kifs* not *the Son*, while the day lafteth, but harden their hearts, will feel to be a certain Truth, when it is too late. To conclude, as faith the Apoftle, *All ought to examin themfelves whether they be in the faith indeed; and try their own felves, for, except Jefus be in them, they are certainly reprobats.* 2 Cor. 13: 5.

§ XXV. Secondly, that, which remaines now to be proved, is, *that by the operation of this Light and Seed fome have been, and may yet be faved, to whom the Gofpel is not outwardly preached, nor the hiftory of Chrift outwardly known.* To make this the eafier, we have already fhewn how that Chrift hath dyed for all men, and confequently thefe are inlightened by Chrift, and have a meafur of Saving Light and Grace; yea that the Gofpel, though not in any outward difpenfation, is preached to them, and *in* them: fo that thereby they are ftated in a poffibility of Salvation. From which I may thus argue,

To whom the Gofpel, the Power of God unto Salvation, is manifeft, they may be faved, whatever outward knowledg they want: Arg.

But this Gofpel is preached *in* every creatur, in which is certainly comprehended many, that have not the outward knowledg:

Therefore of thofe, many may be faved.

But to thofe arguments, by which it hath been proved that all men have a meafur of Saving Grace, I fhall add one, and that very obfervable, not

yet

yet mentioned, *viz*, that excellent saying of the Apostle Paul to *Titus*, c. 2 : v. 11. *The Grace of God, that brings Salvation, hath appeared to all men, teaching us, that denying ungodlyness and worldly lusts, we should live soberly, righteously, and godlyly in this present world.* Than which there can be nothing more clear, it comprehending both the parts of the controversy. First it testifys that it is no natural principle or light, but saith plainly, *it brings Salvation.* Secondly, it says not, that it hath appeared to a few, but unto *all* men. The fruit of it declares also how efficacious it is, seing it comprehends the whole duty of man. It both teacheth us first, to forsake evil, to deny ungodlyness and worldly lusts; and then it teacheth us our whole duty. First, to live *soberly*, that comprehends temperance, chastity, meekness, and those things, that relate unto a man's self. Secondly, *righteously*, that comprehends equity, justice, and honesty, and those things, which relate to our neighbours. And lastly, *godlyly*, which comprehends piety, faithfulnes, and devotion, which are the dutys relating to God. So then there is nothing required of man, or needfull to man, which this Grace teacheth not. Yet I have heard a publick Preacher, one of those, that are accounted zealous men, to evite the strength of this text, deny *this Grace to be saving*, and say, *it was onely intended of common favours and graces, such as is the heat of the fire and outward light of the Sun* Such is the darkness and ignorance of those, that oppose the Truth, whereas the text saith expressly, that it is *Saving.* Others, that can not deny but it is saving, alledg this [*all*] comprehends not every individual, but onely all kinds. But is a bare negation, sufficient to overturn the strength of a positive assertion ? If the Scripturs may be so abused, what so absurd as may not be pleaded for from them? or what so manifest as may not be denyed? But, we have not reason to be staggered by their denying, so long as our faith is found in express termes of the Scriptur, they may as wel seek to perswade us that we do not intend that, which we affirm, though we know the contrary, as make us believe, that, when the Apostle speaks forth our doctrin in plain words, yet he intends theirs ; which is the quite contrary, and indeed can there be any thing more absurd, than to say, where the word is plainly [*all*], *few* is onely intended. For they will not have [*all*] taken here, for the greater number. Indeed, as the case may be sometimes, by a figur, [*all*] may be taken, of two numbers, for the greater number, but let them shew us, if they can, either in Scriptur or profane or ecclesiastical writings, that any man, that wrote sense, did

ever

ever uſe the word [all] to expreſs, of two numbers, the leſſer. Whereas they affirm, that the farr leſs number have received ſaving Grace, and yet will they have the Apoſtle by [all] to have ſignified ſo. Though this might ſuffice, yet to put it further beyond all queſtion, I ſhall inſtance another ſaying of the ſame Apoſtle, that we may uſe him as his own commentator, Rom. 5 : 18. *Therefore as by the offence of One, judgment came upon all men to condemnation, even ſo by the Righteouſneſß of One, the Free Gift came upon all men to juſtification of life.* Here, no man of reaſon, except he will be obſtinately ignorant, will deny but this ſimilitive particle [as] makes the [all], which goes before, and comes after, to be of one and the ſame extent. Or elſe let them ſhew us one example, either in Scriptur, or elſewhere, among men, that ſpeak proper language, where it is otherwiſe. We muſt then either affirm that this loſs, which leads to condemnation, hath not come upon all, or ſay, that this Free Gift is come upon all by Chriſt. Whence I thus argue, Firſt,

If all men have received a loſs, from Adam, which leads to conde-mnation, then all men have received a Gift from Chriſt, which leads to Juſtification: *Arg.*

But the Firſt is true:

Therefore alſo the Laſt.

From all which it naturally followes, that all men, even the Heathens, may be ſaved : for Chriſt was given, as a *Light, to inlighten the Gentiles,* Iſa. 49 : 6. Now, to ſay, that, though they might have been ſaved, yet none were, is to judg too uncharitably. I ſee not what reaſon can be al-ledged for it, yea, though it were granted, which never can be, that none of the Heathens were ſaved; it will not from thence follow, that they could not have been ſaved : or that none now in their condition can be ſaved. For, *à non eſſe ad non poſſe non datur ſequela*, i. e. that conſequence is falſe, that concludes a thing can not be, becauſe it is not.

But if it be objected, which is the great objection, *That there is no name under heaven, by which Salvation is known, but by the Name JESUS :*   *Obj.*

Therefore they (not knowing this) can not be ſaved.

I anſwer : though they know it not outwardly, yet, if they know it in-wardly, by feeling the vertue and power of it, the Name *Jeſus* indeed (which ſignifies a *Saviour*) to free them from ſin and iniquity *in* their hearts, they are ſaved by it. I confeſs there is no other name to be ſaved by; but Salvation lieth not in the literal, but in the experimental know- *Anſw.*

ledg,

ledg, albeit thofe, that have the literal knowledg, are not faved by it, without this real experimental knowledg. Yet thofe, that have rhe real knowledg, may be faved without the external; as by the arguments here-after brought will more appear. For, if the outward diftinct knowledg of him, by whofe means I receive benefit, were neceffary for me, before I could reap any fruit of it, then, by the rule of *Contrarys*, it would fol-low, that I could receive no hurt, without I had alfo the diftinct knowledg of him, that had occafioned it; whereas, experience proves the contra-ry. How many are injured by Adam's fall, that know nothing of ever there being fuch a man in the world? or of his eating the forbidden fruit? why may they not then be faved by the Gift and Grace of Chrift *in* them, making them righteous and holy, though they know not diftinctly how that was purchafed unto them by the death and fufferings of Jefus, that was crucified at Jerufalem; efpecially feing God hath made that know-ledg fimply impoffible to them? As many men are killed by poifon infufed into their meat, though they neither know what the poifon was, nor who infufed it: fo alfo on the other hand, how many are cured of their dif-eafes by good remedys, who know not how the medicin is prepared, what the ingredients are, nor often times who made it? The like may alfo hold in Spiritual things, as we fhall hereafter prove.

§ XXVI. Firft, If there were fuch an abfolute neceffity for this out-ward knowledg, that it were even of the effentials of Salvation, then none could be faved without it; whereas our adverfarys deny not, but readily confefs, that many infants and deaf perfons are faved without it. So that, here they break that general rule, & make Salvation poffible with-out it. Neither can they alledg, that it is, becaufe fuch are free from fin, feing they alfo affirm, that all infants, becaufe of Adam's fin, deferve eternal condemnation, as being really guilty in the fight of God; and of deaf people it is not to be doubted, and experience fhewes us, that they are fubject to many common iniquitys, as wel as other men.

Obj.   If it be faid, *that thefe children are the children of believing parents,*

Anfw.   What then? They will not fay, that they tranfmitt grace to their children. Do they not affirm, that the children of believing parents are guilty of original fin, and deferve death, as wel as others? How prove they, that that makes up the lofs of all explicit knowledg?

Obj.   If they fay, *Deaf people may be made fenfible of the Gofpel by fignes,*

Anfw.   All the fignes can not give them any explicit knowledg of the hiftory
of

of the death, ſufferings, and reſurrection of Chriſt.   For what ſignes can inform a deaf man, that *the Son of God took on him man's natur? was born of a Virgin, and ſuffered under Pontius Pilat?*

And, if they ſhould further alledg, *that they are within the boſome of the* Obj.
viſible Church, and partakers of the Sacraments;

All that gives no certainty of Salvation, for (as the Proteſtants con- Anſw.
feſs) they confer not Grace *ex opere operatô.*   And will not they acknowledg, that many are in the boſom of the Church, who are viſibly no
members of it?   But if this charity be extended towards ſuch, who are
where the Goſpel is preached, ſo that they may be judged capable of Salvation, becauſe they are under a ſimple impoſſibility of diſtinctly knowing the means of Salvation; what reaſon can be alledged, why the like
charity may not be had to ſuch, as though they can hear, yet are under
a ſimple impoſſibility of hearing, becauſe it is not ſpoken unto them. Is
not a man in *China* or in *India* as much to be excuſed for not knowing a
thing, which he never heard of, as a deaf man here, who can not hear?
For, as the deaf man is not to be blam'd, becauſe God hath been pleaſed
to ſuffer him to lie under this infirmity, ſo is the *Chinees* or the *Indian* as
excuſable, becauſe God hath with-held from him the opportunity of hearing. He, that can not hear a thing, as being neceſſarily abſent, and he,
that can not hear it, as being naturally deaf, are to be placed in the ſame
category.

Secondly, this manifeſtly appears by that ſaying of Peter, Act. 10:34.
*Of a truth I perceive that God is no reſpecter of perſons : But in every nation, he,
that feareth him, and worketh righteouſneſs, is accepted of him.* Peter was before liable to that miſtake, that the reſt of the Jewes were in, judging
that all were unclean except themſelves, and that no man could be ſaved
except they were proſelyted to their religion, and circumciſed. But God
ſhewed Peter other wayes, in a viſion, and taught him to call nothing
common or unclean; and therefore, ſeing that God regarded the prayers
of *Cornelius*, who was a ſtranger to the Law, and to Jeſus Chriſt, as to the
outward; yet Peter ſaw that God had accepted him. And he is ſaid to
fear God, before he had this outward knowledg, therefore Peter concluds
that every one, that, in every nation, without reſpect of perſons, feareth
God, and worketh righteouſneſs, is accepted of him. So he makes the
fear of God and the working of righteouſneſs, and not an outward hiſto-
rical knowledg, the qualification; They then, that have this, wherever
R
they

they be, they are faved. Now we have already proved, that to every man that Grace is given, whereby he may live godlyly and righteoufly, and we fee that by this Grace *Cornelius* did fo, and was accepted, and his prayers came up for a memorial before God, before he had this outward knowledg. Alfo was not *Job a perfect and upright man, that feared God and efchewed evil?* Who taught Job this? how knew Job Adam's fall? And from what Scriptur learned he that excellent knowledg he had, and that faith, by which he knew his *Redeemer lived?* For, many make him as old as Mofes, was not this by an inward Grace *in* the heart? was it not that inward Grace, that taught Job to efchew evil, and to fear God? and was it not by the workings thereof that he became a juft and upright man? how doth he reprove the wickednefs of men, chap. 24? and, after he hath numbred up their wickednefs, doth he not condemn them, vers 13. for *rebelling* againft this *Light*, for not knowing the way thereof, nor abiding in the paths thereof? It appears then Job believed that men had a Light, and that becaufe they rebelled againft it, therefore they knew not its wayes, and abod not in its paths, even as the Pharifees, who had the Scripturs, are faid to err, not knowing the Scripturs. And alfo Job's friends, though in fome things wrong, yet who taught them all thofe excellent fayings, and knowledg, which they had? Did not God give it them in order to fave them, or was it meerly to condemn them? Who taught Elihu that *the Infpiration of the Almighty giveth underftanding, that the Spirit of God made him, and the Breath of the Almighty gave him life?* And did not the Lord accept a facrifice for them? And who dare fay that they are damned? But further, the Apoftle puts this controverfy out of doubt, for, if we may believe his plain affertions, he tells us, Rom. 2. that the *Heathens did the things contained in the Law.* From whence I thus argue,

Arg.   In every nation, he, that feareth God, and worketh righteoufnefs, is accepted:

    But many of the Heathens feared God, and wrought righteoufnefs:

    Therefore they were accepted.

The *minor* is proved from the example of *Cornelius.* But I fhall further prove it thus:

    He, that doth the things contained in the Law, feareth God, and worketh righteoufnefs:

    But the Heathens did the things contained in the Law:

    Therefore they feared God, and wrought righteoufnefs.

Can

Can there be any thing more clear ? For, if to doe the things contained in the Law be not to fear God and work righteoufnefs, then what can be faid to doe fo, feing the Apoftle calls the Law *fpiritual*, *holy*, *juft* and *good*? But this appears manifeftly by another *medium* taken out of the fame chapter, vers 13. So that nothing can be more clear. The words are, *The doers of the Law fhall be juftified*, from which I thus argue, without adding any word of my own :

The doers of the Law fhall be juftified: Arg.

But the Gentiles doe the things contained in the Law.
All, that know but a conclufion, do eafily fee what followes from thefe exprefs words of the Apoftle. And indeed, he, through that whole chapter, labours, as if he were contending now with our adverfarys, to confirm this doctrin, ver. 9, 10, 11. *Tribulation and anguifh upon every Soul of man, that doth evil, to the Jew firft, and alfo to the Gentile. For there is no refpect of perfons with God.* Where the Apoftle clearly homologats the fentence of Peter before mentioned, and fhewes that Jew and Gentile, or, as he himfelf explains in the following verfes, both they, that have an outward Law, and they, that have none, when they doe good, fhall be juftified, And, to put us out of doubt, in the very following verfes, he tells, that *the doers of the Law are juftified*, and that the *Gentiles did* the Law. So that, except we think he fpake not what he intended, we may fafely conclude, that fuch Gentiles were juftified, and did partake of that *honour*, *glory* and *peace*, *which comes upon Every one that doth good* : even the Gentiles, that are without the Law, when they work good, feing with God there is no refpect of perfons ; fo, as we fee that it is not the having of the outward knowledg that doth fave, without the inward ; fo neither doth the want of it, to fuch, to whom God hath made it impoffible, who have the inward, bring condemnation. And many, that have wanted the outward, have had a knowledg of this inwardly, by vertue of that inward Grace and Light given to *every* man, working *in* them, by which they forfook iniquity, and became juft and holy, as is above proved; who, though they knew not the hiftory of Adam's fall, yet were fenfible *in* themfelves of the lofs, that came by it, feeling their inclinations to fin, and the body of fin in them : and, though they knew not the coming of Chrift, yet were fenfible of that inward Power and Salvation, which came by him, even before, as wel as fince, his appearance in the flefh. For I queftion whether thefe men can prove that all the Patriarchs and Fathers before Mofes

R 2

had

had a diftinct knowledg either of the one or the other, or that they knew the hiftory of the tree of knowledg of good and evil, and of Adam's eating the forbidden fruit : farr lefs that Chrift fhould be born of a Virgin, fhould be crucified, and treated in the manner he was. For it is juftly to be believed that what Mofes wrot of Adam, and of the firft times, was not by tradition, but by revelation : yea we fee that, not onely after the writing of Mofes, but even of David and all the Prophets, who prophefied fo much of Chrift, how little the Jewes, that were expecting and wifhing for the Meffiah, could thereby difcern him, when he came, that they crucified him as a blafphemer, not as the Meffiah, by miftaking the prophecys concerning him; for Peter faith expresfly, Act. 3 : 17. to the Jewes, that both *they and their rulers did it through ignorance.* And Paul faith, 1 Cor. 2 : 8. that *had they known it, they would not have crucified the Lord of Glory.* Yea Mary her felf, to whom the Angel had fpoken, and who had laid up all the miraculous things accompanying his birth, *in* her heart, fhe did not underftand how, when *he difputed with the doctors in the temple,* that *he was about his Father's bufineß.* And the Apoftles, that had believed him, converfed daily with him, and faw his miracles, could not underftand neither believe thofe things, which related to his death, fufferings, and refurrection, but were, in a certain refpect, ftumbled at them.

§ XXVII. So, we fee how that it is the inward work, and not the outward hiftory and Scriptur, that gives the true knowledg, and by this inward Light many of the Heathen Philofophers were fenfible of the lofs received by Adam, though they knew not the outward hiftory : Hence *Plato* afferted, that *man's Soul was faln into a dark cave, where it onely converfed with fhaddowes.* *Pythagoras* faith, *man wandereth in this world, as a ftranger, banifhed from the Prefence of God.* And *Plotinus* compareth *man's Soul, faln from God, to a cinder, or dead coal, out of which the fire is extinguifhed.* Some of them faid, that the *the wings of the Soul were clipped, or faln off, fo that they could not flee unto God.* All which, and many more fuch expreffions, that might be gathered out of their writings, fhew they were not without a fenfe of this lofs. Alfo they had a knowledg and difcovery of Jefus Chrift inwardly, as a remedy *in* them, to deliver them, from that evil feed, and the evil inclinations of their own hearts, though not under that particular denomination.

Some called him a *Holy Spirit,* as Seneca, Epift. 41. who faid, *there is a Holy Spirit in us, that treateth us, as we treat him.* Cicero calleth it an *innate Light,*

Light, in his book *de Republica,* cited by *Lactantius,* 6. Inſtit. where he calls
this; *Right Reaſon given unto all, conſtant and eternal, calling unto duty by command-*
ing, and deterring from deceit, by forbidding. Adding, that it can not be abrogated,
neither can any be freed from it, neither by Senat nor people; that it is one eternal, and
the ſame always to all nations, ſo that there is not one at Rome, and another at
Athens: who ſo obey it not, muſt flee from himſelf, and in this is greatly torment-
ed, although he ſhould eſcape all other puniſhment. Plotinus alſo calls him
Light, ſaying, that *as the Sun can not be known but by its own Light, ſo God can*
not be known but with his own Light: and as the eye can not ſee the Sun, but by re-
ceiving its image, ſo man can not know God, but by receiving his Image, and
that it behoved man to come to purity of heart, before he could know God. Calling
him alſo *Wiſdom,* a name frequently given him in Scriptur. See Prov. 1:
v. 20. to the end and Prov. 8: 9, 34. where *Wiſdom* is ſaid to cry, intreat,
and invite all, to come unto her, and learn of her. And what is this
Wiſdom, but Chriſt? hence ſuch as came; among the Heathen, to
forſake evil, and cleave to righteouſneſs, were called *Philoſophers,* that is
lovers of Wiſdom. They knew this *Wiſdom* was *nigh* unto them, and that
the beſt knowledg of God and Divine Myſteries was by the Inſpiration of the Wiſdom
of God, Phocylides affirmed, that *the Word of the Wiſdom of God was the*
beſt. His words in the Greek are, Τῆς δ Θεοπνεύστης σοφίας λόγος ἐστὶν ἄριστος.

And much more of this kind might be inſtanced, by which it appears
they knew *Chriſt,* and by his work working *in* them, were brought from
unrighteouſneſs to righteouſneſs, and to love that Power, by which they
felt themſelves redeemed; ſo that, as ſaith the Apoſtle, *they ſhew the*
work of the Law written in their hearts, and *did the things contained in the Law,*
and therefore, as *all doers of the Law are, were no doubt juſtified,* and ſaved
thus by the Power of Chriſt in them. And, as this was the judgment of
the Apoſtle, ſo was it of the primitive Chriſtians. Hence Juſtin Martyr
ſtuck not to call *Socrates a Chriſtian,* ſaying, that *all ſuch as lived according*
to the Divine Word in them, which was in all men, were Chriſtians, ſuch as So-
crates and Heraclitus and others among the Greeks, &c. That, *ſuch as live with*
the Word, are Chriſtians without fear or anxiety.

Clemens Alexandrinus ſaith, Apol. 2. Strom. lib. 1. that *this Wiſdom*
or Philoſophy was neceſſary to the Gentiles, and was their ſchool maſter to lead them
unto Chriſt, by which of old the Greeks were juſtified.

Nor do I think, ſaith Auguſtin, in his book of the City of God, lib. 18.
cap. 47. *that the Jewes dare affirm that none belonged unto God, but the Iſra-*
elites.

elits. Upon which place Ludovicus Vives faith, that *thus the Gentiles not having a Law, were a Law unto themselves, and the Light of so living is the Gift of God, and proceeds from the Son: of whom it is written, that he inlighteneth every man, that cometh into the world.*

Augustin also testifys in his Confessions, lib. 7. cap. 9. that *he had read in the writings of the Platonists, though not in the very same words, yet that, which by many and multiplied reasons did persuade, that in the beginning was the Word, and the Word was with God, this was in the beginning with God, by which all things were made, and without which nothing was made, that was made: In him was Life, and the Life was the Light of men; and the Light shined in the darkness, and the darkness did not comprehend it. And, albeit the Soul gives testimony concerning the Light, yet it is not the Light, but the Word of God, for GOD is the true LIGHT, which inlighteneth every man, that cometh into the world;* and so repeats to the 14 verse of the 1 chapter of John, adding, *these things have I there read.*

Yea there is a book translated out of the Arabick, which gives an account of one Hai Ebn Yokdan, who, without converse of man, living in an island alone, attained to such a profound knowledg of God, as to have immediate converse with him, and to affirm *that the best and most certain knowledg of God is not that, which is attained by premisses premised, and conclusions deduced, but that, which is enjoyed by conjunction of the mind of man with the Supream Intellect, after the mind is purified from its corruptions, and is separated from all bodily images, and is gathered into a profound stilness!*

§ XXVIII. Seing then it is by this inward Gift, Grace and Light that both those, that have the Gospel preached unto them, come to have Jesus brought forth *in* them, and to have the saving and sanctified use of all outward helps and advantages: and also by this same Light that all may come to be saved, and that God calls, invites, and strives with all, in a day, and saveth many, to whom he hath not seen meet to conveigh this outward knowledg; therefore we having the experience of the inward and powerfull work of this Light *in* our hearts, even *Jesus* revealed *in* us, can not cease to proclaim the day of the Lord, that it is arisen in it, crying-out with the woman of Samaria, *Come, and see One, that hath told me all, that ever I have done, Is not this the Christ?* that others may come and feel the same *in* themselves, and may know that that little small thing, that reproves them *in* their hearts, however they have despised it, and neglected it, is nothing less, than the Gospel preached *in* them, *Christ* the

Wis-

Wifdom and *Power of God*, being *in* and *by* that Seed, feeking to fave their Soules.

Of this *Light* therefore Auguftin fpeaks, in his Confeffions, lib. 11. cap. 9. *In this beginning, O God! thou madeft the heaven and the earth, in thy Word, in thy Son, in thy Vertue, in thy Wifdom, wonderfully faying, and wonderfully doing, who fhall comprehend it? who fhall declare it? what is that, which fhineth-in unto me, and fmites my heart without hurt, at which I both tremble, and am inflammed, I tremble in fo farr as I am unlike unto it, and I am inflammed in fo farr as I am like unto it? It is Wifdom, which fhineth-in unto me, and difpelleth my cloud, which had again cover'd me, after I was departed from that darknefs and rampier of my punifhments.* And again he faith, lib. 10. cap. 27. *It is too late that I have loved thee, O thou Beautifulnefs, fo ancient, and fo new; late have I loved thee, and behold thou waft within and I was without, and there was feeking thee, thou didft call, thou didft cry, thou didft break my deafnefs, thou glanç-edft, thou didft fhine, thou chafedft away my darknefs.*

Of this alfo our countrey-man *George Buchanan* fpeaketh thus, in his book De Jure Regni apud Scotos : *Truely I underftand no other thing at prefent, than that Light, which is divinely infufed into our Soules, for, when God formed man, he not onely gave him eyes to his body, by which he might fhun thofe things, that are hurtfull to him, and follow thofe things, that are profitable. But alfo hath fet before his mind, as it were, a certain Light, by which he may difcern things, that are vile, from things that are honeft: Some call this Power, Natur, others the Law of Natur, I truely judg it to be Divine, and am perfwaded that Natur and Wifdom never fay different things. Moreover God hath given us a compend of the Law, which in few words comprehends the whole to wit, that we fhould love him from our hearts, and our neighbours as our felves. And of this Law all the books of the Holy Scripturs, which pertain to the forming of manners, contain no other, but an explication.*

This is that Univerfal, Evangelical Principle, in, and by which this Salvation of Chrift is exhibited to *all* men, both Jew and Gentile, Schythian and Barbarian, of whatfoever countrey or kindred he be. And therefore God hath raifed up unto himfelf, in this our age, faithfull witneffes and Evangelifts to preach again his Everlafting Gofpel, and to direct *all*, as wel the high Profeffors, who boaft of the Law and the Scriptur, and the outward knowledg of Chrift, as the Infidels and Heathens, that know not him the way, that they may all come to mind the Light *in* them, and know Chrift *in* them, the *Juft One*, τòγ Δίκαιον, *whom they have fo long kill-*
ed,

ed, and made merry over, and he hath not resisted, Ja. 5 : 6. and give up their
sins, iniquitys, false faith, professions and out-side righteousness to be
crucified by the Power of his Cross *in* them, so as they may know Christ
within, to be the *Hope of Glory*, and may come to walk in his Light, and be,
saved, who is that *True Light, that inlighteneth Every man that cometh into
the world.*

The Seventh Proposition,

Concerning Iustification.

As many as resist not this *Light*, but receive the same, it
becomes *in* them, a Holy, Pure and Spiritual birth,
bringing forth holyness, righteousness, purity, and all
those other blessed fruits, which are acceptable to God,
by which holy birth, to wit, *Iesus Christ formed within us*,
and working his works *in* us, as we are sanctified, so are
we justified in the sight of God, according to the Apostl's words; *But ye are washed, but ye are sanctified, but ye
are justified in the Name of the Lord Iesus, and by the Spirit of
our God*, 1 Cor. 6:11. Therefore it is not by our works,
wrought in our will, nor yet by good works, considered as of themselves, but by *Christ*, who is both the *Gift*
and the *Giver*, and the Cause produceing the effects *in*
us, who, as he hath reconciled us, while we were enemies, doth also in his Wisdom save us, and justify us,
after this manner, as saith the same Apostle elsewhere,
*according to his mercy he hath saved us, by the washing of rege-
neration and the renewing of the Holy Ghost*, Tit. 3: 5.

§ I.   THe doctrin of Justification comes wel in order after
the discussing of the extent of Christ's death, and of the
Grace thereby communicated; some of the sharpest
contests concerning this having from thence their rise.
Many are the disputs, among those called *Christians*,
concerning this point; and indeed, if all were truely minding that, which
justi-

juſtifieth, there would be leſs noyſe about the notions of Juſtification. I
ſhall briefly review this controverſy, as it ſtands among others, and as I
have often ſeriouſly obſerved it: then in ſhort ſtate the controverſy, as
to us, and open our ſenſe and judgment of it: and laſtly, prove it (if the
Lord will) by ſome Scriptur teſtimonys, and the certain experience of all,
ever were truely juſtified.

§ II. That this doctrin of *Iuſtification* hath been, and is greatly, vitiated, in the Church of Rome, is not by us queſtioned, though our adverſarys, who, for want of better arguments, do often make lyes their
refuge, have not ſpared, in this reſpect, to ſtigmatize us with Popery,
but how untruely, will hereafter appear. For to ſpeak little of their *meritum ex condignô*, which was, no doubt a very common doctrin of the
Romiſh Church, eſpecially before *Luther*, though moſt of their modern
writers, eſpecially in their controverſys with Proteſtants, do partly
deny it, partly qualify it, and ſeem to ſtate the matter onely, as if they
were propagators and pleaders for good works, by the others denyed.
Yet, if we look to the effects of this doctrin among them, as they appear in the generality of their Church members, not in things diſapprov-
ed, but highly approved, and commended by their father the *Pope*, and
all his clients, as the moſt beneficial caſuality of all his revenue, we ſhall
find that *Luther* did not without great ground oppoſe himſelf to them in
this matter, and, if he had not himſelf run into another extream (of
which hereafter) his work would have ſtood the better. For in this, as
in moſt other things, he is more to be commended for what he pulled
down of Babylon, than for what he built of his own. Whatever then the
Papiſts may pretend, or even ſome good men among them may have
thought, experience ſheweth, and it is more than manifeſt by the univerſal and approved practice of their people, that they place not their
juſtification ſo much in works, that are truely and morally good, and in
the being truely renewed and ſanctified in the mind, as in ſuch things as
are either nor good nor evil, or may truely be called evil, and can no
otherwayes be reckoned good, than becauſe the *Pope* pleaſes to call them
ſo. So that, if the matter be wel ſifted, it will be found, that the greateſt part of their juſtification depends upon the authority of his *Bulls*, and
not upon the Power, Vertue, and Grace of Chriſt revealed *in* the heart,
and renewing of it. As will appear, Firſt, from their principle concerning their *Sacraments*, which, they ſay, *confer grace, ex opere operatô.* So

S

that,

that, if a man partake but of them, he thereby obtaines remiſſion of ſin, though he remain as he was; the vertue of the Sacraments making up the want, that is in the man.   So that this act of ſubmiſſion and faith to the Lawes of the Church, and not any real inward change, is that, which juſtifieth him. As for example, if a man make uſe of the *Sacrament* (as they call it) *of Pennance*, ſo as to tell over his ſins to a prieſt, though he have not true *contrition*; which the Lord hath made abſolutely neceſſary for penitent ſinners, but onely *attrition*, a *figment* of their own, that is, If he be ſorry he hath ſinned, not out of any love to God, or his Law, which he hath tranſgreſſed, but for fear of puniſhment, yet doth the vertue of the Sacrament (as they affirm) procure to him remiſſion of ſins; ſo that, being abſolved by the prieſt, he ſtands accepted and juſtified in the ſight of God.   This man's juſtification then proceedeth not from his being truely penitent, and in any meaſur inwardly changed and renewed by the working of God's Grace *in* his heart, but meerly from the authority of the prieſt, and vertue of the Sacrament, who hath pronounced him *abſolved*, ſo that his juſtification is from ſomewhat without him, and not within him.

Secondly, this will yet more appear in the matter of *Indulgences*, where remiſſion of all ſins, not onely paſt, but for years to come, is annexed to the viſiting ſuch and ſuch Churches and reliques, ſaying ſuch and ſuch prayers: ſo that the perſon, that ſo doth, is preſently cleared from the guilt of his ſin, and juſtified and accepted in the ſight of God. As for example, he, that in the great Jubilee, will go to Rome, and preſent himſelf before the gate of Peter and Paul, and there receive the Pop's bleſſing, or he, that will go a pilgrimage to James's ſepulchre in Spain, or to Mary of Lorreta, is, upon the performance of thoſe things, promiſed forgiveneſs of ſins.   Now, if we ask them the reaſon, how ſuch things, as are not morally good in themſelves, come to have vertue, they have no other anſwer but becauſe of the Church and Pop's authority; who, being the great treaſurer of the magazin of Chriſt's merits, lets them out, upon ſuch and ſuch conditions. Thus alſo the invention of ſaying *Maſſe* is made a chief inſtrument of Juſtification; for in it they pretend to offer Chriſt daily to the Father, a Propitiatory Sacrifice for the ſins of the living and the dead: ſo that a man, for money, can procure Chriſt thus to be offered for him, when he pleaſes, by which offering he is ſaid to obtain remiſſion of ſins, and to ſtand juſtified in the ſight of God.

From

From all which, and much more of this natur, which might be mentioned, it doth appear, that the Papifts place their juftification, not fo much in any work of holynefs, really brought forth in them, and real forfaking of iniquity, as in the meer performance of fome ceremonys, and a blind belief, which their teachers have begotten in them, that the Church and the Pope having the abfolute difpenfation of the merits of Chrift, have power to make thefe merits effectual for the remiffion of fins, and juftification of fuch as will perform thofe ceremonys. This is the true and real method of juftification taken by the generality of the Church of Rome, and highly commended by their publick preachers, efpecially the Monks, in their fermons to the people, of which I my felf have been an ear-and an eye-witnefs. However fome of their modern writers have laboured to qualify it in their controverfys. This doctrin *Luther* and the Proteftants then had good reafon to deny and oppofe, though many of them ran into another extream, fo as to deny *good works to be neceffary to juftification*, and to preach up *not onely remiffion of fins, but juftification by faith alone, without all works however good*. So that men do not obtain their juftification, according as they are inwardly fanctified and renewed, but are juftified meerly by believing that Chrift dyed for them, and fo fome may perfectly be juftified, though they be lieing in grofs wickednefs, as appears by the example of David, whom they fay was fully and perfectly juftified, while he was lieing in the grofs fins of murder and adultery. As then the Proteftants have fufficient ground to quarrel and confute the Papifts concerning thofe many abufes in the matter of juftification, fhewing how the doctrin of Chrift is thereby vitiated and overturned, and the Word of God made voyd by many and ufelefs traditions, the Law of God neglected, while foolifh and needlefs ceremonys are prized and followed, through a falfe opinion of being juftified by the performance of them; and the merits and fufferings of Chrift (which is the *Onely Sacrifice* appoynted of God for remiffion of fins) derogated from, by the feting up of a *daily facrifice*, never appoynted by God, and chiefly devifed out of covetoufnefs to get money by: fo the Proteftants, on the other hand, by not rightly eftablifhing and holding forth the doctrin of Juftification, according as it is delivered in the Holy Scripturs, have opened a door for the Papifts to accufe them, as if they were neglecters of good works, enemies to mortificaton and holinefs, fuch as efteem themfelves juftified, while lieing in great fins, by which

                                              kind

kind of accusations (for which too great ground hath been given out of the writings of some rigid Protestants) the Reformation hath been greatly defamed and hindered, and the Souls of many insnared. Whereas who will narrowly look into the matter, may observe these debates to be more *in specie*, than *in genere*, seing both do upon the matter land in one, and like two men in a circle, who, though they go sundry wayes, yet meet at last in the same centre.

For the *Papists*, they say, *they obtain remission of sins, and are justified by the merits of Christ, as the same are applyed unto them, in the use of the Sacraments of the Church: and are dispensed in the performance of such and such ceremonys, pilgrimages, prayers and performances, though there be not an inward renewing of the mind, nor knowing of Christ inwardly formed, yet they are remitted, and righteous, ex opere operatô, because of the power and authority accompanying the Sacraments and the dispensators of them.*

So saith the Westminster confession of Faith, chap. 11. sect. 1.

The *Protestants* say, *that they obtain remission of sins, and stand justified in the sight of God, by vertue of the merits and sufferings of Christ, not by infusing righteousnesß into them, but by pardoning their sins, and by accounting and accepting their persons as righteous: they resting on him and his righteousnesß by faith, which faith, the act of believing, is not imputed unto them for righteousnesß.*

So the justification of neither here is placed, in any inward renewing of the mind, or by vertue of any Spiritual birth or formation of Christ *in* them; but onely by a bare application of the death and sufferings of Christ outwardly performed for them: whereof the one lays hold on a faith resting upon them, and hoping to be justified by them alone; the other by the saying of some outward prayers and ceremonys, which they judg makes the death of Christ effectual unto them. I except here (being unwilling to wrong any) what things have been said as to the necessity of inward holynesß, either by some modern Papists, or some modern Protestants, who, in so farr as they have laboured after a midst betwixt these two extreams, have come near to the Truth, as by some citations out of them, hereafter to be mentioned, will appear, though this doctrin hath not, since the apostasy, so farr as ever I could observe, been so distinctly and evidently held forth according to the Scripturs testimony, as it hath pleased God to reveal it, and preach it forth, in this day by the witnesses of his Truth, whom he hath raised to that end: which doctrin, though it be briefly held forth and comprehended in the *thesis* it self, yet I shall a little more fully explain the state of the controversy, as it stands betwixt us and those, that now oppose us.　　　　　§ III.

§ III. Firſt then, as by the explanation of the former Theſis appears, we renounce all natural power, and ability in our ſelves, in order to bring us out of our loſt and faln condition, and firſt natur: and confeſs, that of our ſelves we are able to doe nothing, that is good; ſo neither can we procure remiſſion of ſins, or juſtification, by any act of our own, ſo as to merit it, or draw it as a debt from God, due unto us, but we acknowledg all to be *of* and *from his Love*, which is the original and fundamental cauſe of our acceptance.

Secondly, God manifeſted this love towards us, in the ſending of his Beloved Son the Lord Jeſus Chriſt into the world, who gave himſelf for us an Offering and a Sacrifice to God, for a ſweet ſmelling ſavour: and having made peace through the blood of his Croſs, that he might reconcile us unto himſelf, and by the Eternal Spirit offered himſelf, without ſpot unto God, and ſuffered for our ſins, the *juſt* for the *unjuſt*, that he might bring us unto God.

Thirdly then, foraſmuch as all men, who have come to man's eſtate (the Man Jeſus onely excepted) have ſinned, therefore all have need of this Saviour, to remove the wrath of God from them, due to their offences, in this reſpect, he is truely ſaid to *have born the iniquitys of us all, in his body on the tree*; and therefore is the Onely Mediator, having qualified the wrath of God towards us, ſo that our former ſins ſtand not in our way being, by vertue of his moſt ſatisfactory Sacrifice, removed and pardoned. Neither do we think that remiſſion of ſins is to be expected, ſought, or obtained any other way, or by any woiks or ſacrifiçe whatſoinever: (though, as has been ſaid formerly, they may come to partake of this remiſſion, that are ignorant of the hiſtory) So then Chriſt by his death and ſufferings hath reconçiled us to God, even while we are enemies, that is, he offers reconçiliation unto us, we are put into a capaçity of being reconçiled, God is willing to forgive us cur iniquitys, and to acçept us, as is wel expreſſed by the Apoſtle, 2 Cor. 5: 19. *God was in Chriſt reconçiling the world unto himſelf, not imputing their treſpaſſes unto them, and hath put in us the Word of reconçiliation.* And therefore the Apoſtle, in the next verſes, treats them *in Chriſt's ſtead to be reconçiled to God*, intimating, that, the wrath of God being removed by the obediençe of Chriſt Jeſus, he is willing to be reconçiled unto them, and ready to remitt the ſins, that are paſt, if they repent.

We conſider then our Redemption in a twofold reſpect or ſtate, both

S 3

which

which in their own natur are perfect, though in their application to us, the one is not, nor can not be without respect to the other.

The first is the redemption performed and accomplished by Christ *for us*, in his crucified body, without us. The other is the redemption wrought by *Christ in us*, which no less properly is called and accounted a redemption than the former. The first then is that, whereby man, as he stands in the fall, is put into a capacity of Salvation, and hath conveighed unto him a measur of that Power, Vertue, Spirit, Life and Grace, that was in Christ Jesus: which, as the Free Gift of God, is able to counterballance, overcome and root-out the evil seed, wherewith we are naturally, as in the fall, leavened.

The second is that, whereby we witness, and know this pure and perfect redemption *in* our selves, purifying, cleansing and redeeming us from the power of corruption, and bringing us into unity, favour and friendship with God. By the first of these two, we, that were lost in Adam, plunged in the bitter and corrupt seed, unable, of our selves, to doe any good thing, but naturally joyned and united to evil, forward and propense to all iniquity, servants and slaves to the power and spirit of darkness, are, notwithstanding all this, so farr reconciled to God by the death of his Son, while enemies, that we are put into a capacity of Salvation; having the glad tidings of the Gospel of peace offered unto us: and God is reconciled unto us, in Christ, calls and invites us to himself, in which respect, we understand these Scripturs * *He slew the enmity in himself. He loved us first, seing us in our blood, he said unto us live, he, who did not sin his own self, bare our sins in his own body on the tree, and he dyed for our sins, the Just for the unjust.*

By the second we witness this capacity brought into act, whereby receiving, and not resisting, the purchase of his death, to wit, the Light, Spirit, and Grace of Christ revealed to us, we witness and possess a real true and inward redemption from the power and prevalency of sin, and so come to be truely and reaily redeemed, justified and made righteous, and to a sensible union and friendship with God. Thus he dyed *for us, that he might redeem us from all iniquity,* and thus, *we know him and the Power of his Resurrection, and the fellowship of his Sufferings, being made conformable to us.* This last followes the first in order, and is a consequence of it, proceeding from it, as an *effect* from its *cause.* So as none could have enjoyed the last, without the first had been, (such being the will of God) so also can none now partake of the first, but as he witnesseth the last. Wherefore,

fore, as to us, they are both cauſes of our Juſtification. The firſt the *pro-curing, efficient,* the other the *formal cauſe.*

Fourthly, we underſtand not by *this juſtification by Chriſt,* barely the *good works, even as wrought by the Spirit of Chriſt,* for they, as Proteſtants truely affirm, are rather an *effect* of *juſtification,* than the *cauſe* of it. But we underſtand *the formation of Chriſt in us, Chriſt born and brought forth in us,* from which good works as naturally proceed, as fruit from a fruitfull tree. It is *this inward birth in us bringing forth righteouſueß and holyneß in us, that doth juſtify us,* which, having removed and done away the contrary natur and ſpirit, that did bear rule, and bring condemnation, now is in dominion, over all, *in* our hearts. Thoſe then, that come to know Chriſt thus formed *in* them, do enjoy him wholly and undivided, who is *The LORD our RIGHTEOUSNESS,* Jer. 23 : 6. This is to be cloathed with Chriſt and to have put him on, whom God therefore truely accounteth righteous and juſt. This is ſo farr from being the doctrin of Papiſts, that, as the generality of them do not underſtand it, ſo the learned among them oppoſe it, and diſpute againſt it, and particularly *Bellarmin.* Thus then, as I may ſay, the formal cauſe of juſtification is not the works, to ſpeak properly, they being but an effect of it ; but this inward birth, this Jeſus brought forth *in* the heart, who is the Wel-beloved, whom the Father can not but accept, and all thoſe, who thus are ſprinkled with the *blood* of *Jeſus,* and waſhed with it. By this alſo comes that communication of the goods of Chriſt unto us, *by which we come to be made partakers of the Divine natur,* as ſaith Peter, ep. 2. c. 1: v. 4. are made one with him, as the branches with the vine, and have a title and right to what he hath done and ſuffered for us. So that his obedience becomes ours, his righteouſneſs ours, his death and ſufferings ours. And by this nearneſs we come to have a ſenſe of his Sufferings, and to ſuffer with his Seed, that yet lies preſſed and crucified *in* the hearts of the ungodly, and ſo travel with it, and for its redemption, and for the repentance of thoſe Soules, that in it are crucifying as yet the *Lord of Glory.* Even as the Apoſtle Paul, *who by his ſufferings is ſaid to fill up that, which is behind of the afflictions of Chriſt for his Body, which is the Church.* Though this be a myſtery ſealed up from all the wiſe men, that are yet ignorant of this Seed *in* themſelves, and oppoſe it, neverthelefs ſome Proteſtants ſpeak of this juſtification by Chriſt inwardly put-on, as ſhall hereafter be recited in its place.

· Laſtly, though we place remiſſion of ſins *in the righteouſneſs and obedi-*
ence

ence of *Chrift performed by him* , *in the flefh* , as to what pertaines to the remote procuring caufe , and that we hold our felves *formally juftified by Chrift
Jefus formed and brought forth in us*; yet can we not (as fome Proteftants
have unwarily done) *exclude works from Juftification*: for, though properly
we be not juftified *for them* , yet are we juftified *in them* , and they are neceffary, even as *caufa fine quâ non*, i. e. *the caufe* , *without which none
are juftified*. For the denying of this , as it's contrary to the Scripturs teftimony , fo it hath brought a great fcandal to the Proteftant Religion ,
opened the mouths of Papifts , and made many too fecure , while they
have believed to be juftified without good works. Moreover , though it
be not fo fafe to fay *they are meritorious* , yet , feing they are rewarded , many of thofe , called *the Fathers* , have not fpared to ufe the word [*merit*]
which fome of us have perhaps alfo done , in a qualified fenfe , but no
wayes to inferr the Popifh abufes above mentioned.   And laftly , if we
had that notion of *good works* , which moft Proteftants have , we could
freely agree to make them , not onely not neceffary , but reject them, as
hurtfull : viz , *that the beft works* , *even of the Saints* , *are defiled and polluted*.
For though we judg fo of the beft works performed by man , endeavour-
ing a conformity to the outward Law , by his own ftrength , and in his
own will ; yet we believe , that fuch *works* as naturally proceed from this
Spiritual birth , and formation of Chrift *in us* , are *pure* and *holy* , even as
the *Root*, from which they come , and therefore God accepts them , ju-
ftifies us *in them* , and rewards us *for* them , of his own Free Grace. The
ftate of the controverfy being thus ftated , thefe following pofitions do
hencefrom arife , in the next place to be proved.

§ IV. Firft, *that the obedience* , *fufferings*, *and death of Chrift is that* , *by
which the Soul obtaines remiffion of fins* , *and is the procuring caufe of that Grace* ,
by whofe inward workings Chrift comes to be formed inwardly , *and the Soul to be
made conformable unto him* , *and fo juft and juftified*. And that therefore , in
refpect of this capacity and offer of Grace , *God* is faid to be *reconciled*,
not as if he were actually reconciled , or did actually juftify , or account
any juft , fo long as they remain in their fins , really impure and unjuft.

Secondly , *that it is by this inward birth of Chrift in man* , *that man is made
juft* , *and therefore fo accounted by God* , wherefore to be plain , we are
thereby , and not till that be brought forth *in us* , *formally* (if we muft
ufe that word) juftified in the fight of God : becaufe *Juftification* is, both
more properly and frequently in Scriptur , taken in its proper fignification ,

tion, for making one juft, and not reputing one meerly fuch, and is all one with *Sanctification.*

Thirdly, *that*, fince *good works* as naturally follow from this birth, as heat from fire, therefore are they *of abfolute neceffity to juftification*, as *caufa fine qu.t non*, i. e. though not as the caufe *for which* yet as that, *in which* we are and without which we can not be, juftified. And though they be *not meritoriou*, and draw no debt upon God, yet he can not but accept and reward them, for it is contrary to his natur to deny his own : Since they may be perfect in their kind, as proceeding from a Pure, Holy birth and Root. Wherefore their judgment is falfe, and againft the Truth, that fay, that *the holyeft works of the Saints are defiled and finfull in the fight of God* : for thefe good works are not the works of the Law, excluded, by the Apoftle, from juftification.

§ V. As to the firft, I prove it from Rom. 3: 25. *whom God hath fet forth to be a Propitiation through faith in his blood, to declare his righteoufnefs for the remiffion of fins, that are paft through the forbearance of God.* Here the Apoftle holds forth the extent and efficacy of Chrift's death fhewing that thereby and by faith therein, remiffion of fins, that are paft, is obtained : as being that, wherein the forbearance of God is exercifed towards mankind. So that, though men for the fins, they daily committ, deferve eternal death, and that the wrath of God fhould lay hold upon them ; yet, by vertue of that *moft fatisfactory Sacrifice of Chrift Jefu*, the Grace and Seed of God moves in love towards them, during the day of their vifitation : yet not fo, as not to ftrick againft the evil, for that muft be burned-up and deftroyed, but to redeem man out of the evil.

Secondly, if God were perfectly reconciled with men, and did efteem them juft, while they are actually unjuft, and do continue in their fins, Then fhould God have no controverfy with them : * How comes he then fo often to complain, to expoftulat fo much, throughout the whole Scriptur, with fuch as our adverfarys confefs to be juftified, telling them, that *their fins feparat betwixt him* and *them* ? Ifa. 59: 2. For, where there is a perfect and full reconciliation, there there is no feparation. Yea from this doctrin it neceffarily followes, either that fuch for whom Chrift dyed,

I do not onely fpeak concerning men before converfion, who afterwards are converted,

T

whom yet fome of our antagonifts, called *Antinomians*, do averr were juftifed from the beginning, but alfo touching thofe, who, according to the common opinion of Proteftants have been converted ; whom, albeit they confefs they perfift alwayes in fome misdeeds and fometimes in hinous fins, as is manifeft in David's adultery and murder, yet they affert to be perfectly and wholly juftified.

ed, and whom he hath thus reconciled, never sin, or that, when tey so doe, they are still reconciled, and their sins make not the least separation from God, yea that they are justified in their sins. From whence also would follow this abominable consequence, that the good works and greatest sins of such are all alike in the sight of God, seing neither the one serves to justify them, nor the other to break their reconciliation, which occasions great security, and opens a door to every lewd practice.

Thirdly, this would make void the whole practical doctrin of the Gospel, and make faith it self needless; for, if faith and repentance, and the other conditions, called for throughout the Gospel, be a qualification upon our part, necessary to be performed, then, before this be performed by us, we are either fully reconciled to God, or but in a capacity of being reconciled to God, he being ready to reconcile and justify us, as these conditions are performed: which latter, if granted, is according to the Truth we profess; and, if we are already perfectly reconciled and justified, before these conditions are performed, (which conditions are of that natur, that they can not be performed at one time, but are to be done all one's life time) then can they not be said to be absolutely needfull; which is contrary to the very express testimony of Scriptur, which is acknowledged by all Christians. *For without faith it is impossible to please God. They, that believe not, are condemn'd already, because they believe not in the Onely begotten Son of God. Except ye repent, ye cannot be saved. For, if ye live after the flesh, ye shall dye.* And of those, that were converted: *I will remove your candle-stick from you, and unless ye repent.* Should I mention all the Scripturs, that positively and evidently prove this, I might transcribe much of all the doctrinal part of the Bible. For, since Christ said *It is finished*, and did finish *his work* sixteen hundred years agoe, and upwards, if he so fully perfected redemption then, and did then actually reconcile every one, that is to be saved, not simply opening a door of mercy for them, offering the Sacrifice of his Body, by which they may obtain remission of their sins, when they repent, and communicating unto them a measur of his Grace, by which they may see their sins, and be able to repent: but really make them to be reputed as just, either before they believe, (as say the *Antinomians*) or after they have assented to the Truth of the history of Christ, or are sprinkled with the baptism of water, while nevertheless they are actually unjust, so that no part of their redemption is to be wrought by him now, as to their reconciliation and justification,

then

Heb. 11:6
Joh. 3:18
Luc. 13:3
Apoc. 2:5
Rom. 8:13.

then the whole doctrinal part of the Bible is uselefs and of no profit; in vain were the Apoftles fent forth to preach repentance and remiffion of fins, and in vain do all the preachers beftow their labour, fpend their lungs, and give forth writings, yea much more in vain do the people fpend their money, which they give them for preaching, feing it is all but *actum agere*, but a vain and uneffectual effay to doe that, which is already perfectly done, without them.

But laftly, to pretermitt their humane labours, as not worth the di-fputing, whether they be needfull or not, fince (as we fhall hereafter fhew) themfelves confefs the *beft* of them is *finfull* ; this alfo makes void the prefent interceffion of Chrift for men. What fhall become of that great article of faith, by which *we affirm that he fits at the right hand of God daily making interçeffion for us, and for which end the Spirit it felf maketh interçef-fion for us with groanings which can not be uttered?* For Chrift maketh not inter-ceffion for thofe, that are not in a poffibility of Salvation ; that is abfurd. Our adverfarys will not admitt that he prayed for the world at all. And to pray for thofe that are already reconciled, and perfectly juftified, is to no purpofe: to pray for remiffion of fins is yet more needlefs, if all be remitted paft, prefent, and to come. Indeed there is not any folid folving of this, but by acknowledging, according to the Truth, that Chrift by his death remo-ved the wrath of God, fo farr as to obtain remiffion of fins for as many as receive that *Graçe* and *Light*, that he communicats unto them, & hath pur-chafed for them by his *Blood*: which as they believe in, they come to know remiffion of fins paft, and power to fave them from fin, and to wipe it away fo often as they may fall into it by unwatchfulnefs or weaknefs, if, applying themfelves to this Grace, they truely repent : for *to as many as receive him he gives power to become the fons of God.* So none are fones, none are juftified, none reconciled, untill they thus receive him *in* that little *Seed* in their hearts. *And life eternal is offered to thofe, who by patient continu-ance in wel-doing feek glory, honour, and immortality. For, if the righteous man depart from his righteoufnefs, his righteoufnefs fhall be remembred no more*; and therefore, on the other part, none are longer fons of God, and juftified, than they patiently continue in righteoufnefs and wel doing. And there-fore Chrift lives alwayes making interceffion, during the day of every man's vifitation, that they may be converted : and, when men are in fome meafur converted, he makes interc.ffion, that they may continue, and go-on, and not faint, nor go back again. Much more might be faid

to confirm this truth, but I go on to take notice of the common objections against it, which are the arguments made use of to propagat the
errors contrary to it.

§ VI. The firſt and chief is drawn from that ſaying of the Apoſtle,
before mentioned, 2 Cor. 5: 18, 19. *God hath reconciled us to himſelf by
Jeſus Chriſt: God was in Chriſt reconçiling the world unto himſelf, not imputing
their treſpaſſes unto them.*

Obj.   From hence they ſeek to inferr *that Chriſt fully perfeĉted the work of reconçiliation, while he was on earth.*

Anſw.   I anſwer: If by [*Reconçiliation*] be underſtood the removing of wrath,
and the purchaſe of that Graçe, by which we may come to be reconciled, we agree to it; but that that place ſpeaks no more, appears from the
place it ſelf; for, when the Apoſtle ſpeaks in the *perfeĉt time*, ſaying,
He hath reconçiled us, he ſpeaks of himſelf and the Saints, who, having
received the Graçe of God purchaſed by Chriſt, were, through faith in
him, aĉtually reconciled. But as to the *World*, he ſaith [*reconçiling,*] not
[*reconçiled,*] which reconciling, though it denotat a time ſomewhat paſt,
yet it is by the *imperfeĉt time*, denoting that the thing begun was not perfeĉted. For this work Chriſt began towards *all*, in the dayes of his fleſh,
yea and long before: for *he was the Mediator from the beginning, and the Lamb
ſlain from the foundation of the world.* But in his fleſh, after he had *perfeĉtly
fulfilled the Law*, and the *righteouſneſs* thereof, and *rent the* vail, and made
way for the more clear and univerſal revelation of the Goſpel to *all*, both
Jew and *Gentile*, he *gave up himſelf a muſt ſatisfaĉtory Sacrifiçe for ſin*, which
becomes effeĉtual to as many as receive him in his inward appearance in
his Light in the heart. Again, this very place ſheweth that no other reconciliation is intended, but the opening of a door of mercy, upon God's
part, and a removing of wrath for ſins, that are paſt, ſo as men, notwithſtanding their ſins, are ſtated in a capacity of Salvation. For the Apoſtle, in
the following verſe, ſaith, *Now then we are Ambaſſadors for Chriſt, as though
God did beſeech you by us; we pray you in Chriſt's ſtead, be ye reconciled
to God.* For, if their reconciliation had already been perfeĉtly accompliſ -
ed, what need any intreating then to be reconciled? Ambaſſadors are
nor ſent, after a peace already perfeĉted, and reconciliation made, to intreat for a reconciliation, for that implies a manifeſt contradiĉtion.

Secondly, they objeĉt, verſe 21 of the ſame chapter, *For he hath made
him to be ſin, for us, who knew no ſin, that we might be made the righteouſneſs
of God in him.*   From

From whence they argue; *that, as our sin is imputed to Christ, who had* Obj.
no sin, so Christ's righteousness is imputed to us, without our being righteous.

But this interpretation is easily rejected, for, though *Christ bare our* Answ.
sins, and *suffered for us,* and was, among men, *accounted a sinner,* and
numbred among transgressors; yet that God reputed him a sinner, is no
where proved. For it is said *he was found before him holy, harmeless, and un-* Heb. 7:26
defiled, neither was there found any guile in his mouth. That *We* deserved these 1 Pet. 2:
things, and much more for our sins, which he endured in obedience to the 22.
Father, and, according to his counsel, is true, but that ever God reputed
Him a sinner, is denyed. Neither did he ever dye, that we should be reputed righteous, though no more really such, than he was a sinner
(as hereafter appears). For indeed, if this argument hold, it might be
stretched that length, as to become very pleasing to wicked men, that
love to abide in their sins : For, if we be made *righteous, as Christ was made
a sinner, meerly by imputation, Then, as there was no sin, not in the least, in
Christ,* so it would follow *that there needed no more righteousnes, no more ho-
lynes, no more inward sanctification in us, than there was sin in him.* So then,
by his [*being made sin for us*] must be understood his suffering for our sins,
that we might be made partakers of the Grace purchased by him, by the
workings whereof we are made the righteousnes of God in him. For, that
the Apostle understood here a being made really righteous, and not meerly a being reputed such, appears, by what followes, seing in the 14, 15,
and 16 verses of the following chapter he argues largely against any supposed *agrement of Light and darknes, righteousnes and unrighteousnes,* which
must needs be admitted, if men be to be reckoned ingrafted *in* Christ, and
real members of him, meerly by an imputative righteousnes, wholly
without them, while they themselves are actually unrighteous. And indeed it may be thought strange, how some men have made this so fundamental an article of their faith, which is so contrary to the whole strain of
the Gospel. A thing Christ in none of all his sermons and gratious speeches
ever willed any to relie upon, always recommending to us *works,* as in-
strumental in our justification ; and the more 't is to be admired at, because that that sentence or term (so frequent in their mouths, and so often
pressed by them, as the very *basis* of their hope and confidence) to wit,
the imputed righteousnes of Christ, is not to be found in all the Bible, at
lest as to my observation. Thus have I past through the first part, and
that the more briefly, because many, who assert this justification by bare

T 3

im-

imputation, do neverthelefs confefs, that even the elect are not juftified, untill they be converted, that is, not, untill this imputative juftification be applied to them by the Spirit.

§ VII. I come then to the fecond thing propofed by me, which is, *that it is by this inward birth, or Chrift formed within, that we are, fo to fpeak, formally juftified in the fight of God.* I fuppofe I have faid enough already to demonftrat how much we afcribe to the death and fufferings of Chrift, as that, whereby fatisfaction is made to the Juftice of God, remiffion of fins obtained, and this *Grace* and *Seed* purchafed, by and from which this birth proceeds. The thing now to be proved is, *that by Chrift Jefus formed in us we are juftified, or made juft.* Let it be marked I ufe *juftification* in this fenfe upon this occafion.

First then I prove this by that of the Apoftle Paul, 1 Cor. 6: 11. *And fuch were fome of you, but ye are wafhed, but ye are fanctified, but ye are juftified in the Name of the Lord Jefus, and by the Spirit of our God.* Firft this [*juftified*] here underftood muft needs be *a being really made juft,* and not *a being meerly imputed fuch,* elfe [*Sanctified*] and [*wafhed*] might be reputed a being efteemed fo, and not a being really fo; and then it overturns the whole intent of the context. For the Apoftle fhewing them, in the preceeding verfes, how the unrighteous *can not inherit the Kingdom of God,* and defcending to the feveral *fpecies of wickednefs,* fubfumes, that they *were fometimes fuch, but now are not any more fuch.* Wherefore, as they are now wafhed and fanctified, fo are they juftified; For, if this juftification were not real, then it might be alledged that the Corinthians had not forfaken thefe evils, but were, though ftill they continued in them, notwithftanding juftified. Which, as in it felf, it is moft abfurd, fo it luculently overturneth the very import and intent of the place, as if the Corinthians turning Chriftians had not wrought any real change in them, but had onely been a belief of fome barren notions, which had wrought no alteration in their affections, will, or manner of life. For my own part, I neither fee any thing, nor could ever yet hear or read any thing, that with any colour of reafon did evince [*juftified*] in this place to be underftood any other ways, than in its own proper and genuin interpretation of being *made juft.* And for the more clear underftanding hereof let it be confidered, that this word [*juftify*] is derived either from the Subftantive *juftice,* or the Adjective *juft.* Both which words import the Subftantive, that true and real *vertue in the Soul,* as it is in it felf, to wit, it fignifies really, and
                                                                                not

not fuppofitively, that excellent quality expreffed and underſtood among men by the word [*juftice,*] and the Adjective [*juft*] as applied fignifies a man or woman, who is juft, that is, in whom this quality of *Juftice* is ftated; for it would not onely be great impropriety, but alfo manifeft falſity, to call a man *juft,* meerly by fuppofition, efpecially if he were really unjuft. Now this word [*juftify*] formed or from *juftice,* or *juft,* doth beyond all queftion fignify *a making juft,* it being nothing elfe, but a compofition of the Verb *facio* and the Adjective *juftus,* which is nothing elfe, than thus *juftifico,* i. e. *juftum facio,* to make juft; and [*juftified*] of *juftus* and *fio,* as *juftus fio,* I become juft, & *juftificatus* i. e. *juftus factus* I am made juft. Thus alfo is it with Verbs of this kind, as *fanctifico,* from *fanctus* holy, and *facio*; *honorifico* from *honos* and *facio*; *facrifico* from *facer* and *facio*: all which are ftill underftood of the Subject really and truely endued with that vertue and quality, from which the verb is derived. Therefore, as none are faid to be fanctified, that are really unholy, while they are fuch; fo neither can any be truely faid to be juftified, while they actually remain unjuft. Onely this Verb *juftify* hath, in a metaphorical and figurative fenfe, been otherwayes taken, to wit, in a Law fenfe; as when a man really guilty of a crime is freed from the punifhment of his fin, he is faid to be *juftified,* that is, put in the place, as if he were *juft.* · For this ufe of the word hath proceeded from that true fuppofition, that none ought to be acquited but the innocent. Hence alfo that manner of fpeaking, *I will juftify fuch a man,* or *I will juftify this or that,* is ufed from the fuppofition, that the perfon and thing is really juftifiable. And where there is an error and abufe in the matter, fo farr there is alfo in the expreffion.

This is fo manifeft, and apparent, that *Paraus,* a chief Proteftant, and a Calvinift alfo in his opinion, acknowledges this, *We never at any time faid* (faith he) *nor thought that the Righteoufnes of Chrift was imputed to us, that by him we fhould be named formally juft, and be fo, as we have divers times already fhewed; for that would no lefs foundly fight with right Reafon, than if a guilty man abfolved in judgment fhould fay that he himfelf were formally juft by the clemency of the judg granting him his life.* Now is it not ftrange, that men fhould be fo facile in a matter of fo great concernment, as to build the ftrefs of their acceptance with God upon a meer borrowed and metaphorical fignification, to the excluding, or at leſt eftceming that not neceffary; without which, the Scriptur faith exprefsly, *no man fhall ever fee God?* For, if *holynefs* be requifit and neceffary, of which this is faid, then

De Juft.
con. Bell.
lib. 2.
cap. 7.
pag. 469.

muft

muſt *good works* alſo, unleſs our adverſarys can ſhew us a holy man without good works. But moreover, [*juſtified*] in this figurative ſenſe is uſed for *approved*, and indeed for the moſt part, if not always in Scriptur, when the word [*juſtify*] is uſed, it is taken in the worſt part, that is, that, as the uſe of the word, that way, is an uſurpation, ſo it is ſpoken of ſuch as uſurp the thing to themſelves, while it properly doth not belong unto them, as will appear to thoſe, that will be at the pains to examine theſe places, Exod. 23: 7. Job. 9: 20. 27: 5. Prov. 17: 15. Iſa. 5: 23. Jer. 3: 11. Ezech. 16: 51, 52. Luk. 10: 29. 16: 15. which are all ſpoken of men *juſtifying the wicked*, or of *wicked men juſtifying themſelves*, that is, approving themſelves in their wickedneſs. If it be at any time in this ſignification taken in good part, it is very ſeldom comparatively, and that ſo obvious and plain by the context, as leaves no ſcruple. But the queſtion is not ſo much the uſe of the word, where it is paſſingly or occaſionally uſed, as where the very doctrin of *juſtification* is handled. Where indeed to miſtake it, *viz*, in its proper place, ſo as to content our ſelves with an *imaginary* juſtification, while God requires a *real*, is of moſt dangerous conſequence, for the diſquiſition of which, let it be conſidered, that in all theſe places to the Rom. Corinth. Gal. and elſewhere, where the Apoſtle handles this theam, the word may be taken in its own proper ſignification, without any abſurdity : as, where it is often aſſerted in the above mentioned epiſtles to the Rom. and Gal. that *a man can not be juſtified by the Law of Moſes, nor by the works of the Law*, there is no abſurdity nor danger in underſtanding it, according to its own proper ſignification, to wit, that a man can not be *made juſt* by the Law of Moſes, ſeing this ſo wel agrees with that ſaying of the ſame Apoſtle, that *the Law makes nothing perfect*. And alſo where it is ſaid *We are juſtified by faith*, it may very wel be underſtood of being *made juſt*, ſeing it is alſo ſaid, that *faith purifies the heart*, and no doubt the *pure in heart are juſt*, and *The juſt live by faith*. Again, where it is ſaid, *We are juſtified by Grace, We are juſtified by Chriſt, We are juſtified by the Spirit*, it is no wayes abſurd to underſtand it of being *made juſt*, ſeing by his Spirit and Grace he doth make men *juſt*. But to underſtand it univerſally the other way, meerly for *acceptance* and *impuration*, would inferr great abſurditys, as may be proved at large, but, becauſe I judged it would be acknowledged, I forbear at preſent, for brevity's ſake. But further, in the moſt weighty places, where this word *juſtify* is uſed in Scriptur with an immediate relation to the doctrin of *juſtification*, our adverſary

verſarys muſt needs acknowledg it to be underſtood of *making juſt*, and not
barely in the legal acceptation, as firſt in that of the 1 Cor. 6: 11. *But ye*
are waſhed, but ye are ſanſtified, but ye are juſtified, as I before have proved; which alſo many Proteſtants are forced to acknowledg. *Neither diffide*
we, ſaith Thyſius, *becauſe of the moſt great and ſtrict connexion, that juſtifi-* Diſp. de
cation doth ſometimes ſeem alſo to comprehend ſanctification, as a conſequençe, Iuſt.
as in Rom. 8: 30. Tit. 3: 7. 1 Cor. 6: 11. And ſuch ſometimes were ye, but Theſ. 3.
ye are waſhed, &c. Zanchius having ſpoken concerning this ſenſe of juſti- In cap. 2.
fication, adds, ſaying, *There is another ſignification of the word*, viz, *for a man* ad Eph.
from unjuſt to be made juſt, even as ſanctified, ſignifys from unholy to be made holy. ver. 4.
In which ſignification the Apoſtle ſaid (in the place above cited) *and ſuch were* Iuſt.
ſome of you, &c. that is, *of unclean ye are made holy, and of unjuſt ye are made*
juſt by the Holy Spirit, for Chriſt's ſake, in whom ye have believed. Of this ſignifi-
cation is that, Rev. 22: 11. *Let him, that is juſt, be juſt ſtill*, that is, *really from*
juſt become more juſt, even as from unjuſt he became juſt. And according to this
ſignification the Fathers, and eſpecially Auguſtin, have interpreted this word.
Thus farr he. H. Bullinger on the ſame place 1 Cor. 6. ſpeaketh thus, *By*
divers words (ſaith he) *the Apoſtle ſignifies the ſame thing, when he ſaith, ye are*
waſhed, ye are ſanctified, ye are juſtified.

Secondly, in that excellent ſaying of the Apoſtle ſo much obſerved,
Rom. 8: 30. *Whom he called, them he alſo juſtified, and whom he juſtified them*
he alſo glorified. This is commonly called the *golden chain*, as being acknowledged to comprehend the method and order of Salvation. And therefore, if [*juſtified*] were not underſtood here in its proper ſignification,
of being *made juſt*, ſanctification would be excluded out of this chain.
And truely it is very worthy of obſervation, that the Apoſtle, in this ſuc-
cinct and compendious account, makes the word [*juſtified*] to comprehend all betwixt *calling* and glorifying; thereby clearly inſinuating that
the being really *righteous* is that onely *medium*, by which from our *calling* we
paſs to glorification. All for the moſt part do acknowledg the word to be
ſo taken in this place, and not onely ſo, but moſt of thoſe, who oppoſe,
are forced to acknowledg, that, as this is the moſt proper, ſo the moſt
common, ſignification of it, thus divers famous Proteſtants do acknow-
ledg. *We are not*, ſaith D. Chamierus, *ſuch impertinent eſteemers of words, as to* Tom. 3.
be ignorant, nor yet ſuch importunat Sophiſts, as to deny that the words of juſtifica- de Sanct.
tion and ſanctification do inferr one another ; yea we know that the Saints are chiefly lib. 10.
for this reaſon ſo called, becauſe that in Chriſt they have received remiſſion of ſins : and cap. 1.

we read in the Revelation, Let him, that is juſt, be juſt ſtill; *which can not be under-ſtood, except of the fruit of inherent righteouſneſ.* Nor do we deny but perhaps in other places they may be promiſcuouſly taken, eſpecially by the Fathers, I take, ſaith Beza, *the name of juſtification largely, ſo as it comprehends whatſoever we acquire from Chriſt, as wel by imputation, as by the efficacy of the Spirit in ſanctiſing us. So likewiſe is the word of juſtification taken,* Rom. 8: 30. Melancthon ſaith that *to be juſtified by faith ſignifies in Scriptur not onely to be pronounçed juſt, but alſo of unrighteous to be made righteous.* Alſo ſome chief Proteſtants, though not ſo clearly, yet in part, hinted at our doctrin, whereby we aſcribe unto the death of Chriſt remiſſion of ſins, and the work of juſtification unto the Grace of the Spirit acquired by his death. *Martinus Boræus* explaining that place of the Apoſtle, Rom. 4. 25. *Who was given for our ſins, and roſe again for our juſtification,* ſaith: *There are two things beheld in Chriſt, which are neceſſary to our juſtification, the one is his death, the other is his ariſing from the dead. By his death, the ſins of this world behoved to be expiated. By his riſing from the dead, it pleaſed the ſame goodneſ of God to give the Holy Spirit, whereby both the Goſpel is believed, and the righteouſneſ loſt by the fault of the firſt Adam is reſtor-ed.* And afterwards he ſaith, *The Apoſtle expreſſeth both parts in theſe words,* who was given for our ſins, &c. *In his death is beheld the ſatisfaction for ſin; in his reſurrection the Gift of the Holy Spirit, by which our juſtification is perfected.* And again the ſame man ſaith elſewhere, *both theſe kinds of righteouſneſ are therefore contained in juſtification, neither can the one be ſeparat from the other. So that in the definition of juſtification, the merit of the blood of Chriſt is included both with the remiſſion of ſins and with the gift of the Holy Spirit of juſtification and re-generation.* Martinus Bucerus ſaith, *Seing by one ſin of Adam the world was loſt, the Grace of Chriſt hath not onely aboliſhed that one ſin, and death, which came by it, but hath together taken away thoſe infinit ſins, and alſo led into full juſtification as many as are of Chriſt, ſo that God now not onely remitts unto them Adam's ſin and their own, but alſo gives them therewith the Spirit of a ſolid and perfect righ-teouſneſ, which renders us, conſorme unto the Image of the Firſt-Begotten.* And upon theſe words [*by Jeſus Chriſt*] he ſaith, *We always judge that the whole benefit of Chriſt tends to this, that we might be ſtrong through the Gift of righte-ouſneſ, being rightly and orderly adorned with all vertue, that is, reſtored to the Image of God.* And laſtly, William Forbes our countrey-man, Biſhop of Edinburgh, ſaith, *Whenſoever the Scriptur makes mention of the juſtification before God, as ſpeaketh Paul, and from him, beſides others, Auguſtin, it appears that the word* [*juſtify*] *neceſſarily ſignifies not onely to pronounçe juſt, in a Law*

ſenſe,

sense, but also really and inherently to make just, because that God doth other wayes justify a wicked man, than earthly judges. For he, when he justifies a wicked or unjust man, doth indeed pronounce him, as these also do, but by pronouncing him just, because his judgment is according to Truth, he also makes him really, of unjust to become just. And again, the same man upon the same occasion answering the more rigid Protestants, who *say that God first justifies, and then makes just*, he adds, *But let them have a care, lest by too great and empty subtilty, unknown both to the Scripturs and the Fathers, they lessen and diminish the weight and dignity of so great and Divine a benefit, so much celebrated in the Scriptur, to wit, justification of the wicked. For, if to the formal reason of justification of the ungodly doth not at all belong his justification, (so to speak) i. e. his being made righteous, then in the justification of a sinner, although he be justified, yet the stain of sin is not taken away, but remaines the same in his Soul, as before justification. And so, notwithstanding the benefit of justification, he remaines, as before, unjust and a sinner, and nothing is taken away, but the guilt and obligation to pain, and the offence and enmity of God through non-imputation. But both the Scripturs and Fathers do affirm, that, in the justification of a sinner, their sins are not onely remitted, forgiven, covered, not imputed, but also taken away, blotted out, cleansed, washed, purged, and very farr removed from us, as appears from many places of the Holy Scripturs.* The same Forbes shewes us at length, in the following chapter, that this was the confessed judgment of the Fathers, out of the writings of those, who hold the contrary opinion, some whereof out of him I shall note, as First, Calvin saith, *that the judgment of Augustin, or* *at left his manner of speaking, is not throughout to be received, who, although he took from man all praise of righteousness, and ascribed all to the Grace of God, yet he refers Grace to Sanctification, by which we are regenerat through the Spirit unto newness of life.* Chemnitius saith, *that they do not deny but that the Fathers take the word* [justify] *for renewing, by which, works of righteousness are wrought in us by the Spirit.* And pag. 130 *I am not ignorant that the Fathers indeed often use the word* [justify] *in this signification, to wit, of making just.* Zanchius saith, *that the Fathers, and chiefly Augustin, interpret the word* [justify] *according to this signification, to wit, of making just, so that, according to them, to be justified was no other, than of unjust to be made just, through the Grace of God for Christ.* He mentioneth more, but this may suffice to our purpose.

Inst.lib.3.
cap. 11.
Sect 15.
In exam.
Concil.
Trid de
Iust.
pag. 129.
In cap. 2.
ad Eph.
ver. 4.
loc de
Iust.
Thes. 15.

§ VIII. Having thus sufficiently proved that by *justification* is to be understood a really being *made righteous*, I do boldly affirm, and that not onely from a notional knowledg, but from a real inward experimental

 feel-

feeling of the thing, that the immediat, neareft, or formal caufe (if we muft, in condefcendence to fome, ufe this word) of a man's juftification, in the fight of God, is the *revelation of Jefus Chrift in the Soul*, changing, altering and renewing the mind, by whom (even the Author of this inward work) thus formed and revealed, we are truely juftified and accepted in the fight of God. For it is as we are thus covered and cloathed with him, in whom the Father is always wel pleafed, that we may *draw near to God*, and ftand with confidence before his throne, being *purged* by the *blood* of *Iefus* inwardly poured into our Souls, and cloathed with his life and righteoufnefs therein revealed. And this is that order and method of Salvation held forth by the Apoftle in that Divine faying, Rom. 5: 10. *For, if, when we were enemies, we were reconciled to God, by the death of his Son; much more being reconciled, we fhall be faved by his Life.* For the Apoftle firft holding forth the reconciliation wrought by the death of Chrift, wherein God is near to receive and redeem man, holds forth his *Salvation* and *juftification* to be by the *Life of Jefus.* Now that this Life is an inward Spiritual thing revealed *in* the Soul, whereby it is renewed and brought forth out of death, where it naturally has been, by the fall; and fo quickened and made alive unto God. The fame Apoftle fhewes, Eph. 2: 5. *Even when we were dead in fins and trefpaffes, he hath quickened us together in Chrift, (by whofe Grace ye are faved) and hath raifed us up together.* Now, this none will deny to be the inward work of renovation, and therefore the Apoftle gives that reafon of their being *faved by Grace*, which is the inward Vertue and Power of Chrift *in* the Soul: but of this place more hereafter. Of the revelation of this inward Life the Apoftle alfo fpeaketh, 2 Cor. 4: 10. *That the Life alfo of Jefus might be made manifeft in our bodys*, and vers 11. *That the Live alfo of Jefus might be made manifeft in our mortal flefh.* Now, this inward *Life* of *Jefus* is that, *whereby*, as is before obferved, he faith *We are faved.*

Secondly: *That it is by this revelation of Jefus Chrift, and the new creation in us, that we are juftified*, doth evidently appear from that excellent fayirg of the Apoftle included in the Propofition it felf, Tit. 3: 5. *according to his mercy he hath faved us, by the wafhing of regeneration and renewing of the Holy Ghoft*, &c. Now that, whereby we are faved, that we are alfo no doubt juftified by, which words are, in this refpect, fynonimous. Here the Apoftle clearly afcribes the immediat caufe of juftification to this inward work of regeneration, which is Jefus Chrift revealed *in* the Soul, as being that, which formally ftates us in a capacity of being reconciled with God,

the

the waſhing or regeneration being that inward Power and Vertue, whereby the Soul is cleanſed and cloathed with the righteouſneſs of Chriſt, ſo as to be made fit to appear before God.

Thirdly, this doctrin is manifeſt from 2 Cor. 13 : 5. *Examin your own ſelves whether ye be in the faith , prove your own ſelves, know ye not your own ſelves how that Jeſus Chriſt is in you , except ye be reprobats?* Firſt, it appears here how earneſt the Apoſtle was, that they ſhould know *Chriſt in them,* ſo that he preſſes this exhortation upon them, and inculcats it three times. Secondly, he makes the cauſe of reprobation or not-juſtification the want of Chriſt thus revealed and known *in* the Soul : whereby it neceſſarily followes by the rule of *Contrarys*, where the parity is alike, (as in this caſe it is evident) that, where Chriſt is inwardly known, there the perſons ſubjected to him are approved and juſtified. For there can be nothing more plain than this, that if we muſt know Chriſt *in* us, except we be reprobats or unjuſtified perſons, that, if we do know him in us, we are not reprobats, and conſequently juſtified ones. Like unto this is that other ſaying of the ſame Apoſtle, Gal. 4 : 19. *My little children, of whom I travel in birth again untill Chriſt be formed in you,* and therefore the Apoſtle termes this *Chriſt within the hope of glory*, Col. 1: 27, 28. Now that, which is the hope of glory can be no other, than that, which we immediately and moſt nearly relie upon for our juſtification, and that, whereby we are really and truely made juſt. And, as we do not hereby deny, but the original and fundamental cauſe of our juſtification is the love of God manifeſted in the appearance of Jeſus Chriſt in the fleſh, who by his life, death, ſufferings and obedience made a way for our reconciliation, and became a Sacrifice for the remiſſion of ſins, that are paſt, and purchaſed unto us this *Seed* and *Grace*, from which this birth ariſes, and in which Jeſus Chriſt is inwardly received, formed and brought forth *in* us, in his own pure and holy Image of righteouſneſs ; by which our Souls live unto God, and are cloathed with him, and have put him on, even as the Scriptur ſpeaks, Eph. 4: 23, 24. Gal. 3 : 27. We ſtand *juſtified* and *ſaved in* and *by him* and by his *Spirit* and *Grace*, Rom. 3 : 24. 1 Cor. 6 : 11. Tit. 3 : 7. So again reciprocally we are hereby made partakers of the fulneſs of his *merits*, and his cleanſing *blood* is near, to waſh-away every ſin and infirmity, and to heal all our *back ſlidings*, as often as we turn towards him by unfeigned repentance, and become renewed by his Spirit. Thoſe then, that find him thus raiſed and ruling *in* them, have a true ground of hope to believe that

they

they are *juſtified* by his *blood.* But let not any deceive themſelves, ſo as to foſter themſelves in a vain hope and confidence, that by the death and ſufferings of Chriſt they are juſtified, ſo long as *ſin lies at their door*, Gen. 4: v, 7. iniquity prevailes, and they remain yet unrenewed and unregencrat, left it be ſaid unto them *I know you not.* Let that ſaying of Chriſt be remembred, *not every one, that ſaith Lord, Lord, ſhall enter, but he, that doth the will of my Father*, Matth. 7:21. To which let theſe excellent ſayings of the beloved diſciple be added, *Little children, let no man deceive you, he, that doth righteouſneſß, is righteous, even as he is righteous. He, that committeth ſin, is of the devil, becauſe, if our heart condemn us, God is greater than our heart, and knoweth all things,* 1 Joh. 3:7. & 20.

In Gen.
pag 162.   Many famous Proteſtants bear witneſs to this inward juſtification by Chriſt inwardly revealed and formed *in* man, as 1. *M. Borrhæus*, ,, In
,, the imputation (ſaith he) wherein Chriſt is aſcribed and imputed to
,, believers for righteouſneſs, the merit of his blood, and the Holy
,, Ghoſt given unto us, by vertue of his merits, are equally included.
,, And ſo it ſhall be confeſſed that *Chriſt is our Righteouſneſß* as wel from
,, his merit, ſatisfaction, and remiſſion of ſins obtained by him, as from
,, the Gifts of the Spirit of righteouſneſs. And, if we doe this, we ſhall
,, conſider whole Chriſt, propoſed to us for our Salvation, and not any
,, ſingle part of him. The ſame man, pag. 169. In our juſtification then
,, Chriſt is conſidered, who breaths and lives *in* us, to wit, by his Spirit
,, put-on by us, concerning which putting-on the Apoſtle ſaith, *Ye have*
,, *put on Chriſt.* And again, pag. 171. We endeavour to treat, in juſtifi-
,, cation, not of part of Chriſt, but him wholly., in ſo farr as he is our
,, righteouſneſs every way. And a little after, As then bleſſed Paul, in
,, our juſtification, when he ſaith, *whom he juſtified, them he glorified*, com-
,, prehends all things, which pertain to our being reconciled to God the
,, Father, and our renewing, which fits us for attaining unto glory, ſuch
,, as faith, righteouſneſs, Chriſt, and the gift of righteouſneſs exhibited
,, by him, whereby we are regenerated to the fulfilling of the juſtifica-
,, tion, which the Law requires; ſo we alſo will have all things com-
,, prehended in this cauſe, which are contained in the recovery of righte-
,, ouſneſs and innocency. And pag. 181. The form (ſaith he) of our
,, juſtification is the Divine Righteouſneſs it ſelf, by which we are form-
,, ed juſt and good. This is Jeſus Chriſt, who is eſteem'd our Righteouſ-
,, neſs, partly from the forgiveneſs of ſins, and partly from the renew-
,, ing

,, ing and the restoring of that integrity, which was lost by the fault of
,, the first Adam: so that this New and Heavenly Adam being put-on
,, by us, of which the Apostle saith *Ye have put on Christ*, ye have put him
,, on, I say, as the form, so the righteousness, wisdom, and Life of God.
So also affirmeth *Claudius Alberius Inuncanus*, see his orat. apodeict. Lau-
saniæ excus. 1587. orat. 2. pag. 86, 87. *Zuinglius* also in his epistle to the
Princes of Germany, as cited by *Himelius*, c. 7. p. 60. saith, that *the Sanctification of the Spirit is true justification, which alone suffices to justify.* Essius,
upon 1 Cor. 6: 11. saith, *Lest Christian righteousness should be thought to consist in the washing alone, that is, in the remission of sins, he addeth the other degree
or part, [but ye are sanctified,] that is, ye have attain'd to purity, so that ye are
now truely holy before God. Lastly expressing the summe of the benefit received in
one word, which includs both the parts, But ye are justified, the Apostle adds, in the
Name of the Lord Jesus Christ, that is, by his merits, and in the Spirit of our
God, that is the Holy Spirit proceeding from God, and communicated to us by Christ.*
And lastly *Richard Baxter* a famous English Preacher, who yet liveth, in
his book called Aphorisms of *justification*, pag. 80. saith, that *some ignorant wretches gnash their teeth at this doctrin, as if it were flat Popery, not understanding the nature of the righteousness of the New Covenant, which is all out of
Christ in our selves, though wrought by the Power of the Spirit of Christ in us.*

§ IX. The third thing proposed to be considered is, concerning *Good
Works their necessity to Justification.* I suppose there is enough said before to
clear us from any imputation of being Popish in this matter.

But if it be queried, *Whether we have not said, or will not affirm, that a man
is justified by Works?* Quest.

I answer, I hope none need, neither ought, to take offence, if in this Answ.
matter we use the plain language of the Holy Scriptur; which saith expressly in answer hereunto, Ja. 2: 24. *Ye see then how that by works a man is
justified, and not by faith onely.* I shall not offer to prove the truth of this
saying, since what is said in this chapter by the Apostle is sufficient to
convince any man, that will read and believe it, I shall onely from this
derive this one argument,

If no man can be justified without faith, and no *faith* be *living*, nor yet Arg.
available to justification without works, Then *works are necessary to justification:*

But the First is true:
Therefore also the Last.

For

For this Truth is so apparent and evident in the Scripturs, that, for the proof of it, we might transcribe most of the precepts of the Gospel. I shall instance a few, which, of themselves, do so clearly assert the thing in question, that they need no commentary, nor further demonstration. And then I shall answer the objections made against this, which indeed are the arguments used for the contrary opinion, Heb. 12: 14. *Without holyness no man shall see God.* Matth. 7: 21. *not every one, that saith unto me, Lord, Lord! shall enter into the Kingdom of heaven, but he, that doth the will of my Father, which is in heaven.* Joh. 13: 17. *If ye know these things, happy are ye, if ye doe them.* 1 Cor. 7: 19. *Circumcision is nothing, and uncircumcision is nothing, but the keeping of the commandments of God.* Rev. 22: 14. *Blessed are they, that doe his commandments, that they may have right to the Tree of Life, and through the gates may enter into the City:* and many more, that might be instanced; From all which I thus argue,

Arg.   If those onely can *enter into the Kingdom*, that *doe the will of the Father*; If those be accounted onely the *wise builders* and *happy*, that *doe* the sayings of Christ; If no observations avail, but onely the *keeping* of the *Commandments*; and if they be blessed, that *doe the commandments*, and thereby have right to the *Tree of Life*, and entrance through the gate into the City, Then *works* are absolutely *necessary* to *Salvation* and *justification:*

But the First is true:

And *therefore* also the Last.

The *consequence* of the *antecedent* is so clear and evident, that I think no man of sound reason will call for a proof of it.

Obj.   § X. But they object that works are not necessary to justification, First, because of that saying of Christ, Luk 17: 10. *When ye shall have done all these things, that are commanded you, say, We are unprofitable servants, &c.*

Answ.   Answer, As to God, we are indeed unprofitable, for he needeth nothing, neither can we add any thing unto him; but as to our selves, we are not unprofitable, else it might be said, that it is not profitable for a man to keep God's commandments, which is most absurd, and would contradict Christ's doctrin throughout. Doth not Christ, Matth. 5. through all those beatituds pronounce men blessed for their purity, for their meeknefs, for their peaceableness, &c? And is not then that, for which Christ pronounceth men blessed, profitable unto them? Moreover, Matth. 25: 21, 23, doth not Christ pronounce the men good and

faith-

faithfull ſervants, that improved their talents? Was not their doing of
that then profitable unto them? and vers 30. it is ſaid of him, that hid his
talent, and did not improve it, *caſt ye the unprofitable ſervant into utter darkneſs.* If then their not improving of the talent made the man unprofitable,
and he was therefore caſt into utter darkneſs, it will follow by the
Rule of *Contraries*, ſo farr at leſt, that the improving made the other profitable ; ſeing, if our adverſarys will allow us to believe Chriſt's words,
this is made a *reaſon*, and ſo at leſt a *cauſe inſtrumental* of their acçeptançe,
*Wel done , good and faithfull ſervant , thou haſt been faithfull over a few things ,
I will make thee ruler over many things , enter thou into the joy of thy Lord.*

  Secondly, they object thoſe ſayings of the Apoſtle, where he excluds
the deeds of the Law from juſtification, as firſt, Rom. 3: 20. *becauſe by
the deeds of the Law there ſhall be no fleſh juſtified in his ſight.* and vers 28. *therefore we conclude that a man is juſtified by faith without the deeds of the Law.*

  Anſw: We have ſhewn already what plaçe we give to *works,* even to
the *beſt* of *works,* in *juſtification ,* and how we aſcribe its immediat and formal cauſe to the *worker* brought forth *in* us, but not to the *works.* But, in
anſwer to this objection, I ſay, there is a great differençe betwixt the
works of the *Law,* and thoſe of *Graçe* or of the *Goſpel.* The firſt are excluded,
the ſecond not, but are neçeſſary. The firſt are thoſe, which are performed
in man's own will and by his ſtrength, in a conformity to the outward Law
and letter, and therefore are man's own imperfect works, or works of the
Law, which *makes nothing perfect.* And to this belong all the çeremonys, purifications, waſhings, and traditions of the Jewes. The ſecond are the
works of the Spirit of Graçe *in* the heart wrought in conformity to the Inward and Spiritual Law : which works are not wrought in man's will, nor
by his power and ability, but in and by the Power and Spirit of Chriſt *in* us,
and therefore are *pure* and *perfect* in their kind ; as ſhall hereafter be
proven : and may be called Chriſt's works, for that he is the immediat
author and worker of them. Such *works* we affirm *abſolutely neceſſary to juſtification,* ſo that a man can not be juſtified without them, and all *faith* without them is *dead* and uſeleſs, as the Apoſtle *James* ſaith. Now that ſuch a
diſtinction is to be admitted, and that the works excluded by the Apoſtle,
in the matter of juſtification, are of the firſt kind, will appear, if we conſider the occaſion of the Apoſtle mentioning this, as wel here, as throughout in his epiſtle to the Galatians, where he ſpeaks of th s matter, and to
this purpoſe, at large : which was this, That, whereas many of the Gen-

W

tiles ,

tiles, that were not of the race nor feed of Abraham, as concerning the flesh, were come to be converted to the Christian faith, and believe in him, some of those, that were of the Jewish proselyts thought to subject the faithfull and believing Gentiles, to the legal ceremonys and observations as necessary to their justification. This gave the Apostle Paul occasion at length in his Ep. to the Rom. Gal. and elsewhere, to shew the use and tendency of the Law, and of its works, and to contradistinguish them from the faith of Christ and righteousness thereof; shewing how the former was ceased, and become ineffectual; the other remaining, and yet necessary. And that the works excluded by the Apostle are of this kind of works of the Law, appears by the whole strain of his epistle to the Galatians, chap. 1, 2, 3 & 4. for after, in the 4 chapter, he upbraideth them for their returning unto the observation of days and times, and that in the beginning of the 5 chapter he sheweth them their folly and the evil consequence of adhering to the ceremonys of circumcision, then he adds v. 6. *For in Christ Jesus neither circumcision nor uncircumcision availeth, but faith, which worketh by love*; and thus he concluds again, chap. 6: v. 15. *For in Christ Jesus neither circumcision availeth, nor uncircumcision, but a new creatur.* From which places appeareth that distinction of works afore-mentioned, whereof the one is excluded, the other necessary to justification. For the Apostle sheweth here that circumcision, which word is often used to comprehend the whole ceremonys and legal performances of the Jewes, is not necessary, nor doth avail. Here are then the works, which are excluded, by which *no man is justified*: but *faith*, which *worketh by love*, but *the new creatur*, this is that, which *availeth*, which is *absolutely necessary*; for *faith*, that *worketh by love*, can not be without *works*, for, as is said in the same 5 chapter, vers 22. *Love is a work of the Spirit.* Also the new creatur, if it avail and be necessary, can not be without works, seing it is natural for it to bring forth works of righteousness. Again, that the Apostle no wayes intends to exclude such good works, appears, in that in the same epistle he exhorts the Galatians to them, and holds forth the usefulness and nessity of them, and that very plainly, c. 6: v. 7, 8, 9. *Be not deceived*, saith he, *God is not mocked, for whatsoever man soweth, that shall he also reap: for he, that soweth to the flesh, shall of the flesh reap corruption; but he, that soweth in the Spirit, shall of the Spirit reap life everlasting. And let us not be weary of wel doing, for in due season we shall reap, if we faint not.* Doth it not hereby appear, how necessary the Apostle would have the Galatians

know

know that he esteemed good works to be? to wit, not the outward ceremonys and traditions of the Law, but the fruits of the Spirit, mentioned a little before, by which Spirit he would have them to be led, and walk in those good works. As also how much he ascribeth to these good works, by which he affirms life everlasting is reaped. Now, that can not be useless to man's justification, which capacitats him to reap so rich a harvest.

But lastly, for a full answer to this objection, and for the establishing of this doctrin of *good works*, I shall instance another saying of the same Apostle Paul, which our adversarys also in the blindness of their minds make use of against us, to wit, Tit. 3 : 5. *not by works of righteousness, which we have done, but according to his mercy he saved us, by the washing of regeneration and renewing of the Holy Ghost.* It is generally granted by all, that [*saved*] is here all one as is if it had been said [*justified*]. Now, there are two kinds of *works* here mentioned, one, by which we are not saved, that is, not justified, and another, by which we are saved, or justified. The first, the works of righteousness, which we have wrought, that is, which we in our first, faln natur, by our own strength, have wrought, our own legal performances; and therefore may be truely and properly called ours, whatever specious appearances they may seem to have. And that it must needs, and ought so to be understood, doth appear from the other part, *But by the washing of regeneration and renewing of the Holy Ghost*; seing regeneration is a work, comprehensive of many good works, even of all those, which are called *the fruits of the Spirit*.

Now, in case it should be objected that *these may also be called ours, be* Obj. *cause wrought in us, and also by us, many times as instruments.*

I answer, It is far otherwise than the former: for in the first we are yet Answ. alive in our own natural state, unrenewed, working of our selves, seeking to save our selves, by imitating and endeavouring a conformity to the outward letter of the Law, and so wrestling and striving, in the carnal mind, that is enmity to God, and in the cursed will not yet subdued. But in this second we are *crucified with Christ*, we are become *dead with him*, have *partaken of the fellowship of his sufferings*, are made *conformable to his death*, and our first man, our *old man with all his deeds*, as wel the openly wicked, as the seeming righteous, our legal endeavours and foolish wrestlings, are all buried and nailed to the cross of Christ, and so it is no more *we*, but *Christ alive in us*, the Worker *in* us. So that, though it be *we*, in a sense, yet it is according to that of the Apostle to the same Gal.

c. 2: v. 20. *I am crucified, yet neverthelefs I live, yet not I, but Chrift liveth in me, not I, but the Grace of Chrift in me.* Thefe works are efpecially to be afcribed to the Spirit of Chrift, and Grace of God *in* us, as being immediately thereby acted and led in them, and enabled to perform them. And this manner of fpeech is not ftrained, but familiar to the Apoftles, as appears, Gal. 2 : 8. *For he, that wrought effectually in Peter to the apoftlefhip of the circumcifion, the fame was mighty in me,* &c. Phil. 2 : 13. *For it is God, which worketh in you, both to will and to doe,* &c. So that it appears by this place, that, fince the wafhing of regeneration is neceffary to juftification, and that regeneration comprehends works, works are neceffary; and that thefe works of the Law, that are excluded, are different from thefe, that are neceffary, and admitted.

§ X I. Thirdly they object, that *no works, yea not the works of Chrift in us, can have plaçe in juftification, becaufe nothing, that is impure, can be ufefull in it; and all the works wrought in us are impure.* For this they alledge that faying of the Prophet Ifaiah c. 64. : v. 6. *All our righteoufnefs are as filthy rags,* adding this reafon, *that, feing we are impure, fo muft our works be, which, though good in themfelves, yet as performed by us, they reçeive a tinctur of impurity, even as a clean water paffing through an unclean pipe is defiled.*

That no impure works are ufefull to juftification is confeffed, but that all the works wrought *in* the Saints are fuch is denyed. And for anfwer to this the former diftinction will ferve, We confefs that the firft fort of works, above mentioned, are impure; but not the fecond; becaufe the firft are wrought *in* the unrenewed ftate, but not the other. And as for that of Ifaiah, it muft relate to the firft kind, for, though he faith *all our righteoufnefs are as filthy rags,* yet that will not comprehend the righteoufnefs of Chrift *in* us, but onely that, which we work *of* and *by* our felves. For, fhould we fo conclud, then it would follow that we fhould throw away all holynefs and righteoufnefs, finçe that, which is filthy rags, and as a menftruous garment, ought to be thrown away; yea it would follow that all the fruits of the Spirit, mentioned Gal. 4. were as filthy rags: whereas, on the contrary, fome of the works of the Saints are faid to have a *fweet favour in the noftrils of the Lord,* are faid to be an *ornament of great priçe in the fight of God,* are faid to *prevail with him,* and to be *açceptable to him,* which filthy rags and a menftruous garment can not be. Yea many famous Proteftants have acknowledged that this plaçe is not, therefore, fo to be underftood.   *Calvin* upon this place faith, that it is pfed to be cited

by

Obj.
Anfw.

, by ſo me, that they may prove there is ſo little merit in our works, that
,, they are, before God, filthy and defiled; but this ſeemes to me to be
,, different from the Prophet's mind, (ſaith he) ſeing he ſpeaks not here
,, of all mankind. *Muſculus* upon this place ſaith, that it was uſual for
,, this people to preſume much of their legal righteouſneſs, as if thereby
,, they were made clean; nevertheleſs they had no more cleanneſs than
,, the unclean garment of a man. Others expone this place concerning
,, all the righteouſneſs of our fleſh, that opinion indeed is true. Yet I
,, think that the Prophet did rather accommodat theſe ſayings to the im-
,, purity of that people, in legal terms. The Author (commonly ſuppoſed
Bertius) ſpeaking concering the true ſenſe of the 7 chapter of the epiſtle to
the Romans, hath a digreſſion touching this of Iſaiah, ſaying, *This place
is commonly corrupted by a pernicious wreſting: for it is ſtill alledged, as if the
meaning thereof inferred the moſt excellent works of the beſt Chriſtians,* &c. *James
Coret* a French miniſter in the Church of *Baſil*, in his Apology concerning
Juſtification, againſt *Aleſcales*, ſaith, *Neverthelfs, according to the counſil of
certain good men, I muſt admoniſh the Reader, that it never come into our minds
to abuſe that ſaying of* Iſa. 64: 6. *againſt good works, in which it is ſaid, that
all our righteouſneſs are as filthy rags, as if we would have that, which is
good in our good works, and proceedeth from the Holy Spirit, to be eſteemed as a
filthy and unclean thing.*

§ XII. As to the other part, that, ſeing the beſt of men are ſtill impure
and imperfect, therefore their works muſt be ſo. It is to begg the queſtion,
and depends upon a propoſition denyed, and which is to be diſcuſſed at
further length in the next propoſition. But, though we ſhould ſuppoſe a
man not throughly perfect in all reſpects, yet will not that hinder but
good and perfect works in their kind may be brought forth *in* them by the
Spirit of Chriſt; neither doth the example of water going through an
unclean pipe hitt the matter: becauſe, though water may be capable to
be tinctured with uncleanneſs, yet the Spirit of God can not, whom we
aſſert to be the immediat author of thoſe works, that avail in juſtification;
and therefore Jeſus Chriſt his works in his children are pure and perfect,
and he worketh in and through that pure thing of his own forming and
creating *in* them. Moreover, if this did hold, according to our adverſarys ſuppoſition, that no man ever was or can be perfect, it would follow
that the very miracles and works of the Apoſtles, which Chriſt wrought
in them, and they wrought *in* and *by* the Power, Spirit, and Grace of

W 3   Chriſt,

Chrift, were alfo impure and imperfect, fuch as their converting of the Nations to the Chriftian faith, their gathering of the Churches, their writing of the Holy Scriptur, yea and their offering up and facrificing of their lives for the teftimony of Jefus. What may our adverfarys think of this argument, whereby it will follow that the Holy Scriptur, whofe perfection and excellency they feem fo much to magnify, are proved to be impure and imperfect, becaufe they came through impure and imperfect veffels? It appears by the confeffions of Proteftants, that the Fathers did frequently attribut unto works of this kind, that inftrumental work, which we have fpoken, of, in juftification, (albeit fome ignorant perfons cry out that it is *Popery*) and alfo divers, and that famous, Proteftants, do of themfelves confefs it. *Amandus Polanus* in his fymphonia catholica, cap. 27. de remiffione peccatorum, pag. 651. places this Thefe as the common opinion of Proteftants moft agreable to the doctrin of the Fathers. „ We obtain the remiffion of fins by repentance, confeffion, „ prayers and tears proceeding from faith, but do not merit, to fpeak „ properly, and therefore we obtain remiffion of fins, not by the merit „ of our repentance and prayers, but by the mercy and goodnefs of God. *Innocentius Gentiletus*, a Lawyer of great fame among Proteftants in his

Impreff.
Genevæ
1536.

examen of the Council of *Trent*, pag. 66, 67, of juftification, having before fpoken of faith and works, adds thefe words: *But feing the one can not be without the other, we call them both conjunctly inftrumental caufes.* Zanchius in his 5 book de Naturâ Dei, faith, *We do not fimply deny that good works are the caufe of Salvation, to wit, the inftrumental, rather than the efficient caufe, which they call [fine quâ non.]* And afterwards, *Good works are the inftrumental caufe of the poffeffion of life eternal, for by thefe, as by a means and a lawfull way, God leads unto the poffeffion of life eternal.* G. Amefius faith, *that our obedience,*

In medul-
lâ S. The-
ologiæ
lib. 2.
cap 1.
thefi 30.

albeit it be not the principal and meritorious caufe of life eternal, is neverthelefs a caufe, in fome refpect, adminiftring, helping and advancing towards the poffeffion of the life. Alfo Richard Baxter in the book above cited, pag. 155. faith, *that we are juftified by works in the fame kind of caufality, as by faith, to wit, as being both caufes fine quâ non, or conditions of the New Covenant on our part requifit to juftification.* And pag. 195. he faith, *It is needlefs to teach any fcholar, who hath read the writings of Papifts, how this doctrin differs from them.*

But laftly, becaufe it is fit here to fay fomething of the *merit* and *reward* of *works*, I fhall add fomething in this place of our fenfe and belief concerning that matter, We are farr from thinking or believing that man

merits

merits any thing by his works, from God, all being of *Free Graçe*, and therefore do we, and always have denyed that Popiſh notion of *meritum excondigno*, neverthelеſs we can not deny but that God out of his jnfinit goodneſs, wherewith he hath loved mankind, after he communicats to him his holy Graçe and Spirit, doth, according to his own will, recompence and reward the good works of his children : and therefore this *merit* of *congruity* or *reward*, in ſo farr as the Scriptur is plain and poſitive for it, we may not deny ; neither wholly reject the word, in ſo far as the Scriptur makes uſe of it. For the ſame Greek ἄξιον, which ſignifies [*merit*], is alſo in thoſe places, where the tranſlators expreſs it *worth*, or *worthy*, as Matth. 3: 8. 1 Theſs. 2: 12. 2 Theſs. 1: 5, 8. concerning which Richard Baxter ſaith, in the above cited book, pag. 8. *But in a larger ſenſe as promiſe is an obligation, and the thing promiſed is ſaid to be debt, ſo the performers of the conditions are called worthy, and that, which they perform, merit, although properly all be of Graçe, and not of debt.* Alſo thoſe, who are called the Fathers of the Church, frequently uſed this word of *merit*, whoſe ſayings concerning this matter I think not needfull to inſert, becauſe it is not doubted, but evident, that many Proteſtants are not averſe from this word, in the ſenſe that we uſe it. The Apology for the Auguſtan confeſſión, art. 20. hath theſe words, *We agree that works are truely meritorious, not of remiſſion of ſins, or juſtification, but they are meritorious of other rewards corporal and Spiritual, which are indeed as wel in this life, as after this life.* And further, *Seing works are a çertain fulfilling of the Law, they are rightly ſaid to be meritorious, it is rightly ſaid that a reward is due to them.*

In the acts of the conference of Oldenburgh the Electoral Divines, pag. 110. & 265. ſay, In this ſenſe our Churches *also are not averſe from the word* [merit] *uſed by the Fathers, neither therefore do they defend the Popiſh doctrin of merit.*

G. Voſſius, in his theological Theſe concerning the merits of good works, ſaith, *We have not adventured to condemn the word* [merit] *irholly, as being that, which both many of the Antients uſe, and alſo the reformed Churches have uſed, in their confeſſions. Now that God judgeth and açepteth men, according to their works, is beyond doubt to thoſe, that ſeriouſly will read and conſider theſe Scripturs*, Matth. 17: 26. Rom. 2: 6, 7, 10. 2 Cor. 5: 10. Ja. 1: 25. Heb. 10: 35. 1 Pet. 1: 17. Rev. 22: 12.

§ XIII. And to conclude this theam, let none be ſo bold as to mock God, ſupoſing themſelves juſtified and açepted, in the ſight of God, by vertue

of

of Chrift's death and fufferings, while they remain unfanctified and unja-
ftified in their own hearts, and polluted in their fins, left their *hope* prove
that of the *hypocrit,* which *perifheth.* Neither let any foolifhly imagin
that they can, by their own works, or by the performance of any ceremonys or traditions, or by the giving of gold or money, or by afflicting their
bodys, in will-worfhip and voluntary humility, or foolifhly ftriving to
conform their way to the outward letter of the Law, flatter themfelves
that they merit before God, or draw a debt upon him, or that any man,
or men, have power to make fuch kind of things effectual to their juftification, left they be found foolifh boafters, and ftrangers to Chrift and
his righteoufnefs indeed. But bleffed for ever are they, that having truely
had a fenfe of their own unworthynefs and finfulnefs, and having feen all
their own endeavours and performances fruitlefs and vain, and beheld
their own emptynefs, and the vanity of their vain hopes, faith, and confidence, while they remained inwardly pricked, purfued and condemned by *God's Holy Witnefs in* their *hearts,* and fo having applied themfelves
thereto, and fuffered his *Grace* to work *in* them; are become changed and
renewed in the fpirit of their *minds, paft from death to Life,* and know *Jefus*
arifen *in* them, *working both the will and the deed:* and fo having *put on the*
Lord Jefus Chrift, in effect are cloathed with him, and partake of his righteoufnefs and natur, fuch can draw near to the Lord with boldnefs, and
know their acceptance *in,* and *by* him, *in whom,* and in as many as are found
in him, *the Father is wel-pleafed.*

The Eighth Propofition,
Concerning Perfection.

In whom this pure and holy birth is fully brought forth,
the body of death and fin comes to be crucified, and
removed, and their hearts united and fubjected to the
Truth: fo as not to obey any fuggeftions or temptations
of the Evil one, to be free from actual finning and tranfgreffing of the Law of God, and, in that refpect, perfect:
yet doth this perfection ftill admitt of a growth, and
there remaineth always, in fome part, a poffibility of
finning, where the mind doth not moft deligently and
wathfully attend unto the Lord.

§ I. Since

§ I. SInce we have placed juſtification in the revelation of Jeſus Chriſt formed and brought forth *in* the heart, there working his works of righteouſneſs, and bringing forth the fruits of the Spirit. The queſtion is how farr he may prevail *in us*, while we are in this life, or we over our Soul's enemies, *in* and *by* his ſtrength? Thoſe, that plead for juſtification wholly without them, meerly by imputative righteouſneſs, denying the neceſſity of being cloathed with real and inward righteouſneſs, do conſequently affirm, that it is *impoſſible* for a man, even *the beſt of men*, to *be free of ſin in this life*, *which*, they ſay, *no man ever was*, but on the contrary, that *none* can *neither of himſelf*, *nor by any Grace received in this life* (O! wicked ſaying againſt the power of God's Graçe!) *keep the commandments of God perfectly*, *but that every man doth break the commandments in thought, word, and deed*. Whence they alſo affirm, as was a little before obſerved, *That the very beſt actions of the Saints, their prayers, their worſhips, are impure and polluted*. We, on the contrary, though we freely acknowledg this of the natural, faln man, in his firſt ſtate, whatever his profeſſion or pretence may be, ſo long as he is unconverted and unregenerat: yet we do believe that thoſe, in whom Chriſt comes to be formed, and the new man brought forth, and born of the incorruptible Seed, as that birth, and man in union therewith naturally doth the will of God; ſo it is poſſible ſo farr to keep to it, as not to be found daily tranſgreſſors of the Law of God. And for the more clear ſtating of the controverſy, let it be conſidered. Theſe are the words of the Weſtm. larger Catechiſm.

§ II. Firſt, that we place not this poſſibility *in man's own will and capaçity, as he is a man*, the ſon of faln Adam, or as he is in his natural ſtate, however wiſe or knowing, or however much endued with a notional and literal knowledg of Chriſt, thereby endeavouring a conformity to the letter of the Law, as it is outward.

Secondly, that *we attribut it wholly to man, as he is born again*, renewed in his mind, raiſed by Chriſt, knowing Chriſt alive reigning and ruling *in* him, and guiding and leading him by his Spirit, and revealing *in* him the Law of the Spirit of Life, which not onely manifeſts and reproves ſin, but alſo gives power to come out of it.

Thirdly, that by this we underſtand not *ſuch a perfection as may not daily admitt of a growth*, and conſequently mean not, *as if we were to be as pure,*

X

holy,

holy, *and perfeft, as God* in his Divine attributs of Wifdom, Knowledg, and Purity ; but onely *a perfeftion proportionable and anfwerable to man's meafur* , whereby we are kept from tranfgreffing the Law of God , and enabled to anfwer what he requires of us , even as he , that improved his two talents, fo as to make four , of them , perfefted his work , and was fo accepted of his Lord; as to be called a *good and faithfull fervant* nothing lefs than he, that mad his five ten. Even as a little gold is perfect gold in its kind , as wel as a great mafs , and a child hath a perfeft body as wel as a man , though it daily grow more and more.   Thus *Chrift* is faid , Luk 2 : 52. to have *increafed in wifdom and flatur , and in favour with God and man* , though before that time he had *never finned* , and was (no doubt) *perfeft* , in a true and proper fenfe.

Fourthly, though a man may witnefs this for a feafon , and therefore all ought to prefs after it , yet we do not affirm but *thofe , that have attained it in a meafur , may , by the wiles and temptations of the Enemy , fall into iniquity , and lofe it fometimes , if he be not watchfull , and diligently attend not to that of God in the heart.* And we doubt not but many good and holy men , who have not arrived to everlafting life , have had divers ebbings and flowings of this kind , for , though every fin weaken a man in his fpiritual condition , yet it doth not fo as to deftroy him altogether , or render him uncapable of rifing again.

Laftly , though I affirm , that , after a man hath arrived to fuch a condition in which a man may not fin, he yet may fin ; I will neverthelefs not deny but there may be a ftate attainable in this life , in which to doe righteoufnefs may become fo natural to the regenerat Soul , that in the ftability of this condition they can not fin. Others may perhaps fpeak more certainly of this ftate , as having arrived to it. For me, I fhall fpeak modeftly , as acknowledging my felf not to have arrived at it , yet dare I not deny it , for that it feems fo pofitively to be afferted by the Apoftle, in thefe words , 1 Joh. 3 : 9. *He , that is born of God , finneth not , neither can he , becaufe the Seed of God remaineth in him.*

The controverfy being thus ftated , which will ferve to obviat objeftions, I fhall proceed firft to fhew the abfurdity of that doftrin, that pleads for *fin, for term of life,* even in the Saints.

Secondly , prove this doftrin of *perfeftion* from many pregnant teftimonys of the Holy Scriptur.

And laftly, anfwer the arguments and objeftions of our oppofers.

§ III.

§ III. Firſt then, this doctrin, viz, that the *Saints nor can, nor ever will be free of ſinning in this life, is inconſiſtent with the Wiſdom of.God*, and *with his glorious Power and Majeſty*, *Who is of purer eyes than t o behold iniquity*, who, having purpoſed in himſelf to gather to him, that ſhould worſhip him, and be witneſſes for him, on earth, a choſen people, doth alſo no doubt ſanctify and purify them. For God hath no delight in iniquity, but abhorres tranſgreſſion, and, though he regard man in tranſgreſſion, ſo far as to pitty him, and afford him means to come out of it, yet he loves him not, neither delights in him, as he is joyned thereunto. Wherefore, if man muſt alwayes be joyned to ſin, then God ſhould alwoys be at a diſtance with them, as it is written, Iſa. 59 : 2. *your iniquitys have ſeparated between you and your God, and your ſins have hid his ſace from you*; whereas, on the contrary, the Saints are ſaid to *partake*, even while here, *of the Divine Nature*, 2 Pet. 1 : 4. and to be *one ſpirit with the Lord*, 1 Cor. 6 : 17. now no unclean thing can be ſo. It is expresſly written, that *there is no communion betwixt light and darkneß*, 2 Cor. 6 : 14. But *God is Light*, and every ſin is *darkneß* in a meaſur. What greater ſtain then can there be, than this, upon God's Wiſdom? as if he had been wanting to prepare a means, whereby his children might perfectly ſerve and worſhip him; or had not provided a way, whereby they might ſerve him in any thing, but that they muſt withall ſtill ſerve the devil, no leſs, yea more, than himſelf. For *he, that ſinneth, is the ſervant of ſin*, Rom. 6 : 16. and every ſin is an act of ſervice and obedience to the devil. So then, if the Saints ſin daily, in thought, word and deed, yea, if the very ſervice they offer to God, be ſin, ſurely they ſerve the devil more than they do God. For, beſides that they give the devil many intire ſervices without mixtur of the leaſt grain to God, they give God not the leaſt ſervice, in which the devil hath not a large ſhare; and, if their prayers, and all their ſpiritual performances be ſinfull, the devil is as much ſerved by them, in theſe, as God, and in moſt of them much more : Since they confeſs that many of them are performed, without the leadings and influence of God's Spirit. Now, who would not account him a fooliſh maſter, among men, who, being able to doe it, and alſo deſirous that it might be ſo, yet would not provide a way, whereby his children and ſervants might ſerve him more intirely than his avowed enemy, or would not guard againſt their ſerving of him; but be ſo imprudent, and unadviſed in his contrivance, that, whatever way his ſervants and children ſerved him, they ſhould no leſs,

X 2

yea

yea often much more serve his enemy? What may we then think of that doctrin, that would inferr this folly upon the *Omnipotent* and *Onely Wise GOD?*

§ IV. Secondly, *It is inconsistent with the Justice of God.* For, since he requires purity from his children, and commands them to abstain from every iniquity, so frequently and precisely, as shall hereafter appear; and, since *his wrath is revealed against all ungodlyness and unrighteousness of men*, it must needs follow, that he hath capacitated man to answer his will, or else that he requires more than he has given power to perform: which is to declare him openly unjust, and with the slothfull servant, to be a *hard master.* We have elsewhere spoken of the injustice these men ascribe to God, *in making him to damn the wicked, to whom* they alledg *he never afforded any means of being good.* But this is yet an aggravation more irrational and inconsistent, to say, *that God will not afford to those, whom he has chosen to be his own,* (whom they confess he loveth) *the means to please him.* What can follow then from so strange a doctrin? This imperfection in the Saints either proceeds from God, or from themselves. If it proceed from them, it must be, because they are short in improving or making use of the Power given them, whereby they are capable to obey; and so it is a thing possible to them, (as indeed it is by the help of that Power) but this our adversaries deny, they are then not to be blamed for their imperfection and continuing in sin, since it is not possible to them to doe otherwise. If it be not of themselves, it must be of God, who hath not seen meet to allow them Grace in that degree to produce that effect. And what is this but to attribut to God the heighth of injustice, to make him require his children to forsake sin, and yet not to afford them sufficient means for so doing? Surely this makes God more unrighteous than wicked men, *who, if,* as Christ saith, *their children require bread of them, will not give them a stone, or in stead of a fish a serpent.* But these men confess, we ought to seek of God power to redeem us from sin, and yet believe they are never to receive such a power: such prayers then can not be in faith, but are all vain. Is not this to make God as unjust to his children, as Pharaoh was to the Israelits, in requiring brick and not giving them straw? But blessed be God, he deals not so with those, that truely trust in him, and wait upon him, as these men vainly imagin: For such faithfull ones find of a truth; that his Grace is sufficient for them, and know how by his power and Spirit to overcome the Evil one.

§ V. Third-

§ V. Thirdly, This evil doctrin is *highly unjurious to Jesus Christ, and greatly derogats from the Power and Vertue of his Sacrifice, and renders his coming and ministery*, as to the great end of it, *ineffectual.* For Christ (as for other ends) so principally he appeared, for the removing of sin, for gathering a righteous generation, that might serve the Lord, in purity of mind, and walk before him, in fear, and bring-in everlasting righteousnness, and that evangelik perfection, which the Law could not doe. Hence he is said, Tit. 2: 14. *to have given himself for us, that he might redeem us from all iniquity, and purify unto himself, a peculiar people, zealous of good works.* This is certainly spoken of the Saints, while upon earth. But contrary thereunto, these men affirm that we *are never redeemed from all iniquity*, and so make Christ's giving of himself for us, void and ineffectual, and give the Apostle Paul the lye plainly by denying that *Christ purifieth to himself a peculiar people, zealous of good* works. How are they zealous of good works, who are ever committing evil ones ? how are they a purified people, that are still in impurity, as are they, that daily sin, unless sin be accounted no impurity ? Moreover, it is said expressely, 1 Joh. 3. 5: 8. that *For this purpose the Son of God was manifested, that he might destroy the works of the devil, and ye know that he was manifested to take away our sins.* But these men make this purpose of none effect, for they will not have the Son of God to *destroy the works of the devil in his children* in this world. Neither will they at all believe that he was manifest to take away our sins, seing they plead a necessity of always living in them. And lest any should wrest this place of the Apostle, as if it were spoken onely of taking away the guilt of sin, as if it related not to this life, the Apostle, as of purpose to obviat such an objection, adds, in the two following verses, *whosoever abideth in him sinneth not*, &c. I hope then they sin not daily in thought, word and deed. *Let no man deceive you, he, that doth righteousness, is righteous, even as he is righteous, he, that committeth sin is of the devil.* But he, that sinneth daily, in thought, word, and deed, committeth sin. How comes such a one then to be the child of God ? And, if Christ was manifest to take away sin, how strangely do they overturn the doctrin of Christ, that deny that it is ever taken away here ? And how injurious are they to the efficacy and power of Christ's appearance ? Came not Christ to gather a people out of sin into righteousness, out from the kingdom of Satan, into the *Kingdom of the Dear Son of God ?* and are not they, that are thus gathered by him, his servants, his children, his brethren, his friends ? *Woo, as he was, so are they to be in this world, holy, pure,*

X 3

and

and undefiled. And doth not Christ still watch over them, stand by them, pray for them, preserve them by his Power and Spirit, walk in them, and dwell among them; even as the devil, on the other hand, doth among the reprobat ones? How comes it then that the servants of Christ are less his servants, than the devils are his? or is Christ unwilling to have his servants throughly pure? which were gross blasphemy to assert, contrary to many Scripturs. Or is he not able by his Power to preserve, and enable his children to serve him? which were no less blasphemous to affirm of him, concerning whom the Scripturs declare that he has *overcome sin*, *death*, *hell*, and the *grave*, and *triumphed* over them openly, and that *all power in heaven and earth is given to him.* But certainly, if the Saints sin daily, in thought, word and deed, as these men assert, they serve the devil daily, and are subject to his power, and so he prevails more than Christ doth, and holds the servants of Christ in bondage, whether Christ will, or not. But how greatly then doth it contradict the end of Christ's coming? as it is expressed by the Apostle, Eph. 5: 25, 26, 27. *even as Christ also loved the Church, and gave himself for it: That he might sanctifie and cleanse it with the washing of water, by the word, That he might present it to himself a glorious Church, not having spot or wrinkle, or any such thing; but that it should be holy and without blemish.* Now, if Christ hath really thus answered the thing he came for, then the members of this Church are not always sinning, in thought, word, and deed. Or there is no difference betwixt being sanctified and unsanctified, clean & unclean, holy and unholy, being daily blemished with sin and being without blemish.

§ VI. Fourthly, this doctrin renders *the work of the ministery, the preaching of the word, the writing of the Scriptures, and the prayers of the holy men, altogether useless and ineffectual.* As to the first, Eph. 4: 11. *Pastors and teachers are said to be given for the perfection of the Saints*, &c. *till we all come in the unity of the faith and of the knowledg of the Son of God, unto a perfect man, unto a measur of the stature of the fulness of Christ.* Now, if there be a necessity of sinning daily, and in all things, then there can be no perfection. For such, as doe so, can not be esteemed perfect. And, if, for effectuating this perfection in the Saints, the ministery be appointed and disposed of God, do not such, as deny the possibility hereof, render the ministery useless, and of no profit? seing there can be no other true use assigned but to lead people out of sin into righteousness. If so be these ministers assure us, that we need never expect to be delivered from it do not they render their own work needless? what needs preaching against sin, for

the

the reproving of which all preaching is, if it can never be forsaken? Our adverfarys are exalters of the Scripturs, in words, much crying up their ufefulnefs and perfection. Now the Apoftle tells us, 2 Tim. 3:17. that *the Scripturs are for making the man of God perfect.* And, if this be denyed to be attainable in this life, then the Scripturs are of no profit, For in the other life we fhall not have ufe for them. It renders the prayers of the Saints altogether ufelefs, feing themfelves do confefs they ought to pray daily *that God would deliver them from evil, and free them from fin, by the help of his Spirit and Grace, while in this world.* But, though we might fuppofe this abfurdity to follow, that *their prayers are without faith,* yet were not that fo much, if it did not inferr the like upon the holy Apoftles, who prayed earneftly for this end, and therefore (no doubt) believed it attainable, Col. 4: 12. *labouring fervently for you in prayers, that ye may ftand perfect,* & c. 1 Thefs. 3: 13. & 5: 23. & c.

§ VII. But fifthly, this doctrin is *contrary to common reafon and fenfe.* For the two oppofit principles, whereof the one rules, in the children of *darknefs,* the other in the children of *Light,* are, *fin and righteoufnefs.* And, as they are refpectively leavened and acted by them, fo they are accounted either as reprobated, or juftified: feing it is *abomination in the fight of God*   Prov. 17. *either to juftifi the wicked, or condemn the juft.* Now to fay that men can not   ver. 15. be fo leavened with the one as to be delivered from the other, is, in plain words, to affirm that fin and righteoufnefs are confiftent, and that a man may be truely termed righteous, though he be daily finning in every thing he doth. And then, what difference betwixt *good* and *evil?* Is not this to fall into that great abomination of *puting Light for darknefs,* and *calling good evil, and evil good?* fince they fay *the very beft actions of God's children are defiled and polluted,* and that *thofe, that fin daily, in thought, word, and deed, are good men and women, the Saints and holy fervants of the Holy Pure God.* Can there be any thing more repugnant, than this to common Reafon? Since the *fubject* is ftill denominated from that *accident,* that doth moft influence it, as a wall is called white, when there is much whitenefs, and black, when there is much blacknefs, and fuch like. But, when there is more unrighteoufnefs in a man, than righteoufnefs, that man ought rather to be denominated unrighteous than righteous. Then furely, if every man fin daily, in thought, word, and deed, and that in his fins there is no righteoufnefs at all, and that all his righteous actions are polluted and mixed with fin, then there is in every man more unrighteoufnefs than rightcoufnefs,

and

and fo no man ought to be called *righteous*, no man can be faid to be
fanctified, or waſhed. *Where are then the children of God? where are the purified ones? where are they, who were ſometimes unholy, but now holy? that ſometimes were darkneſs, but now are Light in the Lord?* There can none ſuch be
found then at this rate, except that unrighteouſneſs be eſteemed ſo. And
is not this to fall into that abomination above mentioned of juſtifiing the
ungodly? This certainly lands in that horrid blaſphemy of the *Ranters,*
that affirm *there is no difference betwixt good and evil,* and that *all is one in the
fight of God.* I could ſhew many more groſs abſurditys, evil conſequences,
and manifeſt contradictions plied in this *ſinfull doctrin,* but this may ſuffice
at preſent, by which alſo, in a good meaſur, the probation of the Truth
we affirm is advanced. Yet nevertheleſs, for the further evidencing of it,
I ſhall proceed to the ſecond thing propoſed by me, to wit, to prove this
from ſeveral teſtimonies of the Holy Scriptures.

§ VIII. And firſt, I prove it from the peremptory poſitive command of Chriſt and his Apoſtles, ſeing this is a maxime ingraven in every man's heart naturally, that *no man is bound to that, which is impoſſible:*
ſince then Chriſt and his Apoſtles have commanded us to keep *all* the
commandments, and to be perfect in this reſpect, it is poſſible for us ſo
to doe.   Now that this is thus commanded without any commentary or
conſequence, is evidently apparent from theſe plain teſtimonies, Matth.
c. 5: v. 48. 7: 21. Joh. 13: 17. 1 Cor. 7: 19. 2 Cor. 13: 11. 1 Joh.
c. 2: v. 3, 4, 5, 6. & c. 3: v. 2, 3, 4, 5, 6, 7, 8, 9, 10. Theſe Scripturs intimat a poſitive command for it, they declare the abſolut neceſſity
of it, and therefore, as if they had purpoſely been written to anſwer the
objections of our oppoſers, they ſhew the folly of thoſe, that will eſteem
themſelves children or friends of God, while they doe otherwiſe.

Secondly, it is poſſible, becauſe we receive the Goſpel and Law thereof, for that effect, and it's expreſſly promiſed to us, as we are under grace,
as appears by theſe Scripturs, Rom. 6: 14. *ſin ſhall not have dominion over
you: for ye are not under the Law, but under Grace.* and Rom. 8: 3. *For what
the Law could not doe, in that it was weak through the fleſh, God ſending his
own Son, &c. That the righteouſneß of the Law might be fulfilled in us, &c.* For,
if this were not a condition, both requiſit, neceſſary and attainable, under the Goſpel, there were no difference betwixt *the bringing-in of a better
hope* and the *Law, which made nothing perfect,* neither betwixt thoſe, which
are under the Goſpel, or who, under the Law, enjoyed and walked in the
                                                           Life

Life of the Goſpel, and meer Legaliſts. Whereas the Apoſtle through-out that whole ſixth to the Romans, argues not onely the poſſibility, but neceſſity of being free from ſin, from their being under the Goſpel, and under Grace, and not under the Law, and therefore ſtates himſelf and thoſe, to whom he wrot, in that condition, in theſe verſes 2, 3, 4, 5, 6, 7. and therefore, in the 11, 12, 13, 16, 17, 18 verſes, he argues both the poſſibility and neceſſity of this freedom from ſin, almoſt in the ſame manner we did a little before: and in the 22 he declares them in mea-ſur to have attained this condition, in theſe words, *But now being made free from ſin, and become ſervants to God, ye have your fruit unto holyneſſ, and the end everlaſting life.* And, as this perfection or freedom from ſin is attained and made poſſible, where the Goſpel and inward Law of the Spirit is received and known, ſo the ignorance hereof has been, and is, an occaſion of oppo-ſing this Truth. For man not minding the *Light* and *Law within in his heart*, which not onely diſcovers ſin, but leads out of it, and ſo being a ſtranger to the new Life and Birth, that is born of God, which naturally doeth his will, and can not, of its own natur, tranſgreſs the commandments of God, doth, I ſay, in his natural ſtate, look at the commandments, as they are without him, in the letter, and, finding himſelf reproved and convi-ted, is by the letter killed, but not made alive. So man, finding him-ſelf wounded, and not applying himſelf inwardly to that, which can heal, labours in his own will after a conformity to the Law, as it is without him, which he can never obtain, but finds, the more he wreſtles, the more he falleth ſhort. So this is the Jew ſtill, in effect, with his carnal command-ment, with the *Law* without, in the firſt covenant ſtate, which *makes not the comers thereunto perfect, as pertaining to the Conſcience,* Heb. 9: 9. though they may have here a notion of Chriſtianity, and an external faith in Chriſt. This hath made them ſtrain and wreſt the Scripturs for an *impu-tative righteouſneſs,* wholly without them, to cover their impuritys, and this hath made them imagin an acceptance with God poſſible, though they ſuppoſe it impoſſible ever to obey Chriſt's commands. But alas! O de-ceived Soules! that will not avail in the day, wherein *God will judg every man according to his works, whether good or bad.* It will not ſave thee to ſay it was neceſſary for thee to ſin daily, in thought, word, and deed; for ſuch as doe ſo, have certainly obeyed unrighteouſneſs. And what is provided for ſuch, but *tribulation and anguiſh, indignation and wrath,* even as *glory, honour, and peace, immortality and eternal life to ſuch as have done good, and patiently*

Y

con-

continued in wel-doing. So then, if thou defirft to know this perfection and freedom from fin poffible for thee, turn thy mind to the *Light* and *Spiritual Law* of *Chrift in the heart,* and fuffer the reproofs thereof, bear the judgment and indignation of God upon the unrighteous part in thee, as therein it is revealed; which Chrift hath made tolerable for thee; and fo fuffer *judgment in thee* to be *brought forth into victory,* and thus come to *partake* of the *fellowfhip* of *Chrift's fufferings,* and be *made conformable unto his death,* that thou maift feel thy felf *crucified with him to the world,* by the *Power of his crofs in thee,* fo that that life, that fometimes was alive in thee to this world, and the love and lufts thereof, may dye, and a new life be raifed, by which thou mayft live hence-foreward to God, and not to, or for, thy felf, and with he Apoftle thou mayft fay, Gal. 2: 20. *It is no more I, but Chrift alive in me;* and then thou wilt be a Chriftian indeed, and not in name onely, as too many are. Then thou wilt known what it is to have *put off the old man with his deeds,* who indeed fins daily, in thought, word, and deed; and to have *put on the New Man, that is renewed in holynefs after the Image of him, that hath created him,* Eph. 4: 24. and thou wilt witnefs thy felf to be *God's workmanfhip created in Chrift Jefus unto good works,* and fo not to fin always. And to this New Man *Chrift's yoak is eafy, and his burthen is light,* though it be heavy to the old Adam, yea the *commandments of God are not unto this grierous,* For it is his *meat* and *drink* to be found *fulfilling the will of God.*

Matth. 11
vers 30.'
1 Joh. 5:
vers 3.

Laftly, this perfection or freedom from fin is poffible, becaufe many have attained it, according to the exprefs teftimony of the Scriptur. Some before the Law, and fome under the Law, through witneffing and partaking of the benefit and effect of the Gofpel, and much more many under the Gofpel. As firft, it is written of Enoch, Gen. 5: 22, 24. that he *walked with God,* which no man, while finning, can, nor doth the Scriptur record any feeling of his. It is faid of Noah, Gen. 6: 9. and of Job. 1: 8. and of Zachrias and Elizabeth, Luk. 1: 6. that *they were perfect.* But under the Gofpel, befides that of the Rom. above mentioned, fee what the Apoftle faith of many Saints in general. Eph. 2: 4, 5, 6. *But God, who is rich in mercy, for his great love, wherewith he hath loved us, Even when we were dead in fins, hath quickened us together with Chrift (By Grace ye are faved) And hath raifed us up together, and made us fit together in heavenly places in Chrift Jefus,* &c. I judg, while they were fitting in thefe heavenly places, they could not be daily finning, in thought, word, and deed, neither were all their works, which they did there, as *filthy rags,* or as a *menftruous garment.* See what is

fui-further faid to the Hebrewes 12: 22, 23, *Spirits of juft men made perfect.* And to conclud, let that of the *Revelation* 14: 1,2,3,4, 5. be confidered. Where, though their being found without fault be fpoken in the prefent time, yet is it not without refpect to their innocency while upon earth; and their being *redeemed from among men, and no guile found in their mouth* is expresfly mentioned in the time paft. But I fhall proceed now, in the third place, to anfwer the objections, which indeed are the arguments of our oppofers.

§ I X. I fhall begin with their chief and great argument, which is the words of the Apoftle, 1 Joh. 1: 8. *If we fay that we have no fin, we deceive our felves, and the Truth is not in us,* This they think invincible. Obj.

But is it not ftrange to fee men fo blinded with partiality ? How many Scripturs, tenfold more plain, do they reject, and yet ftick fo tenacioufly to this, that can receive fo many anfwers ? As firft, [*If we fay we have no fin,* &c.] will not import the Apoftle himfelf to be included. Sometimes the Scriptur ufeth this manner of expreffion, when the perfon fpeaking can not be included, which manner of fpeech the Grammarians call *Metafchematifmos.* Thus Ja. 3: 9, 10. fpeaking of the tongue, faith, *therewith blefs we God, and therewith curfe we men, adding, thefe things ought not fo to be:* who from this will conclude that the Apoftle was one of thofe curfers ? But fecondly, this objection hitteth not the matter, he faith not *we fin daily, in thought, word, and deed,* far lefs that *the very good works, which God works in us by his Spirit, are fin;* yea the next verfe clearly fhewes, that upon *confeffion* and *repentance* we are not onely *forgiven,* but alfo *cleanfed. He is faithfull to forgive us our fins, and to cleanfe us from all unrighteoufnefs.* Here is both a forgivenefs & removing of the guilt, and a cleanfing or removing of the filth ; for to make forgivenefs and cleanfing to belong both to the removing of the guilt, as there is no reafon for it, from the text, fo it were a moft violent forceing of the words, and would imply a needlefs tautology. The Apoftle having fhewn how that not the guilt onely, but even the filth alfo of fin, is removed, fubfumes his words in the time paft, in the 10 verfe, *If we fay we have not finned, we make him a liar.* Thirdly, as *Auguftin* wel obferved in his expofition upon the Epiftle to the Galatians, *It is one thing not to fin, another thing not to have fin.* The Apoftl's words are not, *If we fay we fin not, or committ not fin daily,* but *if we fay we have no fin.* And betwixt thefe two there is a manifeft difference, for in refpect all have finned, as we freely acknowledg, all may be faid, in a fenfe to have fin. Again, *Sin* may be taken for the *feed of fin,* which may be in thofe, that Anfw.

are redeemed from actual sinning : but as to the temptations, and provocations proceeding from it, being resisted by the servants of God, and not yeelded to, they are the devil's sin, that tempteth, not the man's, that is preserved. Fourthly, this being considered, as also how positive and how plain, once and again, the same Apostle is, in the very same epistle, as in divers places above cited, is it equal, or rational to strain this one place, presently after so qualified, and subsumed in the time past, to contradict, not onely other positive expressions of his, but the whole tendency of his Epistle, and of the rest of the holy commands and precepts of the Scriptur.

Obj.   Secondly, Their second objection is from two places of Scriptur much of one signification. The one is, 1 Kings 8: 46. *For there is no man, that sinneth not.* The other is Eccles. 7: 20. *for there is not a just man upon earth, that doeth good, and sinneth not.*

Answ.   I answer, first; These affirm nothing of a daily and continual sinning, so as never to be redeemed from it, but onely that all have sinned, or that there is none, that doth not sin, though not always, so as never to cease to sin: and in this lies the question. Yea, in that place of the Kings, he speaks, within two verses, of the returning of such *with all* their *Souls* and *hearts*, which implies a possibility of leaving off sin. Secondly there is a respect to be had to the seasons and dispensations; for, if it should be granted that in Solomon's time there was none, that sinned not, it will not follow that there are none such now, or that it is a thing is not now attainable by the Grace of God under the Gospel, for *à non esse ad non posse non valet sequela.* And lastly, this whole objection hangs upon a false interpretation, for the Hebrew word יחטא may be read in the *potential mood,* thus, *There is no man, who may not sin,* as wel as in the *Indicative:* so both the old Latin, *Junius* and *Tremellius* and *Vatablus* have it, and the same word is so used, Psal. 119 : 11. *I have hid thy Word in my heart,* לְמַעַן לֹא אֶחֱטָא-לָךְ: *that is to say, that I may not sin against thee,* in the potential mood, and not in the indicative, as it is in the English; which being more answerable to the universal scope of the Scripturs, the testimony of the Truth, and the sense almost of all interpreters, doubtless ought to be so understood, and the other interpretation rejected as spurious.

Obj.   Thirdly, they *object* some expressions of the Apostle Paul, Rom. 7: 19. *for the good, that I would, I doe not; but the evil, which I would not, that I doe.* And vers 24. *O wretched man that I am! who shall deliver me from the body of this death?*

I anfwer, This place infers nothing, unlefs it were apparent that the   Anfw.
Apoftle here were fpeaking of his own condition, and not rather in the
perfon of others, or what he himfelf had fometimes born, which is frequent in Scriptur, as in the cafe of curfing in *James*, before mentioned.
But there is nothing, in the text, that doth clearly fignify the Apoftle
to be fpeaking of himfelf, or of a condition he was then under, or was always to be under; yea, on the contrary, in the former chapter, as afore
is at large fhewn, he declares they were *dead to fin*, demanding how fuch
fhould yet live any longer therein? Secondly, it appears that the Apoftle
onely perfonated one not yet come to a Spiritual condition, in that he
faith, vers 14. *but I am carnal, fold under fin.*   Now, is it to be imagined
that the Apoftle Paul, as to his own proper condition, when he wrot that
epiftle, was a carnal man, who in the 1 chapter teftifies of himfelf,
that he was *feparated to be an Apoftle, capable to impart to the Romans Spiritual gifts ?* and chapter 8. vers 2. that *the Law of the Spirit of Life in Chrift
Jefus* had made him *free from the Law of fin and death*, fo then he was not carnal. And feing there are Spiritual men in this life, as our adverfarys will
not deny, and is intimated through this whole 8 chapter to the Romans,
it will not be denyed but the Apoftle was one of them.   So then, as his
calling himfelf *carnal*, in the 7 chap. can not be underftood of his own proper ftate, neither can the reft of what he fpeaks there of that kind be fo
underftood; yea after verfe 24, where he makes that exclamation, he
adds, in the next verfe, *I thank God through Jefus Chrift our Lord*, fignifiing
that by him he witneffed deliverance, and fo goeth on, fhewing how he
had obtained it, in the next chapter, viz, 8: v. 35. *Who fhall feparat us from
the love of Chrift ?* and vers 37. *But in all thefe things we are more than conquer-
ers.* And in the laft verfe, *nothing fhall be able to feparat us*; &c. But wherever there is a continuing in fin, there there is a feparation, in fome degree, feing every *fin is contrary to God*, and ἀνομία, i. e. a *tranfgreffion of the
Law*, 1 Joh. 3: 4. and whoever committeth the leaft fin is overcome of it,
and fo, in that refpect, is not a conqueror, but conquered. This condition then, which the Apoftle plainly teftified, he with fome others had obtained, could not confift with continual remaining and abiding in fin.

Fourthly, they object the *faults and fins of feveral eminent Saints, as Noah,*   Obj.
David, &c.

I anfwer, that doth not at all prove the cafe, for the queftion is not   Anfw.
whether good men may not fall into fin, which is not denyed, but *whether it be*

Y 3

not possible for them not to sin? It will not follow, becaufe thefe men finned, that therefore they were never free of fin, but always finned. For, at this rate of arguing it might be urged according to this rule, *contrariorum par ratio*, i. e. *the reafon of contraries is alike*, that, if, becaufe a good man hath finned, once, or twice, he can never be free from fin, but muft always be daily and continually a finner, all his life long, then by the rule of *Contraries*, if a wicked man have done good once or twice, he can never be free from righteoufnefs, but muft always be a righteous man all his life time, which, as it is moft abfurd in it felf, fo it is contrary to the plain teftimony of the Scriptur, Ezech 33: 12. to the 18.

Obj.   Laftly they *object*, that, if perfection or freedom from fin be attainable, this will render mortification of fin ufelefs, and make the blood of Chrift of no fervice to us, neither need we any more pray for forgivenefs of fins.

Anfw.   I anfwer, I had almoft omitted this objection, becaufe of the manifeft abfurdity of it; for can mortification of fin be ufelefs, where the end of it is obtained? feing there is no attaining of this perfection but by mortification, doth the hope and belief of overcoming render the fight unneceffary? Let rational men judg which hath moft fenfe in it, to fay, as our adverfaries do, *It is neceffary that we fight and wreftle, but we muft never think of overcoming. We muft refolve ftill to be overcome.* Or to fay, Let us fight, becaufe we may overcome. Whether do fuch as believe they may be cleanfed by it, or thofe, that believe they can never be cleanfed by it render the *Blood of Chrift* moft *effectual?* If two men were both grievoufly difeafed, and applied themfelves to a phyfician for remedy, which of thofe do moft commend the phyfician and his cure, he, that believeth he may be cured by him, and as he feels himfelf cured, confeffeth that he is fo, and fo can fay This is a fkilfull phyfician, this is good medicin, behold! I am made whole by it? or he, that never is cured, nor ever believes that he can, fo long as he lives? As for praying for forgivenefs, we deny it not, for that *all have finned*, and therefore all need to pray that their fins paft may be blotted out, and that they may be daily preferved from finning. And, if hoping or believing to be made free from fin, hinders praying for forgivenefs of fin, it would follow by the fame inference, that men ought not to forfake murder, adultery, or any of thefe grofs evils, feing the more men are finfull, the more plentifall occafion there would be of afking forgivenefs of fin, and the more work for mortification. But the Apoftle hath fufficiently refuted fuch fin-pleafing cavills, in thefe words, Rom. 6: 1, 2. *Shall we continue in fin, that Grace may abound? God forbid,*   But

But laſtly, it may be eaſily anſwered, by a retorſion, to thoſe, that preſs this, from the words of the Lord's prayer, *forgiven us our debts*, that this militats no leſs againſt perfect juſtification, than againſt perfect ſanctification. For, if all the ſaints, the leaſt, as wel as the greateſt, be perfectly juſtified in that very hour wherein they are converted, as our adverſarys will have it, then they have remiſſion of ſins, long before the dye. May it not then be ſaid to them, What need have ye to pray for remiſſion of ſin, who are already juſtified, whoſe ſins are long ago forgiven, both paſt and to come?

§ X. But this may ſuffice; concerning this poſſibility *Jerom* ſpeaks clearly enough, lib. 3. adver. Pelagium. *This we alſo ſay that a man may not ſin, if he will, for a time and place, according to his bodily weakneß, ſo long as his mind is intent, ſo long as the cords of the cythar relax not by any vice*, and again in the ſame book, *which is that, that I ſaid, that it is put in our power, (to wit, being helped by the Grace of God) either to ſin, or not to ſin.* For this was the error of *Pelagius*, which we indeed reject and abhorr, and which the *Fathers* deſervedly withſtood, that *man by his natural ſtrength, without the help of God's Grace, could attain to that ſtate, ſo as not to ſin.* And *Auguſtin* himſelf, a great oppoſer of the Pelagian hereſy, did not deny this poſſibility, as attainable by the help of God's Grace, as in his book *de Spiritu & literâ*, cap. 2. and his book *de naturâ & Gratiâ* againſt Pelagius, cap. 42. 50, 60, & 63 *de geſtis concilii Palaſtini*, cap. 7. & 11. and *de peccato originali*, lib. 2. cap. 11. *Gelaſius* alſo, in his diſputation againſt *Pelagius*, ſaith, *But if any affirm that this may be given to ſome Saints in this life, not by the Power of man's ſtrength, but by the Grace of God, he doth wel to think ſo confidently, and hope it faithfully : for by the Gift of God all things are poſſible.* That this was the common opinion of the *Fathers*, appears from the words of the Afzanſik council, canon laſt, *We believe alſo this, according to the catholik faith, that all, that are baptized through Grace by baptiſm received, and Chriſt helping them, and co working, may and ought to doe whatſoever belongs to Salvation, if they will faithfully labour.*

§ XI. Bleſſed then are they, that believe in him, who is both able and willing to deliver as many as come to him through true repentance, from all ſin, and do not reſolve, as theſe men do, to be the devil's ſervants all their life time, but daily go on forſaking unrighteouſneſs, and forgeting thoſe things, that are behind, *preſs forwards towards the Mark, for the Prize of the high calling of God, in Chriſt Jeſus:* ſuch ſhall not find their faith

Phil 3. vers 14.

and

and confidence to be in vain, but in due time shall be made conquerors, through him, in whom they have believed, and so, overcoming, *shall be established as pillars in the house of God, so as they shall go no more out*, Rev. 3. ver. 12.

The Ninth Propofition,

Concerning Perseverance, and the possibility of falling from Grace.

Although this Gift, and inward Grace of God be sufficient to work out Salvation, yet in those, in whom it is resisted, it both may, and doth, become their condemnation. Moreover, they, in whose hearts it hath wrought in part to purify and sanctify them, in order to their further perfection, may by disobediënce fall from it, *turn it to wantoness*, 1 Tim. 1:19. *make shipwrack of faith, and after having tasted the heavenly Gift, and been made partakers of the Holy Ghost, again fall away*, Heb. 6: 4, 5, 6, yet such an increafe and ftability in the Truth may, in this life, be attained, from which there can not be a total apostasy.

§ I. THe first sentence of this Propofition hath already been treated of, in the 5 and 6 Propofitions, where it hath been shewn that that *Light*, which is given for Life, and Salvation, becomes the condemnation of those, that refuse it, and therefore is already proved in those places, where did demonstrat the possibility of man's resisting the Grace and Spirit of God; and indeed it is so apparent in the Scripturs, that it can not be denyed, by such as will but seriously confider these testimonies, Prov. 1:24, 25, & 26. Joh. 3: 18, 19, 2 Thess. 2: 11, 12. Act. 7: 51. & 13. 46. Rom. 1: v. 18. As for the other part of it, that, *they, in whom this Grace may have wrought in a good measur, in order to purifie and sanctifie them, tending to their further perfection, may afterwards through disobedience fall away*, &c. The testimonies of the Scriptur included in the Proposition it self are sufficient to prove it, to men of unbyaſſed judgments. But, becauſe, as to this part, our cauſe is common with many other Proteſtants, I ſhall be the more brief in it. For it is not my deſign to doe that, which is done already, neither do I covet to appear knowing, by writing much, but ſimply purpoſe to preſent to the world a faithfull account of our principles, and briefly to let them underſtand what we have to ſay for our ſelves.

§ 11. From theſe Scripturs then included in the Propoſition (not to mention many more, which might be urged) I argue thus.

If men may turn the Graçe of God into wantonneſs, then they muſt once have Arg. 1. *had it :*

But the Firſt is true :

Therefore alſo the Second.

If men may make ſhipwrack of faith, they muſt once have had it, neither could Arg. 2. *they ever have had true faith without the Graçe of God :*

But the Firſt is true :

Therefore alſo the laſt.

If men may have taſted of the heavenly Gift, and been made partakers of the Holy Arg. 3. *Spirit, and afterwards fall away, they muſt needs have known in meaſur the operation of God's Saving Graçe and Spirit, without which no man could taſt the heavenly Gift, nor yet partake of the Holy Spirit :*

But the firſt is true :

Therefore alſo the laſt.

Secondly, Seing the contrary doctrin is built upon this falſe *hypotheſis*, that *Graçe is not given for Salvation to any, but to a certain elect number, which cannot loſe it, & that all the reſt of mankind, by an abſolut decree, are debarred from Graçe and Salvation,* that being deſtroyed, this falls to the ground. Now as that doctrin of theirs is wholly inconſiſtent with the daily practice of thoſe, that preach it, in that they exhort people to believe and be ſaved ; while in the mean time, if they belong to the decree of reprobation, it is ſimply impoſſible for them ſo to doe, and, if to the decree of Election, it is needleſs ; ſeing it is as impoſſible to them to miſs of it, as hath been before demonſtrated : ſo alſo in this matter of *perſeverançe*, their practice and principle are no leſs inconſiſtent and contradictory, for, while they daily exhort people, to be *faithful to the end,* ſhewing them, if they continue not, they ſhall be *cut-off,* and fall ſhort of the *reward:* which is very true, but no leſs inconſiſtent with that doctrin, that affirmes *there is no hazard, becauſe no poſſibility of departing from the leaſt meaſur of true Graçe.* Which it true,

it

it is to no purpose, to beseech them to stand, to whom God hath made it impossible to fall. I shall not longer insist upon the probation of this, seing what is said may suffice to answer my design, and that the thing is also abundantly proved by many of the same judgment. That this was the doctrin of the primitive Protestants, thence appears, that the *Augustan* confession condemns it as an error of the *Anabaptists*, to say, *that who once are justified, they can not lose the Holy Spirit.* Many such like sayings are to found in the common places of *Philip Melancthon. Vossius*, in his Pelagian history, lib 6. testifies, that this was the common opinion of the *Fathers*, in the confirmation of the 12 These, pag. 587. he hath these words, *that this, which we have said, was the common sentiment of antiquity, those at present can onely deny, who other ways perhaps are men not unlearned, but neverthelefs in antiquity altogether strangers, &c.* These things thus observed, I come to the objections of our opposers.

Obj.

§ III. First they *alledg*, that those places mentioned of *making ship-wrack of faith* is onely understood of seeming faith, and not of a real true faith.

Answ.   This objection is very weak, and apparently contrary to the text, 1 Tim. 1 : 19. where the Apostle addeth *to faith a good Conscience*, by way of complaint; whereas, if their faith had been onely seeming and hypo-critical, the men had been better without it, than with it, neither had they been worthy of blame, for losing that, which in it self was evil. But the Apostle expressly adds [*and of a good Conscience*], which shewes it was real, neither can it be supposed, that men could truely attain a *good Conscience*, without the operation of God's *Saving Grace*: far less that a good Con-scien̄ce doth consist with a seeming, false, and hypocritical faith. Again, these places of the Apostle, being spoken by way of regret, clearly import that these attainments, they had faln from, were good and real, not false and deceitfull, else he would not have regreted their falling from them. And so he saith positively, *they tasted of the heavenly Gift, and were made par-takers of the holy Ghost, &c.* not that they seem'd to be so, which sheweth this objection is very frivolous.

Obj.   Secondly they *alledg*, Phil. 1: 6. *Being confident of this very thing, that he, which hath begun a good work in you, will perform it, untill the day of Jesus Christ, &c.* and 1 Pet. 1: 5. *who are kept by the Power of God through faith unto Salvation.*

Answ.   These Scripturs, as they do not affirm any thing positively contrary

to

to us, fo they can not be underftood otherwife than as the condition is performed upon our part, feing Salvation is no other ways propofed there, but upon certain neceffary conditions to be performed by us, as hath been above proved, and as our adverfaries alfo acknowledg, as Rom 8: v. 13. For, *if ye live after the flefh, ye fhall dye: but, if ye, through the Spirit, do mortifie the deeds of the body, ye fhall live.* And Heb. 3:14. *We are made partakers of Chrift, if we hold the beginning of our confidence ftedfaft unto the end.* For, if thefe places of the Scriptur, upon which they build their objection, were to be admitted without thefe conditions, it would manifeftly overturn the whole tenor of their exhortations throughout all their writings. Some other objections there are of the fame nature, which are folved by the fame anfwers, which alfo, becaufe largely treated of by others, I omitt, to come to that teftimony of the Truth, which is more efpecially ours in this matter, and is contained in the latter part of the Propofition, in thefe words, *yet fuch an increafe and ftability in the Truth may in this life be attained, from which there can not be a total apoftafy.*

§ IV. As, in the explanation of the fifth and fixth Propofitions, I obferved that fome, that had denyed the errors of others concerning *reprobation*, and affirmed the *univerfality of Chrift's death*, did notwithftanding fall fhort in fufficiently holding forth the Truth; and fo gave the contrary party an occafion, by their defects, to be ftrengthened in their errors: fo may it be faid in this cafe. As, upon the one hand, they err, that affirm that the leaft degree of true and Saving Grace can not be faln from, fo do they err, upon the other hand, that deny any fuch ftability to be attained, from which there can not be a total and final apoftafy. And betwixt thefe two extrems lieth the Truth, apparent in the Scripturs, which God hath revealed unto us by the teftimony of his Spirit, and which alfo we are made fenfible of, by our own fenfible experience. And, even as in that former controverfy was obferved, fo alfo in this the defence of Truth will readily appear, to fuch as ferioufly weigh the matter: for the arguments upon both hands, rightly applied, will, as to this, hold good, and the objections, which are ftrong, as they are refpectively urged againft the two oppofit falfe opinions, are here eafily folved by the eftablifhing of this Truth. For all the arguments, which thefe alledg, that affirm *there can be no falling away*, may wel be received upon the one part, as of thefe, who have attained to this ftability & eftablifhment, and their objections folved by this conceffion: fo, upon the other hand, the arguments alledged,

from

from Scriptur teſtimonies, by thoſe, that affirm *the poſſibility of falling* away, may wel be received of ſuch as are not come to this eſtabliſhment, though having attained a meaſur of true Graçe.   Thus then the contrary batterings of our adverſaries, who miſs the Truth, do concurr the more ſtrongly to eſtabliſh it, while they are deſtroying each other.   But, leſt this may not ſeem to ſuffice to ſatisfie ſuch as judg it *always poſſible for the beſt of men, before they dye, to fall away*, I ſhall add, ſor the proof of it, ſome brief conſiderations, from ſome few teſtimonies of the Scriptur.

§ V. And firſt, 1 freely acknowledg, that it is good for all to be humble, and in this reſpeçt, not over confident, ſo as to lean to this, to foſter themſelves in iniquity, or lie down in ſecurity, as if they had attained this condition, ſeing *watchfulneſs* and *diligence* is of *indiſpenſible neceſſity* to all mortal men, ſo long as they breath in this world: for God will have this to be the conſtant praçtice of a Chriſtian, that thereby he may be the more fit to ſerve him, and the better armed againſt all the daily temptations of the Enemy.   For, ſince *the wages of ſin is death*, there is no man, while he ſinneth, and is ſubjeçt thereunto, but may lawfully ſuppoſe himſelf capable of periſhing.   Hence the Apoſtle Paul himſelf ſaith, 1 Cor. 9: 27: *But I keep under my body, and bring it into ſubjeçtion ; leſt that by any means, when I have preached to others, I my ſelf ſhould be a caſt-away.*   Here the Apoſtle ſuppoſeth it poſſible for him to be a caſt-away, and yet it may be judged he was far more advanced in the inward work of regeneration, when he wrot that epiſtle, than many, who, now adays, too preſumptuouſly ſuppoſe they can not fall away, becauſe they feel them ſelves to have attained ſome ſmall degree of true Graçe.   But the Apoſtle makes uſe of this ſuppoſition, or poſſibility of his being a *caſt away* (as I before obſerved) as an induçement to him to be watchfull, *I keep under my body, leſt*, &c.   Neverthelefs the ſame Apoſtle at another time, in the ſenſe and feeling of God's Holy Power, and in the dominion thereof, finding himſelf a conqueror therethrough over ſin and his Soul's enemies, maketh no difficulty to aſſirm, Rom. 8: 38. *For I am perſwaded, that neither death nor life*, &c. which clearly ſheweth that he had attained a condition, from which he knew he could not fall away.

But ſecondly, it appears ſuch a condition is attainable, becauſe we are exhorted to it, and, as hath been proved before, the Scriptur never propoſeth to us things impoſſible.   Such an exhortation we have from the Apoſtle, 2 Pet. 1: 10. *Wherefore the rather, brethren, give diligence to make*
your

your calling and election sure.   And though there be a condition here proposed, yet since we have already proved that it is possible to fulfill this condition, then also the promise, annexed thereunto, may be attained. And
since, where assurance is wanting, there is still a place left for doubtings
and despairs, if we should affirm it never attainable, then should there
never be a place known by the Saints in this world, wherein they might
be free of doubting and despair: Which, as it is most absurd in it self, so it's
contrary to the manifest experience of thousands.

Thirdly, God hath given to many of his Saints and children, and is
ready to give unto *all*, a *full* and *certain assurance*, that they are his, and that
no power shall be able to pluck them out of his hand.   But this assurance
would be *no* assurance, if those, who are so *assured* were not *established* and
confirmed beyond all doubt and hesitation.   If so, then surely there is no
possibility for such to miss of that, which God hath assured them of. And
that there is such *assurance*, *attainable* in this life, the Scriptur abundantly
declareth, both in general, and as to particular persons. As first, Rev. 3:
v. 12. *him, that overcometh, will I make a pillar in the temple of my God, and he
shall go no more out*, &c. which containeth a general promise unto all.
Hence the Apostle speaks of some, that are sealed, 2 Cor. 1: 22. *Who
hath also sealed us, and given the earnest of his Spirit in our hearts:* wherefore the
Spirit so *sealing* is called the *earnest* or *pledg of our inheritance*, Eph. 1: 13. *In
whom ye were sealed by the Holy Spirit of promise.*   And therefore the Apostle
Paul, not onely in that of the Romans above noted, declareth himself to
have attained that condition, but 2 Tim. 4: 7. he affirmeth in these words,
I have fought a good fight, &c. which also many good men have, and do witness. And therefore, as there can be nothing more manifest, than that,
which the manifest experience of this time sheweth, and therein is found
agreable to the experience of former times, so we see there have been,
both of old, and of late, that have *turned the Grace of God into wantonness*,
that have *faln from* their *faith* and integrity, thence we may safely conclud
such a *falling away possible.* We also see that some of old and of late have
attained a certain assurance, sometime before they departed, that they
should *inherit eternal life*, and have accordingly dyed in that good hope.
Of and concerning whom the Spirit of God testified, that they are saved.
Wherefore we also see that such a state is attainable in this life, from which
there is not a falling away. For, seing the Spirit of God did so testify, it
was not possible that they should perish, concerning whom *he, who can
not lye*, thus bare witness.   Z 3   The

The Tenth Propofition,
Concerning the Miniftery.

As by this Light or Gift of God all true knowledg in things Spiritual is received and revealed, fo by the fame, as it is manifefted and received in the heart, by the ftrength and power thereof, every true *Minifter* of the Gofpel is ordained, prepared, and fupplied in the work of the *Miniftery* : and by the leading, moving and drawing hereof, ought every *Evangelift* and Chriftian *paftor* to be led and ordered in his labor and work of the Gofpel, both as to the place; *where*, as to the perfons, *to whom*, and as to the time, *wherein* he is to *minifter*. Moreover, who have this *authority*, may and ought to *preach* the *Gofpel*, though *without human commiffion* or literatur, as, on the other hand, who want the Authority of this Divine Gift, however learned or authorized by the commiffion of men and Churches, are to be efteemed, but as deceivers, and not true minifters of the Gofpel.   Alfo, who have received this holy and unfpotted Gift, *as they have freely received it, fo are they freely to give it*, without hire or bar-gaining, far lefs to ufe it as a trade to get money by; yet, if God hath called any one from their employments or trades, by which they acquire their lively-hood, it may be lawfull for fuch, according to the liberty, which they feel given them in the Lord, to receive fuch temporals (to wit, what may be needfull for them for meat and cloathing) as are given them freely, and cordially by thofe, to whom they have communicated Spirituals.

Matth. 10:
verf 8.

§ I. Itherto I have treated of thofe things, which relate to the Chriftian faith, and Chriftians, as they ftand, each in his privat and particular condition, and how and what way every man may be a Chriftian indeed, and fo abide. Now I come in order to fpeak of thofe things, that relate to Chriftians, as they are ftated in a joynt fellowfhip and communion, and come under a vifible and outward fociety, which fociety is called the *Church of God*, and in Scriptur compared to a body, and therefore named the *Body of Chrift*. As then in the natural body there be divers members, all concurring to the common end of preferving and confirming the whole body; fo in this *Spiritual* and *myftical Body* there are alfo divers, according to the different meafurs of *Grace*, and of the *Spirit* diverfly adminiftred unto *each member*; and from this diverfity arifeth that diftinction of perfons in the vifible fociety of Chriftians, as of *Apoftles, Paftors, Evangelifts, Minifters*, &c. That, which in this Propofition is propofed, is, *What makes or conftituts any a Minifter of the Church, what his qualifications ought to be, and how he ought to behave himfelf?* But becaufe it may feem fomewhat prepofterous, to fpeak of the diftinct *offices* of the Church, untill fomething be faid concerning the *Church* in general, though nothing pofitively be faid of it in the Propofition, yet, as here implied, I fhall briefly premife fome thing thereof, and then proceed to the particular members of it.

§ 11. It is not in the leaft my defign to meddle with thofe tedious and many controverfies, wherewith the Papifts and Proteftants do tear one another, concerning this thing, but onely, according to the Truth manifefted to me, and revealed *in* me, by the teftimony of the Spirit, according to that proportion of wifdom given me, briefly to hold forth, as a neceffary introduction both to this matter of the *Miniftery*, and of *Worfhip*, which followeth, thofe things, which I, together with my brethren, do believe, concerning the Church.

The [*Church*] then, according to the grammatical fignification of the word, as it is ufed in the Holy Scriptur, fignifies an *affembly* or *gathering* of *many* into one place, for the fubftantive ἐκκλησία comes from the word ἐκκαλέω *I call out of*, and originally from καλέω *I call*, and indeed as this is the grammatical fenfe of the word, fo alfo it is the real and proper fignification of the thing, the *Church* being no other thing, but the *fociety, gathering*, or *company of fuch as God hath called out of the world, and worldly fpirit, to walk in his LIGHT and LIFE.* The *Church* then fo defigned is to be confidered, as it comprehends all, that are thus *called* and *gathered* truely *by God*, both fuch as are yet in this inferior world, and fuch as, having already laid down the earthly tabernacle, are paffed into their heavenly manfions, which together do make up the One catholik Church, (concerning which there is fo much controverfy) out of which Church we free-

ly

ly acknowledg there can be no Salvation, becaufe under this Church and its denomination are comprehended all, and as many, of whatfoever nation, kindred, tongue, or people, they be, (though outwardly ftrangers and remote from thofe, who profefs Chrift and Chriftianity in words, and have the benefit of the Scripturs) as become obedient to the Holy Light and teftimony of God *in* their hearts, fo as to become fanctified by it, and cleanfed from the evils of their wayes. For this is the univerfal or catholik Spirit, by which many are called from *all the four corners of the earth, and fhall fit down with Abraham, Ifaak and Jacob.* By this the fecret Life and Vertue of Jefus is conveyed into many, that are a farr off, even as by the blood, that runs into the veins and arteries of the natural body, the Life is conveyed from the head and heart unto the extremeft parts. There may be members therefore of this catholik Church both among Heathens, Turks, Jewes, and all the feveral forts of Chriftians, men and women of integrity and fimplicity of heart, who, though blinded in fomething in their underftanding, and perhaps burthened with the fuperftitions and formality of the feveral fects, in which they are ingroffed, yet being upright in their hearts before the Lord, chiefly aiming and labouring to be delivered from iniquity, and loving to follow righteoufnefs, are by the fecret touches of this Holy Light *in* their Souls, inlivened and quickened, thereby fecretly united to God, and there through become true members of this catholik Church. Now the Church, in this refpect, hath been in being in all generations, for God never wanted fome fuch witneffes for him, though many times flighted, and not much obferved by this world. And therefore this Church, though ftill in being, hath been oftentimes, as it were, invifible, in that it hath not come under the obfervation of the men of this world, being, as faith the Scriptur, Jer 3: 14. *one of a city, and two of a family.* And yet, though the Church thus confidered, may be, as it were, hid from wicked men, as not then gathered into a vifible fellowfhip, yea and not obferved even by fome, that are members of it, yet may there notwithftanding many belong to it, as when Elias complained he was *left alone,* 1 Kings 19: 18. God anfwered unto him, *I have referved to my felf feven thoufand men, who have not bowed their knees to the image of Baal,* whence the Apoftle, argues, Rom. 11. the being of a remnant in his day.

§ III. Secondly the Church is to be confidered, as it fignifies a certain number of perfons gathered by God's Spirit, and by the teftimony of

fome

fo ne of his fervants, raifed up for that end, unto the belief of the true principles and doctrines of the Chriftian faith, who, through their hearts being united by the fame love, and their underftanding informed in the fame truths, gather, meet, and affemble together, to *wait upon* God, to worfhip him, and to bear a joynt teftimony for the *Truth* againft error, fuffering for the fame, and fo becoming, through this fellowfhip, as one family and houfhold in certain refpects, do each of them watch over, teach, inftruct, and care for one another, according to their feveral meafurs and attainments. Such were the Churches of the primitive times, gathered by the Apoftles, whereof we have divers mentioned in the Holy Scripturs. And as to the *vifiblity* of the *Church*, in this refpect, there hath been a great interruption fince the Apoftles days, by reafon of the *apoftafy*, as fhall hereafter appear.

§ IV. To be a *member* then of the *catholik Church*, there is need of the *inward calling of God*, by his *Light in* the *heart*, and a being leavened into the natur and Spirit of it, fo as to forfake unrighteoufnefs, and be turned to righteoufnefs; and, in the inwardnefs of the mind to be cut out of the wild olive tree of our own firft faln natur, and ingrafted into Chrift, by his *Word* and *Spirit in the heart*. And this may be done in thofe, who are ftrangers to the hiftory (God not having pleafed to make them partakers thereof) as in the 5 and 6 Propofitions hath already been proved.

To be a *member* of a *particular* Church of Chrift, as this inward work is indifpenfibly neceffary, fo is alfo the outward profeffion of and belief in Jefus Chrift, and thofe holy Truths delivered by his Spirit in the Scripturs, feing the teftimony of the Spirit, recorded in the Scripturs, doth anfwer the teftimony of the fame Spirit *in* the *heart*, even as *face anfwereth face in a glafs*. Hence it followes that the inward work of Holinefs, and forfaking iniquity, is neceffary, in every refpect, to the being a member in the Church of Chrift; and that the outward profeffion is neceffary to be a member of a particular gathered Church, but not to the being a member of the catholik Church; yet it is abfolutely neceffary, where God affords the opportunity of knowing it: the outward teftimony is to be believed, where it is prefented and revealed, the fumme whereof hath upon other occafions been already proved.

§ V. But contrary hereunto, the devil, that worketh, and hath wrought, in the *myftery of iniquity*, hath taught his followers, to affirm, *that no man, however holy, is a member of the Church of Chrift, without the out-*

ward profession, and that he be initiated thereunto by some outward ceremonies.
And again, *that men, who have this outward profession, though inwardly unholy, may be members of the true Church of Christ, yea and ought to be so esteemed.*
This is plainly to put *Light for darkness,* and *darkness for Light,* as if God had a greater regard to words, than actions, and were more pleased with vain professions, than with real holiness: But these things I have sufficiently refuted heretofore. Onely from hence let it be observed, that upon this false and rotten foundation Antichrist hath builded his Babylonish structur, and the anti-Christian Church in the apostasy hath hereby reared her self up to that heighth and grandeur she hath attained, so as to exalt her self above *all, that is called God,* and *sit in the Temple of God, as God.*

For the particular Churches of Christ, gathered in the Apostles dayes, soon after beginning to decay, as to the inward Life, came to be over-grown with several errors, and the hearts of the professors of Christianity to be leavened with the old spirit and conversation of the world. Yet it pleased God, for some centuries, to preserve that *life in* many, whom he imboldned with zeal, to stand and suffer for his Name, through the ten *persecutions.* But these being over, the meeknefs, gentlnefs, love, long-suffering, goodnefs, and temperance of Christianity came to be loft. For, after that the princes of the earth came to take upon them that profession, and that it ceased to be a reproach *to be a Christian,* but rather became a means to preferment, men became such by birth and education, and not by conversion, and renovation of spirit: then there was none so vile, none so wicked, none so profane, who became not a member of the Church. And the teachers and pastors thereof becoming the companions of princes, and so being inriched by their benevolence, and geting vast treafurs and estats, became puffed up, and, as it were, drunken with the vain pomp and glory of this world, and so marshalled themselves in manifold orders, and degrees, not without innumerable contefts and altercations *who should have the* * precedency. So the vertue, life, substance, and kernel of the Christian religion came to be loft, and nothing remained but a shaddow and image, which dead image, or carcafe of Christianity (to make it take the better with the superftitious multitud of Heathens, that became ingroffed in it, not by any inward conversion of their hearts, or by becoming lefs wicked or superftitious, but by a little change in the object of their superftition) not having the inward ornament and life of the Spirit, became decked with many outward and visible orders, and beautified

with

* As was betwixt the Bishop of *Rome* and the Bishop of *Constanti-nople.*

with the gold, silver, precious stones, and the other splendid ornaments
of this perishing world; so that this was no more to be accounted the
Christian Religion and Christian Church, notwithstanding t e outward
profession, than the dead body of man is to be accounted a living man,
which, however cunningly embalmed, and adorned with ever so much
gold, or silver, or most precious stones, or sweet ointments, is but a dead
body still, without sense, life or motion. For that *Apostat* Church of *Rome*
has introduced no less ceremonys and superstitions into the Christian profession, than was either among Jewes, or heathens; and that there is,
and hath been, as much, yea and more pride, covetousness, unclean lust,
luxury, fornication, profanity and atheïsm among her teachers and chief
Bishops, as ever was among any sort of people, none need doubt, that
have read their own authors, to wit, *Platina*, and others.

Now though *Protestants* have reformed from her in some of the most
gross points, and absurd doctrines, relating to the Church and Ministery,
yet (which is to be regreted) they have but lopt the branches, but retain
and plead earnestly for the same root, from which these abuses have
sprung, so that even among them, though all that mass of superstition,
ceremonys and orders be not again established, yet the same prid, covetousness and sensuality is found to have overspread and leavened their
Churches and ministery; and the *life*, *power*, and *vertue* of *true religion* is
lost among them, and the very same death, barrenness, dryness, and
emptyness is found in their ministery, so that in effect they differ from
Papists but in form and some ceremonys, being with them apostatized
from the life and power the true primitive Church and her pastors were
in, so that of both it may be said truely (without breach of charity) that
having onely a form of godlyness (and many of them not so much as that)
they are denyers of, yea enemies to the power of it. And this proceeds,
not simply from their not walking answerable to their own principles,
and so degenerating that way, (which also is true) but, which is worse,
their setting down to themselves and adhering to certain principles,
which naturally, as a cursed root, bring forth these bitter fruits: these
therefore shall afterwards be examined and refuted, as the contrary positions of Truth, in the Proposition are explained and proven.

For, as to the natur and constitution of a Church (abstract from their
disputs concerning its constant visibility, infallibility, and the primacy
of the Church of Rome) the Protestants, as in practice, so in principles,

A a 2

differ

differ not from Papists, for they ingrofs within the compafs of their Church whole nations, making their infants members of it, by fprinkling a little water upon them, fo that there is none fo wicked or profane, who is not a fellow-member, no evidence of holinefs being required to conftitut a member of the Church; and look through the Proteftant nations, and there fhall no difference appear in the lives of the generality of the one, more than of the other, but he, who *ruleth in the children of difobedi-ence*, reigning in both, fo that the reformation, through this detect, is but in holding fome lefs grofs errors, in the notion, but not in having the heart reformed and renewed, in which mainly the life of Chriftianity confifteth.

§ V. I. But the Popifh errors concerning the *miniftery*, which they have retained, are moft of all to be regreted, by which chiefly the life and power of Chriftianity is barred out among them, and they kept in death, barrennefs and drynefs: there being nothing more hurtfull, than an error in this refpect, for, where a falfe and corrupt miniftery entreth, all other manner of evils followes upon it, according to that Scripturs adage, *like people, like prieft*. For by their influence, in ftead of miniftring life and righteoufnefs, they minifter death and iniquity. The whole back-flidings of the Jewifh congregations of old is hereto afcribed. *The leaders of my people have caufed them to err.* The whole writings of the Prophets are full of fuch complaints; and for this caufe, under the New Teftament, we are fo often warned and guarded to *beware of falfe prophets and falfe teach-ers,* &c. What may be thought then, where all, as to this, is out of order, where both the foundation, call, qualifications, maintainance, and whole difciplin is different from, and oppofit to, the *miniftery* of the primitive Church, yea and neceffarily tends to the fhuting out a *Spiritual miniftery*, and the in-bringing and eftablifhing a carnal? This fhall appear by parts.

§ V I I. That then, which comes firft to be queftioned in this matter, is concerning *the Call of a Minifter,* to wit, *what maketh, or how cometh a man to be a minifter, paftor, or teacher in the Church of Chrift?*

We *anfwer,* by the *inward power* and *vertue* of the Spirit of God. For, as faith our propofition, *having received the true knowledg of things Spiritual by the Spirit of God, (without which they can not be known) and being by the fame in meafur purified and fanctified, he comes thereby to be called and moved to minifter to others, being able to fpeak from a living experience, of what he himfelf is a witnefs, and therefore knowing the terror of the Lord, he is fit to perfuade men,*

men,&c. 2 Cor. 5:11.and his words and ministery,proceeding from the inward power and vertue, reaches to the heart of his hearers,and makes them approve of him, and be subject unto him.   Our adversarys are forced to confess that this were indeed desirable, and best, but this they will not have to be absolutely necessary.   I shall first prove the necessity of it; and then shew how much they err in that, which they make more necessary than this Divine and Heavenly call.

First, That, which is necessary to make a man a Christian, so as without-   Arg.
out it he can not be truely one, must be much more necessary to make a man a minister of Christianity, seing the one is a degree above the other, and has it included in it, nothing less than he, that supposeth a *master*, supposeth him first to have attained the knowledg and capacity of a scholar.   They, that are not Christians, can not be Teachers or ministers among Christians :

But this inward call, power and vertue of the Spirit of God is necessary to make a man a Christian, as we have abundantly proven before in the second Proposition, according to these Scripturs, *He, that hath not the Spirit of Christ, is none of his.   As many as are led by the Spirit of God, are the sons of God.*

Therefore this call, moving, and drawing of the Spirit must be much more necessary to make a minister.

Secondly, all *ministers of the New Testament* ought to be *ministers of the Spirit, and not of the letter*, according to that 2 Cor. 3: 6. and as the old Latine hath it, *not by the letter, but by the Spirit*.   But how can a man be a minister of the Spirit, who is not inwardly called by it, and who looks not upon the operation and testimony of the Spirit as essential to his call ? As he could not be a minister of the letter, who had thence no ground for his call, yea that were altogether a stranger to, and unacquainted with it, so neither can he be a minister of the Spirit, who is a stranger to it, and unacquainted with the motions thereof, and knowes it not to draw, act, and move him, and go before him in the work of the *Ministery*.   I would willingly know, how those, that take upon them to be ministers (as they suppose) of the Gospel, meerly from an outward vocation, without so much as being any ways sensible of the work of the Spirit, or any inward call therefrom, can either satisfy themselves or others, that they are *ministers of the Spirit*, or wherein they differ from the *ministers of the Letter*.   For

Thirdly, if this inward call or testimony of the Spirit were not essential and necessary to a minister, then the ministery of the *New Testament* should

not onely be no ways preferable to , but in divers respects far worse than
that of the *Law* : for , under the *Law* , there was a certain tribe alloted for
the ministery , and of that tribe certain families set apart for the priest-
hood and other offices , by the immediat command of God to *Moses* , so
that the people needed not be in any doubt , who should be priests and ministers of the holy things : yea and besides this , God called forth , by the
immediat testimony of his Spirit , severals , at divers times , to teach , instruct , and reprove his people , as Samuel , Nathan , Elias , Elisa , Jeremiah , Amos , and many more of the Prophets : But now under the *New
Covenant* , where the *ministery* ought to be more *spiritual* , the *way* more *certain* , and the *access* more *easy* unto the Lord , our adversarys , by denying
the necessity of this inward and Spiritual vocation , make it quite other
ways ; for there being now no certain family or tribe , to which the ministery is limited , we are left in uncertainty , to chuse and have pastors at a
ventur , without all certain assent of the will of God , having neither an
outward rule nor certainty , in this affair , to walk by ; for that the Scriptur
can not give any certain rule in this matter , hath , in the third Proposition
concerning it , been already shewn.

 Fourthly , Christ proclames them all *thieves and robbers , that enter not by*
him the door into the sheep fold , but climb up some other way whom the sheep ought
not to h ar , but such as come in without the *Call* , *movings* , and *leadings* of
the *Spirit* of *Christ* wherewith he leads his children into all truth , come in
certainly not by *Christ* , who is the *Door* , but some other way , and therefore
are not true shepherds.

Joh. 10 : 1

 § V I I I. To all this they object *the succession of the Church* , alledging ,
that , since Christ gave a call to his Apostles and disciples , they have conveighed that
call to their successors , having power to ordain pastors and teachers , by which power
the authority of ordaining and making ministers and pastors is successively conveighed
to us , so that such , who are ordained and called by the pastors of the Church , are
therefore true and lawfull ministers , and others , who are not so called , are to be
accounted but intruders. Hereunto also some Protestants add *a necessity* ,
though they make it *not as a thing essential , that , besides this calling of the Church ,*
every one being called ought to have the inward call of the Spirit , inclining him , so
chosen , to his work. but this they say is *subjective* , and not *objective* , of which
before.

Obj.

Answ.   As to what is subjoyned of the inward call of the Spirit , in that
they make it not essential to a true call , but a supererogation as it were , it
                                                                                      shew-

sheweth, how little they set by it, since those, they admitt to the ministery, are not so much as questioned, in their trials, whether they have
this or not. Yet, in that it hath been often mentioned, especially by the
primitive Protestants in their treatises of this subject, it sheweth, how
much they were secretly convinced in their minds, that this inward call of
the Spirit was most excellent, and preferable to any other; and therefore
in the most noble and heroïk acts of the reformation they laid claim unto
it, so that many of the primitive Protestants did not scruple both to despise
and disown this outward * call, when urged by the Papists against them.   * succes-
But now Protestants having gon from the testimony of the Spirit, plead   sion.
for the same succession, &, being pressed by those, whom God now raiseth
up by his Spirit to reform these many abuses that are among them, with the
example of their forefathers practice against Rome, they are not at all
ashamed utterly to deny that their fathers were called to their work by the
inward and immediat vocation of the Spirit, cloathing themselves with
that call, which they say their fore-fathers had, as pastors of the Roman
Church. For thus (not to go further) affirmeth * *Nicolaus Arnoldus*, in a   ＋ Who
pamphlet, written against the same Propositions, called a *Theologik Exer-*   gives
citation, sect. 40. averring, that *they pretended not to an immediat act of the*   himself
Holy Spirit, but reformed by the vertue of the ordinary vocation, which they had in   out Do-
the Church, as it then was, to wit, *that of Rome*, &c.   ctor and
                                                                              Professor
§ IX. Many absurditys do Protestants fall into, by deriving their mi-   of the Sa-
nistery thus through the Church of Rome. As first they must acknowledg   cred The-
her to be a true Church of Christ, though onely erroneous in some things,   ology at
which contradicts their fore-fathers so frequently, and yet truely, calling   *Franequer.*
her *anti-Christ*. Secondly, they must needs acknowledg that the priests
and bishops of the Romish church are true ministers and pastors of the
Church of Christ, as to the essential part, else they could not have been
fit subjects, for that power, and authority to have resided in, neither could
they have been vessels capable to receive that power, and again transmitt
it to their successors. Thirdly, it would follow from this, that the priests &
bishops of the Romish Church are yet really true pastors and teachers; for,
if Protestant ministers have no authority, but what they received from
them, & since the Church of Rome is the same, she was at that time of the
reformation, in doctrin and manners, and she has the same power now,
she had then, and if the power lie in the succession, then these priests of
the Romish Church now, which derive their ordination from those bishops,

that ordained the firſt reformers, have the ſame authority, which the ſucceſſors of the reformed have, and conſequently are no leſs Miniſters of the Church than they are. But how ſhall this agree with that opinion, which the primitive Proteſtants had of the Romiſh prieſts and clergy, to whom *Luther* did not onely deny any power or authority, but contrariwiſe affirmed, that it was wickedly done of them, to aſſume, to themſelves onely, this authority to teach, and be prieſts and miniſters, &c. For he himſelf affirmed, *that every good Chriſtian (not onely men, but even women alſo) is a preacher.*

§ X. But againſt this vain ſucceſſion, as aſſerted either by Papiſts or Proteſtants, as a neceſſary thing to the call of a miniſter, I *anſwer*, that ſuch as plead for it, as a ſufficient or neceſſary thing to the call of a miniſter, do thereby ſufficiently declare their ignorance of the natur of Chriſtianity, and how much they are ſtrangers to the Life and Power of a Chriſtian miniſtery, which is not entail'd to ſucceſſion, as an outward inheritance: and herein, as hath been often before obſerved, they not onely make the Goſpel not better than the Law, but even far ſhort of it; for Jeſus Chriſt, as he regardeth not any diſtinct particular family, or nation, in the gathering of his children, but onely ſuch as are joyned to, and leavened with his own *pure* and *righteous Seed*, ſo neither regards he a bare outward ſucceſſion, where his pure, immaculat, and righteous Life is wanting; for that were all one. He took not in the Nations within the New Covenant, that he might ſuffer them to fall into the old errors of the Jewes, or to approve them in theſe errors; but that he might gather unto himſelf a pure people out of the earth. Now, this was the great error of the Jewes, to think they were the Church and People of God, becauſe they could derive their outward ſucceſſion from Abraham, whereby they reckoned themſelves the children of God, as being the off-ſpring of Abraham, who was *the father of the faithfull*. But how ſeverely doth the Scriptur rebuke this vain and frivolous pretence? Telling them, *that God is able of the ſtones to raiſe children unto Abraham*, and that not the outward ſeed, but thoſe, that were found in the faith of Abraham, are the true children of faithfull Abraham. Far leſs then can this pretenſe hold among Chriſtians, ſeing Chriſt rejects all outward affinity of that kind; *Theſe*, ſaith he, *are my mother, brethren, and ſiſters, who doe the will of my Father which is in heaven.* And again: *He looked round about him, and ſaid, who ſhall doe the will of God, theſe (ſaid he) are my brethren.* So then ſuch as doe not the

com-

Matth. 12 v. 48. &c.
Mark 3: ver 33, &c

commands of Chrift, as are not found cloathed with his righteoufnefs,
are not his difciples ; and that, which a man hath not, he can not give
to another ; and it's clear, that no man , nor church, though truely called
of God, and, as fuch, having the authority of a Church and minifter,
can any longer retain that authority, than they retain the power, life,
and righteoufnefs of Chriftianity ; for the form is entailed to the power
and fubftance, and not the fubftance to the form.   So that, when a man
ceafeth inwardly in his heart to be a Chriftian, (where his Chriftianity
muft lie) by turning to Satan, and becoming a reprobat, he is no more a
Chriftian , though he retain the name and form, than a dead man is a
man , though he have the image and reprefentation of one, or than the
pictur or ftatue of a man is a man ; and , though a dead man may ferve to
a painter to retain fome imperfect reprefentation of the man , that fometimes was alive, and fo one pictur may ferve to make another by , yet
none of thofe can ferve to make a true living man again , neither can they
conveigh the life and fpirit of the man, it muft be God, that made the
man at firft, that alone can revive him. As death then makes fuch interruption of an outward natural fucceffion, that no art, nor outward form
can up-hold ; and as a dead man, after he is dead, can have no iffue,
neither can dead images of men make living men , fo that it is the living
that are onely capable to fucceed one another, and fuch as dye, fo foon as
they dye, ceafe to fucced, or to tranfmitt fucceffion. So it is in Spiritual
things, it is the life of Chriftianity, taking place in the heart, that makes
a Chriftian , and fo it is a number of fuch being alive, joyned together in
the life of Chriftianity, that make a Church of Chrift, and it is all thofe,
that are thus alive and quickened, confidered together, that make the
catholik Church of Chrift : therefore where this life ceafeth in one , then
that one ceafeth to be a Chriftian , and all power, vertue, and authority,
which he had as a Chriftian, ceafeth with it ; fo that, if he hath been a
minifter or teacher, he ceafeth to be fo any more ; and though he retain
the form , and hold to the authority in words, yet that fignifies no more ,
nor is it of any more real vertue or authority , than the meer image of a
dead man : and, as this is moft agreable to Reafon, fo is it to the Scripturs teftimony, for it is faid of Judas, Act. 1 : 25. *that Judas fell from his
miniftery and apoftlefhip by tranfgresfion.* So his tranfgreffion caufed him ceafe
to be an apoftle any more ; whereas had the apoftlefhip been entailed to
his perfon, fo that tranfgreffion could not caufe him to lofe it, untill he

B b

had

had been formally degraded by the Church, (which Judas never was, so
long as he lived) Judas had been as really an Apostle, after he betrayed
Christ, as before: and as it is of one, so of many, yea of a whole Church;
for, seing nothing makes a man truely a Christian, but the life of Christianity inwardly ruling *in* his heart, so nothing makes a Church, but the gathering of several true Christians into one body. Now, where all these
members lose this life, there the Church ceaseth to be, though they still
uphold the form, and retain the name; for when that, which made them
a Church, and for which they were a Church, ceaseth, then they cease
also to be a Church: and therefore the Spirit speaking to the Church of
Laodicea, because of her luke-warmness, Rev. 3: 16. threateneth to *spue*
her *out of* his *mouth.* Now, suppose the Church of Laodicea had continu-
in that luke-warmness, and had come under that condemnation and judgment, though she had retained the name and form of a Church, and had
had her pastors and ministers, as no doubt she had at that time, yet surely
she had been no true Church of Christ, nor had the authority of her pastors
and teachers been to be regarded because of any outward succession,
though perhaps some of them had it immediatly from the Apostles. From
all which I inferr, that, since the authority of the Christian Church and
her pastors is always united, and never separated from the inward power,
vertue, and righteous life of Christianity, where this ceaseth, that ceaseth also. But our adversarys acknowledg, that many, if not most of those,
by and through whom they derive this authority, were altogether destitut
of this life and vertue of Christianity. Therefore they could neither receive, have, nor transmitt any Christian authority.

Obj. But if it be *objected,* that, *though the generality of the Bishops and Priests of
the Church of Rome, during the apostasy were such wicked men, yet Protestants affirm, and thou thy self seem'st to acknowledg, that there were some good men among
them, whom the Lord regarded, and who were true members of the catholik Church
of Christ: might not they then have transmitted this authority?*

Answ. I answer: This saith nothing, in respect Protestants do not at all lay
claim to their ministery as transmitted to them by a direct line of such good
men, which they can never shew, nor yet pretend to, but generally place
this succession as inherent in the whole pastors of the apostat church,
neither do they plead their call to be good and valid, because they can
derive it through a line of good men, separat and observable distinguish-
able from the rest of the bishops and clergy of the Romish church, but
they

they derive it, as an authority refiding in the whole ; for they think it herefy to judg that the quality or condition of the adminiſtrator any ways
invalidats or prejudiceth his work.

This vain then and pretended fucceſſion not onely militats againſt, and
fights with the very manifeſt purpofe and intent of Chriſt, in the gathering and calling of his Church, but makes him (fo to fpeak) more blind
and lefs prudent, than natural men are in conveighing and eſtabliſhing
their outward inheritances : for where an eſtate is entailed to a certain
name and family, when that family weareth out, and there is no lawfull
fucceſſor found of it, that can make a juſt title appear, as being really of
blood & affinity to the family, it is not lawfull for any one of another race
erblood, becaufe he affumes the name or armes of that family, to poſſefs the
eſtate, and claime the fuperioritys and priviledges of the family, but by
the law of Nations the inheritance devolves into the Prince, as being
ultimus hares, and fo he giveth it again immediatly to whom he feeth meet,
and makes them bear the name and armes of the family, who then are
entitled to the priviledges and revenues thereof.   So in like manner the
true name and *title* of a *Chriſtian,* by which he *hath right* to the *heavenly inheritance,* and is a member of Jefus Chriſt, is *inward Righteoufnefs* and *Holynefs,*
and the *mind redeemed from the vanitys, luſts,* and *iniquitys* of this *world.* And
a gathering or company made up of fuch members makes a Church ;
where this is loſt, the title is loſt, and fo the true Seed, to which the promife is, and to which the inheritance is due, becomes extinguiſhed in
them, and they become dead as to it, and fo it retires, and devolves it felf
again into *Chriſt,* who is the *righteow heir of Life,* and he gives the title and
true right again immediatly, to whom it pleafeth him, even to as many
as being turned to his *Pure Light in* their *Confciençes,* come again to walk in
his *righteow* and *innoçent life,* and fo become true members of his *body, which
is the Church.*   So the authority, power and heirſhip is not annexed to perfons, as they bear the bare names or retain a form, holding the meer ſhell
or ſhiddow of Chriſtianity : But the promife is to Chriſt, and to the Seed,
in whom the authority is inherent, and in as many as are one with him, and
united unto him, by purity and holynefs, and by the inward renovation
and regeneration of their minds.

Moreover, this pretended fucceſſion is contrary to Scriptur, definitions
and natur of the Church of Chriſt, and of the true members.   For firſt,
the Church is the houfe of God, the pillar and ground of Truth, 1 Tim. 3: 15.

B b 2

But,

But according to this doctrin, the house of God is a polluted nest of all
sort of wickednefs and abominations, made up of the moft ugly, defiled,
and perverfe ftones, that are in the earth, where the devil rules in all
manner of unrighteoufnefs. For fo our adverfarys confefs, and hiftory informes, the Church of Rome to have been, as fome of their hiftorians acknowledg; and, if that be truely the houfe of God, what may we call the
houfe of Satan? or may we call it therefore the houfe of God, notwithftanding all this impiety, becaufe they had a bare form and that vitiated
many ways alfo, and becaufe they pretended to the name of Chriftianity,
though they were anti-Chriftian, devilifh, and athëiftical in their whole
practice and fpirit, and alfo in many of their principles? Would not this
inferr yet a greater abfurdity, as if they had been fomething to be accounted of, becaufe of their hypocrify and deceit, and falfe pretences? Whereas the Scriptur looks upon that as an aggravation of guilt, and calls it blafphemy, Rev. 2: 9. Of two wicked men, he is moft to be abhorred, who
covereth his wickednefs with a vain pretence of God and righteoufnefs;
even fo thefe *abominable beafts,* and *fearfull monfters,* who look upon themfelves to be *bifhops* in the *apoftat church,* were never a whit the better, that
they falfly pretended to be the fucceffors of the Holy Apoftles, unlefs to
lye be commendable, and that hypocrify be the way to heaven. Yea were
not this to fall into that evil, condemned among the Jewes? Jer. 7: 4.
*Truft ye not in lying words, faying, the Temple of the Lord, the Temple of the
Lord, the Temple of the Lord are thefe, throughly amend your ways,* &c. as if fuch
outward names and things were the thing the Lord regarded, and not inward holinefs? or can that then be the pillar and ground of Truth, which
is the very fink and pit of wickednefs, from which fo much error, fuperftition, idolatry, and all abomination fprings? Can there be any thing
more contrary both to Scriptur and Reafon?

 Secondly, The *Church* is defined *to be the Kingdom of the Dear Son of God,
into which the Saints are tranflated, being delivered from the power of darknefs. It
is called the Body of Chrift, which from him by joynts and bands having nourifhment
miniftred, and knit together increafeth with the increafe of God,* Col. 2: 19.
But can fuch members, fuch a gathering, as we have demonftrated that
Church and members to be, among whom they alledg their pretended
authority to have been preferved, and through which they derive their
call, can fuch, I fay, be the body of Chrift, or the members thereof? or
is Chrift the Head of fuch a corrupt, dead, dark, abominable, ftinking

car-

carcafe? If fo, then might we not as wel affirm againft the Apoftle, 2 Cor. 6: 14. *that righteoufnefs hath fellowſhip with unrighteoufnefs, that Light hath communion with darknefs, that Chriſt hath concord with Belial, that a believer hath part with an infidel, and that the temple of God hath agrement with idols?* Moreover, no man is called the temple of God, nor of the Holy Ghoft, but as his veſſel is purified, and fo he fitted and prepared for God to dwell in, and many, thus fitted by Chriſt, become his body, in and among whom he dwells and walks, according as it is written, *I will dwell in them, and walk in them, and I will be their God and they ſhall be my people.* It is therefore that we may become the temple of Chriſt, and people of God, that the Apoftle in the following verfe exhorts, faying out of the Prophet, *Wherefore come out from among them, and be ye feparat, faith the Lord, and touch not the unclean thing, and I will receive you; and I will be a father unto you, and ye ſhall be my fons and daughters, faith the Lord Almighty.* But to what purpofe all this exhortation, and why ſhould we feparat from the unclean, if a meer outward profeffion, and name be enough to make the true Church, and if the unclean and polluted were both the Church and lawfull fucceffors of the Apoftles, inheriting their authority, and tranfmitting it to others? Yea how can the Church be the Kingdom of the Son of God, as contradiftinguifhed from the kingdom and power of darknefs? and what need, yea what poffibility of being tranflated out of the one into the other, if thofe, that make up the kingdom and power of darknefs, be real members of the true Church of Chriſt, and not fimple members onely, but the very paftors and teachers of it? But how do they *increafe in the increafe of God, and receive Spiritual nouriſhment from Chriſt the Head,* that are enemies of him in their hearts, by wicked works, and openly go into perdition? Verily as no metaphyfical and nice diftinctions, (that, though they were practically, as to their own privat ftats, enemies to God and Chriſt, and fo fervants of Satan, yet they were, by vertue of their office, members and minifters of the Church, and fo able to tranfmitt the fucceffion) I fay, as fuch invented and frivolous diftinctions will not pleafe the Lord God, neither will he be deluded by fuch, nor make up the glorious body of his Church with fuch meer out-fide hypocritical fhewes, nor be beholden to fuch painted fepulchres for to be members of his body, which is found, pure and undefiled; and therefore he needs not fuch falfe and corrupt members to make up the defects of it; fo neither will fuch diftinctions fatisfie truely tender and Chriftian Confciences, efpecially confidering the Apoftle

2 Cor. 6: v. 17, 18.

B b 3

is

is so far from desiring us to regard that, as that we are expresly commanded to turn away from such as *have a form of godlines, but deny the Power of it.*
For we may wel *object* against these, as the poor man did against the proud
Prelat, that went about to cover his vain and unchristian like sumptuous-
nes, by distinguishing that *it was not as Bishop, but as Prince, he had all that
splendor.* To which the poor rustik wisely is said to have answered, *When the
Prince goeth to hell, what shall become of the Prelat?* And indeed this were to
suppose the body of Christ to be defective, and, that to fill up these defective places, he puts counterfeit and dead stuff, in stead of real living members; like such as lose their eyes, armes, or legs, make counterfeit ones
of timber or glass, in stead of them. But we can not think so of Christ,
neither can we believe, for the reasons above adduced, that either we are
to account, or that Christ doth account, any man, or men, a whit the
more members of his body, because, though they be really wicked, they
hypocritically and deceitfully cloath themselves with his Name pretended
to it, for this is contrary to his own doctrin, where he saith expresly,
Joh. 15: 1, 2, 3, 4, 5, 6, &c. that *he is the Vine, and his Disciples are the
Branches, that except they abide in him, they can not bear fruit, and, if they be unfruitfull, they shall be cast forth, as a branch, and wither.* Now I suppose these
cut and withered branches are no more true branches, nor members of the
Vine, they can draw no more sap nor nourishment from it, after that they
are cut·off, and so have no more vertue, sap, nor life. What have they
then to boast or glory of any authority, seing they want that life, vertue
and nourishment, from which all authority comes? So such members of
Christ, as are become dead to him through unrighteousnes, and so derive
no more vertue nor life from him, are cut-off by their sins, and wither,
and have no more any true or real authority, and their boasting of any is
but an aggravation of their iniquity by hypocrisy and deceit. But further,
would not this make Christ's body a meer shaddow and phantam? Yea
would it not make him the head of a lifeless, rotten, stinking carcase,
having onely some little outward false shew, while inwardly full of rotten-
nes and dirt? and what a monster would these men make of Christ's body,
by assigning it a real, pure, living, quick Head, full of vertue and life,
and yet tied to such a dead, lifeless body, as we have already described
these members to be, which they alledg to have been the Church of Christ.
Again, the members of the *Church of Christ* are specified by this definition,
to wit, as being *the sanctified in Christ Jesus*, 1 Cor. 1: 2. But this notion of
succes-

ſucceſſion ſuppóſeth not onely ſome unſanctiſied members to be of the Church of Chriſt, but even the whole to conſiſt of unſanctiſied members, yea that ſuch as were profeſſed necromancers, and open ſervants of Satan, were the true ſucceſſors of the Apoſtles, and in whom the Apoſtolik authority reſided, theſe being the veſſels, through whom this ſucceſſion is tranſmitted, though many of them, as all Proteſtants, and alſo ſome Papiſts, confeſs, attained theſe offices in the (ſo called) Church, not onely by ſuch means as *Simon Magus* ſought it, but by much worſe, even by witchcraft, murther, traditions, money, and treachery, which Platina himſelf confeſſeth * of divers Biſhops of *Rome.*

§ X I. But ſuch as *object* not this ſucceſſion of the Church, (which yet moſt Proteſtants begin now to do) diſtinguiſh in this matter, affirming, *that, in a great apoſtaſy, ſuch as was that of the Church of Rome, God may raiſe up ſome ſingularly, by his Spirit, who, from the teſtimony of the Scripturs, perceiving the errors, into which ſuch as bear the name of Chriſtians are faln, may inſtruct and teach them, and then become authorized by the peopl's joyning with, and accepting of their miniſtery onely.* Moſt of them alſo will affirm *that the Spirit herein is ſubjective, and not objective.*

But they ſay, that, *where a Church is reformed,* ſuch as they pretend the Proteſtants Churches are, *there an ordinary orderly call is neceſſary; and that of the Spirit, as extraordinary, is not to be ſought after,* alledging that *res aliter ſe habet in eccleſiâ conſtituendâ, quàm in eccleſiâ conſtitutâ,* that is, *there is a difference in the conſtituting of a Church, and after it is conſtitut.*

I anſwer, this *objection* as to us ſaith nothing, ſeing we accuſe, and are ready from the Scripturs to prove the Proteſtants guilty of groſs errors, and needing reformation, as wel as they did, and do the Papiſts; and therefore we may juſtly lay claim, if we would, to the ſame extraordinary call, having the ſame reaſon for it, and as good evidence, to prove ours, as they had for theirs. As for that maxim, viz, *that the caſe is different in a conſtituting Church, and a Church conſtituted,* I do not deny it, and therefore there may be a greater meaſur of power required to the one, than to the other, and God in his Wiſdom diſtributs the ſame, as he ſeeth meet, but that the ſame immediat aſſiſtance of the Spirit is not neceſſary for miniſters in a gathered Church as wel as in gathering one, I ſee no ſolid reaſon alledged for it. For ſure Chriſt's promiſe was to be *with his children to the end of the world;* and they need him no leſs to preſerve and guide his Church and children, than to gather and beget them. Natur taught the Gentiles this maxim,

Non

Non minor est virtus, quam quærere parta tueri.

Englithed thus,

> For to defend what you attain
> Requires no lefs ftrength, than to gain.

For it is by this inward and immediat operation of the Spirit (which *Chrift* hath promifed to *lead his children* with *into all Truth*, and to *teach them all things*) that Chriftians are to be led in all fteps (as wel laft as firft) which relate to God's Glory and their own Salvation, as we have heretofore fufficiently proven, and therefore need not now repeat it. And truely this device of Satan, whereby he has got people to put the immediat guidings and leadings of God's Spirit, as an extraordinary thing, afar off, which their fore-fathers had, but which they now are neither to wait for, nor expect, is a great caufe of the growing apoftafy upon the many gathered Churches, and is one great reafon why a dry, dead, barren, lifelefs, fpiritlefs miniftery, which leavens the people into the fame death, doth fo much abound, and is fo much overfpreading even the Proteftant nations, that their preachings and worfhips, as wel as whole converfation, is not to be difcerned from Popifh by any frefh living zeal, or lively Power of the Spirit accompanying it, but meerly by the differenfe of fome notions and opinions.

Obj.

§ XII. Some unwife and unwary Proteftants do fometimes *object* to us, *that, if we have fuch an immediat call, as we lay claim to, we ought to confirm it by miracles.*

Anfw.

But this being an objection once and again objected to the primitive Proteftants by the Papifts, we need but fhort return the anfwer to it, that they did to the Papifts, to wit, that *we need not miracles, becaufe we preach no new Gofpel, but that, which is already confirmed by all the miracles of Chrift and his Apoftles, and that we offer nothing, but that, which we are ready and able to confirm by the teftimony of the Scripturs, which both already acknowledg to be true.* And that John the Baptift, and divers of the Prophets did none, that we hear of, and yet were both immediatly and extraordinarily fent. This is the common Proteftant anfwer, therefore may fuffice in this place, though, if need were, I could fay more to this purpofe, but that I ftudy brevity.

§ XIII. There is alfo another fort of Proteftants, to wit, the *Englifh Independents*, who, differing from the *Calviniftical Presbyterians*, and denying the neceffity of this fucceffion, or the authority of any *National Church*, take another way, affirming, *that fuch as have the benefit of the Scri-*

pturs,

ptirs, any company of people, agreing in the principles of Truth, as they find them there declared, may constitut among themselves a Church, without the authority of any other, and may chuse to themselves a pastor, who by the Church thus constitut and consenting, is authorized, requiring onely the assistançe and concurrence of the pastors of the neighbouring Churches, (if any be) not so much as absolutely neçessary to authorize, as decent for order's sake. Also they go so far as to affirm, that, in a Church so constitut, any *gifted brother*, as they call them, if he find himself qualified thereto, may instruct, exhort, and preach in the Church, though, as not having the pastoral office, he can not administer that they call their *Sacraments.*

To this I answer, that this was a good step out of the Babylonish darkness, and, no doubt, did proceed from a real discovery of the Truth, and from the sense of a great abuse of the promiscuous National gatherings. Also this preaching of the *Gifted Brethren* (as they called them) did proceed at first from certain lively touches and movings of the Spirit of God upon many. But, (alas!) because they went not fore-ward, that is much decayed among them, and the motions of God's Spirit begin to be deny-ed and rejected among them now, as much as by others.

But as to their *pretended call from the Scriptur*, I Answer: The Scriptur gives a meer declaration of true things, but no call to particular persons, so that though I believe the things there written to be true, and deny the errors, which I find there testified against, yet, as to these things which may be my particular duty, I am still to seek, and therefore I can never be resolved in the Scriptur, whether I such a one by name ought to be a mini-ster. And for the resolving this doubt, I must needs recurr to the inward and immediat testimony of the Spirit, as in the Proposition conçerning the Scripturs more at large is shewn.

§ XIV. From all this then we do firmly conclude, that not onely in a general apostasy it is needfull, men be extraordinarily called, and raised up by the Spirit of God, but that even when severall assemblys or Churches are gathered by the Power of God, not onely into the belief of the prin-çiples of Truth, so as to deny errors and heresies, but also into the life, Spirit, and Power of Christianity, so as to be the body and house of Christ indeed, and a fit spouse for him, that he who gathers them, doth also, for the preserving them in a lively, fresh, and powerfull condition, raise up, and move among them, by the inward immediat operation of his own Spirit, ministers and teachers to instruct and teach, and watch over them,

C c

who,

who, being thus called, are manifest in the hearts of their brethren, and their call is thus verified in them, who, by the feeling of that life and power, that passeth through them, being inwardly builded up by them daily in the *most holy faith* become the seals of their apostleship, and this is answerable to another saying of the same Apostle Paul, 2 Cor. 13: 3, *Since ye seek a proof of Christ speaking in me, which to you-wards is not weak, but is mighty in you.* So this is that, which gives a *true substantial call* and *title* to a *minister,* whereby he is a real successor of the vertue, life, and power, that was in the Apostles, and not of the bare name; and to such ministers we think the outward ceremony of ordination, or laying-on of hands, not necessary, neither can we see the use of it, seing our adversarys, who use it, acknowledg that the vertue and power of communicating the Holy Ghost by it is ceased among them. And is it not then foolish and ridiculous for them, by an apish imitation, to keep up the shaddow, where the substance is wanting? And may not they by the same rule, where they see blind and lame men, in imitation of Christ and his Apostles, bid them see and walk? yea is it not in them a mocking of God and men, to put-on their hands, and bid men *receive the Holy Ghost,* while they believe the thing impossible, and confess that that ceremony hath no real effect? Having thus far spoken of the *Call,* I shall proceed next to treat of the qualifications and work of a true minister.

§ XV. As I have placed the *true call* of a *minister* in the *motion-of* this *Holy Spirit,* so is the *power,* *life,* and *vertue* thereof, and the *pure Grace of God,* that comes therefrom, the *chief* and *most necessary qualification,* without which he can no ways perform his duty, neither acceptably to God, nor beneficially to men. Our adversarys in this case affirm that three things go to the making up of a minister, viz, 1. *natural parts,* that he be not a fool. 2. *acquired parts,* that he be learned in the languages, in Philosophy, and school-Divinity. 3. *the Grace of God.*

The two first they reckon necessary to the being of a Minister, so as a man can not be one without them: the third they say goeth to the welbeing of one, but not to the being; so that a man may truely be a lawfull minister without it, and ought to be heard and received as such. But we (supposing a natural capacity, that one be not an idiot) judg the Grace of God indispensibly necessary to the very being of a minister, as that, without which any can neither be a true, nor lawfull, nor good minister. As for letter-learning, we judg it not so much necessary to the wel-being of of one, though accidentally sometimes in certain respects it may concurr, but more frequently it is hurtfull than helpfull, as appeared in the example of *Taulerus*, who, being a learned man, and who could make an eloquent preaching, needed nevertheless to be instructed in the way of the Lord, by a poor laik. I shall first speak of the *necessity of Grace*, and then proceed to say something of that literatur, which they judg so needfull.

First then, as we said in the *Call*, so may we much more here. If the *Grace of God* be a necessary qualification to make one a true Christian, it must be a *qualification* much more necessary to constitut a true minister of Christianity. That Grace is necessary to make up a true Christian, I think will not be questioned, since it is *by Grace we are saved*, Eph. 2: 8. it is *the Grace of God, that teacheth us to deny ungodlynes, and the lusts of this world, and to live godlily and righteously,* Tit 2: 11. yea Christ saith expressly, that *without* him we can doe nothing, Joh 15: 5. and the way, whereby Christ helpeth, assisteth, and worketh with us, is by his Grace. Hence saith to Paul, *my Grace is sufficient for thee.* A Christian without Grace is indeed no Christian, but an hypocrit, and a false pretender. Then I say, *If Grace be necessary to a privat Christian, far more to a teacher among Christians, who must be as a father and instructor of others, seing this dignity is bestowed upon such as have attained a greater measur, than their brethren. Even Natur it self may teach us that there is more required in a teacher, than in those, that are taught, and that the master must be above and before the scholar in that art or science, which he teacheth others. Since then Christianity can not be truely enjoyed, neither any man denominated a Christian without the true Grace of God, Therefore neither can any man be a true nor lawfull teacher of Christianity without it.*

Secondly, No man can be a minister of the *Church of Christ,* which is his *body,* unless he be a member of the body, and receive of the vertue and life of the *Head*;

But he, that hath not true Grace, can neither be a member of the body, neither receive of that life and nourishment, which comes from the Head:

Therefore far less can he be a minister to edify the body.

That he can not be a minister, who is not a member, is evident, because who is not a member is shut out, and cut-off, and hath no place in the body, whereas the ministers are counted among the most eminent members of the body; But no man can be a member, unless he receive of the vertue, life, and nourishment of the Head: for the members, that receive

not

not this life and nourishment, decay, and wither, and then are cut-off. And that every true member doth thus receive nourishment and life from the Head, the Apostle expresfly affirmeth, Eph. 4: 16. *From whom the whole body being fitly joyned together, and compacted by that which every joynt supplyeth, according to the effectual working in the measur of every part, makes increase of the body, unto the edifying of it self in love.* Now this, that thus is communicated, and which thus uniteth the whole, is no other than the Grace of God, and therefore the Apostle in the same chapter, vers 7, *But unto every one of us is given Grace according to the measur of the gift of Christ,* and v. 11. he sheweth how that *by this Grace and Gift both Apostles, Prophets, Evangelists, pastors, and teachers are given for the work of the ministery and edifying of the body of Christ.* And certainly then no man, destitut of this Grace, is fit for this work, seing that all, that Christ gives, are so qualified ; and these, that are not so qualified, are not given, nor sent of Christ, are not to be heard, nor received, nor acknowledged as ministers of the Gospel, becaufe his sheep neither ought, nor will hear the voyce of a stranger. This is also clear from 1 Cor. 12. throughout, for the Apostle, in that chapter, treating of the diversity of gifts and members of the body, sheweth how by the working of the same Spirit in different manifestations or measurs in the several members the whole body is edified, saying, v. 13. that *we are all baptized by the One Spirit into one body,* and then v. 28. he numbers out the several dispensations thereof, which by God are set in the Church through the various working of his Spirit, for the edification of the whole.   Then, if there be no true member of the body, which is not thus baptized by this Spirit, neither any thing, that worketh to the edifying of it, but according to a measur of Grace received from the Spirit, surely without Grace none ought to be admitted to work or labour in the body, becaufe their labor and work, without this Grace and Spirit, would be but ineffectual.

§ XVI. Thirdly, that this *Grace* and *Gift* is a *necessary qualification* to a *minister,* is clear from that of the Apostle Peter, 1 Pet. 4: 10, 11. *As every man hath received the Gift, even so minister the same one to another, as good stewards of the manifold Grace of God. If any man speak, let him speak as the oracles of God ; if any man minister, let him doe it as of the ability which God giveth, that God in all things may be glorified through Jesus Christ ; to whom be praise and dominion for ever and ever. Amen.* From which it appears, that these, that minister, must minister according to the Gift and Grace received, but they, that have not such a Gift, can not minister according thereunto.

Secondly,

Secondly, *as good stewards of the manifold Grace of God:* but how can a man be a good steward of that, which he hath not? Can urgedly men, that are not gracious themselves, be good stewards of the manifold Grace of God? and therefore in the following verses he makes an exclusive limitation of such as are not thus furnished, saying, *if any man speak, let him speak as the oracles of God; and if any man minister, let him doe it as of the ability that God giveth,* which is as much, as if he had said, They, that can not thus speak, and thus minister, ought not to doe it: for this [*If*] denotats a necessary condition. Now what this ability is, is manifest by the former words, to wit, the Gift received, and the Grace, whereof they are stewards, as by the immediat context and dependency of the words doth appear: neither can it be understood of a meer natural ability, because man in this condition is said *not to know the things of God,* and so he can not minister them to others. And the following words shew this also, in that he immediately subjoyneth, *that God in all things may be glorified:* but surely God is not glorified, but greatly dishonoured, when natural men from their meer natural ability meddle in Spiritual things, which they neither know nor understand.

Fourthly, that Grace is a most necessary qualification for a minister, appears by these qualifications, which the Apostle expresly requires, 1 Tim. 3: 2. Tit. 1: &c. where he saith, *a bishop must be blameleß, vigilant, sober, of good behaviour, apt to teach, patient, a lover of good men, just, holy, temperat, as the steward of God, holding fast the faithfull Word, as he hath been taught.* Upon the other hand, *he must neither be given to wine, nor a striker, nor covetous, nor proud, nor self willed, nor soon angry.* Now I ask, If it be not impossible, that a man can have all these above named vertues, and be free of all these evils, without the Grace of God? If then these vertues (for the produceing of which in a man Grace is absolutely necessary) be necessary to make a true minister of the Church of Christ, according to the Apostles judgment, surely Grace must be necessary also.

Concerning this thing a learned man, and wel skilled in *Antiquity,* about the time of the reformation, writeth thus, *Whatsoever is done in the Church, either for ornament or edification of religion, whether in chusing magistrats, or instituting ministers of the Church, except it be done by the ministery of God's Spirit, which is, as it were, the Soul of the Church, it is vain and wicked. For whoever hath not been called by the Spirit of God to the great office of God, and dignity of Apostleship, as Aaron was, and hath not entred in by the door which is*

Christ,

* Franciscus Lambertus Avenionensis, in in his book concerning Prophecy, learning, tongues, and the Spirit of Prophecy. Argentorat. excuf. annô 1516 de prov: cap. 24.

Christ, but hath either ways risen in the Church by the window, by the favours of men, &c. truely such a one is not the vicar of Christ and the Apostles, but a thief and a robber, and the vicar of Judas Iscariot, and Simon the Samaritan. Hence it was so strictly appoynted concerning the election of Prelats (which holy Dionysius *calls the Sacrament of Nomination) that the bishops and apostles, who should oversee the service of the Church, should be men of most intire manners and life, powerfull in sound doctrin to give a reason for all things.* So also * another about the same time writeth thus, *Therefore it can never be, that by the tongues or learning any can give a sound judgment concerning the Holy Scripturs and the Truth of God. Lastly (*saith he*) the sheep of Christ seeketh nothing but the voice of Christ, which he knoweth by the holy Spirit, wherewith he is filled : he regards not learning, tongues, or any outward thing, so as therefore to believe this or that to be the voice of Christ his true shepherd, he knoweth that there is need of no other thing, but the testimony of the Spirit of God.*

§ XVII. Against this absolut necessity of grace they object, *that, if all ministers had the saving Grace of God, then all ministers should be saved, seing none can fall away from, or lose Saving Grace.*

Anfw.

But this objection is built upon a false *hypothesis*, purely denyed by us, and we have, in the former Proposition concerning *Perseverance*, already refuted it.

Obj.

Secondly, it may be objected to us, *that, since we affirm that every man hath a measur of true and Saving Grace, there needs no singular qualification neither to a Christian, nor minister, for, seing every man hath this Grace, then no man needs forbear to be a minister, for want of Grace.*

Anfw.

I answer, we have above shewn, that there is necessary, to the making a minister, a special and particular call from the Spirit of God, which is something besides the universal dispensation of Grace to *all*, according to that of the Apostle, *No man taketh this honor unto himself, but he, that is called of God, as was Aaron.* Moreover, we understand by Grace, as a qualification to a minister, not the meer measur of Light, as it is given to reprove, and call him to righteousness : but we understand *Grace*, as it hath converted the Soul, and operateth powerfully in it, as hereafter, concerning the *work of ministers*, will further appear. So we understand not men simply, as having *Grace* in them, as a *Seed*, (which we indeed affirm *all* have, in a measur) but we understand *men*, that are *gratious*, leavened by it, into the natur thereof, so as thereby to bring forth these good fruits of a blameless conversation, and of justice, holyness, patience, and temperance,

Heb. 5: 4.

perance, which the Apostle requires as necessary in a true Christian Bishop and minister.

Thirdly, they * object the *example of the false Prophets, of the Pharisees,
and of Judas.*

But first, As to the false Prophets; there can nothing be more foolish
and ridiculous, as if, because there were false Prophets, truely false,
without the Grace of God, therefore Grace is not necessary to a true Christian minister. Indeed, if they had proven that true Prophets wanted this
Grace, they had said something. But what have false Prophets common
with true ministers? but that they pretend falsely that, which they have
not. And, because false Prophets want true Grace, will it therefore follow, that true Prophets ought not to have it, or need it not? yea doth it not
much rather follow, that they ought to have it, that they may be true,
and not false? The example of the Pharisees and Priests under the Law
will not answer to the Gospel times, because God set apart a particular
tribe for that service, and particular families, to whom it belonged by a
lineal succession; and also their service and work was not purely Spiritual,
but onely the performance of some outward and carnal observations and
ceremonys, which were but a shaddow of the Snbstance, that was to
come, and therefore their work *made not the comers thereunto perfect as pertaining to the Conscience*, seing they were appoynted onely according to
the Law of a carnal commandment, and not according to the power of an
endless life. Notwithstanding, as in the figur they behoved to be *without
blemish*, as to their outward man, and, in the performance of their work,
they behoved to be washed, and purified from their outward pollutions;
so now under the Gospel times the *ministers* in the anti-typ must be inwardly *without blemish in their Soules and spirits*, being, as the Apostle requires, blameless, and in their work and service must be pure, and undefiled, from their inward pollutions, and so clean and holy, *that they may
offer up Spiritual sacrifices, acceptable to God by Jesus Christ*, 1 Pet. 2: 5.
As to Judas, the season of his ministery was not wholly Evangelical, as
being, before the *work was finished*, and while Christ, himself, and his
Disciples were yet subject to the Jewish observances and constitutions,
and therefore his commission, as wel as that, which the rest received with
him at that time, was *onely to the house of Israel*, Matth. 10: 5,6. which
made that by vertue of that commission the rest of the Apostles were not
impowered to go forth and preach after the resurrection, untill they had

wait-

waited at Jerusalem for the pouring-forth of the Spirit. So that it appears, Judas's ministery was more Legal, than *Evangelical.* Secondly, Judas's case, as all will acknowledg, was singular, and extraordinary, he being immediatly called by Christ himself, and accordingly furnished and impowered by him to preach, and doe miracles, which immediat commission our adversaries do not so much as pretend to, and so fall short of Judas, who trusted in Christ's words, and therefore went forth and preached, *without gold or silver, or scrip for his journey, giving freely,* as he had *freely received,* which our adversaries will not do, as hereafter shall be observed; Also, that Judas at that time had not the least measur of God's Grace, I have not as yet heard proved. But is it not sad, that even Protestants should lay aside the eleven good and faithfull Apostles, and all the rest of the holy disciples and ministers of Christ, and betake them to that one, of whom it was testified that he was a devil, for a pattern, and example to their ministery? Alas! it is to be regreted that too many of them resemble this pattern over much.

* Ibid Nic. Arnoldus.

Obj.   Another objection is usually made against the necessity of Grace, * *that, in case it were necessary, then such as wanted it could not truely administer the Sacraments, and consequently the people would be left in doubts and infinit scruples, as not knowing certainly whether they had truely received them, because not knowing infallibly whether the administrators were truely gratious men.*

Answ.   But this objection hitteth not us at all, because the natur of that Spiritual and Christian worship, which we, according to the Truth, plead for, is such as is not necessarily attended with these carnal and outward institutions, from the administring of which the objection ariseth, and so hath not any such absurdity following upon it, as will afterwards more clearly appear

§ XVIII. Though then we make not human learning necessary, yet we are far from excluding true learning, to wit, that learning, which proceedeth from the inward teachings and instructions of the Spirit, whereby the Soul learneth the secret wayes of the Lord, becomes acquainted with many inward travels and exercises of the mind, and learneth by a living experience how to overcome evil and the temptations of it, by *following the Lord,* and *walking in his Light,* and *waiting daily for wisdom and knowledg immediatly from the revelation thereof,* and *so layeth up these heavenly and Divine lessons in the good treasur of the heart,* as honest *Mary* did the sayings, which she heard, and things, which she observed; and also

out

out of this treasur of the Soul, as the good Scribe, brings forth things new and old, according as the same Spirit moves, and gives a true liberty, and as need is for the Lord's glory, whose the Soul is, and for whom, and with an eye to whose glory, she, which is the Temple of God, learneth to doe all things. This is that good learning, which we think neçeffary to a true Minifter, by and through which learning a man can wel inftruct, teach, and admonifh in due feafon, and teftify for God from a certain experience, as did David, Solomon, and the holy Prophets of old, and the bleffed Apoftles of our Lord Jefus Chrift, *who teftified of what they had feen, beard, felt, and handled of the Word of Life*, 1 Joh. 1: 1. *miniftring the Gift, according as they had received the fame, as good ftewards of the manifold Grace of God*, and preached not the uncertain rumors of others, by hear-fay, which they had gathered meerly in the comprehenfion, while they were ftrangers to the thing in their own experience in themfelves: as to teach people how to believe, while themfelves were unbelieving, or how to overcome fin, while themfelves are flaves to it, as all ungracious men are, or to believe and hope for an eternal reward, which themfelves have not as yet arrived at, &c.

§ X I X, But let us examin this literatur, which they make fo neçef-fary to the being of a minifter; as in the firft place, the knowledg of the *tongues*, at leſt of the *Latine*, *Greek*, and *Hebrew*. The reafon for this is, that they may read the Scripturs, which is their onely Rule, in the original languages, and thereby be the more capable to comment upon it, and interpret it, &c. That alfo, which made this knowledg be the more prized by the primitive Proteftants, was indeed that dark Barbarity, that was over the world, in the centurys immediately preceeding the reforma-tion; the knowledg of the tongues being about that time, untill it was even then reftored by *Erafmus* and fome others, almoft loft and extinct. And this barbarity was fo much the more abominable, that the whole worfhip and prayers of the people was in the Latine tongue, and, among that vaft number of priefts, monks and friers, fcarçe one of a thoufand underftood his breviary, or that mafs, that he daily read and repeated. The Scripturs being not onely to the people, but to the greater part of the Clergy, even as to the literal knowledg of it, as a fealed book. I fhall not at all difcommend the zeal, that the firft Reformers had, againft this Babylonifh darknefs, nor their pious endeavours to tranflate the Holy Scripturs, but I do truely believe, according to their knowledg, that they

D d

did

did it candidly : and therefore, to anſwer the juſt deſires of thoſe, that
deſire to read them, and for other very good reaſons, as maintaining a
commerſe and underſtanding among divers nations by theſe common
languages and other of that kind, we judge it neceſſary and commendable, there be publik ſchools, for the teaching and inſtructing youth,
as are inclinable thereunto, in the languages. And, although that *Papal
ignorance* deſerved juſtly to be abhorred and abominated, we ſee nevertheleſs that the true reformation conſiſts not in that knowledg, becauſe,
although, ſince that time, the Papiſts, ſtirred up through emulation of
the Proteſtants, have more applied themſelves unto literatur, and it now
more flouriſheth in their univerſitys, and cloyſters, than before, eſpecially in the Ignatian or Jeſuitik ſect, they are as far now, as ever, from
a true reformation, and more obdured in their pernicious doctrines. But
all this will not make this a neceſſary qualification to a miniſter, far leſs a
more neceſſary qualification, than the Grace of God and his Spirit, becauſe the Spirit and Grace of God can make up this want in the moſt
ruſtik and ignorant. But this knowledg can no ways make up the want of
the Spirit in the moſt learned and eloquent. For all that, which man by
his own induſtry, learning, and knowledg in the languages, can interpret of the Scripturs, or find out, is nothing without the Spirit, he can
not be certain of it, and may ſtill miſs of the ſenſe of it ; but a poor man,
that knoweth not a letter, when he heareth the Scripturs read, by the
ſame Spirit, he can ſay this is true, and by the ſame Spirit he can underſtand, open, and interpret it, if need be : yea he, finding his condition
to anſwer the condition and experience of the Saints of old, knoweth and
poſſeſſeth the Truths there delivered, becauſe they are ſealed and witneſſed in his own heart by the ſame Spirit. And this we have plentifull
experience of, in many of thoſe illiterat men, whom God hath raiſed up to
be miniſters in his Church in this day, ſo that ſome ſuch by his Spirit have
corrected ſome of the *errors* of the *Tranſlators*, as in the third Propoſition,
concerning the Scripturs, I before obſerved. Yea I know my ſelf a poor
ſhoe-maker, that can not read a word, who, being aſſaulted with a falſe
citation of Scriptur, from a publik Profeſſor of Divinity, before the Magi-
ſtrat of a City, when he had been taken preaching to ſome few, that came
to hear him, I ſay, I know ſuch a one, and he yet liveth, who, though
the Profeſſor (who alſo is eſteemed a learned man) conſtantly aſſerted
his ſaying to be a Scriptur ſentence, yet affirmed, not through any certain

letter

letter knowledg he had of it, but from the most *certain evidence of the Spirit in himself*, that the Professor lyed, and that the Spirit of God never said any such thing as the other affirmed, and the Bible being brought, it was found as the poor shoe-maker had said.

§ XX. The second part of their Literatur is *Logik* and *Philosophy*, an art so little needfull to a true minister, that, if one, that comes to be a true minister, hath had it, it is safest for him to forget and lose it; for it is the root and ground of all contention and debate, and the way to make a thing a great deal darker, than clearer. For under the pretence of regulating man's Reason into a certain order and rules, that he may find out, as they pretend, the Truth, it leads into such a labyrinth of contention, as is far more fit to make a *Sceptik* than a Christian, far less a minister of Christ; yea it often hinders man from a clear understanding of things, that his own Reason would give him: and therefore, through its manifold rules and divers inventions, it often gives occasion for a man, that hath little reason, foolishly to speak much to no purpose. Seing a man, that is not very wise, may notwithstanding be a perfect Logician, and then, if ye would make a man a fool to purpose, that is not very wise, do but teach him *Logik* and *Philosophy*, and, whereas before he might have been fit for something, he shall then be good for nothing, but to speak none-sense, for these notions will so swim in his head, that they will make him extreamly busy about nothing. The use, that wise men and solid make of it, is, to see the emptyness thereof; therefore saith one, *It is an art of contention and darkness, by which all other sciences are rendered more obscure, and harder to be understood.*

If it be urged, that *thereby the Truth may be maintained and confirmed, and* Inst. *heretiks confuted*,

I answer, the Truth, in men truely rational, needeth not the help Answ. thereof, and such as are obstinat, this will not convince, for by this they may learn twenty tricks and distinctions, how to shut out the Truth; and * Lucæ the Truth proceeding from an honest heart, and spoken forth from the Osiandri Vertue and Spirit of God will have more influence, and take sooner and epit. hist. more effectually, than by a thousand demonstrations of *Logik*, , as that * Ecclef. Heathen Philosopher acknowledged, who, disputing with the Christian lib. 2. Bishops in the counsil of *Nice*, was so subtile, that he could not be over- cent. 4. come by them, but yet by a few words, spoken by a simple old rustik, was presently convinced by him, and converted to the Christian faith, and

D d 2   being

being inquired how he came to yeeld to that ignorant old man, and not to the Bishops, he said, that *they contended with him in his own way, and he could still give words for words, but there came from the old man that vertue, which he was not able to resist.* This *secret vertue* and *power* ought to be the *Logik* and *Philosophy,* wherewith a true Christian minister ought to be furnished, and for which they need not be beholden to *Aristotel.* As to *natural Logik,* by which rational men, without that art and rules, or sophistical learning, deduce a certain conclusion out of true Propositions, which scarce any man of Reason wants, we deny not the use of it, and I have sometimes used it in this Treatise, which also may ſerve without that *Dialectical* art. As for the other part of *Philosophy,* which is called *Moral,* or *Ethicks,* it is not so necessary to Christians, who have the rules of the holy Scripturs, and the Gift of the Holy Spirit, by which they can be much better instructed. The *Physical* and *Metaphysical* part may be reduced to the arts of *Medicin* and the *Mathematiks,* which have nothing to doe with the essence of a Christian minister. And therefore the Apostle Paul, who wel understood what was good for Christian ministers, and what hurtfull, thus exhorted the Colossians, Col. 2: 8. *Beware lest any man spoil you through Philosophy and vain deceit.* And to his beloved disciple Timothy he writs also thus, 1 Tim. 6: 20. *O Timothy, keep that which is committed to thy trust, avoiding profane and vain bablings, and oppositions of science, falsly so called.*

§ XXI. The third and main part of their literatur is *school Divinity,* a *monster* made up betwixt some Scriptural notions of Truth, and the Heathenish terms and maxims, being, as it were, the *Heathenish Philosophy Christianized,* or rather the *literal external knowledg of Christ Heathenized;* it is man in his first faln natural state, with his devilish wisdom, pleasing himself with some notions of Truth, and adorning them with his own ſerpentin and worldly wisdom, because he thinks the simplicity of the Truth too low and mean a thing for him, and so despiseth that simplicity, wheresoever it is found, that he may set up and exalt himself, puffed up with this his monstrous birth; it is the devil darkening, obscuring, and vailing the knowledg of God with his sensual and carnal wisdom, that so he may the more securely deceive the hearts of the simple, and make the Truth, as it is in it self, despicable and hard to be known and understood, by multiplying a thousand hard and needless questions, and endless contentions and debats, all which whoso perfectly knoweth, he is not a whit

less

lefs the fervant of fin, than he was, but ten times more, in that he is exalted and proud of iniquity, and fo much the further from receiving, underftanding or learning the Truth, as it is in its own naked fimplicity, becaufe he is full, learned, rich, and wife in his own conçeit; and fo thofe, that are moft skilled in it, wear out their day, and fpend their pretious time about the infinit and innumerable queftions they have feigned and invented conçerning it. A certain learned man called it *a two-fold difçiplin, as of the raçe of the centaurs, partly proceeding from Divine fayings, partly from Philofophical reafons.* A thoufand of their queftions they confefs themfelves to be no ways neceffary to Salvation, and yet many more of them they could never agree upon, but are and ftill will be in endlefs janglings about them. The volums, that have been written about it, a man in his whole age, though he lived very old, could fcarce read, and when he has read them all, he has but wrought himfelf a great deal more vexation and trouble of fpirit, than he had before. Thefe certainly are the *words multiplied without knowledg, by which counfil hath been darkened,* Job. c. 38: v. 2. They make the Scriptur the text of all this mafs, and it's concerning the fenfe of it that their voluminous debats arife. But a man of a good upright heart may learn more in half an hour, and be more certain of it by waiting upon *God* and his *Spirit in the heart,* than by reading a thoufand of their volums, which by filling his head with many needlefs imaginations may wel ftagger his faith, but never confirm it; and indeed thofe, that give themfelves moft to it, are moft capable to fall into error, as appeareth by the example of *Origen,* who, by his learning, was one of the firft, that, falling into this way of interpreting the Scripturs, wrot fo many volums, and in them fo many errors, as very much troubled the Church. Alfo *Arius* led by this curiofity and humane fcrutiny, defpifing the fimplicity of the Gofpel, fell into his *error,* which was the caufe of that horrible herefy, which fo much troubled the Church; me thinks the fimplicity, plainnefs, and brevity of the Scripturs themfelves fhould be a fufficient reproof for fuch a fcience; and the Apoftles being honeft, plain, illiterat men, may be better underftood by fuch kind of men now, than with all that mafs of fcholaftik ftuff, which neither Peter, nor Paul, nor John ever thought of.

§ XXII. But this invention of Satan, wherewith he began the apoftafy, hath been of dangerous confequençe, for thereby he at firft fpoiled the fimplicity of Truth, by keeping up the Heathenifh learning, which

occa-

occafioned fuch uncertainty even among thofe, called *Fathers*, and fuch debate, that there are few of them to be found, who, by reafon of this mixtur, do not onely frequently contradict one another, but themfelves alfo. And therefore, when the *apoftafy* grew greater, he, as it were, buried the Truth with this vail of darknefs, wholly fhuting out people from true knowledg, and making the *Learned*, fo accounted, bufy themfelves with idle and needlefs queftions, while the weighty Truths of God were neglected, and, as it were, went into defuetud. Now, though the groffeft of thefe abufes be fwept away by Proteftants yet the evil root ftill remaines, and is nourifhed and upheld, and upon the growing hand, that this fcience is ftill kept up, and deemed neceffary for a minifter; for, while the pure learning of the *Spirit of Truth* is defpifed and neglected, and made ineffectual, man's faln, earthly wifdom is upheld, and fo in that he labours and works with the Scripturs, being out of the *Life* and *Spirit*, thofe that wrot them, were in, by which they are onely rightly underftood, and made ufe of. And fo he, that is to be a *minifter*, muft learn this *art* or *trade* of *merchandizing* with the *Scripturs*, and be that, which the Apoftle would not be, to wit, a trader with them, 2 Cor. 2: 17. That he may acquire a trick from a verfe of Scriptur, by adding his own barren notions and conceptions to it, and his uncertain conjecturs, and what he hath ftoln out of books, (for which end he muft have of neceffity a good many by him) and may each Sabbath day, (as they call it) or oftener make a difcourfe for an hour long, and this is called *the preaching of the word*, whereas the Gift, Grace, and Spirit of God, to teach, open, and inftruct, and to preach a word in feafon, is neglected; and fo man's *arts* and *parts*, and *knowledg* and *wifdom*, which is *from below*, fet up and eftablifhed in the Temple of God, yea and above the little *Seed*: which in effect is anti-Chrift working in the myftery; and fo the devil may be as good and able a minifter, as the beft of them, for he has better skill of languages, and more Logik, Philofophy and fchool Divinity, than any of them, and knowes the Truth in the notion, better than they all, and can talk more eloquently, than all thofe preachers. But what availeth all this? Is it not all but as death, as a painted fepulchre, and dead carcafe without the Power, Life, and Spirit of Chriftianity, which is the marrow and fubftance of a Chriftian miniftery, and he, that hath this, and can fpeak from it, though he be a poor fhepherd, or a fifher man, and ignorant of all that learning, and of all thofe queftions and

notions,

See alfo
2 Pet. 2 :
vers 3.

notions, yet speaking from the Spirit, his ministery will have more influence towards the converting of a sinner unto God, than all of them, learned after the flesh, as in that example of the old man at the Council of *Nice* did appear.

§ XXIII. And if in any age, since the Apostles days, God hath purposed to shew his Power by weak instruments, for the battering down of that carnal and Heathenish wisdom, and restoring again the antient simplicity of Truth, this is it; for in our day God hath raised up witnesses for himself, as he did fisher men of old, many, yea most of whom are labouring and mechanik men, who altogether, without that learning, have by the Power and Spirit of God struk at the very root and ground of Babylon, and in the strength and might of this Power have gathered thousands, by reaching their Consciences, into the same Power and Life; who, as to the outward part, have been far more knowing than they, yet not able to resist the vertue, that proceeded from them. Of which I my self am a true witness, and can declare from a certain experience, because my heart hath been often greatly broken and tendered by that vertuous Life, that hath proceeded from the powerfull ministery of those illiterat men; so that by their very countenance, as wel as words, I have felt the evil in me often chained down, and the good reached to, and raised. What shall I then say to you, who are lovers of learning, and, admirers of knowledg? Was not I also a lover and admirer of it, who also sought after it, according to my age and capacity? But it pleased God in his unutterable love early to withstand my vain endeavours, while I was yet but eighteen years of age, and made me seriously to consider (which I wish also may befall others) that *without holiness and regeneration no man can see God*, and that *the fear of the Lord is the beginning of wisdom, and to depart from iniquity a good understanding.* And how *much knowledg puffeth up*, and leadeth away from that inward quietness, stilness, and humility of mind, where the Lord appears, and his heavenly wisdom is revealed. If ye consider these things, then will ye say with me that all this learning, wisdom, and knowledg gathered in this faln natur is but as *dross* and *dung, in comparison of the Cross of Christ*, especially being destitut of that Power, Life, and Vertue, which I perceived these excellent, though despised, because illiterat, Witnesses of God to be filled with; and therefore, seing that, in and among them, I with many others have found the *heavenly food*, that gives contentment, let my Soul seek after this learning, and wait for it for ever.

Job 28:
vers 28.

§ XXIV.

§ XXIV. Having thus spoken of the *Call* and *qualifications* of a *Gospel minister*, that, which comes next to be considered, is, *What his proper work is, how, and by what rule, he is to be ordered.* Our *adversaries* do all along go upon *outwards*, and therefore have certain prescribe'd rules and methods contrived, according to their human and earthly wisdom. We, on the contrary, walk still upon the same foundation, and lean always upon the immediat assistance and influence of that Holy Spirit, which God hath given his children to teach them all things, and lead them in all things; which Spirit, being the *Spirit of order* and *not of confusion*, leads us, and as many as follow it, into such a comely and decent order, as becometh the Church of God. But our adversaries, having shut themselves out from this immediat counsil and influence of the Spirit, have run themselves into many confusions and disorders, seeking to establish an order in this matter. For some will have first a chief Bishop or *Pope* to rule and be Prince over all, and under him by degree *Cardinals, Patriarchs, arch-Bishops, Priests, deacons, sub-deacons*, and besides these, *acoluthi, tonsorati, ostiarii*, &c. And in their Theology, as they call it, *Professors, bachelors, doctors*, &c. And others are to have every nation *independent* of another, having its own *metropolitan*, or *patriarch*, and the rest in order subject to him, as before. Others again are against all *precedency* among *pastors*, and constitut their subordination not of persons, but of powers, as first the *consistory*, or *session*, then the *classe*, or *presbytery*, then the *provincial*, and then the *national synod* or *assembly*. Thus do they tear one another, and contend among themselves concerning the ordering, distinguishing, and making their several orders and offices, concerning which there hath been no less contest, not onely by way of verbal disput, but even by fighting, tumults, wars, vastations, and blood-shed, than about the conquering, overturning, and establishing of kingdoms. And the historys of late times are as full of the various tragedys, acted upon the account of this *Spiritual* and *Ecclesiastik Monarchy* and *common wealth*, as the historys of old times, that gave account of the wars and contests, that fell out both in the *Assyrian, Persian, Greek*, and *Roman* impires. These last upon this account, though among those, that are called Christians, have been no less bloody and monstrous, than the former among Heathens, concerning their outward impires and governments. Now all this, both among Papists and Protestants, proceedeth, in that they seek in imitation to uphold a form and shaddow of things, though they want the Power, Vertue, and

Sub-

Substance, though for many of their orders and forms they have not so much as the name in the Scriptur. But, in opposition to all this mass of formality and heap of orders, rules and governments, we say, *the Substance is chiefly to be sought after, and the Power, Vertue, and Spirit is to be known, and waited for, which is One* in all the different names and offices the Scriptur makes use of, as appears by 1 Cor. 12. often before mentioned, *There are diversitys of gifts, but the same Spirit.* And after the Apostle throughout the whole chapter hath shewn how one and the self same Spirit worketh *in*, and quickeneth, each member, then in the 28 verse he sheweth how thereby God hath set in the Church, first *Apostles*, secondly *Prophets, teachers*, &c. And likewise to the same purpose, Eph. 4. he sheweth how *by these Gifts he hath given some Apostles, some Prophets, some Evangelists, some pastors, some teachers*, &c. Now it was never Christ's purpose nor the Apostles, that Christians should without this Spirit and Heavenly Gift, set up a shaddow and form of these orders, and so make several ranks and degrees, to establish a carnal ministery of mens making, without the Life, Power, and Spirit of Christ: this is that work of anti-Christ and mystery of iniquity, that hath got up in the dark night of apostasy; but in a true Church of Christ, gathered together by God, not onely unto the belief of the principles of Truth, but also into the Power, Life, and Spirit of Christ, the Spirit of God is the Orderer, Ruler, and Governour, as in each particular, so in the general: and when they assemble together, to wait upon God and worship and adore him, then such as the Spirit sets apart to the ministery by its Divine Power and influence, opening their mouths, and giving them to exhort, reprove, and instruct with vertue and power, these are thus of God ordained and admitted into the ministery, and their brethren can not but hear them, receive them, and also *honour them for their wor'ks sake*, and so this is not monopolized to a certain kind of men, as the Clergy (who are to that purpose educated and brought up, as other carnal artists) and the rest to be despised as laïks: but it is left to the *free Gift of God*, to chuse any, whom he seeth meet thereunto, whether rich, or poor, servant, or master, young, or old, yea male, or female. And such as have this call, verify the Gospel, by *preaching not in speech onely, but also in power, and in the Holy Ghost, and in much fulness*, 1 Thess. 1 : 5. and can not but be received and heard by the sheep of Christ.

§ XXV. But if it be objected here, *that I seem hereby to make no distin-*

ction at all betwixt ministers and others, which is contrary to the Apostle, saying, 1 *Cor.* 12:29. *Are all Apostles? are all Prophets? are all Teachers?* &c. from thence they insinuat, *that I also contradict his comparison, in that chapter, of the Church of Christ with a humane body, as where he saith,* verse 17. *If the whole body were an eye, where were the hearing? If the whole were hearing, where were the smelling,* &c.? *Also the Apostle not onely thus distinguisheth the ministers of the Church in general, from the rest of the members, but also among themselves, as naming them, distinctly and separatly; Apostles, Prophets, Evangelists, Pastors and Teachers,* &c.

Answ.   As to the last part of this objection, to which I shall first answer, it is apparent, that this deversity of names is not for to distinguish separat offices, but to denotat the different and various operations of the Spirit, a manner of speech frequent with the Apostle Paul, wherein he sometimes expatiats to the illustrating of the glory and praise of God's Grace, as in particular, Rom. 12: 6. *Having then gifts, differing according to the Grace, that is given to us, whether prophecy, let us prophesie according to the proportion of faith; Or ministery,* let us wait on our *ministring; or he that teacheth, on teaching; Or he that exhorteth, on exhortation.* Now none will say from all this that these are distinct offices, or do not or may not coincide in one person, as may all these others things mentioned by him, in the subsequent verses, viz, *of loving, being kindly affectioned, fervency of spirit, hospitality, diligence, blessing, rejoycing,* &c. Which yet he numbers forth as different gifts of the Spirit. And, according to this objection, might be placed as distinct and separat offices, which were most absurd.

Secondly, in these very places mentioned it is clear, that it is no real distinction of separat offices, because all acknowledg, that pastors and teachers, which the Apostle there no less separateth and distinguisheth, than pastors and prophets or Apostles, are one and the same, and coincide in the same office and person, and therefore so may be said of the rest. For [*Prophecy,*] as it signifieth *the foretelling of things to come,* is indeed a distinct gift, but no distinct office, and therefore our adversarys do not place it among their several orders, neither will they deny but that both may be and have been given of God to some, that not onely have been pastors and teachers, and that there it hath coincided in one person with these other offices, but also to some of the laiks, and so it hath been found, according to their own concession, without the limits of their *Clergy. Prophecy,* in the other sense, to wit, as it signifieth *a speaking from the*

Spirit

Spirit of Truth, is not only peculiar to pastors and teachers, who ought so to prophesie, but even a common priviledg to the Saints : for, though to inltruct, teach and exhort be proper to such, as are more particularly called to the work of the ministery, yet it is not so proper to them, as not to be, when the Saints are met together, as any of them are moved by the Spirit, common to others : for some acts belong to all in such a relation, but not onely to those within that relation ; *competunt omni, sed non soli* : thus to *see* and *hear* are *proper acts* of a *man* : seing it may be properly predicated of him, that he heareth and seeth, yet are they common to other creaturs also. So to *prophesie*, in this sense, is indeed proper to ministers and teachers, yet not so, but that it is also common and lawfull to other Saints, when moved thereunto, though it be not proper to them by way of relation, because, notwithstanding that motion, they are not particularly called to the work of the ministery, as appears by 1 Cor. 14. where the Apostle at large declaring the order and ordinary method of the Church, saith, ver. 30, 31. *But*, *if any thing be revealed to another, that sitteth by*, *let the first hold his peace. For ye may all prophesie one by one*, *that all may learn*, *and all may be comforted* ; which sheweth that none is here excluded. But yet that there is a subordination according to the various measurs of the Gift received, the next verse sheweth, *And the spirits of the Prophets are subject to the Prophets. For God is not the* author *of confusion*, *but of peace.* Now that *prophecying*, in this sense, may be *common to all Saints*, appears by the 39 verse of the same chapter, where, speaking to [*all*] in general, he saith, *Therefore*, *brethren*, *covet to prophesie* : and verse 1. he exhorts them, saying, *covet Spiritual* gifts, *but the rather that ye may prophesie.*

Secondly, as to Evangelists, the same may be said ; for whoever preacheth the Gospel, is really an Evangelist, and so consequently every true minister of the Gospel is one, else what proper office can they assign to it, unless they should be so foolish, as to affirm, that none were Evangelists, but *Matthew*, *Mark*, *Luk*, and *John*, who wrot the account of Christ's life and sufferings ? And then it were neither a particular office, seing John & Matthew were Apostles, Mark and Luk pastors and teachers, so that there they coincided in one, and indeed it is absurd to think, that, upon that particular account the Apostle used the word [*Evangelist*]. *Calvin* acknowledgeth, th*at such*, *as preach the Gospel in puri*t*y after some time of apostasy*, *may be truely called Evangelists*, and th*ere*for*e* saith, that *there were Apostles in his time* ; and hence the Protestants, at their first coming forth, termed themselves *Evangelici*, or *Evangelists*.   E e 2   La st ‑

Laſtly, an *Apoſtle*, if we look to the etymology of the word, ſignifies one, that is ſent, and in reſpect *every true miniſter is ſent of God*, in ſo far he is an Apoſtle, though theſe twelve, becauſe of their being ſpecially *ſent of* Chriſt, were therefore called *Apoſtles*, κατ' ἐξοχύν, or *per eminentiam*, i. e: by way of excellency. And yet that there was no limitation to ſuch a number, as ſome fooliſhly imagin, it appears, becauſe, after that number was filled up, the Apoſtle Paul was afterwards ſo called; therefore we judg that theſe are no diſtinct ſeparat offices, but onely names, uſed upon occaſions, to expreſs the more eminent ariſing and ſhining forth of God's Grace, as if any miniſter of Chriſt ſhould now proſelyt or turn a whole nation to the Chriſtian faith, though he had no diſtinct office, yet I doubt not but both Papiſts and Proteſtants would judg it tolerable, to call ſuch an one an Apoſtle, or an Evangeliſt. For ſome of the Jeſuits call of their ſect *Apoſtles*, of *India* and of *Japon*, upon this alledged account. And *Calvin* teſtifies that there were Apoſtles and Evangeliſts in his time, upon the account of the Reformation, upon which account we have known *John Knox* often called *the Apoſtle of Scotland,* ſo that we conclud that *miniſters*, *paſtors*, or *teachers*, doth comprehend *all*, and that the *office* is but *one*, and therefore in that reſpect we judg there ought to be no precedency among them; to prove which I ſhall not inſiſt, ſeing it is ſhewn largely and treated of by ſuch as have denyed the *dioceſian epiſcopacy*, as they call it.

§ XXVI. As to the firſt part of the objection, viz, that I ſeem to make no diſtinction betwixt the *miniſter* and people, *I anſwer*, If it be underſtood of a liberty to ſpeak or propheſie by the Spirit, I ſay all may doe that, when moved thereunto, as above is ſhewn; but we do believe and affirm that ſome are more particularly called to the work of the miniſtery, and therefore are fitted of the Lord for that purpoſe, whoſe work is more conſtantly and particularly to inſtruct, exhort, admoniſh, overſee, and watch over their brethren; and that as there is ſomething more incumbent upon them, in that reſpect, than upon every common believer, ſo alſo, as in that relation, there is due to them from the flock ſuch obedience and ſubjection, as is mentioned in theſe teſtimonys of the Scriptur, Heb. 13: 17. 1 Theſs. 5: 12, 13. 1 Tim. 5 17. 1 Pet. 5: 5: Alſo beſides theſe, who are thus particularly called to the miniſtery, and conſtant labor in the Word and doctrin, there are alſo the elders, who, though they be not moved to a frequent teſtimony by way of declaration

in

in words, yet, as such as are grown up in the experiense of the blessed work of Truth *in* their hearts, watch over, and privatly admonish the young, care for the widdows, the poor and fatherless, and care and look that nothing be wanting, but that peace, love, unity, concord and soundness be preserved in the Church of Christ, and this answers to the *deacons* mentioned, Act. 6.

That, which we oppose, is the distinction of *Laïty* and *Clergy* (which in the Scriptur is not to be found) whereby none are admitted unto the work of the ministery, but such as are educated at schools on purpose, and instructed in *Logik* and *Philosophy*, &c. and so are at their apprentiship to learn the *art* and *trade of preaching*, even as a man learns any other art, whereby all other honest *mechanik* men, who have not got this *Heathenish art*, are excluded from having this priviledge; and so he, that is a scholar, thus bred up, must not have any honest trade whereby to get him a livelyhood, if he once intend for the ministery, but he must see to get him a place, and then he hath his *set hire* for a *lively-hood* to him, he must also be distinguished from the rest by the color of his cloaths, for he must onely wear *black*, and must be a *master of arts*: but more of this hereafter.

§ XXVII. As this manner of separating men for the ministery is nothing like the Church in the Apostles dayes, so great evils have and do follow upon it; for first, parents seing both the honor and profit, that attends the Clergy, do allot their children sometimes from their infancy to it, and so breed them up on purpose: and others, come to age, upon the same account betake them to the same trade, and having these natural and acquired parts, that are judged the necessary qualifications of a minister, are thereby admitted, and so are bred up in idleness and pleasur, thinking it a disgrace for them to work with their hands, onely if they study a little out of their books to make a discourse once or twice in a week, during the running of an hour-glass. Whereas the Gift, Grace and Spirit of God to call, gift and qualify for the ministery, is neglected and overlooked. And many *covetous*, *corrupt*, *earthly*, *carnal* men, having a meer shew and form, but strangers to and utterly ignorant of the inward work of Grace upon their hearts, are brought-in, and intrude themselves, and so, through them, death, barrenness and darkness, and by consequence superstition, error and idolatry hath entred, and leavened the Church; and they, that will narrowly observe, shall find that it was thus the apostasy came to take place; of the truth of which I could give many examples, which, for brevity's fake, I omitt. For fo the office, reverence, and refpect due to it, was annexed to the meer name, fo that, when once a man was ordain'd a Bifhop or a Prieft, he was heard and believed, though he had nothing of the Spirit, Power, and Life, that the true Apoftles and minifters were in, that in a fhort time the fucceffion came to be of the name and title, and the office was thereto annexed, and not of the natur, vertue and life. Which in effect made them to ceafe to be the miniftery and minifters of Chrift, but onely a fhaddow and vain image of it, which alfo decaying was in fome ages fo metamorphofed, that not onely the Subftanse was loft, but the very form wholly vitiated, alterated and marred, that it may be far better faid of the pretended Chriftian Church, as was difputed of *Thefeus*'s boat, (which by the piesing of many new pieses of timber was wholly altered) whether indeed it were the fame or another. But in cafe that the firft had been of oak, & the laft pieces put in but of rotten fir, and that alfo the form had been fo far changed, as to be nothing like the firft, I think it would have fuffered no difput, but might have eafily been concluded to be quite another, retaining nothing but the name, and that alfo unjuftly. Secondly, from this diftinction of *Laity* and *Clergy* this abufe alfo followes, that good honeft mechanik men, and others, who have not learned the art and trade of preaching, and fo are not licentiated according to thefe rules they prefcribe unto themfelves, fuch, I fay, being poffeffed with a falfe opinion, that it is not lawfull for them to meddle with the Miniftery, nor that they are any wayes fit for it, becaufe of the defect of that literatur, do thereby neglect the Gift *in* themfelves, and *quench* many times the *pure breathings* of the *Spirit* of *God in* their *hearts*; which, if given way to, might have proved much more for the edification of the Church, than many of the cunned fermons of the learned. And fo by this means the Apoftles command and advise is flighted, who exhorteth, 1 Thef. 5: 19, 20. *not to quench the Spirit, nor defpife prophecying*: and all this is done by men pretending to be Chriftians, who glory that the firft preachers and propagators of their religion were fuch kind of plain mechanik men, and illiterat. And even Proteftants do no lefs than Papifts exclude fuch kind of men from being minifters among them, and thus limit the Spirit and Gift of God, though their fathers, in oppofition to Papifts, afferted the contrary; and alfo their own hiftorys declare, how that kind of illiterat men did, without learning, by the Spirit of God, greatly contribut in divers places to the Reformation.

By

By this it may appear, that, as in calling and qualifiing, so in preaching and praying, and the other particular steps of the ministery, every true minister is to know the Spirit of God, by its vertue and life to accompany and assist him. But, because this relats to worship, I shall speak, of it more largely in the next Proposition, which is concerning *Worship*. The last thing to be considered and inquired into is, concerning the maintainance of a Gospel minister. But before I proceed, I judg it fit to speak something in short concerning the *preaching of women*, and to declare what we hold in that matter.

Seing *male and female are one in Christ Jesus*, and that he gives his Spirit no less to tł e one, than to the other, when God moveth by his Spirit *in a woman*, we judg it no wayes unlawfull for her to preach in the assemblys of Gods people. Neither think we that of Paul, 1 Cor. 14: 34. to reprove the inconsiderat and talkative women among the Corinthians, who troubled the Church of Christ with their unprofitable questions, or that, 1 Tim. 2: 11. that *women ought to learn, in all silence, not usurping authority over the man*, any wayes repugnant to this doctrin, because it's clear, that *women* have *prophesied* and *preached* in the Church, else had the saying of *Joël* been badly applied by *Peter*, Act. 2: 17. And, seing Paul himself, in the same epistle to the Corinthians, giveth rules, how women should behave themselves in their publik preaching and praying, it would be a manifest contradiction, if that place were other wayes taken in a larger sense, and the same Paul speaks of a woman, that laboured with him in the work of the Gospel: and it is written that *Philip* had four *daughters*, that prophesied; and lastly it hath been observed, that *God* hath *effectually* in this day *converted many Soules* by the *ministery* of *women*, and by them also frequently comforted the Soules of his children, which manifest experience puts the thing beyond all controversy: but now I shall proceed to speak of the maintainance of Ministers. Act. 21:9.

§ XXVIII. We freely acknowledg, as the Proposition holds forth, that there is an obligation upon such, to whom God sends, or among whom he raiseth up a minister, that, if need be, they minister to his necessitys. Secondly, that it is lawful for him to receive what is necessary & convenient. To prove this, I need not insist, for our adversaries will readily grant it to us, for the thing we affirm, is, that this is all that these Scriptur testimonys relating to this thing do grant, Gal 6:6. 1 Cor.9: 11,12, 13, 14. 1 Tim. 5: 16. That, which we then oppose in this matter, is first,

firſt, that it ſhould be conſtrained and limited. Secondly, that it ſhould be ſuperfluous, chargeable, and ſumptuous. And thirdly, the manifeſt abuſe hereof, of which I ſhall alſo briefly treat.

As to the firſt, our adverſarys are forced to recurr to the example of the *Law*, a refuge they uſe in defending moſt of their errors and ſuperſtitions, which are contrary to the natur and purity of the Goſpel.

Obj.　　They ſay, *God appointed the Levits the tithes, therefore they belong alſo to ſuch as miniſter in holy things under the Goſpel.*

Anſw.　　I anſwer, all that can be gathered from this, is, that, as the Prieſts had a maintainance allowed them under the *Law*, ſo alſo the miniſters and preachers under the *Goſpel*, which is not denyed: but the compariſon will not hold, that they ſhould have the very ſame, ſince, Firſt, there is no expreſs Goſpel command for it, neither by Chriſt, nor his Apoſtles. Secondly, the parity doth no wayes hold betwixt the *Levits* under the *Law*, and the *preachers* under the *Goſpel*, becauſe the *Levits* were one of the tribes of *Iſraël*, and ſo had a right to a part of the inheritance of the land, as wel as the reſt of their brethren, and having none, had this alloted to them in lieu of it. Next, the tenth of the tithes was onely allowed to the Prieſts that ſerved at the Altar, the reſt being for the Levits, and alſo to be put up in ſtorehouſes for entertaining of the widows and ſtrangers. But theſe prea.hers, notwithſtanding they inherit what they have by their parents, as wel as other men, yet claim the whole tithes, allowing nothing either to widow, or ſtranger. But as to the *tithes*, I ſhall not inſiſt; becauſe divers others have clearly and learnedly treated of it apart, and alſo divers Proteſtants do confeſs them not to be *jure Diviⁿô*, and the parity, as to the *quota*, doth not hold, but onely in general as to the *obligation of a maintainançe*. Which maintainance, though the hearers be obliged to give, and fail of their duty, if they do not, yet that it ought neither to be received nor yet forced, I prove, becauſe Chriſt, when he ſent forth his Apoſtles, ſaid, *Freely ye have reçeived, freely give,* Matth. 10: 8. and yet they had liberty to receive meat and drink from ſuch as offered them to ſupply their need. Which ſhewes that they were not to ſeek or require any thing by force, or to ſtint, or make a bargain before hand, as the preachers, as wel among Papiſts as Proteſtants, do in theſe days, who will not preach to any, untill they be ſure firſt of ſo much a year; but, on the contrary, theſe were to doe their duty and freely to communicat (as the Lord ſhould order them) what they had received, without ſeeking or expecting a reward.

The

The answer of this, given by *Nicolaus Arnoldus*, Exercit. Theolog. Sect. 42, 43. is not to be forgotten, but indeed to be kept upon record for a perpetual remembrance of him and his brethren, for he frankly answers after this manner, *We have not freely received, and therefore are not bound to give it freely.* The answer I confess is ingenuous and good. For, if those, that receive freely, are to give freely, it would seem to follow by the rule of *Contrarys*, that those, who receive not freely, ought not to give freely, and I shall grant it.   Onely they must grant me, that they preach not by and according to the Gift and Grace of God received, nor can they be good stewards of the *manifold Grace of God*, as every true minister ought to be, or then they have gotten this gift or grace by money, as *Simon Magus* would have been compassing it, since they think themselves not bound to give it without money again.   But, to be plain, I believe he intended not that it was from the Gift or Grace of God they were to preach, but from their acquired arts and studys, which hath cost them much labor and also some money at the Univerlity ; and therefore, as he, that puts his stock in the publik bank, expects interest again, so these scholars having spent some money, learning the art of preaching, think they may boldly say, they have it not freely, for it hath cost them both money and pains, and therefore they expect both money and ease again. And therefore as *Arnoldus* gets money for teaching his young students the art and trade of preaching, so he intends they should be repayed, before they give it again to others. It was of old said, *Omnia venalia Romæ*, i. e. *All things are set out to sale at Rome*, but now the same proverb may be applyed to *Franequer*.   And therefore *Arnoldus's* students, when they go about to preach, may safely seek and require hereby, telling their hearers their master's maxim, *Nos gratis non accepimus, ergo neque gratis dare tenemur.* But then they may answer again, that they find them, and their master to be none of his ministers, who, when he senth forth his disciples, give them this command, *Freely ye have received, freely give,* and therefore we will have none of your teaching, because we perceive you to be of the number of those, *that look for their gain from their quarter.*

§ XXIX. Secondly, the Scriptur testimonys, that urge this, are in the same natur of these, that press charity and liberality towards the poor, and command hospitality, &c. But these are not, nor can be stinted to a certain quantity, because they are deeds meerly voluntary, where the obedience to the command lieth in the good-will of the giver, and

Jef. 56: vers 11.

F f   not

not in the matter of the thing given, as Christ shew in the example of the widow's *mite.* So that, though there be an obligation upon Christians to minister of outward things to their ministers, yet there can be no definition of the quantity, but by the givers own consents, and a little from one may more truely fulfill the obligation, than a great deal from another. And therefore as acts of charity and hospitality can neither be limited nor forced, so neither can this.

Obj.		If it be *objected,* that *ministers may and ought to exhort, persuade, yea and earnestly press Christians (if they find them defective therein) to acts of charity and hospitality, and so may they do also to the giving of maintainance.*

Answ.		I answer: All this saith nothing for a stinted and forced maintainance, (for which there can not so much as the shew of one solid argument be brought from Scriptur) I confess, ministers may use exhortation in this, as much as in any other case, even as the Apostle did to the Corinthians, shewing them their duty: but it were fit for ministers, that doe so, that their testimony might have the more weight, and be the freer of all suspicion of covetousness and self-interest, that they might be able to say truely, in the sight of God, that, which the same Apostle subjoyns upon the same occasion, 1 Cor. 9: 15, 16, 17, 18. *But I have used none of these things. Neither have I written these things, that it should be so done unto me; For it were better for me to dye, than that any man should make my glorying void. For, though I preach the Gospel, I have nothing to glory of; for necessity is laid upon me, yea wo is unto me, if I preach not the Gospel. For, if I doe this thing willingly, I have a reward; but, if against my will, a dispensation of the Gospel is committed unto me. What is my reward then? Verily, that when I preach the Gospel, I may make the Gospel of Christ without charge, that I abuse not my power in the Gospel.*

Thirdly, As there is neither precept nor example for this forced and stinted maintainance in the Scriptur, so the Apostle, in his solemn farewel to the Pastors and Elders of the Church of *Ephesus,* guards them against it, Act. 20: 33, 34, 35. But, if the thing had been either lawfull, or practised, he would rather have exhorted them to be content with their stinted hire, and not to covet more ; whereas he sheweth them first by his own example, that they were not to *covet or expect any man's silver or gold.* Secondly, that they ought to *work with their hands* for an honest lively-hood, as he had done. And lastly, he exhorts them so to doe from the words of Christ, *because it is a more blessed thing to give, than to receive* ; shewing that it is so far from a thing that a true minister ought to aim at,

or

or expect, that it is rather a burthen to a true minister, and cross to him, to be brought upon necessity, so to lack.

§ XXX. Fourthly, If a forced and stinted maintainance were to be supposed, it would make the ministers of Christ just one with those hirelings, whom the Prophets cryed out against. For certainly, if a man make a bargain to preach to people for so much a year, so as to refuse to preach, unless he have, and seek to force the people to give it by violence, it can not be denyed, that such a one preacheth for hire, and so *looks for his gain from his quarter*, yea and *prepares war against such as put not into his mouth*: but this is the particular special mark of a false Prophet, and a hireling, and therefore can no ways compet to a true minister of Christ. `Mich. 3:5`

Next, that a superfluous maintainance, that is, more than in reason is needfull ought not to be received by Christian ministers, will not need much proof, seing the more moderat and sober, both among Papists and Protestants, readily confess it, who with one voyce exclame against the excessive revenues of the Clergy: and that it may not want a proof from Scriptur, what can be more plain than that of the Apostle to Timothy? 1 Tim. 6: 7, 8, 9. 10. where he both shewes wherewith we ought to be content, and also the hazard of such as look after more; and indeed, since that very obligation of giving maintainance to a minister is founded upon their need, and such as have opportunity to work, are commended rather in not receiving than in receiving, it can no ways be supposed lawfull for them to receive more than is sufficient, and indeed, were they truely, pious and right, though necessitat, they would rather incline to take too little than to be gaping after too much.

§ XXXI, Now that there is great excess and abuse hereof among Christians, the vast revenues, which the Bishops and Priests have, both Papist and Protestant, do declare, since I judg it may be said without any *hyperbole*, that some particular persons have more paid them yearly, than Christ and his Apostles made use of, their whole life time, who yet wanted not what was needfull as to the outward man, and no doubt deserved it far better, than those that enjoy that fulness. But it is manifest these *Bishops and Priests love their fat benefices, and the pleasur and honor, that attend them, so wel, that they purpose neither to follow Christ nor his Apostles example, nor advice in this matter.*

But it's usually *objected*; that *Christians are become so hard-hearted, and generally so little heed Spiritual things, that, if ministers had not a settled and* `Obj.`

stinted

stinted maintainance secured them by Law, they and their families might starve for want of bread.

Answ. I answer, This objection might have some weight as to a carnal mini-stery, made up of natural men, who have no life, power, nor vertue with them, and so may insinuat some need of such a maintainance for such a ministery: but it saith nothing, as to such, as are called and sent of God, *who sends no man away faring upon his own charges,* and so go forth in the Authority and Power of God, to turn people from *darkness* to *Light,* for such can trust to him, that sendeth them, and do believe that he will *pro-vide* for them, knowing that he requireth nothing of any, but what he giveth power to perform, and so, when they returr, if he inquire, can say they wanted nothing. And such also, when they stay in a place, (being immediately furnished by God, and not needing to borrow and steal what they preach from books, and take up their time that way) fall a working of their lawfull imployments, and labour with their hands, as *Paul* did, when he gathered the Church of Corinth. And indeed, if this objection had any weight, the Apostles and primitive pastors should never had gone forth to convert the nations, for fear of want. Doth not the doctrin of Christ teach us to ventur all, and part with all, to serve God? Can they then be accounted ministers of Christ, who are afraid to preach him, lest they get not money for it, or will not do it, untill they be sure of their payment? What for serves the ministery, but to perfect the Saints, and so to convert them from that hard-heartedness?

Obj. But thou wilt say *I have laboured and preached to them, and they are hard-hearted still, and will not give me any thing.*

Answ. Then surely thou hast either not been sent to them of God, and so thy ministery and preaching hath not been among them in the Power, Vertue, and Life of Christ, and so thou deserv'st nothing: or else they have rejected thy testimony, and so are not worthy, and from such thou ought'st not to expect, yea nor yet to receive any thing, if they would give thee, but thou ought'st to *shake off the dust from thy feet,* and leave them. And how frivolous this objection is, appears, in that in the dark-nest and must superstitious times the Priests revenues increased most, and they were most richly rewarded, though they deserved least. So that he, that is truely sent of God, as he needs not, so neither will he be afraid of want, so long as he serves so good a master, neither will he ever for-bear to do his work for that cause. And indeed, such as make this obje-

Marth 10 vers 14.

ction,

&ion, ſhew truely that they *ſerve not the Lord Chriſt*, but their own belly, and that makes them ſo anxious for want of food to it.

§ XXXII. But laſtly, as to the *abuſes* of this kind of *maintainance*, indeed he, that would go through them all, though he did it paſſingly, might make of it alone an huge volumn, they are ſo great and numerous. For this abuſe, as others, crept-in with the apoſtaſy, there being nothing of this in the primitive times, then the miniſters claimed no tithes, neither ſought they a ſtinted or forced maintainançe, but ſuch as wanted, had their neceſſity ſupplied by the Church, and others wrought with their hands. But the perſecutions being over, and the Emperours and Princes coming under the name of Chriſtians, the zeal of thoſe great men was quickly abuſed by the *covetouſneſs* of the *Clergy*, who ſoon learned to change their cottages with the palaces of Princes, and reſted not, untill by degrees ſome of them came to be Princes themſelves, nothing inferior to them in ſplendor, luxury and magnificence, a method of living, that honeſt *Peter* and *John*, the *fiſher men*, and *Paul*, the *tentmaker*, never coveted. And perhaps as little imagined, that men, pretending to be their ſucceſſors, ſhould have arrived to theſe things; and ſo ſoon as the Biſhops were thus ſeated and conſtitut, forgeting the Life and work of a Chriſtian, they went uſually by the ears together about the *precedency* and *revenues*, each *coveting* the *chiefeſt* and *fateſt benefice*. It is alſo to be regreted to think how ſoon this *miſchief* crept-in among *Proteſtants*, who had ſcarce wel appeared, when the *Clergy* among them began to ſpeak at the old rate, and ſhew, that, though they had forſaken the *Biſhop of Rome*, they were not reſolved to part with their old benefices, and therefore ſo ſoon as any Princes or States ſhook off the Pop's authority, and ſo demoliſhed the *abbeys*, *nunnerys*, and other *monuments* of *ſuperſtition*, the reformed *Clergy* began preſently to cry out to the Magiſtrats, to beware of meddling with the Churches patrimony, ſeverely exclaming againſt making a lawfull uſe of thoſe vaſt revenues, that had been ſuperſtitiouſly beſtowed upon the Church (ſo called) to the good and benefit of the commonwealth, as no leſs than ſacrilege.

But by keeping up of this kind of maintainance for the *miniſtery* and *Clergy men*, ſo called, there is firſt a bait laid for *covetouſneſs*, *which is idolatry*, and of all things moſt hurtfull : ſo that, for covetouſneſs ſake, many, being led by the deſire of *filthy lucre*, do apply themſelves to be miniſters, that they may get a lively-hood by it ; if a man have ſeveral children, he will allot one of them to be a minifter, which if he can get him to be, he reckons it as good as a patrimony, fo that a fat benefice hath always many expectants, and then what bribing, what courting, what induftry, and fhamefull actions are ufed to acquire thefe things, is too openly known, and needs not be proven.

The *fcandal*, that herethrough is raifed among Chriftians, is fo manifeft, that it is become a proverb that *the KIRK is always GREEDT:* Whereby the Gift and Grace of God being neglected, they have for the moft part no other motive or rule, in applying themfelves to one Church more than another, but the greater benefice. For, though they hypocritically pretend, at their accepting of and entring unto their Church, that they have nothing before them, but the Glory of God, and the Salvation of Soules, yet, if a richer benefice offer it felf, they prefently find it more for God's Glory, to remove from the firft, and go thither. And thus they make no difficulty often to change, while notwithftanding they accufe us, that we allow minifters to go from place to place, and not to be tied to one place, but we allow this not, for the gaining of money, but as moved of God; for, if a minifter be called to minifter in a particular place, he ought not to leave it, except God call him from it, and then he ought to obey, for we make *the will of God inwardly revealed*, and *not* the *love of money* and more *gain*, the *ground* of *removing.*

Secondly, From this abufe hath proceeded that *luxury* and *idlenefs*, that moft of the *Clergy* live in, even among Proteftants as wel as Papifts, to the great fcandal of Chriftianity. For not having lawfull trades, to work with their hands, and being fo fuperfluoufly and fumptuoufly provided for, they live in *idlenefs* and *luxury*: and there doth more *pride*, *vanity*, and *worldly glory* appear in their *wives* and *children*, than in moft others, which is open and evident to all.

Thirdly, They become hereby fo *glued* to the *love* of *money*, that there is none like them in *malice*, *rage*, and *cruelty*, if they be denyed their *hire*, they rage like drunken men, fret, fume, and, as it were, go mad. A man may fooner fatisfy the fevereft creditor, than them, the *general* voyce of the poor doth confirm this, for indeed they are far more *exact* in taking up the *tithes* of *fheep*, *geefe*, *fwine*, and *eggs*, &c. and look more narrowly to it, than to the members of their flock; they will mifs the leaft mite, and the pooreft widow can not efcape their avaritious hands: twenty lyes they will hear unreproved, and as many oaths a man may fwear in their

hearing

hearing without offending them, and greater evils than all this they can overlook. But, if thou ow'ft them ought & refuse to pay it, then nothing but *war* will they thunder againft thee, and they will ftigmatize thee with the horrible title of facrilege, & fend thee to hell without mercy, as if thou hadft committed the fin againft the Holy Ghoft. Of all people we can beft bear witnefs to this: for God having fhewn us this corrupt and anti-Chriftian miniftery, and called us out from it, and gathered us unto his own Power and Life, to be a *feparat people*, fo that we dare not joyn with, nor hear thefe anti-Chriftian hirelings, neither yet put into their mouths, or feed them. O! what malice, envy, and fury hath this raifed in their hearts againft us? that, though we get none of their wares, neither will buy them, as knowing them to be nought, yet will they force us to give them money, and becaufe we can not for Confcience fake do it, our fufferings have upon that account been unutterable. Yea to give account of their cruelty and feveral forts of inhumanity ufed againft us, would make no fmall hiftory. Thefe avaritious hirelings have come to that degree of malice and rage, that feveral poor labouring men have been carried hundreds of miles from their own dwellings, and fhut up in prifon, fome two, fome three, yea fome 7 years, together, for the value of one pound fterling, and lefs. I know my felf a poor widow, that for the tithes of her geefe, which amounted not to five fhillings, was about four years kept in prifon, thirty miles from her houfe. Yea they by violence for this caufe have plundered of mens goods the hundredfold, and prejudiced much more, yea hundreds have hereby fpilt their innocent blood, by dying in the filthy noifom holes and prifons, and fome have the Priefts have been fo inraged, that goods thus ravifhed could not fatisfie them, but they muft alfo fatisfie their fury by beating, knocking, and wounding with their hands innocent men and women, for refufing (for Confcience fake) to put into their mouths.

The onely way then foundly to reform and remove all thefe abufes, and take away the ground and occafion of them, is to take away all ftinted and forced maintainance and ftipend: and, feing thofe things were anciently given by the people, that they return again into the publik treafur, and thereby the people may be greatly benefited by them, for that they may fupply for thefe publik taxations, and impofitions, that are put upon them, and may eafe themfelves of them. And whoever call or appoint teachers to themfelves, let them accordingly entertain them. And for fuch as are called and moved to the miniftery by the Spirit of God,

th-fe,

thofe, that receive them, and taſt of the good of their miniſtery, will no doubt provide things needfull for them, and there will be no need of a Law to force a hire for them; for he, that ſends them, will take care

1 Tim. 6: veis 8.

for them, and they alſo *having food and raiment,* will *therewith be content.*

§ XXXIII. The ſum then of what is ſaid, is, that *The miniſtery, that we have pleaded for, and which alſo the Lord hath raiſed up among us, is in all its parts like the true miniſtery of the Apoſtles and primitive Church. Whereas the miniſtery our adverſarys ſeek to uphold and plead for, as it doth in all its parts differ from them, ſo, on the other hand, it is very like the falſe prophets and teachers, teſtified againſt and condemned in the Scriptur,* as may be thus briefly illuſtrated.

1. *The miniſtery and miniſters, we plead for, are ſuch as are immediately called and ſent forth by Chriſt and his Spirit unto the work of the miniſtery,* ſo were the holy Apoſtles and Prophets, as appears by theſe places, Matth 10: verſe 1, 5. Eph. 4: 11. Heb. 5: 4.

1. *But the miniſtery and miniſters, our oppoſers plead for, are ſuch as have no immediat call from Chriſt, to whom the leading and motion of the Spirit is not reckoned neceſſary: but who are called, ſent forth, and ordained by wicked and ungodly men,* ſuch were of old the falſe Prophets and teachers, as appears by theſe places Jer. 14: 14, 15. item chap. 23. 21, and 27: 15.

2. *The miniſters we plead for, are ſuch, as are acted and led by God's Spirit, and by the Power and operation of his Grace in their hearts, are in ſome meaſur converted and regenerate, and ſo are good, holy, and gratious men,* ſuch were the Holy Prophets and Apoſtles, as appears from 1 Tim. 3: 2, 3, 4, 5, 6. Tit. 1: 7, 8, 9.

2. *But the miniſters, our adverſarys plead for, are ſuch, to whom the Grace of God is no needfull qualification, and ſo may be true miniſters according to them, though they be ungodly, unholy, and profligate men,* ſuch were the falſe prophets and apoſtles, as appears from Mic. 3: 5, 11. 1 Tim 6: 5, 6, 7, 8, &c. 2 Tim. 3: 2. 2 Pet. 2: 1, 2, 3.

3. *The miniſters, we plead for, are ſuch, as act, move and labour in the work of the miniſtery, not from their own meer natural ſtrength and ability, but as they are acted, moved, under-proped, aſſiſted, and influenced by the Spirit of Chriſt, and miniſter according to the Gift received, as good ſtewards of the manifold Grace of God,* ſuch were the holy Prophets and Apoſtles, 1 Pet. 4, 10, 11. 1 Cor. 1: 17. 1 Cor. 2: 3, 4, 5, 13. Act. 2: 4. Matth. 10: 20. Mark. 13: 11. Luk. 12: v. 12 1 Cor. 13: 2.

3. *But the miniſters our adverſarys plead for, are ſuch as wait not for, nor expect,*

expect, nor need the Spirit of God, to act and move them in the work of the mini-stery, but what they do, they do from their own meer natural strength and ability, and what they have gathered and stoln from the letter of the Scriptur, and other books, and so speak it forth in the strength of their own wisdom and eloquence, and not in the evidence and demonstration of the spirit and of power : Such were the false prophets and apostles, as appears, Jer. 23 : 30, 31, 32, 34, &c. 1 Cor. 4: 18. Jud. 16.

4. *The ministers we plead for, are such as being holy and humble contend not for precedency and priority, but rather strive to prefer one another, and serve one another in love, neither desire to be distinguished from the rest by their garments and large phylacteries, nor seek the greetings in the market places, nor uppermost rooms at feasts, nor the chief seats in the synagogues, nor yet to be called of men* MASTER, &c. Such were the holy Prophets and Apostles, as appears from Matth. 23: 8, 9, 10. and 20: 25, 26, 27.

4. *But the ministers our adversarys plead for, are such as strive and contend for superiority, and claim precedency over one another, affecting and ambitiously seeking after the forementioned things,* such were the false prophets and apostles in time past, Matth. 23: 5, 6, 7.

5. *The ministers we plead for, are such as having freely received, freely give, who covet no man's silver, gold, or garments, who seek no man's goods, but seek them, and the Salvation of their Soules, whose hands supply their own necessitys, working honestly for bread to themselves and their families: and, if at any time they be called of God, so as the work of the Lord hinder them from the use of their trades, take what is freely given them by such, to whom they have communicated Spirituals, and having food and raiment, are therewith content* ; such were the holy Prophets and Apostles, as appears from Matth. 10: 8. Act. 20 : 33, 34, 35. 1 Tim. 6: 8.

5. *But the ministers our adversarys plead for, are such as not having freely received, will not freely give, but are covetous, doing that, which they ought not, for filthy lucr's sake, as to preach for hire, and divine for money, and look for their gain from their quarter, and prepare war against such as put not into their mouths,* &c. *Greedy dogs, which can never have enough. Shepherds, who feed themselves, and not the flock, eating the fat, and cloathing themselves with the wool, making merchandise of Soules, and following the way of Balaam, that loved the wages of unrighteousness.* Such were the false prophets and apostles, Isa. 56, 11. Ezech. 34: 2, 3, 8. Mic. 3: 5, 11. Tit. 1: 10, 11. 2 Pet. 2: verses 1, 2, 3: 14, 15.

G g

And

And in a word, *We are for a holy, Spiritual, pure and living miniſtery, where the miniſters are both called, qualified, and ordered, acted and influenced in all the ſteps of their miniſtery by the Spirit of God, which being wanting, we judg ceaſe to be the miniſters of Chriſt.*

But they judging this Life, Graçe and Spirit no eſſential part of their miniſtery, are therefore for the upholding of an humane, carnal, dry, barren, fruitleſs and dead miniſtery, of which (alas !) we have ſeen the fruits in the moſt part of their Churches, of whom that ſaying of the Lord is certainly verified, Jer. 23: 32. ---- *I ſent them not, nor commanded them : therefore they ſhall not profit this people at all,* ſaith the *L O R D.*

The Eleventh Propoſition,

Concerning VVorſhip.

All true and acceptable Worship to God is offered in the inward and immediat moving and drawing of his own Spirit, which is neither limited to places, times, nor perſons : for, though we be to worship him always, and that we are continually to fear before him, yet, as to the outward ſignification thereof in prayers, praiſes or preachings, we ought not to do it in our own will, where and when we will; but where and when we are moved thereunto by the ſtirring and ſecret inſpiration of the Spirit of God *in* our hearts; which God heareth and accepteth of, and is never wanting to move us thereunto, when need is, of which he himſelf is the alone proper Judge. All other worship then, both praiſes, prayers or preachings, which man ſets about in his own will and at his own appointment, which he can both begin and end at his pleaſur, do, or leave undone, as himſelf ſeeth meet, whether they be a *preſcribed form,* as a *Liturgy,* &c. or prayers conceived *extempore* by the natural ſtrength and faculty of the mind, they are all

but

but fuperftitions, *will-VVorfhip*, and abominable idolatry in the fight of God, which are now to be denyed
and rejeƈted, and feparated from, in this day of his Spiritual arifing, however it might have pleafed him (*who
winked at the times of ignorance*, with a refpeƈt to the fimplicity and integrity of fome, and of his own innocent
Seed, which lay, as it were, buried *in* the *hearts* of men
under that mafs of fuperftition) to *blow upon the dead and
dry bones*, and to raife fome breathings of his own and
anfwer them; and that untill the day fhould more clearly dawn and break forth.

§ I. THe *duty* of man towards *God* lieth chiefly in thefe two
generals. 1. *In an holy conformity to the pure Law and Light
of God, fo as both to forfake the evil, and be found in the pra-
ƈtiƈe of thefe perpetual and moral precepts of righteoufnefs and*
equity. And 2. *In rendering that reverence, honor and adoration to God, that he
requires, and demands of us,* which is comprehended under *Worfhip.* Of
the former we have already fpoken, as alfo of the different relations of
Chriftians, as they are diftinguifhed by the feveral meafurs of Graƈe
received, and given to every one, and in that refpeƈt have their feveral
offiƈes in the *body of Chrift, which is the Church.* Now I come to fpeak of
Worfhip, or of thofe aƈts, whether privat, or publik, general, or particular, whereby man renders to God that part of his duty, which relates
immediately to him; and as *obedienƈe is better than facrifiƈe,* fo neither is
any facrifiƈe acƈeptable, but that, which is done according to the will
of him, to whom it is offered. But men, finding it eafier to facrifiƈe in
their own wills, than obey God's will, have heaped up facrifiƈes without obedience, and thinking to deceive God, as they do one another,
give him a fhew of reverenƈe, honor and worfhip, while they are both
inwardly eftranged and alienated from his holy and righteous life, and
wholly ftrangers to the pure breathings of his Spirit, in which the acceptable Sacrifice and worfhip is onely offered up. Hence it is, that there
is not any thing, relating to man's duty towards God, which among all
forts of people hath been more vitiated, and in which the devil hath more
prevailed, than in abufing man's mind concerning this thing: and, as

among

among many others, so among those called *Christians*, nothing hath been more out of order, and more corrupted, as some Papists, and all Protestants do acknowledg. As I freely approve whatsoever the Protestants have reformed from Papists in this respect, so I meddle not at this time with their controversys about it; onely it suffices me with them to deny, as no part of the true worship of God, that abominable superstition and idolatry the *Popish mass*, *the adoration of Saints and Angels*, *the veneration of reliques, the visitation of sepulchres*, and all these other superstitious ceremonys, *confraternitys*, and *endless pilgrimages of the* Romish synagogue. Which all may suffice to evince to Protestants, that anti-Christ hath wrought more in this, than in any other part of the Christian religion, and so it concerns them narrowly to consider whether herein they have made a clear and perfect reformation, as to which stands the controversy betwixt them, and us. For we find many of the branches lopped off by them, but the root yet remaining, to wit, a worship acted in and from man's will and spirit, and not by and from the Spirit of God; for the true Christian and Spiritual worship of God hath been so early lost, and man's wisdom and will hath so quickly and throughly mixed it self herein, that both the apostasy in this respect hath been greatest, and the reformation herefrom, as to the evil root, most difficult. Therefore let not the Reader suddenly stumble at the account of our Proposition in this matter, but hear us patiently in this respect explain our selves, and I hope (by the assistance of God) to make it appear, that, though our manner of speaking and doctrin seem most singular and different from all other sorts of Christians, yet it is most according to the purest Christian Religion, and indeed most needfull to be observed and followed; and that there be no ground of mistake (for that I was necessitat to speak in few words, and therefore more obscurely and dubiously in the Proposition it self) it is fit in the first place to explain and hold forth our sense, and clear the state of the controversy.

§ II. And first, let it be considered, that what is here affirmed is spoken of the *worship of God in Gospel times*, and not of the worship, that was under or before the *Law*: For the particular commands of God to men then, are not sufficient to authorize us now to do the same things; else we might be supposed at present acceptably to offer sacrifice, as they did, which all acknowledg to be ceased. So that what might have been both commendable and acceptable under the *Law*, may justly now be

charged

charged with fuperftition, yea and idolatry. So that impertinently in this refpect doth *Arnoldus* rage, againft this Propofition, (*Exercit. Theolog. fect.* 44.) faying, *that I deny all publik worſhip, and that, according to me, ſuch as in Enoch's time publikly began to call upon the Name of the Lord, and ſuch as at the command of God went twice up to Jeruſalem to worſhip, and that Anna, Simeon, Mary, &c. were idolaters, becauſe they uſed the publik worſhip of theſe times.* Such a confequence is moft impertinent, and no lefs foolifh and abfurd, than if I fhould inferr from Paul's expoftulating with the Galatians for their returning to the Jewifh ceremonys, that he therefore condemned *Moſes* and all the Prophets as foolifh and ignorant, becaufe they ufed thofe things : the forward man, not heeding the different difpenfations of times, ran into this impertinency. Though a *Spiritual worſhip* might have been, and no doubt was practifed by many under the *Law* in great fimplicity, yet will it not follow that it were no fuperftition to ufe all thofe ceremonys, that they ufed, which were by God difpenfed to the Jewes, not as being effential to true worfhip, or neceffary as of themfelves for tranfmitting and entertaining an holy fellowfhip, betwixt him and his people, but in condefcenfion to them, who were inclinable to idolatry : albeit then in this, as in moft other things, the Subftançe was enjoyed under the Law by fuch as were Spiritual indeed, yet was it vailed and furrounded with many rites and ceremonys, which is no wayes lawfull for us to ufe now under the Gofpel.

§ III. Secondly, albeit I fay, that this worfhip is neither limited to times, plaçes, nor perfons, yet I would not be underftood, as if I intended the putting away of all fet times and places to worfhip. God forbid I fhould think of fuch an opinion. Nay, we are none of thofe, that *forſake the aſſembling of our ſelves together*, but have even certain times and places, in which we carefully meet together (nor can we be driven therefrom by the threats or perfecutions of men) to *wait upon God*, and worfhip him. To meet together we think neceffary for the people of God, becaufe, fo long as we are cloathed with this outward tabernacle, there is a neceffity to the entertaining of a joynt and vifible fellowfhip, and bearing of an outward teftimony for God, and feing of the faces one of another, that we concurr with our perfons, as wel as fpirits. To be accompanyed with that inward love and unity of fpirit, doth greatly tend to encourage and refrefh the Saints.

But the *limitation*, we condemn, is, that, whereas the Spirit of God

G g 3

fhould

fhould be the immediat actor, mover, perfwader and influencer of man in the particular acts of worfhip, when the Saints are met together, this Spirit is limited in its operations, by feting up a particular man, or men to preach and pray in man's will, and all the reft are excluded from fo much as believing that they are to wait for God's Spirit to move them in fuch things, and fo they neglecting that, which fhould quicken them *in* themfelves, and not waiting to feel the pure breathings of God's Spirit, fo as to obey them, are led meerely to depend upon the preacher, and hear what he will fay.

Secondly, in that thefe peculiar men come not thither to meet with the Lord, and to wait for the inward motions and operations of his Spirit, and fo to pray, as they feel the Spirit to breath *through* them, and *in* them, and to preach, as they find themfelves acted and moved by God's Spirit, and as he gives utterance, fo as to fpeak a word in feafon, to refrefh weary Soules, and as the prefent condition and ftate of the peoples hearts requires, fuffering God by his Spirit both to prepare peoples hearts, and alfo give the preacher to fpeak what may be fit and feafonable for them. But *he* hath hammered together in his clofet, according to his own will, by his humane wifdom and literatur, and by ftealing the words of Truth from the letter of the Scripturs, and patching together other mens writings and obfervations, fo much as will hold him fpeaking an hour, while the glafs runns, and without waiting or feeling the inward influence of the Spirit of God, he declames that by hap-hazard, whether it be fit or feafonable for the peoples condition or no; and when he has ended his fermon, he faith his prayer alfo in his own will and *fo there is an end of the bufinefs.* Which cuftomary worfhip, as it is no wayes acceptable to God, fo how unfruitfull it is and unprofitable to thofe, that are found in it, the prefent condition of the Nations doth fufficiently declare. It appears then that we are not againft fet times for worfhip, as *Arnoldus* againft this Propofition, *fect. 45.* no lefs impertinently alledgeth, offering needlefly to prove that, which is not denyed: onely thefe times being appointed for outward conveniency, we may not therefore think with the Papifts that thefe *dayes* are holy, and lead people into a fuperftitious obfervation of them, being perfwaded that *all days are alike holy in the fight of God.* And, albeit it be not my prefent purpofe to make a long digreffion concerning the debates among Proteftants concerning the firft day of the Week, commonly called *the Lord's day,* yet, forafmuch as it comes fitly in here, I fhall briefly fignifie our fenfe thereof.   § IV.

§ IV. We, not seing any ground in Scriptur for it, can not be so superstitious, as to believe that either the Jewish sabbath now continues, or that the first day of the week is the anti-typ thereof, or the true Christian sabbath, which with *Calvin* we believe to have a more Spiritual sense, and therefore we know no moral obligation, by the fourth command or elsewhere, to keep the first day of the Week more as any other, or any holiness inherent in it. But first, forasmuch as it is most necessary, that there be some time set apart for the Saints to meet together to *wait upon God*. And that, secondly, it is fit at some times they be freed from their other outward affairs. And that thirdly, Reason and Equity doth allow that servants and beasts have some time allowed them, to be eased from their continual labor. And that fourthly, it appears that the Apostles and primitive Christians did use the first day of the week for these purposes. We find our selves sufficiently moved for these causes to do so also, without superstitiously straining the Scripturs for another reason, which that it is not to be there found, many Protestants, yea *Calvin* himself, upon the fourth command hath abundantly evinced. And though we therefore meet, and abstain from working upon this day, yet doth not that hinder us from having meetings also for worship at other times.

§ V. Thirdly, though according to the knowledg of God, revealed unto us by the spirit, through that more full dispensation of Light, which we believe the Lord hath brought about in this day, we judg it our duty to hold forth that *Pure* and *Spiritual worship*, which is acceptable to God, and answerable to the testimony of Christ and his Apostles, and likewise to testifie against, and deny not onely manifest superstition and idolatry, but also all formal will-worship, which stands not in the Power of God, yet, I say, we do not deny the whole worship of all those, that have born the name of *Christians* even in the apostasy, as if God had never heard their prayers, nor accepted any of them. God forbid we should be so void of charity. The latter part of the Proposition sheweth the contrary; and, as we would not be so absurd on the one hand to conclude, because of the errors and darkness, that many were covered and surrounded with, in Babylon, that none of their prayers were heard, or accepted of God, so will we not be so unwary on the other, as to conclude, that, because God heard and pityed them so, we ought to continue in these errors and darkness, and not come out of Babylon, when it is by God discovered unto us. The *Popish mass*, and *vespers*, I do believe to be, as to the matter
of

of them, *abominable idolatry* and *fuperftition*, and fo alfo believe the Proteftants; yet will either I, or they, affirm, that in the darknefs of Popery no upright-hearted men, though zealous in thefe abominations, have been heard of God, or accepted of him? Who can deny, but that both *Bernard* and *Bonaventur*, *Thaulerus*, *Thomas à Kempis*, and divers others have both known and tafted of the love of God, and felt the Power and Vertue of God's Spirit working with them for their Salvation? And yet ought we not to forfake and deny thofe fuperftitions, which they were found in? The Calviniftical Presbyterians do much upbraid (and I fay, not without reafon) the formality and deadnefs of the Epifcopalian and Lutheran liturgys, and yet, as they will not deny but there have been fome good men among them, fo neither dare they refufe, but that, when that good ftep was brought in by them of turning the publik prayers into the vulgar tongues, though continued in a liturgy, it was acceptable to God, & fometimes accompanyed with his Power & Prefence: yet will not the Presbyterians have it from thence concluded, that the common prayers fhould ftill continue; fo likewife, though we fhould confefs, that, through the mercy and wonderfull condefcenfion of God, there have been upright in heart both among Papifts and Proteftants, yet can we not therefore approve of their way in the general, or not go on to the upholding of that *Spiritual worfhip*, which the Lord is calling all to, and fo to the teftifying againft whatfoever ftands in the way of it.

§ VI. Fourthly, to come then to the ftate of the controverfy, as to the publik worfhip, we judge it the duty of all, to be diligent in the affembling of themfelves together, (and what we have been, and are, in this matter, our enemies in Great *Britan*, who have ufed all means to hinder our affembling together to worfhip God, may bear witnefs) and when affembled, the great work of one and all ought to be to wait upon God, and, returning out of their own thoughts and imaginations, to feel the Lord's prefence, and know a *gathering into his Name* indeed, where he is *in the midft* according to his promife. And as every one is thus gathered, and fo met together inwardly in their fpirits, as wel as outwardly in their perfons, there the fecret Power and Vertue of Life is known to refrefh the Soul, and the pure motions and breathings of God's Spirit are felt to arife, from which as words of declaration, prayers, or praifes arife, the acceptable worfhip is known, which edifies the Church, and is wel-pleafing to God, and no man here limits the Spirit of God, nor

bringeth

bringeth forth his own cunned and gathered ſtuff, but every one puts that forth, which the Lord puts into their hearts, and it's uttered forth not in man's will and wiſdom, but *in the evidence and demonſtration of the Spirit and of Power.* Yea though there be not a word ſpoken, yet is the true Spiritual worſhip performed, and the body of Chriſt edified; yea it may and hath often faln out among us, that divers meetings have paſt without one word, and yet our Soules have been greatly edified and refreſhed, and our hearts wonderfully overcome with the ſecret ſenſe of God's Power and Spirit, which without words hath been miniſtred from one veſſel to another. This is indeed ſtrange and incredible to the meer natural and carnally-minded man, who will be apt to judge all time loſt, where there is not ſomething ſpoken, that's obvious to the outward ſenſes; and therefore I ſhall inſiſt a little upon this ſubject, as one, that can ſpeake from a certain experience, and not by meer hear-ſay of this wonderfull and glorious diſpenſation, which hath ſo much the more of the wiſdom and glory of God in it, as it's contrary to the natur of man's ſpirit, will, and wiſdom.

§ VII. As there can be nothing more oppoſit to the natural will and wiſdom of man, than this ſilent waiting upon God, ſo neither can it be obtained nor rightly comprehended by man, but as he layeth down his own wiſdom and will, ſo as to be content to be throughly ſubject to God. And therefore it was not preached, nor can be ſo practiſed, but by ſuch as find no outward ceremony, no obſervations, no words, yea not the beſt and pureſt words, even the words of Scriptur, able to ſatisfie their weary and afflicted Soules, becauſe where all theſe may be, the life, power, and vertue, which make ſuch things effectual, may be wanting. Such, I ſay, were neceſſitat to ceaſe from all outwards, and to be ſilent before the Lord, and being directed to that inward principle of *Life* and *Light in* themſelves, as the moſt excellent teacher, which *can never be removed into a corner*, came thereby to be learned to wait upon God in the meaſur of Life and Grace received from him, and to ceaſe from their own forward words and actings in the natural willing and comprehenſion, and feel after this inward Seed of Life, that, as it moveth, they may move with it, and be acted by its Power, and influenced, whether to pray, preach or ſing. And ſo from this principle of man's being ſilent, and not acting in the things of God, of himſelf, untill thus acted by God's *Light* and *Grace in the heart*, did naturally ſpring that man-

Iſa. 30: vers 20.

H h

ner

ner of fitting filent together, and waiting together upon the Lord. For many thus principled, meeting together in the pure fear of the Lord, did not apply themfelves prefently to fpeak, pray, or fing, &c. being afraid to be found acting forwardly in their own wills, but each made it their work to retire inwardly to the meafur of Grace in themfelves, not onely being filent as to words, but even abftaining from all their own thoughts, imaginations, and difires, fo watching in a holy dependence upon the Lord, and meeting together not onely outwardly in one place, but thus inwardly in *One Spirit*, and in *One Name of Jefus,* which is his Power and Vertue. They come thereby to enjoy and feel the arifings of this *Life,* which, as it prevails *in* each particular, becomes as a flood of refrefhment, & overfpreads the whole meeting, for man and man's part and wifdom being denyed and chained down in every individual, and God exalted, and his Grace in dominion *in* the heart, thus his *Name* comes to be *One in all*, and his Glory breaks forth, and covers all, and there is fuch a holy aw and reverence upon every Soul, that, if the natural part fhould arife *in* any, or the wife part, or what is not one with the Life, it would prefently be chained down and judged out.   And when any are through the breaking forth of this Power conftrained to utter a fentence of exhortation or praife, or to breath to the Lord in prayer, then all are fenfible of it, for the fame Life in them anfwers to it, *as in water face* anfwereth *to face.* This is that *Divine* and *Spiritual worfhip*, which the world neither knoweth, nor underftandeth, which the vulture eye feeth not into.   Yet many and great are the advantages, which my Soul with many others hath tafted of hereby, and which would be found of all fuch as would ferioufly apply themfelves hereunto.   For, when people are gathered thus together, not meerly to hear men, nor depend upon them, but *all are inwardly taught to ftay their minds upon the Lord*, and *wait for his appearance in their hearts,* thereby the forward working of the fpirit of man is ftayed and hindered from mixing it felf with the worfhip of God; and the form of this worfhip is fo naked and void of all outward and worldly fplendor, that all occafion for man's wifdom to be exercifed in that fuperftition and idolatry hath no lodging here; and fo there being alfo an inward quietnefs and retirednefs of mind, the *Witnefs of God* arifeth *in the heart*, and the *Light of Chrift* fhineth, whereby the Soul cometh to fee its own condition.   And there being many joyned together in this fame work, there is an inward travel and wreftling, and alfo, as the meafur of Grace is abode in, an overcoming of the power and

fpirit

Prov. 27:
vers 19.

Ifa 10:20.
&.
26: 3.

ſpirit of darkneſs; and thus we are often greatly ſtrengthened and renewed in the ſpirits of our minds without a word, and we enjoy and poſſeſs the holy fellowſhip and *communion of the body and blood of Chriſt*, by which our inward man is nouriſhed and fed. Which makes us not to dote upon outward water and bread and wine in our Spiritual things. Now as many thus gathered together, grow up in the ſtrength, power, and vertue of Truth, and as Truth comes thus to have victory & dominion in their Soules, then they receive an utterance, & ſpeak ſteadily to the edification of their brethren, and the *pure Life* hath a free paſſage through them, and, what is thus ſpoken, edifieth the body indeed. Such is the evident certainty of that Divine ſtrength, that is communicated by thus meeting together, and waiting in ſilence upon God, that ſometimes, when one hath come in, that hath been unwatchfull, and wandering in his mind, or ſuddenly out of the hurry of outward buſineſs, & ſo not inwardly gathered with the reſt, ſo ſoon as he retires himſelf inwardly, this Power, being in a good meaſur raiſed in the whole meeting, will ſuddenly lay hold upon his ſpirit, & wonderfully help to raiſe up the good *in* him, and beget him into the ſenſe of the ſame Power, to the melting and warming of his heart, even as the warmth would take hold upon a man, that is cold, coming into a ſtove, or as a flame will lay hold upon ſome little combuſtible matter lieing near unto it; yea if it fall out, that ſeverals met together, be ſtraying in their minds, though outwardly ſilent, and ſo wandering from the meaſur of Grace *in* themſelves, (which through the working of the enemy, and negligence of ſome may fall out) if either one come in, or may be in, who is watchfull, and *in* whom the *Life* is raiſed in a great meaſur, as that one keeps his place, he will feel a ſecret travel for the reſt, in a ſympathy with the *Seed*, which is oppreſſed *in* the other, and kept from ariſing by their thoughts and wanderings; and as ſuch a faithfull one waits in the *Light*, and keeps in this Divine work, God often-times anſwers the ſecret travel and breathings of his own Seed through ſuch a one, ſo that the reſt will find themſelves ſecretly ſmitten without words, and that one will be as a midwife, through the ſecret travel of his Soul, to bring forth the life *in* them, juſt as a little water, thrown into a pump brings up the reſt, whereby *Life* will come to be raiſed *in* all, and the vain imaginations brought down, and ſuch a one is felt by the reſt to miniſter life unto them without words; yea ſometimes, when there is not a word in the meeting, but all are ſilently waiting, if one come in, that is rude and wicked, and in whom the power

Eph. 4: vers 23.

of darknefs prevaileth much , perhaps with an intention to mock , or do mifchief, if the whole meeting be gathered into the *Life*, and it be raifed in a good meafur, it will ftrike terror .into fuch an one , and he will feel himfelf unable to refift, but by the fecret ftrength and vertue thereof the power of darknefs in him will be chained down , and, if the day of his vifitation be not expired, it will reach to the meafur of Grace *in* him , and raife it up to the redeeming of his Soul , and this we often bear witnefs of, fo as we had hereby frequent occafion, in this refpect, fince God hath gathered us to be a people, to renew this old faying, of many , *Is Saul alfo among the Prophets?* For not a few have come to be convinced of the Truth, after this manner, of which I my felf in a part am a true witnefs, who not by ftrength of arguments , or by a particular difquifition of each doctrin, and convincement of my underftanding thereby, came to receive and bear witnefs of the Truth , but by being fecretly reached by this *Life*: for, when I came into the filent affemblys of God's people, I felt a fecret power among them, which touched my heart, and as I gave way unto it, I found the evil weakening in me, and the good raifed up, and fo I became thus knit and united unto them, hungering more and more after the increafe of this Power and Life, whereby I might feel my felf perfectly redeemed : and indeed this is the fureft way to become a Chriftian ; to whom afterwards the knowledg and underftanding of principles will not be wanting, but will grow up, fo much as is needfull, as the natural fruit of this good root, and fuch a knowledg will not be barren nor unfruitfull after this manner. We defire therefore all, that come among us, to be profelyted, knowing, that, though thoufands fhould be convinced in their underftandings of all the Truths we maintain, yet, if they were not fenfible of this inward Life, and their Soules not changed from unrighteoufnefs to righteoufnefs, they could add nothing to us; for this is that cement, whereby we are *joyned* as *to the Lord*, fo to one another, and without this none can worfhip with.us. Yea if fuch fhould come among us, and from that underftanding and convincement they have of the Truth, fpeak ever fo true things , and utter them forth with ever fo much excellency of fpeech, if this Life were wanting, it would not edify us at all : but be as *founding brafs, or a tinkling cymbal.* 1 Cor. 13:1.

§ VIII. Our work then and worfhip is, when we meet together for *every* one to *watch,* and *wait upon God in themfelves,* & to be *gathered* from all vifibles thereinto. And as every one is thus ftated , they come to find

the

the *good* arife over the *evil*, and the *pure* over the *impure*, in which *God*
reveals himfelf, and *draweth near* to *every individual*, and fo he in the midft
in the general. Whereby each not onely partakes of the particular refreſhment and ſtrength, which comes from the good *in* himſelf, but is a ſharer
of the whole body, as being a living member of the body, having a joynt
fellowſhip and communion with all; and as this worſhip is ſtedfaſtly
preached, and kept to, it becomes eaſy, though it be very hard at firſt to
the natural man, whoſe roving imaginations, and running worldly defires are not fo eafily brought to filence; and therefore the Lord often-
times, when any turn towards him, and have truē defires thus to wait upon
him, and find great difficulty through the unſtayednefs of their minds,
doth in condeſcenſion and compaſſion cauſe his Power to break forth in a
more ſtrong and powerfull manner; and when the mind finks down, and
waits for the appearance of Life, and that the power of darkneſs in the
Soul wreſtles and works againſt it, then the good Seed, as it ariſeth, will
be found to work, as phyſik, in the Soul, eſpecially if ſuch a weak one be in
the aſſembly of divers others, in whom the Life is ariſen in greater dominion, and through the contrary workings of the power of darkneſs there
will be found an inward ſtriving in the Soule, as really in the myſtery,
as ever *Efau* and *Jacob* ſtrove in *Rebekkah's* womb. And from this inward
travel, while the *darkneſs* ſeeks to obſcure the *Light*, and the *Light* break
through the darkneſs (which always it will do, if the Soul give not its
ſtrength to the darkneſs) there will be ſuch a painfull travel found in the
Soul, that will even work upon the outward man; fo that often-times
through the working thereof the body will be greatly ſhaken, and many
groans and fighs and tears, even as the pangs of a woman in travel, will
lay hold upon it, yea and this not onely as to one, but when the enemy
(who, when the children of God aſſemble together, is not wanting to be
prefent, to fee if he can let their comfort) hath prevailed in any meaſur
in a whole meeting, and ſtrongly worketh againſt it, by ſpreading and
propagating his dark power, and by drawing out the minds of ſuch as are
met, from the Life *in* them, as they come to be ſenfible of this power
of his, that works againſt them, and to wreſtle with it by the *armour of*
Light, fometimes the Power of God will break forth into a whole meeting, and there will be ſuch an inward travel, while each is ſeeking to overcome the evil *in* themſelves, that by the ſtrong contrary workings of theſe
oppoſit powers, like the going of two contrary tides, every individual
H h 3

will

will be ſtrongly exerciſed , as in a day of battel ; and thereby trembling , and a motion of body will be upon moſt , if not upon all , which , as the power of Truth prevailes , will from pangs and groans end with a ſweet ſound of thankſgiving and praiſe , and from this the name of *Quakers*, i. e. *Tremblers*, was firſt reproachfully caſt upon us , which , though it be none of our chooſing , yet in this reſpect we are not aſhamed of it , but have rather reaſon to rejoyce therefore , even that we are ſenſible of this Power , that hath often-times laid hold upon our adverſarys , and made them yeeld unto us , and joyn with us , and confeſs to the Truth , before they had any diſtinct or diſcurſive knowledg of our doctrines , ſo that ſometimes many at one meeting have been thus convinced , and this Power would ſometimes alſo reach to , and wonderfully work even in little children , to the admiration and aſtoniſhment of many.

§ IX. Many are the bleſſed experiences , which I could relate of this *ſilence* and manner of worſhip , yet do I not ſo much commend and ſpeak of *ſilence* , as if we had a law in it to ſhut out praying or preaching , or tied our ſelves thereunto ; not at all : for , as our worſhip conſiſteth not in the words , ſo neither in ſilence , as ſilence , but in an holy dependence of the mind upon God , from which dependence ſilence neceſſarily followes in the firſt place , untill words can be brought forth , which are from God's Spirit ; and God is not wanting to move *in* his children to bring forth words of exhortation or prayer , when it is needfull , ſo that of the many gatherings and meetings of ſuch , as are convinced of the Truth , there is ſcarce any , *in* whom God raiſeth not up ſome or other to mini-ſter to his brethren , that there are few meetings , that are altogether ſilent. For , when many are met together in this one Life and Name , it doth moſt naturally and frequently excite them to pray to , and praiſe God , and ſtirr up one another by mutual exhortation and inſtructions ; yet we judge it needfull there be , in the firſt place , ſome times of ſilence , during which , every one may be gathered inward to the Word and Gift of Grace , from which he , that miniſtreth , may receive ſtrength to bring forth what he miniſtreth , and that they , that hear , may have a ſenſe to diſcern betwixt the *pretious* and the *vile* , and not to hurry into the exerciſe of theſe things , ſo ſoon as the bell rings , as other Chriſtians do ; yea and we doubt not , but aſſuredly know that the meeting may be good and refreſhfull , though , from the ſitting down to the riſing up thereof , there hath not been a word as outwardly ſpoken ; and yet Life may have been

known

known to abound in each particular , and an inward growing up therein ,
and thereby , yea so as words might have been spoken acceptably , and
from the life : yet there being no absolute neceffity laid upon any so to do ,
all might have chosen rather quietly and silently to poffefs and enjoy the
Lord *in* themselves , which is very sweet and comfortable to the Soul ,
that hath thus learned to be gathered out of all its own thoughts and workings , to feel the Lord to bring forth both the will and the deed , which
many can declare by a bleffed experience , though indeed it can not but
be hard for the natural man to receive or believe this doctrin ; and therefore it muft be rather by a fenfible experience , and by coming to make
proof of it , than by arguments that fuch can be convinced of this thing ,
feing it is not enough to believe it , if they come not also to enjoy and
poffefs it ; yet in condefcenfion to , and for the fake of fuch as may be
the more willing to apply themselves to the practice and experience hereof , that they found their underftandings convinced of it , and that it is
founded upon Scriptur and Reafon , I find a freedom of mind to add fome
few confiderations of this kind , for the confirmation hereof , befides what
is before mentioned of our experience.

§ X. That *to wait upon God* , and *to watch before him* , is *a duty incumbent
upon all* , I fuppofe none will deny ; and that this also is *a part of worfhip*
will not be called in queftion , fince there is fcarce any other so frequently
commanded in the Holy Scripturs , as may appear from Pfal. 27: 14. 37:
v. 7 & 34. Prov: 20. 22. Ifa. 30: 18. Hofea 12: 7. Zach. 3 : 8.
Matth. 24: 42. 25 : 13. 26: 41. Marc. 13 : 33, 35 & 37. Luc. 21 : 36.
Act. 1: 4. 20: 31. 1 Cor. 16: 13. Col. 4: 2. 1 Theff. 5: 6. 2 Tim. 4: 5.
1 Pet. 4: 7. Alfo this duty is often recommended with very great and
precious promifes, as, Pfal. 25:3. 37: 9. 69:7. Ifa. 40: 31. Lam. 3:25,26.
they, that wait upon the Lord , *fhall renew their ftrength* , &c. Now, how is this
waiting upon God or watching before him , but by this *filence* , of which
we have fpoken? Which, as it is in it felf a *great and principal duty* , so it
neceffarily in *order* both of *nature* and *time* preceedeth all other. But, that
it may be the better and more perfectly underftood , as it is not onely an
outward filence of the *body* , but an *inward filence* of the *mind* from all its
own imaginations and felf-cogitations , let it be confidered according
to Truth and to the principles and doctrines heretofore affirmed and
proven , that man is to be confidered in a twofold refpect , to wit , in his
natural , *unregenerat* , *and faln ftate* : and in his *Spiritual and renewed* *condition* ,

tion, from whence ariseth that distinction of *the natural* and *Spiritual man,* so much used by the Apostle, and heretofore spoken of, also these two births of the mind proceed from the two *Seeds* in man respectively, to wit, the *good Seed* and the *evil.* And from the evil seed doth not onely proceed all manner of gross and abominable wickedness and profanity, but also hypocrisy, and these *wickednesses,* which the Scriptur calls *spiritual,* because it is the *serpent* working *in* and *by* the natural man in things that are spiritual, which having a shew and appearance of good are so much the more hurtfull and dangerous, as it is *Satan transformed* and *transforming himself into an Angel of Light*; and therefore doth the Scriptur so pressingly and frequently (as we have heretofore had occasion to observe) shut out and exclude the natural man from meddling with the things of God, denying his endeavours therein, though acted and performed by the most eminent of his parts, as of wisdom and utterance.

Also this *spiritual wickedness* is of two sorts, though both one in kind, as proceeding from one root, yet different in their degrees, and in the subjects also sometimes. The one is, when as the natural man is meddling in, and working in the things of Religion, doth from his own conceptions and divinations affirm or propose wrong and erroneous notions and opinions of God and things spiritual, and invent superstitions, ceremonys, observations, and rites in worship, from whence have sprung all the heresies and superstitions, that are among Christians. The other is, when as the natural man, from a meer conviction of his understanding, doth in the forwardness of his own will, and by his own natural strength, without the influence and leading of God's Spirit, go about either in his understanding to imagin, conceive, or think of the things of God, or actually to perform them by preaching or praying. The first is a missing both in matter and form. The second is a retaining of the form without the Life and Substance of Christianity, because Christian Religion consisteth not in a meer belief of true doctrines, or a meer performance of acts good in themselves, or else the bare letter of the Scriptur, though spoken by a drunkard or a devil, might be said to be spirit and life, which I judge none will be so absurd as to affirm : and also it would follow, that, where the form of godlyness is, there the power is also, which is contrary to the express words of the Apostle. For the form of godlyness can not be said to be, where either the notions and opinions believed are erroneous and ungodly, or the acts performed evil and wicked, for then it would

would be the form of ungodlynefs and not of godlynefs. But of this further hereafter, when we fhall fpeak particularly of preaching and praying. Now, though this laft be not fo bad, as the former, yet hath it made way for it; for men having firft departed from the Life and Subftance of true Religion and worfhip, to wit, from the inward Power and Vertue of the Spirit, fo as therein to act, and thereby to have all their actions enlivened, have onely retained the form and fhew, to wit, the true words and appearance, and fo acting in their own natural and unrenewed wills in this form; the form could not but quickly decay and be vitiated, for the working and active fpirit of man could not contain it felf within the fimplicity and plainnefs of Truth, but giving way to his own numerous inventions and imaginations began to vary in the form, and adapt it to his own inventions, untill by degrees the form of godlynefs, for the moft part came to be loft, as wel as the Power. For this kind of idolatry, whereby man loveth, idolizeth and huggeth his own conceptions, inventions, and product of his own brain, is fo incident unto him, and feated in his faln natur, that, fo long as his natural fpirit is the firft author and actor of him, and is that, by which he onely is guided and moved in his worfhip towards God, fo as not firft to wait for another Guide to direct him, he can never perform the pure Spiritual worfhip, nor bring forth any thing, but the fruit of the firft, faln, natural, and corrupt root. Wherefore the time appointed of God being come, wherein by Jefus Chrift he hath been pleafed to reftore the true Spiritual Worfhip, and the outward form of worfhip, which was appointed by God to the Jewes, and whereof the manner and time of its performance was particularly determined by God himfelf, being come to an end, we find that Jefus Chrift, the Author of the Chriftian Religion, prefcribes no fet form of worfhip to his children under the more pure adminiftration of the New Covenant; * fave that he onely
tells

** If any object here, that the Lord's prayer is a prefcribed form of Prayer, and therefore of Worfhip, given by Chrift to his children.*   Obj.

I anfwer, firft, This can not be objected by any fort of Chriftians, that I know, becaufe there are none, who ufe not other prayers, or that limit their worfhip to this. Secondly, this was commanded to the Difciples while yet weak, before they had received the difpenfation of the Gofpel, not that they fhould onely ufe it in praying, but that he might fhew them by one example, how that their prayers ought to be fhort, and not like the long prayers of the Pharifee; and that this was the ufe of it, appears by all the prayers, which divers Saints afterwards made ufe of, whereof the Scriptur makes mention, for none made ufe of   Anfw.

this

thus, neither repeated it, but used other words, according as the thing required, and as the Spirit gave utterance. Thirdly, that this ought so to be understood, appears from Rom. 8: 26. of which afterwards mention shall be made at greater length, where the Apostle saith, We know not what we should pray for as we ought : but the Spirit it self maketh intercession for us, &c. But if this prayer had been such a prescribed form of prayer to the Church, that had not been true, neither had they been ignorant what to pray, nor should they have needed the help of the Spirit to teach them.

tells them, that the *worship, now to be performed*, is *Spiritual*, and in *the Spirit*; and it's especially to be observed, that in the whole New Testament there is no order, nor command given in this thing, but to follow the revelations of the Spirit, save onely that general, of meeting together; a thing dearly owned and diligently practised by us, as shall hereafter more appear. True it is, mention is made of the dutys of praying, preaching, and singing, but what order or method should be kept in so doing, or that presently they should be set about so soon as the Saints are gathered, there is not one word to be found, yea these dutyes (as shall afterwards be made appear) are alwayes annexed to the assistance, leadings and motions of God's Spirit. Since then man in his natural state is thus excluded from acting or moving in things Spiritual, how or what way shall he exercise this first and previous duty of waiting upon God, but by silence, and by bringing that natural part to silence? Which is no other wayes, but by abstaining from his own thoughts and imaginations, and from all the self-workings and motions of his own mind, as wel in things materially good, as evil, that, he being silent, *God* may *speak in him*, and the *Good Seed* may arise. This, though hard to the natural man, is so answerable to Reason and even natural experience in other things, that it can not be denyed. He, that cometh to learn of a master, if he expect to hear his master, & be instructed by him, must not continually, be speaking of the matter to be taught, and never be quiet, otherwise how shall his master have time to instruct him? yea though the scholar were never so earnest to learn the science, yet would the master have reason to reprove him, as untoward & indocile, if he would alwayes be meddling of himself, and still speaking, and not wait in silence patiently to hear his master instructing and teaching him, who ought not to open a mouth, untill by his master he were commanded and allowed so to do. So also, if one were about to attend a great Prince, he would be thought an impertinent and imprudent servant, who, while he ought patiently and readily to wait,

that

that he might anſwer the King, when he ſpeaks, and have his eye upon him to obſerve the leaſt motions and inclinations of his will, and to do accordingly, would be ſtill deafening him with diſcourſe, though it were in praiſes of him, and running to and fro, without any particular and immediat order to do things, that perhaps might be good in them-ſelves, or might have been commanded at other times to others. Would the Kings of the Earth accept of ſuch ſervants, or ſervice? Since then we are commanded to *wait upon God diligently*, and in ſo doing it is pro-miſed, that our *ſtrength ſhall be renewed*, this waiting can not be perform-ed but by a ſilence, or ceſſation of the natural part on our ſide, ſince God manifeſts himſelf not to the outward man or ſenſes ſo much as to the inward, to wit, to the Soul and ſpirit, if the Soul be ſtill thinking and working in her own will, and buſily exerciſed in her own imaginations, though the matters, as in themſelves, may be good concerning God, yet thereby ſhe incapacitats her ſelf from diſcerning the *ſtill ſmall voyce of the Spirit*, and ſo hurts her ſelf greatly, in that ſhe neglects her *chief buſi-neſs of waiting upon the Lord*; nothing leſs then if I ſhould buſy my ſelf crying out and ſpeaking of a buſineſs, while in the mean time I neglect to hear one, who is quietly whiſpering into my ear, and informing me in theſe things, which are moſt needfull for me to hear and know con-cerning that buſineſs. And ſince it is the chief work of a Chriſtian to know the natural will, in its own proper motions, crucified, that God may both move in the act and in the will, the Lord chiefly regards this pro-found ſubjection and ſelf-denial. For ſome men pleaſe themſelves as much, and gratifie their own ſenſual wills and humors in high and curious ſpeculations of religion, affecting a name and reputation that way, or becauſe thoſe things by cuſtom, or other wayes, are become pleaſant and habitual to them, though not a white more regenerated, or inwardly ſanctified in their ſpirits, as others gratifie their luſts in actions of ſenſua-lity; and therefore both are alike hurtfull to men and ſinfull in the ſight of God, it being nothing but the meer fruit and effect of man's natural and unrenewed will and ſpirit. Yea ſhould one (as many no doubt do) from a ſenſe of ſin and fear of puniſhment ſeek to terrifie themſelves from ſin, by multiplying thoughts of death, hell and judgment, and by pre-ſenting to their imaginations the happyneſs and joyes of heaven, and alſo by multiplying prayers and other religious performances, as theſe things could never deliver him from one iniquity without the ſecret and inward

I i 2

Power

Power of God's Spirit and Grace, so would they signifie no more, than the fig-leaves, wherewith *Adam* thought to cover his nakedness; and seing it is onely the product of man's own natural will, proceeding from a self-love, and seeking to save himself, and not arising purely from that *Divine Seed* of *Righteousness*, which is given of God to *all* for *Grace* and *Salvation*, it is rejected of God, and no wayes acceptable unto him, since the natural man, as natural, while he stands in that state, is with all his arts, parts, and actings reprobated by him. This great duty then of waiting upon God must needs be exercised in man's denying *self*, both inwardly and outwardly in a still and meer dependence upon God, in abstracting from all the workings, imaginations and speculations of his own mind, that, being emptyed, as it were, of himself, and so throughly crucified to the natural products thereof, he may be fit to receive the Lord, who will have no copartner nor corrival of his Glory and Power. And man being thus stated, the little Seed of Righteousness, which God hath planted *in* his Soul, and Christ hath purchased for him, even the measur of Grace and Life, (which is burthened and crucified by man's natural thoughts and imaginations) receives a place to arise, and becometh a holy birth, and genitur *in* man, and is that *Divine air*, in, and by which man's Soul and spirit comes to be leavened. And by waiting therein he comes to be accepted in the sight of God, to stand in his presence, hear his voyce, and observe the motions of his Holy Spirit. And so man's place is, to wait in this; and as hereby there are any objects presented to his mind concerning God or things relating to Religion, his Soul may be exercised in them without hurt, and to the great profit both of himself and others, because those things have their rise not from his own will, but from God's Spirit. And therefore, as in the arisings and movings of this, his mind is still to be exercised in thinking and meditating, so also in the more obvious acts of preaching and praying. And so it may hence appear, we are not against meditation, as some have sought falsely to inferr from our doctrin; but we are against the thoughts and imaginations of the natural man in his own will, from which all errors and heresies concerning the Christian Religion, in the whole world, have proceeded. But if it please God at any time, when one or more are waiting upon him, not to present such objects, as gives them occasion to exercise their minds in thoughts and imaginations, but purely to keep them in this holy dependence, and, as they persist there-

in,

in, to caufe his fecret refrefhment and the pure incomes of his holy Life to flow in upon them, then they have good reafon to be content, becaufe by this (as we know by good and bleffed experience) the Soul is more ftrengthened, renewed, and confirmed in the love of God, and armed againft the power of fin, than any wayes elfe: this being a fore-taft of that real and fenfible enjoyment of God, which the Saints in heaven daily poffefs, which God frequently affords to his children here, for their comfort and encouragment, efpecially when they are affembled together to wait upon him.

§ XI. For there are *two contrary powers* or *ſpirits*, to wit, *the power and ſpirit of this world*, in which the Prince of darknefs bears rule, and over as many as are acted by it and work from it, and *the Power or Spirit of God*, in which God worketh and beareth rule, and over as many as act in and from it. So whatever be the things, that a man thinketh of, or acteth in, however Spiritual or religious, as to the notion or form of them, fo long as he acteth and moveth in the natural and corrupt fpirit, and will, and not from, in, and by the Power of God, he finneth in all, and is not accepted of God. For hence both *the ploughing* and praying *of the* Prov. 21: *wicked is fin*: as alfo whatever a man acts in and from the Spirit and Power vers 4. of God, having his underftanding and will influenced and moved by it, whether it be actions religious, civil, or even natural, he is accepted in fo doing in the fight of God, and is *bleffed in them*. From what is faid it Ja. 1: 25. doth appear, how frivolous and impertinent their objection is, that fay, they *wait upon God in praying and preaching*, fince *waiting* doth of it felf imply *a paſſive dependence* rather, than an *acting*; and fince it is, and fhall yet be more fhewn, that preaching and praying without the Spirit is an offending of God, not a waiting upon him, and that praying and preaching by the Spirit prefuppofes neceffarily a filent waiting, for to feel the motions and influence of the Spirit to lead thereunto. And laftly, that in feveral of thefe places, where praying is commanded, as Matth. 26: 41. Mark. 13: 33. Luk. 21: 36. 1 Pet. 4: 7. watching is fpecially prefixed, as a previous preparation thereunto. So that we do wel and certainly conclude, that, fince waiting and watching is fo particularly commanded and recommended, and this can not be truely performed, but in this inward filence of the mind from mens own thoughts and imaginations, this filence is, and muft neceffarily be, a fpecial and principal part of God's worfhip.

I i 3

§ XII.

§ XII. But secondly: The excellency of this silent waiting upon God doth appear, in that it is impossible for the enemy, viz, the devil, to counterfeit it, so as for any Soul to be deceived or deluded by him in the exercise thereof. Now, in all other matters he may mix himself in with the natural mind of man, and so, by transforming himself, he may deceive the Soul, by busying it about things perhaps innocent in themselves, while yet he keeps them from beholding the *Pure Light of Christ*, and so from knowing distinctly his duty, and doing of it. For that envious spirit of man's eternal happyness knoweth wel, how to accommodat himself, and fit his snares for all the several dispositions and inclinations of men; if he find one not fit to be engaged with gross sins or worldly lusts, but rather averse from them, and religiously inclined, he can fit himself to beguile such an one, by suffering his thoughts and imaginations to runn upon Spiritual matters, and so hurry them to work, act, and meditat in their own wills: for he wel knoweth, that, so long as *self* bears rule, and the Spirit of God is not the principal and chief actor, man is not put out of his reach, so therefore he can accompany the priest to the altar, the preacher to the pulpit, the Zelot to his prayers, yea the Doctor and Professor of Divinity to his study, and there he can chearfully suffer him to labour and work among his books, yea and help him to find out and invent subtile distinctions and quidditys, by which both his mind, and others through him, may be kept from heeding *God's Light in the* Conscience, and waiting upon him. There is not any exercise whatsoever, wherein he can not enter and have a chief place, so as the Soul many times can not discern it, except in this alone; for he can onely work in and by the natural man, and his facultys, by secretly acting upon his imaginations and desires, &c. and therefore, when he, to wit, the natural man, is silent, there he must also stand. And therefore, when the Soul comes to this silence, and, as it were, is brought to nothingness, as to her own workings, then the devil is shut out, for the *Pure Presence of God*, and *shining* of his *Light* he can not abide, because so long as a man is thinking and meditating as of himself, he can not be sure, but the devil is influencing him therein, but when he comes wholly to be silent, as the *Pure Light of God* shines in upon him, then he is sure that the devil is shut out, for beyond the imaginations he can not go, which we often find by sensible experience. For he, that of old is said to have come to the gathering together of the children of God, is not wanting to come to our assemblys, and indeed he can

wel

wel enter and work in a meeting, that's filent onely as to words, either by keeping the minds in various thoughts and imaginations, or by ftupifying them, fo as to overwhelm them with a fpirit of heavynefs and flothfulnefs; but, when we retire out of all and are turned in, both by being diligent and watchfull upon the one hand, and alfo filent and retired out of all our thoughts upon the other, as we abide in this fure place, we feel our felves out of his reach; yea often-times the Power and Glory of God will break forth and appear, juft as the bright fun through many clouds and mifts, to the difpelling of that power of darknefs, which will alfo be fenfibly felt feeking to cloud and darken the mind, and wholly to keep it from purely waiting upon God.

§ XIII. Thirdly: The *excellency* of this *worfhip* doth appear, in that it can neither be ftopped, nor interrupted by the malice of men or devils, as all other can. Now interruptions and ftoppings of worfhip may be underftood in a twofold refpect, either as we are hindered from meeting, as being outwardly by violence feparated one from another; or, when permitted to meet together, as we are interrupted by the tumult, noife and confufion, which fuch as are malitious may ufe, to moleft or diftract us. Now in both thefe refpects this worfhip doth greatly overpafs all others; for how far fo ever people be feparate or hindred from coming together, yet as every one is inwardly gathered to the meafur of Life *in* himfelf, there is a fecret unity and fellowfhip enjoyed, which the devil and all his inftruments can never break or hinder. But fecondly, it doth as wel appear, as to thefe moleftations, which occur, when we are met together, what advantage this true and Spiritual Worfhip gives us, beyond all others, feing in defpite of a thoufand interruptions and abufes, one of which were fufficient to have ftopped all other forts of Chriftians, we have been able, through the natur of this worfhip, to keep it uninterrupted as to God, and alfo at the fame time to fhew forth an example of our Chriftian patience towards all, even oftentimes to the reaching and convincing of our oppofers; for there is no fort of worfhip ufed by others, which can fubfift, (though they be permitted to meet) unlefs they be either authorized and protected by the Magiftrate, or defend themfelves with the arme of flefh, but we at the fame time exercife worfhip towards God, and alfo patiently bear the reproaches and ignominys, which Chrift prophefied fhould be fo incident and frequent to Chriftians; for how can the *Papifts* fay their *Mafs*, if there be any there to

disturb

difturb and interrupt them? Do but take away the Mafs book, the calice, the hoft, or the Prieft's garments; yea do but fpill the water or the wine, or blow out the candles, (a thing quickly done) and the whole bufinefs is marred, and no facrifice can be offered. Take from the *Lutherans* or *Epifcopalians* their *Liturgy*, or common prayer book, and no fervice can be faid. Remove from the *Calvinifts*, *Arminians*, *Socinians*, *Independents* or *Anabaptifts* the pulpit, the Bible, and the hour-glafs, or make but fuch a noife, as the voice of the preacher can not be heard, or difturb him but fo, before he come, or ftrip him of his Bible and his books, and he muft be dumb: for they all think it an herefy, to wait to fpeak as the Spirit of God giveth utterance; and thus eafily their whole worfhip may be marred. But when people meet together, and their worfhip confifteth not in fuch outward acts, and they depend not upon any ones fpeaking, but meerly fit down to wait upon God, and to be gathered out of all vifibles, and to feel the Lord in Spirit, none of thefe things can hinder them; of which we may fay of a truth, we are fenfible witnefles; for when the Magiftrates, ftirred up by the malice and envy of our oppofers, have ufed all means poffible, and yet in vain, to deter us from meeting together, and that openly and publikly in our own hired houfes, for that purpofe; both death, bannifhments, imprifonments, finings, beatings, whippings, and other fuch devilifh inventions have proven ineffectual to terrifie us from our holy affemblys, I fay, and we having thus oftentimes purchafed our liberty to meet by deep fufferings, our oppofers have then taken another way, by turning in upon us the worft & wickedeft people, yea the very off-fcourings of men, who by *all manner of inhumane, beaftly*, and *brutifh behaviour* have fought to provoke us, weary us, and moleft us, but in vain. It would be almoft incredible to declare, and indeed a fhame, that, among men pretending to be Chriftians, it fhould be mentioned, what things of this kind mens eyes have feen, and I my felf, with others, have fhared of in fuffering, there they have often beaten us, and caft water and dirt upon us; there they have danced, leaped, fung, and fpoken all manner of profane and ungodly words, offered violence, and fhamefull behaviour to grave women and virgins, jeared, mocked, and fcoffed, asking us, *if the Spirit was not yet come*, and much more, which were tedious here to relate; and all this, while we have been ferioufly and filently fitting together, and waiting upon the Lord, fo that by thefe things our inward and fpiritual fellowfhip with

God

God and one with another in the *pure life* of *Righteoufnefs* hath not been hindered. But on the contrary, the Lord, knowing our fufferings and reproaches for his teftimony's fake, hath caufed his Power and Glory more to abound among us, and hath mightily refrefhed us by the fenfe of his love, which hath filled our Soules, and fo much the rather as we found our felves gathered into *the Name of the Lord*, which is the *ftrong tower of the righteous*, Prov. 18: whereby we felt our felves fheltered from receiving any inward hurt 10. through their malice; and alfo that he had delivered us from that vain name and profeffion of **Chriftianity**, under which our oppofers were not afhamed to bring forth thefe bitter and curfed fruits; yea fometimes in the midft of this tumult and oppofition God would powerfully move fome or other of us by his Spirit, both to teftifye of that joy, which, notwithftanding their malice, we enjoyed, and powerfully to declare in the evidence and demonftration of the Spirit againft their folly and wickednefs, fo as the Power of Truth hath brought them to fome meafur of quietnefs and ftilnefs, and ftopped the impetuous ftreams of their fury and madnefs: that as ever of old Mofes by his rod divided the waves of the red fea, that the Ifraelits might pafs, fo God hath thus by his Spirit made a way for us in the midft of this raging wickednefs, peaceably to enjoy and poffefs him, and accomplifh our worfhip to him. So that fometimes upon fuch occafions feveral of our oppofers and interrupters have hereby been convinced of the Truth, and gatheredfrom being perfecutors to be fufferers with us. And let it not be forgotten, but let it be infcribed and abide for a conftant remembrance of the thing, that in thefe beaftly and brutifh pranks, ufed to moleft us in our Spiritual meetings, none have been more bufy, than the young ftudents of the Univerfitys, who were learning Philofophy, and Divinity, fo called, and many of them preparing themfelves for the miniftery. Should we committ to writing all the *abominations* committed in this refpect by the *young fry* of the *Clergy*, it would make no fmall volumn, as the Churches of Chrift, gathered into his Pure worfhip in *Oxford* and *Cambridge* in *England*, and *Edinburgh* and *Aberdeen* in *Scotland*, where the univerfitys are, can wel bear witnefs.

§ XIV. Moreover, in this we know, that we are partakers of the New covenant's difpenfation, and difciples of Chrift indeed, fharing with him of that Spiritual worfhip, which is performed in the Spirit and in Truth, becaufe, as he was, fo are we in this world. For the old Covenant worfhip had an outward glory, temple, and ceremonys, and was

K k

full

full of outward splendor, and majesty, having an outward tabernacle, and altar beautified with gold, silver and precious stones, and their sacrifices were tied to an outward particular place, even the outward mount *Zion*, and those, that prayed, behoved to pray with their faces towards that outward Temple, and therefore all this behoved to be protected by an outward arm, nor could the Jewes peaceably have enjoyed it, but when they were secured from the violence of their outward enemies, and therefore when at any time their enemies prevailed over them, their glory was darkened, and their sacrifices stopped, & the face of their worship marred; hence they complain, lament, and bewail the destroying of the Temple, as a loss irreparable. But Jesus Christ, the Author and Institutor of the New Covenant worship, testifies, that God is neither to be worshipped in this nor that place, but in the Spirit and in Truth; and forasmuch as his *Kingdom is not of this world*, neither doth his worship consist in it, or need either the wisdom, glory, riches or splendor of this world, to beautifie or adorn it, nor yet the outward power or arm of flesh to maintain, uphold or protect it; but it is and may be performed by those, that are spiritually minded, notwithstanding all opposition, violence, and malice of men; because, it being purely Spiritual, it is out of the reach of natural men to interrupt or molest it; even as Jesus Christ, the Author thereof, did enjoy and possess his *Spiritual Kingdom*, while oppressed, persecuted, and rejected of men, and as, in despite of the malice and rage of the devil, *he spoiled principalitys and powers, triumphing over them, and, through death, destroyed him, that had the power of death, that is, the devil*; so also all his followers both can and do worship him, not onely without the arm of flesh to protect them, but even when oppressed. For their worship, being spiritual, is by the Power of the Spirit defended and maintained: but such worships as are carnal and consist in carnal and outward ceremonys and observations, need a carnal and outward arm to protect them, and defend them, else they can not stand and subsist. And therefore it appears, that the several worships of our opposers both Papists and Protestants are of this kind, and not the true Spiritual and New Covenant worship of Christ, because, as hath been observed, they can not stand without the protection or countenance of the outward Magistrate, neither can be performed, if there be the least opposition: for they are not in the patience of Jesus, to serve and worship him with sufferings, ignominies, calumnies, and reproaches; And from hence have

sprung

Joh. 18:
vers 36.

Col. 2:
vers 15.

fprung all thofe warrs, fightings, and blood-fhed among Chriftians, while each by the arm of flefh endeavoured to defend & protect their own way and worfhip; and from this alfo fprung up that monftrous opinion of *perfecution*, of which we fhall fpeak more at length hereafter.

§ XV. But fourthly, The nature of this worfhip, which is performed by the Operation of the Spirit, the natural man being filent, doth appear from thefe words of Chrift, Joh. 4: 23, 24. *But the hour cometh, and now is, when the true worfhippers fhall worfhip the Father in Spirit and in Truth: for the Father feeketh fuch to worfhip him. God is a Spirit, and they that worfhip him, muft worfhip him in Spirit and in Truth.* This teftimony is the more fpecially to be obferved, for that it is both the firft, chiefeft and moft ample teftimony, which Chrift gives us, of his Chriftian worfhip, as different and contradiftinguifhed from that under the *Law*. For Firft, he fheweth, that the feafon is now come, wherein the *Worfhip* muft be *in Spirit and in Truth, for the Father feeketh fuch to worfhip him*: fo then it is no more a worfhip confifting in outward obfervations, to be performed by man at fet times or opportunitys, which he can do in his own will, and by his own natural ftrength, for elfe it would not differ in matter, but onely in fome circumftances, from that under the *Law*. Next, as for a reafon of this worfhip, we need not to give any other, and indeed none can give a better, than that, which Chrift giveth, which I think fhould be fufficient to fatisfie every Chriftian, to wit, GOD *is a* SPIRIT, *and they, that worfhip him, muft worfhip him in Spirit and in Truth*. As this ought to be received, becaufe it is the words of Chrift, fo alfo it is founded upon fo clear a demonftration of *Reafon*, as fufficiently evidenceth its verity. For Chrift excellently argues from the analogy, that ought to be betwixt the *Object* and the *worfhip* directed thereunto:

God is a Spirit: Arg.
Therefore he muft be worfhipped in Spirit.

This is fo certain, that it can fuffer no contradiction, yea and this analogy is fo neceffary to be minded, that, under the *Law*, when God inftituted and appointed that ceremonial worfhip to the Jewes, becaufe that worfhip was outward, that there might be an analogy, he faw it neceffary to condefcend to them, as in a fpecial manner, to dwell betwixt the Cherubims within the tabernacle, and afterwards to make the Temple of Jerufalem in a fort his habitation, and caufe fomething of an outward

K k 2

glory

and majesty to appear, by causing fire from heaven to consume the sacrifices, and filling the Temple with a cloud, through and by which mediums, visible to the outward eye, he manifested himself proportionably to that outward worship, which he had commanded them to perform. So now under the New Covenant, he seeing meet in his heavenly wisdom to lead his children in a path more heavenly and Spiritual, and in a way both more easy and familiar, and also purposing to disappoynt carnal and outward observations, that his may have an eye more to an *inward glory* and *Kingdom*, than to an outward, he hath given us, for an example hereof, the appearance of his Beloved Son the Lord Jesus Christ, who (in stead that Moses delivered the Israëlits out of their outward bondage, and by outwardly destroying their enemies) hath delivered and doth deliver us by suffering, and dying by the hands of his enemies, thereby triumphing over the devil, and his, and our inward enemies, and delivering us therefrom: he hath also instituted an inward and Spiritual worship, so that God now tieth not his people to the temple of Jerusalem, nor yet unto outward ceremonies and observations, but taketh the *heart* of every Christian for a *Temple* to dwell in, and there immediately appeareth, and giveth him directions, how to serve him in any outward acts. Since, as Christ argueth, *God is a Spirit*, he will now be worshipped in the Spirit, where he reveals himself, and dwelleth with the contrite in heart: Now, since it is the heart of man, that now is become the Temple of God, in which he will be worshipped, and no more in particular outward temples, (since, as blessed *Stephen* said, out of the Prophet, to the professing Jewes of old, *the Most High dwelleth not in temples made with hands*) as, before the glory of the Lord descended to fill the outward temple, it behoved to be purified and cleansed, and all polluted stuff removed out of it, yea and the place for the tabernacle was overlaid with gold, the most pretious, clean, and clearest of metalls; so also, before God be worshipped in the inward temple of the heart, it must also be purged of its own filth, and all its own thoughts and imaginations, that so it may be fit to receive the Spirit of God, and to be acted by it, and doth not this directly lead us to that inward silence, of which we have spoken, and exactly pointed out? And further, This worship must be *in truth*; intimating, that this Spiritual worship thus acted is onely and properly a true worship, as being that, which, for the reasons above observed, can not be counterseited by the enemy, nor yet performed by the hypocrit.

Actor. 7: 48.

§ XVI.

§ XVI. And though this worſhip be indeed very different from the divers eſtabliſhed invented worſhips among Chriſtians, and therefore may ſeem ſtrange to many, yet hath it been teſtiſied of, commended, and practiſed by the moſt pious of all ſorts, in all ages, by many evident teſtimonies might be proved, ſo that from the profeſſing and practiceing thereof the name of *Myſtiks* hath ariſen, as of a certain ſect generally commended by all, whoſe writings are full both of the explanation and of the commendation of this ſort of worſhip, where they plentifully aſſert this *inward introverſion*, and *abſtraction of the mind*, as they call it, *from all images and thoughts*, and the *prayer of the will*, yea they look upon this as *the heighth of Chriſtian perfection*, ſo that ſome of them, though profeſſed Papiſts, do not doubt to affirm, that, ſuch as have attained this method of worſhip, or are aiming at it, (as in a book, called *Sancta Sophia*, put out by the Engliſh Benedictins, printed at *Douay*, anno 1657. Tract. 1. Sect. 2. cap. 5.) *need not, nor ought to trouble or buſy themſelves with frequent and unneceſſary confeſſions, with exerçiſing corporal labors and auſteritys, the uſing of vocal voluntary prayers, the hearing of a number of maſſes, or ſet devotions, or exerciſes to Saints, or prayers for the dead, or having ſoliçiteus and diſtracting cares to gain indulgençes, by going to ſuch and ſuch Churches, or adjoyning ones ſelf to confraternitys, or intangling ones ſelf with vowes and promiſes, becauſe ſuch kind of things hinder the Soul from obſerving the operations of the Divine Spirit, in it, and from having liberty to follow the Spirit, whither it would draw her.* And yet who knowes not, but that in ſuch kind of obſervations the very ſubſtance of the Popiſh religion conſiſteth? Yet neverthelefs it appears by this and many other paſſages, which out of their *Myſtik* writers might be mentioned, how they look upon this worſhip as excelling all other, and that ſuch as arrived hereunto had no abſolute need of the others; yea (ſee the life of *Balthazar Alvares*, in the ſame *Sancta Sophia*, Tract. 3 ſect. 1. cap. 7.) ſuch as taſted of this, quickly confeſſed that the other formes and ceremonies of worſhip were uſeleſs as to them, neither did they perform them as things neceſſary, but meerly for order or exampl's ſake; and therefore thoughſome of them were ſo overclouded with the common darkneſs of their profeſſion, yet could they affirm that this Spiritual worſhip was ſtill to be retained and ſoughtfor, though there be a neceſſity of omitting their outward ceremonys. Hence *Bernard*, as in many other places, ſo in his epiſtle to one *William*, Abbot of the ſame order, ſaith, *Take heed to the rule of God, the Kingdom of God is within you*: and afterwards,

K k 3

ſay-

saying that their outward orders and rules should be observed, he adds, *but otherwise when it shall happen, that one of those two must be omitted in such a case, these are much rather to be omitted, than those former; for by how much the Spirit is more excellent and noble than the body, by so much are Spiritual exercises more profitable than corporal.* Is not that then the best of worships, which the best of men in all ages and of all sects have commended, and which is most suteable to the doctrin of Christ, I say, is not that worship to be followed and performed? And so much the rather as God hath raised a people to testifie for it, and preach it to their great refreshment and strengthening, in the very face of the world, and notwithstanding much opposition, who do not, as these *Mystiks*, make of it a mystery onely to be attained by a few men or women in a cloyster, or, as their mistake was, after wearying themselves with many outward ceremonyes and observations, as if it were the consequence of such a labor. But who in the free love of God (who respects not persons, and was near to hear and reveal himself as wel to *Cornelius* a centurion and a Roman, as to *Simeon* and *Anna*, and who discovered his glory to Mary a poor handmaid, and to the poor shepherds rather than to the high priests and devout proselyts among the Jewes) in and according to his free love finding that God is revealing and establishing this worship, and making many poor tradesmen, yea young boyes and girles, witnesses of it, do intreat and beseech all to lay aside all their own will-worships and voluntary acts performed in their own wills, and by their own meer natural strength and power, without retiring out of their own vain imaginations and thoughts, or feeling the *pure Spirit of God* to move and stir *in* them, that they may come to practise this acceptable worship, which is *in Spirit and in Truth.* But against this worship they object

	 Obj. § XVII. First, *It seemes to be an unprofitable exercise for a man to be doing or thinking nothing, and that one might be much better imployed either in meditating upon some good subject, or otherwise praying to or praising God.*

•   Answ.   I *answer,* That is not unprofitable, which is of absolute necessity, before any other duty can be acceptably performed, as we have shewn this waiting to be. Moreover, those have but a carnal and gross apprehension of God, and of the things of his Kingdom, that imagin that men please him by their own workings and actings, whereas, as hath been shewn, the first step for man to fear God is to cease from his own thoughts and imaginations, and suffer God's Spirit to work in him: for we must *cease to do evil,*

Isa.1: 16, 17.

crc

ere we *learn to do wel*; and this meddling in things Spiritual by man's own natural underftanding is one of the greateft and moft dangerous evils, that man is incident to, being that, which occafioned our firft parents fall, to wit, a forwardnefs to defire to know things, and a meddling with them, both without and contrary to the Lord's command.

Secondly fome *object*, *if your worfhip meerly confift in inwardly retiring to the Lord, and feeling of his Spirit arife in you, and then to do outward acts, as ye are led by it, what need ye have publik meetings at fet times and places, fince every one may enjoy this at home? or fhould not every one ftay at home, untill they be particularly moved to go to fuch a place at fuch a time; fince to meet at fet times and places feemes to be an outward obfervation and ceremony contrary to what ye at other times affert?* .   *Obj.*

I *anfwer* firft, To meet at fet times and places is not any religious act, or part of worfhip, in it felf, but onely an outward conveniency, neceffary for our feing one another, fo long as we are cloathed with this outward tabernacle; and therefore our meeting at fet times and places is not a part of our worfhip, but a preparatory accommodation of our outward man, in order to a publik vifible worfhip, Since we fet not about the vifible acts of worfhip, when we meet together, untill we be led there-unto. Secondly, God hath feen meet, fo long as his children are in this world, to make ufe of the outward fenfes, as a means, to convey Spiritual Life, as by fpeaking, praying, praifing, &c, which can not be done to mutual edification, but when we hear and fee one another, but alfo for to entertain an outward vifible teftimony for his Name in the world: he caufeth the inward Life (which is alfo many times not con-veyed by the outward fenfes) the more to abound, when his children affemble themfelves diligently together to wait upon him; that, *as iron fharpeneth iron*, fo the feing of the face one of another, when both are in-wardly gathered unto the *Life*, giveth occafion for the *Life* fecretly to arife, and pafs from veffel to veffel; and as many candles lighted and put in one place do greatly augment the light, and makes it more to fhine forth; fo when many are gathered together into the fame Life, there is more of the Glory of God, and his Power appears to the refrefhment of each individual, for that he partakes not onely of the *Light* and *Life*, raif-ed *in* himfelf, but in all the reft; and therefore Chrift hath particularly promifed a bleffing to fuch as affemble together *in* his *Name*, feing he will be *in the midft of them*, Matth. 18:20. and the author to the Hebrewes   *Anfw.*

  Prov. 27: vers 17.

doth

doth precisely prohibit the neglect of this duty, as being of very dangerous and dreadfull consequence, in these words, Heb. 10: 24. *And let us consider one another to provoke unto love, and to good works: Not forsaking the assembling of our selves together, as the manner of some is; ---- For if we sin wilfully after that we have received the knowledge of the Truth, there remaineth no more sacrifice for sins.* And therefore the Lord hath shewn, that he hath a particular respect to such as thus assemble themselves together, because that thereby a publik testimony for him is upheld in the earth, and his Name is thereby glorified; and therefore such as are right in their spirits are naturally drawn to keep the meetings of God's people, and never want a Spiritual influence to lead them thereunto. And if any do it in a meer customary way, they will no doubt suffer condemnation for it. Yet can not the appoynting of places and times be accounted a ceremony and observation done in man's will in the worship of God, seing none can say that it is an act of worship, but onely a meer presenting of our persons in order to it, as is above said. Which that it was practised by the primitive Church and Saints all our adversarys do acknowledg.

Obj.   Lastly, some object, *That this manner of Worship in silence is not to be found in all the Scriptur.*

Answ.   I answer, we make not silence to be the sole matter of our worship, since, as I have above said, there are many meetings, which are seldom, if ever, altogether silent, some or other are still moved either to preach, pray, and praise, and so, in this, our meetings can not be but like the meetings of the primitive Churches recorded in Scriptur, since our adversarys confess that they did preach and pray by the Spirit. And then, what absurdity is it to suppose that at some times the Spirit did not move them to these outward acts, and that then they were silent, since we may wel conclude, they did not speak, untill they were moved, and so no doubt had sometimes silence, Act. 2: 1. before the Spirit came upon them, it is said, ---- *they were all with one accord in one place:* and then it is said, *the Spirit suddenly came upon them:* but no mention is made of any one speaking at that time, and I would willingly know what absurdity our adversarys can inferr, should we conclude they were a while silent.

Inst.   But if it be urged, that *a whole silent meeting can not be found in Scriptur.*

Ans.   I answer, supposing such a thing were not recorded, it will not therefore follow that it is not lawfull, seing it naturally followeth from other Scriptur precepts, as we have proven this doth, for seing the

Scrifeing the Scriptur commands to meet together, and, when met, the Scriptur prohibits prayers or preachings, but as the Spirit moveth thereunto: if people meet together, and the Spirit move not to such acts, it will necessarily follow, that they must be silent. But further, there might have been many such things among the Saints of old, though not recorded in Scriptur, and yet we have enough in Scriptur, signifying that such things were. For *Job* sat silent seven dayes with his friends together; Job. 2:13 here was a long silent meeting. See also *Ezra* c. 9: 4. and *Ezechiel* c. 1: 14. & 20: 1. Thus having shewn the excellency of this worship, proven it from Scriptur and Reason, and answered the objections, which are commonly made against it, which, though it might suffice to the explanation and probation of our Proposition: yet I shall add something more particularly of *preaching*, *praying*, and *Singing*, and so proceed to the following Proposition.

§ XVIII. *Preaching*, as it's used both among Papists and Protestants, is for one man to take some place or verse of Scriptur, and thereon speak for an hour or two, what he hath studyed and premeditated in his closet, and gathered together from his own inventions, or from the writings and observations of others, and then having got it by heart, as a school boy doth his lesson, he brings it forth and repeats it before the people: and how much the fertiler and stronger a man's invention is, and the more industrious and laborious he is in collecting such observations, and can utter them with the excellency of speech and humane eloquence, so much the more is he accounted an able and excellent preacher.

To this we oppose, that, when the Saints are met together, and every one gathered to the *Gift* and *Grace of God in themselves*, he, that ministreth, being acted thereunto by the arising of the Grace *in himself*, ought to speak forth what the Spirit of God furnisheth him with, not minding the eloquence and wisdom of words, but the demonstration of the Spirit and of Power, and that either in the interpreting some part of Scriptur, in case the *Spirit*, which is the *good Remembrancer*, lead him so to do, or otherwise words of exhortation, advice, reproof, and instruction, or the sense of some Spiritual experiences, all which will still be agreable to the Scriptur, though perhaps not relative to, nor founded upon any particular chapter or verse, as a text. Now let us examin and consider which of these two sorts of preaching be most agreable to the precepts and practice of Christ and his Apostles, and the primitive Church,

L l

record-

recorded in Scriptur. For First, as to their preaching upon a text, if it were not meerly cuſtomary or premeditated, but done by the immediat motion of the Spirit, we ſhould not blame it, but to do it, as they do, there is neither precept nor practice, that ever I could obſerve in the New Teſtament, as a part of the inſtituted worſhip thereof.

Obj.   But they *alledge*, that *Chriſt took the book of Iſajah, and read out of it, and ſpake therefrom, and that Peter preached from a ſentence of the Prophet Joel.*

Anſw.   I *anſwer* that Chriſt and Peter did it not, but as immediatly acted and moved thereunto by the Spirit of God, and that without premeditation, which I ſuppoſe our adverſarys will not deny; in which caſe we willingly approve of it: but what is this to their cuſtomary conned way, without either, waiting for or expecting the movings, or leadings of the Spirit? Moreover, that neither Chriſt nor Peter did it, as a ſettled cuſtom or form, to be conſtantly practiſed by all the miniſters of the Church, appears, in that moſt of all the ſermons recorded by Chriſt and his Apoſtles in Scriptur, were without this, as appears from Chriſt's ſermon upon the mount, Matth. 5: 1, *&c.* Mark. 4: 1, *&c.* and Paul's preaching to the Athenians and to the Jewes, *&c.* As then it appears that this method of preaching is not grounded upon any Scriptur precept, ſo the nature of it is contrary to the preaching of Chriſt under the New Covenant, as expreſt and recommended in Scriptur: for Chriſt, in ſending forth his Diſciples, expreſſely mentioneth, that they are not to ſpeak of or from themſelves, or to fore-caſt before hand, but that, which *the Spirit in the ſame hour ſhall teach* them, as is particularly mentioned in the three Evangeliſts, Matth. 10: 20. Mark. 13: 11. Luk. 12: 12. Now, if Chriſt gave this order to his Diſciples, before he departed from them, as that, which they were to practiſe, during his abode outwardly with them, much more were they to do it, after his departur, ſince then they were more ſpecially to receive the *Spirit* to *lead* them *in all things*, and to *bring all things to* their remembrance, Joh. 14: 26. And, if they were to do ſo, when they appeared before the Magiſtrates and Princes of the earth, much more in the worſhip of God, when they ſtand ſpecially before him, ſeing, as is above ſhewn, his worſhip is to be performed in Spirit, and therefore, after their receiving of the Holy Ghoſt, it is ſaid, Act. 2: 4. *they ſpake, as the Spirit gave them utterance,* not what they had ſtudyed, and gathered from books in their cloſets in a premeditated way.

Franciſcus

Franciscus Lambertus, before cited, speaketh wel, and sheweth their hypocrisy; *Tract* 5. of *Prophecy*, chap. 3. saying, *Where are they now, that glory in their inventions, who say A brave invention, a brave invention! this they call invention, which themselves have made up, but what have the faithfull to do with such kind of inventions? It is not figments, nor yet inventions, that we will have, but things that are solid, invincible, eternal and heavenly, not which men have invented, but which God hath revealed; for, if we believe the Scriptur, our invention serveth nothing, but to provoke God to our ruin.* And afterwards, *Beware* (saith he) *that thou determine not precisely to speak what before thou hast meditated, whatsoever it be, for, though it be lawfull to determine the text, which thou art to expound, yet not at all the interpretation; lest, if thou so dost, thou take from the Holy Spirit, that, which is his, to wit, to direct thy speech, that thou mayst prophesie in the Name of the Lord, denuded of all learning, meditation and experience, and as if thou hadst studyed nothing at all; committing thy heart, thy tongue, and thy self wholly unto his Spirit, and trusting nothing to thy former studying or meditation, but saying with thy self, in great confidence of the Divine promise, the Lord will give a word with much power unto those, that preach the Gospel. But above all things be carefull thou follow not the manner of hypocrits, who have written almost word by word what they are to say, as if they were to repeat some verses upon a theatre have learned all their preaching, as they do, that act tragedys, and afterwards, when they are in the place of prophesieing, pray the Lord, to direct their tongue: but in the mean time shuting up the way of the Holy Spirit, they determin to say nothing, but what they have written. O unhappy kind of Prophets, yea and truely cursed, which depend not upon God's Spirit, but upon their own writings or meditation! Why prayst thou to the Lord, thou false prophet, to give thee his holy Spirit, by which thou mayst speak things profitable, and yet thou repell'st the Spirit? why prefer'st thou thy meditation or study to the Spirit of God? otherwise why committ'st thou not thy self to the Spirit?*

§ X I X. Secondly, this manner of preaching, as used by them, considering that they also affirm, that it may be and often is performed by men, who are wicked or void of true Grace, can not onely not edifie the Church, beget or nourish true faith, but is destructive to it, being directly contrary to the nature of the Christian and Apostolik ministery, mentioned in the Scripturs: *for the Apostles preached the Gospel not in the wisdom of words, lest the Cross of Christ should be of none effect* 1 Cor. 1: 17. But this preaching, not being done by the actings and movings of God's Spirit but by man's invention and eloquence in his own will, and through

his

his natural and acquired parts and learning, is in the wisdom of words; and therefore the Cross of Christ is thereby made of none effect. *The Apostle's speech and preaching was not with enticing words of man's wisdom, but in demonstration of the Spirit and of Power. That the faith of their hearers should not stand in the wisdom of men, but in the Power of God,* 1 Cor. 2: 3, 4, 5, But this preaching having nothing of the Spirit and Power in it, both the preachers and hearers confessing they wait for no such thing, nor yet are often-times sensible of it, must needs stand in the enticing words of man's wisdom, since it is by the meer wisdom of man it is sought after and the meer strength of man's eloquence and enticing words it is uttered, and therefore no wonder, if the faith of such as hear and depend upon such preachers and preachings stand in the wisdom of men, and not in the Power of God. The Apostles declared that *they spake not in the words, which man's wisdom teacheth, but which the Holy Ghost teacheth,* 1 Cor. 2: 13. But these preachers confess that they are strangers to the Holy Ghost his motions and operations, neither do they wait to feel them, and therefore they speak in the words, which their own natural wisdom and learning teacheth them, mixing them in and adding them to such words as they steal of the Scriptur and other books, and therefore speak not what the Holy Ghost teacheth.

Thirdly, this is contrary to the method and order of the primitive Church, mentioned by the Apostle, 1 Cor. 14: 30, &c. where in preaching every one is to wait for his revelation, and to give place one unto another, according as things are revealed. But here there is no waiting for a revelation, but the preacher must speak, and not that, which is revealed unto him, but what he hath prepared and premeditated before hand.

Lastly, By this kind of preaching, the Spirit of God, which should be the chief instructor and teacher of God's people, and whose influence is that onely, which makes all preaching effectual and beneficial for the edifying of Soules, is shut out, and man's natural wisdom, learning and parts set up and exalted, which (no doubt) is a great and chief reason, why the preaching among the generality of Christians is so unfruitfull and unsuccessfull; yea according to this doctrin the devil may preach, and ought to be heard also, seing he both knoweth the Truth, and hath as much eloquence as any. But what availes excellency of speech, if the demonstration and Power of the Spirit be wanting, which toucheth the

Con-

Conſcience? We ſee, that, when the devil confeſſed to the Truth, yet Chriſt would have none of his teſtimony. And as theſe pregnant teſtimonys of the Scriptur do prove this part of preaching to be contrary to the doctrin of Chriſt, ſo do they alſo prove that of ours, before affirmed, to be conforme thereunto?

XX. But if any *object* after this manner, *Have not many been benefited, yea &* Obj. *both converted and edified by the miniſtery of ſuch as have premeditated their preachings? yea and hath not the Spirit often concurred, by its Divine influence, with preachings thus premeditated, ſo as they have been powerfully born in upon the Soules of the hearers, to their advantage?*

I *anſwer*, though that be granted, which I ſhall not deny, it will not Anſw. inferr that the thing was good in it ſelf, more than, becauſe Paul was met with by Chriſt, to the converting of his Soul, riding to *Damaſcus* to perſecut the Saints, that he did wel in ſo doing ; neither particular actions nor yet whole congregations (as we above obſerved) are to be meaſured by the acts of God's condeſcenſion, in times of ignorance. But beſides, it hath often-times faln out, that God, having a regard to the ſimplicity and integrity either of the preacher or hearers, hath faln in upon the heart of a preacher by his Power and holy influence, and thereby hath led them to ſpeak things, which were not in his premeditated diſcourſe, and which perhaps he never thought of before : and thoſe paſſing ejaculations, and unpremeditated, but living, exhortations, have proved more beneficial and refreſhfull both to preacher and hearers, than all their premeditated ſermons. But all that will not allow them to continue in theſe things, which in themſelves are not approved, but contrary to the practice of the Apoſtles, when God is raiſing up a people to ſerve him according to the primitive purity and ſpirituality ; yea ſuch acts of God's condeſcenſion in times of darkneſs and ignorance ſhould ingage all more and more to follow him, according as he reveals his moſt perfect and Spiritual way.

§ XXI. Having hitherto ſpoken of *Preaching*, now it is fit to ſpeak of *Praying*, concerning which the like controverſy ariſeth. Our adverſarys, whoſe *religion* is all, for the moſt part, *outſide*, and ſuch, whoſe acts are the meer products of man's natural will and abilitys, as they can preach, ſo can they pray, when they pleaſe, and therefore have their ſet particular prayers, I meddle not with the controverſys, among themſelves concerning this, ſome of them being for ſet prayers, as a *liturgy*,

others

others for such as are *ex tempore* conceived; it suffices me, that all of them agree in this, that the motions and influence of the Spirit of God are not necessary to be previous thereunto; and therefore they have set times in their publik worship, as before and after preaching, and in their privat devotion, as morning and evening, and before and after meat, and other such occasions, at which they precisely set about the performing of their prayers, by speaking words to God, whether they feel any motions or influence of the Spirit or not; so that some of the chiefest have confessed that they have thus prayed without the motions or assistance of the Spirit, acknowledging that they sinned in so doing, yet they said they look upon it as their duty to do so, though to pray without the Spirit be sin. We freely confess, that prayer is both very profitable, and a necessary duty, commanded, and fit to be practised frequently by all Christians; but as we can do nothing without Christ, so neither can we pray without the concurrence and assistance of his Spirit. But that the state of the controversy may be the better understood, let it be considered, First, that *Prayer* is twofold, *inward*, and *outward*. *Inward Prayer* is that *secret turning of the mind towards God*, whereby, being secretly touched and awakened by the *Light of Christ in the Conscience*, and so bowed down under the sense of its iniquitys, unworthyness, and misery, it looks up to God, and joyning issue with the secret shinings of the *Seed* of God it breaths towards him, and is constantly breathing forth some secret desires and aspirations towards him. It is in this sense that we are so frequently in Scriptur commanded to *pray continually*, Luk. 18: 1. 1 Thess. 5: 17. Eph. 6: 18. Luk. 21: 36. which can not be understood of outward prayer, because it were impossible that men should be alwayes upon their knees, expressing words of prayer, and this would hinder them from the exercise of those dutys, no less positively commanded. *Outward Prayer* is when as the spirit (being thus in the exercise of inward retirement, and feeling the breathing of the Spirit of God to arise powerfully *in* the Soul) receives strength and liberty, by a supperadded motion and influence of the Spirit, to bring forth either audible sighs, groans, or words, and that either in publik assemblys, or in privat, or at meat, &c.

As then *inward prayer is necessary at all times*, so, so long as the day of every man's visitation lasteth, he never wants some influence, less or more for the practice of it. Because he no sooner retires his mind, and considers himself in God's presence, but he finds himself in the practice of it.

The

The outward exercife of Prayer as needing a greater and fuperadded influence and motion of the Spirit, as it can not be continually practifed, fo neither can it be fo readily, fo as to be effectually performed, untill his mind be fometime acquainted with the inward ; therefore fuch as are diligent and watchfull in their minds, and much retired in the exercife of this inward prayer, are more capable to be frequent in the ufe of the outward, becaufe that this holy influence doth more conftantly attend them, and they being better acquainted with, and accuftomed to the motions of God's Spirit, can eafily perceive and difcern them : and indeed as fuch, who are moft diligent, have a near accefs to God, and he taketh moft delight to draw them by his Spirit, to approach and call upon him. So, when many are gathered together in this watchfull mind, God doth frequently poure forth the Spirit of Prayer among them, and ftir them thereunto, to the edifying and building up of one another in love. But, becaufe this outward prayer depends upon the inward, as that, which muft follow it, and can not be acceptably performed, but as attended with a fuperadded influence and motion of the Spirit, therefore can not we prefix fet times to pray outwardly, fo as to lay a neceffity to fpeak words at fuch and fuch times, whether we feel this heavenly influence and affiftance, or no ; for that we judge were a tempting of God, and a coming before him without due preparation. We think it fit for us to prefent our felves before him by this inward retirement of the mind, and fo to proceed further, as his Spirit fhall help us and draw us thereunto, and we find that the Lord accepts of this, yea and feeth meet fometimes to exercife us in this filent place, for the trial of our patience, without allowing us to fpeak further, that he may teach us not to relie upon outward performances, or fatisfie our felves, as too many do, with the faying of our prayers, and, that our dependence upon him may be the more firm and conftant, to wait for the holding out of his fcepter, and for his allowance to draw near unto him, and with greater freedom and enlargement of Spirit upon our hearts towards him ; yet neverthelefs we do not deny but fometimes God, upon particular occafions, very fuddenly, yea upon the very firft turning-in of the mind, may give power and liberty to bring forth words or acts of outward prayer, fo as the Soul can fcarce difcern any previous motion, but the influence and bringing forth thereof may be, as it were, *fimul & femel* ; neverthelefs that faying of *Bernard* is true, that *All prayer is tepid, which hath not an infpiration preveening it.*

Though

Though we affirm, that none ought to go about prayer without this motion, yet we do not deny but such sin, as neglect prayer; but their sin is in that they come not to that place, where they may feel that, that would lead them thereunto; And therefore we question not but many, through neglect of this inward watchfulness and retirednefs of mind, mifs many precious opportunitys to pray, and thereby are guilty in the fight of God, yet would they fin, if they should fet about the act, untill they firft felt the influence. For, as he grosfly offends his mafter, that lieth in his bed, and fleeps, and neglects to do his mafter's bufinefs, yet, if fuch a one should fuddenly get up, without puting on his cloaths, or taking along with him thofe neceffary tools and inftruments, without which he could not poffibly work, should forwardly fall a doing, to no purpofe, he would be fo far, thereby from repairing his former fault, that he would juftly incurr a new cenfur: and, as one, that is carelefs, and other wayes bufied, may mifs to hear one fpeaking unto him, or even not hear the bell of a clock, though ftriking hard by him, fo may many through negligence, mifs to hear God often-times calling upon them, and giving them accefs to pray unto him, yet will not that allow them, without his liberty, in their own wills to fall to work.

And laftly, though this be the onely true, and proper method of prayer, as that, which is alone acceptable to God, yet fhall we not deny, but he often-times anfwered the prayers, and concurred with the defires of fome, efpecially in the times of darknefs, who have greatly erred herein, fo that fome, that have fit down in formal prayers, though far wrong in the *matter*, as wel as *manner*, without the affiftance or influence of God's Spirit, yet have found him to take occafion there-through to break in upon their Soules, and wonderfully tender and refrefh them; yet, as in preaching and elfewhere hath afore been obferved, that will not prove any fuch practices, or be a juft let to hinder any from coming to practife that pure Spiritual and acceptable prayer, which God is again reftoring and leading his people into, out of all fuperftitious and meer empty formalitys. The ftate of the controverfy, and our fenfe thereof being thus clearly ftated, will both obviat many objections, and make the anfwer to others more brief and eafy, I fhall firft prove this Spiritual prayer, by fome fhort confiderations from Scriptur, and then anfwer the objections of our oppofers, which will alfo ferve to refute their method and manner thereof.

§ XXII.

§ XXII. And firſt, that there is a neceſſity of this inward retirement of the mind, as previous to prayer, that the Spirit may be felt to draw
thereunto, appears, for that in moſt of thoſe places, where *Prayer* is commanded, *watching* is prefixed thereunto as neceſſary to go before, as
Matth. 24: 42. Mark 13: 33. 14: 38. Luk 21: 36. from which it is evident that this *watching* was to go before *prayer.* Now to what end is this
watching, or what is it, but a waiting to feel God's Spirit to draw unto
prayer, that ſo it may be done acceptably? For, ſince we are to *pray alwayes*   Eph. 6:18
in the Spirit, and can not pray, of our ſelves, without it, acceptably,
this watching muſt be, for this end, recommended to us as preceeding
prayer, that we may watch and wait for the ſeaſonable time to pray, which
is when the Spirit moves thereunto.

Secondly, this neceſſity of the Spirits moving and concurrence appears abundantly from that of the Apoſtle Paul, Rom. 8: 26, 27. *Like-*
wiſe the Spirit alſo helpeth our infirmities: for we know not what we ſhould pray
for as we ought: but the Spirit it ſelf maketh intercesſion for us with groanings,
which can not be uttered. And he that ſearcheth the hearts, knoweth what is the
mind of the Spirit, becauſe he maketh interceſſion for the Saints, according to the
will *of God.* Which *firſt,* holds forth the incapacity of men, as of themſelves, to pray or call upon God in their own wills, even ſuch as have
received the faith of Chriſt, and are, in meaſur, ſanctified by it, as was
the Church of Rome, to whom the Apoſtle then wrot. *Secondly,* it
holds forth that, which can onely help and aſſiſt men to pray, to wit, the
Spirit, as that, without which they can not do it acceptably to God, nor
beneficially to their own Soules. *Thirdly,* the manner and way of the
Spirits interceſſion, *with ſighs and groans, which are unutterable.* And *fourth-*
ly, that God receiveth gratiouſly the prayers of ſuch, as are preſented
and offered unto himſelf by the Spirit, *knowing it to be according to his will.*
Now, it can not be conceived, but this order of prayer, thus aſſerted
by the Apoſtle, is moſt conſiſtent with thoſe other teſtimonys of Scriptur
commending and recommending to us the uſe of prayer. From which I
thus argue,

If man know not how to pray, neither can do it, without the help of   Arg.
the Spirit, then it is to no purpoſe for him, but altogether unprofitable,
to pray without it:

But the firſt is true:

Therefore alſo the laſt.

M m

Thirdly,

Thirdly, this necessity of the Spirit to true Prayer, appears from Eph. 6: verse 18. and Jude ver. 20. where the Apostle commands *to pray alwayes in the Spirit*, and *watching thereunto*; which is as much, as if he had said, that we were never to pray without the Spirit, or watching thereunto. And *Jude* sheweth us that such prayers, as are *in the Holy Ghost*, onely tend to the *building up of our selves in our most holy faith*.

Fourthly, the Apostle Paul saith expresly, 1 Cor. 12: 3. that *no man can say that Jesus is the Lord*; *but by the Holy Ghost*. If then Jesus can not be thus rightly named, but by the Holy Ghost, far less can he be acceptably called upon. Hence the same Apostle declares, 1 Cor. 14: 15. that he *will pray with the Spirit*, &c. A clear evidence, that it was none of his method to pray without it !

But Fifthly, all *prayer* without the Spirit is *abomination*, such as are *the prayers of the wicked*, Prov. 28: 9. and the *confidence*, that the Saints have, that *God will hear them*, is, if they *ask any thing according to his will*, 1 Joh. 5: verse 14. So, if the prayer be not according to his will, there is no ground of confidence that he will hear. Now our adversarys will acknowledge, that prayers without the Spirit are not according to the will of God; and therefore such, as pray without it, have no ground to expect an answer: for indeed to bid a man pray, without the Spirit, is all one, as to bid one' see without eyes, work without hands, or go without feet. And to desire a man to fall to prayer, ere the Spirit, in some measur, less or more, move him thereunto, is to desire a man to see, before he open his eyes, or to walk, before he rise up, or to work with his hands, before he move them.

§ XXIII. But lastly, from this false opinon of praying without the Spirit, and not judging it necessary to be waited for, as that, which may be felt to move us thereunto, hath proceeded all the superstition and idolatry, that is among those, called Christians, and those many abominations, wherewith the *Lord* is *provoked*, and his *Spirit grieved*; so that many deceive themselves now, as the Jewes did of old, thinking it sufficient, if they pay their daily sacrifices, and offer their customary oblations, from thence thinking all is wel, and creating a false peace to themselves, as the whore in the Proverbs, because they have offered up their *Sacrifices* of morning and evening prayers. And therefore it's manifest, that their constant use of things doth not a whit influence their lives and conversations, but they remain, for the most part, as bad as ever, yea it is frequent both among Papists and Protestants for

them

Prov. 7:
vers 14.

them firſt to leap, as it were, out of their vain, light, and profane con-
verſations, at their ſet houres and ſeaſons, and fall to their cuſtomary
devotion, and then, when it is ſcarce finiſhed, and the words to God
ſcarce out, the former profane talk comes after it, ſo that the ſame wicked profane ſpirit of this world acts them in both. If there be any ſuch
thing, as vain oblations, or prayers, that are abomination, which
God heareth not, (as is certain there are, and the Scriptur teſtifies,
Iſa. 66: 3. Jer. 14: 12.) certainly ſuch prayers, as are acted in man's will,
and by his own ſtrength, without God's Spirit, muſt be of that number.

§ XXIV. Let this ſuffice for probation. Now, I ſhall proceed to
anſwer their objections, when I have ſaid ſomething concerning *joyning
in prayer with others*: Thoſe, that pray together with one accord, uſe not
onely to concurr in their ſpirits, but alſo in the geſtur of their body, which
we alſo willingly approve of. It becometh thoſe, who approach before
God to pray, that they do it with bowed knees, and with their heads
uncovered, which is our practice.

But here ariſeth a controverſy, *Whether it be lawfull to joyn with others,* Obj.
*(by thoſe external ſignes of reverence, albeit not in heart) who pray formally,
nor waiting for the motion of the Spirit, nor judging it neceſſary.*

We anſwer, Not at all: and for our teſtimony in this thing we have Anſw.
ſuffered not a little, for, when it hath faln out, that either accidentally,
or to witneſs againſt their worſhip, we have been preſent, during the
ſame, and have not found it lawfull for us to bow with them thereunto,
they have often perſecuted us not onely with reproaches, but alſo with
ſtroaks and cruel beatings; for this cauſe they uſe to accuſe us of pride,
profanity and madneſs, as if we had no reſpect or reverence to the worſhip of God, and, as if we judged none could pray, or were heard of God,
but our ſelvs. Unto all which and many more reproaches of this kind
we *anſwer* briefly and modeſtly, that it ſufficeth us, that we are found ſo
doing neither through pride, nor madneſs, nor profanity, but meerly
leſt we ſhould hurt our Conſciences: the reaſon of which is plain and
evident, for, ſince our principle and doctrin obligeth us to believe that
the *prayers* of thoſe, who themſelves confeſs they are *not acted by the
Spirit*, are *abominations*, how can we, with a ſafe Conſcience, joyn with
them?

If they urge, *that this is the heighth of uncharitablneſs and arrogancy, as if we* Obj.

                    judged

judged our selves alwayes to pray by the Spirits motion, but they never ; as if we were never deceived by praying without the motion of the Spirit, and that they were never acted by it : seing, albeit they judge not the motion of the Spirit always necessary, they confess nevertheless that it is very profitable and comfortable, and they feel it often influencing them, which that it sometimes falls out we can not deny.

Answ, To all which I answer distinctly, if it were their known and avowed doctrin, not to pray without the motion of the Spirit, and that seriously holding thereunto they did not bind themselves to pray at certain prescribed times precisely (at which times they determin to pray, though without the Spirit) then indeed we might be accused of uncharitableness and pride, if we never joyned with them ; and if they so taught and practised, I doubt not but it should be lawfull for us so to do, unless there should appear some manifest and evident hypocrify or delusion. But, seing they profess that *they pray without the Spirit*, and seing God hath perfwaded us that such prayers are abominable, how can we, with a safe Conscience, joyn with an abomination? That God sometimes condescends to them, we do not deny, (albeit now, when the Spiritual worship is openly proclaimed, and all are invited unto it, the case is otherwise, than in those old times of Apostafy and darkness) and therefore, albeit any should begin to pray in our presence, not expecting the motion of the Spirit, yet, if it manifestly appear, that God in condescension did concurr with such a one, then, according to God's will, we should not refuse to joyn also ; but this is rare, lest thence they should be confirmed in their false principle. And albeit this seem hard in our profession, nevertheless it is so confirmed, by the authority both of Scriptur and right Reason, that many, convinced thereof, have embraced this part before other, among whom is memorable of late years *Alexander Skein*, a Magistrate of the City of Aberdeen, a man very modest, and very averse from giving offence to others, who nevertheless, being overcome by the Power of Truth in this matter, behoved for this cause to separat himself from the publik assemblys and prayers, and joyn himself unto us ; Who also gave the reason of his change, and likewise succinctly, but yet substantially, comprehended this controversy concerning Worship in some short questions, which he offered to the publik Preachers of the City, which I think meet to insert in this place.

Query   1. *Whether or not should any act of God's worship be gone about, without the motions, leadings and actings of the Holy Spirit ?*

2. If

2. If the motions of the Spirit be neceſſary to every particular duty, whether ſhould he be waited upon, that all our acts and words may be, according as he gives utterance and aſſiſtance?

3. Whether every one, that bears the name of a Chriſtian, or profeſſes to be a Proteſtant, hath ſuch an uninterrupted meaſur thereof, that he may, without waiting, go immediately about the duty?

4. If there be an indiſpoſition and unfitneſs, at ſome times, for ſuch exerçiſes, at leſt as to the Spiritual and lively performance thereof, whether ought they to be performed in that caſe and at that time?

5. If any duty be gone about, under pretence that it is in obedience to the external command, without the Spiritual Life and motion neçeſſary, whether ſuch a duty, thus performed, can in faith be expected to be accepted of God, and not rather reckoned as a bringing of ſtrange fire before the Lord, ſeing it is performed (at beſt) Levit 10 *by the ſtrength of natural and acquired parts, and not by the ſtrength and aſſiſtance* vers 1. *of the Holy Ghoſt, which was typified by the fire, that came down from heaven, which alone behoved to conſume the ſacrifiçe and no other?*

6. Whether dutys, gon about in the meer ſtrength of natural and acquired parts, (whether in publik or in privat) be not as really, upon the matter, an image of man's invention, as the Popiſh worſhip, though not ſo groſs in the outward appearance? And therefore whether it be not as real ſuperſtition to countenance any worſhip of that nature, as it is to countenance Popiſh worſhip, though there be a differençe in the degree?

7. Whether it be a ground of offence, or juſt ſcandal, to countenançe the worſhip of thoſe, whoſe profeſſed prinçiple it is, neither to ſpeak for edification, nor to pray, but as the Holy Ghoſt ſhall be pleaſed to aſſiſt them, in ſome meaſur, leſs or more, without which they rather chuſe to be ſilent, than to ſpeak without this influence?

Unto theſe they anſwered but very coldly and faintly, whoſe anſwers likewiſe long ago he refuted.

Seing then God hath called us to his Spiritual worſhip, and to teſtifie againſt the humane and voluntary worſhips of the apoſtaſy, if we did not, this way, ſtand immoveable to the Truth revealed, but ſhould joyn with them, both our teſtimony for God would be weakened and loſt, and it would be impoſſible ſteadily to propagat this worſhip in the world, whoſe progreſs we dare neither retard nor hinder by any act of ours; though therefore we ſhall loſe not onely worldly honor, but even our lives. And truely many Proteſtants, through their unſteadineſs in this thing, for

                    politik

politik ends, complying with the Popish abominations, have greatly
scandalized their profession, and hurt the Reformation; as appeared in
the example of the Elector of *Saxony*, who, in the convention at *Ausburg*,
in the year 1530, being commanded by the Emperour *Charles* the Fifth,
to be present at the *Mass*, that he might carry the sword before him, according to his place; which when he justly scrupled to perform, his
preachers, taking more care for their Princes honor, than for his Conscience, perswaded him that it was lawfull to do it, against his Conscience,
which was both a very bad example, and great scandal to the Reformation, and displeased many, as the Author of the history of the Council
of *Trent*, in his first book, wel observes.   But now I hasten to the objections of our adversarys against this method of praying.

Obj.

§ XXV. First. They object, that, *if such particular influences were
needfull to outward acts of worship, then they should also be needfull to inward
acts, as to wait, desire and love God:*

    But this is absurd:

    Therefore also that from whence it followes.

Answ.

I answer, that, which was said in the state of the controversy, clear-
eth this, because, as to those general dutys, there never wants an influence, so long as the day of a man's visitation lasteth, during which time
God is *alwayes near* to him, and *wrestling* with him by his Spirit, to turn
him to himself, so that, if he do but stand still, and cease from his evil
thoughts, the Lord is near to help him, *&c.* But as to the outward acts
of Prayer, they need a more special motion and influence, as hath been
proven.

Obj.

Secondly, they object, *that it might be also alledged, that men ought not
to do Moral dutys, as children to honor their parents, men to do right to their neighbours, except the Spirit moved them to it.*

Answ.

I answer, there is a great difference betwixt these general dutys betwixt
man and man, and the particular express acts of worship towards God:
the one is meerly Spiritual, and commanded by God to be performed by
his Spirit; the other answer their end, as to them, whom they are immediatly directed to, and concern, though done from a meer natural principle
of self-love, even as beasts have natural affections one to another, and
therefore may be thus performed, though I shall not deny but that they
are not works accepted of God, or beneficial to the Soul, but as they
are done in the fear of God, and in his blessing, in which his children do

all

all things, and therefore are accepted and bleffed in whatfoever they do.

Thirdly, they object, *that, if a wicked man ought not to pray without a motion of the Spirit, becaufe his prayer would be finfull, neither ought he to plough by the fame reafon, becaufe the ploughing of the wicked, as wel as his praying is fin.*   Obj. prov. 21: vers 4.

This objection is of the fame nature with the former, and therefore may be anfwered the fame way, feing there is a great difference betwixt *natural acts*, fuch as *eating, drinking, fleeping,* and *feeking for fuflenance for the body*, which things man hath common with beafts, and fpiritual acts. And it doth not follow, becaufe man ought not to go about Spiritual acts without the Spirit, that therefore he may not go about natural acts with-out it: The analogy holds better thus, and that for the proof of our affir-mation, that, as man, for the going about natural acts, needs his natu-ral Spirit, fo to perform Spiritual acts, he needs the Spirit of God. That the natural acts of the wicked and unregenerat are finfull, is not denyed, though not as in themfelves, but in fo far as man in that ftate is in all things, reprobated in the fight of God.   Anfw.

Fourthly, they *object,* that *wicked men may, according to this doctrin, forbear to pray for years together, alledging they want a motion to it.*   Obj.

I anfwer, the falfe pretences of wicked men do nothing invalidat the truth of this doctrin: for at that rate there is no doctrin of Chrift, which men might not turn by. That they ought not to pray without the Spirit is granted, but then they ought to come to that place of watching, where they may be capable to feel the Spirits motion. They fin indeed, in not praying, but the caufe of this fin is their not watching; fo their neglect proceeds not from this doctrin, but from their difobedience to it: feing, if they did pray without this, it would be a double fin, and no fulfilling of the command to pray, nor yet would their prayer, without this Spirit, be ufefull unto them, and this our adverfarys are forced to acknowledg in another cafe: for they fay, *it is a duty incumbent on Chriftians to frequent the Sacrament of the Lord's fupper.* (as they call it) Yet they fay, *No man ought to take it unworthily,* yea they plead that fuch, as find themfelves unprepared, muft abftain, and therefore do ufually excommunicat them from the Table. Now, though, according to them, it be neceffary to partake of this Sacrament, yet it is alfo neceffary, that thofe, that do it, do firft examin themfelves, left they eat and drink their own condemna-tion, and, though they reckon it finfull for them to forbear, yet they account it more finfull for them to do it without this examination.   Anfw.

Fifthly,

Obj.   Fifthly, they *object* Act. 8: 22. where *Peter commanded Simon Magus,* *that wicked forçerer, to pray,* from thence inferring that *wicked men may and* *ought to pray.*

Anſw.   I *anſwer*, that, in the citing of this place, as I have often obſerved, they omitt the firſt and chiefeſt part of the verſe, which is thus, Act. 8: verſe 22. *Repent therefore of this thy wickedneſs, and pray God, if perhaps the* *thought of thine heart may be forgiven thee.* So here he bids him firſt *repent*, now the leaſt meaſur of true repentance can not be without ſomewhat of that inward retirement of the mind, which we ſpeak of, and indeed where true repentance goeth firſt, we do not doubt but the Spirit of God will be near to concurr, with and influence ſuch, to pray to, and call upon God.

Obj.   And laſtly, they *object*, that *many prayers, begun without the Spirit, have* *proved effectual, and that the prayers of wicked men have been heard and found ac-* *ceptable, as Achab's.*

Anſw.   This objection was before ſolved: for the acts of God's compaſſion and indulgence, at ſome times, and to ſome perſons, upon ſingular extraordinary occaſions, are not to be a rule of our actions. For if we ſhould make that the meaſur of our obedience, great inconveniençys would follow, as is evident, and will be acknowledged by all. Next, we do not deny but wicked men are ſenſible of the motions and operations of God's Spirit often-times, before their day be expired; from which they may at times pray acceptably, not as remaining altogether wicked, but as entring into piety, from whence they afterwards fall away.

§ XXVI. As to the *ſinging* of *Pſalmes*, there will not be need of any long diſcourſe, for that the caſe is juſt the ſame, as in the two former of *preaching* and *prayer*. We confeſs this to be a part of God's worſhip, and very ſweet and refreſhfull, when it proceeds from a true ſenſe of God's love *in* the heart, and ariſes from the Divine influence of the Spirit, which leads Soules to breath forth either a ſweet harmony, or words ſutable to the preſent condition, whether they be words formerly uſed by the Saints, and recorded in Scriptur, ſuch as the Pſalmes of David, or other words, as were the hymnes and ſongs of *Zacharias, Simeon* and the *bleſſed Virgin Mary.* But as for the formal cuſtomary way of ſinging, it hath in Scriptur no foundation, nor any ground in true Chriſtianity: yea beſides all the abuſes incident to prayer and preaching, it hath this more peculiar, that often-times great and horrid lyes are ſaid in the

ſight

fight of God, for all manner of wicked profane people take upon them to perfonat the experiences and conditions of blefled David, which are not onely falfe, as to them, but alfo as to fome of more fobriety, who utter them forth: as, where they will fing fometimes, Pfal. 22:14. --- *my heart is like vvax, it is melted in the midft of my bovvels.* and verfe 15. *My ftrength is dried up like a pot-fherd: and my tongue cleaveth to my javvs; and thou haft brought me into the duft of death.* and Pfal. 6: 6. *I am vveary vvith my groaning, all the night make I my bed to fwim: I vvater my couch vvith my tears.* And many more, which thofe, that fpeak, know to be falfe, as to them. And fometimes will confefs, juft after, in their prayers, that they are guilty of the vices, oppofit to thofe vertues, which but juft before they have afferted themfelves endued with. Who can fuppofe that God accepts of fuch jugling? And indeed fuch finging doth more pleafe the carnal ears of men, than the pure ears of the Lord, who abhorrs all lying and hypocrify.

That finging then, that pleafeth him, muft proceed from that, which is *P U R E in* the *heart,* (even from the *Word of Life* therein) in and by which richly dwelling *in* us, fpiritual fongs and hymns are returned to the Lord, according to that of the Apoftle, Col. 3: 16.

But as to their artificial mufik, either by organs, or other inftruments, or voice, we have neither example nor precept for it in the New Teftament.

§ X X V I I. But laftly, the great advantage of this true worfhip of God, which we profefs and practife, is, that it confifteth not in man's wifdom, arts, or induftry, neither needeth the glory, pomp, riches, nor fplendor of this world to beautifie it, as being of a Spiritual and heavenly nature, and therefore too fimple and contemptible to the natural mind and will of man, that hath no delight to abide in it, becaufe he finds no room there for his imaginations and inventions, and hath not the opportunity to gratifie his outward and carnal fenfes; fo that this form being obferved, is not like to be long kept pure, without the Power: for it is, of it felf, fo naked, without it, that it hath nothing in it to invite and tempt men to dote upon it, further than it is accompanyed with the Power. Whereas the worfhip of our adverfarys, being performed in their own wills, is *felf-pleafing,* as in which they can largely exercife their natural parts & invention: and (as to moft of them) having fomewhat of an outward and worldly fplendor, delectable to the carnal and worldly fenfes, they can

N n

pleafantly

pleafantly continue in it , and fatisfie themfelves , though without the Spirit and Power, which they make no ways effential to the performance of their worfhip, and therefore neither wait for , nor expect it.

§ XXVIII. So that to conclude, *the Worfhip, preaching, praying, and finging , which we plead for , is fuch, as proceedeth from the Spirit of God, and is alwayes accompanyed vvith its influence , being begun by its motion, and carryed on by the Povver and ftrength thereof ; and fo is a vrorfhip purely Spiritual* , fuch as the Scriptur holds forth , Joh. 4 : 23, 24. 1 Cor. 14 : 15. Eph. 6 : 18. *&c.*

But *the vvorfhip, preaching, praying and finging , vvhich our adverfarys plead for , and vvhich vve oppofe, is a vrorfhip, vvhich is both begun, carryed on and concluded in man's ovvn natural vvill, and ftrength , vvithout the motion or influence of God's Spirit , vvhich they judge they need not vvait for , and therefore may be truely acted , both as to the matter and manner , by the vvickedeft of men,* Such was the worfhip and vain oblations , whish God alwayes rejected , as appears from Ifa. 66 : 3. Jer. 14 : 12, &c. Ifa. 1 : 13. Prov. 15 : 29. Joh. 9 : verfe 31.

The Twelfth Propofition ,

Concerning Baptism.

As there is one Lord, and *one Faith,* fo there is *one Baptism, which is not the putting away the filth of the flesh , but the anfwer of a good Confcience before God , by the Refurrection of Iefus Chrift* , and this Baptifm is a Pure and Spiritual thing, to wit, the *Baptism* of the *Spirit* and *fire* , by which we are buried with him, that being washed and purged from our fins, we may *walk in newnefs of Life* , of which the Baptifm of *Iohn* was a figure, which was Commanded for a time, and not to continue for ever; as to the Baptifm of Infants it is a meer humane Tradition, for which neither Precept nor Practice is to be found in all the Scripture.

Eph. 4. 5.
1 Pet. 3. 21
Rom. 6. 4
Gal. 3 : 27
Col. 2:12
Joh. 3. 30
1Cor. 1: 17

§ I. I Did fufficiently demonftrat , in the explanation and probation of the former Propofition, how greatly the Profeffors of Chriftianity, as wel Proteftants , as Papifts , were degenerated in the matter of worfhip, and how much ftrangers to, and averfe from

from that true and acceptable worship, that is performed in the Spirit of
Truth, because of man's natural propensity, in his faln state, to exalt
his own inventions, and to intermix his own work and product in the
service of God; and from this root sprung all the idle worships, idola-
trys, and numerous superstitious inventions among the Heathens. For,
when God, in condescension to his chosen people, the Jewes, did prescribe to them, by his servant Moses, many ceremonys and observations,
as typs and shaddows of the Substance, which in due time was to be revealed, which consisted for the most part, in washings, outward purifications, and cleansings, which were to continue, untill the time of
the *Reformation*, untill the *Spiritual* worship should be set up, and that
God, by the more powerfull pouring forth of his Spirit, and guiding of
that *Anoynting*, which was to *lead* his children *into all Truth*, and teach
them to worship him in a way more Spiritual and acceptable to him,
though less agreable to the carnal and outward senses: notwithstanding
God's condescension to the Jewes, in such things, we see that that part
in man, which delights to follow its own inventions, could not be re-
strained, nor yet satisfied with all these observations, but that oftentimes
they would be either declining to the other superstitions of the Gentiles,
or adding some new observations and ceremonys of their own, to which
they were so devoted, that they were still apt to prefer them before the
commands of God, and that under the notion of zeal and piety. This we
see abundantly in the example of the Pharisees, the chiefest Sect among
the Jewes, whom Christ so frequently reproves for *making void the commandments of God by their traditions*, Matth. 15: 6, 9. *&c.* This complaint
may at this day be no less justly made, as to many bearing the name of
Christians, who have introduced many things of this kind, partly borrowed from the Jewes, which they more tenaciously stick to; and more
earnestly contend for, than for the weightyer points of Christianity: because that *self*, yet alive, and ruling in them, loves their own inventions
better than God's commands. But, if they can by any means stretch any
Scriptur practice, or conditional precept, or permission; fitted to the
weaknefs or capacity of some, or appropriat to some particular difpenfation, to give some color for any of these their inventions, they do then
so tenaciously stick to them, and so obstinatly and obstreperoufly plead
for them, that they will not patiently hear the most solid Christian reasons against them. Which zeal, if they would but seriously examin it,

N n 2

they

they would find to be but the prejudice of education and the love of *self*, more than of God, or his Pure worship.   This is verified concerning those things, which are called *Sacraments*, about which, they are very ignorant in religious controversys, who understand not, how much debate, contention, jangling, and quarreling there has been among those, called Christians, so that I may safely say, the controversy about them, to wit, about their number, nature, vertue, efficacy, administration, and other things, hath been more than about any other doctrin of Christ, whether as betwixt Papists and Protestants, or among Protestants betwixt themselves, and how great prejudice these controversys have brought to Christians, is very obvious, whereas the things, contended for among them, are, for the most part, but empty shaddows, and meer out-side things; as I hope hereafter to make appear to the patient and unprejudicat Reader.

§ 11. That, which comes first under observation, is the Name [*Sacrament*,] which is strange that Christians should stick to, and contend so much for; since it is not to be found in all the Scriptur, but was borrowed from the military oaths among the Heathens, from whom the Christians, when they began to apostatize, did borrow many superstitious termes and observations, that they might thereby ingratiat themselves, and the more easily gain the Heathens to their Religion, which practice (though perhaps intended by them for good, yet, as being the fruit of humane policy, and not according to God's Wisdom) has had very pernicious consequences.   I see not how any, whether Papists, or Protestants, especially the latter, can, in reason, quarrel us, for denying this term, which it seemes the Spirit of God saw not meet to inspire the pen-men of the Scripturs to leave unto us.

Obj.   But if it be said, that *it is not the name*, *but the thing*, *they contend for?*

Answ.   I *answer*, Let the name then, as not being Scriptural, be laid aside, and we shall see at first entrance how much benefit will redound by laying aside this traditional term, and betaking us to plainness of Scriptur language, for presently the great contest, about the number of them, will evanish: since there is no term, used in Scriptur, that can be made use of, whether we call them *institutions, ordinances, precepts, commandments, appoyntments*, or *lavvs*, &c. that would afford ground for such a debate, since neither will Papists affirm, that there are onely *seven*, or Protestants onely *tvvo*, of any of these forementioned.

If

If it be ſaid, that this *controverſy ariſes from the definition of the thing, as rvel as from the name.* **Obj.**

It wil' be found otherwiſe, for whatever way we take their definition of a *Sacrament*, whether as *an outvvard viſible ſign, vvhereby invvard Grace is conferred, or onely ſignified.* This definition will agree to many things, which neither Papiſts nor Proteſtants will acknowledge to be *Sacraments.* If they be expreſſed under the name of *ſealing ordinances*, as ſome do: I could never ſee neither by Reaſon, nor Scriptur, how this title could be appropriat to them, more than to any other Chriſtian religious performance: for that muſt needs properly be a *ſealing ordinance*, which makes the *perſons*, receiving it, *infallibly certain* of the *promiſe*, or tl.ing *ſealed* to them. **Anſw.**

If it be ſaid, *it is ſo to them, that are faithfull.* **Obj.**

I *anſvver:* So is praying, and preaching, and doing of every good work. Seing the partaking, or performing of the one gives not to any a more certain title to heaven, yea (in ſome reſpect) not ſo much, there is no reaſon to call them ſo, more than the other. **Anſw.**

Beſides we find not any thing, called the *Seal* and *Pledge* of our *inheritance,* but the *Spirit of God,* it is by that we are ſaid to be *ſealed,* Eph. 1:14. & 4:30. which is alſo termed *the earneſt of our inheritançe*, 2 Cor. 1:22. and not by outward water, or eating, and drinking, which as the wickedeſt of men may partake of, ſo many, that do, do notwithſtanding it go to perdition: for it is not outward waſhing with water that maketh the *heart clean*, by which men are fitted for heaven; and as *that vvhich goeth into the mouth, doth not defile a man, becauſe it is put forth again*, and ſo goeth to the dung-hill, neither doth any thing, which man eateth, purifie him, or fit him for heaven. What is ſaid here in general may ſerve for an introduction, not onely to this Propoſition, but alſo to the other, concerning the *Supper.* Of theſe Sacraments (ſo called) *Baptiſm* is alwayes firſt numbered, which is the ſubject of the preſent Propoſition, in whoſe explanation I ſhall firſt demonſtrat and prove our judgment, and then anſwer the objections, and refute the ſentiments of our oppoſers. As to the firſt part, theſe things following, which are briefly comprehended in the Propoſition, come to be propoſed and proved.

§ 11 I. Firſt, *that there is but one Baptiſm,* as wel as but One Lord, one faith, *&c.*

Secondly, *that this one Baptiſm, which is the Baptiſm of Chriſt, is not a*

           vvaſhing

washing with, or dipping in, water, but a being baptized by the Spirit.

Thirdly, *that the baptism of John was but a figur of this, and therefore, as the figure (to give place to the Substance) which, though it be to con'inue, yet the other is ceased.*

As for the first, viz, *that there is but one Baptism*, there needs no other proof, than the words of the Text, Eph. 4: 5. *One Lord, one Faith, one Baptism*; where the Apostle positively and plainly affirmes, that, as there is but one body, one Spirit, one faith, One God, &c. so there is but one Baptism.

Obj.   As to what is commonly alledged by way of explanation upon the text, *that the Baptism of Water and of the Spirit make up this one Baptism, by vertue of the sacramental union.*

Answ.   I answer, This exposition hath taken place, not because grounded upon the testimony of the Scriptur, but because it wrests the Scriptur, to make it sute to their principle of water-baptism, and so there needs no other reply, but to deny it, as being repugnant to the plain words of the Text, which saith not *that there are two baptisms*, to wit, one of *water*, the other of the *Spirit*, which do make up the one baptism, but plainly, that *there is one baptism*, as there is *one faith*, and *One God.* Now there goeth not two faiths, nor two Gods, nor two spirits, nor two bodys, whereof the one is outward and elementary, and the other Spiritual and pure, to the making up of the one faith, the One God, the one body, and the one Spirit; so neither ought there to go two baptisms to make up the one baptism.

Obj.   But secondly, if it be said, *the baptism is but one, whereof water is the one part, to wit, the sign, and the Spirit, the thing signified, the other.*

Answ,   I answer, this yet more confirmeth our doctrin, for, if water be onely the sign, it is not the matter of the one Baptism (as shall further hereafter by its definition in Scriptur appear) and we are to take the one baptism for the matter of it, not for the sign, or figur, and type, that went before, even as where *Christ* is called the *One Offering*, in Scriptur, though he was typified by many sacrifices and offerings under the Law, we un-stand onely by the *One Offering*, his offering himself upon the Cross, whereof though those many offerings were signes and types, yet we say not that they go together with that Offering of Christ, to make up the one Offering; so neither, though water-baptism was a sign of Christ's baptism, will it follow, that it goeth now to make up the baptism of Christ.

If

If any fhould be fo *abfurd*, as to affirm, *that this one baptifm here vvere the baptifm of vvater, and not of the Spirit*: that were foolifhly to contradict the pofitive teftimony of the Scriptur, which faith the contrary, as by what followeth will more amply appear.

Secondly, *that this one baptifm, vvhich is the baptifm of Chrift, is not a vvafhing vvith vvater*, appears, *firft*, from the teftimony of John, the proper and peculiar adminiftrator of water baptifm, Matth. 3: 11. *I indeed baptize you vvith vvater, unto repentance; but he, that cometh after me, is mightier then I, vvhofe fhoes I am not vvorthy to bear: he fhall baptize you vvith the Holy Ghoft, and with fire.* Here John mentions two manners of baptifings, and two different baptifms, the one with water, and the other with the Spirit, the one whereof he was the minifter of, the other whereof Chrift was the minifter of: and fuch, as were baptized with the firft, were not therefore baptized with the fecond, *I indeed baptize you, but he fhall baptize you.* Though in the prefent time they were baptized with the baptifm of water, yet they were not as yet, but were to be, baptized with the Baptifm of Chrift. From all which I thus argue,

If thofe, that were baptized with the baptifm of water, were not therefore baptized with the Baptifm of Chrift, Then the baptifm of water is not the Baptifm of Chrift : Arg. 1.

But the firft is true:

Therefore alfo the laft.

And again,

If he, that truely and really adminiftred the baptifm of water, did not-withftanding declare, that he neither could, nor did baptize with the Baptifm of Chrift, Then the baptifm of water is not the Baptifm of Chrift: Arg. 2.

But the firft is true:

Therefore, *&c.*

And indeed to underftand it otherwife would make John's words void of good fenfe; for, if their baptifms had been all one, why fhould he have fo precifely contradiftinguifhed them? Why fhould he have faid that thofe, whom he had already baptized, fhould yet be baptized by another baptifm?

If it be *urged*, that *Baptifm vvith vvater vvas the one part, and that vvith the Spirit* the other part, or effect onely of the former. Obj.

I *anfvver*: this expofition contradicts the plain words of the text, for
he

he faith not, *I baptize you vvith vvater, and he, that cometh after fhall pro-duce the effects of this my Baptifm in you by the Spirit, &c.* or *he fhall accomplifh this baptifm in you*; but *he fhall baptize you.* So then, if we underftand the word truely and properly, when he faith, *I baptize you,* as confenting that thereby is really fignified that he did baptize with the baptifm of water, we muft needs, unlefs we offer violence to the Text, underftand the other part of the fentence the fame way; that where he adds prefently, *but he fhall baptize you,* &c. that he underftood it of their being truely to be baptized with another baptifm, than what he did baptize with: Elfe it had had been non-fenfe for him thus to have contradiftinguifhed them.

Secondly, this is further confirmed by the faying of Chrift himfelf, Act. 1: 4, 5. --- *but vvait for the promife of the Father, vvhich,* faith he, *ye have heard of me. For John truely baptized vvith vvater, but ye fhall be baptized vvith the Holy Ghoft, not many dayes hence.* There can fcarce two places of Scriptur run more parallel, than this doth with the former, a little before mention-ed, and therefore concludeth the fame way, as did the other. For Chrift here grants fully, that John compleated his baptifm, as to the matter and fubftance of it: *John,* faith he, *truely baptized vvith vvater,* which is as much, as if he had faid, John did truely and fully adminifter the ba-ptifm of water, *But ye fhall be baptized vvith* &c. This fheweth that they were to be baptized with fome other baptifm, than the baptifm of water, and that, although they were formerly baptized with the baptifm of wa-ter, yet not with that of Chrift, which they were to be baptiz'd with.

Thirdly, Peter obferves the fame diftinction, Act. 11: 16. *Then remembred I the vvord of the Lord, hovv that he faid, John indeed baptized vvith vvater; but ye fhall be baptized vvith the Holy Ghoft.* The Apoftle ma-kes this application upon the Holy Ghoft's falling upon them. Whence he infers, that they were then baptized with the baptifm of the Spirit. As to what is urged from his calling afterwards for water, to it fhall be hereafter fpoken. From all which three fentences relative one to another, firft of *John,* fecondly of *Chrift,* and thirdly of *Peter,* it doth evidently follow, that fuch, as were truely and really baptized with the *baptifm of vvater;* were notwithftanding not baptized with the *baptifm* of the Spirit; which is that of Chrift; and fuch as truely and really did adminifter the *baptifm of vvater,* did, in fo doing, not adminifter the *Baptifm of Chrift,* fo that, if there be now but *one baptifm,* as we have already proved, we

may

may fafely conclude, that it is that of the *Spirit*, and not of *water*; elfe it would follow, that *the one baptifm*, which now continues, were the *baptifm of water*, i. e. *John*'s, baptifm, and not the *baptifm of the Spirit*, i. e. *Chrift's*, which were moft abfurd.

If it be faid further, that, *though the baptifm of John, before Chrift's was* Obj. *adminiftred, was different from it, asbeing the figur onely, yet now that both it, as the figur, and that of the Spirit, as the Subftance, is neceffary to make up the one baptifm.*

I anfwer: this urgeth nothing, unlefs it be granted alfo that both of Anfw. them belong to the effence of baptifm, fo that baptifm is not to be accounted as truely adminiftred, where both are not: which none of our adverfarys will acknowledg, but, on the contrary, account, not onely all thofe truely baptized, with the baptifm of Chrift, who are baptized with water, though they be uncertain whether they be baptized with the Spirit, or not; but they even account fuch truely baptized, with the baptifm of Chrift, becaufe fprinkled, or baptized with water, though it be manifeft and moft certain, that they are not baptized with the Spirit, as being enemies thereunto, in their hearts, by wicked works. So here, by their own confeffion, *baptifm with water* is without the Spirit: Wherefore we may far fafer conclude, that the *baptifm of the Spirit*, which is that of *Chrift*, is, and may be without that of *water*, as appears in that Act. 11. where Peter teftifys of thefe men, that *they were baptized with the Spirit, though not then baptized with water*; and indeed the controverfy in this, as in moft other things, ftands betwixt us and our oppofers, in that they not onely often-times prefer the form and fhaddow, to the Power and Subftance, by denominating perfons, as inheritors and poffeffors of the thing, from their having the form and fhaddow, though really wanting the Power and Subftance; and not admitting thofe to be fo denominated, who have the Power and Subftance, if they want the form and fhaddow. This appears evidently, in that they account thofe truely baptized, with the *one baptifm of Chrift*, who are not baptized with the *Spirit*, which, in Scriptur, is particularly called the *baptifm of Chrift*, if they be onely baptized with water, which themfelves yet confefs to be but the fhaddow, or figur. And moreover, in that they account not thofe, who are furely baptized with the *baptifm of the Spirit*, baptized, neither will they have them fo denominat, unlefs they be alfo fprinkled with, or *dipped in water*. But we, on the contrary, do alwayes prefer the Power to the form, the

O o

Sub-

Subſtance to the ſhaddow; and where the Subſtance and Power is, we doubt not to denominat the perſon accordingly, though the form be wanting: and therefore we alwayes ſeek firſt, and plead for, the Subſtance and Power, as knowing that to be indiſpenſibly neceſſary; though the Form ſometimes may be diſpenſed with, and the figur or type may ceaſe, when the Subſtance and Anti-type comes to be enjoyed, as it doth in this caſe, which ſhall hereafter be made appear.

§ I V. Fourthly, that the *one Baptiſm* of Chriſt is not a waſhing with water, appears from 1 Pet. 3: 21. *The like figure whereunto, even baptiſm, doth alſo now ſave us, (not the putting away of the filth of the fleſh, but the anſwer of a good Conſcience towards God) by the reſurrection of Jeſus Chriſt.* So plain a definition of *Baptiſm* is not in all the Bible, and therefore, ſeing it is ſo *plain,* it may wel be preferred to all the coyned definitions of the Schoolmen. The Apoſtle tells us, *firſt, negatively,* what it is not, viz, *not a putting away of the filth of the fleſh,* then ſurely it is not a *waſhing with* water, ſince that is ſo. Secondly, he tells us *affirmatively,* what it is, viz, *the anſwer of a good Conſcience towards God, by the reſurrection of Jeſus Chriſt:* where he affirmatively defines it to be *the anſwer* [or *confeſſion*] (as the *Syriak* verſion hath it) *of a good Conſcience.* Now, this anſwer can not be, but where the Spirit of God hath purified the Soul, and the fire of his judgment hath burned up the unrighteous nature; and thoſe, in whom this work is wrought, may be truely ſaid to be baptized with the *baptiſm of Chriſt,* i. e. *of the Spirit and of fire.* Whatever way then we take this definition of the Apoſtle of Chriſt's baptiſm, it confirmeth our ſentence; fer, if we take the firſt or negative part, viz, *that it is not a putting away of the filth of the fleſh,* then it will follow, that water-baptiſm is not it, becauſe that is a putting away of the filth of the fleſh. If we take the ſecond and affirmative definition, to wit, *that it is the anſwer,* or *confeſſion, of a good Conſcience,* &c. then water-baptiſm is not it; ſince, as our adverſarys will not deny, water-baptiſm doth not alwayes imply it, neither is it any neceſſary conſequence thereof. Moreover, the Apoſtle, in this place, doth ſeem eſpecially to guard againſt thoſe, that might eſteem *water-baptiſm* the true *baptiſm of Chriſt;* becauſe, (leſt by the compariſon induced by him, in the preceeding verſe, betwixt the Soules, that were ſaved in Noah's ark, and us, that are now ſaved by baptiſm, leſt, I ſay, any ſhould have thence haſtily concluded, that, becauſe the former were ſaved by water, this place muſt needs be taken to ſpeak of

water-

water-baptifm) to prevent fuch a miftake, he plainly affirmes, that it is not that, but another thing. He faith not, that *it is the water*, or *the putting away of the filth of the flefh*, *as accompanyed with the anfwer of a good Confcience*, *whereof the one, viz, the water, is the Sacramental element adminiftred by the minifter, and the other, the Grace or thing fignified, conferred by Chrift*; but plainly, *that it is not the putting away*, &c. than which there can be nothing more manifeft to men unprejudicat and judicious. Moreover, Peter calls this here, which faves, the ἀντίτυπον the *Anti-type*, or the thing figured, whereas it is ufually tranflated, as if *the like figure did now fave us*, thereby infinuating, that, as they were faved by water in the Ark, fo are we now by water-baptifm. But this interpretation croffeth his fenfe, he prefently after declaring the contrary, as hath above been obferved: and likewife it would contradict the opinion of all our oppofers. For Proteftants deny it to be abfolutely neceffary to Salvation. And, though Papifts fay, none are faved without it, yet in this they admitt an exception, as, of Martyrs, &c. and they will not fay, that all, that have it, are faved by *water-baptifm*: for, feing we are faved by *this baptifm*, as thofe, that were in the Ark, *were faved by water*, and that all thofe, that were in the Ark, *were faved by water*, it would then follow, that all thofe, that have *this baptifm*, are faved by it. Now this confequence would be falfe, if it were underftood of *water-baptifm*, becaufe many, by the confeffion of all, are baptized *with water*, that are not faved: but this confequence holds moft true, if it be underftood, as we do, of the Baptifm of the Spirit, fince none can have this anfwer of a good Confcience, and, abiding in it, not be faved by it.

Fifthly, *that the One Baptifm of Chrift is not a wafhing with vvater*, as it hath been proved by the definition of *the One baptifm*, fo it is alfo manifeft from the neceffary fruits and effects of it, which are three-times particularly expreffed by the Apoftle Paul, as firft, Rom. 6: 3, 4. where he faith, that *fo many of them as vvere baptized into Jefus Chrift, vvere baptized into his death: buried vvith him by baptifm into death: that they fhould walk in newnefs of life*. Secondly, to the Gal. 3: 27. he faith pofitively, *For as many of you as have been baptized into Chrift, have put on Chrift*. and Thirdly, to the Col. 2: 12. he faith, that they were *Buried with him in baptifm*, and rifen with him *through the faith of the operation of God* It is to be obferved here, that the Apoftle fpeaks generally, without any exclufive term, but comprehenfive of all: he faith not *fome of you, that were baptized into*

Chrift,

Chrift, *have put on Chrift*, but *as many of you*, which is as much, as if he had faid, *every one of you*, *that hath been baptized into Chrift*, *hath put on Chrift*. Whereby it is evident, that this is not meant of *water-baptifm*, but of the *baptifm of the Spirit*; becaufe elfe it would follow, that, whofoever had been baptized with water-baptifm, had put on Chrift, and were rifen with him, which all acknowledg to be moft abfurd. Now, fuppofing all the vifible members of the Churches of Rome, Galatia, and Coloff, had been outwardly baptized with water, (I do not fay, they were, but our adverfarys will not onely readily grant it, but alfo contend for it) fuppofe, I fay, the cafe fo, they will not fay, they had all put on Chrift, fince divers expreffions, in thefe Epiftles to them, fhew the contrary; fo that the Apoftle can not mean baptifm *with water*, and yet that he meaneth the *baptifm of Chrift*, i. e. *of the Spirit*, can not be denyed, or that the baptifm, wherewith thefe were baptized (of whom the Apoftle here teftifies, that they had *put on Chrift*) was the *one baptifm*, I think none will call in queftion. Now admitt, as our adverfarys contend, that many, in thefe Churches, who had been baptized with water had not put on Chrift, it will follow, that, notwithftanding that *water-baptifm*, they were not baptized *into Chrift*, or with the baptifm *of Chrift*, feing *as many of them*, *as were baptized* into *Chrift*, *had put on Chrift*, &c. From all which I thus argue,

Arg. 1.   *If the baptifm with water were the one baptifm*, i. e. *the baptifm of Chrift*, *as many*, *as were baptized with water*, *would have put on Chrift* :
But *the laft is falfe* :
Therefore alfo the firft.
And again,

Arg. 2.   *Since as many*, *as are baptized into Chrift*, i. e. *with the one baptifm*, *which is the baptifm of Chrift*, *have put on Chrift*, *Then water-baptifm is not the one baptifm*, viz, *the baptifm of Chrift* :
But the firft is true :
Therefore alfo the laft.

§ V. Thirdly, *fince John's baptifm was a figur*, *and feing the figur gives way to the Subftance*, *albeit the thing figured remain*, *to wit*, *the one baptifm of Chrift*, *yet the other ceafeth*, *which was the baptifm of John.*

That John's baptifm was a figur of Chrift's baptifm, I judge will not readily be denyed: but in cafe it fhould, it can eafily be proved from the nature of it; John's baptifm was *a being baptized with water*, but Chrift's
is

is *a baptizing with the Spirit.* Therefore John's baptiſm muſt have been a figure of Chriſt's. But further, that *vvater-baptiſm* was *John's* baptiſm, will not be denyed : that *vvater baptiſm* is not *Chriſt's* baptiſm, is already proved. From which doth ariſe the confirmation of our Propoſition, thus;

There is no baptiſm to continue now, but the one baptiſm of Chriſt: Arg.

Therefore water-baptiſm is not to continue now ; becauſe it is not the baptiſm of Chriſt.

That John's baptiſm is ceaſed, many of our adverſarys confeſs : but, if any ſhould alledge it otherwiſe, it may be eaſily proved, by the expreſs words of John, not onely as being inſinuated there, where he contra-diſtinguiſheth his baptiſm from that of Chriſt ; but particularly, where he ſaith, Joh. 3: 30. *he* [Chriſt] *muſt encreaſe, but I* [John] *muſt decreaſe.* From whence it clearly followes, that the encreaſing or taking place of Chriſt's baptiſm is the decreaſing or aboliſhing of John's baptiſm ; ſo that, if water-baptiſm was a particular part of John's miniſtery, and is no part of Chriſt's baptiſm, as we have already proved, it will neceſ-ſarily follow, that it is not to continue.

Secondly, *if water-baptiſm had been to continue a perpetual ordinance of Chriſt in his Church, he would either have practiſed it himſelf, or commanded* Arg. *his Apoſtles ſo to do :*

But that he practiſed it not, the Scriptur plainly affirmes, Joh. 4: 2. And that he commanded his Diſciples to baptize with water, I could never yet read. As for what is alledged, that Matth. 28. 19, &c. (where he bids them baptize) is to be underſtood of water-baptiſm, that is but to beg the queſtion, and the grounds for that ſhall be hereafter examined.

Therefore to baptize with water is no perpetual ordinance of Chriſt to his Church.

This hath had the more weight with me, becauſe I find not any ſtand-ing ordinance, or appoyntment of Chriſt, neceſſary to Chriſtians, for which we have not either Chriſt's own practice, or command, as to obey all the commandments, which comprehend both our duty towards God and man, *&c.* and where the *Goſpel* requires more than the *Law,* which is abundantly ſignified in the 5 and 6 chapters of Matthew and elſewhere. Beſides, as to the durys of worſhip, he exhorts us to meet,

O o 3

pro-

promiſing his preſence, commands to pray, preach, watch, *&c.* and gives precepts concerning ſome temporary things, as the waſhing of one anothers feet, the breaking of bread, hereafter to be diſcuſſed. onely for this one thing of baptiſing with water (though ſo earneſtly contended for) we find not any precept of Chriſt.

§ V I. But to make water-baptiſm a neceſſary inſtitution of the Chriſtian Religion, which is pure and Spiritual, and not carnal and ceremonial, is to derogat from the New Covenant diſpenſation, and ſet up the Legal rites and ceremonys, of which this of baptiſm, or waſhing with water, was one, as appears from Heb. 9: 10. where the Apoſtle ſpeaking thereof, ſaith, that it ſtood *onely in meats, and drinks, and divers baptiſms, and carnal ordinances impoſed, untill the time of reformation.* If then the time of Reformation, or the diſpenſation of the Goſpel, which puts an end to the ſhaddowes, be come, then ſuch baptiſms and carnal ordinances are no more to be impoſed. For how baptiſm with water comes now to be a Spiritual ordinance, more than before in the time of the Law, doth not appear: ſeing it is but water ſtill, and a waſhing of the outward man, and a putting away of the filth of the fleſh ſtill; and, as before, thoſe, that are ſo waſhed, were not thereby made perfect, as pertaining to the Conſcience, neither are they at this day, as our adverſarys muſt needs acknowledg, and experience abundantly ſheweth. So that the matter of it, which is a waſhing with water, and the effects of it, which is onely an outward cleanſing, being ſtill the ſame. How comes water-baptiſm to be leſs a carnal ordinance now than before ?

Obj.   If it be ſaid, that *God confers inward Grace upon ſome, that are now baptized.*

Anſw.   So no doubt he did alſo upon ſome, that uſed thoſe baptiſms among the Jewes.

Obj.   Or if it be ſaid, *becauſe 'tis commanded by Chriſt now, under the New Covenant.*

Anſw.   I anſwer *firſt*, that's to beg the queſtion, of which hereafter.

But ſecondly, we find, that, where the matter of Ordinances is the ſame, and the end the ſame, they are never accounted more or leſs Spiritual, becauſe of their different times. Now, was not God the Author of the purifications and baptiſms under the Law? Was not water the matter of them, which is ſo now? Was not the end of them to ſignifie

an inward purifying by an outward wafhing? And is not that alledged
to be the end ftill? And are the neceffary effects or confequences of it any
better now than before, fince men are now by vertue of water-baptifm,
as a neceffary confequence of it, no more, than before, made inwardly
clean? And, if fome by God's Grace, that are baptized with water,
are inwardly purified, fo were fome alfo under the Law; fo that this is
not any neceffary confequence, nor effect, neither of this nor that baptifm: it is then plainly repugnant to right Reafon, as wel as to the
Scriptur teftimony, to affirm, That to be a Spiritual ordinance now,
which was a carnal ordinance before. If it be ftill the fame both as to its
Author, matter, and end, however made to vary in fome fmall circumftances. The Spirituality of the New Covenant, and of its worfhip eftablifhed by Chrift, confifted not in fuch fuperficial alterations of circumftances, but after another manner, therefore let our adverfarys fhew
us, if they can, (without beging the queftion, and building upon fome
one or other of their own principles, denyed by us) where ever Chrift
appoynted or ordained any inftitution or obfervation, under the New
Covenant, as belonging to the nature of it, or fuch a neceffary part of
its worfhip, as is perpetually to continue, which, being one, in fubftance, and effects, (I fpeak of *neceffary* not *accidental* effects) yet, becaufe of fome fmall difference in form or circumftance, was before carnal, notwithftanding it was commanded by God under the Law, but
now is become Spiritual, becaufe commanded by Chrift under the Gofpel. And if they can not do this, then, if water-baptifm was once a
carnal ordinance, as the Apoftle pofitively affirmes it to have been, it
remaines a carnal ordinance ftill; and, if a carnal ordinance, then no
neceffary part of the Gofpel, or New Covenant difpenfation, and if no
neceffary part of it, then not needfull to continue, nor to be practifed
by fuch, as live and walk under this difpenfation. But in this, as in moft
other things (according as we have often obferved) our adverfarys Ju-
daize, and, renouncing the Glorious and Spiritual priviledges of the
New Covenant, are fticking in, and cleaving to the rudiments of the old,
both in doctrin and worfhip, as being more futed and agreable to their
carnal apprehenfions, and natural fenfes. But we, on the contrary,
travel above all to lay hold upon, and cleave unto the *Light* of the *Glo-*
rious Gofpel, revealed unto us. And the harmony of the Truth we profefs in this may appear, by briefly obferving how in all things we follow
the

the Spiritual Gospel of Christ, as contradistinguished from the carnality of the legal dispensation, while our adversarys, through rejecting this Gospel, are still labouring under the burthen of the Law, which neither they, nor their fathers were able to bear.

For the Law and rule of the old Covenant, and Jewes, was outward, written in tables of stone and parchments. So also is that of our adversarys. *But the Law of the New Covenant is inward and perpetual, written in the heart;* so is ours.

The worship of the Jewes was outward and carnall, limited to set times, places, and persons, and performed according to set prescribed forms and observations; so is that of our adversarys. *But the worship of the New Covenant is neither limited to time, place, nor person, but is performed in the Spirit, and in Truth, and is not acted according to set forms and prescriptions, but as the Spirit of God immediately acts, moves, and leads, whether it be to preach, pray, or sing;* and such is also our worship.

So likewise the Baptism among the Jewes under the Law was an outward washing with outward water, onely to typifie an inward purification of the Soul, which did not necessarily follow upon those that were thus baptized: But the Baptism, *of Christ under the Gospel, is the Baptism of the Spirit, and of fire, not the putting away of the filth of the flesh, but the answer of a good conscience towards God,* and such is the Baptism that we labour to be baptized withall and contend for.

§ VII. But again, If water-baptism had been an ordinance of the Gospel, then the Apostle Paul would have been sent to administer it, but he declares positively, 1 Cor. 1: 17. *That Christ sent him not to baptize, but to preach the Gospel.* The reason of that consequence is undenyable, because the Apostle Paul's *commission* was as large as that of any of them; and consequently he being in special manner the Apostle of Christ to the Gentiles, if water-baptism (as our adversaryes contend) be to be accounted the badge of Christianity, he had more need than any of the rest to be sent to baptize, with water, that he might mark the Gentiles converted by him, with that Christian sign. But indeed the reason holds better thus, that, since Paul was the Apostle of the Gentiles, and that in his ministery he doth through all (as by his epistles appears) labour, to wean them from the former Jewish ceremonies and observations, (though in so doing he was sometimes undeservedly judged by others of his brethren, who were unwilling to lay aside those ceremonies) therefore

fore his commiffion (thoug as full, as to the preaching of the Gofpel and New Covenant difpenfation, as that of the other Apoftles) did not require of him that he fhould lead thofe converts into fuch Jewifh obfervations, and baptifms, however that practice was indulged in, and practifed by the other Apoftles, among their Jewifh profelyts; for which caufe *he thanks* 1 Cor. 1:14 *God that he baptized fo few*; intimating that what he did therein, he did not by vertue of his Apoftolik commiffion, but rather in condefcendence to their weaknefs, even as at another time, he circumcifed Timothy.

Our adverfaries, to evade the Truth of this teftimony, ufually alledge, Obj. *that by this is onely to be underflood, that he was not fent, principally to baptize, not that he was not fent at all.*

But this expofition, fince it contradicts the pofitive words of the text, Anfw. and has no better foundation, than the affirmation of its affertors, is juftly rejected, as fpurious, untill they bring fome better proof for it, he faith not *I was not fent principally to baptize*, but *I was not fent to baptize.*

As for what they urge by way of confirmation from other places of Confir. Scripture, where [*not*] is to be fo taken, as where it's faid, *I will have* Matth. 9: *mercy, and not facrifice*, which is to be underftood, that God requires 13. principally mercy, not excluding facrifices.

I fay this place is abundantly explained by the following words [*and* Refut. *the knowledge of God more then burnt offerings*] by which it clearly appears, that burnt-offerings, which are one with facrifices, are not excluded, but there is no fuch word, added in that of Paul, and therefore the parity is not demonftrated to be alike, and confequently the inftance not fufficient, unlefs they can prove that it ought fo to be admitted here: elfe we might interpret, by the fame rule, all other places of Scriptur the fame way, as where the Apoftle faith, 1 Cor. 2: 5. *that your faith might not ftand in the wifdom of men, but in the Power of God*; it might be underftood, it fhall not ftand principally fo. How might the Gofpel, by this liberty of interpretation, be perverted?

If it be faid, *that the abufe of this baptifm among the Corinthians, in dividing* Obj. *themfelves, according to the perfons, by whom they were baptized, made the Apoftle fpeak fo, but that the abufe of a thing doth not abolifh it.*

I anfwer, it is true, it doth not, provided the thing be lawfull and ne- Anfw. ceffary; and that, no doubt, the abufe above faid, gave the Apoftle occafion

fion fo to write. But let it, from this, be confidered, how the Apoftle excludes *baptizing*, not *preaching*, though the abufe [mark] proceeded from that, no lefs then from the other. For thefe Corinthians did denominat themfelves from thofe different perfons, by whofe preaching (as wel as from thofe, by whom they were baptized) they were converted, as by the 4, 5, 6, 7, and 8 vers of the third chap. may appear : and yet, for to remove that abufe, the Apoftle doth not fay, he was not fent to preach, nor yet doth he rejoyce that he had onely preached to a few, becaufe *preaching*, being a ftanding ordinance in the Church, is not, becaufe of any abufe, that the devil may tempt any to make of it, to be forborn, by fuch as are called to perform it, by the Spirit of God. Wherefore the Apoftle, accordingly chap. 3 : 8, 9. informes them, as to that, how to remove that abufe; but as to water-baptifm, for that it was no ftanding ordinance of Chrift, but onely practifed as in condefcendence to the Jewes, & by fome Apoftles to fome Gentiles alfo, there fo foon as the Apoftle perceived the abufe of, he let the Corinthians underftand how little ftrefs was to be laid upon it, by fhewing them that he was glad that he had adminiftred this ceremony to fo few of them, and by telling them plainly that it was no part of his commiffion, neither that, which he was fent to adminifter.

Queft.   Some ask us, *how we know that* baptizing *here is meant of* water, *and not of* the Spirit, *which if it be, then it will exclude baptifm of the fpirit, as wel as of water.*

Anfw.   I anfwer, fuch as ask the queftion, I fuppofe fpeak it, not as doubting that this was faid of water-baptifm, which is more then manifeft : for fince the Apoftle Paul's meffage was *to turn people from darknefs to Light, and convert them to God*; and that as many as are thus turned and converted (*fo as to have the anfwer of a good confcience towards God, and to have put on Chrift, and be arifen with him in newnefs of life*) are baptized with the baptifm of the *Spirit.* But who will fay, that onely thefe few mentioned there to be baptized by Paul, were come to this ? Or that, to turn or bring them to this condition, was not (even admitting our adverfarys interpretation) as principally a part of Paul's miniftery, as any other ? Since then our adverfaries do take this place for water-baptifm (as indeed it is) we may lawfully, taking it fo alfo, urge it upon them. Why the word *baptifm* and *baptizing* is ufed by the Apoftle, where that of *water*, and not of the *Spirit*, is onely underftood, fhall hereafter be fpoken to.

I come

I come now to confider the reafons alledged by fuch as plead for water-baptifm, which are alfo the objections ufed againft the difcontinuance of it.

Firft, fome object, *that Chrift, who had the Spirit above meafur, was* Joh. 3 : verfe 34. *notwithftanding baptized with water.* As Nic. Arnold. againft this Thefe, Sect. 46 of his Theological Exercitation.

I anfwer, fo was he alfo circumcifed ; it wil not follow from thence, that circumcifion is to continue ; for it behoved Chrift to fulfill all righteoufnefs, not onely the miniftery of John, but the Law alfo. Therefore did he obferve the Jewifh feafts and rites, and kept the paffover : it will not then follow, that Chriftians ought to do fo now ; and therefore Chrift Matth. 3: 15. gives John this reafon of his being baptized, defiring him *to fuffer it to be fo novv*: whereby he fufficiently intimats that he intended not thereby to perpetuate it, as an ordinance to his difciples.

Secondly, they object, Matth. 28: 19. *Go ye therefore, and teach all* Obj. *nations, baptizing them in the Name of the Father, and of the Son, and of the holy Ghoft.*

This is the great objection, and upon which they build the whole Anfw. fuperftructure, whereunto the firft general and found anfwer is, by granting the whole, but putting them to prove that water is here meant, fince the Text is filent of it. And though in reafon it be fufficient upon our part that we concede the whole expreffed in the place, but deny that it is by water, which is an addition to the text. Yet I fhall premife fome reafons why we do fo, and then confider the reafons alledged by thofe, that will have water to be here underftood,

The firft is a maxime yeelded to by all, that *We ought not to go from the* Arg. *literal fignification of the Text, except fome urgent necefsity force us thereunto :*
But no urgent neceffity in this place forceth us thereunto :
Therefore we ought not to go from it.

Secondly, That baptifm, which Chrift commanded his Apoftles, was Arg. *the one Baptifm, id eft*, his own Baptifm :
But the *one Baptifm*, which is Chrift's Baptifm, is not with water, as we have already proved :
Therefore the Baptifm commanded by Chrift to his Apoftles was not water-baptifm.

Thirdly, that Baptifm, which Chrift commanded his Apoftles, was Arg.

such, that as many as were therewith baptized *did put on Christ,*

But this is not true of water-baptism :

Therefore, *&c.*

Fourthly, the Baptism commanded by Christ to his Apostles was not John's Baptism :

But Baptism with water was John's Baptism :

Therefore , *&c.*

Allega-tion.   But first, they alledg, *that Christ's Baptism, though a Baptism with water, did differ from John's, because John onely baptized with water unto repentance, but Christ commands his Disciples to baptize in the Name of the Father, Son, and Holy Ghost, reckoning, that in this form, there lieth a great difference betwixt the Baptism of John, and that of Christ.*

Answ.   I answer, as to that, *John's Baptism* was unto repentance, the difference lieth not there, because so is *Christ's* also ; for our adversaries will not deny, but that adult persons, that are baptized, ought, ere they be admitted to it, to repent, and confess their sins, yea and that infants, with a respect to, and consideration of their Baptism, ought to repent and confess : So that the difference lieth not here ; since this of repentance and confession agrees as well to *Christ's*, as to *John's Baptism.* But in this our adversaries are divided, for *Calvin* will have *Christ's* and *John's* to be all one ; *Inst. lib. 4. cap. 15.* Sect. 7, 8. Yet they do differ, and the difference is, in that the one is by water, the other not, &c.

Secondly, as to what Christ saith, in commanding them *to baptize in the Name of the Father, Son, and Spirit,* I confess that states the difference, & it is great ; but that lies not only in admitting water-baptism in this different forme, by a bare expressing of these words : for as the text saith no such thing, neither do I see how it can be inferred from it. For the Greek is εἰς τὸ ὄνομα, that is, *into the Name*, now the *Name of the Lord* is often taken in Scriptur for something else, than a bare sound of words, or literal expression, even for his Vertue and Power, as may appear from Psal. 54: 3. Cant. 1: 3. Prov. 18: 10. and in many more. Now, that the Apostles were, by their ministery, to baptize the nations *into this Name, Vertue* and *Power* ; and that they did so, is evident, by these testimonies of Paul, above mentioned, where he saith, that *as many of them as were baptized into Christ, have put on Christ*, this must have been a baptizing *into the Name*, i. e. *Power* and *Vertue* ; and not a nicer formal expression of words, adjoyned with water-baptism, because, as hath been above

observ-

obſerved, it doth not follow, as a natural or neceſſary conſequence of it. I would have thoſe, who deſire to have their faith built upon no other foundation, than the teſtimony of God's Spirit, and Scriptures of Truth, throughly to conſider, whether there can be any thing further alledged for this interpretation, than what the prejudice of education and influence of Tradition hath impoſed; perhaps it may ſtumble the unwary and inconſiderate Reader, as if the very character of Chriſtianity were aboliſhed, to tell him plainly that this Scripture is not to be underſtood of baptizing with water, and that this form of baptizing in the Name of Father, Son, and Spirit, hath no warrant from Matth. 28. *&c.*

For which, beſides the reaſon taken from the ſignification of [*the Name*] as being the *Vertue* and *Power* above expreſſed, let it be conſidered, that, if that had been a form preſcribed by Chriſt to his Apoſtles, then ſurely they would have made uſe of that form in the adminiſtring of water-baptiſm, to ſuch as they baptized with water; but though particular mention be made in divers places of the Acts, who were baptized, and how; and though it be particularly expreſſed, that they baptized ſuch and ſuch, as, Acts. 2: 41. 8: 12. 13, 38. 9: 18. 10: 48. 16: 15. 18: 8. yet there is not a word of this form; and in two places, Acts. 8: 16. 19: 5. it is ſaid of ſome, that they were *baptized in the name of the Lord Jeſus*, by which it yet more appears, that either the author of this hiſtory hath been very defective, who having ſo often occaſion to mention this, yet omitteth ſo ſubſtantial a part of baptiſm, (which were to accuſe the Holy Ghoſt, by whoſe guidance Luke wrot it) or elſe that the Apoſtle did no ways underſtand, that Chriſt by his commiſſion, Matth. 28. did injoyn them ſuch a form of water-baptiſm, ſeing they did not uſe it, and therefore it is ſafer to conclude, that what they did in adminiſtring water-baptiſm, they did not by vertue of that commiſſion; elſe they would have ſo uſed it: for our adverſaries, I ſuppoſe, would judge it a great hereſy to adminiſter water-baptiſm without that; or onely in the Name of Jeſus, without mention of Father or Spirit, as it is expreſly ſaid they did, in the two places above cited.

Secondly, they ſay, *if this were not underſtood of water-baptiſm, it would be a tautology, and all one with teaching.*

I ſay nay: baptizing with the ſpirit is ſomewhat further then teaching or informing the underſtanding: for it imports a reaching to, and melting the heart, whereby it is turned, as well as the underſtanding in-

formed

formed: besides, we find often in the Scripture, that *teaching* and *in-structing* are put together without any absurdity or needless tautology, and yet these two have a greater affinity, than teaching and baptizing with the Spirit.

Obj.

Thirdly, they say, *Baptism, in this place, must be understood with water; because it is the action of the Apostles, and so cannot be the baptism of the Spirit, which is the work of Christ, and his Grace, not of man, &c.*

Answ.

I answer, Baptism with the Spirit, though not wrought without Christ and his Grace, is instrumentally done by men fitted of God, for that purpose, and therefore no absurdity followes, that Baptism with the Spirit should be expressed, as the action of the Apostles: for, though it be Christ by his Grace, that gives spiritual gifts, yet the Apostle, Rom. 1: 11. speaks of his *imparting to them spiritual gifts,* and he tells the Corinthians, that he *had begotten them, through the Gospel,* 1 Cor. 4: verse 15. and yet to beget people unto the faith is the work of Christ and his Grace, not of men; to convert the heart is properly the work of Christ, and yet the Scriptur often-times ascribes it to men, as being the instruments: And since Paul's commission was *to turn people from darkness to light,* though that be not done without Christ coöperating by his Grace, so may also baptizing with the Spirit be expressed as performable by man, as the instrument, though the work of Christ's Grace, be needfull to concurr thereunto; so that it is no absurdity, to say, that the Apostles did administer the Baptism of the Spirit.

Obj.

Lastly, they say, *that since Christ saith here, that he will be with his disciples to the end of the world, therefore water-baptism most continue so long.*

Answ.

If he had been speaking here of water-baptism, then that might have been urged; but seing that is denyed, and proved to be false, nothing from thence can be gathered, he speaking of the Baptism of the Spirit, which we freely confess doth remain to the end of the world, yea so long as Christ's presence abideth with his children.

Obj.

§ IX. Thirdly, they object *the constant practice of the Apostles in the primitive Church, who,* they say, *did alwayes administer water-baptism to such as they converted to the faith of Christ, and hence also they further urge that of Matth. 28. to have been meant of water, or else the Apostles did not understand it, in that, in baptizing they used water; or that in so doing they walked without a commission.*

I an-

I anſwer, that it was the conſtant practice of the Apoſtles, is denyed, for we have ſhewn, in the example of Paul, that it was not ſo, ſince it were moſt abſurd to judge, that he converted onely theſe few, even of the Church of Corinth, whom he ſaith he baptized ; nor were it leſs abſurd to think that that was a conſtant Apoſtolik practice, which he, that was not inferior to the chiefeſt of the Apoſtles, and who declares, he laboured as much as they all, rejoyceth he was ſo little in. But further, the concluſion, inferred from the Apoſtles practice of baptizing with water, to evince, that they underſtood Matth. 28. of water-baptiſm, doth not hold : for, though they baptized with water, it will not follow, that either they did it by vertue of that commiſſion, or that they miſtook that place, nor can there be any *medium* brought ; that will infer ſuch a concluſion. As to the other inſinuated abſurdity, *that they did it without a commiſſion*. It is none at all, for they might have done it by a permiſſion, as being in uſe, before Chriſt's death. And becauſe the people, nurſed up with outward ceremonys, could not be weaned wholly from them. And thus they uſed other things, as circumciſion, and legal purifications, which yet they had no commiſſion from Chriſt to do, (to which we ſhall ſpeak more at length in the following Propoſition concerning the *Supper*).

But if, from the ſameneſs of the word, becauſe Chriſt bids them baptize, *Obj.* and they afterwards, in the uſe of water, are ſaid to baptize, it be judged probable, that they did underſtand that commiſſion, Matth. 28. to authorize them to baptize with water, and accordingly practiſed it.

Although it ſhould be granted, that, for a ſeaſon, they did ſo far miſtake *Anſw.* it, as to judge that water belonged to that baptiſm, (which however I find no neceſſity of granting) yet I ſee not any great abſurdity would thence follow; for it is plain they did miſtake that commiſſion, as to a main part of it, for a ſeaſon, as where he bids them *go teach all nations*, ſince ſome time after they judged it unlawfull to teach the Gentiles, yea Peter himſelf ſcrupled it, untill, by a viſion, conſtrained thereunto, for which, after he had done it, he was for a ſeaſon (untill they were better informed) judged by the reſt of his brethren. Now, if the education of the Apoſtles, as Jewes, and their propenſity to adhere and ſtick to the Jewiſh religion, did ſo far influence them, that, even after Chriſt's reſurrection and the pouring forth of the Spirit, they could not receive, nor admitt of the teaching of the Gentiles, though Chriſt, in his commiſſion to them, commanded them to preach to them: What further abſurdity

ſurdity

furdity were it to fuppofe, that through the like miftake, the chiefeft of them, having been the difçiples of John, and his Baptifm being fo much prized there among the Jewes, that they alfo took Chrift's baptifm, intended by him of the Spirit to be that of water, which was John's, and accordingly practifed it, for a feafon, it fuffices us, that, if they were fo miftaken, (though I fay not that they were fo)they did not alwayes remain under that miftake, elfe Peter would not have faid of the *Baptifm*, *vvhich now faves*, *that it is not a putting avvay of the filth of the flefh*, which certainly water-baptifm is.

But further they urge much *Peter's baptifing Cornelius*: in which they prefs two things, Firft, *that water-baptifm is ufed*, *even to thofe*, *that had received the Spirit*. Secondly, *that it is faid pofitively*, *he commanded them to be baptized*, Act. 10: 47, 48.

But neither of thefe doth neceffarily infer water-baptifm to belong to the New Covenant difpenfation, nor yet to be a perpetual ftanding ordinance in the Church. For *firft*, all, that this will amount to, was, that Peter at that time baptized thefe men, but that he did it by vertue of that commiffion, Matth. 28. remaines yet to be proved. And how doth the baptifing with water, after the receiving of the holy Ghoft prove the cafe, more then the ufe of circumcifion and other legal rites acknowledged to have been acted by him afterwards; alfo no wonder if Peter that thought it fo ftrange (notwithftanding all that had been profeffed before and fpoken by Chrift) that the Gentiles fhould be made partakers of the Gofpel, and with great difficulty, not without a very extraordinary impulfe thereunto, was brought to come to them and eat with them, was apt to put this ceremony upon them, which being, as it were, the particular difpenfation of John the *fore-runner* of Chrift, feemed to have greater affinity with the Gofpel, than the other Jewifh ceremonyes, then ufed by the Church, but that will no wayes infer our adverfaries conclufion. Secondly, as to thefe words *and he commanded them to be baptized*, it declareth matter of *fact*, not of *right*, and amounteth to no more, than that Peter did at that time *pro hic & nunc*, command thofe perfons to be baptized with water, which is not denyed, but it faith nothing that Peter commanded water-baptifm to be a ftanding and perpetual ordinance to the Church; neithercan any man of found reafon fay, if he heed what he fayes, that a command in matter of fact to particular perfons, doth infer the thing commanded to be of general obligation to all; if it be not other

wayes

wayes bottomed upon ſome poſitive precept; why doth *Peter's* commanding *Cornelius* and his houſhold to be baptized at that time, infer
water-baptiſm to continue, more than his conſtraining (which is more
than commanding) the Gentiles in general to be circumciſed, and obſerve the Law? We find that at that time, when Peter baptized Cornelius, it was not yet determined, whether the *Gentiles* ſhould *not* be *circumciſed*; but, on the contrary, it was the moſt general ſenſe of the
Church, that *they ſhould.* And therefore no wonder, if they thought it
needfull at that time, that they ſhould be baptized, which had more
affinity with the Goſpel, and was a burthen leſs grievous.

§ X. Fourthly, they *objeſt* from *the ſignification of the word* [baptize,]   **Obj.**
which is as much as to dip *and* waſh *with water*, *alledging thence that the very
word imports a being baptized with water.*

This objection is very weak. For, ſince baptizing with water was   **Anſw.**
a rite among the Jewes, as *Paulus Riccius* ſheweth, even before the coming of John, and that the ceremony received that name from the nature
of the practice, as uſed both by the Jewes and by John. Yea we find
that Chriſt and his Apoſtles frequently make uſe of theſe termes to a
more ſpiritual ſignification; *Circumciſion* was onely uſed and underſtood,
among the Jewes, to be that of the *fleſh.* But the Apoſtle tells us of the
circumciſion of the heart and Spirit, *made without hands.* So that, though
baptiſm was uſed, among the Jewes, onely to ſignify a waſhing with
water, yet both John, Chriſt, and his Apoſtles ſpeak of a being *baptized
with the Spirit and with fire*, which they make the peculiar baptiſm of
Chriſt, as contradiſtinguiſhed from that of water, which was John's
(as is above ſhewn.) So that, though baptiſm, among the Jewes, was
onely underſtood of water, yet, among Chriſtians, it is very wel underſtood of the Spirit without water, as we ſee Chriſt and his Apoſtles ſpiritually to underſtand things, under the terms of what had been ſhaddowes before. Thus *Chriſt*, ſpeaking of his *body*, (though the Jewes
miſtook him) ſaid, he would *deſtroy* this *temple, and build it again in three
dayes*, and many more, that might be inſtanced. But, if the etymology
of the word ſhould be tenaciouſly adhered to, it would militat againſt
moſt of our adverſarys, as wel as againſt us, for the Greek βαπτίζω ſignifies *immergo*, that is, to *plunge* and *dip in*, and that was the proper uſe
of water-baptiſm among the Jewes, and alſo by John, and the primitive
Chriſtians, who uſed it; whereas our adverſarys, for the moſt part, onely

Q q

ſprinkle

fprinkle a little water upon the fore-head, which doth not at all anfwer to the word [*baptifm.*] Yea thofe of old among Chriftians, that ufed water-baptifm, thought this dipping and plunging fo needfull, that they thus dipped children. And forafmuch as it was judged, that it might prove hurtfull to fome weak conftitutions, *fprinkling*, to prevent that hurt, was introduced; yet then it was likewife appoynted, that fuch, as were onely fprinkled, and not dippped, fhould not be admitted to have any office in the Church, as not being fufficiently baptized. So that, if our adverfarys will ftick to the word, they muft alter their method of fprinkling.

Obj.   Fifthly they object, Joh. 3: 5. *Except a man be born* again *of Water and of the Spirit*, &c. *hence inferring the neceffity of water-baptifm, as wel as of the Spirit.*

Anfw.   But, if this prove any thing, it will prove water-baptifm to be of abfolute neceffity; and therefore Proteftants rightly affirm, when this is urged upon them by Papifts, to evince the abfolute neceffity of water-baptifm, that [*water*] is not here underftood of outward water, but myftically of an inward cleanfing and wafhing, even as where Chrift fpeaks of being *baptized with fire*, it is not to be underftood of outward material fire, but onely of purifying, by a *metonymie*; becaufe to *purifie* is a proper *effect* of *fire*, as to *wafh* and *make clean* is of *water*; where it can as little be fo underftood, as where we are faid to be *faved by the wafhing of regeneration*, Tit. 3: 5. Yea Peter faith expresfly, in the place often cited, as * *Calvin* wel obferves, that *the baptifm, which faves, is not the putting away of the filth of the flefh:* fo that, fince [*water*] can not be underftood of outward water, this can ferve nothing to prove water-baptifm.

*In the 4 book of his Inftit. chap. 15

    If it be *faid*, that [*water*] *imports here* neceffitatem præcepti, *though not medii.*

Obj.

Anfw.   I anfwer, that is firft to take it for granted that outward water is here underftood, the contrary whereof we have already proved. Next, *water* and the *Spirit* are placed here together, [*Except a man be born of water and the Spirit*] where the neceffity of the one is urged, as much as of the other. Now, if the Spirit be abfolutely neceffary, fo will alfo water, and then we muft either fay, that *to be born of the Spirit*, is not abfolutely neceffary, which all acknowledg to be falfe; or elfe that water is abfolutely neceffary, which, as Proteftants, we affirm, and have proved, is

falfe:

falfe : elfe we muft confefs that *water* is not here underftood of outward water. For to fay, that when *water* and the *Spirit* are placed here juft together, and in the fame manner, though there be not any difference, or ground for it, vifible in the Text, or deduceable from it, that the *neceffity* of water is here *pracepti*, but not *medii*, but the *neceffity* of the *Spirit* is both *medii* and *pracepti*, is indeed confidently to affirm, but not to prove.

Sixthly, and laftly, they *object*, that *the baptifm of water is a vifible fign, or badge, to diftinguifh Chriftians from Infidels, even as Circumçifion did the Jewes.*   Obj.

I anfwer, This faith nothing at all, unlefs it be proved to be a *necef-* *fary precept*, or part of the New Covenant difpenfation; it not being law-full to us to impofe outward ceremonys and rites, and fay, they will di-ftinguifh us from Infidels. *Circumçifion* was pofitively commanded, and faid to be *a feal of the firft Covenant*, but, as we have already proved, that there is no fach command for *baptifm*, fo there is not any word in all the New Teftament, calling it *a badge of Chriftianity*, or *feal of the New Covenant*; and therefore, to conclude, it is fo, becaufe circumcifion was fo, (unlefs fome better proof be alledged for it) is miferably to beg the queftion. *The profeffing of faith in Chrift, and a holy life anfwering thereunto, is a far better badge of Chriftianity, than any outward wafhing,* which yet anfwers not to that of Circumcifion; fince that affixed a character in the flefh, which this doth not; fo that a Chriftian is not known to be a Chri-ftian by his being baptized, efpecially when he was a child, unlefs he tell them fo much; and may not the profeffing faith in Chrift fignify that as wel. I know there are divers of thofe, called *Fathers*, that fpeak much of water-baptifm, calling it *character Chriftianitatis*, but fo did they alfo of *the fign of the Crofs*, and other fuch things, juftly rejected by Pro-teftants. For the myftery of iniquity, which began to work even in the Apoftles dayes, foon fpoiled the fimplicity and purity of the Chriftian worfhip, fo that not onely many Jewifh rites were retained, but many heathenifh cuftoms and ceremonys introduced into the Chriftian wor-fhip, as particularly that word [*Sacrament*,] fo that it is great folly, efpecially for Proteftants, to plead any thing of this from *Tradition* or *Anti-quity*; for we find that neither Papifts nor Proteftants ufe thefe rites ex-actly, as the *Antients* did, who, in fuch things, not walking by the moft certain Rule of God's Spirit, but doting too much upon outwards,

     were

were very uncertain : for moſt of them all, in the primitive time, did *wholly plunge* and *dip* thoſe they baptized, which neither Papiſts nor Proteſtants do : yea ſeveral of the *Fathers* accuſed ſome as heretiks in their
dayes for holding ſome principles common with Proteſtants concerning
it ; as particularly *Auguſtin* doth the *Pelagians,* for ſaying, that *infants
dying unbaptized may be ſaved.* And the *Manichees* were condemned, for
denying that *Grace is univerſally given by baptiſm ;* and *Julian* the *Pelagian* by
Auguſtin, for denying *exorciſm and inſufflation in the uſe of baptiſm* : all which
things Proteſtants deny alſo. So that Proteſtants do but fooliſhly to upbraid
us, as if we could not ſhew any among the *Antients,* that denyed water-
baptiſm, ſeing they can not ſhew any, whom they acknowledg not to
have been heretical in ſeveral things, to have uſed it, nor yet who uſing
it did not uſe alſo *the ſign of the Croſs,* and other things with it, which
they deny. There were ſome nevertheleſs in the darkeſt times of Popery, who teſtified againſt water-baptiſm. For one *Alanus,* pag. 103,
104, 107. ſpeaks of ſome in his time, that were burnt for the denying
of it : for they ſaid, that *baptiſm had no efficacy either in children, or adult
perſons ; and therefore men were not obliged to take baptiſm.* Particularly *ten
Canoniks,* ſo called, *were burnt for that crime by the order of King* Robert *of*
France. And *P. Pithæu* tells in his fragments of the hiſtory of Guienne,
which is alſo confirmed by one *Johannes Floracenſis* a monk, who was
famous at that time, in his Epiſtle to *Oliva,* Abbot of the *Auſonian* Church.
I will (ſaith he) *give you to underſtand concerning the hereſy, that was in the
City of* Orleans *on childer-maſs day, for it was true, if ye have heard any thing,
that King Robert cauſed to be burnt alive, nigh fourteen of that City, of the chief
of their Clergy, and the more noble of their laiks, who were hatefull to God,
and abominable to heaven and earth, for they did ſtiffly deny the Grace of Holy baptiſm, and alſo the conſecration of our Lord's body and blood.* The time of this
deed is noted in theſe words by *Papir. Maſſon.* in his Annals of *France,*
lib. 3. in *Hugh* and *Robert, actum Aureliæ publicè annô incarnationis Domini*
1022, regni Roberti Regis 28. *indictione* 5. *quando Stephanus hæreſiarcha &*
complices ejus damnati ſunt & exuſti Aureliæ.

Now for their calling them *heretiks* and *Manichees,* we have nothing
but the teſtimony of their accuſers, which will no more invalidat their
teſtimony for this Truth, againſt *the uſe of vvater-baptiſm,* or give more
ground to charge us as being one with *Manichees,* than, becauſe ſome, cal'd
by them *Manichees,* do agree with Proteſtants in ſome things, that there-

fore

fore Proteſtants are *Manichees* or *heretiks*, which Proteſtants can no
wayes ſhun. For the queſtion is, whether, in what they did they walked according to the Truth teſtified of by the Spirit in the Holy Scripturs;
ſo that the controverſy is brought back again to the Scripturs, according
to which I ſuppoſe I have formerly diſcuſſed it.

As for the latter part of the Theſis, denying *the uſe of Infant-baptiſm*,
it neceſſarily followes from what is above ſaid, for, if water-baptiſm be
ceaſed, then ſurely baptizing of Infants is not warrantable. But thoſe,
that take upon them to oppoſe us in this matter, will have more to do,
as to this latter part: for, after they have done, what they can, to prove
water-baptiſm, it remaines for them to prove that infants ought to be
baptized. For he, that proves water-baptiſm ceaſed, proves that Infant-baptiſm is vain. But he, that ſhould prove that water baptiſm continues, has not thence proved that Infant-baptiſm is neceſſary. That
needs ſomething further, and therefore it was a pitifull ſubterfuge of
Nic. Arnoldus againſt this, to ſay, that *the denying of infant-baptiſm belonged
to the gangrene of Anabaptiſts*, without adding any further probation.

The Thirteenth Propoſition,

Concerning the Communion or participation of the body and blood of Chriſt.

The *Communion* of the Body and Blood of Chriſt is *inward*
and *Spiritual*, which is the participation of his fleſh
and blood, by which the *inward man* is daily nouriſhed
in the hearts of thoſe in whom Chriſt dwells, of which
things the *breaking of bread* by Chriſt with his Diſciples
was a *figure*, which they even uſed in the Church for a
time, who had received the Subſtance, for the ſake
of the weak: even as *abſtaining from things ſtrangled*, and
from blood, the waſhing one anothers feet, and the *anointing
of the ſick with Oyl*, all which are commanded with no
leſs authority and ſolemnity than the former; yet ſe-

1 Cor. 10.
16, 17.
Jo. 6: 32,
33, 35.
1Cor. 5:8

Acts. 15:
vers 20.
Joh 13:14
Ja. 5: 14.

ing

ing they are but the *shaddows* of better things, they ceafe in fuch as have obtained the *Subftance.*

§ I HE *Communion* of the body and blood of Chrift is a *my-ftery* hid from all natural men in their firft faln and degenerat ftate, which they can not underftand, reach to, nor comprehend, as they there abide, neither, as they there are, can they be partakers of it, nor yet are they able to *difcern the Lord's body*: And forafmuch as the Chriftian world, fo called, for the moft part hath been ftill labouring, working, conceiving, and imagining in their own natural and unrenewed underftandings about the things of God and Religion, therefore hath this myftery much been hid and fealed up from them, while they have been contending, quarreling, and fighting one with another about the meer fhaddow, outfide, and form, but ftrangers to the Subftance, Life, and Vertue.

§ II. The *body* then of Chrift, which believers partake of, is *Spiri-tual*, and not *carnal*, and his *blood*, which they drink of, is *pure* and *hea-venly*, and not *humane* or *elementary*, as *Auguftin* alfo affirmes of the body of Chrift, which is eaten, in his Tractat. Pfal. 98. *Except a man eat my flefh, he hath not in him life eternal, and he faith, the vvords, vvhich I fpeak unto you, are Spirit and Life, underftand fpiritually vvhat I have fpoken. Te fhall not eat of this body, vvhich ye fee, and drink this blood, vvhich they fhall fpill, that crucify me --- I am the living bread, vvho have defcended from heaven; he called himfelf the bread, vvho defcended from heaven, exhorting that vve might believe in him*, &c.

Queft. If it be *afked* then what that *body*, what that *flefh* and *blood* is?

Anfw. I *anfvver*, it is that *heavenly Seed*, that *Divine, Spiritual, celeftial Sub-ftance*, of which we fpake before, in the 5 and 6 Propofitions. This is that *vehiculum Dei*, or *Spiritual body of Chrift*, whereby and wherethrough he communicateth *Life* to men, and *Salvation to as many as believe in him*, and *receive him*, and whereby alfo man comes to have fellowfhip and communion with God. This is proved from the 6 of John, from *verfe* 32, to the end, where Chrift fpeaks more at large of this matter, than in any other place: and indeed this Evangelift and beloved difçiple, who lay in the bofom of our Lord, gives us a more full account of the Spi-ritual fayings and doctrin of Chrift, and it's obfervable, that, though he fpeaks nothing of the ceremony, ufed by Chrift, of breaking bread with

his

his Difciples, neither in his evangelical account of Chrift's life and fufferings, nor in his epiftles, yet he is more large in this account of the participation of the body, flefh, and blood of Chrift, than any of them all.
For Chrift, in this chapter, perceiving that the Jewes did follow him
for love of the loavs, defires them (ver. 27.) to *labour, not for the meat,
vvhich perifheth,* but *for that meat, vvhich endureth for ever*; but forafmuch
as they, being carnal in their apprehenfions, and not underftanding the
Spiritual language and doctrin of Chrift, did judge the *Manna,* which
Mofes gave their fathers, to be the moft excellent bread, as coming
from heaven. Chrift, to rectify that miftake, and better inform them,
affirmeth, firft, *that is is not Mofes, but his Father, that giveth the true bread
from heaven,* ver. 32 & 48. Secondly, *This bread he calls himfelf,* ver. 35.
I am the bread of Life. And ver. 51. *I am the living bread, vvhich came dovvn
from heaven.* Thirdly, he declares that this *bread* is his *flefh,* ver. 51.
The bread, that I vvill give, is my flefh. And ver. 55. *For my flefh is meat indeed, and my blood is drink indeed.* Fourthly, the neceffity of partaking
thereof, ver. 53. *Except ye eat the flefh of the Son of man, and drink his blood,
ye have no life in you.* And laftly, ver. 33. the bleffed fruits and neceffary
effects of this communion of the body and blood of Chrift, *This bread
giveth life to the vvorld.* ver. 50. *He, that eateth thereof, dyeth not.* ver. 58.
he, that eateth of this bread, fhall live for ever. ver. 51. *vvhofo eateth this flefh,*
and drinketh this blood, fhall live for ever. ver. 54. *and he dvvelleth in Chrift,
and Chrift in him.* ver. 56. and *fhall live by Chrift.* ver. 57. From this large
defcription of the origin, nature, and effects of this body, flefh, and
blood of Chrift, it is apparent, that it is Spiritual, and to be underftood
of a Spiritual body, and not of that body, or Temple of Jefus Chrift,
which was born of the Virgin *Mary,* and in which he walked, lived and
fuffered in the land of Judea; becaufe that it is faid both that it came
down from heaven, yea that it is he, that came down from heaven.
Now all Chriftians at prefent generally acknowledge, that the outward
body of Chrift came not down from heaven, neither was it that part of
Chrift, which came down from heaven. And to put the matter out of
doubt, when the carnal Jewes would have been fo underftanding it, he
tells them plainly, ver. 63. *It is the Spirit, that quickeneth, but the flefh
profiteth nothing.* This is alfo founded upon moft found and folid reafon,
becaufe that it is the Soul, not the body, that is to be nourifhed by this flefh
and blood. Now outward flefh can not nourifh nor feed the Soul, there

is no proportion, nor analogy betwixt them, neither is the communion of the Saints with God by a conjunction and mutual participation of flesh but of the Spirit, *He, that is joyned to the Lord, is One Spirit,* not by flesh, (I mean outward flesh, even such as was that, wherein Christ lived and walked, when upon earth, and not flesh, when transposed by a metaphor, to be understood Spiritually) can onely partake of flesh, as Spirit of Spirit, as the body can not feed upon Spirit, neither can the Spirit feed upon flesh: and that the flesh, here spoken of, is spiritually understood, appears further, in that, that, which feedeth upon it, shall never dye: but the bodys of all men once dye, yea it behoved the body of Christ himself to dye, that this body and Spiritual flesh and blood of Christ is to be understood of that *Divine* and *heavenly Seed*, before spoken of by us, appears both by the nature and fruits of it: First, it's said, *it is that, which cometh down from heaven, and giveth life unto the world:* now, this answers to that *Light* and *Seed,* which is testified of, Joh. 1. to be the *Light of the world, and the Life of men.* For that *Spiritual Light* and *Seed,* as it receives place in mens hearts, and room to spring up there, is as bread to the hungry and fainting Soul, that is, as it were, buried and dead in the lusts of the world, which receives life again, and revives, as it tasteth and partaketh of this heavenly bread, and they, that partake of it, are said to come to Christ; neither can any have it, but by coming to him, and believing in the appearance of his *Light in their hearts,* by receiving which, and believing in it, the participation of this body and bread is known. And that Christ understands the same thing here by his body, flesh, and blood, which is understood, Joh. 1. by the *Light inlightening every man,* and the *Life,* &c. appears, for the *Light* and *Life,* spoken of, Joh. 1. is said to be *Christ, he is the true Light;* and the *bread* and *flesh,* &c. spoken of, in this 6 of John, is called *Christ, I am the bread of Life,* saith he. Again, *they, that received that Light and Life,* John. 1: 12. *obtained power to become the sons of God, by believing in his Name:* so also here, Joh. 6: 35. *he, that cometh unto this bread of life, shall not hunger: and he, that believes in him, who is this bread, shall never thirst.* So then, as there was the outward visible body and temple of Jesus Christ, which took its origin from the Virgin Mary, so there is also the Spiritual body of Christ, by and through which he, that was the *Word in the beginning with God,* and was, and is *GOD,* did reveal himself to the sons of men in all ages, and whereby men, in all ages, come to be made partakers of eternal life,

and

and to have communion and fellowſhip with God and Chriſt. Of which body of Chriſt, and fleſh and blood, if both Adam, and Seth, and Enoch, and Noah, and Abraham, and Moſes, and David, and all the Prophets and holy men of God had not eaten, they had not had life *in* them, nor could their inward man have been nouriſhed. Now, as the outward *body* and *temple* was called *Chriſt*, ſo was alſo this Spiritual body, no leſs properly, and that long before that outward body was in being. Hence the Apoſtle faith, 1 Cor. 10: 3, 4. that the Fathers *did all eat the ſame ſpiritual meat; And did all drink the ſame ſpiritual drink: (for they drank of that Spiritual Rock that followed them: and that Rock was Chriſt.)* This can not be underſtood otherwiſe than of this Spiritual body of Chriſt: which Spiritual body of Chriſt, though it was the ſaving food of the righteous, both before the Law, and under the Law, yet under the Law it was vailed and ſhaddowed, and covered under divers types, ceremonys and obſervations, yea and not onely ſo, but it was vailed and hid, in ſome reſpect, under the outward temple and body of Chriſt, or during the continuance of it: ſo that the Jewes could not underſtand Chriſt's preaching about it, while on earth. And, not the Jewes onely, but many of his Diſciples judged it an *hard ſaying, murmured at it, and many from that time went back* [Joh.6:60] *from him, and walked no more with him.* I doubt not, but there are many [ver. 66.] alſo at this day profeſſing to be Diſciples of Chriſt, that do as little underſtand this matter, as thoſe did, and are as apt to be offended and ſtumble at it, while they are *gazing* and following after the outward body, and look not to that, by which the Saints are daily fed and nouriſhed. For, as *Jeſus Chriſt*, in obedience to the will of the Father, did, *by the eternal Spirit offer up* that *body* for a *propitiation* for the *remiſſion of ſins*, and finiſhed his teſtimony upon earth thereby, in a moſt perfect example of patience, reſignation and holyneſs, that all might be made partakers of the fruit of that Sacrifice, So hath he likewiſe poured forth *into* the *hearts* of *all men* a meaſur of that *Divine Light* and *Seed*, wherewith he is cloathed, that thereby, reaching unto the Conſciences of *all*, he may raiſe them up out of *death* and *darkneſs*, by his *Life* and *Light*, and thereby may be made partakers of his body, and therethrough come to have fellowſhip with the Father and with the Son.

§ 111. If it be aſked, *how, and after what manner man comes to partake of* [Queſt.] *it, and to be fed by it?*

I anſwer in the plain and expreſs words of Chriſt, *I am the bread of* [Anſw.]

R r

Life,

Joh.6:35 & 55.
Life, (faith he) *he, that cometh to me, shall never hunger, he, that believeth in me, shall never thirst:* and again, *for my flesh is meat indeed, and my blood is drink indeed.* So whosoever thou art, that askest this question, or readst these lines, whether thou accountst thy self a believer, or really feelst, by a certain and sad experience, that thou art yet in the unbelief, and findst that the outward body & flesh of Christ is so far from thee, that thou canst not reach it, nor feed upon it: yea, though thou hast often swallowed down and taken-in that, which the Papists have perswaded thee to be the real flesh and blood of Christ, and hast believed it to be so, though all thy senses told thee the contrary: or (being a *Lutheran*) hast taken that bread, in, and with, and under which, the Lutherans have assured thee that the flesh and blood of Christ is: or (being a *Calvinist*) hast partaken of that, which the Calvinists say (though a figure onely of the body) gives them, that take it, a real participation of the body, flesh, and blood of Christ, though they neither know how, nor what way. I say, if, for all this, thou findst thy Soul yet barren, yea hungry, and ready to starve, for want of something thou longest for; Know, that that *Light,* that discovers thy iniquity to thee, that shewes thee thy barrenness, thy nakedness, thy emptyness, is that body, that thou must partake of, and feed upon; but that till, by forsaking iniquity, thou turnst to it, comst unto it, receiv'st it, thoug thou mayst hunger after it, thou canst not be satisfied

2 Cor. 6: ver. 14.
with it; for it *hath no communion with darkness, nor canst thou drink of the cup of the Lord, and the cup of devils, and be partaker of the Lord's table, and the table of devils,* 1 Cor. 10:21. But, as thou sufferst that small *Seed of righteousness* to arise *in* thee, and to be formed into a birth, that new substantial birth, that's brought forth in the Soul, naturally feeds upon, and is nourished by this Spiritual body: yea, as this outward birth lives not, but as it sucks-in breath by the outward elementary air, so this new birth lives not *in* the Soul, but as it drawes-in and breaths by that Spiritual air, or vehicle: and as the outward birth can not subsist without some outward body to feed upon, some outward flesh, and some outward drink, so neither can this inward birth, without it be fed by this inward body, by this inward flesh and blood of Christ, which answers to it after the same manner, by way of analogy. And this is most agreeable to the doctrin of Christ concerning this matter, for, as without outward food the natural body

Joh.6:53 hath not life, so also saith Christ, *Except ye eat the flesh of the Son of man, and drink his blood, ye have no life in you.* And as the outward body, eating
outward

outward food , lives thereby , so Christ saith, that *he, that eateth him,* Joh.6:57
shall live by him. So it is this inward participation of this inward man , of
this inward and Spiritual body , by which man is united to God , and has
fellowship and communion with him. *He , that eateth my flesh , and drink-* Joh.6:56
eth my blood (saith Christ) *dwelleth in me, and I in him.* This can not be
understood of outward eating of outward bread , and as by this the Soul
must have fellowship with God , so also in so far as all the Saints are *par-*
takers of this one body , and this one blood , they come also to have a *joynt com-*
munion. Hence the Apostle , 1 Cor. 10: 17. in this respect saith , that
they *being many are one bread , and one body :* and to the *wise* among the Corinthians he saith , *the bread , which we break , is the communion of the body*
of Christ. This is the true and Spiritual supper of the Lord , which men   ver. 16.
come to partake of , by hearing the voyce of Christ , and opening the
door of their hearts , and so leting him in , in the manner above said ,
according to the plain words of the Scriptur , Rev. 3: 20. *Behold , I stand*
at the door , and knock: if any man hear my voice , and open the door , I will
come in to him , and will sup with him , and he with me. So that the *supper of*
the Lord , and the supping with the Lord , and partaking of his flesh and
blood is no wayes limited to the ceremony of breaking bread , and drinking wine at particular times ; but is truely and really enjoyed , as often as
the Soul retires into the Light of the Lord , and feels and partakes of
that heavenly Life , by which the inward man is nourished , which
may be , and is often witnessed by the faithfull at all times , though
more particularly , when they are assembled together to wait upon the
Lord.

§ IV. But what confusion the Professors of Christianity have runn
into concerning this matter , is more than obvious , who , as in most
other things they have done , for want of a true Spiritual understanding ,
have sought to tie this supper of the Lord to that ceremony (used by
Christ before his death) of breaking bread and drinking wine with his
Disciples. And though they for most part agree in this general , yet how
do they contend , and debate , one against another ? How strangely are
they pinched , pained and straitned to make this Spiritual mystery agree
to that ceremony ? And what monstrous and wild opinions and conceiv-
ings have they invented to inclose or affix the body of Christ to their bread
and wine ? From which opinion not onely the greatest and fiercest and
most hurtfull contests, both among the professors of Christianity in gene-

ral, and among Protestants in particular, have arisen, but also such absurditys, irrational and blasphemous consequences have ensued, as makes the Christian Religion odious and hatefull to Jewes, Turks, and Heathens. The professors of Christianity do chiefly divide, in this matter, into three opinions.

The *first is of those, that say, the substance of the bread is transubstantiated into the very Substance of that same body, flesh, and blood of Christ, which was born of the Virgin Mary, and crucified by the Jewes: so that, after the words of consecration (as they call them) it is no more bread, but the body of Christ.*

The *second is of such, as say, the substance of the bread remaines, but that also that body is in, and with, and under the bread: so that both the substance of the bread and of the body, flesh, and blood of Christ is there also.*

The *third is of those ⸪ that (denying both these) do affirm that the body of Christ is not there corporally, or substantially, but yet that it is really and sacramentally received, by the faithfull, in the use of bread and wine; but how, or what way it's there, they know not, nor can they tell, onely we must believe it is there, yet so that it is onely properly in heaven.*

It is not my design to enter into a refutation of these several opinions; for each of their authors and assertors have sufficiently refuted one another, and are all of them no less strong both from Scriptur and Reason, in refuting each their contrary party's opinion, than they are weak in establishing their own; for I often have seriously observed in reading their respective writings (and so it may be have others) that all of them do notably, in so far as they refute the contrary opinions, but that they are mightily pained, when they come to confirm and plead for their own: Hence I necessarily to conclude, that none of them had attained to the Truth and Substance of this mystery. Let us see, if *Calvin,* * after he hath refuted the two former opinions, be more successfull, in what he affirmes and asserts for the truth of his opinion, who, after he hath much laboured in overturning and refuting the two former opinions, plainly confesseth, that he knowes not what to affirm in stead of them, for, after he has spoken much, and at last concluded *that the body of Christ is there, and that the Saints must needs partake thereof,* at last he lands in those words, sect. 32. *But if it be asked me, how it is, I shall not be ashamed to confess that it is a secret, too high for me to comprehend in my spirit, or ex-*

plain

* Inst.
lib. 4.
cap. 17.

plain in words. Here he deals very ingenuoufly, and yet who would have thought that fuch a man would have been brought to this ftrait, in the confirming of his opinion; confidering but a little before, in the fame chapter, fect. 15. he accufeth the fchool-men among the *Papifts*, (and I confefs, truely) *in that they neither underftand, nor explain to others how Chrift is in the Euchanft*, which fhortly after he confeffeth himfelf he can not do. If then the fchool-men among the Papifts do neither underftand, nor yet can explain to others their doctrin in this matter, nor *Calvin* can comprehend it in his fpirit, (which I judge is as much as not to underftand it) nor exprefs it in words (and then furely he can not explain it to others) then no certainty is to be had from either of them. There have been great endeavours ufed for reconcilement in this matter, both betwixt Papifts and Lutherans, Lutherans and Calvinifts, yea and Calvinifts and Papifts, but all to no purpofe: and many formes and manners of expreffions drawn up, to which all might yeeld, which in the end proved in vain, feing every one underftood them, and interpreted them their own way, and fo they did thereby but equivocat and deceive one another. The reafon of all this contention is, becaufe they all wanted a clear underftanding of the myftery, and were doting about the fhaddow and the externals. For both the ground and matter of their conteft lies in things extrinfic from, and unneceffary to the main matter; and this hath been often the policy of Satan to bufy people, and amufe them with outward fignes, fhaddows and formes, making them contend about that, while in the mean time the *Subftance* is neglected, yea and in contending for thefe fhaddows, he ftirs them up to the practice of malice, heat, revenge, and other vices, by which he eftablifheth his kingdom of darknefs among them, and ruins the *life of Chriftianity*: for there has been more animofity and heat about this one particular, and more blood-fhed and contention, than about any other. And furely they are little acquainted with the ftate of Proteftants affairs, who know not that their contentions about this have been more hurtfull to the Reformation, than all the oppofition they met with from their common adverfarys. Now all thefe uncertain and abfurd opinions and the contentions therefrom arifing have proceeded from their all agreing in two general errors concerning this thing. Which being denyed and receded from, as they are by us, there would be an eafy way made for reconciliation, and we fhould all meet in the one Spiritual and true underftanding of this myftery; and, as the

R r 3

con-

contentions, so would also the absurditys, which follow from all the three forementioned opinions, cease and fall to the ground.

The *first* of these *errors* is, in making the communion or participation of the body, flesh, and blood of Christ to relate to that outward body, vessel, or Temple, that was born of the Virgin Mary, and walked and suffered in Judea, whereas it should relate to the Spiritual body, flesh, and blood of Christ, even that *heavenly* and *celestial Light* and *Life*, which was the food and nourishment of the regenerat in all ages, as we have already proved.

The *second error* is, in tieing this participation of the body and blood of Christ to that ceremony, used by him with his Disciples, in the breaking of bread, *&c.* as if it had onely a relation thereto, or were onely enjoyed in the use of that ceremony, which it neither hath nor is. For this is that bread, which Christ in his prayer teaches to call for, terming it ὁ ἄρτον ὁ ἐπιούσιον, i.e. the *supersubstantial bread*, as the Greek hath it, and which the Soul partakes of, without any relation or necessary respect to this ceremony, as shall be hereafter proved more at length.

These two errors being thus laid aside, and the contentions arising therefrom buried, all are agreed in the main positions, *viz,* first, that *the body, flesh, and blood of Christ is necessary for the nourishing of the Soul.* Secondly, that *the Soules of believers do really and truely partake and feed upon the body, flesh, and blood of Christ.* But while men are not content with the spirituality of this mystery, going, in their own wills, and according to their own inventions, to strain and wrest the Scriptures, for to tie this Spiritual communion of the flesh, and blood of Christ, to outward bread and wine, and such like carnal ordinances, no wonder, if, by their carnal apprehensions, they run into heaps and confusion. But because it hath been generally supposed that the communion of the body and blood of Christ had some special relation to the ceremony of breaking bread, I shall first refute that opinion, and then proceed to consider the *nature* and *use* of that *ceremony,* and whether it be now *necessary to continue,* answering the reasons and objections of such as plead its continuance, as a necessary and standing ordinance of Jesus Christ.

§ V. First it must be understood, that I speak of a necessary and peculiar relation, otherwise than in a general respect: for, forasmuch as our communion with Christ is, and ought to be our greatest and chiefest work, we ought to do all other things with a respect to God, and our

fellow-

fellowſhip with him ; but a ſpecial and neceſſary reſpect or relation is
ſuch, as where the two things are ſo tied and united together, either *of
their own nature*, or *by the command of God*, that the one can not be
enjoyed, or at leſt is not (except very extraordinarily) without the other.
Thus *Salvation* hath a neceſſary reſpect to *holyneſs*, becauſe *without holyneſs
no man ſhall ſee God.* And *the eating of the fleſh and blood of Chriſt* hath a neceſſary reſpect to our having life, becauſe, if we eat not his fleſh, and
drink not his blood, we can not have *life :* and our *feeling of* God's *preſence*
hath a neceſſary reſpect to our being found meeting in his Name, by Divine precept, becauſe he has promiſed, *where two or three are met together in
his Name, he will be in the midſt of them*; in like manner our receiving *benefits*
and *bleſſings from God*, has a neceſſary reſpect to our praying, becauſe if we
ask, *he hath promiſed we ſhall receive.* Now the communion or participation of the fleſh and blood of Chriſt hath no ſuch neceſſary relation to the
breaking of bread and *drinking of wine.* For, if it had any ſuch neceſſary relation, it would either be *from the nature of the thing*, or *from ſome Divine precept :* But we ſhall ſhew it is from neither : Therefore, &c. Firſt, it is not
from the nature of it, becauſe to partake of the fleſh and blood of Chriſt is
a Spiritual exerciſe ; and all confeſs that it is by the Soul and Spirit that
we become real partakers of it, as it is the Soul, and not the body, that
is nouriſhed by it : but to eat bread and drink wine is a natural act, which,
in it ſelf, adds nothing to the Soul, neither has any thing, that is Spiritual,
in it, becauſe the moſt carnal man, that is, can as fully, as perfectly,
and as wholly eat bread and drink wine, as the moſt Spiritual. Secondly,
their relation is not *by nature*, elſe they would infer one another : but
all acknowledge that many eat of the bread, and drink of the wine ,even
that, which, they ſay, is *conſecrat* and *tranſubſtantiat into the very body of Chriſt*,
who notwithſtanding have not life eternal, have not Chriſt dwelling in
them, nor do live by him, as all do, who truely partake of the fleſh and
blood of Chriſt, *without the uſe of this ceremony*, as all the Patriarchs and
Prophets did, before this ordinance (as they account it) was inſtituted : neither was there any thing under the Law, that had any direct or
neceſſary relation hereunto, though to partake of the fleſh and blood of
Chriſt in all ages was indiſpenſibly neceſſary to Salvation. For as for the
Paſchal Lamb, the whole end of it is ſignified particularly ; Exod. 13 : 8.9.
to wit, that *the Jewes might thereby be kept in remembrance of their deliverance out of Egypt.* Secondly it has no relation by Divine precept, for, if it
had;,

had, it would be mentioned in that, which our adverſarys account the inſtitution of it, or elſe in the practice of it, by the Saints recorded in Scriptur, but ſo it is not. For as to the inſtitution, or rather narration of Chriſt's practice in this matter, we have it recorded by the Evangeliſt Matthew, Mark and Luke. In the firſt two there is onely an account of the matter of fact, to wit, *that Chriſt brake bread, and gave it his Diſciples to eat, ſaying, this is my body, and bleſſing the cup, he gave it them to drink, ſaying, this is my blood;* but nothing of any deſire to them to do it. In the laſt, after the bread (but before the bleſſing or giving them the wine) he bids them *do it in remembrance of him;* what we are to think of this practice of Chriſt ſhall be ſpoken of hereafter. But what neceſſary relation hath all this to the believers partaking of the fleſh and blood of Chriſt ? The end of this for which they were to do it (if at all) is to remember Chriſt, which the Apoſtle yet more particularly expreſſes, 1 Cor. 11: 26. *to ſhew forth the Lord's death.* But to remember the Lord, or declare his death, which are the ſpecial and particular ends annexed to the uſe of this ceremony is not at all to partake of the fleſh and blood of Chriſt, neither have they any more neceſſary relation to it, than any other two different Spiritual dutys. For, though they, that partake of *the fleſh and blood of Chriſt,* can not but *remember him;* yet the *Lord* and his *death* may be remembred (as none can deny) where his *fleſh and blood* is not truely *partaken* of. So that, ſince the very particular and expreſs end of this ceremony may be witneſſed (to wit, the remembrance of the Lord's death) and yet the fleſh and blood of Chriſt not partaken of, it can not have had any neceſſary relation to it, elſe the partaking thereof would have been the end of it, and could not have been attained without this participation. But, on the contrary, we may wel infer hence, that, ſince the poſitive end of this ceremony is not the partaking of the fleſh and blood of Chriſt, and that whoever partakes of the fleſh and blood of Chriſt, can not but remember him; that therefore ſuch need not this ceremony to put them in remembrance of him.

But if it be ſaid, *that Jeſus Chriſt calls the bread here his body, and the wine his blood; therefore he ſeems to have had a ſpecial relation to his Diſciples partaking of his fleſh and blood, in the uſe of this thing.*

I *Anſwer,* his calling the bread his body, and the wine his blood, would yet infer no ſuch thing : though it is not denyed but that Jeſus Chriſt, in all things he did, yea and from the uſe of all natural things, took occaſion to

raiſe

raife the minds of his Difciples and hearers to Spirituals. Hence from the woman of *Samaria* her drawing *water*, he took occafion to tell her of that *Living Water*, which *whofo drinketh of fhall never thirft*, which indeed is all one with his *blood*, here fpoken of. Yet it will not follow that that well or water had any neceffary relation to the living water, or the living water to it, *&c.* So Chrift takes occafion, from the Jewes following him for the loavs, to tell them of this *Spiritual bread* and *flefh* of his *body*, which was more neceffary for them to feed upon. It will not therefore follow, that their following him for the loavs had any neceffary relation thereunto. So alfo Chrift, here being at fupper with his Difciples, takes occafion from the *bread* and *wine*, which was before them, to fignify unto them, that, as *that bread*, which he brake unto them, and *that wine*, which he bleffed and gave unto them, did contribute to the preferving and nourifhing of their bodys, fo was he alfo to give his *body*, and fhed his *blood* for the *Salvation* of their *Soules*; and therefore the very *end* propofed in this ceremony, to thofe, that obferve it, is to be a *memorial of his death*.

But if it be faid, that the Apoftle, 1 Cor. 10:16. *calls the bread, which he brake, the communion of the body of Chrift, and the cup, the communion of his blood*.

I do moft willingly fubfcribe unto it, but do deny that this is underftood of the outward bread, neither can it be evinced, but the contrary is manifeft from the context, for the Apoftle in this chapter fpeaks not one word of that ceremony; for, having in the beginning of it fhewn them, how the Jewes of old were made partakers of the *Spiritual food*, and *water*, which was *Chrift*, and how feverall of them, through *difobedience* and *idolatry*, fell from that good condition, he exhorts them by the example of thofe Jewes, whom God deftroyed of old, to flee thofe evils, fhewing them, that they, to wit, the Corinthians, are likewife partakers of the body and blood of Chrift, of which communion they would rob themfelves, if they did evil, *becaufe they could not drink of the cup of the Lord, and the cup of devils, and partake of the Lord's table and of the table of devils*, ver 21. which fhewes, that he underftands not here the ufing of *outward bread* and *wine*; becaufe thofe, that do drink the cup of devils, and eat of the table of devils, yea the wickedeft of men, may partake of the outward bread and outward wine. For there the the Apoftle calls *the bread one*, ver. 17. and he faith, *we being many are one bread and one body, for we are all partakers of that one bread*. Now, if the

Joh. 4:
ver. 14.

S s

bread

bread be one, it can not be the *outward*, or the *inward* would be excluded, whereas it can not be denyed, but that it's the partaking of the *inward bread*, and not the *outward*, that makes the *Saints* truely *one body*, and *one bread*. And whereas they say, that the *one bread* here comprehendeth both the *outward* and *inward*, *by vertue of the Sacramental union*; that indeed is to affirm, but not to prove. As for that *figment of a Sacramental union*, I find not such a thing in all the Scriptur, especially in the New Testament, nor is there any thing can give a rise for such a thing in this chapter, where the Apostle, as is above observed, is not at all treating *of that ceremony*, but onely, *from the excellency of that priviledg*, which the Corinthians had, as believing Christians, *to partake of the flesh and blood of Christ*; dehorts them *from idolatry* and *partaking of the Sacrifices* offered to *idols*, so as thereby to offend or hurt their weak brethren.

Obj.   · But that, which they most of all cry out for in this matter, and are alwayes noysing, is from 1 Cor. 11. where the Apostle is particularly treating of this matter, and therefore from some words here they have the greatest appearance of Truth for their assertion, as ver. 27. where he calls *the cup, the cup of the Lord*, and saith, *that they, who eat of it, and drink it unworthily, are guilty of the body and blood of the Lord*, and ver. 26. *eat and drink their own damnation*, intimating thence that this hath an immediat or necessary relation to the body, flesh, and blood of Christ.

Answ.   Though this, at first view, may catch the unwary Reader, yet being wel considered, it doth no wayes evince the matter in controversy. As for the Corinthians being in the use of this ceremony, why they were so, and how that obliges not Christians now to the same, shall be spoken of hereafter: it suffices at this time to consider that they were in the use of it. Secondly, that in the use of it they were guilty of, and committed divers abuses. Thirdly, that the Apostle here is giving them directions how they may do it aright, in shewing them the right and proper use and end of it.

These things being premised, let it be observed that the very express and particular use of it, according to the Apostle, is *to shew forth the Lord's death*, &c. But *to shew forth the Lord's death and partake of the flesh and blood of Christ* are different things. He saith not, *as often as ye eat this bread and drink this cup, ye partake of the body and blood of Christ*, but, *ye shew forth the Lord's death*. So I acknowledge, that this ceremony by those, that practise it, hath an *immediat relation to the outward body* and *death of Christ*

upon

upon the **Cross**, as being properly a memorial of it , but it doth not thence follow , that it hath any *inward* or *immediat relation to believers communicating or partaking of the Spiritual body and blood of Christ , or that Spiritual supper* , spoken of , Rev. 3: 20. for , though in a general way, as every religious action , in some respect, hath a common relation to the Spiritual communion of the Saints with G d , so we shall not deny but this hath a relation , as others.   Now for his calling *the cup, the cup of the Lord* , and saying *they are guilty of the body and blood of Christ , and eat their own damnation , in not discerning the Lord's body* , &c. I answer , that this infers no more necessary relation , than any other religious act ; and amounts to no more , than this , that , since the Corinthians were in the use of this ceremony , and so performed it , as a religious act , they ought to do it worthily , else they should bring condemnation upon themselves.   Now , this will not more infer the thing , so practised by them , to be a necessary *religious act* obligatory upon others , than when Rom. 14: 6. the Apostle saith , *He , that regardeth the day , regardeth it unto the Lord* , it can be thence inferred , that the dayes , that some esteemed and observed , did lay an obligation upon others to do the same : but yet as he , that *esteemed a day* , and placed Conscience in keeping it , was to *regard it to the Lord*, and so it was to him , in so far as he dedicated it unto the Lord , *the Lord's day* , he was to do it worthily , and if he did it unworthily , he would be guilty of the Lord's day , and so keep it to his own damnation : so also such as observe *this ceremony of bread and wine* , it is to them *the bread of the Lord* , and *the cup of the Lord* , because they use it as a religious act , and forasmuch as their end therein is *to shew forth the Lord's death* , and *remember his body* , that was *crucifi d* for them , and his *blood* , that was *shed* for them. If notwithstanding they believe it is their duty to do it , and make it a matter of Conscience to forbear , if they do it without that due preparation and examination , which every religious act ought to be performed in , then , in stead of truely remembring the Lord's death , and his body and his blood , they render themselves *guilty* of it , as being in one spirit with those that crucified him , and shed his blood , though pretending with thanks-giving and joy to remember it. Thus the *Scribes* and *Pharisees* of old , though in memory of the Prophets they garnished their sepulchres , yet are said by Christ to be *guilty of their blood.*   And that no more can be hence inferred , appears from another saying of the same Apostle , Rom. 14: 23. *he , that doubteth , is damned , if he eat* , &c. where he , speaking of those ,

that

that judged it unlawfull to eat flesh, *&c.* faith, if they eat doubting, they eat their own *damnation.* Now it is manifest for all this, that either the doing or forbearing of this was, to another, that placed no Conscience in it, of no moment. So I fay, he, that eateth that, which in his Conscience he is perſwaded is not lawfull for him to eat, doth eat his own damnation: ſo he alſo, that placeth Conscience in eating bread and wine, *as a religious act,* if he do it unprepared, and without that due reſpect, wherein ſuch acts ſhould be gone about, he eateth and drinketh his own *damnation,* *not diſcerning the Lord's body,* i. e. not minding what he doth, to wit, with *a ſpecial reſpect to the Lord, and by way of ſpecial commemoration of the death of Chriſt.*

§ VI. I having now ſufficiently ſhewn, what the true communion of the body and blood of Chriſt is, how it is partaken of, and how it has no neceſſary relation to that ceremony of *bread* and *wine,* uſed by Chriſt with his Diſciples, it is fit now to conſider the *nature and conſtitution of that ceremony* (for as to the *proper uſe* of it, we have had occaſion to ſpeak of before) whether it be a *ſtanding ordinance* in the Church of Chriſt, obligatory upon all, or indeed whether it be any neceſſary part of the Worſhip of the New-Covenant-diſpenſation, or hath any better or more binding foundation, than ſeveral other ceremonys appoynted and practiſed about the ſame time, which the moſt of our oppoſers acknowledg to be ceaſed, and now no wayes binding upon Chriſtians. We find this ceremony onely mentioned in Scriptur in four places, to wit, Matthew, Mark, and Luke, and by Paul to the Corinthians. If any would infer any thing from the frequency of the mentioning of it, that will add nothing, for it being a matter of fact is therefore mentioned by the Evangeliſts; and there are other things leſs memorable as often, yea oftener, mentioned. Matthew and Mark give onely an account of the matter of fact, without any precept to do ſo afterward, s ſimply declaring, that Jeſus, at that time, did deſire them to eat of the bread, and drink of the cup. To which Luke adds theſe words, *This do in remembrance of me.* If we conſider this action of Chriſt with his Apoſtles, there will appear nothing ſingular in it, for a foundation to ſuch a ſtrange ſuperſtructor, as many in their airy imaginations have ſought to build upon it; for both Matthew and Mark preſs it as an act done by him, as he was eating, Matthew ſaith *and as they were eating;* and Mark, *and as they did eat, Jeſus took bread,* &c. Now this act was no ſingular thing, neither any ſolemn in-

Mat. 26:
ver. 26.
Mar. 14:
ver. 22.
Luk 22:
ver. 19.
1Cor. 11
ver. 23.

ſtitution

ftitution of a Gofpel ordinançe , becaufe it was a conftant cuftom among
the Jewes , as *Paulus Ricçius* obferves at length in his *Celeflial Agri-
cultur*; that, when they did eat the *Paffover* , the mafter of the family did
take bread , and blefs it , and breaking it gave of it to the reft , and likewife taking wine did the fame ; fo that there can nothing further appear
in this , than that *Jefus Chrift , who fulfilled all righteoufnefs* , and alfo obferved the Jewifh feafts and cuftoms , ufed this alfo among his Difciples ,
onely , that , as in moft other things , he laboured to draw their minds
to a further thing , fo , in the ufe of this , he takes occafion to put them in
mind of his death and fufferings , which were fhortly to be , which he
did the oftener inculcat unto them , for that they were averfe from believing it. And as for that expreffion of Luke , *Do this in remembrançe of
me* , it will amount to no more , than being the laft time that Chrift did
eat with his Difciples , he defired them , that in their eating and drinking they might have regard to him , and by the remembring of that opportunity be the more ftirred up to follow him diligently through fufferings and death , *&c.* But what man of reafon , laying afide the prejudice
of education , and the influence of Tradition , will fay , that this account
of the matter of faét , given by Matthew and Mark , or this expreffion
of Luke, to *do that in remembrançe of him*,will amount to thefe confequences,which the generality of Chriftians have fought to draw from it, as calling it , *auguftiffimum euchariftia Sacramentum, venerabile altaris Sacramentum ,
the principal feal of the covenant of Graçe, by which all the benefits of Chrift's death
are fealed to believers*, and fuch like things. But to give a further evidence
how thefe confequences have not any bottom from the praétice of that
ceremony , nor from the words following, *Do this,* & c. let us confider another of the like nature, as it is at length expreffed by John, c. 13. ver. 3,4,
8,13,14,15. *Jefus rifeth from fupper,and laid afide his garments,and took a towel,and girded himfelf. After that he poureth water into a bafon , and began to wafh
the Difciples feet , and to wipe them with the towel, wherewith he was girded.
Peter faith unto him, Thou fhalt never wafh my feet. Jefus anfwered him, If I
wafh thee not, thou haft no part with me. So after he had wafhed their feet ,
--- he faid, Know ye what I have done to you? If I then your Lord and Mafter have
wafhed your feet , ye alfo ought to wafh one anothers feet. For I have given you
an example , that ye fhould do as I have done to you.* As to which let it be obferved, that John relates this paffage to have been done at the fame time,
with the other of *breaking bread.* Both being done the night of the *paffover,*

S s 3.

after

after supper. If we regard the Narration of this, and the circumstances attending it, it was done with far more solemnity, and prescribed far more punctually and particularly, than the former. It is said onely, *as he was eating, he took bread*, so that this would seem to be but an *occasional* business. But here *he rose up, he laid by his garments, he girded himself, he poured out the water, he washed their feet, he wiped them with the towel. He did this to all of them*, which are circumstances surely far more observable, than those noted in the other. *The former was a practice common among the Jewes, used by all masters of families, upon that occasion:* but *this, as to the manner, and person acting it, to wit, for the Master to rise up, and wash the feet of his servants and Disciples, was more singular and observable.* In the breaking of bread, and giving of wine, *it is not pleaded by our adversarys, nor yet mentioned in the Text, that he particularly put them into the hands of all, but breaking it, and blessing it, gave it the nearest, and so they from hand to hand.* But *here it is mentioned that he washed not the feet of one or two, but of many.* He *saith not in the former, that, if they do not eat of that bread, and drink of that wine, they shall be prejudiced by it:* but here *he saith expressly to* Peter, *that, if he wash not him, he hath no part with him; which, being spoken upon* Peter's *refusing to let him wash his feet, would seem to import no less, than not the continuance onely, but even the necessity of this ceremony.* In the former he saith, as it were, passingly, *Do this in remembrance of me:* but here *he sitteth down, again he desires them to consider what he hath done, tells them positively, that as he hath done to them, so ought they to do to one another, and yet again he redoubles that precept, by telling them, he has given them an example, that they should do so likewise.* If we respect the nature of the thing, it hath as much in it, as either baptism, or the breaking of bread, *seing it is an outward element of a cleansing nature, applyed to the outward man, by the command and the example of* Christ, *to signify an inward purifying.* I would willingly propose this seriously to men, that will be pleased to make use of that reason and understanding, that God hath given them, and not be imposed upon, nor abused by the custom or tradition of others, *whether this ceremony, if we respect either the time, that it was appoynted in, or the circumstances, wherewith it was performed, or the command, enjoyning the use of it, hath not as much to recommend it for a standing ordinance of the Gospel, as either water baptism, or bread and wine, or any other of that kind?* I wonder then, what reason the Papists can give, why they have not numbred it among their Sacraments, except meerly *voluntas Ecclesia & traditio Patrum.*

But

But if they say, *that it is used among them, in that the Pope and some other* Obj.
persons among them use to do it 1nce a year to some poor people.

I would willingly know what reason they have why this should not be Answ.
extended to *all*, as wel as that of the *Eucharist*, (as they term it) or whence
it appears from the Text, that [*Do this in remembrançe of me*] should
be interpreted, that the bread and wine were every day to be taken
by all priests, or the bread every day, or every week by the people:
and that that other command of Christ, *ye ought to do, as I have done to
you*, &c. is onely to be understood of the Pope, or some other persons
to be done onely to a few, and that once a year. Surely there can be no
other reason, for this difference assigned from the Text. And as to Protestants, who use not this ceremony at all, if they will but open their
eyes, they may see, how that by custom and tradition they are abused in
this matter, as were their Fathers in divers Popish traditions. For, if
we look into the plain Scriptur, what can be thence inferred to urge the
one, which may not be likewise pleaded for the other, or for laying aside
the one, which may not be likewise said against the continuance of the
other? If they say, *that the former of washing the feet, was onely a ceremony.*
What have they whence they can shew that this breaking of bread is
more? If they say, *that the former was onely a sign of humility and purifying,*
What have they to prove that this was more? If they say, *the one was onely*
for a time, and was no Evangelical ordinance. What hath this to make it such,
that the other wanted? Surely there is no way of Reason to evite this,
neither can any thing be alledged that the one should cease, and not the
other, or the one continue, and not the other; but the meer opinion of
the affirmers, which, by custom, education and tradition, hath begotten in the hearts of people a greater reverence for and esteem of the
one, than the other, which, if it had faln out to be as much recommended to us by Tradition, would, no doubt, have been as tenaciously pleaded for, as having no less foundation in the Scriptur. But, since the
former, to wit, the washing of one anothers feet, is justly laid aside,
as not binding upon Christians, so ought also the other for the same
reason.

§ VII. But I strange, that those, that are so clamorous for this
ceremony, and stick so much to it, take liberty to dispense with the
manner or method, that Christ did it in, since none, that ever I could
hear of, who now do it, use it in the same way, that he did it; Christ
did

did it at supper, while they were eating, but they do it in the morning.
onely by it self. What rule walk they by in this change?

Obj.   If it be said, *these are but circumstances, and not the matter, and if the matter be kept to, the alteration of circumstances is but of small moment.*

Answ.   What if it should be said, the whole is but a circumstance, which fell out at the time, when Christ eat the *Passover?* For, if we have regard to that, which alone can be pleaded for an institution, viz, these words, *Do this in remembrance of me*, it doth as properly relate to the manner, as matter. For what may, or can they evince in reason, that these words, *Do this*; onely signify, *eat bread, and drink wine*; but it is no matter, *when ye eat, nor how ye eat it*, and not, *as ye have seen me eat it at supper with you, who take bread, and break it, and give it you, and take the cup, and bless it, and give it you, so do ye likewise?* And seing Christ makes no distinction in those words, *Do this*, it can not be judged in reason but to relate to the whole. Which if it do, all those, that at present use this ceremony among Christians, have not yet obeyed this precept, nor fulfilled this institution, for all their clamors concerning it.

Obj.   If it be said, *that the time and manner of doing it by Christ was but accidentally, as being after the Jewish Passover, which was at supper.*

Answ.   Besides that it may be answered and easily proved, *that the whole was accidental*, as being *the practice of a Jewish ceremony*, as is above observed: May it not the same way be urged, that *the drinking of wine was accidental*, as being the natural product of that countrey, and so be pleaded, that, in those countryes, where wine doth not grow, as in our nation of *Scotland*, we may make use of *beer* or *ale* in the use of this ceremony, or *bread made of other grain*, than that, which Christ used? And yet would not our adversarys judge this an abuse, and not right performing of this *Sacrament?* Yea have not scruples of this kind occasioned no little contention among the Professors of Christianity? What great contest and strife hath been betwixt the *Greek* and *Latine Churches* concerning the *bread?* While the one will have it *unleavened*, reckoning, because the Jewes made use of unleavened bread in the Passover, that it was such kind of bread, that Christ did break to his Disciples, the other *leavened*; therefore the *Lutherans* make use of unleavened bread, the *Calvinists* of *leavened*: and this contest was so hot, when the Reformation was beginning at *Geneva*, that *Calvin* and *Farellus* were forced to flee for it. But do not Protestants by these uncertaintys open a door to Papists for their excluding

cluding *the people from the cup?* Will not [*Do this*] infer pofitively, that they fhould do *in the fame manner, and at the fame time,* which Chrift did it, as wel as that they fhould ufe *the cup,* and *not the bread onely?* Or what reafon have they to difpenfe with the one, more than the Papifts have to do with the other? O! What ftrange abfurditys and inconveniencys have Chriftians brought upon themfelves, by fuperftitioufly adhering to this ceremony? Out of which difficultys it is impoffible for them to extricat themfelves, but by laying it afide, as they have done others of the like nature. For, befides what is above mentioned, I would gladly know how from the words they can be certainly refolved, that thefe words [*Do this*] muft be underftood to the Clergy, *take, blefs and break this bread, and give it to others,* but to the Laïty onely, *take, and eat,* but do not blefs, *&c.*

If it be faid, *that the Clergy was onely prefent.*

Then will not that open a door for the popifh argument *againft the adminiftration of the cup to the people?* Or may not another from thence as eafily infer *that onely the Clergy ought to partake of this ceremony,* becaufe they were onely thofe prefent, to whom it was faid, Do *this?* But if this [*Do this*] be extended to *all,* how comes it *all have not liberty to obey it in both bleffing, breaking* and *diftributing,* as wel as *taking* and *eating?* Befides all thefe, even the *Calvinian Proteftants of Great Britann* could never yet accord among themfelves about the *manner of taking it,* whether *fitting, ftanding,* or *kneeling;* whether it fhould be given to the *fick,* and *thofe, that are ready to dye,* or not. Which controverfys, though they may be efteemed of fmall moment, yet have greatly contributed, with other things, to be the occafion not onely of *much contention,* but alfo of *blood-fhed* and *devaftation,* fo that in this laft refpect the *Prelatik Calvinifts* have termed the *Presbyterians fchifmatical* and *pertinacious,* and they them again *fuperftitious, idolatrous* and *Papiftical.* Who then, that will open their eyes, but may fee, that the devil hath ftirred up this contention and zeal, to bufy men about things of *fmall moment,* that *greater matters* may be neglected, while he keeps them in fuch adoe about this ceremony, while they lay afide others of the like nature, *as pofitively commanded, and as punctually* practifed, and from the obfervation of which, half fo many difficultys will not follow?

§ VIII. How then? Have we not reafon, not finding the nature of this practice to be obligatory upon us, more than thofe other our ad-

T t

verfarys

verfarys have laid afide, to avoid all this confufion, fince thofe, that ufe it, can never agree, neither concerning the *nature*, *efficacy*, nor *manner of doing* it? And this proceeds, becaufe they take it not plainly, as it lies in the Scriptur, but have fo much mixed-in their own inventions. For, would they take it as it lies, it would import no more, than that *Jefus Chrift at that time did thereby fignify unto them, that his body and blood was to be offered for them,* and defired them, that, *whenfoever they did eat or drink, they might do it in remembranfe of him, or with a regard to him, whofe blood was fhed for them.* Now that the primitive Church, gathered immediately after his afcenfion, did fo underftand it, doth appear from their ufe and practice, if we admitt thofe places of the *Acts,* where *breaking of bread* is fpoken of, to have relation hereto, which as our adverfarys do, fo we fhall willingly agree to. As firft, Act. 2 · 42. *And they continued ftedfaftly in the Apoftles doctrin, and fellowfhip, and in breaking of bread, &c.* This can not be underftood of any other, than of their ordinary eating; for, as nothing elfe appears from the text, fo the context makes it plain; for they had all things in common, and therefore it is faid, ver. 46. *And they continuing daily with one accord in the Temple, and breaking bread from houfe to houfe, did eat their meat with gladnefs and finglenefs of heart.* Who will not wilfully clofe their eyes, may fee here, that their *breaking* being joyned with their *eating*, fhewes, that nothing elfe is here expreffed, but that, having all things in common, and fo continuing together, they alfo did break their bread, and eat their meat together. In doing whereof I fhall not doubt, but they remembred the Lord, to follow whom they had, with fo great zeal and refignation, betaken themfelves. This is further manifeft from *Act.* 6. For the Apoftle, having the care and diftribution of that money, which the believers having fold their poffeffions gave unto them, finding themfelves overcharged with that burthen, appoynted deacons for that bufinefs, that they might give themfelves continually to prayer, and to the miniftery of the Word, not leaving that, to ferve tables. This can not be meant of any *Sacramental eating,* or *religious act of worfhip;* feing our adverfarys make the diftributing of that the proper act of minifters, not of deacons; and yet there can be no reafon alledged, that that *breaking of bread,* which they are faid to have continued in, and to have done from houfe to houfe, was other, than thofe tables, that the Apoftles ferved; but here gave over, as finding themfelves overcharged with it: now as the increafe of the Difciples

did.

did incapacitat the Apoſtles any more to manage this, ſo it would ſeem their further increaſe and diſperſing in divers places hindered the continuance of that practice of having things in common. But notwithſtanding, ſo far at leſt to remember or continue that ancient *community*, they did at certain times come together and break bread together. Hence it is ſaid, Act. 20:7. that Paul coming to *Troas*, *And upon the firſt day of the week, when the diſciples came together to break bread, Paul preached unto them, ready to depart on the morrow, and continued his ſpeech untill midnight.* Here is no mention made of any *ſacramental eating*, but onely, that Paul took occaſion from their being together to preach unto them. And it ſeemes it was a ſupper they intended, (not a morning bitt of bread and ſup of wine) elſe it's not very probable, that Paul would from the morning have preached untill midnight. But the 11 verſe puts the matter out of diſpute, which is thus, *When he therefore was come up again, and had broken bread, and eaten, and talked a long while even till break of day, ſo he departed.* This ſhewes that the breaking of bread was differed till that time: for thoſe words [*and when he had broken bread, and eaten*] do ſhew that it had a relation to the breaking of bread aforementioned, and that that was the time he did it. Secondly, theſe words joyned together, [*and when he had broken bread, and eaten, and talked*] ſhew, it was no religious act of worſhip, but onely an eating for bodyly refreſhment, for which the Chriſtians uſed to meet together ſome time, and doing it in God's fear and ſingleneſs of heart, doth notwithſtanding difference it from the eating or feaſting of *profane perſons*, and this by ſome is called *a love-feaſt*, or a being together, not meerly to feed their bellys, or for outward ends, but to take thence occaſion to eat and drink together in the dread and preſence of the Lord, as his people; which cuſtom we ſhall not condemn; but let it be obſerved, that in all the *Acts* there is no other, nor further mention of this matter. But if that *ceremony* had been ſome *ſolemn ſacrifice*, as ſome will have it, or ſuch a *ſpecial ſacrament*, as others plead it to be, it is ſtrange, that that hiſtory, that in many leſſer things gives a particular account of the Chriſtians behaviour, ſhould have been ſo ſilent in the matter. Onely we find, that they uſed ſometimes to meet together to break bread, and eat. Now, as the primitive Chriſtians began by degrees to depart from that primitive purity and ſimplicity, ſo alſo to accumulat ſuperſtitious traditions, and vitiat the innocent practices of their predeceſſors, by the intermixing either of Jewiſh or heatheniſh

T t 2

rites,

rites, so also, in the use of this, very early abuses began to creep in among Christians, so that it was needfull for the Apostle Paul to reform them, and reprove them therefore, as he doth at large, 1 Cor. 11. from ver. 17. to the end, which place we shall particularly examin, because our adversarys lay the chief stress of their matter upon it, and we shall see whether it will infer any more, than we have above granted. First, because they were apt to use that practice in a superstitious mind beyond the true use of it, as to make of it some mystical supper of the Lord, he tells them, ver. 20, that their *coming together into one place is not to eat the Lord's Supper*, he saith not, *this is not the right manner to eat*, because the *Supper of the Lord is Spiritual, and a mystery.* Secondly, he blames them, in that they come together for the worse, and not for the better, the reason he gives of this, is, ver. 21. *For in eating, every one hath taken before his own supper: and one is hungry, and another is drunken.* Here it is plain, that the Apostle condemnes them for that, because this custom of supping in general was used among Christians, for to increase their love, and as a memorial of Christ's supping with the Disciples, that they should have so vitiated it, to eat it apart, and to come full, who had abundance, and hungry, who had little at home. Whereby the very use and end of this practice is lost and perverted, and therefore he blames them, that they do not either eat this in common at home, or reserve their eating, till they come all together to the publik assembly: this appears plainly by the following verse 22. *have ye not houses to eat and to drink in? or despise ye the Church of God, and shame them that have not?* Where he blames them for their irregular practice herein, in that they despised to eat orderly, or reserve their eating to the publik assembly, and so shaming such as not having houses, nor fulness at home, came to partake of the common table, who, being hungry, thereby were ashamed, when they observed others come thither full and drunken. Those, that without prejudice will look to the place, will see this must have been the case among the Corinthians; for, supposing the use of this to have been then, as now used either by Papists, Lutherans, or Calvinists, it is hard making sense of the Apostl's words, or indeed to conceive, what was the abuse, the Corinthians committed in this thing. Having thus observed what the Apostle said above, because this custom of *eating and drinking together some time* had its rise from Christ's act with the Apostles the night he was betrayed, therefore the Apostle proceeds, ver. 23. to give them an ac-

count

count of that. *For I have received of the Lord that which also I delivered unto you, that the Lord Jesus, the same night in which he was betrayed, took bread, &c.* Those, that understand the difference betwixt a *narration* of a thing and a *Command*, can not but see, if they will, that there is no command in this place, but onely an account of matter of fact; he saith not, *I received of the Lord, that, as he took bread, so I should command it to you to do so also,* there is nothing like this in the place; yea, on the contrary, ver. 25. where he repeats Christ's imperative words to his Apostles, he placeth them so as they import no command, *this do ye, as oft as ye drink it, in remembrance of me.* And then he adds, *For as often as ye eat this bread, and drink this cup, ye do shew the Lord's death, till he come.* But these words [*as often*] imports no more a *command*, than to say, *as often as thou goest to Rome, see the Capitol,* will infer a command to me, to go thither.

But whereas they urge the last words *ye shew forth the Lord's death, till* Obj. *he come,* insinuating, that *this imports a necessary continuance of that ceremony, untill Christ come at the end of the world to judgment.*

I answer, they take two of the chief parts of the controversy here for Answ. granted, without proof. First, that [*as often*] imports a *command*, the contrary whereof is shewn, neither will they ever be able to prove it. Secondly, that this *coming* is understood of *Christ's last outward coming,* and not of his *inward* and *spiritual*: that remaines to be proven, whereas the Apostle might wel understand it of his *inward coming* and *appearance,* which perhaps some of those carnal Corinthians, that used to come drunken together, had not yet known; and others, being weak among them, and inclinable to dote upon outwards, this might have been indulged to them for a season, and even used by those, who knew Christ's appearance in Spirit, (as other things were, of which we shall speak hereafter) especially by the Apostle, who became weak to the weak, and all to all, that he might save some. Now those weak and carnal Corinthians might be permitted the use of this, to shew forth or remember Christ's death, till he come to arise *in* them; for, though such need those outward things, to put them in mind of Christ's death; yet such, as are dead with Christ, and not only dead with Christ, but buried, and also arisen with him, need not such *signs*, to remember him, and to such therefore the Apostle saith, Col. 3: 1. *If ye then be risen with Christ, seek those things which are above, where Christ sitteth on the right hand of God:* but bread and wine are not these things, that are above, but are things of

T t 3

the

the earth. But that this whole matter was a meer act of indulgence and condescendence of the Apostle Paul to the weak and carnal Corinthians appears yet more by the *Syriak* coppy, which, ver. 17. in his entring upon this matter, hath it thus, *In that, concerning which I am about to command you (or instruct you,) I commend you not, because ye have not gone foreward, but are descended unto that, which is less, (or of less consequence.)* Clearly importing, that the Apostle was grieved that such was their condition, that he was forc'd to give them instructions concerning those outward things, and doting upon which they shew, they were not gone forward in the life of Christianity, but rather sticking in beggerly elements. And therefore ver. 20. the same version hath it thus, *when then ye meet together, ye do not do it, as it is just ye should do in the day of the Lord, ye eat and drink.* Thereby shewing to them, that to meet together to eat and drink *outward bread and wine,* was not the labor and work of that day of the Lord; but, since our adversarys are so zealous for this ceremony, because used by the Church of Corinth, (though, with how little ground, is already shewn) how come they to pass over far more positive commands of the Apostles, as matters of no moment? As first, Act. 15:26. where the Apostles peremptorily command even the Gentiles, as that, which was the mind of the Holy Ghost, *to abstain from things strangled, and from blood.* And Ja. 5:14. where it is expressly commanded, *that the sick be anointed with oil in the Name of the Lord.*

Obj.   If they say, *these were only temporary things, but not to continue.*

Answ   What have they more to shew for this, there being no express repeal of them?

Obj.   If they say, *the repeal is implied, because the Apostle saith, We ought not to be judged in meats and drinks.*

Answ.   I admitt the answer, but how can it be evited to militat the same way against the other practice? Surely not at all: nor can there be any thing urged for the one, more than for the other, but custom and tradition.

Obj.   As for that of *James,* they say, *there followed a miracle upon it, to wit, the recovery of the sick: But this being ceased, so should the ceremony.*

Answ.   Though this might many ways be answered, to wit, that *prayer* then might as wel be *forborn,* to which also the saving of the sick is there ascribed, yet I shall accept of it, because I judge indeed that ceremony is ceased, only me thinks, since our adversarys, and that rightly, think a ceremony

mony

mony ought to ceafe, where the vertue failes, they ought by the fame rule to forbear the laying on of hands, in imitation of the Apoftles, fince the gift of the Holy Ghoft doth not follow upon it.

§ I X. But fince we find, that feveral teftimonys of Scriptur do fufficiently fhew, that *fuch external rites are no neceffary part of the New Covenant difpenfation, therefore not needfull now to continue,* however they were for a feafon practifed of old, I fhall inftance fome few of them, whereby from the nature of the thing, as wel as *thofe teftimonys,* it may appear, that the *ceremony of bread and wine is ceafed,* as wel as thofe other things, confeffed by our adverfarys to be fo. The firft is Rom. 14:17 *For the Kingdom of God is not meat and drink; but righteoufnefs and peace, and joy in the Holy Ghoft.* Here the Apoftle evidently fhewes, that the *Kingdom of God,* or Gofpel of Chrift, ftands not *in meats and drinks,* and fuch like things, but *in righteoufnefs,* as by the context doth appear, where he is fpeaking of *the guilt and hazard* of judging one another about meats and drinks. So then, if the Kingdom of God ftand not in them, nor the Gofpel, nor work of Chrift, then the eating of *outward bread* and *wine* can be no neceffary part of the Gofpel worfhip, nor any perpetual ordinance of it. Another is yet more plain, of the fame Apoftle, Col. 2:16. the Apoftle through out this whole fecond chapter doth clearly plead *for us,* and againft the *formality* and *fuperftition of our oppofers:* for in the beginning he holds forth the great priviledges Chriftians have by Chrift, who are come indeed to the *life of Chriftianity,* and therefore he defires them, ver. 6. *as they have received Chrift, fo to walk in him, and to beware left they be fpoiled through Philofophy and vain deceit, after the rudiments or elements of the world, becaufe that in Chrift whom they have received, is all fulnefs. And that they are circumcifed with the circumcifion made without hands, which he cal's the circumcifion of Chrift, and being buried with him by baptifm are alfo arifen with him through the faith of the operation of God.* Here alfo they did partake of the *true baptifm of Chrift,* and, being fuch as are arifen with him, let us fee, whether he thinks it needfull, they fhould make ufe of fuch *meat* and *drink,* as *bread* and *wine, to put them in remembrance of Chrift's death,* or whether they ought to be judged, that they did it not, ver. 16. *Let no man therefore judge you in meat or drink* Is not *bread* and *wine meat* and *drink?* But why? *Which are a fhaddow of things to come: but the body is of Chrift.* Then, fince our adverfarys confefs that their *bread* and *wine* is a *fign* or *fhaddow,* therefore, according to the Apoftl's doctrin, we ought not to be judged in the ob-

fervation

servation of it. But is it not fit for those, that are dead with Christ, to be subject to such ordinances? See what he saith, ver. 20. *Wherefore, if ye be dead with Christ from the rudiments of the world, why, as though living in the world, are ye subject to ordinance.?* (*Touch not, taste not, handle not: Which all are to perish with the using*) *after the commandments and doctrines of men:* What can be more plain? if this serve not to take away the absolute necessity of the use of *bread* and *wine*, what can it serve to take away? Sure I am, the reason here given is applicable to them, which all do perish with the using, since bread and wine perisheth with the using, as much as other things. But further, if the use of *water* and *bread* and *wine* were that, wherein the very *seals* of the *New Covenant* stood, and did pertain to the chief *Sacraments* of the Gospel and evangelical ordinances, (so called) then would not the Gospel differ from the Law, or be preferable to it? Whereas the Apostle shewes the difference, Heb. 9: 10. in that such kind of observations of the Jewes were as a sign of the Gospel, for that this *stood onely in meats and drinks, and divers washings.* And now, if the Gospel worship and service stand in the same, where is the difference?

Obj.   If it be said, *These under the Gospel have a spiritual signification.*

Answ.   So had those under the Law, God was the Author of those, as wel as Christ is pretended to be Author of these. But doth not this contending for the use of *water*, *bread* and *wine*, as necessary parts of the Gospel worship, destroy the nature of it, as if the Gospel were a dispensation of *shaddows*, and not of the *Substance*, whereas the Apostle in that of the *Collossians* above mentioned argues against the use of these things, as needfull to those, that are dead and arisen with Christ, because they are but *shaddows*; and since, through the whole epistle to the Hebrewes, he argues with the Jewes, to wean them from their *worship*, for this reason, because it was *typical* and *figurative*. Is it agreable to right Reason to bring them to another of the same nature? What ground from Scripture or Reason can our adversarys bring us, to evince, that one shaddow or figur should point to another shaddow or figur, and not to the Substance. And yet they make the figure of *Circumcision* to point to *water baptism*, and the *Paschal Lamb to bread and wine.* But was it ever known, that one *figure* was the *antitype* of the other, especially seing Protestants make not these their *antityps* to have any more vertue or efficacy than the *type* had? For, since, as they say, and that truely, *that their Sacraments confer not Grace, but that is conferred according to the faith of the receiver* , it will not be denyed,

ed, but the faithfull among the Jewes received alfo Grace in the ufe of their *figurative worſhip.* And though Papifts boaft that their Sacraments confer Grace *ex opere operatô*, yet experience abundantly proveth the contrary.

§ X. But fuppofing the ufe of *water-baptiſm*, and *bread* and *wine* to have been in the primitive Church, as was alfo that of *abſtaining from things ſtrangled, and from blood, the uſe of Legal purifications*, Act. 21: 23, 24, 25. and *anointing of the ſick with oil*, for the reafons and grounds before mentioned. Yet it remaines for our adverfarys, to fhew us, how they come by power or authority to adminifter them; It can not be from the letter of the Scriptur, elfe they behoved alfo to do thofe other things, which the letter declares alfo they did, and which in the letter have as much foundation. Then their *Power* muft be *derived from the Apoſtles*, either *mediately*, or *immediately*; but we have fhewn before, in the tenth Propofition, that they have no *mediat Power*, becaufe of the interruption made by the *Apoſtaſy.* And for an *immediat power* or command by the Spirit of God, to adminifter thefe things, none of our adverfarys pretend to it. We know, that in this, as in other things, they make a noyfe of the *conſtant conſent of the Church and of Chriſtians* in all ages; but, as *tradition* is not a fufficient ground for faith, fo, in this matter efpecially, it ought to have but fmall weight, for that, in this point of ceremonys and fuperftitious obfervations, the apoftafy began very early, as may appear in the epiftles of Paul to the Galathians and Coloffians; and we have no ground to imitat them in thofe things, whofe entrance the Apoftle fo much withftood, fo heavily regreted, and fo fharply reproved. But, if we look to *Antiquity*, we find, that, in fuch kind of obfervances and traditions they were very uncertain and changeable, fo that neither Proteftants nor Papifts do obferve this ceremony, as they did, both in that they gave it to young boys and to little children, and for ought can be learned, the ufe of this and infant-baptifm are of alike age, though the one be laid afide both by Papifts and Proteftants, and the other, to wit, baptifm of Infants be ftuck to: and we have fo much the lefs reafon to lay weight upon *Antiquity*, for that, if we confider their profeffion of Religion, efpecially as to worfhip and the ceremonial part of it, we fhall not find any Church now, whether Popifh or Proteftant, who differ not widely from them in many things, as *Dallew*, in his Treatife concerning *the uſe of the Fathers*, wel obferveth and demonftrateth. And why they

fhould

should obtrude this upon us, becaufe of the *Antients practice*, which they themfelves follow not, or why we may not reject this, as wel as they do other things, no lefs zealoufly practifed by the *Antients*, no fufficient reafon can be affigned.

I fhall not neverthelefs doubt, but many, whofe underftandings have been clouded with thefe ceremonys, have notwithftanding, by the Mercy of God, had fome fecret fenfe of the myftery, which they could not clearly underftand, becaufe it was fealed from them, by their fticking to fuch outward things, and that, through that fecret fenfe, diving in their comprehenfions, they ran themfelves into thefe carnal apprehenfions, as imagining the fubftance of the bread was changed, or that, if the fubftance was not changed, yet the body was there, *&c.* : and indeed I am inclinable very favorably to judge of *Calvin* in this particular, in that he deals fo ingenuoufly, to confefs he neither comprehends it, nor can exprefs it in words, but yet by a feeling experience can fay, *the Lord is fpiritually prefent.* Now, as I doubt not, but *Calvin* fometimes had a fenfe of this prefence, without the ufe of this ceremony, fo as the underftanding given him of God made him juftly reject the falfe notions of *Tranfubftantiation* and *confubftantiation*, though he knew not, what to eftablifh in ftead of them, if he had fully waited in that *Light*, that *makes all*

Eph. 5 :
ver. 13.

things manifeft, and had not laboured, in his own comprehenfion, to fettle upon that external ceremony, by affixing the Spiritual prefence as chiefly or principally, though not onely (as he wel knew by experience) there, or efpecially to relate to it, he might have reached further unto the knowledg of this myftery, than many, that went before him.

§ XI. Laftly, if any now at this day, from a true tendernefs of Spirit, and with real Confcience towards God, did practife this ceremony in the fame way, method, and manner, as did the primitive Chriftians, recorded in Scriptur (which yet none, that I know, now do) I fhould not doubt to affirm, but they might be indulged in it, and the Lord might regard them, and for a feafon appear to them, in the ufe of thefe things, as many of us have known him to do to us in the time of our ignorance, providing alwayes they did not feek to obtrude them upon others, nor judge fuch, as found themfelves *delivered,* or that they do not pertinacioufly adhere to them. For we certainly know that the *day* is *dawned,* in which God hath arifen, and hath difmiffed all thofe ceremonys and rites, and

is

is onely to be *worfhipped in Spirit*, and that he appears to them, who wait upon him, and that to feek God in thefe things is, with *Mary*, at the fepulchre, to *feek the living among the dead*, for we know that he is arifen and revealed in Spirit, leading his children oot of thefe rudiments, that they may walk with him in his *Light*, to whom be Glory for ever. Amen.

The Fourteenth Propofition,

Concerning the Power of the Civil Magiftrate in matters purely religious and pertaining to the Confcience.

Since God hath affumed to himfelf the Power and Dominion of the Confcience, who alone can rightly inftruct and govern it, therefore it is not lawful for any whofoever, by vertue of any Authority or Principality they bear in the Government of this World, to force the Confciences of others; and therefore all Killing, Banifhing, Fining, Imprifoning, and other fuch things, which are inflicted upon men for the alone exercife of their Confcience or difference in Worfhip, or Opinion, proceedeth from the Spirit of *Cain*, the murtherer, and is contrary to the Truth, providing always that no man, under the pretence of Confcience, prejudice his Neighbour, in his life or eftate, or do any thing deftructive to, or inconfiftent with humane Society, in which cafe the Law is for the tranfgreffor, and Juftice is to be adminiftred upon all without refpect of Perfons.

Luk 9: v. 55,56. Matth. 7 v. 12,13, 29. Tit. 3: ver. 10.

§ I. **L**IBERTY *of Confcience* from the power of the Civil Magiftrate hath been of late years fo largely and learnedly handled, that I fhall not need but to be brief in it; yet it is to be lamented, that few have walked anfwerably to this principle, each pleading it for themfelves, but fcarce

allow-

allowing it to others, as hereafter I shall have occasion more at length to observe.

It will be fit in the first place, for clearing of mistakes, to say something of the state of the controversy, that what followes may be the more clearly understood.

By [*Conscience*] then, as in the explanation of the 5 and 6 Propositions I have observed, is to be understood *that perswasion of the mind, which arises from the understandings being possessed with the belief of the Truth or falsity of any thing,* which, though it may be false or evil upon the matter, yet, if a man should go against his perswasion, or Conscience, he should committ a sin, because what a man doth contrary to his faith, though his faith be wrong, is no ways acceptable to God; hence the Apostle saith, *whatsoever is not of faith is sin; and he, that doubteth, is damned, if he eat,* though the thing might have been lawfull to another, and that this *doubting* to eat some kind of *meats* (since all the creaturs of God are good, and for the use of man, *if received with thanksgiving,* might be a superstition, or at left a weakness, which were better removed.   Hence *Ames De Caf. Conf.* saith, *The Conscience, although erring, doth evermore bind, so as that he sinneth, who doth contrary to his Conscience, because he doth contrary to the will of God, although not materially and truely, yet formally and interpretatively.*

So the question is, First, *Whether the Civil Magistrate hath power to force men in things religious, to do contrary to their Conscience, and, if they will not, to punish them in their goods, libertys or lives?* this we hold in the negative. But secondly, as we would have the Magistrate avoiding this extream of incroaching upon mens Consciences, so, on the other hand, we are far from joyning with, or strengthening such libertines, as would stretch the liberty of their Consciences to the prejudice of their neighbours, or to the ruin of humane society. We understand therefore by *matters of Conscience,* such, as *immediately* relate *betwixt God and man,* or *men and men,* that are under the same perswasion, as to meet together, and worship God in that way, which they judge is most acceptable unto him, and not to incroach upon or seek to force their neighbours otherwise than by reason, or such other means, as Christ and his Apostles used, *viz.* preaching and instructing such as will hear and receive it, but not at all for men, under the notion of Conscience, to do any thing contrary to the moral and perpetual statuts generally acknowledged by all Christians: in which case the Magistrate.

strate.

ftrate may very lawfully ufe his Authority, as on thofe, who, under a pretext of *Confcience*, make it a principle, to kill and deftroy all the wicked,
id eft, all, that differ from them, that they, to wit, the Saints, may rule,
and that therefore feek to make all things common, and would force their
neighbours to fhare their eftates with them, and many fuch wild notions,
as is reported of the *Anabaptifts of Munfter*, which evidently appears to proceed from pride and covetoufnefs, and not from purity or Confcience,
and therefore 1 have fufficiently guarded againft that, in the latter part of
the Propofition. But the *Liberty*, we lay claim to, is fuch, as the primitive
Church juftly fought, under the heathen Emperors, to wit, for men of
fobriety, honefty, and a peaceable converfation to enjoy the *liberty* and
exercife of their *Confcience* towards God and among the mfelves, and to
admitt among them fuch, as, by their perfwafion and influence, come
to be convinced of the fame Truth with them, without being therefore
molefted by the Civil Magiftrate. Thirdly, though we would not have
men hurt in their temporals, nor robbed of their priviledges, as men,
and members of the common-wealth, becaufe of their inward perfwafion,
yet we are far from judging, that in the Church of God there fhould not
be cenfurs exercifed againft fuch as fall into error, as wel as fuch as committ open evils; and therefore we believe it may be very lawfull for a
Chriftian Church, if fhe find any of her members fall into any error, after
due admonitions and inftructions, according to Gofpel order, if fhe find
them pertinacious, to cutt them off from her fellowfhip, by the *fword* of
the *Spirit*, and denude them of thefe priviledges, which they had as fel-
low-members, but not to cutt them off from the world by the *temporal
fword*, or rob them of their common priviledges, as men, feing they enjoy
not thefe, as Chriftians or under fuch a fellowfhip, but as men, and members of the Creation. Hence *Chryfoftom* faith wel, de Anath. *We muft
condemn and reprove the evil doctrines, that proceed from heretiks, but fpare the
men, and pray for their Salvation.*

§ 11. But that no man, by vertue of any Power or principality,
he hath in the government of this world, hath power over the Confciences of men, is apparent, becaufe *the Confcience of man is the feat
and throne of God in him*, of which *God* is the alone *proper* and
infallible Judge, who, by his Power and Spirit, can alone rectify the miftakes of *Confcience*, and therefore hath referved to himfelf the
power of punifhing the errors thereof, as he feeth meet.   Now for the

Y v 3

Magiftrate to affume this , is to take upon him to meddle with things not within the compafs of his jurifdiction, for, if this were within the compafs of his jurifdiction, he fhould be the proper judge in thefe things , and alfo it were needfull to him, as an effential qualification of his being a Magiftrate, to be capable to judge in them. But that the Magiftrate, as a Magiftrate, is neither proper Judge in thefe cafes, nor yet that the capacity fo to be is requifit in him, as a Magiftrate, our adverfarys can not deny, or elfe they muft fay, that all the heathen Magiftrates were either no lawfull Magiftrates, as wanting fomething effential to Magiftracy, and this were contrary to the exprefs doctrin of the Apoftles, Rom. 13. or elfe, which is more abfurd, that thofe heathen Magiftrates were proper judges in matters of Confcience amongft Chriftians. As for that evafion, that the Magiftrate ought to punifh according to the Church cenfur and determination, which is indeed no lefs, than to make the *Magiftrate* the *Churches hang-man*, we fhall have occafion to fpeak of it hereafter. But if the chief members of the Church, though ordained to inform, inftruct, and reprove, are not to have dominion over the faith nor Confciences of the faithfull, as the Apoftle expreffely affirmes, 2 Cor. 1: 24. then far lefs ought they to ufurp this dominion, or ftir up the Magiftrate to perfecute and murder thofe, who can not yeeld to them therein.

Secondly, this pretended power of the Magiftrate is both contrary unto and inconfiftent with the nature of the Gofpel, which is a thing altogether extrinfic from the rule and government of political ftates, as Chrift expresfly fignified, faying, his *Kingdom* was *not of this world*, and if the propagating of the Gofpel had had any neceffary relation thereunto, then Chrift had not faid fo; But he abundantly hath fhewn by his example, whom we are chiefly to imitate in matters of that nature, that its by *perfwafion and the Power of God*, not by whips, imprifonments, banifhments and murderings that the Gofpel is to be propagated, and that thofe, that are the propagators of it, are often to fuffer by the wicked, but never to caufe the wicked to fuffer. When he fends forth his Difciples, he tells them, he fends them forth, as *Lambs among wolves*, to be willing to be devoured, not to devoure; he tells them of their being whipped, imprifoned and killed for their Confcience, but never that they fhall either whip, imprifon, or kill; and indeed, if *Chriftians* muft be as *Lambs*, it is not the nature of Lambs to deftroy or devour any. It ferves

nothing

Mat. 10:
ver. 16.

nothing to alledge, That in Chriſt and his Apoſtles times the Magiſtrates were *heathens*, and therefore Chriſt and his Apoſtles, (nor yet any of the *believers*) being no Magiſtrate they could not exercife the power: Becauſe it can not be denyed, but Chriſt, being the Son of God, had a true right to all kingdoms, and was righteous heir of the earth. Next, as to his Power, it can not be denyed, but he could, if he had feen meet, have called for legions of Angels to defend him, and have forced the Princes and Potentats of the earth to be ſubjeſt unto him, Matth. 26: 53. ſo that it was onely, becauſe it was contrary to the nature of Chriſt's Goſpel and miniſtery, to uſe any force or violence in the gathering of Soules to him. This he abundantly expreſſed in his reproof to the ſons of *Zebedee*, who would have been calling for *fire from heaven* to burn thoſe, that refuſed to receive Chriſt. It is not to be doubted, but this was as great a crime, as now to be in an error conserning the faith and doſtrin of Chriſt. That there was not Power wanting to have puniſhed thoſe refuſers of Chriſt, can not be doubted, for they, that could do other miracles, might have done this alſo, and moreover, they wanted not the preſident of a holy man under the Law, to wit, *Elias*; yet we fee what Chriſt ſaith to them, *Ye know not what ſpirit ye are of*, Luk 9: 55. *for the Son of man is not come to deſtroy mens lives, but to ſave them.* Here Chriſt ſhewes, that ſuch kind of zeal was no ways approved of him, and ſuch as think to make way for Chriſt, or his Goſpel, by this means, do not underſtand what ſpirit they are of. But if it was not lawfull to call for fire from heaven to deſtroy ſuch, as refuſed to receive Chriſt, it is far leſs lawfull to kindle fire upon earth, to deſtroy thoſe, that believe in Chriſt, becauſe they will not believe, nor can believe, as the Magiſtrates do, for Confcience ſake : and if it was not lawfull for the Apoſtles, who had ſo large a meaſur of the Spirit, and were ſo little liable to miſtake, to force others to their judgment, it can be far leſs lawfull now for men, that, as experience declareth, and many of themſelves confeſs, are fallible, and often miſtaken, to kill and deſtroy all ſuch, as can not (becauſe otherwiſe perſwaded in their minds) judge and believe in matters of Confcience, juſt as they do. And, if it was not according to the wiſdom of *Chriſt*, who was, and is, *King of Kings*, by outward force to conſtrain others to believe him, or receive him, as being a thing inconſiſtent with the nature of his *miniſtery* and *Spiritual Government* ; do not they groſly effend him, that will needs be wiſer than he, and think to force men againſt their perſwaſion to con-

form

form to their doctrine and worship? The word of the Lord saith, *not by power, and by might, but by the Spirit of the Lord,* Zach. 4.: 6. But these say, *not by the Spirit of the Lord,* but *by might and carnal power.* The Apostle saith plainly *we wrestle not with flesh and blood,* and *the weapons of our warfar are not carnal, but Spiritual:* but these men will needs wrestle with flesh and blood, when they can not prevail with the Spirit and the understanding, and not having Spiritual weapons go about with carnal weapons, to establish Christ's Kingdom, which they can never do; and therefore, when the matter is wel sifted, it is found to be more out of *love to self,* and from a principle of *pride* in man, to have all others to bow to him, than from the *love* of *God.* Christ indeed takes another method, for he saith, *he will make his people a willing people in the day of his Power,* but these men labour against mens wills and Consciences, *not by Christ's Power,* but by the *outward sword,* to make men the people of Christ, which they can never do, as shall hereafter be shewn.

1 Cor. 10 ver. 4

Pf. 110: 3

But thirdly, Christ fully and plainly declareth to us his sense in this matter, in the parable of the *tares,* Matth. 13. of which we have himself the interpreter, ver. 38, 39, 40, 41. where he expounds them to be the *children of the wicked one,* and yet he will not have the servants to meddle *with them,* left they pull up the *wheat* therewith. Now it can not be denyed, but *heretiks* are here included, but these servants saw *the tares;* and had a certain discerning of them, yet Christ would not they should meddle, left they should hurt the wheat, thereby intimating, that that capacity in man, *to be mistaken,* ought to be a bridle upon him, to make him wary in such matters; and therefore, to prevent this hurt, he gives a positive prohibition, *But he said, Nay,* ver. 29. So that they, that will notwithstanding be pulling up that, which they judge is *tares,* do openly declare that they make no bones to break the commands of Christ. Miserable is that evasion, which some of our adversarys use here, in alledging these *tares* is meant of *hypocrits,* and not of *heretiks!* But how to evince that, seing *heretiks,* as wel as *hypocrits,* are *children of the wicked one,* they have not any thing, but their own bare affirmation, which is therefore justly rejected.

Obj.

If they say, *because hypocrits can not be discerned, but so may not heretiks.*

Answ.

This is both false, and a begging of the question. For those, that have a Spiritual discerning, can discern both hypocrits and heretiks;

and

and thofe, that want it, can not certainly difcern either: feing the queftion will arife, *Whether that is a herefy, which the Magiftrate faith is fo?*
And feing it is both poffible, and confeffed by all, to have often faln
out, that fome Magiftrates have judged that *herefy*, which was not,
punifhing men accordingly for *Truth*, in ftead of *error* : there can no
argument be drawn from the obvioufnefs or evidence of herefy, unlefs
we fhould conclude *herefy* could never be miftaken for *Truth*, nor *Truth*
for *herefy*, whereof experience fhewes daily the contrary, even among
Chriftians. But neither is this fhift applicable to this place, for the fervants did difcern the *tares*, and yet were liable to hurt the *wheat*, if they
had offered to pull them up.

§ I I I. But they object againft this *Liberty of Confcience*, Deut. 1 3: 5. Obj.
*where falfe prophets are appoynted to be put to death, and accordingly they give
example thereof.*

The cafe no ways holds parallel, thofe particular commands to the Anfw.
Jewes, and practices following upon them, are not a rule for Chriftians,
elfe we might, by the fame rule, fay, It were lawfull for us to borrow
from our neighbours their goods, and fo carry them away, becaufe the
Jewes did fo, by God's command; or that it is lawfull for Chriftians to
invade their neighbours kingdoms, and cut them all off, without
mercy, becaufe the Jewes did fo to the Canaanites, by the command of
God.

If they urge, *that thefe commands ought to ftand, except they be repealed in* Obj.
the Gofpel.

I fay, thefe precepts and practices of Chrift and his Apoftles Anfw
mentioned, are a fufficient repeal; for, if we fhould plead, that every
command, given to the Jewes, is binding upon us, except there be a
particular repeal, then would it follow, that, becaufe it was lawfull for
the Jewes, if any man killed one, for the neareft of kindred prefently
to kill the murderer, without any order of Law, it were lawfull for us
to do fo alfo. And doth not this command of Deut. 1 3: 9. openly order
him, who is entifed by another to forfake the Lord, though he were his
brother, his fon, his daughter, or his wife, prefently to kill him, or
her? *Thou fhalt furely kill him, thy hand fhall be firft upon him, to put him to
death.* If this command were to be followed, there needed neither inquifition, nor Magiftrate, to do the bufinefs; and yet, there is no reafon
why they fhould fhuffle by this part, and not the other; yea to argue

W w

this

this way from the practice among the Jewes were to overturn the very Gospel, and to set up again the carnal ordinances among the Jewes, to pull down the Spiritual ones of the Gospel. Indeed we can far better argue from the *analogy* betwixt the *figurative* and *carnal* state of the Jewes, and the *real* and *Spiritual* one, under the Gospel. That, *as Moses delivered the Jewes out of outward Egypt, by an outward force, and established them in an outward Kingdom, by destroying their outward enemies for them; so Christ, not by overcoming outwardly, and killing others, but by suffering and being killed, doth deliver his chosen ones, the inward Jewes, out of mystical Egypt, destroying their Spiritual enemies before them, and establishing among them his Spiritual Kingdom, which is not of this world. And, as such, as departed from the fellowship of outward Israël, were to be cut off by the outward sword, so those, that depart from the inward Israël, are to be cut off by the sword of the Spirit;* for it answers very wel, that, as the Jewes were to cut off their enemies outwardly, to establish their kingdom and outward worship, so they were to uphold it the same way. But, *as the Kingdom and Gospel of Christ was not to be established nor propagated, by cutting off, or destroying the Gentiles, but by perswading them, so neither is it to be upheld otherwise.*

Obj. But secondly they urge Rom. 13. where the *Magistrate* is said *not to bear the sword in vain, because he is the minister of God, to execute wrath upon such as do evil. But heresy,* say they, *is evil.* Ergo.

Answ. But so is hypocrisy also, yet they confess he ought not to punish that. Therefore this must be understood of moral evils, relative of affaires betwixt man and man, not of matters of judgment or worship, or else what great absurditys would follow, considering that Paul wrot here to the Church of Rome, who was under the government of *Nero*, an *impious heathen*, and *persecutor* of the Church? Now, if a power to punish, in poynt of *heresy*, be here included, it will necessarily follow, that *Nero* had this power, yea and that he had it of God; for, because the *power* was of *God*, therefore the Apostle urges their obedience. But can there be any thing more absurd, than to say, that *Nero* had power to judge in such cases? Surely if Christian Magistrates be not to punish for *hypocrisy*, because they can not outwardly discern it, far less could *Nero* punish any body for *heresy*, which he was uncapable to discern. And, if *Nero* had not power to judge, nor punish in poynt of heresy, then nothing can be urged from this place: since all, that's said here, is spoken as applicable to *Nero* with a particular relation to whom it was written.

And,

And, if *Nero* had such a power, surely he was to exercise it, according to his judgment and Conscience, and in doing thereof he was not to be blamed; which is enough to justify him in his persecuting of the Apostles, and murdering the Christians.   Obj.

Thirdly they object that saying of the Apostle to the Gal. 5: 12. *I would they were even cutt off, which trouble you.*   Answ.

But how this imports any more, than a cutting off from the Church, is not, nor can be shewn. *Beza*, upon the place, faith, *We can not understand that otherwise, than of excommunication: Such as was that of the incestuous Corinthian. And indeed, it is madness, to suppose it otherwise; for Paul would not have these cut off otherwise, than he did* Hymenæus *and* Philetus, *who were blasphemers; which was by giving them over to Satan, not by cutting off their heads.*

The same way may be answered that other argument drawn from Rev. 2: 20. where *the Church of Thyatira is reproved for suffering the woman Jezebel.* Which can be no other ways understood, than that they did not excommunicat her, or cutt her off by a Church censur: for as to corporal punishment, it is known, that at that time the Christians had not power to punish heretiks so, if they had had a mind to it.   Obj.

Fourthly, they alledge, that *heresys are numbred among the works of the flesh,* Gal. 5: 20. *Ergo,* &c.

That Magistrates have power to punish all the works of the *flesh,* is Answ. denyed, and not yet proved. Every *evil* is a work of the flesh, but every *evil* comes not under the Magistrat's cognisance. Is not *hypocrisy,* a work of the flesh, which our adversarys confess the Magistrates ought not to punish? yea, is not *hatred* and *envy,* there mentioned, as the works of the *flesh?* and yet the Magistrate can not punish them, as they are in themselves, untill they exert themselves in other acts, which come under his power. But, so long as *heresy* doth not exert it self in any act destructive to humane society, or such like things, but is kept within the sphere of those dutys of doctrine or worship, which stand betwixt a man and God, they no ways come under the Magistrat's power.

§ IV. But secondly, this forceing of mens Consciences is contrary to found *Reason,* and to the very law of *Nature.* For man's understanding can not be forced by all the bodily sufferings another man can inflict upon him, especially in matters Spiritual and Supernatural: *'t is arguments and evident demonstrations of Reason, together with the power of God reaching the heart, that can change a man's mind from one opinion to another, and not knocks and blows, and such like things, which may wel destroy the body, but can never inform the Soul, which is a free agent, and must either accept or reject matters of opinion, as they are born in upon it by something proportional to its own nature.* To seek to force minds, in any other manner, is to deal with men, as if they were brutes, void of understanding, and at last is but to lose ones labor, and, as the proverb is, *to seek to wash the Black-More white.* By that course indeed men may be made *hypocrits,* but can never be made *Christians;* and surely the products of such *compulsion* (even where the end is obtained, to wit, an outward assent, or conformity, whether in doctrine or worship) can be no ways acceptable to God, who desireth not any sacrifice, except that, which cometh throughly from the *heart,* and will have no constrained ones: so that men, so constrained, are so far from being members of the Church, that they are made ten-times more the servants of Satan, than before, in that to their *errors* is added *hypocrisy,* the worst of *evils* in matters of Religion, and that, which above all things the Lord's Soul most abhorrs.

Obj. But if it be said; *their error notwithstanding is thereby suppressed, and the scandal removed.*

Answ. I answer, besides that this is a method no ways allowed by Christ, as is above proved, surely the Church can be no ways better'd by the accession of *hypocrits,* but greatly corrupted and endangered, for open heresys-men may be aware of, and shun such, as profess them, when they are separated from the Church by her censurs, but secret *hypocrits* may putrify the body, and leaven it, ere men be aware. And if the dissenters prove resolute, and suffer boldly for the opinions they esteem right, experience sheweth, that such sufferings often tend to the commendation of the sufferers, but never of the persecutors: for such suffering ordinarily breeds compassion, and begets a curiosity in others, to inquire the more diligently into the things, for which they see men suffer so great losses so boldly, and is also able to beget an opinion, that it is for some good, they do so suffer, it being no ways probable, that men will ventur all, meerly to acquire fame, which may as wel be urged to detract from the reputation of all the *Martyrs,* unless some better arguments be brought against it, than a halter or a faggot. But supposing this principle, *that the Magistrate hath power to force the Consciences of his subjects and to punish them, if they will not comply:* very great inconveniencys and absurditys will

follow,

follow, and even ſuch as are inconſiſtent with the nature of the Chriſtian Religion.

For firſt it will naturally follow, that the Magiſtrate ought to do it, and ſinneth by omiſſion of his duty, if he do it not. Will it not then hence be inferred, that Chriſt was defective to his Church, who, having power to force men, and to call for legions of Angels ſo to do, did notwithſtanding not exert that power, but left his Church to the mercy of the wicked without ſo neceſſary a bulwark.

Secondly, ſeing every Magiſtrate is to exerciſe his power, according to the beſt underſtanding he hath, being obliged ſo to do, for the promoting of what he in Conſcience is perſwaded to be Truth, Will not this juſtify all the heathen Emperors in their perſecutions againſt Chriſtians? Will not this juſtify the *Spaniſh inquiſition*, which yet is *odious* not onely to Proteſtants, but to many moderat Papiſts? How can Proteſtants in reaſon condemn the Papiſts for perſecuting them, ſeing they do but exerciſe a *lawfull power*, according to their *Conſcience*, and beſt underſtanding, and do no more to them, than the ſufferers profeſs they would do to them, if they were in the like capacity? Which takes away all ground of commiſeration from the ſufferers, whereas that was the ground, that gained, of old, reputation to the Chriſtians, that they, being innocent, ſuffered, who neither had, nor by principle could, hurt any. But there is little reaſon to pity one, that is but dealt by according as he would deal with others. For to ſay, *they have not reaſon to perſecut us, becauſe they are in the wrong, and we in the right*, is but miſerably to beg the queſtion. Doth not this doctrine ſtrengthen the hands of perſecutors every where, and that rationally, from a principle of ſelf-preſervation? For who can blame me for deſtroying him, that I know waits but for an occaſion to deſtroy me, if he could? Yea this makes all ſuffering for Religion, which of old was the glory of Chriſtians, to be but of pure neceſſity; whereby they are not led as *Lambs to the ſlaughter* as was the *Captain* of their *Salvation*, but rather as *wolves* catched in the ſnare, who onely bite not again, becauſe they are not able, but, could they get force, would be as ready to lead thoſe the ſame way, that lead them. Where is here the faith and patience of the Saints? For indeed it is but a ſmall glory to make a vertue of neceſſity, and ſuffer becauſe I can not help it. Every thief and murtherer is a martyr at that rate; experience hath abundantly proved this in theſe laſt centurys. For, however each party talk of paſ-

W w 3,

ſively.

vely obeying the Magiſtrate in ſuch caſes, and that the powe: reſides in him, yet it is apparent, that from this principle it naturally followes that any party, ſuppoſing themſelves right, ſhould, ſo ſoon as they are able, endeavour, at any rate, to get uppermoſt, that they might bring under thoſe of another opinion, and force the Magiſtrate to uphold their way, to the ruin of all others. What engine the Pope of *Rome* uſed to make, of his pretended power in this thing, upon any pretence of diſlike to any Prince or State, even for very ſmall hereſies, in their own account, to depoſe Princes, and ſet up their ſubjeċts againſt them, and give their dominions to other Princes to ſerve his intereſt, they can not be ignorant, that have read the life of *Hildebrand*; and how Proteſtants have vindicated the liberty of their Conſciences, after this ſame manner, is apparent. They ſuffered much in *France*, to the great increaſe and advantage of their party, but how ſoon they found themſelves conſiderable, and had gotten ſome Princes upon their ſide, they began to let the King know, that they muſt either have the liberty of their Conſciences, or elſe they would purchaſe it, not by ſuffering, but by fighting. And the experience of other Proteſtant States ſhewes, that, if *Henry* the fourth, to pleaſe the Papiſts, had not quitted his Religion, to get the Crown the more peaceably, and ſo the Proteſtants had prevailed with the ſword, they would as wel have taught the Papiſts with the faggot, and led them to the ſtake; ſo that this princ̨iple of *Perſecution*, on all hands, is the ground of all thoſe miſerys and contentions : for ſo long as any party is perſwaded, that it is both lawfull for them, and their duty, if in power, to deſtroy thoſe, that differ from them, it naturally followes, they ought to uſe all means poſſible to get that power, whereby they may ſecure themſelves in the ruin of their adverſarys. And that neither Papiſts nor Proteſtants judge it unlawfull to compell the Magiſtrate, if they be ſtrong enough to do it, to effeċt this. Experience ſhewes it to be a known Popiſh principle, that *the Pope may depoſe an heretik Prince, and abſolve the people from the oath of fidelity*, and the Pope, as is above ſaid, hath done ſo to divers Princes ; and this doċtrin is defended by *Bellarmin* againſt *Barclay.* The *French* refuſed *Henry* the fourth, till he quitted his religion. And as for Proteſtants, many of them ſcruple not to affirm, that *wicked Kings and Magiſtrates may be depoſed and killed*; yea our Scotch Presbyters are as poſitive in it as any Jeſuits, who would not admitt this preſent *Charles* the ſecond, though otherwiſe a Proteſtant,

Prince

Prince, unleſs he would ſwear to renounce Epiſcopacy, a matter of no great difference, though contrary to his Conſcience. Now how little proportion theſe things bear with the primitive Chriſtians and the Religion propagated by Chriſt and his Apoſtles, needs no great demonſtration; and it is obſervable, that, notwithſtanding many other ſuperſtitions crept into the Church, very early, yet this of perſecution was ſo inconſiſtent with the nature of the Goſpel, and liberty of Conſcience, as we have aſſerted it, ſuch an innate and natural part of the Chriſtian Religion, that almoſt all the Chriſtian writers, for the firſt three hundred years, earneſtly contend for it, condemning the contrary opinion.

§ V. Thus Athanaſius, *It is the property of piety not to force, but to perſwade, in imitation of our Lord, who forced no body, but left it to the will of every one to follow him; &c. But the devil, becauſe he hath nothing of Truth, uſes knocks and axes to break up the doors of ſuch as receive him. But our Saviour is meek, teaching the Truth; Whoſoever will come after me, and whoſoever will be my diſciple, &c. but conſtraining none, coming to us, and knocking rather, and ſaying, My ſiſter, my ſpouſe, open to me, &c. and entreth when he is opened to, and retires, if they delay, and will not open unto him, becauſe it is not with ſwords, nor darts, nor ſouldiers, nor armour, that Truth is to be declared, but with perſuaſion and counſel.* And it is obſervable, that it was the impious *Arians*, who firſt of all brought-in this doctrine to perſecut others, among Chriſtians, whoſe ſucceſſors both Papiſts and Proteſtants are in this matter, whom *Athanaſius* thus reproveth further. *Where (ſaith he) have they learned to perſecut? Certainly they can not ſay, they have learned it from the Saints; but this has been given them, and taught them of the devil. The Lord commanded indeed ſometimes to flee, and the Saints ſometimes fled, but to perſecut is the invention and argument of the devil, which he ſeeks againſt all.* And after, he ſaith, *in ſo far as the Arians banniſh thoſe, that will not ſubſcribe their decrees, they ſhew, that they are contrary to Chriſtians, and friends of the devil.*

But now, O lamentable! (ſaith Hilarius) *it is the ſuffrages of the earth, that recommend the religion of God, and Chriſt is found naked of his vertue, while ambition muſt give credit to his Name. The Church reproves and fights by baniſhments and priſons, and forceth her ſelf to be believed, which once was believed, becauſe of the impriſonments and baniſhments her ſelf ſuffered. She, that once was conſecrated by the terror of her perſecutors, depends now upon the dignity of thoſe,*

that

Athan. in epiſt. ad ſolit. vit. ag. ibid.

Athan. Apol. 1 de fuga ſua, tom. 1.

Hil. contra Aux.

that are in her communion. She, that once was propagated by her banished priests, now banisheth the priests. And she boasts now that she is loved of the world, who could not have been Christ's, if she had not been hated of the world.

Hieron.
epist. 62.
ad The.

Ambr.
epist. 32.
tom. 3.

Ambr.
epist 27.

Marc.
epist. ad
Archi-
mand, &c

Mon.
Eg. in
acta con-
cil. Chal-
ced.
tom. 2.
conc. gen.
* Hosi.
epist. ad
Constit.
apud Ath
in epist ad
solit. vit.
tom. 1.
‡ Hil. l. 1.
ad Const.
† Ambr.
comm. in
Luc. l. 7.
¶ Cypr.
epist. 62.
* Tertull.
Apolog.
cap. 24.
Id. Apo-
log. c. 28.

The Church (saith Hierom) *was founded by sheding of blood, and by suffer-ing, and not in doing of hurt. The Church increased by persecutions, and was crowned by martyrdoms.*

Ambrose speaking of *Auxentius,* saith thus, *whom he (viz, Auxentius) could not deceive by discourse, he thinks ought to be killed by the sword, making bloody laws with his mouth, writing them with his hands, and imagining that an edict can command faith*

And the same *Ambrose* saith, *that going into France, he would not commu-nicat with those Bishops, that required that heretiks should be put to death.*

The Emperor *Marçio,* who assembled the Council of *Chalçedon,* pro-tests, *that he would not force, nor constrain any one to subscribe the Council of Chalçedon, against his will.*

* *Hosius,* Bishop of Cordua, testifies, *that the Emperor Constans would not constrain any to be orthodox.*

‡ *Hilarius* saith further, *that God teacheth, rather than exacteth, the know-ledge of himself, and authorizing his commandments by the miracles of his heavenly works, he wills not that any should confess him with a forced will, &c. He is the God of the whole Universe, he needs not a forced obedience, nor requires a con-strained confession.*

† *Christ* (saith Ambrose) *sent his Apostles to sow faith, not to constrain, but to teach; not to exercise coërçive power, but to extoll the doctrine of hu-mility.*

¶ Hence *Cyprian,* comparing the old Covenant with the New, saith, *then were they put to death with the outward sword, but now the proud and con-tumacious are cut off with the Spiritual sword, by being cast out of the Church:* and this answers very wel that objection, before observed, taken from the practice of the Jewes under the Law.

* *See,* (saith Tertullian to the Heathens) *if it be not to contribute to the renown of irreligion, to seek to take away the liberty of Religion, and to hinder men their choyse of God, that I may not be admitted to adore, whom I will, but must be constrained to serve him, whom I will not. There is none, nay not a man, that desires to be adored by any, against their will. And again,* It's a thing, that easi-ly appears to be unjust, to constrain and force men to sacrifiçe against their wills:

seing,

seing, to do the service of God, there is required a willing heart.   And again, *It is an humane right, and natural power, that every one worship what he esteemes; and one mans religion doth nor profit nor hurt another. Neither is it any piece of Religion, to enforce religion, which must be undertaken by consent, and not by violence, seing that the sacrifices themselves are not required but from a willing mind.*   Idem *ad* Scapul. *cap.* 2.

Now, how either Papists or Protestants (that boast of *Antiquity*) can get by these plain testimonys, let any rational man judge. And indeed I much question, if, in any one poynt, owned by them, and denyed by us, they can find all the old *Fathers* and writers so exactly unanimous. Which shewes, how contrary all of them judged this to be, to the nature of Christianity, and that in the poynt of *persecution* lay no small part of the Apostasy, which, from little to more, came to that, *that the Pope, upon every small discontent, would excommunicat Princes, absolve their subjects from obeying them, and turn them in and out, at his pleasur.*   Now, if Protestants do justly abhorr these things, among Papists, is it not sad, that they should do the like themselves? A thing, that, at their first appearance, when they were in their primitive innocency, they did not think on, as appears by that saying of *Luther. Neither Pope, nor Bishop, nor any other man, hath power to oblige a Christian to one syllable, except it be by his own consent.*   And again, *I call boldly to Christians, that neither man, nor Angel, can impose any Law upon them, but so far as they will; for we are free of all.*   And, when he appeared at the diet of *Spiers*, before the Emperor, in a particular conference he had, before the Arch-bishop of *Triers*, and *Joachim* Elector of *Brandenburgh*, when there seem'd no possibility of agreeing him with his opposers, they asking him, *what remedy seemed to him most fit?* He answered, *the counsel, that Gamaliel proposed to the Jewes*, to wit, *that, if this design was of God, it would stand, if not; it would evanish, which,* he said, *ought to content the Pope:* he did not say, *because he was in the right, he ought to be spared.*   For this counsel supposeth, that those, that are tolerated, may be wrong; and yet how soon did the same *Luther*, ere he was wel secure himself, press the Elector of *Saxony*, to bannish poor *Carolostadius*, because he could not, in all things, submitt to his judgment; and certainly it is not without ground reported, that it smot *Luther* to the heart, (so that he needed to be comforted) when he was informed, that *Carlstadius*, in his letter to his congregation, styled himself *a man bannished for Conscience, by the procurement of Martin Luther.* And since, both the   *Luth. lib. de Capti- vit. Baby- lonicâ.*

History of the Coun- cil of Trent.

X x

Luthe-

Lutherans and Calvinists not admitting one another to worship, in those respective dominions, sheweth how little better they are, that either Papists, or Arians, in this particular.   And yet *Calvin* saith, that *the Conscience is free from the power of all men.* If so, why then did he cause *Castellio* to be bannisht, because he could not, for Conscience sake, believe, as he did, *that God had ordained men to be damned?* and *Servetus* to be burned, for denying the Divinity of Christ, if *Calvin*'s report of him be to be credited, which opinion, though it was indeed to be abominated, yet no less was *Calvin*'s practice, in causing him to be burned, and afterwards defending that it was lawfull to burn *heretiks*, by which he encouraged the Papists to lead his followers the more confidently to the stake, as having, for their warrant, the doctrine of their own *sect-master*, which they omitted not frequently to twit them with, and indeed it was to them unanswerable.   Hence, upon this occasion, the judicious author of the history of the Council of Trent (in his fifth book, where, giving an account of several Protestants, that were burned for their religion) wel and wisely observeth it, *as a matter of astonishment, that those of the new Reformation did offer to punish in the case of Religion:*   And afterwards, taking notice, that *Calvin* justifies the punishing of heretiks, he adds, *But since the name of Heresy may be more or less restricted, yea or diversly taken, this doctrine may be likewise taken in divers senses, and may at one time hurt those, whom at another time it may have benefited.*

So that this doctrine of *Persecution* can not be mentioned by Protestants, without strengthening the hands of Popish inquisitors, and indeed, in the end, lands in direct Popery. *Seing, if I may not profess and preach that Religion, which I am perswaded of in my Conscience is true, it is to no purpose to search the Scripturs, or to seek to chuse my own faith by convictions thence derived, since whatever I there observe, or am perswaded of, I must either subject to the judgment of the Magistrate and Church of that place I am in, or else resolve to remove, or dye.* Yea doth not this *heretical* and *anti-Christian* doctrine both of Papists and Protestants at last resolve into that cursed policy of *Mahomet, who prohibited all reason or discourse about Religion, as occasioning factions and divisions?* And indeed, those, that press *persecution,* and deny *liberty of Conscience,* do thereby shew themselves more the disciples of *Mahomet,* than of *Christ,* and that they are no ways followers of the Apostles doctrin, who desired the Thessalonians, 1 Thess. 5: 21. to *prove all things, and hold fast that, which is good:* and also saith, ----*unto*

Calvin.
Inst. c. 19
sect. 14,

ſuch as are otherwiſe minded, God ſhall reveal it, Phil. 3 : 15. not, that by beatings and banniſhments it muſt be knocked into them.

§ VI. Now the *ground* of *Perſecution*, as hath above been ſhewn, is an *unwillingneſ to ſuffer*; for no man, that will perſecut another, for his *Conſcience*, would ſuffer for his own, if he could avoid it, ſeing his principle obliges him, if he had power, by force to eſtabliſh that, which he judges is the *Truth*, and ſo to force others to it. Therefore I judge it meet, for the information of the Nations, briefly to add ſomething in this place concerning the *nature of true Chriſtian ſufferings*, whereunto a very faithfull teſtimony has been born by God's Witneſſes, which he hath raiſed up in this age, beyond what hath been generally known or practiſed for theſe many generations, yea ſince the Apoſtaſy took place. Yet 'tis not my deſign here in any wiſe to derogat from the *ſufferings* of the *Proteſtant Martyrs*, whom I believe to have walked in faithfulneſs towards God, according to the diſpenſation of *Light* in that day appearing, and of which many were utter enemies to *perſecution*, as by their teſtimonys againſt it, might be made appear.

But the true, faithfull, and Chriſtian ſuffering is, *for men to profeſ what they are perſwaded is right, and ſo practiſe and perform their worſhip towards God, as being their true right ſo to do, and neither to do more in that becauſe of outward encouragement from men, nor any whit leſ, becauſe of the fear of their Laws and acts againſt it.* Thus for a Chriſtian man to vindicat his juſt liberty, with ſo much boldneſs and yet innocency, will, in due time, though through blood, purchaſe peace, as this age has, in ſome meaſur, experienced, and many are witneſſes of it, which yet ſhall be more apparent to the world, as Truth takes place in the earth. But they greatly ſin againſt this excellent rule, that, in time of perſecution, do not profeſs their own way, ſo much as they would, if it were other ways; and yet, when they can get the Magiſtrate upon their ſide, not onely ſtretch their own liberty to the utmoſt, but ſeek to eſtabliſh the ſame, by denying it to others. But of this excellent patience and ſufferings, the Witneſſes of God, in ſcorn called *Quakers*, have given a manifeſt proof; for, ſo ſoon as God revealed his Truth among them, without regard to all oppoſition, or what they might meet with, they went up and down, as they were moved of the Lord, preaching and propagating the Truth in market-places, high-ways, ſtreets, and publik Temples, though daily beaten, whipped, bruiſed, haled, and impriſoned therefore. And, when

X x 2

there

there was any where a Church or aſſembly gathered, they taught them
to keep their meetings openly, and not to ſhut the door, nor do it by
ſtealth, that all might know it, and, who would, might enter: and,
as hereby all juſt occaſion of fear of plotting againſt the Government
was fully removed, ſo this their courage and faithfulneſs, in not giving
over their meeting together, (but more eſpecially the Preſence and
Glory of God, manifeſted in the meeting, being terrible to the Conſciences of the Perſecutors) did ſo weary out the malice of their adverſarys, that often-times they were forced to leave their work undone. For,
when they came to break up a meeting, they were forc'd to take every
individual out by force, they not being free to give up their liberty, by
diſſolving, at their command: and, when they were haled out, unleſs
they were kept forth by violence, they preſently returned peaceably to
their place. Yea when ſometimes the Magiſtrates have pulled down
their meeting-houſes, they have met the next day, openly upon the rubbiſh, and ſo by innocency kept their poſſeſſion and ground, being properly their own, and their right to meet and worſhip God being not
forfeited to any. So that, when armed men have come to diſſolve them,
it was impoſſible for them to do it, unleſs they had killed every one, for
they ſtood ſo cloſe together, that no force could move any one to ſtirr,
untill violently pulled down: ſo that, when the malice of their oppoſers
ſtirred them to take ſhovels and throw the rubbiſh upon them, there
they ſtood unmoved, being willing, if the Lord ſhould ſo permitt, to
have been there buried alive, witneſſing for him. As this patient, but
yet couragious, way of ſuffering made the perſecutors work very heavy,
and wearyſom unto them, ſo the courage and patience of the ſufferers
uſing no reſiſtance, nor bringing any weapons to defend themſelves,
nor ſeeking any ways revenge upon ſuch occaſions, did ſecretly ſmite the
hearts of the perſecutors, and make their chariot wheels go on heavily.
Thus after much and many kind of ſufferings thus patiently born, which
to rehearſe would make a volumn of it ſelf, which may in due time be
publiſhed to the Nations (for we have them upon record) a kind of negative liberty has been obtained, ſo that at preſent, for the moſt part,
we meet together without diſturbance from the Magiſtrate. But, on
the contrary, moſt Proteſtants, when they have not the allowance and
tolerance of the Magiſtrate, meet onely in ſecret, and hide their teſtimony: and, if they be diſcovered, if there be any probability of making
their

their escape, by force, though it were by cutting-off those, that seek them out, they will do it, whereby they lose the glory of their sufferings by not appearing as the innocent followers of Christ, nor having a testimony of their harmelessness, *in* the hearts of their pursuers, their fury, by such resistence, is the more kindled against them. As to this last part of resisting such as persecut them, they can lay claim to no precept from Christ, nor any example of him or his Apostles approved.

But as to the first part for fleeing, and meeting secretly, and not openly testifying for the Truth, they usually object that saying of Christ, Matth. 10:23. *when they persecute you in this city, flee ye into another.* And *Act.* 9:4. *that the disciples met secretly for fear of the Jewes.* And *Act.* 9: v. 25. *that Paul was let out of Damascus in a basket down by the wall.*   Obj.

To all which I answer, First, as to that saying of Christ, it is a question, if it had any further relation than to that particular message, with which he sent them to the Jewes, yea the latter end of the words seem expresly to hold forth so much, *for ye shall not have gone over the citys of Juda, till the Son of man be come.* Now a particular practice or command, for a particular time, will not serve for a *president* to any, at this day, to shun the Cross of Christ. But, supposing this precept to reach further, it must be so understood, to be made use of onely according as the Spirit giveth liberty, else no man, that could flee, might suffer persecution. How then did not the Apostles John and Peter flee, when they were the first time persecuted at Jerusalem? But, on the contrary, went the next day, after they were discharged, by the Council, and preached boldly to the people. But indeed many are but too capable to stretch such sayings as these, for self-preservation, and therefore have great ground to fear, when they interpret them, that they shun to witness for Christ, for fear of hurt to themselves, lest they mistake them. As for that privat meeting of the Disciples, we have onely an account of the matter of fact, but that suffices not to make of it a president for us, and mens aptness to imitat them in that, (which, for ought we know, might have been an act of weakness) and not in other things of the contrary nature, shewes, that it is not a true zeal to be like those Disciples, but indeed a desire to preserve themselves, which moves them so to do. Lastly, as to that of Paul's being conveyed out of Damascus, the case was singular, and is not to be doubted, but it was done by a special allowance from God, who having designed him to be a principal minister of his Gospel, saw meet,   Answ.

in his Wisdom, to disappoint the wicked counsel of the Jewes. But our adversarys have no such pretext for fleeing, whose fleeing proceeds from self-preservation, not from immediat revelation. And that Paul made not this the method of his procedur, appears, in that at another time, notwithstanding the perswasion of his friends, and certain prophecys of his sufferings to come, he would not be disswaded to go up to Jerusalem, which, according to the fore-mentioned rule, he should have done.

But lastly, to conclude this matter, Glory to God and our Lord Jesus Christ, that now these twenty five years, since we were known to be a distinct and separat people, hath given us faithfully to suffer for his *Name*, without shrinking or fleeing the Cross; and what liberty we now enjoy, it is by his Mercy, and not by any outward working or procuring of our own, but 'tis he has wrought upon the hearts of our opposers; nor was it any outward interest hath procured it unto us, but the testimony of our harmelesness in the hearts of our Superiors : for God hath preserved us hitherto in the patient suffering of Jesus, that we have not given away our cause by persecuting any, which few, if any, Christians, that I know, can say. Now against our unparalleled, yet innocent and Christian cause, our malicious enemies have nothing to say, but that, if we had power, we would do so likewise. This is a piece of meer unreasonable malice, and a priviledg they take to judge of things to come, which they have not by immediat revelation; and surely it is the greatest heighth of harsh judgment, to say, men would do contrary to their *professed Principle*, if they could, who have, from their practice, hitherto given no ground for it, and wherein they onely judge others by themselves : such conjecturs can not militat against us, so long as we are innocent. And, if ever we prove guilty of *persecution*, by forcing other men by corporal punishment, to our way, then let us be judged the greatest of hypocrits, and let not any spare to persecute us. *A M E N saith my Soul.*

The Fifteenth Proposition,

Concerning Salutations and Recreations, &c.

Seing the chief end of all Religion is to redeem men from
the

the Spirit and vain converſation of this world, and to lead into inward communion with God, before whom, if we fear always, we are accounted happy, therefore all the vain cuſtoms and habits thereof, both in word and deed, are to be rejected and forſaken by thoſe who come to this fear; ſuch as the taking off the Hat to a man, the bowings and cringings of the body, and ſuch other Salutations of that kind, with all the foolish and ſuperſtitious formalities attending them, all which man has invented in his degenerate ſtate to feed his pride in the vain pomp and glory of this world, as alſo the unprofitable Plays, frivolous Recreations, Sportings and Gamings which are invented to paſs away the pretious time, and divert the mind from the witneſs of God in the heart, and from the living ſenſe of his fear, and from that Evangelical Spirit wherewith Chriſtians ought to be leavened, and which leads into ſobriety, gravity, and Godly fear, in which as we abide, the bleſſing of the Lord is felt to attend us in thoſe actions, which we are neceſſarily engaged, in order to the taking care for the ſuſtenance of the outward man.

Eph. 5:
vers 11.
1 Pet. 1:
vers 14.
Joh. 5: 44
Jer. 10: 3
Acts 10:
vers 26.
Matth 15
vers 13.
Col. 2: 8.

§ I. **H**Aving hitherto treated of the Principles of Religion, both relating to Doctrine and Worſhip; I am now to ſpeak of ſome practices, which have been the product of this Principle, *in* thoſe Witneſſes, whom God hath raiſed up in this day, to teſtify for his *Truth*. It will not a little commend them (I ſuppoſe) in the judgment of ſober and judicious men, that, taking them generally, (even by the confeſſion of their adverſarys) they are found to be free of thoſe abominations, which abound among other profeſſors, ſuch as are *ſwearing, drunkenneß, whoredom, riotouſneß,* &c. and that generally the very coming among this People, doth naturally work ſuch a charge, ſo that many vitious and profane perſons have been known, by coming to this Truth, to become ſober and vertuous; and many light, vain, and wanton ones, to become

grave

* *after this manner the Papists used to disapprove the sobriety of the Waldenses of whom Reinerius a Popish author so writeth, But this sect of the Leonists hath a great shew of Truth, for that they live righteously, before men, and believe all things wel of God, and all the articls, which are contained in the creed, only they blasphem and hate the church of Rome.*

grave and serious, as our adversarys dare not deny, * yet, that they may not want something to detract us for, cease not to accuse us for those things, which, when found among themselves, they highly commend; thus our *gravity* they call *sullenneß*; our *seriousneß, melancholy*; our *silence, sottishneß*. Such as have been vitious and profane among them, but by coming to us have left off those evils, lest they should commend the truth of our profession, they say, that whereas they were *profane* before, they are *now become worse in being hypocritical and spiritually proud*. If any, before *diſſolute* and *profane* among them, by coming to the Truth with us, become *frugal* and *diligent*, then they will charge them with *covetouſneß*. And if any *eminent* among them for *seriouſneß, piety,* and *discoverys of God*, come unto us, then they will say, they were always subject to *melancholy* and to *enthusiasm*, though before, when among them, it was esteem'd neither *melancholy* nor *enthusiasm*, in an evil sense, but *Christian gravity* and *Divine revelation*. Our *boldneß* and *Christian suffering*, they call *obstinacy* and *pertinacy*, though half as much, if among themselves, they would account *Christian courage*, and *nobility*. And, though thus, by their envy, they strive to read all, relating to us, backwards, counting these things *vices in us*, which in themselves they would extoll, as *vertues*, yet hath the strength of Truth extorted this confession often from them, that *we are generally a pure and clean people as to the outward converſation*.

But this, they say, is but in policy to commend our hereſy.

But such policy it is, say I, as Christ and his Apostles made use of, and all good Christians ought to do; yea so far hath Truth prevailed by the purity of its followers, that, if one, that is called a *Quaker*, do but that, which is common among them, as to laugh and be wanton, speak at large, and keep not his word punctually, or be overtaken with hastyneß or anger, they presently say, O! *this is against your profession!* As if indeed so to do were very consistent with theirs, wherein, though they speak the Truth, yet they give away their cause. But if they can find any, under our name, in any of those evils, common among themselves, (as who can imagine, but among so many thousands there will be some chaf, since of twelve Apostles one was found to be a devil) O! how will they insult, and make more noise of the escape of one Quaker, than of an hundred among themselves!

§ II. But there are some singular things, which most of all our adversarys plead for the lawfulneß of, and allow themselves in, as no ways
inconsi-

inconfiftent with the Chriftian Religion , which we have found to be no ways lawfull unto us, and have been commanded of the Lord to lay them afide , though the doing thereof hath occafioned no fmall fufferings and buffetings , and hath procured us much hatred and malice from the world. And becaufe the nature of thefe things is fuch, that they do upon the very fight diftinguifh us, & make us known, fo that we can not hide our felves from any , without proving unfaithfull to our teftimony: our tryals and exercifes have herethrough , proved the more numerous and difficult , as will after appear.   Thefe I have laboured briefly to comprehend in this Propofition , but they may more largely be exhibited in thofe fix fol‑ lowing Propofitions.

1. *That it is not lawfull to give to men fuch flattering Titles , as , Your Ho‑ lynefs , Your Majefly , Your Eminency , Your Excellency , Your Grace , Your Lordfhip , Your Honor , &c. nor ufe thofe flattering words , commonly called* [COMPLEMENTS.]

2. *That it is not lawfull for Chriftians to kneel , or proftrat themfelves to any man , or to bow the body , or to uncover the head to them.*

3. *That it is not lawfull for a Chriftian to ufe fuperfluitys in apparel , as are of no ufe fave for ornament and vanity.*

4. *That it is not lawfull to ufe games , fports , plays , nor , among other things , Comedys among Chriftians , under the notion of Recreations , which do not agree with Chriftian filence , gravity , and fobriety : for laughing , fporting , gaming , mocking , jefting , talking , &c. is nor Chriftian liberty , nor harmlefs mirth.*

5. *That it is not lawfull for Chriftians to fwear at all under the Gofpel , not onely not vainly , and in their common difcourfe , which was alfo forbidden under the Mofaical Law , but even not in Judgment before the Magiftrate.*

6. *That it is not lawfull for Chriftians to refift evil , or to warr or fight in any cafe.*

Before I enter upon a particular difquifition of thefe things, I fhall firft premife fome general confiderations , to prevent all miftakes , and next add fome general confiderations , which equally refpect all of them. I would not have any judge , that hereby we intend to deftroy the *mutual relation* , that either is betwixt *Prince* and *people* , *Mafter* and *fervant* , *Parents* and *children* , nay not at all. We fhall evidence that our Principle in thefe things hath no fuch tendency , and that thefe natural relations are rather better eftablifhed , than any ways hurt by it.   Next , let not any judge ,
Y y
that ,

that, from our opinion in these things, any necessity of levelling will follow, or that all men must have things in common. Our Principle leaves every man to enjoy that peaceably, which either his own industry, or parents have purchased to him, onely he is thereby instructed to use it aright, both for his own good, and that of his brethren, and all to the Glory of God: In which also his acts, are to be voluntary, and no ways constrained. And further, we say not hereby, that no man may use the creation more, or less than another. For we know, that, as it hath pleased God, to dispense it diversly, giving to some more, and to some less, so they may use it accordingly. The several conditions, under which men are diversly stated, together with their educations answering thereunto, do sufficiently shew this: the *servant* is not the same way educated as the *Master*, nor the *tennant* as the *land-Lord*, nor the *rich* as the *poor*, nor the *Prince* as the *peasant*. Now, though it be not lawfull for any, however great abundance they may have, or whatever their education may be, to use that which is meerly superfluous: yet, seing their *education* has accustomed them thereunto, and their *capacity* enables them so to do, without being profuse or extravagant, they may use things better in their kind, than such, whose education hath neither accustomed them to such things, nor their capacity will reach to compass them. For it is beyond question, that whatever thing the Creation affords, is for the use of man, and the moderat use of them is lawfull, yet *per accidens* they may be unlawfull to some, and not to others. As for instance, who by reason of his estate and education hath been used to eat *flesh* and drink *wine*, to be cloathed with the *finest wool*, if his estate bear it, and he use it neither in superfluity, nor immoderatly, he may do it, and perhaps, if he should apply himself to feed or be cloathed, as are the peasants, it might prejudice the health of his body, and nothing advance his Soul. But, if a man, whose estate and education had accustomed to both courser food and rayment, should stretch himself beyond what he had or were used to, to the manifest prejudice of his family and children, no doubt, it would be unlawfull to him, even so to eat or be cloathed, as another, (in whom it is lawfull) for that that other may as much mortified, and have denyed himself as much in coming down to that, which this aspires to, as he in willing to be like him, aspires beyond what he either is able or hath accustomed to do. The safe place then is for such as have fulness to watch over themselves, that they use it moderatly, and rescind all superfluitys, being willing so far

as they can, to help the need of those, to whom Providence hath al-
lotted a smaller allowance.   *Let the brother of high degree rejoyce in that he
is abased, and such as God calls in a low degree to be content with their condition,
not envying those brethren, who have greater abundance,* knowing *they have
received abundance as to the inward man,* which is chiefly to be regarded.
And therefore beware of such a temptation, as to use their calling as an
engine to be richer, knowing they have this advantage beyond the *rich*
and *noble,* that are called, that the Truth doth not any ways abase them,
nay not in the esteem of the world, as it doth the other, but that they
are rather exalted thereby, in that as to the inward and spiritual fellowship of the Saints they become the brethren and companions of the Greatest and richest, and in this respe&t *let him of low degree rejoyce that he is exalted.*

These things premised, I would seriously propose unto all such as
mind, in reality, to be Christians indeed, and that in *nature,* and not
in *name* onely, whether it were not desirable, and would not greatly
contribute to the commendation of Christianity, and to the encrease of
the life and vertue of Christ, if *all superfluous titles of honor, profusness and
prodigality in meat and apparel, excess of gaming, sporting and playing* were
laid aside and forborn? And whether such as lay them aside, in so doing,
walk not more like the Disciples of Christ and his Apostles, and are
therein nearer their example than such as use them? Whether the laying
them aside would hinder any from being good Christians, or if *Christians*
might not be better without them, than with them? Certainly the *sober*
and *serious,* among all sorts, will say yea. Then surely such as lay them
aside, as reckoning them unsutable for Christians, are not to be blamed, but rather commended for so doing : because that both in principle, &
practice, they effe&tually advance that, which others acknowledg were
desirable ; but can never make effe&tuall, so long as they allow the use
of them, as lawfull. And God hath made it manifest in this age, that
by discovering the evil of such things, and leading his Witnesses out
of them, and to testify against them, he hath produced effe&tually, *in*
many, that *mortification* and *abstraction from the love* and *cares of this world,*
who daily are conversing in the world (but inwardly redeemed out of it)
both in wedlock, and in their lawfull imployments, which was judged could onely be obtained by such as were shut up in cloysters and mona-
sterys. This much in general.

Y y 2

§ I I I.

§ III. **As** to the first, we affirm positively; that *it is not lawfull for Christians either to give or receive these titles of honor*, as, *Your Holyness, Your Majesty, Your Excellency, Your Eminency*, &c.

First, because these *titles* are no part of that obedience, which is due to Magistrates or Superiors, neither doth the giving them add to, nor diminish from that subjection we ow to them, which consists *in obeying their just and lawfull commands*, not in *titles* and designations.

Secondly, we find not, that, in the *Scriptur* any such *titles* are used either under the *Law*, or the *Gospel*: but, that in the speaking to *Kings Princes*, or *Nobles*, they use onely a simple compellation, as *O King*, and that without any further designation, save perhaps the name of the person, as, *O King Agrippa*, &c.

Thirdly, It lays a necessity upon Christians most frequently to *lye*; because the persons, obtaining these *titles*, either by election, or hereditarily, may frequently be found to have nothing really *in them*, deserving them, or answering to them: as some, to whom it is said *Your Excellency*, having nothing of *Excellency in them*: and who is called *Your Grace*, appear to be an enemy to *Grace*: and he who is called *Your Honor*, is known to be base and ignoble. I wonder what Law of man, or what patent ought to oblige me to make a lye, in *calling good, evil, and evil, good*? I wonder what Law of man can secure me, in so doing from, the just judgment of God, that will make me count for *every idle word*, and to *lye*, is something more! Surely Christians should be ashamed, that such Laws, manifestly crossing the Law of God, should be among them.

Obj.   If it be said, *We ought in charity to suppose, that they have these vertues, because the King has bestowed those titles upon them, or that they are descended of such as deserved them.*

Answ.   I answer, *Charity* destroys not *knowledge*: I am not obliged, by *charity*, either to believe or speak a *lye*. Now it is apparent, and can not be denyed by any, but that those vertues are not in many of the persons, expressed by the *titles* they bear, neither will they allow to speak so to such, in whom these vertues are, unless they be so dignified by outward Princes. So that such as are truely vertuous must not be styled by their vertues, because not priviledged by the Princes of this world, and such, as have them not, must be so called, because they have obtained a patent so to be; and all this is done by those, who pretend to be his followers, that commanded his Disciples *not to call any man Master*, and told them
                                                                                                such,

fuch *could not believe as received honor one from another, and fought not the honor, which cometh from God onely.* This is fo plain to fuch as will indeed be Chriftians, that it needs no confequence.

Fourthly, as to thofe *titles of Holynefs, Eminency* and *Excellency*, ufed among the Papifts to the *Pope* and *Cardinals*, &c. and *Grace, Lordfhip* and *Worfhip* ufed to the *Clergy* among the *Proteftants*, it is a moft blafphemous ufurpation. For, if they ufe *Holynefs* and *Grace*, becaufe thefe things ought to be in a *Pope* or in a Bifhop, how come they to ufurp that peculiarly to themfelves? Ought not *Holynefs* and *Grace* to be in every Chriftian? And fo every Chriftian fhould fay *Tour Holynefs* and *Tour Grace one to another.* Next, how can they in reafon claim any more *titles*, than were practifed, and received by the Apoftles and primitive Chriftians, whofe fucceffors they pretend they are, and as whofe fucceffors (and no otherwife) themfelves, I judge, will confefs, any honor they feek is due to them? Now, if they neither fought, received, nor admitted fuch *honor*, nor *titles*, how came thefe by them? If they fay they did, Let them prove it, if they can; we find no fuch thing in the Scriptur. The Chriftians fpeak to the Apoftles without any fuch denominations, neither faying, *If it pleafe Tour Grace, Tour Holynefs, Tour Lordfhip*, nor *your Worfhip*: they are neither called *My Lord Peter*, nor *My Lord Paul*, nor yet *Mafter Peter*, nor *Mafter Paul*, nor *Doctor Peter*, nor *Doctor Paul*, but fingly *Peter* and *Paul*, and that not onely in the Scriptur, but for fome hundreds of years after. So that, this appears to be a manifeft fruit of the Apoftafy: for, if thefe *titles* arife either from the *office* or *worth* of the *perfons*, it will not be denyed, but the Apoftles deferved them better, than any now, that call for them. But the cafe is plain, the Apoftles had *the Holynefs, the excellency, the grace*, and becaufe they were *holy, excellent* and *gracious*, they neither ufed nor admitted of fuch *titles*: but thefe, having neither *holynefs, excellency*, nor *grace*, will needs be fo called, to fatisfie their ambitious and oftentive minds, which is a manifeft token of their hypocrify.

Fifthly, as to that *title of Majefty*, ufually afcribed to Princes, we do not find it given to any fuch in the holy Scriptur. But that it is fpecially and peculiarly afcribed unto God, as, 1 Chron. 29: 11. Job 37: 22. Pfal. 21: 5. 29: 4. 43: 3. 63: 1. 96: 6. Ifa. 2: 10. 24: 14. 26: 10. Heb. 1: ver 3. 2 Pet. 1: 16. and many more places: Hence faith *Jude*, ver. 25. *To the onely Wife God our Saviour be glory, and Majefty*, &c. not to men.

Y y 3

Wi.

We find in Scriptur the proud *King Nebuchadnezar* assuming this *title to* himself, Dan. 4: 30. who at that time received a sufficient reproof, by a sudden judgment, which came upon him.   Therefore in all the compellations used to Princes in the old Testament, "it is not to be found, nor yet in the New. Paul was very civil to *Agrippa*, yet he gives him no such *title*: neither was this *title* used among Christians in the primitive times. Hence the Ecclesiastik history of the Reformation of *France* relating the speech of the Lord *Rochefort*, at the assembly of the Estate of *France*, held under *Charles* the ninth, in the year 1560, saith, *that this barrang was wel remarked, in that he used not the word* [Majesty,] *invented by flatterers of late years*, and yet this Author minded not how his Master *Calvin* used this *flattering title* to *Francis* the first, King of *France*, and not onely so, but calls him *most Christian King*, in the Epistle to his *Institutions*, though, by his daily persecuting of the Reformers, it was apparent, he was far from being such, even in *Calvin's* own esteem. Surely the complying with such vain *titles*, imposed and introduced by Antichrist, greatly tended to stain the *Reformation*, and to render it defective in many things.

Eclef. hist. lib. 4. Pag. 445.

  Lastly all these *titles* and *styls* of *honor* are to be rejected by Christians ; because they are to seek the *honor*, *that comes from above*, and not the *honor*, that is from below. But these honors are not that honor, that comes from above, but are from below. For we known wel enough what industry, and what pains men are at, to get these things, and what part it is that seeks after them, to wit, the *proud*, *insolent*, *haughty*, *aspiring*, *mind*. For judge, is it the *meek* and *innocent Spirit of Christ*, that covets that honor ? Is it that Spirit, that must be *of no reputation in this world*, that has its *conversation in heaven*, that comes to have *fellowship with the sones of God* ? is it that Spirit, I say, that loves that honor, that seeks after that honor, that pleads for the upholding of that honor, that frets and rages and fumes, when it is denyed that honor ? Or is it not rather the lordly insulting Spirit of *Lucifer*, the *Prince of this world*, he, that of old affected and sought after this honor, and loved not to abide in the submissive low place ? And so all his children are possessed with the same ambitious proud mind, seeking and coveting *titles of honor*, which indeed belong not to them. For let us examin, *who are they, that are honorable indeed* ? Is it not the *righteous man*? Is it not the *holy man*? Is it not the *humble-hearted man*? the *meek-spirited man*? And are not such those, that ought to be *honoured*

Phil. 3: ver. 20.

1 Sam. 2: ver. 30.

among

among *Christians?* Now, of these, may there not be poor men? laboures? silly fisher men? And if so, how comes it that the *titles* of *honor* are not bestowed upon such? But who are they, that generally receive and look for this honor? Are they not the rich ones? such as have abundance of the earth? as be like they rich glutton? such as are proud and ambitious? such as are oppressors of the poor? such as swell with lust and vanity? and *all superfluity of naughtiness?* who are the very abomination and plague of the Nations, are not these they, that are accounted the honorable? that require and receive the titles of honor, proud *Hamans?* Now whether is this the honor, that comes from God, or the honor from below? Doth God honor such as daily dishonor him, and disobey him? And if this be not the honor, that comes from God, but the honor of this world, which the children of this world give, and receive one from another, how can the children of God, such as are Christians indeed, give or receive that honor among themselves, without coming under the reproof of Christ, who saith, that *such as do so, can not believe?* But further, if we respect the cause, that most frequently procures to men these *titles* of honor, there is not one of a thousand, that shall be found to be, because of any Christian vertue. But rather for things to be discommended among Christians. As by the favor of Princes procured by flattering, and often by worse means, yea the most frequent, and accounted among men most honorable, is *fighting*, or some great martial exploit, which can add nothing to a Christian's worth: since, sure it is, it were desirable there were no fightings among Christians at all, and in so far as there are, it shewes they are not right Christians. And *James* tells us, that *all fighting proceeds from the lusts,* so that it were fitter for Christians by the sword of God's Spirit to fight against their lusts, than by the prevalency of their lusts to destroy one another. Whatever honor any might have attained of old, under the *Law*, this way, we find under the *Gospel*, Christians commended for *suffering*, not for *fighting*, neither did any of Christ's Disciples, save one, offer outward violence by the sword, in cutting-off *Malchus's* ear, for which he received no title of honor, but a just reproof. Finally, if we look either to the *nature* of this *honor*, the *cause* of it, the *way* it's conveyed, the *termes* in which it is delivered, it can not be used by such as mind to be *Christians* in good earnest,

§. I V. Now besides these general *titles* of honor, what gross abuses are crept-in among fuch, as are called *Chriſtians*, in the uſe of *Comple-ments*, wherein, not ſervants to maſters, or others, with reſpect to any ſuch kind of relations, do ſay and write to one another, at every turn, *Your humble ſervant*, *Your moſt obedient ſervant*, &c. Such wicked cuſtoms have, to the great prejudice of Soules, accuſtomed Chriſtians to lye, and to uſe lying is now come to be accounted civility. O horrid apoſta-ſy! For it is notoriouſly known that the uſe of theſe *complements* imports not any deſign of ſervice, neither are any ſuch fools as to think ſo, for, if we ſhould put them to it, that ſay ſo, they would not doubt to think we abuſed them, and would let us know they gave us words in courſe, and no more. It is ſtrange, that ſuch, as pretend to Scriptur as their Rule, ſhould not be aſhamed to uſe ſuch things: ſince Elihu, that had not the Scri-pturs, would, by the *Light* within him, which theſe men think inſuffici-ent, ſay, Job 32: 21, 22. *Let me not accept any mans perſon, neither let me give flattering titles unto man. For I know not to give flattering titles*, in ſo do-ing *my Maker would ſoon take me away.*   * A certain antient devot man in the primitive time ſubſcribed himſelf, to a Biſhop, *your humble ſervant*, wherein, I doubt not, but he was more real, than our uſual *comple-menters*; and yet he was ſharply reproved for it.

But they uſually object, to defend themſelves, *that Luke ſaith, Moſt excellent Theophilus, and Paul, Moſt Noble Feſtus.*

I anſwer, ſince Luke wrot that, by the dictats of the *infallible Spirit* of God, I think it will not be doubted, but Theophilus did deſerve it, as being really endued with that vertue, in which caſe we ſhall not condemn thoſe, that do it by the ſame Rule. But it is not proved, that Luke gave Theophilus this title, as that, which was inherent to him, either by his father, or by any patent Theophilus had obtained from any of the Princes of the Earth, or that he would have given it him, in caſe he had not been truely *excellent*, and without this be proved, which never can, there can nothing hence be deduced againſt us. The like may be ſaid of that of Paul to Feſtus, whom he would not have called ſuch, if he had not been truely *noble*; as indeed he was, in that he ſuffered him to be heard
in

*This hi-ſtory is reported by *Caſau-bonus*, in his book of *man-ners* and *cuſtoms*, pag. 169. In this laſt age he is eſteemed an uncivil man, who will not, either to his infe-rior, or equal, ſubſcribe himſelf ſervant.

But Sulpitius Severus was heretofore ſharply reproved by Paulinus Biſhop of Nola, becauſe, in his epiſtle, he had ſubſcribed himſelf his *ſervant*, ſaying, *Beware thou ſub-ſcribe not thy ſelf his ſervant, who is thy brother, for flattery is ſinfull, not a teſtimony of humility, to give their honors to men, which are only due to the One Lord, Maſter, and GOD.*

in his own cauſe, and would not give way to the fury of the Jewes againſt him, it was not becauſe of any outward title beſtowed upon *Feſtus*, that he ſo called him, elſe he would have given the ſame compellation to his predeceſſor *Felix*, who had the ſame office, but being a covetous man we find he gives him no ſuch ſtyle.

§ V. It will not be unfit in this place, to ſay ſomething concerning the uſing of the *ſingular number* to *one perſon*; of this there is no controverſy in the *Latine*, for, when we ſpeak to one, we always uſe the Pronoun [T U,] and he, that would do otherwiſe, would break the rules of Grammar. For what boy, learning his rudiments, is ignorant, that it is incongruous, to ſay, [*vos amas*, *vos legis*,] that is [*you lov'ſt*, *you readſt*,] ſpeaking to *one*? But the pride of man, that hath corrupted many things, refuſes alſo to uſe this *ſimplicity* of ſpeaking in the vulgar languages. For, being puff'd up with a vain opinion of themſelves, as if the *ſingular number* were not ſufficient to them, they will have others to ſpeak to them in the *plural*. Hence *Luther*, in his plays, reproves and mocks this manner of ſpeaking, ſaying, *Magiſter vos eſ iratus*. Which corruption *Eraſmus* ſufficiently refutes in his Colloquys. Concerning which likewiſe *James Howel*, in his epiſtle to the Nobility of *England*, before the French and Engliſh Dictionary, takes notice, *that both in France and in other Nations the word* [THOU] *was uſed in ſpeaking to one, but, by ſucceſs of time, when the Roman common-wealth grew into an Empire, the Courtiers began to magnify the Emperor, (as being furniſhed with power to confer dignitys and offices) uſing the word* [You,] *yea and deifying him with more remarkable titles; concerning which matter we read in the Epiſtles of* Symmachus *to the Emperors* Theodoſius *and* Valentinianus, *where he uſeth theſe forms of ſpeaking* Veſtra æternitas, *Your eternity,* Veſtrum numen, *Your Godhead,* Veſtra ſerenitas, *Your ſerenity,* Veſtra clementia, *Your clemency. So that the word* [You,] *in the plural number, together with the other titles and compellations of honor, ſeem to have taken their riſe from Monarchical government, which afterwards by degrees came to be derived to privat perſons.*

The ſame is witneſſed by *John Mareſius*, of the French Academy, in the preface of his Clovis. *Let none wonder* (ſaith he) *that the word* [Thou] *is uſed in this work to Princes and Princeſſes. For we uſe the ſame to God: and of old the ſame was uſed to* Alexanders, Ceſars, Queens, *and* Empereſſes. *The uſe of the word* [You,] *when one perſon is ſpoken to, was onely introduced by theſe baſe flatterys of men of latter ages, to whom it ſeemed good to uſe the plural number to one person, that he may imagine himself alone to be equal to many others in dignity and worth, from whence at last it came to persons of lower quality.*

To the same purpose speaketh also M. *Godeau,* in his preface to the New Testament translation. *I had rather (saith he) faithfully keep to the express words of Paul, than exactly follow the polished style of our tongue. Therefore I always use that form of calling God in the singular number, not in the plural, and therefore I say rather [Thou,] than [You]. I confess indeed, that the civility and custom of this world requires him to be honoured after that manner, but it is likewise, on the contrary, true, that the original tongue of the New Testament hath nothing common with such manners and civility, so that not one of these many old versions we have, doth observe it. Let not men believe, that we give not respect enough to God, in that we call him by the word [Thou;] which is nevertheless far otherwise, for I seem to my self (may be by the effect of custom) more to honour his Divine Majesty, in calling him after this manner, than if I should call him after the manners of men, who are so delicat in their forms of speech.*

See how clearly and evidently these men witness, that this form of speaking, and these profane titles derive their origin from the base flattery of these last ages, and from the delicat haughtyness of *wordly men,* who have invented these *noveltys,* that thereby they might honor one another under, I know not what, pretence of *civility* and *respect.* From whence many of the present Christians, so accounted, are become so perverse, in commending most wicked men, and wicked customs, that the *simplicity* of the *Gospel* is wholly lost, so that the giving of men and things their own names is not onely worn out of custom, but the doing thereof is accounted absurd and rude, by such kind of *delicat parasits,* who desire to ascribe to this flattery and abuse the name of *civility.* Moreover, that this way of speaking proceeds from a high and proud mind, hence appears, because that men usually use the *singular number* to *beggars,* and to their *servants,* yea and in their *prayers* to *God.* Thus the *superior* will speak to his *inferior,* who yet will not bear that the *inferior* so speak to him, as judging it a kind of reproach unto him. So hath the *pride of men* placed *God* and the *beggar* in the same *category* I think I need not use arguments to prove to such, as know congruous language, that we ought to use the *singular number,* speaking to *one;* which is the common dialect of the whole Scriptur, as also the most interpreters do translate it. Seing there-

therefore it is manifeſt to us, that this form of ſpeaking to men, in the
pural number, doth proceed from pride, as wel as that it is, in it ſelf, a
lye, we found a neceſſity upon us, to teſtify againſt this corruption, by
uſing the *ſingular* equally unto *all*.   And albeit no reaſon can be given,
why we ſhould be perſecuted upon this account, eſpecially by Chriſtians,
who profeſs to follow the rule of Scriptur, whoſe dialect this is, yet it
would perhaps ſeem incredible, if I ſhould relate how much we have
ſuffered for this thing, and how theſe proud ones fume, fret, and gnaſh
their teeth, frequently beating and ſtriking us, when we ſpeak to them
thus in the *ſingular number* : whereby we are the more confirmed in our
judgment, as ſeing that this teſtimony of Truth, which God hath given
us to bear, in all things, doth ſo vex the ſerpentin nature in the *children of
darkneſs*.

§ V I. Secondly Next unto this of *titles* the other part of *honor*, uſed
among Chriſtians, is the *kneeling*, *bowing*, and *uncovering of the head* to
one another. I know nothing our adverſarys have to plead for them in
this matter, ſave ſome few inſtances of the *old Teſtament*, and the *cuſtom*
of the *countrey*.

The firſt are ſuch as *Abraham's bowing himſelf to the children of Heth*, and
Lot to the two Angels, &c

But the practice of theſe patriarchs, related as matter of fact, are not
to be a rule to Chriſtians now : neither are we to imitat them in every
practice, which has not a particular reproof added to it, for we find not
Abraham reproved for taking *Hagar*, &c. and indeed to ſay, all things
were lawfull for us, which they practiſed, would produce inconveniencys obvious enough to all. And as to the *cuſtoms of the Nations*, it's a very
ill argument for a Chriſtians's practice. We ſhould have a better rule to
to walk by, than the *cuſtom* of the *Gentiles*, the Apoſtles deſire us not to be
conformed *to this world*, &c. We ſee how little they have to ſay for themſelves in this matter. Let it be obſerved then, whether our reaſons for
laying aſide theſe things be not conſiderable, and weighty enough to uphold us, in ſo doing.

Firſt, We ſay, *that God, who is the Creator of man, and he, to whom
he oweth the dedication both of Soul and body, is over all to be worſhipped and
adored, and that not onely by the Spirit, but alſo with the proſtration of body.*
Now *kneeling*, *bowing*, and *uncovering of the head* is the alone outward ſignification of our *adoration* towards God, & *therefore it is not lawfull to give it*

Rom. 12:
ver. 2.

unto man. He that kneeleth or proftrats himfelf to man, what doth he more to God? He that boweth and *uncovereth his head* to the *creatur*, what hath he referved to the *Creator*? Now the Apoftle fhewes us that the *uncovering of the head* is that, which God requires of us in our worfhipping of him, 1 Cor. 11. But if we make our addref to men in the fame manner, where lieth the difference? Not in the outward *fignification*, but meerly in the *intention*, which opens a door for the *Popifh veneration* of *images*, which hereby is neceffarily excluded.

Secondly, *Men, being alike by creation*, (though their being ftated under their feveral relations requires from them mutual fervices, according to thofe refpective relations) *ow not worfhip to one another, but all equally are to return it to God: becaufe it is to him and his Name alone, that every knee muft bow, and before whofe Throne the four and twenty elders proftrat themfelves.* Therefore for men to take this one from another is to rob God of his Glory: fince all the dutys of relations may be performed one to another, without thefe kind of bowings, which therefore are no effencial part of our duty to man, but to God: all men, by an inward inftinct, in all Nations have been led to proftrat and bow themfelves to God. And it is plain, that this bowing to men took place from a flavifh fear poffeffing fome, which led them to fet up others as Gods, when alfo an ambitious proud fpirit got up *in* thofe others to ufurp the place of God over their brethren.

Thirdly, *We fee that Peter refufed it from Cornelius*, faying, *he was a man.* Are then the *Popes* more, or more excellent, than *Peter*, who fuffer men daily to fall down at their feet, and kifs them? This repoof of Peter to Cornelius doth abundantly fhew, that fuch manners were not to be admitted among Chriftians. Yea we fee, that the Angel twice refufed this kind of *bowing* from John, *Rev.* 19:10. 22:9. for this reafon, *becaufe I am thy fellow fervant, and of thy brethren;* abundantly intimating, that it is *not lawfull* for *fellow-fervants* thus to proftrat themfelves one to another. (and in this refpect all men are fellow-fervants.)

Obj.   If it be faid, *John intended here a religious worfhip, and not a civil.*

Anfw   I anfwer, that is to fay, not to prove: neither can we fuppofe John at that time of the day fo ill inftructed, as not to know it was unlawfull to worfhip Angels; onely it fhould feem, becaufe of thefe great and myfterious things revealed to him by that Angel, he was willing to fignify fome more then ordinary teftimony of refpect, for which he was reprov-

ed.

ed. These things being thus confidered, it is remitted to the judgment of fuch as are defirous to be found Chriftians indeed, whether we be found worthy of blame for waving it to men. Let thofe then, that will blame us, confider whether they might not as wel accufe *Mordecai* of uncivility, who was no lefs fingular, than we, in this matter. And forasmuch as they accufe us herein of rudenefs and pride, though the teftimony of our Confciences, in the fight of God, be a fufficient guard againft fuch calumnys, yet there are of us, known to be men of fuch education, as forbear not thefe things, for want of that they call *good breeding*, and we fhould be very void of reafon to purchafe that pride, at fo dear a rate, as many have done the exercife of their Confcience in this matter, many of *us* having been *forely beaten* & *buffeted*, yea & feveral moneths *imprifoned*, for no other reafon, but becaufe we could not fo fatisfy the *proud unreafonable humors of proud men*, as to *uncover* our *heads*, and *bow* our *bodys*. Nor doth our innocent practice in ftanding ftill, though upright, not puting off our *hats* any more than our *fhoes*, the one being the *covering* of our *heads*, as wel as the other of our *feet*, fhew fo much rudenefs as their beating or knocking us, *&c.* becaufe we can not *bow* to them, contrary to our Confciences. Which certainly fhewes lefs *meeknefs* and *humility* upon their part, than it doth of rudenefs or pride upon ours. Now fuppofe it were our weaknefs, and we really under a miftake in this thing, fince it is not alledged to be the breach of any Chriftian precept, are we not to be indulged, as the Apoftle commanded fhould be done to fuch as fcrupled to eat flefh? And doth not perfecuting us and reviling us upon this account fhew them to be more like unto proud *Haman*, than the Difciples or followers of the *meek felf-denying Jefus*? And this I can fay boldly, in the fight of God, from my own experience, and that of many thoufands more, that however fmall or foolifh this may feem, yet we behoved to chufe death rather than do it, and that for Confcience fake: and that, in its being fo contrary to our natural fpirits, there are many of us, to whom the forfaking of thefe bowings and ceremonys was as death it felf. Which we could never have left, if we could have enjoyed our peace with God in the ufe of them, *though it be far from us to judge all thofe, to whom God hath not fhewn the evil of them, under the like hazard*, yet neverthelefs, we doubt not, but to fuch, as will prove *faithfull Witneffes* to Chrift's *Divine Light in* their *Confciences*, God will alfo fhew the evil of thefe things.

Z z 3.   § VII.

§ VII. The third thing, to be treated of, is the *ranity and superfluity of Apparel*, in which first two things are to be considered, the *condition of the person*, and the *countrey, he lives in*. We shall not say, that all persons are to be cloathed alike, because it will perhaps neither sute their bodys, nor their estates. And if a man be cloathed soberly and without superfluity, though they may be finer, than that, which his servant is cloathed with, we shall not blame him for it: the abstaining from superfluitys, which his condition and education hath accustomed him to, may be, *in* him, a greater act of mortification, than the abstaining from finer cloaths in the servant, who never was accustomed to them. As to the *countrey*, what it naturally produces may be no vanity to the inhabitants to use, or what is commonly imparted to them by way of exchange, seing it is without doubt that the Creation is for the use of man. So where *Silk* abounds, it may be worn, as wel as wool; and were we in those countreys, or near unto them, where gold or silver were as common as iron or brass, the one might be used as wel as the other. The iniquity lies then here, First, when, from a lust of vanity, and desire to adorn themselves, men and women, not content with what their condition can bear, or their countrey easily affords, do stretch to have things, that, from their rarity, and the price, that's put upon them, seem to be pretious, and so feed their lust the more, and this all sober men of all sorts will readily grant to be evil.

Secondly, when men are not content to make a true use of the Creation, whether the things be fine or course, and do not satisfy themselves with what need & conveniency calls for, but add thereunto things meerly superfluous, such as is the use of *ribbands* and *lace*, and much more of that kind of stuff, as *painting the face, plaiting the hair*, which are the fruits of the faln, lustfull and corrupt nature, and not of the new Creation, as all will acknowledge. And though sober men, among all sorts, will say, that it were better these things were not, yet will they not reckon them unlawfull, and therefore do admitt the use of them, among their Church members: But we do account them altogether unlawfull, and unsutable to Christians, and that for these reasons

First, *the use of cloaths came originally from the fall,* if man had not faln, it appears he would not have needed them. But this miserable state made them necessary, in two respects, 1. *to cover his nakedness*, and 2. *to keep him from the cold,* which is both the proper and principal use of them.

Now,

Now, for man to delight himſelf in that, which is the fruit of his iniquity, and is the conſequence of ſin, can be no ways lawfull for him; ſo to extend things beyond their real uſe, or to ſuperadd things wholly ſuperfluous, is a manifeſt abuſe of the Creation, and therefore not lawfull to Chriſtians.

Secondly, thoſe, that will needs ſo adorn themſelves in the uſe of their cloaths, as to beſet them with things having no real uſe nor neceſſity, but meerly for ornament's ſake, do openly declare, that the end of it is either to pleaſe their *luſt*, (for which end theſe things are chiefly invented and contrived) or otherwiſe to gratify a *vain, proud and oſtentive mind*; and it is obvious theſe are their general ends in ſo doing. Yea we ſee, how eaſily men are puft'd up with their garments, and how proud and vain they are, when adorned to their mind. Now, how far theſe things are below a true Chriſtian, and how unſutable, it needs not great probation. Hereby, thoſe, that love to be *gaudy* and *ſuperfluous* in their cloaths, ſhew they concern themſelves little with *mortification* and *ſelf-denial*, and that they mind to beautify their bodys more than their Soules, which proves they mind little upon *mortality*, and ſo certainly are more *nominal* than *real* Chriſtians.

Thirdly, the Scriptur ſeverely reproves ſuch practices, both commending and commanding the contrary, as Iſa. 3. how ſeverely doth the Prophet reprove the daughters of Iſrael for their *tinkling ornaments*, their *cauls*, and their *round tiars*, their *chaines* and *bracelets*, &c. and yet is it not ſtrange to ſee Chriſtians allow themſelves in theſe things, from whom a more ſtrict and exemplary converſation is required? Chriſt deſires us not to be *anxious* about our *cloathing*, Matth. 6 : 25. and, to ſhew the vanity of ſuch as glory in the ſplendor of their cloathing, tells them, *that even Solomon in all his glory was not to be compared to the lily of the field, which to day is, and to morrow is caſt into the oven.* But ſurely they make ſmall reckoning of Chriſt's words and doctrine, that are ſo curious in their cloathing, and ſo induſtrious to deck themſelves, and ſo earneſt to juſtify it, and ſo mad, when they are reproved for it, the Apoſtle *Paul* is very poſitive in this reſpect, 1 Tim. 2 : 8, 9, 10 *I will therefore in like manner alſo, that women adorn themſelves in modeſt apparel, with ſhamefaſtneſs and ſobriety, not with broidered hair, or gold, or pearls, or coſtly aray: But (which becometh women, profeſsing godlineſs) with good works.* To the ſame purpoſe ſaith Peter, 1 Pet. 3 : 3, 4. *Whoſe adorning, let it not be that out-*
ward

ward adorning, *of plaiting the hair, and of wearing of gold, or of putting on of apparel. But let it be the hidden man of the heart, in that, which is not corruptible,* even the ornament *of a meek and quiet spirit,* &c. Here, both the *Apostles* do very positively and expresly assert two things, First, That the adorning of Christian women (of whom it is particularly spoken, I judge, because that sex is most naturally inclined to that vanity, and that it seems that Christian men, in those days, deserved not in this respect so much to be reproved) ought not to be outward, nor to consist in the apparel. Secondly, that they ought not to use *the plaiting of the hair,* or *ornaments,* &c. which was at that time the custom of the Nations. But is it not strange, that such, as make the Scriptur their Rule, and pretend they are guided by it, should not onely be so frequently and ordinarily in the use of these things, which the Scriptur so plainly condemns, but also should allow themselves in so doing? For the Apostles not onely commend the forbearance of these things, as an attainment commendable in Christians, but condemn the use of them as unlawfull, and yet may it not seem more strange, that, in contradiction to the Apostles doctrin, as if they had resolved to slight their testimony, they should condemn those, that, out of Conscience, apply themselves seriously to follow it, as if, in so doing, they were singular, proud, or superstitious? This certainly betokens a sad *apostasy* in those, that will be accounted Christians, that they are so offended with those, that love to follow Christ and his Apostles, in denying of, and departing from, the *lying vanitys* of this *perishing world,* and so doth much evidence their affinity with such, as *hate to be reproved,* and *neither will enter themselves, nor suffer those, that would.*

§ VIII. Fourthly, let us consider the use of *games, sports, comedys* and other such things, commonly and indifferently used, by all the several forts of Christians, under the notion of *diversisment* and *recreation,* and see whether these things can consist with the *seriousnss, gravity,* and *godly fear,* which the Gospel calls for: Let us but view and look over the notions of them, that call themselves Christians, whether Popish or Protestant, and see, if generally there be any difference, save in meer name and profession, from the Heathen; doth not the same *folly,* the same *vanity,* the same *abuse* of *pretious* and *irrevocable time* abound? The same *gaming, sporting, playing,* and, from thence, *quarrelling, fighting, swearing, ranting, revelling?* Now, how can these things be remedied, so long as the *Preachers* and *Professors,* and those who are the leaders of
the

the people, do allow thefe things, and account them not inconfiftent with the profeffion of Chriftianity? And it is ftrange to fee that thefe things are tolerated every where, the inquifition lays no hold on them, neither at *Rome*, nor in *Spain*, where, in their *mafcarads* all manner of ob-fcenity, *folly*, yea and *atheifm* is generally praƈtifed, in the face of the world, to the great fcandal of the *Chriftian* name: but if any man reprove them in thefe things, and forfake their fuperftitions, and come ferioufly to *ferve God*, and *worfhip him in* the *Spirit*, he is made a prey, and pre-fently made liable to cruel fufferings. Doth this bear any proportion to Chriftianity? Do thefe things look any thing like the Churches of the primitive Chriftians? Surely not at all. I fhall firft cite fome few Scriptur teftimonys, being very pofitive precepts to Chriftians, and then fee whether fuch, as obey them, can admitt of thefe forementioned things. The Apoftle commands us, that, *whether we eat, or drink, or whatever we do, we do it all to the glory of God.* But I judge none will be fo impudent, as to affirm, that, in the ufe of thefe *fports* and *games*, God is glorified. If any fhould fo fay, they would declare they neither knew God nor his Glory: and experience abundantly proves, that, in the praƈtice of thefe things, men mind nothing lefs, than the glory of God, and nothing more than the fatisfaƈtion of their own *carnal lufts, wills* and *appetits.* The Apoftle defires us, 1 Cor. 7: 29, 31. *becaufe the time is fhort, that they, that buy, fhould be, as though they poffeffed not. And they, that ufe this world, as not abufing it,* &c. But how can they be found in the obedience of this precept, that plead for the ufe of thefe *games* and *fports?* who, it feems, think the time fo long, that they can not find oc-cafion enough to employ it, neither in taking care for their Soules, nor yet in the neceffary care for their bodys, but invent thefe games and fports, to pafs it away, as if they wanted other work to ferve God, or be ufefull to the Creation in. The Apoftle Peter defires us to *pafs the time of our fojourning here in fear*, 1 Pet. 1: 17. But will any fay, that fuch, as ufe *danceing* and *comedys, carding*, and *dicing*, do fo much as mind this precept in the ufe of thefe things? where there is nothing to be feen, but *lightnefs* and *vanity, wantonnefs* and *obfcenity*, contrived, to hinder men from *fear*, or being *ferious*, and therefore no doubt calculat for the fervice of the devil. There is no duty more frequently commanded, nor more incumbent upon Chriftians, than *the fear of the Lord*, to *ftand in aw before him*, to *walk* as *in his prefence*, but if fuch, as ufe thefe games

A a a

and

and sports, will speak from their Consciences, they can, I doubt not, experimentally declare, that this fear is forgotten in their gaming: and if God, by his *Light* secretly touch them, or mind them of the *vanity* of their way, they strive to shut it out, and use their gaming, as an engine to put away from them that troublsom guft, and thus *make merry over the Just One, whom they have flain and crucified in themfelves.* But further, if Chrift's reafoning be to be heeded, who faith, Matth. 12: 35, 36. that *the good man out of the good treafur of the heart, bringeth forth good things: and an evil man out of the evil treafur, bringeth forth evil things:* And that *of every idle word* we *fhall give an account in the day of Judgment*, it may be eafily gathered from what *treafur* thefe *inventions* come, and it may be eafily proved, that it is from the *evil*, and not the *good.* How many *idle words* do they neceffarily produce? Yea what are *comedys* but a *ftudyed complex of idle* and *lying words?* Let men, that believe their *Soules* are *immortal,* and that there will be a day of judgment, in which thefe words of Chrift will be accomplifhed, anfwer me, how all thefe will make account in that great and terrible day, of all thefe *idle words,* that are neceffarily made ufe of, about danceing, gaming, carding, and comedys acting? And yet how is it that, by Chriftians not condemning thefe things, but allowing of them, many, that are accounted Chriftians, take up their whole time in them, yea make in their trade and employment, fuch as the *dancing-mafters* and *comedians,* &c. whofe hellifh converfations do fufficiently declare what mafter they ferve, and to what end thefe things contribute, and it can not be denyed, as being obvioufly manifeft by experience, that fuch as are mafters of thefe trades, and are moft delighted in them, (if they be not open atheifts and profligats) are fuch, at beft, as make Religion, or the care of their Soules, their leaft bufinefs. Now, if thefe things were difcountenanced by *Chriftians,* or inconfiftent with their profeffion, it would remove thefe things; for thefe *wretches* would be neceffitated then to betake themfelves to fome more honeft livelyhood, if they were not fed and upholden by thefe. And, as hereby a great fcandal and ftumbling-block would be removed from off the Chriftian Name, fo alfo would that, in part, be taken out of the way, which provokes the Lord to withhold his bleffing, and by occafion of which things the *minds* of many remain *chained* in *darknefs,* and drowned in *luft, fenfuality,* and *worldly pleafurs,* without any fenfe of God's fear, or their own Soules Salvation. Many of thofe, called *Fathers*

of

of the Church, and other ferious perfons, have fignified their regrete for thefe things, and their defires they might be remedied, of whom many citations might be alledged, which for brevity's fake I have omitted.

§ IX. But they object, *that mens fpirits could not fubfift, if they were* Obj. *always intent upon ferious and fpiritual matters, and that therefore there is need of fome divertifement to recreat the mind a little, whereby it, being refreſhed, is able, with greater vigor, to apply it felf to thefe things.*

I anfwer, though all this were granted, it would no ways militat againft Anfw. us, neither plead the ufe of thefe things, which we would have wholly laid afide. For that men fhould be always in the fame intentivenefs of mind we do not plead, knowing how impoffible it is, fo long as we are cloathed with this tabernacle of clay. But this will not allow us at any time fo to reced from the memory of God and of our Soules chief concern, as not ftill to retain a certain fenfe of his fear, which can not be fo much as rationally fuppofed to be in the ufe of thefe things, which we condemn. Now the neceffary occafions, which all are involved into, in order to the care and fuftentation of the outward man, are a relaxation of the mind from the more ferious dutys ; and thofe are performed in the bleffing, as the mind is fo leavened with the love of God and fenfe of his prefence, that, even in doing thefe things, the Soul carryeth with it that *Divine influence* and *Spiritual habit*, whereby, though thefe acts, as of *eating*, *drinking*, *fleeping*, *working*, be, upon the matter, one with what the wicked do, yet they are done in another fpirit, and, in doing of them, we pleafe the Lord, ferve him, and anfwer our end in the Creation, and fo feel, and are fenfible of his bleffing. Whereas the wicked and profane, being not come to this place, are, in whatfoever they do, curfed, and their *ploughing*, as wel as *praying*, *is fin!* Now, if any will *plead*, that, for relaxation of mind, there may be a liberty allowed beyond thefe things, which are of abfolute need to the fuftenanance of the outward man ; I fhall not much *contend* againft it, provided thefe things be not fuch as are wholly fuperfluous, or in their proper nature and tendency lead the mind into *luft*, *vanity*, and *wantonnefs*, as being chiefly contrived and framed for that end, or generally experienced to produce thefe effects, or being the common engines of fuch as are fo minded to feed one another therein, and to propagat their wickednefs, to the impoyfoning of others ; feing there are other innocent

A a a 2

di-

divertifements, which may fufficiently ferve for relaxation to the mind, fuch as for *friends to vifit one another*, *to hear or read hiftory*, *to fpeak foberly of the prefent or paft tranfactions*, *to follow after gardnering*, *to ufe Geometrical and Mathematical experiments*, and fuch other things of this nature: in all which things we are not fo to forget God, (*in whom we both live and are moved*, Act. 10: 26.) as not to have always fome fecret referve to him, and fenfe of his fear and prefence, which alfo frequently exerts it felf in the midft of thefe things, by fome fhort afpiration and breathings, and that this may neither feem ftrange nor troublefome, I fhall clear it by one manifeft inftance, anfwerable to the experience of all men, it will not be denyed, but that men ought to be more in the love of God, than of any other thing, for we ought to *love God above all things*. Now, it is plain, that men, that are taken with love, whether it be of a woman, or any other thing, if it hath taken deep place *in* the heart, and poffefs the mind, it will be hard for the man, fo in love, to drive out of his mind the perfon or thing fo loved, yea in his eating, drinking and fleeping his mind will always have a tendency that way, and, in bufinefs or recreation, however intent he be in it, there will but a very fhort time be permitted to pafs, but the mind will let fome ejaculation forth towards its beloved. And, albeit fuch a one muft be converfant in thofe things, that the care of this body, and fuch like things call for, yet will he avoid, as death it felf, to do thofe things, that may offend the party fo beloved, or crofs his defign in obtaining the thing fo earneftly defired, though there may be fome fmall ufe in them, the great defign, which is chiefly in his eye, will fo ballance him, that he will eafily look over & difpenfe with fuch petty neceffitys, rather than endanger the lofs of the greater, by them. Now that men ought to be thus *in love* with *God* and the *life to come*, none will deny, and the thing is apparent from thefe Scripturs, Matth. 6: 20. *But lay up for your felves treafures in heaven*, Col. 3: 2. *Set your affection on things above*, &c. And that this hath been the experience and attainment of fome, the Scriptur alfo declares, Pfal. 63: 1. 84: 2. Cor. 5: 14.

And again, that thefe *games, fports, plays, dancing, comedys*, &c. do naturally tend to draw men from God's fear, to make them forget heaven, death and judgment, to fofter *luft, vanity*, and *wantonnefs*, and therefore are moft loved as wel as ufed by fuch kind of perfons, experience abundantly fhewes, and the moft ferious and Confcientious among all will fcarcely deny, wich if it be fo, the application is eafy.

§ X.

§ X. Fifthly, the use of *Swearing* is to be considered, which is so frequently practised almost among all Christians, not onely profane *oaths* among the profane, in their common discourses, whereby the *most HOLY NAME of GOD* is, in a horrible manner, daily blasphemed, but also *solemn oaths* with those, that have some shew of piety, whereof the most part do defend *swearing* before the Magistrate, with so great zeal, that not onely they are ready themselves to do it upon every occasion, but also stirr up the Magistrates to persecut those, who, out of obedience to Christ, their Lord and Master, judge it unlawfull to swear: upon which account not a few have suffered imprisonment, and the spoiling of their goods.

But considering these clear words of our Saviour, Matth 5: 33, 34. *Again, ye have heard that it hath been said by them of old time, Thou shalt not forswear thy self, but shalt perform unto the Lord thine oaths. But I say unto you, SWEAR NOT AT ALL, neither by heaven, &c. But let your communication be Yea, Yea: Nay, Nay: for whatsoever is more than these, cometh of evil.* As also the words of the Apostle *James* 5 : 12. *But above all things, my brethren, Swear not, neither by heaven, neither by the earth, neither by any other oath: but let your Yea be Yea, and your Nay, Nay: lest ye fall into condemnation.* I say, considering these clear words, it is admirable, how any one, that professeth the Name of Christ, can pronounce any *oath* with a quiet Conscience; far less to persecut other Christians, that dare not swear, because of their Master Christ his Authority. For did any one purpose seriously, and in the most rigid manner, to forbid any thing, comprehended under any general, can they use a more full and general prohibition, and that without any exception? I think not. For Christ, First, proposeth it to us negatively, *Swear not at all, neither by Heaven, nor by the earth, nor by Jerusalem, nor by thy head,* &c. And again, *Swear not by heaven, nor by earth, nor by* any other *oath.* Secondly, he presseth it affirmatively, *But let your communication be Yea, Yea: and Nay, Nay: for whatsoever is more than these cometh of evil.* And saith James, *lest ye fall into condemnation.*

Which words both all and every one of them do make such a full prohibition, and so free of all exception, that it is strange, how men, that boast the *Scriptur* is the *Rule* of their *faith* and *life*, can counterfeit any exception. Certainly Reason ought to teach every one, that it is not lawfull to make void a general prohibition, coming from God, by such opposition, unless the exception be as clearly and evidently expressed as the

pro--

prohibition; neither is it enough, to endeavour to confirm it by confequences and probabilitys, which are obfcure and uncertain, and not fufficient to bring quiet to the Confcience. For, if they fay, that there is therefore an exception and limitation in the words, becaufe there are found exceptions in the other general prohibition of this fifth chapter, as in the forbidding of *divorçment,* where Chrift faith, *It hath been faid, Whofoever fhall put away his wife, let him give her a writing of divorçment. But I fay unto you, That whofoever fhall put away his wife, faving for the caufe of fornication, caufeth her to committ adultery;* If, I fay, they fay this, they not onely labour in vain, but alfo fight againft themfelves, becaufe they can produçe no exçeption of this general command of *not fwearing,* expreffed by God to any under the New Covenant, after Chrift gave this prohibition, fo clear, as that, which is made in the prohibition it felf: moreover, if Chrift would have exçepted *oaths,* made before *Magiftrates,* certainly he had then expreffed, adding, *exçept in judgment, before the Magiftrate,* or the like; as he did in that of divorçment, by thefe words, *faving for the caufe of fornication:* which being fo, it is not lawfull for us to except or diftinguifh, or, (which is all one) make void this general prohibition of Chrift; it would be far lefs agreable to Chriftian holynefs, to bring upon our heads the crimes of fo many *oaths,* which, by reafon of this corruption and exception, are fo frequent among Chriftians.

Neither is it to be omitted, that, without doubt, the moft learned Doctors of each Sect know, that thefe forementioned words were underftood, by the antient Fathers of the firft three hundred years after Chrift, to be a prohibition of all forts of *oaths:* it is not then without reafon, that we wonder, that the Popifh Doctors and Priefts bind themfelves by an *oath,* to interpret the Holy Scripturs according to the univerfal expofition of the holy Fathers, who notwithftanding underftood thofe controverted texts quite contrary to what thefe modern Doctors do: and from thence alfo doth clearly appear the vanity and foolifh certainty (fo to fpeak) of Popifh traditions; for, if by the writings of the *Fathers,* fo called, the faith of the Church of thefe ages may be demonftrated, it is clear, they have departed from the faith of the Church of the firft three ages in the poynt of *fwearing.* Moreover, becaufe not onely Papifts, but alfo Lutherans and Calvinifts, and fome others, do reftrict the words of *Chrift* and *James,* I think it needfull to make manifeft the vain foundation, upon which their prefumption in this matter is built.

§ XI.

§ XI. Firſt they objeſt, *that Chriſt onely forbids theſe oaths, that are made* Obj. *by creaturs, and things created*; and they prove it thence, becauſe he numbers ſome of theſe things.

Secondly, *All raſh and vain oaths in familiar diſcourſes; becauſe he ſaith, Let your communication be Yea, Yea, and Nay, Nay.*

To which I anſwer, Firſt, that the *Law* did forbid all oaths made by Anſw. 1. the creaturs, as alſo all vain and raſh oaths in our common diſcourſes, commanding, that men ſhould onely ſwear by the Name of God, and that neither falſly, nor raſhly, for that is to take his Name in vain.

Secondly, it is moſt evident, that Chriſt forbids ſomewhat, that was Anſw. 2. permitted under the Law, to wit, to ſwear by the Name of God, becauſe it was not lawfull for any man to ſwear but by God himſelf, and becauſe he ſaith, *neither by heaven, becauſe it is the throne of God*, therefore he excludes all other oaths, even thoſe, which are made by God ; for he ſaith, chap. 23 : ver. 22. *he, that ſhall ſwear by heaven, ſweareth by the throne of God, and by him, that ſitteth thereon* : which is alſo to be underſtood of the reſt.

Laſtly, that he might put the matter beyond all controverſy, he adds, Anſw. 3. *neither by any other oath* : Therefore, ſeing to ſwear, before the Magiſtrate, by God, is an oath, it is here without doubt forbidden.

Secondly, they objeſt, *that by theſe words oaths by God's Name can not be* Obj. *forbidden, becauſe the heavenly Father hath commanded them, for the Father and the Son are One, which could not be, if the Son did forbid that, which the Father commanded.*

I anſwer, They are indeed One, and can not contradiſt one another ; Anſw. neverthelefs the Father gave many things to the Jewes, for a time, becauſe of their infirmity under the old Covenant, which had onely a ſhaddow of good things to come, not the very Subſtance of things, untill Chriſt ſhould come, who was the Subſtance, and by whoſe coming all theſe things evaniſhed, to wit, Sabbaths, Circumciſior, the Paſchal Lamb, men uſed then ſacrifices, who lived in controverſy with God, & one with other, which all are abrogated in the coming of the Son, who is the Subſtance, Eternal Word, and eſſential oath and Amen, in whom *the promiſes of God are Yea and Amen* : who came, that men might be redeemed out of ſtrife, and might make an end of controverſy.

Thirdly, they objeſt, *But all oaths are not ceremonys, nor any part of the* Obj. *ceremonial Law.*

I anſwer, Except it be ſhewn to be an eternal, immutable, and moral Anſw.

pre-

precept, it withſtands not; neither are they of ſo old an origin as tithes and the offering of the firſt fruits of the ground, which by *Abel* and *Cain* were offered, long before the ceremonial Law, or the uſe of oaths, which, whatever may be alledged againſt it, were no doubt ceremonys, and therefore no doubt unlawfull now to be practiſed.

Obj. Fourthly, they object, *that to ſwear by the Name of God is a moral precept of continual duration; becauſe it is marked with his eſſential and moral worſhip,* Deut. 6: 13. and 10: 20. *Thou ſhalt fear the Lord thy God, and ſerve him alone: thou ſhalt cleave to him, and ſwear by his Name.*

Anſw. I anſwer, this proves not, that it is a moral and eternal precept; for *Moſes* adds that to all the precepts and ceremonys in ſeveral places: as Deut. 10:12,13. ſaying, *And now, Iſrael, what doth the Lord thy God require of thee, but to fear the Lord thy God, to walk in all his ways, and to love him, and to ſerve the Lord thy God with all thy heart, and with all thy Soul. To keep the commandments of the Lord, and his ſtatutes, which I command thee this day?* And chap. 14: ver. 23. the fear of the Lord is mentioned together with the tithes. And ſo alſo Lev. 19: 2, 3, 6. the Sabbaths and regard to parents are mentioned with ſwearing.

Obj. Fifthly, they object, *that ſolemn oaths, which God commanded, can not be here forbidden by Chriſt, for he ſaith, that they come from evil: But theſe did not come from evil, for God never commanded any thing, that was evil, or came from evil.*

Anſw. I anſwer, there are things, which are *good, becauſe commanded,* and *evil, becauſe forbidden* : other things are *command, becauſe good,* and *forbidden, becauſe evil.* As *Circumciſion* and *oaths,* which were *good,* when and becauſe they were commanded, and in no other reſpect; and again, when and becauſe prohibited under the Goſpel, they are *evil.*

And in all theſe Jewiſh conſtitutions, however ceremonial, there was ſomething of good, to wit, in their ſeaſon, as prefiguring ſome good: as by Circumciſion, the purifications, and other things, the holyneſs of God was typified, and that the Iſraelits ought to be *holy, as their God was holy.* In the like manner *oaths* under the *ſhaddows* and *ceremonys* ſignified the *verity* of God, his faithfulneſs and certainty, and therefore that we ought in all things to ſpeak and witneſs the Truth. But the *Witneſs of Truth* was before all oaths, and remaines, when all oaths are aboliſhed; and this is the morality of all oaths, and ſo long as men abide therein, there is no

neceſſi-

neceffity of, nor place for, oaths, as *Polybius* witneffed, who faid, *The use of oaths in judgment were rare among the Antients, but by the growing of perfidiousnefs so grew also the use of oaths.* To which agreeth *Gratious,* faying, *An Oath is onely to be used, as a medicin, in cafe of neceffity: a solemn oath is not used but to supply defect. The lightnefs of men and their inconstancy begot diffidence, for which swearing was sought out as a remedy.* Bafil the Great faith, *that swearing is the effect of fin.* And Ambrofe, that *Oaths are onely a condefcendency for defect.* Chryfoftom faith, *that an oath entred, when evil grew, when men exercifed their frauds, when all foundations were overturned: that oaths took their beginning from the want of Truth.* Thefe and the like are witneffed by many others with the forementioned authors. But what need of teftimonys, where the evidence of things fpeaks it felf? For who will force another to fwear, of whom he is certainly perfwaded, that he abhorrs to lye in his words? And again, as Chryfoftom and others fay, *For what end wilt thou force him to swear, whom thou believst not that he will speak the Truth.*

§ XII. That then, which was not from the beginning, which was of no ufe in the beginning, which had not its beginning firft from the will of God, but from the work of the devil, occafioned from evil, to wit, from *unfaithfulnefs, lying, deceit*; and which was at firft onely invented by man as a mutual remedy of this evil, in which they called upon the names of their idols; yea that, which (as *Hierom, Chryfoftom*, and others teftify) was given to the Ifraelits by God, as unto children, that they might abftain from the *idolatrous oaths* of the Heathens, Jer. 12: 16. whatfoever is fo, is far from being a moral and eternal precept; and laftly, whatfoever by its profanation an abufe is polluted with fin, fuch as are abundantly the oaths of thefe times, by fo often fwearing, and forfwearing, far differs from any neceffary and perpetual duty of a Chriftian: But oaths are fo: Therefore, *&c.*

Sixthly, they object, that *God fwore, Therefore to swear is good.*

I anfwer with Athanafius, *Seing it is certain, it is proper in swearing to swear by another, thence it appears, that God, to speak properly, did never swear, but onely improperly: whence speaking to men he is said to swear; becaufe thefe things, which he speaks, becaufe of the certainty and immutability of his will, are to be efteemed for oaths.* Compare Pfal. 110: 4. where it is faid, *The Lord did swear, and it did not repent him,* &c. And *I swore* (faith he) *by my felf: and this is not an oath, for he did not swear by another,*

B b b   *which*

which is the property of an oath, but by himself. Therefore God swears not according to the manner of men, neither can we be induced from thence to swear, but let us so do and say, and shew our selves such by speaking and acting, that we need not with our hearers an oath, and let our words of themselves have the testimony of Truth: for so we shall plainly imitat God.

Obj.   Seventhly, they object: *Christ did swear, and we ought to imitat him.*

Answ.   I answer, that Christ did not swear; and albeit he had sworn, being yet under the Law, this would no ways oblige us under the Gospel, as neither Circumcision, or the celebration of the Paschal Lamb. Concerning which *Hierom* saith, *All things agree not to us, who are servants, that agreed to our Lord, &c. The Lord swore, as Lord, whom no man did forbid to swear: but unto us, that are servants, it is not lawfull to swear, because we are forbidden by the Law of our Lord. Yet, lest we should not suffer scandal by his example, he hath not sworn, since he commanded us not to swear.*

Hier. lib.
Ep. part.
3. tract. 1
Ep. 2.

Obj.   Eighthly, they object, *that Paul swore, and that often,* Rom. 1:9. Phil. 1: 8. saying, *For God is my witness.* 2 Cor. 11: 10. *As the Truth of Christ is in me.* 2 Cor. 1: 23. *I call God for a record upon my Soul. I speak the Truth in Christ, I lye not.* Rom. 9:1. *behold, before God, I lye not,* Gal. 1: 20. *And so requires oaths of others. I obtest you,* saith he, *before God and our Lord Jesus Christ,* 1 Thess. 5: 27. *I charge you by the Lord, that this Epistle be read to all the brethren. But Paul would not have done so, if all manner of oaths had been forbidden by Christ, whose Apostle he was.*

Answ.   To all which I answer, First, that the using of such forms of speaking are neither oaths, nor so esteemed by our adversarys: for, when, upon occasion, in matters of great moment we have said, *We speak the Truth in the fear of God, and before him, who is our Witness, and the searcher of our hearts,* adding such kind of serious attestations, which we never refused in matters of consequence, nevertheless an oath hath moreover been required of us, with the ceremony of putting our hand upon the book, the kissing of it, the lifting up of the hand or fingers, together with this common form of imprecation, *So help me God,* or *So truely let the Lord God Almighty help me.* Secondly, This contradicts the opinion of our adversarys; because that Paul was neither before a Magistrate, that was requiring an oath of him; nor did he himself administer the office of a Magistrate, as offering an oath to any other. Thirdly, the question is not, what Paul or Peter did, but what their and our Master taught to be done; and if Paul did swear, (which we believe not) he had sinned against the command of

Christ,

Chrift; even according to their opinion, becaufe he fwore not before a Magiftrate, but in an Epiftle to his Brethren.

Ninthly, they objeét, Ifa. 65: 16. where fpeaking of the Evangeli- Obj.
cal times, he faith, *That he who bleffeth himfelf in the earth fhall blefs himfelf in the God of Truth, and he that fweareth in the earth, fhall fwear by the God of Truth; becaufe the former troubles are forgotten, and becaufe they are hid from mine eyes. For behold, I creat new heavens, and a new earth: Therefore in thefe times we ought to fwear by the Name of the Lord.*

I anfwer, It is ordinary for the Prophets, to exprefs the greateft du- Anfw.
tys of Evangelical times in Mofaical terms, as appears, among others, from Jer. 31: 38, 39, 40. Ezech. 36: 25. and 40. and Ifa. 45: 23. *I have fworn by my felf, that unto me every knee fhall bowe, every tongue fhall fwear.* Where the righteoufnefs of the New Jerufalem, the purity of the Gofpel with its Spiritual worfhip, and the profeffion of the Name of Chrift, are expreffed under forms of fpeaking ufed to old Jerufalem, under the wafh-ings of the Law, under the names of ceremonys, the Temple, fervices, facrifices, oaths, *&c.* Yea that, which the Prophet fpeaks here of fwear-ing, the Apoftle Paul interprets it exprefsly of confeffion, faying, Rom. 14: 11. *For it is written, As I live, faith the Lord, Every knee fhall bowe to me, and every tongue fhall confefs to God.* Which being rightly confidered, none can be ignorant, but thefe words, which the Prophet writes under the Law, when the ceremonial oaths were in ufe, to wit, *Every tongue fhall fwear,* were by the Apoftle being under the Gofpel, when thofe oaths became abolifhed, expreffed by *Every tongue fhall confefs.*

Tenthly, they objeét, *But the Apoftle Paul approves oaths ufed among men, when he writes,* Heb. 6: 16. *For men verily fwear by the Greater, and* Obj.
an oath for confirmation is to them an end of all ftrife. But there are as many con-tefts, fallacys, and diffidences at this time, as there were ever: Therefore the neceffity of oats doth yet remain.

I anfwer, the Apoftle tells indeed in this place, what men at that time did, who lived in controverfys and incredulity, not what they ought Anfw.
to have done, nor what the Saints did, who were redeemed from ftrife and incredulity, and had come to Chrift, the Truth and Amen of God. Moreover, he onely alluds to a certain cuftom ufual among men, that he might exprefs the firmity of the Divine promife, that he might excite in the Saints fo much the more *confidence* in God, promifing to them, not

that he might inſtigat them to ſwear againſt the Law of God, or confirm them in that: no not at all, for neither doth 1 Cor. 9: 24. teach Chriſtians the vain races, whereby men often-times, even to the deſtruction of their bodys, are wearied to obtain a corruptible prize. So neither doth *Chriſt*, who is the *Prince of Peace*, teach his Diſciples to fight, albeit he takes notice, Luke 14: 31. what it behoveth ſuch Kings to do, who are accuſtomed to fight, as prudent warriors therein. Secondly, as to what pertains to conteſts, perfidys, and diffidences among men, which our adverſarys affirm to have grown to ſuch an height, that ſwearing is at preſent as neceſſary, as ever; that we deny not at all, for we ſee, and daily experience teacheth us, that all manner of deceit and malice doth encreaſe among worldly men and falſe Chriſtians, but not among true Chriſtians: but, becauſe men can not truſt one another, and therefore require oaths one of another, it will not therefore follow, that true Chriſtians ought to do ſo, whom Chriſt has brought to true faithfulneſs and honeſty, as wel towards God, as one towards another, and therefore has delivered them from conteſts, perfidys, and conſequently from oaths.

Obj. Eleventhly, they object, *We grant, that, among true Chriſtians, there is not need of oaths, but by what means ſhall we infallibly know them? It will follow then, that oaths are at preſent needfull, and that it is lawfull for Chriſtians to ſwear, to wit, that ſuch may be ſatisfied, who will not acknowledge this and the other man to be a Chriſtian.*

Anſw. I anſwer, It is no ways lawfull for a Chriſtian to ſwear, whom Chriſt hath called to his eſſential Truth, which was before all oaths, forbidding him to ſwear, and, on the contrary, commanding him to ſpeak the Truth in all things, to the honor of Chriſt, who called him; that it may appear, that the words of his Diſciples may be as truely believed, as the oaths of all other worldly men. Neither is it lawfull for them to be unfaithfull in this, that they may pleaſe others, for that they may avoid their hurt: for thus the primitive Chriſtians for ſome ages remained faithfull, who, being required to ſwear, did unanimouſly anſwer, *I am a Chriſtian, I ſwear not.* What ſhall I ſay of the Heathens, ſome of whom arrived to that degree? For *Diodoris Siculus*, relates, lib. 16. that *the giving of the right hand was, among the Perſians, a ſign of ſpeaking the Truth:* and the *Scythians*, as Qu. *Curtius*, relates, ſaid, in their conferences with *Alexander* the Great, *Think not, that the Scythians confirm their friendſhip by ſwearing, they ſwear by*

keepiŋg

keeping their promiſes. Stobæus, in his third ſermon, tells, that Solomon ſaid, *A good man ought to be in that eſtimation, that he need not an oath, becauſe it is to be reputed a leſſening of his honor, if he be forced to ſwear.* Pythagoras, in his oration, among other things, hath this maxime, as that, which concerns the adminiſtration of the Common-wealth : *Let no man call God to witneſs by an oath, no not in judgment; but let every man ſo accuſtom himſelf to ſpeak, that he may become worthy to be truſted even without an oath.* Baſil the Great commends *Clinias* an Heathen, *that he had rather pay three talents, which are about three thouſand pound, than ſwear.* Socrates, as *Stobæus* relates, Serm. 14. had this ſentence, *the duty of good men requires, that they ſhew to the world, that their manners and actions are more firm than oaths :* the ſame was the judgment of *Iſocrates.* Plato alſo ſtood againſt oaths in his judgments *De Leg.* 12. *Quintilianus* takes notice, *that it was of old a kind of infamy, if any was deſired to ſwear; but to require an oath of a noble man, was like an examining him by the hangman.* Marcus Aurelius Antonius, the Emperor of Rome, ſaith in his deſcription of *a good man, Such is his integrity, that he needs not oaths.* So alſo ſome Jewes did witneſs, as *Grotius* relates out of *Maimonides, It is beſt for a man to abſtain from all oaths.* The Eſſeans, as *Philo Judæus* relates, *did eſteem their words more firm than oaths; and oaths were eſteemed among them as needleſs things.* And *Philo* himſelf, ſpeaking of the third commandment, explaines his mind thus, viz, *It were better altogether not to ſwear, but to be accuſtomed always to ſpeak the Truth, that naked words might have the ſtrength of an oath.* And elſewhere he ſaith, *It is more agreable to natural Reaſon, altogether to abſtain from ſwearing;* perſwading, *that whatſoever a good man ſaith, may be equivalent with an oath.*

Who then needs further to doubt, but that, ſince Chriſt would have his Diſciples attain the higheſt pitch of Perfection, he abrogated oaths, as a rudiment of infirmity, and, in place thereof, eſtabliſhed the uſe of Truth ? Who can now any more think, that the holy Martyrs and antient Fathers of the firſt three hundred years, and many others ſince that time have ſo oppoſed themſelves to oaths, that they might onely rebuke vain and raſh oaths by the creaturs, or heathen idols, which were alſo prohibited under the Moſaical Law; and not alſo ſwearing by the True God in truth and righteouſneſs, which was there commanded ? As *Polycarpus,* *Juſtin Martyr* Apolog 2. and many Martyrs, as *Euſebius* relates. Tertullian in his Apolog, cap. 32 ad *Scap.* cap. 1 of Idolatry. c. 11. *Clemens.* *Alexandrinus,* Strom. lib. 7. Origen. in Matth. Tract. 25. Cyprianus, lib. 3.

B b b 3

Athanaſ.

Athanaſ. in paſſ. & cruc. Domini Chriſti. *Hilarius* in Matth. 5. 34. *Baſi-lius Magn.* in Pſal. 14. *Greg. Nyſſenus* in Cant. Orat. 13. *Greg. Nazianzenus* in dialog. contra juramenta. *Epiphanius* adverſus hæreſ. lib. 1. *Ambroſ.* de Virg. lib. 3. Idem in Matth. 5. *Chryſoſtom* in Geneſ. homil. 15. Idem homil. in Act. Apoſt. cap. 3. *Hieronymus* Epiſtol. lib. part. 3. Ep. 2. Idem in Zach. lib. 2. cap. 8. Idem in Matth. lib. 1. cap. 5. *Auguſtinus* de ſerm. Dom. ſerm. 28. *Cyrillus* in Jerem. 4. *Theodoretus* in Deut. 6. *Iſi-dorus Peluſiota* Ep. lib. 1. Epiſt. 155. *Chromatius* in Matth. 5. *Johannes Damaſcenus* l. 3. c. 16. *Caſſiodorus* in Pſal. 94. *Iſidorus Hiſpalenſis* cap. 31. *Antiochus* in Pandect. ſcript. hom. 62. *Beda* in Jac. 5. *Haimo* in Apoc. *Ambroſius Ansbertus* in Apoc. *Theophylactus* in Matth. 5. *Paſcaſius Ratbertus* in Matth. 5. *Otho Brunsfelſius* in Matth. 5. *Druthmarus* in Matth. 5. *Eu-thymius Eugubinus* Bibliotheca vet. patr. in Matth. 5. *OEcumenius* in Jac. c. 5: v. 12. *Anſelmus* in Matth. 5. *Waldenſes, Viclevus, Eraſmus* in Matth. 5. & in Jac. 5.   Who can read theſe places, and doubt longer of their ſenſe in this matter? And who, believing that they were againſt all *oaths*, can bring ſo great an indignity to the Name of Chriſt, as to ſeek to ſub-ject again his followers to ſo great an indignity? Is it not rather time, that all good men labour to remove this abuſe and infamy from Chri-ſtians?

Obj.   Laſtly, they object, *This will bring-in fraud and confuſion, for impoſtors will counterfeit probity, and under the benefit of this diſpenſation will be without fear of puniſhment.*

Anſw.   I anſwer, There are two things onely, which oblige a man to ſpeak the Truth: Firſt, Either the fear of God *in* his heart and love of Truth, for, where this is, there is no need of oaths to ſpeak the Truth. Or Se-condly, the fear of puniſhment from the Judge. Therefore let there be the ſame or rather greater puniſhment appoynted to thoſe, who pretend ſo great truth in words, and ſo great ſimplicity *in* heart, that they can not lye, and ſo great reverence towards the Law of Chriſt, that for Con-ſcience ſake they deny to ſwear in any wiſe, if they fail, and ſo there ſhall be the ſame good order, yea greater ſecurity againſt deceiv-ers, as if oaths were continued, and alſo by that more ſevere puniſh-ment, to which theſe falſe diſſemblers ſhall be liable. Hence wicked men ſhall be more terrified, and good men delivered from all oppreſſion, both in their liberty, and goods: for which cauſe, for their tender Con-ſciences, God hath often a regard to Magiſtrates and their ſtate, as a
thing

thing moſt acceptable to him. But if any can further doubt of this thing, to wit, if without confuſion it can be practiſed in the Common-wealth, let him conſider the ſtate of the united Nether-lands, and he ſhall ſee the good effect of it, for there, becauſe of the great number of merchants, more than in any other place, there is moſt frequent occaſion for this thing, and though the number of thoſe, that are of this mind, be conſiderable, to whom the States theſe hundred years have condeſcended, and yet daily condeſcend, yet neverthleſs there has nothing of prejudice followed thereupon to the Common-wealth, government, or good order, but rather great advantage to trade, and ſo to the Common-wealth.

§ XIII. Sixthly, The laſt thing, to be conſidered, is *revenge* and *warr*, an evil as oppoſit and contrary to the Spirit and doctrin of Chriſt, as *Light to darkneſs*. For as is manifeſt, by what is ſaid, through contempt of Chriſt's Law, the whole world is filled with various oaths, curſings, blaſphemous profanations, and horrid perjurys, ſo likewiſe through contempt of the ſame Law the world is filled with violence, oppreſſion, murders, raviſhing of women and virgins, ſpoilings, depredations, burnings, vaſtations, and all manner of laſciviouſneſs and cruelty: ſo that it is ſtrange, that men, made after the Image of God, ſhould have ſo much degenerated, that they rather bear the image and nature of roaring lions, tearing tygers, devouring wolves, and raging boars, than of rational creaturs endued with reaſon: and is it not yet much more admirable, that this horrid monſter ſhould find place and be fomented among thoſe men, that profeſs themſelves Diſciples of our *peaçable* Lord & Maſter Jeſus Chriſt, who by *excellency* is called *the Prinçe of Peaçe*, and hath expresſly prohibited his children all violence, and, on the contrary, commanded them, that according to his example, they ſhould follow patience, charity, forbearance, and other vertues worthy of a Chriſtian.

Hear then what this great Prophet ſaith, whom every Soul is commanded to hear under the pain of being cutt-off, Matth. 5: from ver. 38. to the end of the chapter. For thus he ſaith: *Ye have heard, that it hath been ſaid, An eye for an eye, and a tooth for a tooth. But I ſay unto you, That ye Reſiſt not evill: but whoſoever ſhall ſmite thee on thy right cheek, turn to him the other alſo. And if any man will ſue thee at the law, and take away they coat, let him have thy cloak alſo. And whoſoever ſhall compell thee to go a mile, go with him twain. Give to him that asketh thee; and from him that would borrow of*
thee,

thee, turn not thou away. Ye have heard, that it hath been said. Thou shalt love thy neighbour, and hate thine enemy : But I say unto you, Love your enemies, bless them that curse you, do good to them that hate you, and pray for them which despitefully use you, and prosecute you. That ye may be the children of your Father which is in heaven : for he maketh his Sun to rise on the evil, and on the good, and sendeth rain on the just, and on the unjust. For if ye love them which love you, what reward have ye ? Do not even the Publicanes the same ? And if ye salute your brethren onely, what do you more than others ? Do not even the Publicanes so ? Be ye therefore perfect, even as your Father which in heaven is perfect.

These words with a respect to *revenge*, as the former, in the case of *swearing*, do forbid somethings, which were formerly lawfull to the Jewes, considering their condition and dispensation, and command unto such, as will be the Disciples of Christ, a more perfect, eminent, and ful signification of charity, as also patience and suffering, than was required of them in that time, state, and dispensation by the Law of Moses. This is not only the judgment of most, if not all, the Antient *Fathers*, so called, the first three hundred years after Christ, but also of many others, and in general of all those, who have rightly understood and propagated the Law of Christ, concerning *swearing*, as appears from *Justin Mart.* in Dialog. cum Tryph. ejusdemque Apolog. 2. Item ad Zenam. *Tertull.* de Coronâ Militis. It. Apolog. cap. 21. & 37. It. lib. de Idolol. c. 17, 18, 19. It. ad Scapulam cap. 1. It. adversus Jud. cap. 7 & 9. It. adv. Gnost. 13. It: adv. Marc. c. 4. It. lib. de patientia. c. 6. 10. *Orig.* cont. Celsum, lib. 3. 5. 8. It. in Josuam, hom. 12. cap. 9. It. in Mat. cap. 26. Tract. 36. *Cypr.* Epist. 56. It. ad Cornel. Lactan. de just. lib. 5. c. 18. lib. 6. c. 20. *Ambr.* in Luc. 22. *Chrysost.* in Matth. 5. hom. 18. It. in Matth. 26. hom. 85. It. lib. 2. de sacerdotio. It. 1 Cor. 13. *Chromat.* in Matth. 5. *Hieron.* ad Ocean. It. lib. Epist. p. 3. Tom. 1. Ep. 2. *Athan.* de Inc. Verb. Dei. *Cyrill. Alex.* lib. 11. in Johan. cap. 25, 26. Yea *Augustin*, although he vary much in this matter, notwithstanding in these places he did condemn *fighting.* Epist. 158, 159, 160. It ad Judices, Epist. 263. It. ad Darium, & lib. 21. It. ad Faustum, cap. 76. lib. 22. de Civit. ad Marc. cap. 6. as *Sylburgius* relates. *Euthym.* in Matth. 26. and, among others of this last age, *Erasmus* in Luc. cap. 3. & 22. *Ludor. Vives* in introd. ad Sap. *J. Ferus*, lib. 4. Comment. in Matth. 7. & Luc. 22.

From hence it appears, that there is so great a connexion betwixt these two precepts of Christ, that, as they were uttered and commanded by

him

him at one and the same time, so the same way they were received by men of all ages, not onely in the first promulgation, by the little number of the Disciples, but also after the Christians encreased in the first three hundred years, even so also in the Apostasy the one was not left and rejected without the other, and now again in the restitution and renewed preaching of the Eternal Gospel, they are acknowledged as eternal and unchangeable laws, properly belonging to the Evangelical state and perfection thereof, from which if any withdraw, he falls short of the perfection of a Christian man.

And truly the words are so clear in themselves, that, in my judgment, they need no illustration, to explain their sense: for it is more easy to reconcile the greatest contradictions, as these Laws of our Lord Jesus Christ with the wicked practice of *warrs*, for they are plainly inconsistent. Whoever can reconcile this, *Resist not evil*, with *Resist violence by force*; again, *Give also thy other cheek*, with *strick again*; also, *Love thine enemies*, with *spoile them*, *make a prey of them*, *pursue them with fire and sword*, or, *pray for those*, *that persecute you*, *and those*, *that calumniat you*, which *persecute them by fines*, *imprisonments and death it self*, and not onely such, as do not *persecute you*, but *who heartily seek and desire your eternal and temporal welfare*; whoever, I say, can find a means to reconcile these things may be supposed also to have found a way to reconcile *God* with the *Devil*, *Christ* with *Antichrist*, *Light* with *Darkness*, and *good* with *evil*. But if this be impossible, as indeed it is impossible, so will also the other be impossible, and men do but deceive both themselves and others, while they boldly adventure to establish such absurd and impossible things.

§ XIV. Nevertheless because some, perhaps through *inadvertency*, and by the force of *custom* and *Tradition*, do transgress this command of Christ, I shall briefly shew, how much *warr* doth contradict this precept, and how much they are inconsistent with one another, and consequently, that *warr is no ways lawfull to such*, *as will be the Disciples of Christ*. For

First, Christ commands, *that we should love our enemies*: But warr, on the contrary, teacheth us to hate and destroy them.

Secondly the Apostle saith, that *we warr not after the flesh*, and that *we fight not with flesh and blood*: But outward warr is according to the flesh, and against flesh and blood, for the shedding of the one, and destroying of the other.

Matth. 5: ver. 43.

Eph. 6: ver. 12.

C c c

Third-

2 Cor. 10; ver. 4.

Thirdly, the Apostle saith, that *the weapons of our warfare are not carnal, but Spiritual*: But the weapons of outward warfare are carnal, such as cannon, muskets, spears, swords, *&c.* of which there is no mention in the armour described by Paul.

Ja. 4: 1. Galat. 5: ver. 24.

Fourthly, because *James* testifies, that *warrs and strifes come from the lusts, vvhich vvarr in the members of carnal men*: But Christians, that is, those, that are truely Saints, *have crucified the flesh vvith its affections and lusts*: Therefore they can not indulge them by waging war.

Jes. 2: 4. Mich. 4: 3

Fifthly, because the Prophets *Isaiah* and *Micah* have expresly prophesied, that, *in the mountain of the house of the Lord, Christ shall judge the Nations, and then they shall beat their svvords into plow-shares*, &c. and the antient *Fathers* of the first three hundred years after Christ did affirm these prophecys to be fulfilled in the Christians of their times, who were most averse from warr, concerning which *Justin Martyr, Tertullian,* and others, may be seen: which need not seem strange to any, since *Philo Judæus* abundantly testifies of the *Esseans*, that *there vvas none found among them, that vvould make instruments of vvarr.* But how much more did Jesus come, *that he might keep his follovvers from fighting, and might bring them to patience and charity?*

Isf. 65: 25

Sixthly, because the Prophet foretold, that *there should none hurt nor kill, in all the Holy Mountain of the Lord*: But outward warr is appoynted for killing and destroying.

Joh. 18. ver. 36.

Seventhly, because Christ said, that *his Kingdom is not of this world*, and therefore that *his servants shall not fight*: Therefore those, that fight, *are not his Disciples nor servants.*

Matth. 26 ver. 52.

Eightly, because he reproved Peter for the use of the svvord, saying, *Put up again thy svvord into his place*: for all they, that take the svvord, shall perish vvith the svvord. Concerning which *Tertullian* speaks wel, lib. de idol. *Hovv shall he fight in peace vvithout a svvord, vvhich the Lord did take avvay? For although souldiers came to John and received a form of observation, if also the centurion believed aftervvards, he disarmed every souldier in disarming of Peter.* Idem de Coro. Mil. asketh, *shall it be lavvfull to use the svvord, the Lord saying, that he, that useth the svvord, shall perish by the svvord.*

Rom. 12: ver. 19.

Ninthly, because the Apostle admonisheth Christians, *that they defend not themselves, neither revenge by rendring evil for evil, but give place unto wrath, because Vengeance is the Lord's: Be not overcome of evil, but overcome evil vvith good. If thine enemy hunger, feed him: if he thirst, give him drink:*

But

But warr throughout teacheth and injoyneth the quite contrary.

Tenthly, becaufe *Chrift calls his children to bear his crofs, not to crucify or kill others: to patience not to revenge : to Truth and fimplicity, not to fraudulent ftratagems of vvarr, or to play the fycophant,* which John himfelf forbids *: to flee the glory of this vvorld;* not *to acquire it by vvarlike endeavours:* Therefore warr is altogether contrary unto the Law and Spirit of Chrift.

§ XV. But they object, *that it is lawfull to warr, becaufe Abraham did warr before the giving of the Law, and the Ifraelits after the giving of the Law.*

I anfwer as before, 1. that Abraham offered facrifices at that time, and circumcifed the males : which neverthelefs are not lawfull for us under the Gofpel.

2. That neither defenfive nor offenfive warr was lawfull to the Ifraelits, of their own will, or by their own counfel or conduct, but they were obliged at all times, if they would be fuccefsfull, firft to inquire the oracle of God.

3. That their wars, againft the wicked Nations, were a figure of the inward warr of the true Chriftians againft their Spiritual enemies, in which we overcome the devil, the world, and the flesh.

4. Something is expresfly forbidden by Chrift, Matth. 5 : 26. which was granted to the Jewes in their time, becaufe of their hardnefs; and, on the contrary, we are commanded that fingular patience and exercife of love, which Mofes commanded not to his Difciples. From whence *Tertullian* faith wel againft Marc. *Chrift truely teacheth a new patience, even forbidding the revenging of an injury, which was permitted by the Creator.* And lib. de patien. *The Law finds more than it loft, by Chrift faying, Love your enemies.* And in the time of *Clem. Alex.* Chriftians were fo far from warrs, that he teftified, that they had no marks or figns of violence among them, faying, *Neither are the faces of idols to be painted, to which fo much as to regard is forbidden : neither fword nor bow to them, that follow peace, nor cups to them, who are moderat and temperat,* as Sylvius Difc. de Rev. Belg.

Secondly, they object, *that Defence is of natural right, and that Religion deftroys not nature.*

I anfwer, Be it fo, but to obey God, and commend our felves to him in faith and patience, is not to deftroy nature, but to exalt and perfect it; to wit, to elevat it from the natural to the fupernatural life, by Chrift living therein, and comforting it, that it may do all things, and be rendered more than conqueror.   C c c 2   Third-

Obj.   Thirdly, they object, *that John did not abrogat or condemn warr, when souldiers came unto him.*

Answ.   I answer, What then? the question is not concerning John's doctrine, but Christ's, whose Disciples we are, not John's: for Christ, and not John, is that Prophet, whom we ought all to hear: and albeit that Christ said, *that a greater than John the Baptist was not among men born of women*, yet he adds, *that the least in the Kingdom of God is greater than he.* But what was John's answer, that we may see, if it can justify the souldiers of this time? For, if it be narrowly minded, it will appear, that, what he proposeth to souldiers, doth manifestly forbid them that employment, for he commands them, *not to do violence to any man, not to defraud any man,* but that they *be content with their wages.* Consider then what he dischargeth to souldiers, viz, not to use violence or deceit against any, which being removed, let any tell how souldiers can warr? For is not *craft, violence*, and *injustice*, three propertys of *warr*, and the natural consequences of battels?

Luc. 7:
ver. 28.

Luc. 3:
ver. 14.

Obj.   Fourthly, they object, *that Cornelius, and that centurion, of whom there is mention made*, Matth. 8 : 5. *were souldiers, and there is no mention that they laid down their military employments.*

Answ.   I answer, Neither read we that they continued in them. But it is most probable, that, if they continued in the doctrine of Christ, (and we read not any where of their falling from the faith) that they did not continue in them; especially if we consider, that two or three ages afterwards Christians altogether rejected warr, or at left a long while after their time, if the Emperor *Marc. Aurel. Anton.* be to be credited, who writes thus : — — *I prayed to my countrey Gods. But when I vvas neglected by them, and observed my self pressed by the enemy, considering the fevvneß of my forces, I called to one; and entreated those, vvho vvith us are called Christians, and I found a great number of them: and I forced them vvith threats: vvhich ought not to have been; because aftervvards I knevv their strength and force; therefore they betook themselves neither to the use of darts, nor trumpets, for they use not to do so, for the cause and Name of their God, vvhich they bear in their Consciences.* And this was done about an hundred and sixty years after Christ. To this add those words, which in *Justin Martyr* the Christians answer, ὐ πλεμῦμιν τῶς ἐχϑροῖς, that is, *We fight not vvith our enemies* : and moreover the answer of *Martin* to *Julian* the Apostat, related by *Sulpitius Severus* : *I am a souldier of Christ, therefore I can not fight*, which was the ee
                                                                hu—

hundred years after Chrift. It is not therefore probable, that they continued in warlik employments. How then is *Vincentius Lyrinenfis* and the
Papifts confiftent with their maxime, *That, vvhich alvvays, every vvhere,
and by all vvas received*, &c.? And what becomes of the priefts with their
oath, *that they neither ought, nor will, interpret the Scriptur, but according to
the univerfal confent of the Fathers, fo called? For it is as eafy to obfcure the
fun at mid-day, as to deny that the primitive Chriftians renounced all revenge and
vvarr.*

And albeit this thing be fo much known to al, yet it is as wel known, that
all the modern fects live in the neglect & contempt of this Law of Chrift,
and likewife opprefs others, who in this agree not with them for Confcience fake towards God, even as we have fuffered much in our countrey,
becaufe *We neither could our felves bear armes, nor fend others in our place, nor
give our money for the buying of drums, ftandards, and other military attire*: and
laftly, *becaufe we could not hold our doors, windows, and fhops clofe, for Confcience fake, upon fuch days as fafts and prayers vvere appoynted, for to defire a
bleffing upon, and fucceß for, the armes of that Kingdom or Common-Wealth, under
vvhich vve live) neither give thanks for the victorys acquired by the effufion of much
blood.* By which forceing of the Confcience, they would have conftrained
our brethren living in divers Kingdoms, at war together, to have im-
plored our God for contrary and contradictory things, and confequently
impoffible; for it is impoffible, that two partys fighting together fhould
both obtain the victory. And becaufe we can not concurr with them in
this contufion, therefore are we fubject to *perfecution*. Yea and others,
who with us do witnefs that the ufe of armes is unlawfull to Chriftians,
do look afquint upon us: but which of us two do moft faithfully obferve
this teftimony againft armes? either they, who at certain times at the
Magiftrates order do clofe up their fhops and houfes, and meet in their
affembly, praying for the profperity of their armes, or giving thanks for
fome victory or other, whereby they make themfelves like to thofe,
that approve warrs and fighting? Or we, which can not do thefe things,
for the fame caufe of Confcience, left we fhould deftroy, by our works,
what we eftablifh in words; we fhall leave to the judgment of all prudent
men?

 Fifthly, they object, *that Chrift*, Luk. 22:36. *fpeaking to his Difciples,* Obj.
*commands them, that he, that then had not a fword, fhould fell his coat, and
buy a fword: Therefore,* fay they; *Armes are lawfull.*
C c c 3

I an-

Anſw.   I anſwer, Some indeed underſtand this of the *outward ſvvord*, nevertheleſs regarding onely that occaſion, otherwiſe judging that Chriſtians are prohibited wars under the Goſpel: among which is *Ambroſe*, who upon this place ſpeaks thus: *O Lord! Why commandſt thou me to buy a ſword, who forbidſt me to ſmite vvith it? vvhy commandſt thou me to have it, vvhom thou prohibitſt to dravv it? Unleſs perhaps a defence be prepared, not a neceſſary revenge, and that I may ſeem to have been able to revenge, but that I would not. For the Law forbids me to ſmite again: and therefore perhaps he ſaid to Peter, offering two ſwords,* [It is enough,] *as if it had been lawfull, untill the Goſpel time, that, in the Law, there might be a learning of equity, but in the Goſpel a perfection of goodneſs.* Others judge Chriſt to have ſpoken here myſtically, and not according to the letter, as *Origen* upon Matth. 19. ſaying, *If any looking to the letter, and not underſtanding the will of the words, ſhall ſell his bodily garment, and buy a ſword, taking the words of Chriſt contrary to his vvill, he ſhall periſh. But concerning vvhich ſvvord he ſpeaks is not proper here to mention.* And truely when we conſider the anſwer of the Diſciples, *Maſter, behold, here are tvvo ſvvords,* underſtanding it of outward ſwords; and again Chriſt's anſwer, *It is enough;* it ſeems, that Chriſt would not, that the reſt, who had not ſwords, (for they had only two ſwords) ſhould ſell their coats, and buy an outward ſword. Who can think, that, matters ſtanding thus, he ſhould have ſaid *two was enough?* But however it is ſufficient, that the uſe of Armes is unlawfull, under the Goſpel.

Obj.   Sixthly, they object, *that the Scripturs, and old Fathers, ſo called, did onely prohibit privat revenge, not the uſe of armes, for the defence of our countrey, body, wives, children, and goods, when the Magiſtrate commands it, ſeing the Magiſtrates ought to be obeyed: Therefore albeit it be not lawfull for privat men to do it, of themſelves, nevertheleſs they are bound to do it by the command of the Magiſtrate.*

Anſw.   I anſwer, If the Magiſtrate be truely a Chriſtian, or deſires to be ſo, he ought himſelf in the firſt place to obey the command of his Maſter, ſaying, *Love your enemies,* &c. and then he could not command us to kill them: but if he be not a true Chriſtian, then ought we to obey our *Lord* and *King Jeſus Chriſt*, to whom he ought alſo to obey: for in the Kingdom of Chriſt all ought to ſubmitt to his Lawes, from the higheſt to the loweſt, that is, from the King to the Beggar, and from *Ceſar* to the Clown. But (alas!) where ſhall we find ſuch an obedience? O deplorable

plorable fall! Concerning which *Ludov. Viv.* writes wel, lib. de con. vit. Chrift. fub Turc. by relation of Fredericus Sylvius, Difc. de Revol. Belg. p. 85. *The Prince entred into the Church, not as a true and plain Chriftian: which had indeed been moft happy and defirable, but he brought in with him his nobility, his honors, his ARMES, his enfigns, his triumphs, his haughtynefs, his pride, his fupercilioufnefs,* that is, *He came into the houfe of Chrift accompanyed with the devil, and which could no wayes be done, he would have joyned two houfes and two citys together, God's and the Devils, which could not more be done, than* Rome *and* Conftantinople, *which are diftant by fo long a tract both of fea and land.* (What communion, *faith* Paul, is there betwixt Chrift and Belial?) *Their zeal cooled by degrees, their faith decreafed, their whole piety degenerated, in ftead whereof we make novv ufe of fhaddovvs and images, and, as he faith, I vvould vve could but retain thefe!* Thus far *Vives.* But laftly, as to what relates to this thing, fince nothing feemes more contrary to man's nature, and feing, of all things, the defence of ones felf feems moft tolerable, as it is moft hard to men, fo it is the moft perfect part of the Chriftian Religion, as that, wherein the *denial of felf* and *intire confidence in God* doth moft appear, and therefore Chrift and his Apoftles left us hereof a moft perfect example. As to what relates to the prefent Magiftrates of the Chriftian world, albeit we deny them not altogether the name of *Chriftians*, becanfe of the publik profeffion they make of Chrift's Name, yet we may boldly affirm, that they are far from the perfection of the Chriftian Religion; becaufe in the ftate, in which they are, (as in many places before I have largely obferved) they have not come to the pure difpenfation of the Gofpel, and therefore, while they are in that condition, we fhall not fay, that warr, undertaken upon a juft occafion, is altogether unlawfull to them. For even as Circumcifion and the other ceremonys were for a feafon permitted to the Jewes, not becaufe they were either neceffary, or of themfelves, or lawfull at that time after the refurrection of Chrift, but becaufe that Spirit was not yet raifed up in them, whereby they could be delivered from fuch rudiments; fo the prefent confeffors of the Chriftian name, who are yet in the mixtur, and not in the patient fuffering fpirit, are not yet fitted for this form of Chriftianity, and therefore can not be undefending themfelves, untill they attain that perfection: but for fuch, whom Chrift has brought hither, it is not lawfull to defend themfelves by *armes*, but they ought over all to truft to the Lord.

§. X.VI. But laftly, to conclude, If to give and receive flattering

titles,

titles, which are not used because of the vertues inherent in the persons, but are for most part bestowed by wicked men upon such as themselves; If to bow, scrape and cringe to one another; If at every time to call one another *humble servant*, and that most frequently, without any design of real service, if this be the honor, that comes from God, and not the honor, that is from below, then indeed our adversarys may be said to be believers, and we condemned as proud and stubborn in denying all these things. But if with *Mordecai* to refuse to bowe to proud *Haman*, and with *Elihu* not to give *flattering titles to men, lest we should be reproved of our Maker*; and if according to Peters's example and the Angel's advice, to bowe onely to God, and not to our fellow-servants; and if to call no man Lord, nor Master, except under particular relations, according to Christ's command, I say, if these things be not to be reproved, then are we not blame-worthy in so doing. If to be vain and gaudy in apparel, if to paint the face, and plait the hair; if to be cloathed with gold and silver and pretious stones, and if to be filled with ribbands and lace, be to be cloathed in modest apparel; and if these be the ornaments of Christians, and if that be to be humble, meek, and mortified, Then are our adversarys good Christians indeed, and we proud, singular, and conceited in contenting our selves with what need and conveniency calls for, and condemning, what is more, as superfluous : but not otherwise. If to use games, sports, plays; if to card, dice, and dance; if to sing, fidle, and pipe; if to use stage-plays and comedys, and to lye, counterfeit, and dissemble, be to fear always; and if that be to do all things to the glory of God; and if that be to pass our sojourning here in fear; and if that be to use this world, as if we did not use it; and if that be not to fashion our selves according to our former lusts; to be not conformable to the spirit and vain conversation of this world; then are our adversaries, notwithstanding they use these things, and plead for them, very good, sober, mortified, and self-denyed Christians, and we justly to be blamed for judging them, but not otherwise. If the profanation of the Holy Name of God, if to exact oaths one from another upon every light occasion; if to call God to witness in things of such a nature, in which no earthly King would think himself lawfully and honorably to be a witness, be the dutys of a Christian man; I shall confess, that our adversaries are excellent good Christians, & we wanting in our duty : but if the contrary be true, of necessity our obedience to God in this thing must be acceptable. If to revenge our selves,

or

or to render injury, evil for evil, wound for wound, to take eye for eye, tooth for tooth; If to fight for outward and perishing things, to go a warring one against another, whom we never saw, nor with whom we never had any contest, nor any thing to do, being moreover altogether ignorant of the cause of the war, but onely that the Magistrates of the Nations foment quarrells one against another, the causes whereof are, for the most part, unknown to the souldiers, that fight, as wel as upon whose side the right or wrong is; and yet to be so furious, and rage one against another, to destroy and spoil all, that this or the other worship may be received or abolished; If to do this, and much more of this kind, be to fulfill the Law of Christ, Then are our adversaries indeed true Christians, and we miserable heretiks, that suffer our selves to be spoiled, taken, imprisoned, banished, beaten, and evilly entreated, without any resistance, *placing our trust onely in GOD*, that he may defend us, and lead us by this way of the *Cross* unto his *Kingdom*. But if it be other ways, we shall certainly receive the *reward*, which the Lord hath promised to those, that *cleave to him*, and, in denying themselves, *confide in him*.

And, to summ up all, If to use all these things, and many more, that might be instanced, be to walk in the *strait way*, that *leads to Life*, be to *take up the Cross of Christ*; be to *dye with him to the lusts* and *perishing vanitys* of this *world*; and to *arise with him in newness of Life*; and *fit down with him in the heavenly places*; Then our adversarys may be accounted such, and they need not fear, they are in the *broad way*, that *leads to destruction*; and we are greatly mistaken, that have laid aside all these things, for Christ's sake, to the crucifying of our own lusts, and to the procuring to our selves shame, reproach, hatred, and ill-will from the men of this world : not as if by so doing we judged to merit heaven, but as knowing they are contrary to the will of him, who redeems his children from the love of this world, and its lusts, and leads them in the ways of *Truth* and *Holyness*, in which they take delight to walk.

The

The CONCLUSION.

IF in God's fear, candid Reader, thou apply'ft thy felf to confider this Syftem of Religion, here delivered, with its confiftency and harmony, as wel in it felf, as with the Scripturs of Truth; I doubt not, but thou wilt fay with me and many more, that this is the Spiritual day of Chrift's appearance, wherein he is again revealing the antient paths of Truth and Righteoufnefs. For thou mayft obferve here the Chriftian Religion, in all its parts, truely eftablished and vindicated, as it is a living, inward, Spiritual, Pure, and Subftantial thing, and not a meer form, shew, shaddow, notion, and opinion, as too many have hitherto held it, whofe fruits declare they wanted that, which they bear the name of, and yet many of thofe are fo in love with their empty forms and shaddows, that they ceafe not to calumniat us, for commending, and calling them to the Subftance, as if we therefore denyed or neglected the true form and outward part of Chriftianity, which indeed is (as God the fearcher of hearts knowes) a very great flaunder. Thus, becaufe we have defired people earneftly to feel after God near and in themfelves, telling them, that their notions of God, as he is beyond the clouds, will little avail them, if they do not feel him near: hence they have fought malitioufly to infer, that we deny any God, except that, which is within us. Becaufe we tell people, that it is the Light and the Lavv vvithin, and not the letter without, that can truely tell them their condition, and lead them out of all evil: hence they fay, we vilify the Scripturs, and fet up our own imaginations above them. Becaufe we tell them, that it is not their talking, or believing of Chrift's outward life, fufferings, death, and refurrection no more, than the Iewes crying, the Temple of the Lord, the temple of the Lord, that will ferve their turn, or juftify them in the fight of God, but that they muft know Chrift in them, whom they have crucified, to be raifed, and to juftify them, and redeem them from their iniquitys: hence they fay, we deny the life, death,

and

and sufferings of Christ, justification by his blood, and remission of sins through him. Because we tell them, while they are talking and determining about the Resurrection, that they have more need to know the Just One, whom they have slain, raised in themselves, and to be sure they are partakers of the first resurrection, and that, if this be, they will be the more capable to judge of the second: hence they say, that we deny the resurrection of the body. Because, when we hear them talk foolishly of heaven, and hell, and the last judgment, we exhort them to come out of that hellish condition they are in, and come down to the judgment of Christ in their own hearts, and believe in the Light, and follow it, that so they may come to sit in the heavenly places, that are in Christ Iesus, hence they maliciously say, that we deny any heaven or hell, but that, which is within us, and that we deny any general judgment: which slaunders the Lord knowes are fouly cast upon us, whom God hath raised for this end, and gathered us, that, by us, he might confound the wisdom of the wise, and bring to nought the understanding of the prudent, and might, in and by his own Spirit and Power in a despised People, (that no flesh might glory in his presence) pull down that dead, dark, corrupt image, and meer shaddow, and shell of Christianity, wherewith Antichrist hath deceived the Nations, for which end he hath called us to be a first-fruits of those, that serve him, and worship him, no more in the oldness of the letter, but in the newness of the Spirit. And though we be few in number, in respect of others, and weak as to outward strength, which we also altogether reject; and foolish, if compared with the wise ones of this world, yet as God hath prospered us, notwithstanding much opposition, so will he yet do, that neither the art, wisdom, nor violence of men or devils shall be able to quench that little spark, that hath appeared, but it shall grow to the consuming of whatsoever shall stand up to oppose it. The mouth of the Lord hath spoken it, yea he, that hath arisen in a small remnant, shall arise, and go-on by the same Arme of Power in his Spiritual manifestation, untill he hath con-

D d d 2

quered

quered all his enemies, untill all the Kingdoms of the Earth become the Kingdom of Chrift Iefus.

Unto him, that hath begun this work, not among the rich, or great ones, but among the poor and fmall, and hath revealed it not to the wife and learned, but unto the poor, unto babes and fucklings, even to him the Onely-Wife and Omnipotent GOD be honor, glory, thanksgiving, and renown, from henceforth and for ever. *Amen.* *Halelu* - J A H.

A

Passages of
SCRIPTUR,
Occurring in this book.

MATTHEW.

Chap.	Verf.	Pag
	14	236
	16	350
	20	240. 274
	23	365
XI	27	11
	30	178
XII	35, 36	386
	48	200
XIII		114
	14	109
	18, 19	90
	31, 32	122
	29, to 41	352
XV	6, 9	291
	13	367
XVII	26	167
XVIII	7	83
	20	271
	32, 34	108
XIX		406
XX	25, 26, 27	241
XXI	33	107
	42	123
XXIII	5, 6, 7	241
	8, 9, 10	241
	22	391
	37	108
XXIV	27	101
	42	255. 281
XXV		115
	13	255
	15	90
	21, 23	160
	26	109
	30	161
XXVI	26	328 332
	41	255. 261
	52	402
XXVIII		301. 309
	18	351
	19	301

MARK.

Chap.	Verf.	Pag
III	33, 34	200
IV		114
	1	274
	12	109
VIII	34	403
XII	1	107
	10	123
XIII	11	240. 274
	33	261. 281
	33, 35, 37	25
XIV	22	328. 332
	38	281
XVI	15	79

LUKE.

Chap.	Verf.	Pag
I	6	178
II	10	75
	52	170
III	14	404
VII	28	404
VIII	10	109
	11	114
IX	55	351
	55, 56	347
X	22	11
	29	152
XII	12	240. 274
	48	115
XIII	3	146
	34, &c.	108
XIV	31	396
XVI	15	152
XVII	10	160
	20, 21	122
XVIII	1	277
XIX	41, 42	101
	42	93
XX	9	107
	17	123
XXI	36	255. 261
	36	277
XXII	19	328. 332
	36	405

JOHN

Chap.	Verf.	Pag.
I.		320
	1, 2, 3	10
	7	118
	9	110
	12	320
III	3	121
	5	314
	8	101
	16, 17	81
	18	146
	18, 19	184
	20	123
	30	290. 301
	34	307
IV	2	301
	14	329
	23, 24	267, 290
V	39	56
	44	367
VI	16	323
	27, 32, &c.	317, 318
	35	317, 320
	35	322
	45	50
	53	322
	55	322
	56, 57	323
	60	321
	63	22
	66	321
VII	7	83
	48, 49	2
VIII	26	83
IX	31	290
X	1	198
XII	19	83
	36	112
	40	109
	47	82
XIII	3, 4, &c	83
	14	317
	17	160. 170

I. CORINTHIANS.

CHAP.	Verſ.	Pag.
	9, 10, 12, 14	12
	9, 10	23
	12	83
	13	276
	14	66
III	4 to 8, 19	306
	16	99
IV	15	310
	18	241
V	8	317
VI	2	83
	11	136.150
	17	171.252
	17	320
	19	21
VII	19	160.176
	29, 30	385
IX	11, &c.	231
	15	234
	18	234
	24	396
	27	188
X	3, 4	321
	16	329
	16, 17	317
	17	323
	21	322
XI		380
	17, 20	342
	17 to 32	340
	23	332
	26	328
	26, 27	330
XII		47
	3	282
	4	225
	4, 5, 6	19
	7	72.90
	8, 9, 10, 13	23
	9, 10, 11	21
	13	13.212
	17, 29	226

I. CORINTHIANS.

CHAP.	Verſ.	Pag.
XIII	2	240
XIV	15	282
	30	276
	30, 31, 33	227
	34	231
XVI	13	255

II. CORINTHIANS.

CHAP.	Verſ.	Pag.
I	22	189.293
	23	394
	24	350
II	17	222
III	6	197
IV	10, 11	156
V	11	197
	14	388
	16, 17	121
	18, 19, 21	148
	19	141
VI	14	171.322
	14, 15, 16	149
	16	97
	17, 18	205
X	4	352.402
XI	10	394
XIII	3	210
	5	48.125
		157
	11	176

GALATIANS.

CHAP.	Verſ.	Pag.
1, &c.		162
	8, 9	59
	16	12
	20	394
II	8	164
	20	164.178
III	27	157.290
IV		164
	19	157

GALATIANS.

CHAP.	Verſ.	Pag.
V	12, 20	355
	24	402
VI	6	231
	14	83

EPHESIANS.

CHAP.	Verſ.	Pag.
I	13	189
	14	293
II		68
	4, 5, 6	178
	5	156
	8	211
	15	142
III	9	10
IV		225
	5	18.290
	7, 11, 16	212
	11	174.225
	23	251
	23, 24	157
	24	178
	30	293
V	8	112
	11	367
	13	90.100
		346
	25, 26, 27	174
VI	12	401
	18	281, 282

PHILIPPIANS

CHAP.	Verſ.	Pag.
I	6	186
	8	394
	21	70
II	13	164
III	10	142
	14	183
	15	363
	20	74

COLOSSIANS.

I. THESSALONIANS.

II. THESSALONIANS.

I. TIMOTHY.

I. TIMOTHY.

II. TIMOTHY.

TITUS.

HEBREWS.

HEBREWS.

JAMES.

I. PETER.

II. PETER.

CHAP.	Verf.	Pag.
I	4	143.171
	10	48.188
	12, 13	53
	16	373
II	1, 2, 3	240
	3	122
	1, 3, 14, 15	241
	20	83
III	9	77.82
	15	106

I. JOHN.

CHAP.	Verf.	Pag.
I	1	217
	7	110
	8	179
II	1, 2	83

I. JOHN.

CHAP.	Verf.	Pag.
	2 to 6	176
	15	83
	27	29
III	1, 13	83
	2 to 10	176
4		181
	5, 8	173
	7, 20	158
	9	170
IV	4, 5	38
	9	81
	10	142
	13	37.49
V	3	178
	6	37.49
	14	282
	19	84

JUDE.

CHAP.	Verf.	Pag.
I	16	241
	20	282

REVELATION.

CHAP.	Verf.	Pag.
II	5	146
	9	204
	20	355
III	12	189.184
	16	202
	20	12.331
XIV	to 5	179
XIX	10	380
XXII	9	380
	14	160
	18	60

A
TABLE
Of the chief things.

Chri-

Name.

Q.

R.

 without

F I N I S.

9 783337 404994